JEWISH CULTURAL STUDIES

VOLUME THREE

The Jewish Cultural Studies series is sponsored by the Jewish Folklore and Ethnology Section of the American Folklore Society in co-operation with the Council on the Anthropology of Jews and Judaism of the American Anthropological Association.

Members of the Section receive volumes as a privilege of membership. For more information see <http://afsnet.org/sections/jewish>.

The Section is also the sponsor of the Raphael Patai Prize, given to an outstanding student essay in English on Jewish folklore and ethnology. The chapters in this volume by Irit Koren of Bar-Ilan University (Israel), entitled 'The Power of Discourse', and Jillian Gould of Memorial University of Newfoundland (Canada), entitled 'Shiva as Creative Ritual in an Institutional Home', received the prize in 2008 and 2009, respectively. For more information, see the website listed above or <http://littman.co.uk/jcs/index.html>.

This volume has benefited from the financial support of
THE ROTHSCHILD FOUNDATION (EUROPE)

THE LITTMAN LIBRARY OF
JEWISH CIVILIZATION

*The Littman Library of Jewish Civilization is a registered UK charity
Registered charity no. 1000784*

JEWISH CULTURAL STUDIES

VOLUME THREE

Revisioning Ritual
Jewish Traditions
in Transition

Edited by
SIMON J. BRONNER

Oxford · Portland, Oregon
The Littman Library of Jewish Civilization
2011

The Littman Library of Jewish Civilization

Chief Executive Officer: Ludo Craddock
Managing Editor: Connie Webber

PO Box 645, Oxford OX2 0UJ, UK
www.littman.co.uk

Published in the United States and Canada by
The Littman Library of Jewish Civilization
c/o ISBS, 920 NE 58th Avenue, Suite 300
Portland, Oregon 97213-3786

A catalogue record for this book is available from the British Library

Revisioning ritual : Jewish traditions in transition / edited by Simon J. Bronner.
p. cm.—(The Littman library of Jewish civilization)
Includes bibliographical references and index.
1. Judaism—Customs and practices. I. Bronner, Simon J.
BM700.R375 2011   296.4–dc22   2010047712

ISBN 978–1–904113–47–8

Publishing co-ordinator: Janet Moth
Copy-editing: Agnes Erdos
Proofreading: Mark Newby
Index: Bonnie Blackburn
Designed and typeset by Pete Russell, Faringdon, Oxon.
Production: John Saunders
Printed in Great Britain on acid-free paper by
the MPG Books Group, Bodmin and King's Lynn

*The editor dedicates this volume to
the memory of*

RABBI HENRY A. FISCHEL
(1913–2008)

*late Professor Emeritus of Near Eastern Languages and
Cultures at Indiana University (USA), and founding
father of its Jewish studies programme*

*He inspired many a student in ethnology and folklore with
his broad knowledge of Jewish texts and cultures*

Editor and Advisers

EDITOR

Simon J. Bronner

The Pennsylvania State University

ADVISORY BOARD

Acknowledgements

I HAVE HAD THE PRIVILEGE of working with a stellar international cast of advisers, who also laboured as reviewers of essays. I want to extend my special gratitude to advisers who served on the Raphael Patai Prize committee: Dan Ben-Amos, Haya Bar-Itzhak, and Steve Siporin. Other colleagues who provided professional service by evaluating manuscripts were Stephen Blank, Shifra Epstein, Ari Y. Kelman, Rabbi Peter Kessler, Laura Levitt, Andrea Lieber, Ilana Rosen, Shalom Sabar, Matthew Singer, Rabbi Stephen Stern, Mickey Weems, and Steven Zeitlin. Matti Bunzl also serves the cause well in his leadership of the Council on the Anthropology of Jews and Judaism. My appreciation goes out to Timothy Lloyd, Executive Director of the American Folklore Society, for working so well with the organization's Jewish Folklore and Ethnology section, sponsor of the Jewish Cultural Studies series. At the Littman Library, Connie Webber, Janet Moth, and Ludo Craddock are always in my corner.

Contents

Note on Transliteration

THE transliteration of Hebrew in this book reflects consideration of the type of book it is, in terms of its content, purpose, and readership. The system adopted therefore reflects a broad approach to transcription, rather than the narrower approaches found in the *Encyclopaedia Judaica* or other systems developed for text-based or linguistic studies. The aim has been to reflect the pronunciation prescribed for modern Hebrew, rather than the spelling or Hebrew word structure, and to do so using conventions that are generally familiar to the English-speaking reader.

In accordance with this approach, no attempt is made to indicate the distinctions between *alef* and *ayin*, *tet* and *taf*, *kaf* and *kuf*, *sin* and *samekh*, since these are not relevant to pronunciation; likewise, the *dagesh* is not indicated except where it affects pronunciation. Following the principle of using conventions familiar to the majority of readers, however, transcriptions that are well established have been retained even when they are not fully consistent with the transliteration system adopted. On similar grounds, the *tsadi* is rendered by 'tz' in such familiar words as bar mitzvah, mitzvot, and so on.

The distinction between *ḥet* and *khaf* has been retained, using ḥ for the former and *kh* for the latter; the associated forms are generally familiar to readers, even if the distinction is not actually borne out in pronunciation, and for the same reason the final *heh* is indicated too. As in Hebrew, no capital letters are used, except that an initial capital has been retained in transliterating titles of published works (for example, *Shulḥan arukh*).

Since no distinction is made between *alef* and *ayin*, they are indicated by an apostrophe only in intervocalic positions where a failure to do so could lead an English-speaking reader to pronounce the vowel-cluster as a diphthong—as, for example, in *ha'ir*—or otherwise mispronounce the word.

The *sheva na* is indicated by an *e*—*perikat ol, reshut*—except, again, when established convention dictates otherwise. The *yod* is represented by *i* when it occurs as a vowel (*bereshit*), by *y* when it occurs as a consonant (*yesodot*), and by *yi* when it occurs as both (*yisra'el*).

Names have generally been left in their familiar forms, even when this is inconsistent with the overall system.

Ritualizing Jewishness

SIMON J. BRONNER

SETTING THE TONE for a theme that pervades Judaism as well as this volume, the first question posed in the Mishnah concerns the flexibility of Jewish ritual. The query in the opening tractate, *Berakhot*, 'From what time may they recite the Shema in the evening?', is the starting point probably because it deals with a prayer that structures the day and defines the collective referred to as 'they', or Jews. The opening question, followed quickly by a discussion about the latest time the Shema can be recited, may seem to require a straightforward answer, but it elicits a raft of responses, including 'until the end of the first watch', 'until midnight', and 'until the rise of dawn', with accompanying commentaries. Several of the replies refer to the 'obligation' to recite the prayer ritually—that is, to perform it repeatedly according to a set order with an understanding of its essential role as practice and symbol in daily life. The Mishnah does not specify that fulfilling this obligation need occur in a synagogue or in a special part of the home. The precept of the tractate is that Jews repeat the recitation daily and this action is viewed as central to Jewish life. Its repetition in the morning and evening represents a pattern of living marking time from beginning to end.

The Mishnah describes the details of Jewish practices, but it also reflects on the meaning of traditions such as reciting the Shema, explaining that recitation as a ritual has a meaning that goes beyond the spoken text in that it serves 'to protect man from sin'. The implication is that its performance has a function within a larger system of interrelated action and belief. Broadly speaking, in this way of thinking ritual structures Jewish life and also comes to symbolize it. A major lesson from the exchange in the Mishnah is that although Judaism follows a number of laws that were created in response to God's commandments, religious practice is often subject to variation and is open to interpretation. This also creates the possibility of debate and controversy over the appropriate or effective variant to adopt.

Complicating the application of a social model by which Jewish practices comply with ancient scriptural dictates, even while leaving details subject to revision, is the fact that many people who call themselves Jewish do not recite the Shema twice daily, or maybe ever. They may not recognize a scriptural basis to Jewish identity but nonetheless participate in customs that they perceive as setting them apart as Jewish—observing holidays, lighting sabbath candles, eating kosher meat, or installing a *mezuzah*, to name some examples cited in Jewish social surveys (Sheskin 2001: 72–103). The possibility remains that someone calls him- or herself 'just Jewish' without having an awareness of any Jewish customs they practice, although others may attribute apparently Jewish habits to them. Jews may also define themselves by practices that they do not follow, because they perceive such practices as essentially 'not Jewish'—such as holding bridal showers (although some do), bringing flowers to a cemetery (although in fact this is standard in Israel), or eating pork (though of course there are Jews who do that too). Beyond the concept that ritual negation, or prohibitions, mark social boundaries and draw attention to the distinctive cognate customs that the group holds, one might further include under cultural self-awareness identity-forming practices that have modern secular overtones or are self-consciously created to provide new spiritual ceremonies (Boris 2008: 36–8; Bronner 2008: 16–18; Ochs 2007; Silver 1998: 60–78; Whitfield 2008). For example, what about attending a Holocaust commemoration annually? Or participating in an Israeli folk dance at a festival? Or performing a *mitsvah* by helping others on Mitzvah Day or other occasions? Or eating Chinese food and attending a movie at Christmas? Or forming a women's Rosh Hodesh group and reciting a blessing over Miriam's cup? Or composing a script for a new commitment or naming ceremony (for example Simhat Bat, a name-giving ceremony for a newborn daughter introduced in the late twentieth century, or Zeved Habat, a Sephardi and Italian ritual dating to the seventeenth century)?

Our awareness of the different ways of constructing Jewishness might be further nuanced by calling to mind boundary-setting practices that suggest ethnic or intrasectarian differences within the Jewish world, such as eating rice at Passover (a Sephardi custom), holding a Feast of Jethro (identified as distinctively Tunisian in the first chapter), or observing Simhat Kohen (known in Morocco and India, to celebrate on the day after Yom Kippur the safe return of the high priest or Kohen Gadol from the sanctuary, based upon the description in the Mishnah (*Yoma* 7: 4), 'And they celebrate a festival for all his friends when he has come forth whole from the sanctuary'). If these examples suggest intentional constructions of ritual, what about expressive behaviour that appears ritualistic and characteristically Jewish to observers but of which the actors themselves may be unaware? One might notice, for example, personal rituals suggesting Jewishness such as reflexively uttering 'Oy vey!', starting a meeting late with the explanation that the convener operates on 'Jewish time', or making excessive amounts of food for a social occasion with the declaration 'I'm a Jewish mother.' Finally, what of consciously inventing or adapting ritual to serve a personal or community need, such as creating a menstrual or menopausal ceremony for women or organizing an Irish Jewish seder in Boston or Dublin?

These kinds of questions, posed in modern discourse and ancient texts about the source, perpetuation, adaptation, change, and invention of rituals representing Jewishness, spin off ultimately from a central query that this volume addresses: how and why do Jews repeat themselves and perform symbolic acts? The contributors recognize that the ritual process in Jewish tradition is manifestly a way that many Jews define themselves and are often defined by outsiders. However, it is more than a classificatory device: in the Jewish context, ritual can also be seen as a strategy for perpetuating peoplehood and the values that it suggests. Scholars may encapsulate this idea of a people's collective outlook in psychological terms as 'world-view', or consider, from a sociological perspective, the particular context that gives meaning to ritual texts specific to a given location. Whether looking inside the participants' heads or outside to social and historical conditions, writers in this volume share the assumption that ritual is subject to change across time and space. Methodologically, they pursue evidence of the loss and gain of customs in an attempt to interpret the contexts, rationales, and world-views that constitute versions of the Jewish experience.

Religion is one aspect of a broader process that people engage in to create Jewish associations. Others may be found in social situations where ritualized, repeated practices such as play, dance, drama, and narrative evoke Jewishness. In other words, in focusing their analytical lens on the revision of ritual practices, the contributors to this volume seek an explanation for the visions of life that Jews hold. This approach differs from an earlier emphasis in Jewish studies on the origin and diffusion of customs, often treating ritual practices as relics from antiquity (see F. L. Cohen 1900; Grunwald 1923; Jacobs 1890; Yoffie 1916). The contributors to this volume examine ritual situationally, often as a diverse, emergent social and intellectual construction, rather than presuming it to be inherited as a limited set of scripturally derived practices. As such, the concept of ritual expands from remarkably persistent and stable religious rites to symbolic practices that are contextualized culturally and analysed for their changes. The authors look as much at contemporary secular discontinuity, controversy, and initiative as they do at the conventional idea of long-standing religious continuity and survival. The lesson they offer from their studies is not all that far, however, from the one drawn from the opening exchange in the Mishnah: the traditionality of Jewishness correlates with the variability and even creativity of Jewish practice. As cultural studies, the essays in this volume are especially concerned with rituals as expressive forms incorporated rhetorically and strategically into a multilayered Jewish cultural system. This system is not isolated but emanates from the immediate community and individuals engaging in a ceremony to the broader Jewish and non-Jewish worlds.

A precedent for an approach to the dynamism of Jewish ritual lies in the discourse about *minhag* (custom), encompassing the dualism of scripturally derived rite and adapted or invented post-biblical ritual (Chill 1978: pp. xix–xxii; Tabory 1997: 466). In rabbinic writing, it is distinguished from *mitsvot* (commandments), conceived as divinely instituted rules of conduct such as the Decalogue; rabbinical *mitsvot* are instructions of religious authorities such as reading the

Scroll of Esther on Purim and ritually washing hands before eating. *Minhagim* come from the people and exhibit variation across localities. *Minhag* includes localized performances of prayer rituals and the liturgical variations that developed between the Ashkenazi and Sephardi communities. It can also suggest variations of religious practices between localities and sects, including rites and festivals of hasidic, Karaite, German, Polish, Yemenite, Ethiopian, Bukharan, and Italian Jews, to name a few prominent regional traditions (Raisin 1907: 79–123). The bulk of references to *minhagim* are related to life-course rituals, or rites of passage (Fox 1978: p. vii). *Minhag* could also refer to customs that arose from popular usage rather than being introduced by a rabbinical authority or taken from biblical writ. Customs often attach to a community or region, although they can also be widely adopted, even becoming binding as rules or norms, such as eating apples and honey on Rosh Hashanah or men wearing head coverings. The concern in much of the discourse on *minhag* is not so much an explanation of the process of attachment as judging the appropriateness of a custom, and especially its characterization as functional, primitive, or even heretical (Chill 1978: pp. xx–xxi; Linke 1999: 12–15; Tabory 1997: 467).

The use of *minhag* in the Bible differs from its meaning in rabbinic discourse. Originally, *minhag*—from the Hebrew root associated with leading—refers to the way that Jehu, son of Nimshi, handles a chariot (2 Kgs 9: 20). The figurative meaning of *minhag* refers to practices that people adopt in order to identify themselves religiously, and presumably to lead, or conduct, themselves through life. With the Jewish emphasis on following ancestral traditions the concept of *minhag* allowed Judaism to be conceived as a religion evolving organically in relation to its cultural context (Gaster 1978: 3–5). The lines between law and custom are often blurry. Writing the foreword to *The Minhagim*, Marvin Fox gives 'folkway' as the quick definition of *minhag*, but adds that 'it is more than just folkway' (1979: p. vii). He explains:

Established custom is seen, in some instances, as a source of law embodied in the practice of the people. If the original legal basis of the practice has been lost to us, the *minhag* still preserves a correct pattern of practice. Even when we are dealing with pure custom [a practice not mentioned in any sacred texts], the practices of established Jewish communities express deeply felt and authentic Jewish values. (Fox 1979: p. vii)

The Mishnah comments on the priority of *minhag* in several places, such as the directive for Passover that 'a person should not vary from *minhag* [in the sense of local custom] so as to avoid contentiousness' (*Pes.* 4: 1). An oft-cited passage concerns the repetition of verses when reciting Hallel during Sukkot: 'Everything follows the *minhag* of the locality' (*Suk.* 3: 11). Not coincidentally, the passage underscores the rhetorical connection between ritual repetition and the idea of *minhag* becoming widespread or binding through long-standing social usage. Attempts to integrate these customs that have the quality of law have emerged since the geonic period, most notably the *Shulḥan arukh*, a sixteenth-century legal code comprising 13,602 halakhic rules as well as *minhagim* by Rabbi Yosef Karo, including judgements of the customs themselves (Chill 1978: pp. xx–xxi; A. Davis 2006). Karo's text led to a host of published commentaries, with the authors often commenting on the appropriateness of the customs or noting a particular local usage (Raisin 1907: 111–23).

Rooted in the concern to show non-Jews as well as Jews that Jewish practices held meaning for the present, works such as *Ta'amei haminhagim* (Reasons for our Customs) by Rabbi Avraham Yitzhak Sperling (1999 [1890]), translated into several languages, became popular in the wake of modernism and opened symbolic as well as historical associations for scrutiny. The corpus of Jewish customs was still limited, however, to religious or synagogue ceremonies. Translating Sperling's work into English in the mid-twentieth century, for example, Rabbi Abraham Matts dismissed the ethnic or nationalistic uses of tradition with the comment that 'These ceremonial acts of course, are but the means to an end, namely the religious life. If they fail to achieve that objective, they are useless' (Matts 1968: 7).

Aware of Christian criticism of some Jewish practices as old-fashioned or superstitious, Sperling responds to the question 'Why is it customary in some communities for those whose parents are still living to leave the synagogue when *Yizkor* is begun, and stay outside until after the memorial service is over?' with a practical as well as an ethical answer: 'It is awkward to stand quietly and not join the rest of the congregation in its prayers. Also, one should not put himself in a position where he may be the object of envy for still having his parents' (Sperling 1968: 198).

Also referring to Sperling's work rationalizing certain aspects of tradition, Shmuel Pinchas Gelbard called his compilation of customs *Rite and Reason: 1050 Jewish Customs and their Sources* (1998). His intention, he wrote, was to review 'many practices [that] have fallen into disuse and, more importantly, many of the reasons and rationales given for them [that] have become tarnished by time' (1998: p. vii). The categories of ceremony that fell under the rubric of *minhag* in these works were primarily historical: first, the ancient customs that had universally become integrated into halakhah; second, customs practised by specific communities (Gelbard delineates Ashkenazim, Sephardim, hasidim, German Jews, communities in Erets Yisra'el, and the Jews of Jerusalem). These rabbinic writers were clearly defensive about the social challenge to rabbinic authority posed by *minhagim* that emerged from popular usage, and they reflected more on the codification of law than on the analysis of Jewish cultural patterns (Ben-Menahem 1996: 431–2; Chill 1978: pp. xx–xxi; Ginzberg 1955: 153–86). In his 1903 lectures on *Jewish Ceremonial Institutions and Customs*, for example, Rabbi William Rosenau extolled the value of codes 'framed to meet all violations of sanctity' as a bulwark against 'a marked tendency in the Synagogue to de-rabbinize

Judaism, by laying less emphasis on the forms and more on the spirit of the faith'
(1903: 43, 11). He warned about bending too much to local preferences such as
cutting short the length of shiva observance or extending bar mitzvah celebrations. He called for a reconfirmation of rabbinical *mitsvot* in viewing Judaism as a
formula for living.

Even as codification strengthened a rule-centred religious tradition adminis-
tered by rabbinic authority, support for the inclusion of *minhagim* in the codes
also implied what Jewish historian Theodor Gaster dubbed a 'progressive' world-
view in Judaism—'the Torah itself is dynamic, not static, unfolding itself continuously throughout the ages' (Gaster 1978: 4). Calling for the interpretation of
practices by successive generations and recognizing rituals adapted in the present gave power to the living rather than the dead. It sanctioned the multiplicity of
Jewish experience. This view is evident in the summative Yiddish saying, *a minhag brekht a din* (custom supersedes a law), invoked by prominent liberal rabbinic
figures such as Philip David Bookstaber, who broadened its meaning to include
the relationship of Jews to non-Jews in writing that 'Rabbinic literature is very
insistent upon the maintenance of "custom" and, likewise, with equal insistence,
careful to exhort the Jew to revere and honor the customs of others within his own
community or of the community into which he may come as a visitor. So strong
and so important are these "customs"—yea—these "mores," that for no idle reason has the following phrase been made classic in Jewish life: "*Minhag brecht ein
Din*"' (Bookstaber 1939: 15; see also Chill 1978: p. xxi). Bookstaber called for Jewish practices evolving with the times. A counter-view expressed as an aphorism is
'ancestral custom is Torah', suggesting, in Joseph Tabory's words, a rabbinic
'protest against slavish adherence to senseless or even objectionable customs'
that arose in the post-biblical period (Tabory 1997: 466). In this view, which
Byron Sherwin refers to as 'monolithic' as opposed to the progressive 'dialogic'
perspective where present custom is in dialogue with ancient precedent, universally accepted, long-standing customs that come out of Torah deserve rabbinical
endorsement (1990: 34).

The problem that the concept of *minhag* raises is that despite the appearance
of social acceptance, entrenched customs such as *kaparot* (literally 'atonements'
in Hebrew, referring to moving fowl around the head three times on the eve of
Yom Kippur and symbolically transferring one's sins to the rooster or hen) may
be subject to rabbinical derision, or worse, condemnation by non-Jewish society,
as dated, backward, superstitious, and irreverent. The *kaparot* ritual is accompanied by the declaration, 'This is my substitute, this is my exchange, this is my
atonement. This fowl shall go unto death, and I will go, and enter, into a good and
long life, and into peace' (Rappoport 1937: 114–16; Stern 1987: 123–6; Unterman
1999: 164). The animal is then ritually slaughtered to complete the expiatory
process. Mentioned first in ninth-century Babylonia and associated today primarily with Orthodox Ashkenazim, the custom has aroused calls for its abolish-

ment, or for revision, for example by using money instead of a bird and then giving the money to charity, or replacement by the *minhag* of *tashlikh* ('casting off') comprising the throwing of crumbs into water to discharge sins (D. N. Cohen 2009). Some, however, argue that *kaparot* is a compulsory practice in keeping with the theme of atonement on Yom Kippur. Objections to *kaparot* focused for centuries on its similarity to pagan sacrifice, on the cruelty to the bird, or on the fact that the ritual does not appear in the Torah.

In a modern twist to the debate, the animal rights movement got involved in 2008 with a widely publicized complaint from People for the Ethical Treatment of Animals (PETA) that chickens were abused before the ritual (*Jewish Journal* 2008). In addition to objecting to swinging the fowl and slicing their throats, PETA charged that chickens used in the ritual waited for days in cramped cages, lacking food, water, and protection from inclement weather. The implication was that the humane tradition that Orthodox Jews referred to in justifying this ritual was belied by actual practice. Rabbi Avi Shafran, director of public affairs for Agudat Yisrael of America, answered that rabbinic authorities had taken steps to prevent chickens from being treated without 'the sensitivity to animals' comfort that halacha mandates'. He further addressed the underlying objection from both Jews and non-Jews that 'the custom itself is "primitive"'. Calling the *minhag* indispensable for Orthodox Jews, Shafran cited the belief that 'the day of ultimate reckoning may be upon us far sooner than we imagine, just as fish swimming freely in the water may find themselves captured suddenly in the hungry fishmonger's net—and . . . we dare not live lives of spiritual leisure on the assumption that there will always be time for repentance when we grow old'. He argued on religious grounds that the ritual 'is an opportunity for self-sensitization to our need for repentance'. He counted himself as modern as the next person, but complained:

All too often we moderns tend to view ancient Jewish laws, customs and rituals as quaint relics of the distant past evoking, at most, warm and nostalgic feelings of ethnic identity. But, as a closer look at Kapporos and Tashlich suggest, there is a world of difference between Tevya's celebration of 'Tradition!' for tradition's sake [in *Fiddler on the Roof*] and the deep meanings that lie in the rites and rituals of Jewish religious life. (Shafran 2010)

An issue, at least for cultural scholars, is that the broad term *minhag* does not discriminate between rites, rituals, initiations, ceremonies, and customs that are enacted as parts of localized traditions. Much as the *minhag* compilations provide a rich source of centuries-old evidence of ethnic practices for Jewish cultural studies, ethnological distinctions are useful for objectifying and broadening the understanding of tradition as lived experience. Emphasis on 'custom' in *minhag* may imply a practice that people follow unthinkingly rather than performing it with the idea of conveying symbols and values. Rituals are typically regarded as events condensed in time that are repeatable, structured, expressive, performed, and intentionally symbolic (Bronner 2004: 17–29; Rappaport 1992: 249, and 1996 [1979]; Snoeck 2006). Ritual exaggerates and symbolizes relationships by putting them on display in an event that is separated from mundane activity; it is often framed as 'time out of time' in which participants and their audiences expect words and actions to be symbolically significant (see e.g. Beattie 1966: 65; Bell 1992: 197–223; Leach 1968: 524; Shepard 1973: 196). Embracing this notion of ritual involving symbolic action and embodying social contract, anthropologist Roy Rappaport asserts that ritual is the 'fundamental social act upon which human society is founded' (Rappaport 1992: 254). While custom is an activity that is performed with regularity, and could include rituals, it is commonly, as folklorist Richard Sweterlitsch has noted, 'a vast aggregate of human behavior' that is usually described as part of the ordinary routine in people's lives (1997: 168). Ritual breaks everyday routine, creates a different space and time, and establishes an *extra*ordinary action or symbol as a guide to daily practice (Abrahams 1986).

An application of this idea is evident in the so-called Lubavitch Mitzvah Mobile: a brightly coloured van driven through or parked in Jewish neighbourhoods with the purpose of attracting Jews to relate to their Jewish identity by performing a ritual act. The yeshiva students travelling in the vehicle ask passers-by if they are Jewish; if the answer is yes, they request the individual to engage in a ritual, such as putting on *tefilin* or making a *berakhah* (blessing). Ethnographer Debra Renee Kauffman observes that these repeated scenes convey the message that ritual observances, apparently out of step with everyday routine, actually define daily living and personal identity. She finds it significant that unselfconscious engagement with tradition in the ritual is essential to the deepening of Jewish self-awareness: 'Dressed in their black suits and hats and with untrimmed beards, these recruiters offer no explanations for ritual behavior—potential recruits are just encouraged to act' (1991: 26). The actions are supposed to be transformative, signalling an expressive moment.

Ritual acts also hold social attention and can be organized with outcomes in mind to rally a community behind a cause or publicize a group's values and concerns. Modern institutions and individuals often create rituals by introducing, scripting, and staging symbolic events within a ceremonial frame (Belasco 2009; Ochs 2007; Rubin 2009; Ruttenberg 2009; Schwartzman and Francesca 2004). Rather than imagining that rituals are repeated by blindly following precedent, the idea of individuals and groups scripting and framing events to communicate meaning through ceremony introduces agency to the cultural process (Bronner 2010a; Handelman 2006; Mechling 1980; Sax 2006). Yael Zerubavel (1997) provides an example of ritual innovation in her historical ethnography, namely the introduction by secular Israeli youth of the holiday eve bonfire into Lag Ba'omer celebrations. The Talmud refers to a plague that wiped out 24,000 of Rabbi Akiva's students between Passover and Shavuot, also known as the *omer* period

(BT *Yev.* 62b). Lag Ba'omer is celebrated on the thirty-third day because on that day the plague ended and students stopped dying. An alternative historical connection to Lag Ba'omer with Zionist overtones is the legendary reconquering of Jerusalem by Bar Kokhba's army during the Jewish revolt in the second century CE (Zerubavel 1997: 97). Organizers of the bonfires in the 1920s explained their significance as a representation of fires kindled by Hebrew 'freedom fighters' during the revolt, camping on mountains and communicating by beacons with other rebel groups to inform them of the movements of Roman legions (Zerubavel 1997: 101).

Zerubavel points out that Bar Kokhba's army was ultimately defeated on the fast day of Tishah Be'av, the day commemorating the destruction of the First and Second Temples. The joyous lighting of bonfires in honour of Bar Kokhba's Jerusalem victory shifts the ritual context of the revolt from a grim fast day to a festive occasion, thus transforming lamentation over Bar Kokhba's ultimate defeat into the celebration of a victorious moment in the Zionist discourse of the struggle for liberation. The ritual of bonfire kindling takes on added significance because wood is a relatively scarce resource in the Middle East, and Israeli culture treats the planting of trees as a major patriotic act. The gathering of wood in preparation for the ritual becomes a sign of empowerment for Israeli youth. Zerubavel observes that 'In the days preceding Lag ba-Omer, children begin to look for scraps of wood and carefully hide or protect their findings because of the harsh competition over a limited supply. Humorous Lag ba-Omer lore describes the parents' need to protect their furniture from their children's overly zealous efforts to find materials for the bonfire' (1997: 102). The point is that the memory of the Bar Kokhba revolt merges with the 'zealous' spirit of the Zionist youth movement: Zerubavel finds that the ritual reinforces the symbolic continuity between the ancient fighters and Hebrew youth. An added dimension is the frequent burning of the effigy of a leading enemy in the bonfires (Hitler during the 1940s, Abdel Nasser during the 1950s). The symbolic burning of villainous destroyers of the Jews may have a precedent of burning effigies of the Jews' archenemy Haman on Purim, but in the new context it is introduced as a novel, festive component. Zerubavel concludes that the result is that 'The themes of courage, success, and revenge have become central to the commemoration of the Bar Kokhba revolt, thereby blurring the memory of the massacre, destruction, and exile it brought upon the Jews' (1997: 102). Supporting the Zionist themes are songs and stories that narrate the redefinition of the holiday and highlight the bonfire as its central ritual observance (Zerubavel 1997: 99).

The term 'initiation' is important in the terminology of ritual because it refers specifically to changes in status and therefore draws attention to the transformative power of ritual. Initiation expresses a transition from one life stage to another or from outsider to insider, and for some Jewish commentators, it is the main source of *minhagim* (Fox 1979: p. vii). Rites constitute another subset of ritual fulfilling religious or magical functions (Pentikäinen 1997: ii. 734–5), but the concept of 'rite of passage', introduced by Arnold van Gennep in 1908, suggests a specific tripartite structure for initiatory events that move through distinct phases of separation, transition (or liminality), and incorporation or return (Bronner 2008–9; Myerhoff 1982; Van Gennep 1960). In the analysis of Jewish experience, rite connotes a sacred or magico-religious connection to transformation, while ritual as a symbolic form expressively embodying the social contract can be secularized and objectified (Bell 1997: 61–90; Burkert 1996 [1983]; Girard 1997 [1977]; V. W. Turner 1967, 1969, 1982).

Ethnologists often refer to ceremony, in conjunction with ritual, as an organized event, such as a commemoration requiring reverence or special attention (Bronner 2008–9). A ceremony's defining characteristic is that it is a formal act or observance, although as a whole it may not exhibit the structure or sacred qualities of rites. Nonetheless, along with festival, celebration, and holiday as cultural genres, ceremony may contain a number of discrete rituals (Turner 1982: 22–3). Of all the terms related to *minhag*, 'tradition' represents most broadly the precedence of certain actions or ideas, or more generally stands for continuity with the past. It differs from laws and rules by being socially constituted (its derivation from the Latin *tradere*, for handing down or over, suggests oral or socially informal exchange) rather than officially inscribed, and it is often expressed as cultural norms or conventional knowledge (Bronner 1998: 9–72, and 2009). Tradition is often coupled with ritual because both connote the precedence and repetition of localized social convention. They both feed the perception that conduct of life, and the cultural norms, symbols, and expectations guiding it, are subject to variation, change, and innovation.

In many societies Jewish ritual often stands out among the different ethnic traditions because of its deviation from prevalent national customs by working with a distinctive calendar (lunar), by its life-course milestones (circumcision and bar mitzvah), and by origin (ancient Israel). If rabbinic sources underscore the importance of custom in giving practical expression to Jewish beliefs and in framing Jewish identity as an all-encompassing experience, a related argument is that popular and anthropological literature implies the exoticism, anachronism, and clannishness of Jews by assigning their practices to the category of ritual (Boyarin 1996: 138–9; Bronner 1998: 132–7; Judd 2007; Moltke 1997). Recognizing the importance of distinctive rituals, particularly in museum displays, nineteenth-century Jewish scholars could appear defensive about characterizing Jews by their rituals because of the association of these with secrecy and even diabolicalness. In response, they strove to present the Jewish world as a civilization marked by artistic and intellectual contributions or as a tradition and faith comparable to other modern religions (J. Cohen and R. I. Cohen 2008; Glick 1982; Kirshenblatt-Gimblett 1998: 79–130). The tendency to categorize Jewish practice as naturally ritualized is evident, however, in the popular taxonomy of Jewish activities as prefaced by 'ritual': bath, slaughter, head covering, dress, food, object, law—and, in antisemitic literature, murder.

With the modern shift in defining ritual from an exotic event suggesting superstitious, controlled, or irrational content to the behavioural basis for organizing experiences that all people undergo out of social and psychological necessity, scholars applied a more neutral and expansive rhetoric involving terms such as interaction, framing, social construction, and identity. Introducing the field of ritual studies, Ronald L. Grimes observed in 1996 that 'Much that would not have been regarded as ritual three decades ago now appears, either literally or metaphorically, to be ritual. Ritual can seem to exist in strictly circumscribed spaces (as if it were hiding in the corners of decrepit churches), and yet, almost magically, it can be everywhere, functioning as the very lifeblood of individuals and societies' (Grimes 1996: p. xiv). In the period in which Grimes observed a change in ritual studies, an elastic conceptualization of ritual arose that emphasized the repetitive framing of symbolic activity rather than the criteria of ancient lineage or magico-religious context. Examples interpreted as Jewish ritual events whose ritualistic qualities imbue the activities with transformative significance include Jewish summer campfire programmes as identity renewals and Israeli youth embarking on backpacking pilgrimages at an expected time in the life course (C. Noy 2006; Sales and Saxe 2003; Zerubavel 1997: 114–37). While this elastic approach emphasizing process and context has broadened the range of practices considered as ritual by freeing the notion from religious and historical restrictions, it has also raised questions about how self-conscious participants are in the organization of such events and in communicating their meaning as ritual.

With process and context as its defining characteristics among other forms of framed, repetitive behaviour, ritual is evident throughout daily life and critical to the principles that guide that life as cultural experience. Frequently cited in this volume for epitomizing attention to process and context in interpretations of cultural events as ritual, even if participants in those events do not recognize them as such, is the work of social scientists Victor Turner, Erving Goffman, and Clifford Geertz. These figures at the forefront of the pivotal 'interactionist' ethnographic movement of the 1960s and 1970s placed ritual at the centre of cultural analysis, labelling its symbols as representative of the conflicts and paradoxes of the larger society (Grimes 2006: 384–7). Scholars in the movement commonly applied the dramaturgical rhetoric of actors, stages, and audiences to describe these scenes as examples of symbolized performance (Bronner 1988). The new analytical rhetoric suggested that participants' behaviour and communication with one another and with the audience created meaning anew, rather than following a predefined script. Instead of separating the spoken word as text from the actions that it was accompanied by, these scholars encouraged the treatment of the whole scene as a cultural text that could be read for symbolism and structure. Using their work, a host of daily non-religious activities were analysed as ritual and interactive cultural text, including play, dance, drama, and joking in modern industrialized societies (McCurdy et al. 2004; Silverman and Rader 2005).

Twenty-first-century museum exhibitions at major institutions such as the Jewish Museum in New York, the Jewish Historical Museum in Amsterdam, the Contemporary Jewish Museum in San Francisco, and the Philadelphia Museum of Jewish Art, particularly of new artistic (and often abstract) interpretations of ritual objects, have fuelled interactionist thinking about ritual among public viewers who were formerly accustomed to musing on historic Judaica suggestive of continuity from an ancient past (Belasco 2009; Contemporary Jewish Museum 2009; Sachs and van Voolen 2004; Singer 2007, 2009). Arnold Eisen, chancellor of the Jewish Theological Seminary, commented in a catalogue for the Jewish Museum's exhibition entitled *Reinventing Ritual*:

Ritual has made a comeback of late. After decades (indeed, centuries) of denigration in the West as behavior that is hopelessly stereotyped, formulaic, repetitive, and largely boring, after unceasing put-down as rote action that stifles creativity and innovation, or as legalism that inhibits genuine feeling, or as mere 'ritualism' that stands in the way of true human relationship and blocks the way to authentic encounter with God—after all of that, we find ourselves in 2009 at a moment when ritual is once again receiving its due as an essential element of culture . . . The abiding chutzpa of Judaism—its central claim that the world is not good enough and that we can make it and ourselves better, with God's help—imperceptibly inspires contemporary Jewish creativity and performance. (Eisen 2009: pp. xi, xiii)

The interactionist movement in cultural studies also owed a debt to the analytical work on Jewish ritual by Theodor Gaster and Raphael Patai who, working in different parts of the Jewish world, highlighted the importance of the performative context of the events and of the relationship to local societies (Gaster 1955; Patai 1960: 20–2, 1983: 17–44). They were concerned about the survival of traditions more than about innovation, but they helped promote the understanding of the process of ritualization as a social action strategically applied in various situations, and countered the popular view of Jewish ritual as primitive or functionless (Grimes 1982: 133–59). Gaster, for example, in *Thespis* (1961), linked Jewish ritual and myth to dramas circulating in Middle Eastern communities about seasonal transitions. In *The Holy and the Profane* (1955) he insisted that 'The Jews were not mere "copycats" and did not borrow mechanically. The characteristic trait of Jewish folklore is a genius for infusing into originally "alien" material a new and more spiritual meaning and significance born of their own distinctive heritage and tradition' (Gaster 1955: p. xi). Patai meanwhile declared the ethnographic priority involved in the study of Jewish culture: 'The ethnologist working on a Jewish community has to take into account the special circumstances in which such a community lives', or in other words its local context and intercultural relations (Patai 1983: 27).

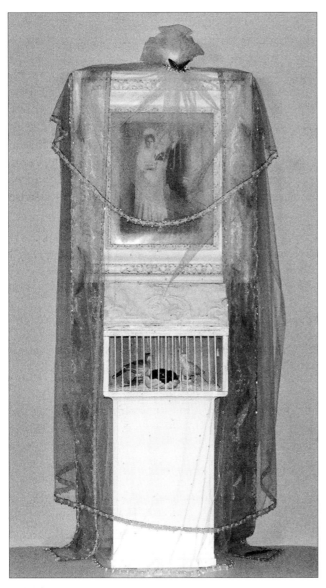

Figure 1 *To Part No More*. Mixed media art by Kym Hepworth of Savannah, Georgia, featured in the exhibition *Wimpel! Wrapped Wishes* at the Philadelphia Museum of Jewish Art, 2010. Hepworth explains her representation of the *wimpel* (sash used for binding the Torah scroll) in the piece as part of a wedding canopy with paradoxes characteristic of ritual: 'Here, the house/ birdcage motif represents continuity, security, and hope for the future. However, there are cracks in this foundation and the overall stability of the structure is threatened by the tension of entrapment and anxiety of abandonment.' *Photo: Robin Miller. Reproduced by courtesy of Kym Hepworth*

Other connections to the interactionist perspective on ritual and culture emerge from research into Jewish ritual or from theorizing that is contextualized by the ethnographer's Jewish background. Israeli scholar Dan Ben-Amos's influential definition of 'folklore in context' as 'artistic communication in small groups', which came as a response to the emphasis on textual sources in the interpretation of folk traditions, was undoubtedly influenced by his familiarity with the complexities of Jewish communities and of ritual performances (Ben-Amos 1971, 1982). Ben-Amos was a contributor to a paradigm-shifting volume, *Toward*

New Perspectives in Folklore (Paredes and Bauman 1972) that heralded approaches focusing on culture as performance, along with German Jewish folklorist Roger D. Abrahams, who referred to rituals as enactments to be analysed situationally and rhetorically (Abrahams 1980: 14; see also Abrahams 1968, 1972, 1977, 2005). The contextual orientation in more recent works is evident in historical studies, too, such as Ivan Marcus's study of medieval Jewish rituals of childhood, in which he conceptualizes ritual broadly as 'gestures' in his reference to ritual as 'all conventional gestures that are routinely expressed in the life of a particular group', rather than restricting himself to religious events in the synagogue (1996: 4; see also Geffen 1993; Goldberg 2003; Marcus 2004). The Jewish subject, having been stripped of its physical, racial component, raises questions for contemporary cultural studies scholars of boundary and identity maintenance, evident in anthropologist Harvey E. Goldberg's important twenty-first-century analysis of Jewish life-cycle rituals: 'Can one speak of "the Jews" in the absence of a centralized authority with the power to determine "what Judaism is," and when scholars writing about "Jewish tradition" now recognize that they are dealing with phenomena whose contents and boundaries are fluid?' (2003: 11).

Influenced by a preoccupation with difference and boundary maintenance, both Jewish and non-Jewish commentators often overlook the way that Jews adapt to, or participate in, local traditions and deal with the controversies that arise from hybridizing or acculturative processes (see Agnieszka Jagodzińska's chapter on Polish Jewish funerary tradition). Indeed, one of the issues that arises from the interpretation of ritual revision is the way that shared or imported practices become judaized, ethnicized, exalted, or stigmatized (Abrahams 1980). Such practices may be perceived as Jewish by both Jews and non-Jews, even though the structures and symbols are similar to those in non-Jewish culture (see Michael Hoberman's chapter on Jewish traditions at New England boarding schools, and Rachel Sharaby's chapter on Ethiopian marriage rituals in Ethiopia and Israel). With the additional connection made between Jewish practice and ancient lineage, particularly in the Middle East, emergent rituals that are either socially constituted or individually composed, and that serve non-sacred as well as religious purposes, may not receive the analytical attention they deserve for an understanding of Jewish identity (see Gail Labovitz's chapter on the feminist liturgy of *berit ahuvim*, and Nina Spiegel's chapter on the Dalia dance festivals in Israel). In sum, contextualizing the changes and adaptations of, and the conflicts and debates over, ritual reveals various transitions—between generations, among contemporary factions, between homeland and destination, between religious and secular functions, and among sources of authority, for example—that make up the cultural experience that people call Jewish.

When viewed from the perspective of interaction and lived experience, Jewish rituals take on a different look and forms of analysis that are far more complex than the mere bifurcation of *minhag* into biblical and post-biblical custom, or the engrossment in pre-modern sources (Eisen 1998: 8–10). Taking away the organizing principle of biblical source, rituals can be alternatively summarized by their cultural connection to contexts of (1) liturgy and prayer, (2) time and yearly cycle, (3) passage (or life course) and initiation, and (4) performance and practice. This is not to say that the sources in text and antiquity are immaterial; they have a strong bearing on the perception and enactment of rituals. A factor in the integration of text and context in analysis is the growth of Jewish field-based studies of the multiplicity of Jewish culture, defined as people's daily life and conduct at home and in the street as well as in the synagogue (Avrutin et al. 2009; Bronner 2010b; Gonen 1994; Mikdash-Shamilov 2002; Shwartz-Be'eri 2000; Slapak 2003). In Harvey E. Goldberg's survey of ethnographic approaches to Jewish culture, he notes that 'Anthropology was suspicious in its formative period of attaching too much weight to written sources, or to the interpretations offered by literati of the rituals and mores of their own traditions' (Goldberg 2003: 6; see also Hertzog et al. 2010; D. Noy 1980; Patai 1960), but disciplinary changes, including the scholarly acceptance of group members studying themselves close to home and the de-emphasis of racial factors in cultural analysis, encouraged more Jewish ethnography promulgated by Jews. Goldberg notes that these shifts allowed Jewish cultural researchers to view 'texts as formative components in social life', while incorporating the 'basic insight of social science that thought, speech, and writing often follow from behavior, rather than being the "reason why" people do things' (Goldberg 2003: 6). Accordingly, contributors to this volume have religio-historical as well as ethnological perspectives, but they primarily ask questions about process, function, symbol, and constructed meaning. In asking how and why Jews create rituals, they also examine the ways in which Jews revise, and transform, their world (Sax 2006: 474–6).

Liturgy and Prayer

The concern for textual sources is most evident in the ritual category of liturgy and prayer. It includes the forms of congregational and individual prayer, as well as the attire, gestures, and incantations that ritualize the content of worship. Much of the attention to liturgy and prayer has focused on the synagogue as an institutional context that frames the ritual components of services materially and socially (Elbogen 1993). The material aspects of ritualized behaviour include the exterior of the synagogue that sets it apart from domestic architecture, and within the interior, the physical guides to practice, such as the expectations of expressive behaviour around the ark, the *bimah* (Torah-reading platform), and the Torah. Changing social factors that have received attention for structuring synagogue practice, and for raising controversy over gender relations, include the constitution of the *minyan* (traditionally ten adult males 13 years of age or older) and the existence of a *meḥitsah* separating men and women. Noticeable as a sign of transition in ritual participation is the growing trend among women in some circles to wear yarmulkes, *talit*, and *tefilin*—previously an exclusively male practice.

The connection between gendered ritual dress and prayer has led to considerable discussion, also found in this volume, on the role of the body in framing Jewish practice. This might include the regard for the deceased body in funerary rituals (see Jagodzińska's chapter on nineteenth-century debates in Polish Jewish communities); the body movements of Jewish *daven*ing as a contrast to the constrained, kneeling devotion in Catholic prayer; texts related to the laws of *nidah* (menstrual impurity), pregnancy, and childbirth (Wasserfall 1992; Weissler 1992); and the definition of the synagogue service as a male space—and by extension of other spaces such as the *mikveh* (ritual bath) as primarily female locations (Anijar 1999; Eilberg-Schwartz 1992; Gilman 1991; Konner 2009).

Ritual as symbolic knowledge and action figures prominently not only in the gendering of Jewish liturgical practice, but also in boundary maintenance between Jews and non-Jews and Orthodox and non-Orthodox Jews. This is especially evident in patterns such as the *ba'al teshuvah* movement (literally 'men of repentance' but figuratively, people who were not religious previously but have come to embrace Orthodox Judaism) that defy the modernist expectation that ritual observance should decline with modernization. In Debra Renee Kauffman's study of newly Orthodox women, known as *ba'alot teshuvah*, for example, Miriam tells her:

'*I have found meaning in all this ritual* . . . meaning I have never really had at any other time in my life. Torah has so much to say to me as a woman. My feelings about myself as a sexual person . . . the family purity laws are so in line with me as a woman . . . it is commanded that I not be sexually taken for granted, that I have two weeks each month for myself . . . It is mind-boggling to me to think that this wonderful Torah has known who I am as a woman for centuries.' (1991: 45; emphasis added)

She connects this meaning to *tseniut* (modesty) and sees its ritual presentation of a bodily self as a strategy for boundary maintenance:

'It's [*tseniut*] such a wonderful way of presenting oneself . . . it means modesty. It means you should present yourself as caring, soft-spoken, gentle, you know . . . in a feminine way. That's what orthodoxy is really all about. Tznius doesn't just apply to women; it's meant for all Jews. We are supposed to be separate, different, apart . . . different from a world that can do such things as a Holocaust.' (Kauffman 1991: 45; see also Falk 1998)

Questions about the ritual texts of the congregational service include the selection and performance of prayers, especially at the opening and closing of sections of the various services to mark time. One example is the prevalent use of the Kaddish for closing public services, since liturgical scholars point out that in antiquity it was not part of the synagogue ritual (Eisenberg 2004: 394; Lamm 1969: 149–74). As Ronald Eisenberg notes, 'The ancient custom of dismissing the assembly with the words of the *Kaddish* is still preserved in the *Kaddish de-*

Rabbanan (*Kaddish* of the Rabbis), which is recited in the synagogue after communal study. However, instead of being uttered by the teacher, the *Kaddish de-Rabbanan* is now recited by those mourners who are in attendance' (Eisenberg 2004: 394). In the tradition of the *minhagim* compilers, Eisenberg describes the emergence of the custom 'out of the practice of honoring a deceased scholar, at the close of the seven-day shivah period', although cultural studies scholars may note in the congregational response and in the rhetorical importance of the mourner's Kaddish in the service (and its relation to the *yizkor* [remembrance] memorial service) a symbolic value placed upon generational continuity as a key to reproducing Jewishness (Eisenberg 2004: 394; Lamm 1969: 153–61). Indeed, Kaddish is a ritual that carries over into the home and into individual practice, for example in lighting candles on the anniversary of the death of a relative (Lamm 1969: 201–5; Syme 2004: 207–8).

'Modeh ani', the thanksgiving blessing upon awakening, which precedes the ritual washing of hands for purity, can be said in bed because it does not contain divine names. Yet some sources suggest that before washing hands, one meditates on the prayer and then says it audibly after washing hands (Nulman 1993: 252). Observers have interpreted the ritual recitation upon awakening in different ways: Macy Nulman, in *The Encyclopedia of Jewish Prayer*, links its utterance, particularly popular with children, to an awareness of God with the beginning of each day, but Ronald Eisenberg in *The JPS Guide to Jewish Traditions* finds its enactment symbolic of a 'mini-resurrection' that occurs as the soul is returned to the body after sleep in keeping with Orthodox 'belief in both the future resurrection of the dead as part of the messianic redemption and in some form of immortality of the soul after death' (Eisenberg 2004: 120). Another thanksgiving benediction, 'Sheheheyanu' (the first distinctive word of the blessing meaning 'who has kept us in life'), is often featured in coming-of-age events and inventive ceremonies such as Simhat Bat, and is part of a recent trend to enrich joyous occasions with newly composed blessings and recitations (Cardozo 1982: 210; Marcus 2004: 106, 112; Wolowelsky 1997: 43–50).

Beyond the matter of the content and agency of the text there are questions of performance that have arisen in the synagogue as context and in the liturgy as content. Music as a ritual device, especially when accompanied by instruments or choirs, has raised debates since the early nineteenth century about attitudes towards halakhic issues relating to music and, by extension, to dance. In addition to spiritual and scriptural questions about the role of music and dance in Jewish liturgy (and about ritual specialists for them), their performance within that framework could be viewed as an ethnic boundary marker, and their exclusion contributed to the view that Jews were not creative or modern (Gilman 2008). Jewish historian Jonathan D. Sarna notes that 'questions concerning music in the synagogue have stood second only to questions concerning women in the synagogue as prime sources of disputation, dividing synagogues and sometimes even landing up in court' (2003: 195). The two issues overlapped in the rise of female cantors as ritual specialists in the late twentieth century (Heskes 1997; Slobin 2002: 112–34), but well before the liturgical disputes between the liberal and Orthodox wings of Judaism, controversies had broken out over the character of the music performed in the synagogue, and later about the role of instruments, especially the organ associated with Protestant churches. Music became a flash-point for intra-ethnic disputes, according to Sarna, because it was 'as tightly regulated as the synagogue ritual. Indeed, the music was inseparable from the ritual. Both were hallowed by tradition, what was called in Hebrew the *minhag*, the synagogue's ritual or custom as passed down from generation to generation' (2003: 195). The symbolic upshot of the disputes was that despite the hope that agreement on a musical standard in the liturgy would unite Jews in a common tradition, music, perhaps because of its performative ritual associations, had come to represent the division of Jews from one another, and from non-Jews, or lack thereof (Sarna 2003: 203; see also J. M. Cohen 2009; Hoffman and Walton 1993; Levine 1989; Shiloah 1992).

Outside the synagogue, various ritualized public commemorations after the Second World War in the Jewish world regularly included music and recitations for the victims of the Holocaust, Israeli independence, and the reunification of Jerusalem (Flam 1992: 170–8; Handelman and Katz 1990; Schuman et al. 2003). The new question that Seth Ward takes up in this volume is the rabbinic discourse over incorporating ritual components into synagogue liturgy for these modern events. Inside the synagogue, the question arose whether the memorialization of the major events could be included in the *yizkor* service that recognizes martyrs or whether they necessitated a separate liturgical ritual. In the case of Israel Independence Day, the blessings and activities (such as blowing the shofar) introduced into the service inside the synagogue provide a contrast to the parades, fireworks, fairs, and barbecues of the public celebration. Although prayer books were generally slow to change over time, the impact of the Holocaust and the formation of the State of Israel precipitated some of the most noticeable changes in newly composed siddurs for all the wings of Judaism (Harlow 1993). Focusing on the interaction of the rabbis as reflected in their discussion of the different ritualized texts, Ward traces the geographical, historical, and religious negotiation of the founding of the modern State of Israel by Jewish tradition.

Gail Labovitz, herself an ordained Conservative rabbi, engages in this volume what Sarna calls the major liturgical disputes of the modern period concerning the ritual roles and expertise of women. She focuses on the new feminist vision represented by Rachel Adler's revision of liturgy in her *berit ahuvim* for synagogue weddings (Adler 1998: 169–208). The implication of the revision is the resetting of the process of adjudicating Jewish law or halakhah. Labovitz notes that the intention behind using narratives found in prophetic texts, notably the

Figure 2 An example of the synagogue appropriation of Holocaust remembrance is the annual Reading of the Names, a twenty-four-hour vigil during which the names of Holocaust victims are read continuously. In this image, taken in the 1990s in Harrisburg, Pennsylvania, a member of the congregation reads names while the rabbi sitting behind her oversees the event. The display reads 'Unto Every Person There is a Name', a phrase from a poem by Ukrainian-born Israeli writer Zelda Shneurson Mishkowsky (1914–84). The six candles represent the *yahrzeit* memorials of the 6 million Jewish victims, and there are six plants symbolizing new life. *Reproduced by courtesy of the Jewish Federation of Greater Harrisburg*

book of Hosea, regarding the metaphorical marriage between God and Israel is to create halakhah as a communal practice ritually grounded in Jewish stories. She analyses the texts from a rhetorical perspective and considers, from a theological vantage point, their ritualized inclusive functions with a view to interpreting the connection of feminist halakhah to the changing notion of Jewish community.

Time and Yearly Cycle

Ritual's function of marking time is particularly evident in the reference of many Jewish practices to daily, weekly, and yearly recurrence. Ritual does more than structure quantities of time before and after the ritual; it reassures participants that the ordering of time will be ever-renewing and infuses this order with symbolic connections to nature and culture (Bell 1997: 102). A symbolic division is apparent in the establishment of the Jewish weekly cycle moving from the sacred to the profane, represented by the duality of the sabbath and workaday week (Eisenberg 2004: 125–54; Linke 1999: 81–100). Dietrich Harth notes the irony of rituals serving to suspend time and yet to emphasize it 'in order to establish that continuity of order called "tradition" that is meant to form a bulwark against the disintegration of community' (Harth 2006: 31). Mythological connections bet-ween Scripture and the organization of time have often been made using the story of the creation of day and night in Genesis (1: 1). In a form of metafolklore, Jews relate the Genesis narrative to the start of Jewish holidays on the evening before the calendrical day. Other ritual periods take their names from the time allotted for their completion: shiva and *sheloshim* are practices of seven and thirty days of mourning, respectively. Yet, as Jillian Gould points out in her essay, sitting shiva is a ritual that the residents of Jewish senior care institutions deem flexible, particularly in the context of dealing with their own mortality. The alternative popular choice, despite rabbinical protests, of three days as sufficient indicates supplanting one ritual number with another. Three, as folklorist Alan Dundes has pointed out, joins a quantity representing completeness (evident in the say-ing 'to begin on the count of three') to its magical associations in incantations (1968).

In her essay on Purim theatricals Jean Freedman examines the Jewish concep-tion of time—past and present, suspended and real—enacted in the ritualized drama associated with the holiday. She points out that Purim is a time of ritual reversal: participants revel in a lack of self-restraint customary in daily life and laugh at the sacred. Actors often publicly mock the rabbi in the skit (*purimshpil*) they perform, and congregants may ritually kidnap him or her and then raise a ransom from the congregation. Yet in referring to a historic event involving a Jew-ish response to oppression, Purim encourages the contemplation of present con-ditions: in recent times, for example, it has frequently invited references to the Holocaust. The stage is literally set with the reading of the Megillah, and the scripted play contains riffs of, and costumes from, contemporary popular culture. The hilarity dramatizes in a playful frame repressed conflicts about maintaining Jewishness while being assimilated into the accelerating modern world. Freed-man uses psychological ideas of projection to explain the revitalization of the *purimshpil* as a strategy of ritualizing modern Jewishness. She finds in her ethno-graphic case study of a Washington, DC performance that the new *purimshpil* is not so much re-creation as it is re-visioning.

The maintenance of Jewishness through the adaptation of ritual is also a cen-tral theme in Michael Hoberman's essay on Jews in New England boarding schools. Once excluded from these predominantly Protestant elite institutions, Jews might view their growing presence there as a sign of success. Faced with the double consciousness of being seen as 'like everyone else' and at the same time 'standing out' with a Jewish identity, even if it is secular, Jews in these boarding schools have relied on the 'time out of time' represented by the sabbath ritual to maintain balance in a precarious social environment that Hoberman suggests is a microcosm of complex modern society. Examining the hybridization of

Figure 3 Performers in a *purimshpil* from Foehrenwald, an international displaced persons camp in the American zone of occupation in Germany, pose after the Second World War. Their play script focused on the theme of combating antisemitism. *Reproduced by courtesy of Linda Schwab*

boarding-school and Jewish traditions, he emphasizes the importance of small-group dialogue centred on the ritualized meal rather than on candle-lighting and blessings. In this ritual process, Hoberman observes a grassroots strategy at work to revise the boarding-school legacy and thereby transform the elite cultural experience.

Whereas the sabbath meal is universally known in the Jewish world, Harvey E. Goldberg and Hagar Salamon draw attention to a celebration, Se'udat Yitro, that appears to be unique to Tunisian Jewry. It occurs on the Thursday of the week approaching the reading of the *parashah* (weekly portion) called 'Yitro', in January or February. Incorporating textual sources, their field-based study indicates that the celebration is associated with a personal life-cycle moment, marking the first time that boys hear the reading of the Ten Commandments. The essay reveals a subcategory of ritual in the yearly cycle that appears to be localized. Such rituals, including the previously mentioned Simhat Kohen (Goldberg and Salamon also mention the Sigd of the Beta Israel Ethiopian community and the Mimuna among Moroccan Jews), raise questions about the relationship of customs to local conditions, and about their perpetuation (or abandonment) as communities relocate or experience new social and economic circumstances. These rituals often present puzzles for which pieces are missing from the historical record. Goldberg and Salamon find that the ambiguity of the tradition attracted conscious intervention and structuring by local rabbis, resulting in regional variation. They weigh the various meanings given by the participants and chroniclers who emphasize Jewish time out of time, the overarching narrative of the Exodus that creates peoplehood, a religious coming of age, or relate a subcultural Tunisian heritage. Instead of lamenting the inability to pinpoint a definite origin or spell out a single meaning, the authors find that the vagueness surrounding the event and the variations it invites add to its attractiveness.

Because many Jewish observances in the yearly cycle are intended to be conducted in the home, participants may reinterpret the text or add symbolic actions to convey values of the gathered group. Cultural studies of Passover, in particular, have focused on variant performances of the Haggadah intended to convey social and political messages. An early model for the analysis of Jewish cultural adaptation and of changes in holiday rituals, for example, was produced by Beatrice S. Weinreich with data from probably the first systematic ethnographic questionnaire projects conducted by YIVO in 1928 and 1949. She reported in the post-war period amendments to Haggadot adding passages about the Holocaust in keeping with the theme of remembering in the seder. She also noted the invention in the 1920s of a 'new tradition', the Third Seder, framed as a secular ritual for Zionist and other political causes (Weinreich 1960: 355–60). But why would a group wanting, in Weinreich's words, 'to renounce the religious content of Judaism' retain the seder model of Passover? The answer is in part that the symbolic overlay of religion gave their political cause a Jewish character; another factor was the appropriation of the freedom theme of Exodus for a non-religious application. 'The development of the Third Seder', she insightfully wrote,

is an interesting illustration of the 'de-dogmatizing' of a religious holiday, plus the selection of certain formal elements of traditional ritual (the use of *a* Haggada) coupled with the invention of new ritual. In this development, we see very clearly reflected the situation of those Jews who, though continuing to renounce the intellectual and practical (or instrumental) aspects of the Jewish religion, seem to feel a need for some of its emotional content. (1960: 362; italics in original)

David Shuldiner has followed the Third Seder to the end of the twentieth century as a ritual of Jewish radicalism as much as a play on liberation, and Muky Tsur has analysed the process of composing Haggadot to express a collective memory of kibbutzim in Israel (Shuldiner 1999: 119–40; Tsur 2007). The rituals often have a transgressive quality because alterations to the expected actions of holiday observance draw attention to their symbolic content. Rabbi Rebecca T. Alpert, for example, reported the emergence of transgressive rituals in the 1980s in the first and second seders among lesbian Jews, who claim that 'there is as much place for lesbians in Judaism as for leavened bread at the Seder table' (1989: 2). What began as a response to a remark at a public lecture became formalized as the 'Crust of Bread at the Seder Table' midrash incorporated into Jewish lesbian Haggadot around the United States (Alpert 1997: 2). For some groups that felt that placing bread on the seder plate was too great a transgression, alternatives included leaving an open space on the seder plate marked as *makom* (place), a name for God that lacks gender, and placing an orange on top of the matzot to represent the status of homosexuals in Judaism (Alpert 1997: 2–3). These early examples of ritual as intentional social action, as well as the analysis of the strategic 'invention of new ritual', influenced many scholars, such as Shaul Kelner in this volume, who not only examine the function of marking time but also the representation of power relations and transformative intentions in ritual.

Passage and Initiation

In 'rites of passage' a kind of transformation takes place from one stage of life or social status to another. The changes that are marked by the ritual may be conspicuous transitions such as birth and death that participants feel compelled to mark, or else they are created through ritual, such as naming and consecration ceremonies. A processual question about both types is how the structure of these rituals facilitates passage; a psychological point can also be raised about why people feel that passage needs ritual help and why some communities ritualize some status changes that others do not. An example is the relatively modern haircutting ceremony for boys, usually at the age of 3. Called an *upshern* (Yiddish: 'to shear off') or *ḥalaka* (Arabic: 'haircut'), the ritual marks the beginning of formal Hebrew and Torah study, when the child is presented with cookies in the form of Hebrew letters, often covered in honey, to signify the sweetness of learning. Emphasizing a change in status from infant to student, the initiate will regularly wear a yarmulke and *tsitsit* after the ritual. This custom has not been universally adopted, but it is popular among the hasidim who particularly embrace the ceremony's symbolism of Torah study. The social construction of the ritual is evident in the fact that it is celebrated at home, and many families will hold it not on the boy's birthday but on the occasion of Lag Ba'omer, conceptualized as the 'scholars' holiday' and symbolically connected to the image of three as a quantity representing completeness because it falls on the thirty-third day of the *omer* period. Families may design the ceremony to include family members and rabbis taking turns cutting the child's hair and making charitable acts with the hair such as donating it to cancer victims or contributing money equivalent to the weight of the hair. Psychologically, the symbolism of cutting (as a sign of independence and maturity, as in cutting 'ties that bind'; as an expression of submission to social constraint by human shaping rather than letting hair go natural or wild; or in Freudian terms viewing the cutting of the upraised hair as a castrative act) comes into question, as well as the significance of shortening the hair to clearly distinguish a boy from a girl. A symbolic association is apparent of cutting as ritualized

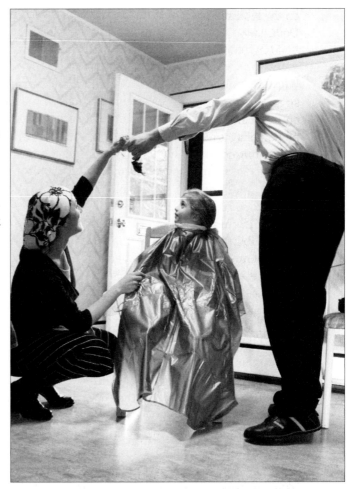

Figure 4 *Ḥalaka* ritual enacted by an Orthodox Sephardi family in Harrisburg, Pennsylvania, in 2009. The child's father on the right cut the hair while the mother on the left watched. Family members and rabbis were also called up to cut a lock of hair. *Photo: Simon Bronner*

action with the previous rite of passage of circumcision, particularly among some strictly Orthodox groups concerned for the maintenance of ethnic boundaries (Bilu 2003).

But then what is the relationship of haircutting to constructing a life-stage passage with entrance into formal schooling? Marc-Alain Ouaknin and Françoise-Anne Ménager suggest that the immersion in books is symbolically consistent with the gendering of cutting rituals: 'He goes from the maternal language, which is oral, to the paternal language, which is written' (2005: 48). In the speech typically made by the boy's father at the *upshern*, it is common to mention biblical allusions to human life as a tree and to apply the prohibition on eating fruit that grows on a tree for the first three years to cutting a child's hair (Lev. 19: 23). In staging the *upshern*, which is usually perceived as distinguishing Orthodox affiliation from others, parents communicate a passage not only in age, but also in piety. The child may echo this sentiment with the singing of a Hebrew song based on the biblical verse *Torah tsivah lanu mosheh* ('Moses prescribed the Torah to us'; Deut. 33: 4).

Many rituals condense a larger experience into a sequence of events that symbolize the desirability of certain changes or replace a real trauma with a manageable task that expresses the ability to overcome a challenge. Van Gennep (1960) suggests that life-cycle changes necessitate a tripartite structure representing entrance alone through the ritual separation of the individual, the symbolic completion of a task in the transitional phase, and status change with the support of a welcoming community (incorporation phase). The rites function as guides to the initiates and their communities in the process of transition. Gennep postulates, for example, that birth rites at the beginning of life emphasize incorporation into the community while at the end of life, separation from the deceased becomes central. In rites relating to the move from childhood to adulthood, when family responsibilities are especially significant, the liminal or transitional phase will be prominent. Mircea Eliade argues that the symbolism packed into initiatory rituals represents an enactment of birth, death, and rebirth in an altered state, thus marking a fresh start in the new phase of life (1958). Often in this process, the past life is labelled profane and the new one sacred. To hold attention and to lend symbolic significance to the event, the paradoxes or conflicts of the society are frequently made evident in the transitional stage, suggesting that emergence into the new status promises clarity and unity (Myerhoff 1982).

The complexity of rites of passage can be seen as evidence of the stress associated with the transition. Therefore, the wedding is often elaborate and multi-episodic because of the perception that the move from being an individual to forming a union—and family—involves greater risk than other transitions in life. The special dress and number of attendants for the bride have been interpreted in many ritual observances as conveying the meaning that the woman bears extra risk, especially if she is the one moving into the groom's family household (Bar'am-Ben Yossef 1998; Cohen Grossman 2001). At the end of life, the complexity of burial and mourning shows the strain that the loss of a community member, exalted as a deceased ancestor, places on the living left behind. Ritual, then, compensates for conflict in the society as well as potentially creating tension and exhibiting contradiction.

Life-cycle rituals such as *berit milah* and bar and bat mitzvah have drawn cultural attention for defining ethnic affiliation and yet they are also among the most contested of Jewish rituals for different reasons (Bronner 2008–9; S. J. D. Cohen 2005; Glick 2005; Gollaher 2001; Mark 2003; Sabar 2006; Kline Silverman 2006). The more durable tradition is ritual circumcision (Schauss 1950: 11–62). In anthropological literature, it has gained notice for being so resistant to change and for highlighting the symbolic importance of male genital alteration as a sign of Jewishness. Anthropologist Leonard Glick steps away from a typical cultural relativist position by arguing that parents do not have the right to 'impose nonessential, irreversible surgery on him before he is able to decide for himself that he wants his genitals permanently altered' (Glick 2005: 280). He is puzzled by the fact that 'practices mandated or sanctioned in the Hebrew Scriptures—animal sacrifice, slavery, polygamy, rites of purification' have been abandoned, but circumcision remains a pillar of Jewish identity in many locations, particularly in the West (Glick 2005: 281). Leaving aside the issue of ritual circumcision, which has its own separate bookshelf, his query about the choices and negotiations that occur between the application of textual sources and modern practice is one that authors in this volume take up.

The subject of bar and bat mitzvah, with its own extensive bibliography, is also not a focus here, although its relatively recent rise as a localized *minhag* (see further below) makes it worthy of attention in connection to the discussion of structure and process. Questions concerning gender, family relations, secularization, materialism, and coming of age that circulate about this custom are also apparent in the controversies and functions of the Jewish wedding and funeral, which are approached from fresh ethnographic perspectives by the contributors to this volume. Unlike *berit milah*, the bar mitzvah is not prescribed in the Torah and has not become universally adopted in the Jewish world. The scholarly consensus is that as a religious ceremony it goes back to medieval German local practices which diffused to eastern Europe, but there it did not acquire the elevated or standardized status it now has in western Europe and America (Marcus 1996: 119–26, 2004: 82–123; Pollack 1971: 59–62). In the West it gained reputation in the twentieth century as a rare ritual for passage from adolescence into adulthood in industrialized societies and for its flexible, often individualized, exhibition of material excess in the manner of a wedding for a family member considered by the host societies to be under-age (Bronner 2008–9; Joselit 1994: 89–118).

The interpretations heaped on the bar mitzvah provide a benchmark for the meaning of weddings and funerals perceived by different parts of society—Jewish and non-Jewish. Frequently interpreted sociologically as a sign of economic arrival for Jews, a persecuted minority group, showing success through material display and the last opportunity to declare Jewishness publicly (in capitulation to the possibility of an interfaith wedding later), the bar mitzvah has also received psychological analysis as a ritual embodying father–son conflicts and the crisis of masculinity for Jewish boys feminized, or perceived as such, by modern complex society (Arlow 1951; Bronner 2008–9; J. Davis 2003). Furthermore, for Jews it is another ritual that brought into the open the tension between home and synagogue (especially with early rabbinic opposition to the popular bar mitzvah on the grounds that it did not have a basis in Torah or it signalled for participants an end to religious education) as well as between the different levels of acceptance and preparation in various wings of Judaism (Sherwin 1990: 150; Spiro 1977). It also begs comparison with the Jewish wedding, with its parallel rituals such as lifting

Figure 5 In this scene from a bar mitzvah reception in New York City in 2009, the father is lifted in a chair in the style of a wedding custom after his bar mitzvah son. But in a symbolic distinction, the father positions himself to 'ride the chair like a bull'. *Photo by Simon Bronner*

up the child coming of age in a chair, showering him or her with sweets, and, in some traditions, candle-lighting by relatives.

Although the bar mitzvah is often called a rite of passage because it is popularly viewed as an entrance into adulthood through reaching religious majority, the ceremony does not follow the conventional model of ritual passage with its tripartite structure of separation, transition, and incorporation. One would expect much transition in a coming-of-age practice, but the bar mitzvah involves an inordinately long preparation time. The boy is not separated during the event and is not presented as being in a liminal state. His main religious task is to read a Torah portion and give a speech rather than to engage in an initiatory act with male elders. The ceremony also lacks the stage of incorporation in most non-Orthodox settings: as sociologist Judith Davis noted (2003), it fails to mark a change in status or passage to another stage, for the initiate is not granted adult privileges outside congregational life. It is nevertheless symbolically significant in it thematizing of the boy's and girl's special interests, thereby relating the tensions between Jewish identity and popular cultural expectations of the youngster. For many commentators, the bar mitzvah represents a ritual of finality rather than transition, as in many circles it marks the end of Jewish education (Marcus 2004: 122; Rosenberg 1965; Spiro 1977: 397; Telushkin 1991: 612).

This volume contains several related studies of the structure, function, and symbolism of passage in weddings and funerary practices, particularly as they raise controversies as revised rituals in different national contexts. Vanessa Ochs discusses the contemporary rise of legal same-sex commitment ceremonies and the emerging discourse on judaizing such ceremonies when they involve Jewish participants, again both inside and outside the synagogue. Following her influential book *Inventing Jewish Ritual* (2007), on modern ritual innovations, particularly in North America, she details here the rhetorical strategies evident in ceremonies adapted from heterosexual Jewish weddings and from what she calls the evolving tradition of 'reconstructed' ceremonies that supplant the standard structure and symbolism with 'liberal' values while still being invested in Jewish tradition. She locates a longer timeline for same-sex ceremonies than may be apparent from recent legalization, and finds that marriage ritual over that period was a central arena where ethical battles over the compatibility of homosexuality with Jewish law and identity were fought (Alpert 1998; Balka and Rose 1989; Kaplan-Mayer 2004: 11; Schwartzman and Francesca 2004: 58–60). The background for ritual controversies over commitment and revised marriage ceremonies is the community's response to the formation of separate gay Jewish congregations and the acceptance of openly homosexual rabbis who are redefining, and re-visioning, the 'normality' of this Jewish sexual taboo (Eisenberg 2004: 58–61; Greenberg 2005).

Both Irit Koren and Gail Labovitz deal with the impact of feminist thinking in reshaping Jewish marriage. Labovitz, as described earlier, examines the effect of narratives in a revised feminist liturgy for marriage. Koren looks at the special case of Israel, where she finds Modern Orthodox brides taking agency in shifting the content of the traditional wedding to be more empowering for women. She analyses the negotiation among, and outlooks of, the different participants in the ritual process, including parents, groom, and rabbis. Rachel Sharaby also examines the Israeli context where Jews constitute a majority culture to assess the accommodations and symbolic shifts made by Ethiopian immigrants and their children in marriage rituals, which they consider to be the most critical identity marker among all the rites of passage. She finds that the change in the ritual epitomized the contrast between the Ethiopian experience and that of other groups absorbed into Israeli society, and she analyses the ways in which young people have established a hybridized Ethiopian wedding to navigate between inherited and newly adopted traditions.

Another multi-contextual study is provided by Alanna E. Cooper, who considers the mourning rituals of Bukharan Jews in Uzbekistan, Israel, and the United States. She looks at the evolution of what Bukharan Jews call a *yushva*, a mourning event that differs from sitting shiva. Unlike American and western European mourning rituals, which are conducted as affairs that are relatively cut off from the everyday flow of life, among Bukharan Jews they are tightly woven into the fabric of daily living. Despite changes in cultural life from Uzbekistan to Israel and the United States, the *yushva* has been a constant presence, and Cooper asks why it has endured while other rituals have faded away. She finds that the *yushva*, which serves as a specific occasion for reflection on the past through spontaneous, public oration, also promotes contemplation about lost eras in communal life. In the ritual space and time it creates, ethnic Bukharan Jews have a renewable forum to cope with the imminence of change.

Whereas Cooper moves across continents to trace the same ritual in different contexts, Jillian Gould views the evolution of a socially shared memorial event at a single institution in Toronto. The broad significance of her work is her recording of the dialogue among participants in an institutional context that moved the urge to memorialize the dead in a Jewish manner from a traditional shiva to a 'gathering' (see Lamm 1969). By focusing her analytical lens on a specific situation within the senior centre, she can pinpoint the factors that guided the ritual process for a group segregated by age. Their older status meant that the meaning of the traditional shiva to which they were accustomed shifted as the mourners confronted their own imminent death and found the symbolism of the shiva potentially disturbing; their agency to revise what was at first introduced by younger institutional staff into a memorial gathering revealed a new modern context in which the elderly constitute a separate community with its own symbolically significant rituals.

Taking the reader back in time to explore the possibilities of a historical ethnography of ritual, Agnieszka Jagodzińska examines nineteenth-century documents and objects revealing contentious interaction among the different Jewish factions in Warsaw. She discovers in Polish Jewish periodicals a fierce running debate over the conduct of funerary ritual. At issue was the Jewish response to the idea of progress promoted in the European Enlightenment and its Jewish version, the Haskalah. The discourse reveals a double consciousness characteristic of diaspora minority groups in which the formation of identity and world-view is influenced by the conflict between the self-awareness, heritage, and values of the group, on the one hand, and reaction to the way that outsiders perceive the group on the other (Allen 2002; Bial 2005: 16–21; Daval 1996). Jagodzińska finds that factionalism arose in the mid-nineteenth century between the traditional forces and the progressive, upwardly aspiring Jews, who weighed the social and economic implications of an elite Catholic majority viewing them as backward or superstitious against the need to maintain their community through the continuity of tradition. Jewish rituals of burial became central to this issue because of the public view of cemeteries, the symbolic value of attitudes towards the body, the cultural contrast in the question of religious authority over the handling of the deceased, and the political contexts of Polish nationalism and class relations. Besides its exposure of an often overlooked debate over progressivism and Enlightenment in Poland, Jagodzińska's essay adds an important consideration of the intellectual construction and myriad perceptions of *ritualism*, as well as giving a historical ethnography of ritual within a group.

Performance and Practice

Many of the rituals described so far have audiences oriented towards a staged activity, be it in the ritual space of the *bimah* in a synagogue or at the formalized dinner table of a home seder. Roles are assigned and enacted, often by ritual specialists such as the rabbi and cantor, or by ordinary members of the group such as a mourner reciting Kaddish (see Heilman 1998; Starr Sered 1992). Participants may not be aware of the function of performative roles and settings in the ritual because of the cognitive tendency to separate ritual, considered meditative or replicative, from theatre, with its associations of being artistic or individualistic (Grimes 2006: 381). Ritual draws much of its power, however, not only from its patterned repetition, but also from its dramatic, affective quality. On occasions such as Passover and Purim, social expectations of improvisation and adaptation of enacted texts rendered in a personalized style within a sequenced order of events make performers out of participants. Performance, in the sense of stylized actions that draw attention to themselves by their contrast to mundane gesture and speech, can also act to signify a symbolic message of fellowship and spirituality (Heilman 1987). If those reading the Haggadah out loud at Passover around the dinner table are unwitting performers, the intentional staging of activities as ritual occasions, such as the dance festivals described by Nina Spiegel that are meant to be annual events, and the political street rallies discussed by Shaul Kelner that invoke Jewish holidays normally observed at home or in the synagogue, bring into analytical view the emotionally affective, and socially effective, theatricals of ritual organized as a strategy of persuasion.

The organizers of staged events often do not promote them with the label of ritual even though they intend them to be ritualesque by engaging audience and participants together in a shared purpose (Goffman 1967: 5–45, 1974: 43–58; Handelman 2006: 571–8; Santino 2009; see also Michael Hoberman's use of the 'ritualesque' concept in his chapter). In the use of ritual components, they often aim to elevate the event from fleeting entertainment or demonstration to a momentous occasion, and a question that arises in Shaul Kelner's chapter is about the interactional and contextual factors that rendered the political movement for Soviet Jewry effective. An example is the linking of the ritual event of *hakafot* (dancing in circles with the Torah) on Simhat Torah with exuberant street demonstrations to allow emigration for Soviet Jews during the 1970s. Part of the political message given was that the Soviet Union prevented Jews from participation and rejoicing on the festival. Besides the rare use of demonstrative dancing in Jewish religious holiday observance, the Save Soviet Jewry movement made a textual connection with the traditional Sukkot invocation of *hoshia na* ('save us').

Theatrical and ritual performance can typically be distinguished by the expectation, in the case of ritual, of a repeated, stylized sequence of events that invites audience participation. Theatre implies a unique statement of artistry whereas

ritual invokes tradition and socially shared purpose. With the theatrical organization of a ritual, it is possible to envision secular dramatized ceremonies suggesting collective Jewish identity, whether in the staged performance of Israeli music
at a Jewish arts festival, or in storytelling at the kitchen table (Shavit and Sitton
2004: 84–105; Zeitlin 1997: 17–24), or at a Jewish camping or scouting experience (Sales and Saxe 2003); in a military induction ceremony at the top of Masada
and in retirement rituals joined to the secular observance of Hanukah (Ben-
Yehuda 1995: 147–62; Rubin 2009: 134–75; Zerubavel 1997: 60–113), or in
organized pilgrimage tours such as the March of the Living and Birthright Israel
(Kelner 2010; Saxe and Chazan 2008; Shevelev and Schomer 1996).

Whereas ritual performance exaggerates the distance between everyday activity and staged action, ritualized practice draws attention to identity markers in the
structure of daily living. Popular guides to Jewish living often identify activities in
the worldly realm that tie Jews together socially and culturally. *The How To Handbook for Jewish Living* by Kerry M. Olitzky and Ronald H. Isaacs, for example,
includes 'How to Dance the Hora' and 'Making a Family Tree' along with 'How to
Make Aliyah to the Torah' and 'Putting on Tefillin' (1993: 15–24, 106–10). The
rhetoric of 'practice' to mark Jewish life implies constant usage, but one which is
ritualized because it involves self-conscious patterning. A handbook such as *The
Rituals and Practices of a Jewish Life* (2002) by Kerry Olitzky and Daniel Judson
(the foreword was written by Vanessa Ochs, a contributor to this volume)
includes *kashrut*, covering the head, and Torah study under the rubric of practice.
Other advisers dwell on dress and hair practices as keys to the Jewish values of
modesty, community, and devotion (Falk 1998; Schreiber 2003), and these cultural fashions commonly serve to signify and maintain sectarian boundaries and
piety (Behrouzi 1991; Goldman Carrel 1999; Landau 1993: 32–40; Lowenstein
2000: 149–74; Yoder 2001: 144–6).

The cultural significance of practices lies in the way in which, in their patterned repetition, they connote values to the practitioner as well as to the potential
viewer. When actions take on collectively shared connotations, such as covering
(the head or limbs), cutting (hair and foreskin), and carrying (on the sabbath) in
the Jewish context, analysts such as Gail Labovitz in this volume may refer to
them as 'praxis' to identify their behavioural significance as cultural paradigms
(see Bauman 1999 [1973]; Bernstein 1971; Bourdieu 1977; Bronner 1988; Wulf
2006). They may especially draw public as well as analytical notice when they
symbolize ethnic and moral differences, as in the political controversy over
shehitah explored by Sander Gilman in this volume (see also Alderman 2008:
111–36; Judd 2007). If slaughtering as praxis attracts critical attention, many less
public practices are worthy of analysis because they present opportunities for per-
sonalizing and innovating meaning. Individuals may ritualize their Jewishness
by having food they remember from their parents and grandparents, by adorning
their yarmulke with personal symbols, and by producing creative works on a

Jewish theme. A question that arises from practices that skirt the line between out of the ordinary ritual activity and everyday routine concerns how and why actions become ritualized, if they indeed do. Nina Spiegel, for example, examines the development of the Dalia Dance Festival from a localized event into an annual national tradition. She argues that, by being staged on open kibbutz fields, the dance festival became a prime opportunity for ritualizing secular, socialist Zionism with the symbolism of reclaiming the land.

In sum, the complexities of ritual, especially its interactive and processual dynamics involving negotiations of the religious and the secular, the old and the new, the traditional and the modern, the social and the political, and performance and practice, command the attention of the contributors to this book. The volume opens with ritual's manifest role of marking time and community under the general heading of 'ritual year', a term increasingly used by comparative ethnologists to refer to the cultural divisions formed by ritual performance (Mifsud-Chircop 2005). This part of the volume includes the unique calendrical observance among Tunisian Jews of Jethro's Feast and more widely celebrated rituals of Purim. It also has investigations of ritual innovation and adaptation: Seth Ward on liturgical inclusions of Israel Independence Day observances and Michael Hoberman on a small group's alterations of sabbath rituals in a syncretic process combining the traditions of an elite Protestant boarding school with Jewish domestic rituals.

The second part of the volume focuses on changes in the wedding ceremony, often considered the most complex ritual in the life cycle. Authors in this section examine various phenomena that have posed a challenge to the traditional ceremony: same-sex marriages, the transformation of gender relations in Modern Orthodoxy, and migration from Ethiopia to Israel. Another complex and often contentious set of rituals centres on mourning and death, including preparation for burial, funeral and mourning, and cemetery interment. Essays on this theme form Part III of the book. The closing section brings together analyses of different activities that have become ritualized—and politicized. These include the contemporary political battles in Europe over the legality of ritual slaughtering practised by Jews and Muslims, the rallies and campaigns of the Save Soviet Jewry movement of the 1970s, and, finally, the most overtly performative event that has become organized and framed as a secular, nationalistic ritual in Israel: the Dalia Dance Festival.

All told, the contributors show ritual action, from that steeped in ancient scriptures to modern innovative festivals and ceremonies, to be the key to the continuation of culture and to the expression of world-view. Often overlooked as routine or dismissed as bizarre abnormality, ritual in its many forms, conflicts, and guises embodies experience that is lived, imagined, and even negated. For Jewish cultural studies, examining textual and contextual revisions is especially meaningful for understanding what is Jewish about Jewishness. The analysis of changes in ritual content, and of the responses of both participants and non-participants to those changes, is critical to illuminating the centrality of perception that has often been omitted from the documentation of customs. With the understanding of variations in perception, the meaning of ritual events—liturgies, holidays, life-cycle events, and political rallies—for a given group may be discerned. This also allows reflection on the uses of ritual, and the context of tradition, in everyday life set against the background of modernity and community. Jews are hardly alone in relying on ritual to provide them with an inventory of social meanings that have to be constantly negotiated, but as this volume shows, they are keenly aware of the duality of the perception and enactment of ritual from within their community and from outside it. Jews know and express themselves by their rituals. Whether or not they begin their day with the recitation of the Shema, they are aware of the importance of repetition—and of the possibility of variation—in Jewish practice. The agency, interaction, and construction by which rituals persist, change, and transform provide the core of this book.

References

ABRAHAMS, ROGER D. 1968. 'Introductory Remarks to a Rhetorical Theory of Folklore', *Journal of American Folklore*, 81: 143–58.

——1972. 'Personal Power and Social Restraint in the Definition of Folklore'. In Américo Paredes and Richard Bauman, eds., *Toward New Perspectives in Folklore*, 16–30. Austin, Tex.

——1977. 'Toward an Enactment-Centered Theory of Folklore'. In William Bascom, ed., *Frontiers of Folklore*, 79–120. Boulder, Colo.

——1980. 'Folklore in the Definition of Ethnicity: An American and Jewish Perspective'. In Frank Talmage, ed., *Studies in Jewish Folklore*, 13–20. Cambridge, Mass.

——1986. 'Ordinary and Extraordinary Experience'. In Victor W. Turner and Edward M. Bruner, eds., *The Anthropology of Experience*, 45–72. Urbana, Ill.

——2005. *Everyday Life: A Poetics of Vernacular Practices*. Philadelphia.

ADLER, RACHEL. 1998. *Engendering Judaism: An Inclusive Theology and Ethics*. Boston.

ALDERMAN, GEOFFREY. 2008. *Controversy and Crisis: Studies in the History of the Jews in Modern Britain*. Brighton, Mass.

ALLEN, ERNEST, JR. 2002. 'Du Boisian Double Consciousness: The Unsustainable Argument'. *Massachusetts Review*, 43: 217–53.

ALPERT, REBECCA. 1997. *Like Bread on the Seder Plate: Jewish Lesbians and the Transformation of Tradition*. New York.

ANIJAR, KAREN. 1999. 'Jewish Genes, Jewish Jeans: A Fashionable Body'. In Linda B. Arthur, ed., *Religion, Dress and the Body*, 181–200. Oxford.

ARLOW, JACOB. 1951. 'A Psychoanalytic Study of a Religious Initiation Rite: Bar Mitzvah'. In Ruth Eissler, Anna Freud, Heinz Hartmann, and Ernst Kris, eds., *The Psychoanalytic Study of the Child*, vol. vi, pp. 353–74. New York.

AVRUTIN, EUGENE M., VALERI DYMSHITS, ALEXANDER IVANOV, ALEXANDER LVOV, HARRIET MURRAV, and ALLA SOKOLOVA. 2009. *Photographing the Jewish Nation: Pictures from S. An-Sky's Ethnographic Expeditions*. Lebanon, NH.

BALKA, CHRISTIE, and ANDY ROSE, EDS. 1989. *Twice Blessed: On Being Lesbian or Gay and Jewish*. Boston.

BAR'AM-BEN YOSSEF, NOAM. 1998. *Brides and Betrothals: Jewish Wedding Rituals in Afghanistan*. Jerusalem.

BAUMAN, ZYGMUNT. 1999 [1973]. *Culture as Praxis*. London.

BEATTIE, JOHN. 1966. 'Ritual and Social Change', *Man*, NS 1: 60–71.

BEHROUZI, NITZA. 1991. *Head Adornment: Festive and Ceremonial Headdresses*. Tel Aviv.

BELASCO, DANIEL. 2009. 'Chopping Noodles: The Art of Jewish Practice'. In Daniel Belasco, ed., *Reinventing Ritual: Contemporary Art and Design for Jewish Life*, 1–45. New Haven.

BELL, CATHERINE. 1992. *Ritual Theory, Ritual Practice*. New York.

——1997. *Ritual: Perspectives and Dimensions*. New York.

BEN-AMOS, DAN. 1971. 'Toward a Definition of Folklore in Context', *Journal of American Folklore*, 84: 3–15.

——1982. *Folklore in Context: Essays*. New Delhi.

BEN-MENAHEM, HANINA. 1996. 'Postscript: The Judicial Process and the Nature of Jewish Law'. In N. S. Hecht, B. S. Jackson, S. M. Passamaneck, D. Piatelli, and A. M. Rabello, eds., *An Introduction to the History and Sources of Jewish Law*, 421–38. Oxford.

BEN-YEHUDA, NACHMAN. 1995. *The Masada Myth: Collective Memory and Mythmaking in Israel*. Madison, Wis.

BERNSTEIN, RICHARD J. 1971. *Praxis and Action: Contemporary Philosophies of Human Activity*. Philadelphia.

BIAL, HENRY. 2005. *Acting Jewish: Negotiating Ethnicity on the American Stage and Screen*. Ann Arbor, Mich.

BILU, YORAM. 2003. 'From *Milah* (Circumcision) to *Milah* (Word): Male Identity and Rituals in the Jewish Ultraorthodox Community', *Ethos*, 31: 172–203.

BOOKSTABER, PHILIP DAVID. 1939. *Judaism and the American Mind in Theory and Practice*. New York.

BORIS, STACI. 2008. *The New Authentics: Artists of the Post-Jewish Generation*. Chicago.

BOURDIEU, PIERRE. 1977. *Outline of a Theory of Practice*. Cambridge.

BOYARIN, JONATHAN. 1996. *Thinking in Jewish*. Chicago.

BRONNER, SIMON J. 1988. 'Art, Performance, and Praxis: The Rhetoric of Contemporary Folklore Studies', *Western Folklore*, 47: 75–102.

——1998. *Following Tradition: Folklore in the Discourse of American Culture*. Logan, Ut.

——2004. '"This is Why We Hunt": Social-Psychological Meanings of the Traditions and Rituals of Deer Camp', *Western Folklore*, 63: 11–50.

——2008. 'The Chutzpah of Jewish Cultural Studies'. In Simon J. Bronner, ed., *Jewish Cultural Studies*, 1: *Jewishness: Expression, Identity, Representation*, 1–28. Oxford.

——2008–9. 'Fathers and Sons: Rethinking the Bar Mitzvah as an American Rite of Passage', *Children's Folklore Review*, 31: 7–34.

——ed. 2010a. 'Framing Folklore: Essays in Honor of Jay Mechling', *Western Folklore*, special issue, 69, nos. 2–3.

——ed. 2010b. *Jewish Cultural Studies, 2: Jews at Home: The Domestication of Identity*. Oxford.

BURKERT, WALTER. 1996 [1983]. 'The Function and Transformation of Ritual Killing'. In Ronald L. Grimes, ed., *Readings in Ritual Studies*, 62–71. Upper Saddle River, NJ.

CARDOZO, ARLENE ROSSEN. 1982. *Jewish Family Celebrations*. New York.

CHILL, ABRAHAM. 1978. *The Minhagim: The Customs and Ceremonies of Judaism, their Origins and Rationale*. New York.

COHEN, DEBRA NUSSBAUM. 2009. 'PETA's Kaparot Protest: Gelt, Not Guilt', *Jewish Daily Forward*, 9 Oct. < http://www.forward.com/articles/115595/, accessed 30 Aug. 2010.

COHEN, FRANCIS L. 1900. 'Folk-Song Survivals in Jewish Worship-Music', *Journal of the Folk-Song Society*, 1: 32–8, 52–9.

COHEN, JEREMY, and RICHARD I. COHEN, eds. 2008. *The Jewish Contribution to Civilization: Reassessing an Idea*. Oxford.

COHEN, JUDAH M. 2009. *The Making of a Reform Jewish Cantor: Musical Authority, Cultural Investment*. Bloomington, Ind.

COHEN, SHAYE J. D. 2005. *Why Aren't Jewish Women Circumcised? Gender and Covenant in Judaism*. Berkeley, Calif.

CONTEMPORARY JEWISH MUSEUM. 2009. *New Works, Old Story: 80 Artists at the Passover Table: The Dorothy Saxe Invitational*. San Francisco.

DAVAL, SAMIR. 1996. 'Diaspora and Double Consciousness', *Journal of the Midwest Modern Language Association*, 29: 46–62.

DAVIS, AVRAHAM. 2006. *Kitzur Shulchan Aruch*, 3 vols. Lakewood, NJ.

DAVIS, JUDITH. 2003. 'Mazel Tov: The Bar Mitzvah as a Multigenerational Ritual of Change and Continuity'. In Evan Imber-Black, Janine Roberts, and Richard A. Whiting, eds., *Rituals in Families and Family Therapy*, 182–216. New York.

DUNDES, ALAN. 1968. 'The Number Three in American Culture'. In Alan Dundes, ed., *Every Man His Way: Readings in Cultural Anthropology*, 401–24. Englewood Cliffs, NJ.

EILBERG-SCHWARTZ, HOWARD, ed. 1992. *People of the Body: Jews and Judaism from an Embodied Perspective*. Albany, NY.

EISEN, ARNOLD M. 1998. *Rethinking Modern Judaism: Ritual, Commandment, Community*. Chicago.

——2009. Preface to Daniel Belasco, ed., *Reinventing Ritual: Contemporary Art and Design for Jewish Life*, pp. xi–xiii. New Haven, Conn.

EISENBERG, RONALD L. 2004. *The JPS Guide to Jewish Traditions*. Philadelphia.

ELBOGEN, ISMAR. 1993. *Jewish Liturgy: A Comprehensive History*. Philadelphia.

ELIADE, MIRCEA. 1958. *Rites and Symbols of Initiation: The Mysteries of Birth and Rebirth*. New York.

FALK, PESACH ELIYAHU. 1998. *Modesty, an Adornment for Life: Halachos and Attitudes Concerning Tznius of Dress and Conduct*. Gateshead.

FLAM, GILA. 1992. *Singing for Survival: Songs of the Lodz Ghetto, 1940–1945*. Urbana, Ill.

FOX, MARVIN. 1978. Foreword to Abraham Chill, *The Minhagim: The Customs and Ceremonies of Judaism, their Origins and Rationale*. New York.

GASTER, THEODOR H. 1955. *The Holy and the Profane: Evolution of Jewish Folkways*. New York.

——1961. *Thespis: Ritual, Myth, and Drama in the Ancient Near East*. Garden City, NY.

——1978. *Festivals of the Jewish Year: A Modern Interpretation and Guide*. New York.

GEFFEN, RELA M., ed. 1993. *Celebration and Renewal: Rites of Passage in Judaism*. Philadelphia.

GELBARD, SHMUEL PINCHAS. 1998. *Rite and Reason: 1050 Jewish Customs and their Sources*, trans. R. Nachman Bulman. Petach Tikvah.

GILMAN, SANDER L. 1991. *The Jew's Body*. New York.

——2008. 'Are Jews Musical? Historical Notes on the Question of Jewish Musical Modernism'. In Philip V. Bohlman, ed., *Jewish Musical Modernism, Old and New*, pp. vii–xvi. Chicago.

GINZBERG, LOUIS. 1955. *Jewish Law and Lore*. Philadelphia.

GIRARD, RENÉ. 1997 [1977]. 'Violence and the Sacred: Sacrifice'. In Ronald L. Grimes, ed., *Readings in Ritual Studies*, 239–56. Upper Saddle River, NJ.

GLICK, LEONARD B. 1982. 'Types Distinct from Our Own: Franz Boas on Jewish Identity and Assimilation', *American Anthropologist*, 84: 545–65.

——2005. *Marked in Your Flesh: Circumcision from Ancient Judea to Modern America*. Oxford.

GOFFMAN, ERVING. 1967. *Interaction Ritual: Essays in Face-to-Face Behavior*. Garden City, NY.

——1974. *Frame Analysis: An Essay on the Organization of Experience*. New York.

GOLDBERG, HARVEY E. 2003. *Jewish Passages: Cycles of Jewish Life*. Berkeley, Calif.

GOLDMAN CARREL, BARBARA. 1999. 'Hasidic Women's Head-Coverings: A Feminized System of Hasidic Distinction'. In Linda B. Arthur, ed., *Religion, Dress and the Body*, 163–80. Oxford.

GOLLAHER, DAVID L. 2001. *Circumcision: A History of the World's Most Controversial Surgery*. New York.

GONEN, RIVKA, ed. 1994. *Back to the Shtetl: An-Sky and the Jewish Ethnographic Expedition, 1912–1914*. Jerusalem.

GREENBERG, STEVEN. 2005. *Wrestling with God and Men: Homosexuality in the Jewish Tradition*. Madison, Wis.

GRIMES, RONALD L. 1982. *Beginnings in Ritual Studies*. Lanham, Md.

——1996. 'Introduction'. In Ronald L. Grimes, ed., *Readings in Ritual Studies*, pp. xiii–xvi. Upper Saddle River, NJ.

——2006. 'Performance'. In Jens Kreinath, Jan Snoek, and Michael Strausberg, eds., *Theorizing Rituals: Issues, Topics, Approaches, Concepts*, 379–94. Leiden.

GRUNWALD, MAX. 1923. 'Zur Vorgeschichte des Sukkothrituals und verwandeter Kultformen'. In id., ed., *Jahrbuch für Jüdische Volkskunde*, 427–72. Berlin.

HANDELMAN, DON. 2006. 'Framing'. In Jens Kreinath, Jan Snoek, and Michael Strausberg, eds., *Theorizing Rituals: Issues, Topics, Approaches, Concepts*, 413–28. Leiden.

——and ELIHU KATZ. 1990. 'State Ceremonies of Israel: Remembrance Day and Independence Day'. In Don Handelman, ed., *Models and Mirrors: Toward an Anthropology of Public Events*, 191–233. Cambridge.

HARLOW, ILANA. 1993. '"We Are Bound to Tradition Yet Part of that Tradition is Change": The Development of the Jewish Prayerbook', *Folklore Forum*, 26: 30–41.

HARTH, DIETRICH. 2006. 'Ritual and Other Forms of Social Action'. In Jens Kreinath, Jan Snoek, and Michael Strausberg, eds., *Theorizing Rituals: Issues, Topics, Approaches, Concepts*, 15–36. Leiden.

HEILMAN, SAMUEL C. 1987. *The People of the Book: Drama, Fellowship, and Religion*. Chicago.

——1998. *Synagogue Life: A Study in Symbolic Interaction*. New Brunswick, NJ.

HERTZOG, ESTHER, ORIT ABUHAV, HARVEY E. GOLDBERG, and EMANUEL MARX. 2010. 'Introduction: Israeli Social Anthropology: Origins, Characteristics, and Contributions'. In Esther Hertzog, Orit Abuhav, Harvey E. Goldberg, and Emanuel Marx, eds., *Perspectives on Israeli Anthropology*, 1–16. Detroit.

HESKES, IRENE. 1997. 'Cantors'. In Paula E. Hyman and Deborah Dash Moore, eds., *Jewish Women in America: An Historical Encyclopedia*, 202–5. New York.

HOFFMAN, LAWRENCE A., and JANET R. WALTON, EDS. 1993. *Sacred Sound and Social Change: Liturgical Music in Jewish and Christian Experience*. Notre Dame, Ind.

JACOBS, JOSEPH. 1890. 'Jewish Ideals', *Jewish Quarterly Review*, 2: 494–508.

Jewish Journal. 2008. 'PETA Slams N. Y. Kapparot Ritual.' *Jewish Journal* website (26 Aug.), <http://www.jewishjournal.com/religion/article/peta_slams_ny_kapparot_ritual_video_20080826>, accessed 10 Feb. 2010.

JOSELIT, JENNA WEISSMAN. 1994. *The Wonders of America: Reinventing Jewish Culture, 1880–1950*. New York.

JUDD, ROBIN. 2007. *Contested Rituals: Circumcision, Kosher Butchering, and Jewish Political Life in Germany, 1843–1933*. Ithaca, NY.

KAPLAN-MAYER, GABRIELLE. 2004. *The Creative Jewish Wedding Book: A Hands-on Guide to New and Old Traditions, Ceremonies, and Celebrations*. Woodstock, Vt.

KAUFFMAN, DEBRA RENEE. 1991. *Rachel's Daughters: Newly Orthodox Jewish Women*. New Brunswick, NJ.

KELNER, SHAUL. 2010. *Tours That Bind: Diaspora, Pilgrimage, and Israeli Birthright Tourism*. New York.

KIRSHENBLATT-GIMBLETT, BARBARA. 1998. *Destination Culture: Tourism, Museums, and Heritage*. Berkeley, Calif.

KLINE SILVERMAN, ERIC. 2006. *From Abraham to America: A History of Jewish Circumcision*. Lanham, Md.

KONNER, MELVIN. 2009. *The Jewish Body*. New York.

LAMM, MAURICE. 1969. *The Jewish Way in Death and Mourning*. New York.

LANDAU, DAVID. 1993. *Piety and Power: The World of Jewish Fundamentalism*. New York.

LEACH, EDMUND. 1968. 'Ritual'. In David L. Sills, ed., *International Encyclopedia of the Social Sciences*, vol. xiii, pp. 520–6. New York.

LEVINE, JOSEPH A. 1989. *Synagogue Song in America*. Crown Point, Ind.

LINKE, STUART. 1999. *Psychological Perspectives on Traditional Jewish Practices*. Northvale, NJ.

LOWENSTEIN, STEVEN M. 2000. *The Jewish Cultural Tapestry: International Jewish Folk Traditions*. New York.

MCCURDY, DAVID W., JAMES P. SPRADLEY, and DIANNA J. SHANDY. 2004. *The Cultural Experience: Ethnography in Complex Society*. Long Grove, Ill.

MARCUS, IVAN G. 1996. *Rituals of Childhood: Jewish Acculturation in Medieval Europe*. New Haven, Conn.

——2004. *The Jewish Life Cycle: Rites of Passage from Biblical to Modern Times*. Seattle.

MARK, ELIZABETH WYNER, ed. 2003. *The Covenant of Circumcision: New Perspectives on an Ancient Jewish Rite*. Lebanon, NH.

MATTS, ABRAHAM. 1968. Preface to Rabbi Abraham Isaac Sperling, *Reasons for Jewish Customs and Traditions*, trans. Abraham Matts, 7. New York.

MECHLING, JAY. 1980. 'The Magic of the Boy Scout Campfire', *Journal of American Folklore*, 93: 35–56.

MIFSUD-CHIRCOP, GEORGE. 2005. 'The Ritual Year Working Group: A Shared Experience To Be Remembered', *SIEF (International Society for Ethnology and Folklore) Newsletter*, 4(1): 8–12.

MIKDASH-SHAMAILOV, LIYA. 2002. *Mountain Jews: Customs and Daily Life in the Caucasus*. Jerusalem.

MOLTKE, JOHANNES VON. 1997. 'Identities on Display: Jewishness and the Representational Politics of the Museum'. In Jonathan Boyarin and Daniel Boyarin, eds., *Jews and Other Differences: The New Jewish Cultural Studies*, 79–107. Minneapolis.

MYERHOFF, BARBARA. 1982. 'Rites of Passage: Process and Paradox'. In Victor Turner, ed., *Celebration: Studies in Festivity and Ritual*, 109–35. Washington, DC.

NOY, CHAIM. 2006. *A Narrative Community: Voices of Israeli Backpackers*. Detroit.

NOY, DOV. 1980. 'Introduction: Eighty Years of Jewish Folkloristics: Achievements and Tasks'. In Frank Talmage, ed., *Studies in Jewish Folklore*, 1–12. Cambridge, Mass.

NULMAN, MACY. 1993. *Encyclopedia of Jewish Prayer*. Northvale, NJ.

OCHS, VANESSA L. 2007. *Inventing Jewish Ritual*. Philadelphia.

OLITZKY, KERRY M., and DANIEL JUDSON, eds. 2002. *The Rituals and Practices of a Jewish Life: A Handbook for Personal Spiritual Renewal*. Woodstock, Vt.

——and RONALD H. ISAACS. 1993. *The How To Handbook for Jewish Living*. Hoboken, NJ.

OUAKNIN, MARC-ALAIN, and FRANÇOISE-ANNE MÉNAGER. 2005. *Bar Mitzvah: A Guide to Spiritual Growth*. New York.

PAREDES, AMÉRICO, and RICHARD BAUMAN, eds. 1972. *Toward New Perspectives in Folklore*. Austin, Tex.

PATAI, RAPHAEL. 1960. 'Jewish Folklore and Jewish Tradition'. In Raphael Patai, Francis Lee Utley, and Dov Noy, eds., *Studies in Biblical and Jewish Folklore*, 11–28. Bloomington, Ind.

——1983. *On Jewish Folklore*. Detroit.

PENTIKÄINEN, JUHA. 1997. 'Ritual'. In Thomas A. Green, ed., *Folklore: An Encyclopedia of Beliefs, Customs, Tales, Music, and Art*, vol. ii, pp. 733–6. Santa Barbara, Calif.

POLLACK, HERMAN. 1971. *Jewish Folkways in Germanic Lands (1648–1806): Studies in Aspects of Daily Life*. Cambridge, Mass.

RAISIN, J. S. 1907. *Sect, Creed and Custom in Judaism: A Study in Jewish Nomology*. Philadelphia.

RAPPAPORT, ROY A. 1992. 'Ritual'. In Richard Bauman, ed., *Folklore, Cultural Performances, and Popular Entertainments: A Communications-Centered Handbook*, 249–60. New York.

——1996 [1979]. 'The Obvious Aspects of Ritual'. In Ronald L. Grimes, ed., *Readings in Ritual Studies*, 427–40. Upper Saddle River, NJ.

RAPPOPORT, ANGELO S. 1937. *The Folklore of the Jews*. London.

ROSENAU, WILLIAM. 1903. *Jewish Ceremonial Institutions and Customs*. New York.

ROSENBERG, STUART E. 1965. 'The Right Age for Bar Mitzvah', *Religious Education*, 60: 298–300.

RUBIN, NISSAN. 2009. *New Rituals, Old Societies: Invented Rituals in Contemporary Israel*. Brighton, Mass.

RUTTENBERG, DANYA. 2009. 'Heaven and Earth: Notes on New Jewish Ritual'. In Daniel Belasco, ed., *Reinventing Ritual: Contemporary Art and Design for Jewish Life*, 71–93. New Haven, Conn.

SABAR, SHALOM. 2006. *The Life Cycle* [Ma'agal haḥayim]. Jerusalem.

SACHS, ANGELI, and EDWARD VAN VOOLEN, eds. 2004. *Jewish Identity in Contemporary Architecture*. Munich.

SALES, AMY L., and LEONARD SAXE. 2003. *'How Goodly Are Thy Tents': Summer Camps as Jewish Socializing Experiences*. Waltham, Mass.

SANTINO, JACK. 2009. 'The Ritualesque: Festival, Politics, and Popular Culture', *Western Folklore*, 68: 9–26.

SARNA, JONATHAN D. 2003. 'The Question of Music in American Judaism: Reflections at 350 Years', *American Jewish History*, 91: 195–203.

SAX, WILLIAM S. 2006. 'Agency'. In Jens Kreinath, Jan Snoek, and Michael Strausberg, eds., *Theorizing Rituals: Issues, Topics, Approaches, Concepts*, 473–81. Leiden.

SAXE, LEONARD, and BARRY CHAZAN. 2008. *Ten Days of Birthright Israel: A Journey in Young Adult Identity*. Waltham, Mass.

SCHAUSS, HAYYIM. 1950. *The Lifetime of a Jew: Throughout the Ages of Jewish History*. New York.

SCHREIBER, LYNNE. 2003. *Jewish Women and Hair Covering*. New York.

SCHUMAN, HOWARD, VERED VINITZKY-SEROUSSI, and AMIRAM D. VINOKUR. 2003. 'Keeping the Past Alive: Memories of Israeli Jews at the Turn of the Millennium', *Sociological Forum*, 18: 103–36.

SCHWARTZMAN, ANA, and ZOË FRANCESCA. 2004. *Make Your Own Jewish Wedding: How to Create a Ritual that Expresses Your True Selves*. San Francisco.

SHAFRAN, AVI. 2010. 'Wings and Prayers'. Jewish America website, <http://www.jewishamerica.com/ja/content/amechad/amarch17.cfm#Wings%20and%20Prayers>, accessed 10 Feb. 2010.

SHAVIT, YAACOV, and SHOSHANA SITTON. 2004. *Staging and Stagers in Modern Jewish Palestine: The Creation of Festive Lore in a New Culture, 1882–1948*, trans. Chaya Naor. Detroit.

SHEPARD, PAUL. 1973. *The Tender Carnivore and the Sacred Game*. Athens, Ga.

SHERWIN, BYRON L. 1990. *In Partnership with God: Contemporary Jewish Law and Ethics*. Syracuse, NY.

SHESKIN, IRA M. 2001. *How Jewish Communities Differ: Variations in the Findings of Local Jewish Population Studies*. New York.

SHEVELEV, RAPHAEL, and KARINE SCHOMER. 1996. *Liberating the Ghosts: Photographs and Text from the March of the Living*. Anacortes, Wash.

SHILOAH, AMNON. 1992. *Jewish Musical Traditions*. Detroit.

SHULDINER, DAVID P. 1999. *Of Moses and Marx: Folk Ideology and Folk History in the Jewish Labor Movement*. Westport, Conn.

SHWARTZ-BE'ERI, ORA. 2000. *The Jews of Kurdistan: Daily Life, Customs, Arts and Crafts*. Jerusalem.

SILVER, MITCHELL. 1998. *Respecting the Wicked Child: A Philosophy of Secular Jewish Identity and Education*. Amherst, Mass.

SILVERMAN, JONATHAN, and DEAN RADER. 2005. *The World is a Text: Writing, Reading, and Thinking about Culture and its Contexts*. Upper Saddle River, NJ.

SINGER, MATTHEW, ed. 2007. *A Kiss for the Mezuzah*. Philadelphia.

——2009. *Wimpel! Wrapped Wishes*. Philadelphia.

SLAPAK, ORPA. 2003. *The Jews of India: A Story of Three Communities*. Jerusalem.

——2002. *Chosen Voices: The Story of the American Cantorate*. Urbana, Ill.

SNOEK, JAN A. M. 2006. 'Defining "Rituals"'. In Jens Kreinath, Jan Snoek, and Michael Strausberg, eds., *Theorizing Rituals: Issues, Topics, Approaches, Concepts*, 3–14. Leiden.

SPERLING, AVRAHAM YITZHAK. 1968. *Reasons for Jewish Customs and Traditions*, trans. Abraham Matts. New York.

——1999 [1890]. *Sefer ta'amei haminhagim umekorei hadinim*. Jerusalem.

SPIRO, JACK D. 1977. 'The Educational Significance of the Bar Mitzvah Initiation', *Religious Education*, 72: 383–99.

STARR SERED, SUSAN. 1992. *Women as Ritual Experts: The Religious Lives of Elderly Jewish Women in Jerusalem*. New York.

STERN, J. 1987. 'Modes of Reference in the Rituals of Judaism', *Religious Studies*, 23: 109–28.

SWETERLITSCH, RICHARD. 1997. 'Custom'. In Thomas A. Green, ed., *Folklore: An Encyclopedia of Beliefs, Customs, Tales, Music, and Art*, vol. i, pp. 168–72. Santa Barbara, Calif.

SYME, DANIEL B. 2004. *The Jewish Home: A Guide for Jewish Living*. New York.

TABORY, JOSEPH. 1997. 'Minhag'. In R. J. Zwi Werblowsky and Geoffrey Wigoder, eds., *The Oxford Dictionary of the Jewish Religion*. Oxford.

TELUSHKIN, JOSEPH. 1991. *Jewish Literacy: The Most Important Things to Know about the Jewish Religion, its People and its History*. New York.

TSUR, MUKY. 2007. 'Pesach in the Land of Israel: Kibbutz Haggadot', *Israel Studies*, 12: 74–103.

TURNER, VICTOR W. 1967. *The Forest of Symbols: Aspects of Ndembu Ritual*. Ithaca, NY.

——1969. *The Ritual Process: Structure and Anti-Structure*. Chicago.

——1982. Introduction to id., ed., *Celebration: Studies in Festivity and Ritual*, 11–32. Washington, DC.

UNTERMAN, ALAN. 1999. *The Jews: Their Religious Beliefs and Practices*. Portland, Oreg.

VAN GENNEP, ARNOLD. 1960. *The Rites of Passage*. Chicago.

WASSERFALL, RAHEL. 1992. 'Menstruation and Identity: The Meaning of Niddah for Moroccan Women Immigrants to Israel'. In Howard Eilberg-Schwartz, ed., *People of the Body: Jews and Judaism from an Embodied Perspective*, 309–28. Albany, NY.

WEINRICH, BEATRICE S. 1960. 'The Americanization of Passover'. In Raphael Patai, Francis Lee Utley, and Dov Noy, eds., *Studies in Biblical and Jewish Folklore*, 329–66. Bloomington, Ind.

WEISSLER, CHAVA. 1992. '*Mizvot* Built into the Body: *Tkhines* for *Niddah*, Pregnancy, and Childbirth'. In Howard Eilberg-Schwartz, ed., *People of the Body: Jews and Judaism from an Embodied Perspective*, 101–15. Albany, NY.

WHITFIELD, STEPHEN J. 2008. 'Between Memory and Messianism: A Brief History of American Jewish Identity'. In Staci Boris, *The New Authentics: Artists of the Post-Jewish Generation*, 44–55. Chicago.

WOLOWELSKY, JOEL B. 1997. *Women, Jewish Law and Modernity: New Opportunities in a Post-Feminist Age*. Hoboken, NJ.

WULF, CHRISTOPH. 2006. 'Praxis'. In Jens Kreinath, Jan Snoek, and Michael Strausberg, eds., *Theorizing Rituals: Issues, Topics, Approaches, Concepts*, 395–411. Leiden.

YODER, DON. 2001. 'Sectarian Costume Research in the United States'. In id., *Discovering American Folklife: Essays on Folk Culture and the Pennsylvania Dutch*, 143–72. Mechanicsburg, Pa.

YOFFIE, LEAH R. C. 1916. 'Present-Day Survivals of Ancient Jewish Customs', *Journal of American Folklore*, 29: 412–17.

ZEITLIN, STEVE. 1997. *Because God Loves Stories: An Anthology of Jewish Storytelling*. New York.

ZERUBAVEL, YAEL. 1997. *Recovered Roots: Collective Memory and the Making of Israeli National Tradition*. Chicago.

PART I

The Ritual Year

The Riddle of Se'udat Yitro: Interpreting a Celebration among Tunisia's Jews

HARVEY E. GOLDBERG AND HAGAR SALAMON

BOTH POPULAR AND LEARNED understanding assume that Jewish holidays and their component rituals are intimately linked to sacred texts. Discovering a calendar-based celebration that seems to have no parallel elsewhere within an established Jewish community invites questions from a variety of directions. Examples of such festivities are the Saharaneh of the Kurdish communities, the Sigd of the Beta Israel Ethiopian community, and the Mimuna celebrated among Moroccan Jews.[1] In each of these cases, the historical development of the holiday is unclear, and parts of it reflect local dialogues with the cultural environment in which these groups lived. At the same time, we witness an engagement in an active process of Judaization where a practice with an origin external to Jewish religious life is assigned Jewish meaning, often by connecting it to other customs or to textual traditions. Such processes must have occurred at earlier periods of Jewish history in various cultural contexts, but the sources available usually yield only 'final' outcomes, showing little of the actual intricate dynamics that go into the Judaization of celebrations.

In this essay, we introduce the case of Se'udat Yitro, a little-known holiday that appeared in the annual cycle of Jewish life in Tunisia and became a central event for those celebrating it. Se'udat Yitro, or Jethro's festive meal, is considered mysterious even by those committed to its practice. The lack of ability to point to its origin or to spell out its meaning does not make it any less significant. On the contrary, the vagueness surrounding the festive event, and the varying ways that it is enacted, seem to add to its attractiveness.

Both participants in the event and scholars reflecting upon it assume Se'udat Yitro to be relatively recent, probably emerging only during the nineteenth century. The historical data available, which include aspects of general Tunisian history along with accounts of the celebration among Jews there, combined with our field interviews among Jews from Tunisia now living in Israel, provide an opportunity to examine the dynamics and negotiations which link the original local circumstances to the process of making the celebration Jewish. We thus see that the creation, reshaping, and revisioning of rituals is not only a contemporary process, but was part and parcel of traditional society in which the interplay of popular practice and textual culture was in perpetual motion.

Young boys who have only recently begun their elementary Torah education stand at the centre of the celebration, which takes place on the Thursday night before the weekly portion—*parashah*—named 'Yitro' is read in the synagogue on sabbath morning (in accordance with the way his name was pronounced in Tunisia, we use the Hebrew form rather than 'Jethro' throughout the chapter). This is a key *parashah* in Jewish tradition, because the Ten Commandments are included within it (Exod. 19). The *parashah* begins, however, by telling how Yitro—Moses' father-in-law—came to visit Moses at Sinai in the days before the revelation there. Exodus 18: 12 describes how 'Aaron and all the Children of Israel' joined them 'to eat bread . . . before the Lord'. One standard explanation of the Tunisian *se'udah* (meal or feast) is that it marks the first time that young boys will hear the reading of the Decalogue.

The very term Se'udat Yitro may be understood in various ways. At the most mechanical level, it serves as a linguistic condensation of *se'udat parashat yitro*—the feast occurring before the reading of the *parashah* named 'Yitro'. This usage simply indicates the time at which it is celebrated within the annual Torah-reading cycle, typically in January.[2] It would not necessarily engage the biblical figure Yitro in terms of content.[3] In contrast to this is the interpretation that the modern festival celebrates the biblical event in which Moses and Yitro sat down and dined together. Later in the essay we address the question of what aspects of the 'textual Yitro' may be relevant to understanding the celebration; here we present some of the main features of Se'udat Yitro as they appeared in our field descriptions.

Within the Tunisian communities, there exist two models of the *se'udah*, one characterizing Tunis and the north and the other prominent in Jerba and the south. We present these briefly and elaborate upon them below. The 'Tunis model' highlights a celebration at home with an elaborate meal, characterized by a unique aesthetic of smallness: the cooking utensils, dinnerware, and table and chairs are small, as are the portions served. The standard entrée is stuffed squab. Accompanying the main course are all sorts of delicacies specially prepared in miniature fashion by the women of the household.

The 'Jerba model' takes the synagogue as the major locus of the celebration and elaborates the link to Torah study and the Ten Commandments. The rabbi who teaches the young boys in the *kuttab* (school of elementary Torah education) plays a salient part in the goings-on, and it is his wife who prepares a festive meal for the children.[4] While in some cases, according to our interviewees, an additional celebratory meal took place in individual homes (including squab in some cases), the central theme of the celebration was study, interpretation of Torah texts, and the relationship between the figure of Yitro and the glory of God and his revelation to Israel at Sinai.

These standard practices and explanations notwithstanding, Se'udat Yitro remains 'mysterious' for several reasons. First, except for sparse references regarding possible parallels elsewhere (to be discussed below), this ritual is known only among Jews in Tunisia. Second, there is no adequate tracing or satisfactory account of its origin or history, even though there is a general notion of its being connected to an epidemic among Jews in Tunis about a century earlier. Third, although the context of its practice is linked to a central textual segment of Jewish life—*parashat* 'Yitro', including the image of Yitro with his affiliation to Israel and the Ten Commandments—there is no biblical verse or rabbinic source mandating this celebration. Only during the past century have rabbis commented upon it, reflecting the fact that it has become established within the Tunisian community. A fourth puzzling feature is that it is always in close proximity to another feast that did become widespread in the Jewish world subsequent to the sixteenth century—that of Tu Bishvat. These features, including the fact that there was significant variation as to how the celebration was carried out, make it a case in point for examining the question of how customs that are popularly practised and perceived as being part of Jewish tradition interact with textual traditions and their exponents in situations where the linkage between these is uncertain, at best. Our exploration examines some processes regarding the interplay among customs, texts, cultural contexts, and forms of communal authority.

In our fieldwork interviews, as well as in the relevant literature we discovered, we were impressed by the fuzziness and partial nature of the information regarding both the origin of the celebration and its meanings. While at first frustrated, as scholars seeking a key to unlock mysteries, we gradually came to view this ambiguity as a basic fact, and perhaps even the essence of the story of Se'udat Yitro. As our informants shared with us recollections of the *se'udah* in Tunisia (and also from their life after immigrating to Israel) they communicated its puzzling nature and incorporated explanations that they had heard from a variety of sources. Many of them were explicit about their uncertainty, and specified the information as coming from personal experience, learned acquaintances, lectures by rabbis, and most recently internet sites concerning Tunisian Jewry.[5] They often prefaced their explanations with a caveat. This moving back and forth between historical and ethnographic data proved illuminating but also left many puzzles open, encouraging further speculation as to the history and meanings of the celebration.

The above situation invited us to seek connections between what we learned about Se'udat Yitro and other cultural articulations that were both concrete and free-floating. The data collected, as well as the written sources we found, had the quality of 'shreds and patches', to invoke a classic anthropological image, while it was striking that our interlocutors were content to leave their speculations vague. This ambiguity is epitomized in the very name and character attached to the celebration, that of the biblical figure Yitro, whose ethnic identity as a Midianite priest and the father-in-law of Moses remains puzzling, as does his relationship to what our interlocutors felt was a robust Jewish holiday. In this essay we seek to contribute to the search to understand Se'udat Yitro without pretending to solve the mystery fully. We thus add illuminating pieces to the puzzle by supplying a specific historical background, highlighting cultural kernels that lend significance to the celebration, and trace how these cultural-historical elements flow into perceptions of the festival as narrated to us by Jews from Tunisia whom we have encountered. This interpretative strategy is based on three levels of research: interview materials, written sources, and classic texts in which the figure of Yitro plays a role. We begin by presenting some of the main written sources that discuss the celebration.

Sources Describing Se'udat Yitro

The challenge posed by the custom of Se'udat Yitro is reflected in the writings of several scholars, all of Tunisian origin, who have discussed it as part of their work.[6] David Cohen's linguistic-ethnographic study of the Judaeo-Arabic of Tunis provides a brief description of the custom in Tunis:

It is during the second two weeks of the month of *Shvat* that there takes place a solemn rite which is purely Tunisian, the *se'uda* of Yitro, in honor of the young children. The *se'uda* is thus named because it takes place the Thursday of the week approaching the ritual reading of the *parashah* called Yitro (Exodus 18–20). The origin and primary meaning of that *se'uda* are not known with any certainty, and neither is the date at which it was established in Tunisia. Two explanations are given for the subject:

1. According to one of these explanations, it was instituted by a collective vow following an epidemic that decimated Jewish infants.

2. Another tradition is that the *se'uda* is aimed at celebrating the young boys who are about to read the Decalogue for the first time, which is precisely contained in the *parashah* of Yitro (Exodus 20: 2–17).

This *se'uda* is characterized by the fact that it constitutes a kind of a miniature dinner setting, made up of small servings in children's plates on a table lit up by small candles. A recent tradition invokes the slaughter [and consumption] of pigeons. (1964: 79–80)

In his brief discussion Cohen remarks that this practice is known only in Tunis, and the closest parallel he has to offer are family celebrations in late medieval and early modern Ashkenaz that precede a boy's circumcision. This speculative comment places Se'udat Yitro conceptually in the context of other ceremonies in Jewish life highlighting both Torah and young boys.[7]

A second scholar, Michal Malakhi (Saraf), has studied and made available little-known and unpublished texts of Tunisian writers—usually rabbis. A posthumous collection of her writings contains a description and discussion of the celebration (Malakhi 2002: 25–36). In it, she provides a description very close to that presented by Cohen: one explanation is historical—an epidemic in the nine-teenth century—and a second has a textual-liturgical emphasis with two inter-linked aspects—the *parashah* named 'Yitro', and the content of the Ten Commandments contained within it.

Malakhi also expands upon the material in Cohen's account. She indicates that there is variation in the names attached to the occasion: in certain places it was called Hag Yitro (Hebrew: the festival of Yitro), while some of our inter-viewees mentioned the term *festat lulad* (the holiday of the young boys, in Judaeo-Arabic). She notes the existence of a related celebration in Algeria, citing Eisenstein's Hebrew encyclopaedia (1909: 176) and his entry—*siyum*[8]—that describes a festive gathering before *parashat* 'Yitro'. That brief account, however, does not mention children. Eisenstein takes the Hebrew term *siyum* and inter-prets it as an acronym of the words *se'udat yitro umosheh*—the feast of Yitro and Moses. It is not clear what the source of his information is, but it may simply be a linguistic play on a standard Hebrew word rather than the source of the term. Malakhi indicates that the same word appears in what she regards as a mistaken form in the writings of Nahum Slouschz, in his discussion of the customs of both Tunis and Jerba (Malakhi 2002: 27). He refers to *ḥag tsiyon* (the holiday of Zion) which Malakhi corrects to *ḥag siyum*, but the former may in fact be a regional vari-ation (see Bahloul 1996: 111), or be another example of language play with a word whose meaning has become obscure. The indeterminacy of the very name also reinforces the event's mysterious background that continues to generate explana-tions.

That the uncertainty surrounding the celebration was a source of rabbinic ambivalence is made clear by Malakhi:

It is worth mentioning that the rabbis of Tunisia did not always look upon the holiday favorably, and some even tried to eliminate it from communal life. The reason is that there is no halakhic basis for the holiday, and it is anchored in a popular custom whose true and precise source is shrouded in uncertainty. Despite this, the Jews of Tunisia, more than any other community, insisted on maintaining the custom. (2002: 31)

There was thus some tension between apparently varying rabbinic attitudes that took into account textual traditions, and a deep attachment of Jews in Tunisia to the details of the celebration, many of which seem to have ludic or play-like aspects as well as magical features.

While Malakhi recognizes the probability of non-Jewish origins for Se'udat Yitro, her discussion reveals the desire to accord it as much traditional legitimacy as possible.[9] The tendency to 'digest' the custom by adding Jewish ingredients is found not only among rabbis but also others who value rabbinic authority and contribute to discourse underlining it. Thus, interviewees from Tunis made a connection between the epidemic, the intercession of rabbis through prayers and fasting, and the date of the *se'udah*. Some people were quite conscious of this process. One Jerba-born man, when asked about Se'udat Yitro, stated that wherever there is an opening, the rabbis enter with their interpretations.

Given the probability that the origin of Se'udat Yitro does not lie solely within the age-old cycle of Jewish life, its Judaization emerges as a central concern. This is true for many ritualized practices. In the present case, however, we also have an opportunity to work with sources that may provide a fuller picture of the complex historical setting within which the dynamics of Judaization operated. Part of this setting consists of elemental Jewish materials, 'building blocks' (Goldberg 1987a: 322–3) that existed within the broad horizons of Jewish North Africa. Added to these is the Muslim environment to which Jews in Tunisia were selectively exposed, both in terms of cultural patterns and of specific defining events. The availability of both these elements enables us to follow the interplay between the various influences.

At times the link between ethnographic work and concern with the past has been characterized as 'doing history backwards'.[10] We have found that unravelling the riddle of Se'udat Yitro has entailed moving not only forwards and backwards but at times also 'horizontally'. Therefore, having presented a basic outline of the festival, we next look at ethnographic sources from various geographical regions of North Africa, elements of which resonate with certain features of Yitro events. We then return to Tunis to examine in detail aspects of its nineteenth-century history that might have played a direct role in the emergence of the celebration. Next, we draw more fully on our interview materials, and while doing so follow the lead of many interviewees in referring to textual materials as they impinge upon the practices and understandings shared with us. In the conclusion, we further open up this direction, while suggesting the broader implications of piecing together a cultural puzzle.

Scattered References: Between Jewish Traditions and Local Scenarios

In this cultural-historical excursus, it will be helpful to locate Se'udat Yitro between two sets of concerns: a broad comparative view of rituals related to Torah education, on the one hand, and the specific history of Tunis and Jews in Tunisia on the other. We believe that it is reasonable to hypothesize about plausible scenarios for the emergence of the celebration, or, perhaps more precisely, to envision the parameters that make it meaningful.

Above, we noted the parallel drawn by Cohen between Se'udat Yitro and celebrations in Ashkenaz relating to an upcoming circumcision. More recently, Ivan Marcus (1996) has provided an extended discussion of life-cycle ceremonies, with special emphasis on rites associated with the early education of boys in ḥeder (Jewish religious school for young children). While focusing on Ashkenaz,

Marcus presents a broad view of childhood rituals in the Jewish world, including some examples from North Africa (1996: 21–5). He cites one reference, regarding southern Morocco, to a custom with parallels in Europe in which the young boy is exposed to the 'sweetness' of the Hebrew alphabet by licking it after it has been written on a school slate in honey. He also calls attention to an unusual custom in Ghardaia in southern Algeria, which we will consider here in some detail.

Marcus cites an ethnographic study of the latter community which was carried out intensively between 1961 and 1962 by two people who were not specialists in Jewish culture but were aware that this remote Jewish community would disappear when Algeria gained independence (Briggs and Guède 1964). They devote several pages (1964: 28–31) to a ceremony that took place during the period between Passover and Shavuot, stressing that it held great importance to the local community even though, like Se'udat Yitro, it was not anchored in any canonical source. The ceremony was called *kittab*, and the authors indicate that 'in the Sahara it meant primarily a free religious school maintained by a Jewish community' (1964: 29). This might be an alternative (or mistaken?) rendering of *kuttab*, the standard word in Tunisia denoting a school for elementary Torah education. Here, too, one gets the impression of a distinct local practice (the authors claim that 'this was a unique Saharan custom apparently unknown anywhere in the Jewish world except possibly in southeastern Morocco'), with hints that it may be part of a larger pattern found in the region.

Consider the description of the final stages of this ceremony:

each father took his son in his arms and carried him up onto the platform running along the far wall, beneath the Tablets of the Law.[11] Here they all strutted back and forth, showing off their progeny and shouting to call attention to them . . . Three times the men all broke into a loud prayer in unison, led by the chief rabbi, after which the women would applaud with a whooping 'you-you' cry. (Briggs and Guède 1964: 30)

These boys were all approaching the age of 5 (Briggs and Guède 1964: 29 n.), and the ceremony highlighted the physical contiguity with the Torah scrolls. Beyond that, a man from the community of Ghardaia who had moved to Strasbourg provided us with an additional perspective on its significance in 1981. He said that the ceremony marked the 'survival' of these children: they had passed the age of childhood diseases and parents felt more confident about their future health. This does not make the ceremony any less of a Torah initiation ritual, and is in accord with the perspective of Victor Turner who stressed the interpenetration of normative and emotional elements in rituals (Turner 1964). Practices growing out of the 'great tradition' of Judaism may also resonate strongly with other planes of existence (Goldberg 1987b). The Ghardaia ceremony may thus represent the merging of a fluid tradition of symbolic forms appropriate to the socialization of young boys with the concretely felt concerns of a particular community.

With regard to such symbolic forms, Marcus surmises 'that a Spanish Mediterranean initiation *tradition* existed which both resembled and differed substantially from the Ashkenazic ritual' (1996: 24–5; emphasis added). From the few examples available, it is not clear what might be meant by the term 'tradition'. Is one to envision a widespread tradition that has either disappeared or of which only a few instances have survived in ethnographic and historical records? Or, relating again to older ethnological notions, can we speak here of a case of independent invention, in which Torah initiation ceremonies cropped up in an autonomous manner in diverse locales? In this context, it is also worth putting into question Marcus's gloss of the tradition being Spanish. Examples he cites are in the southern reaches of the Maghreb, with no clear indication (thus far) of a continuous distribution of such practices from the Mediterranean coast southward. An intermediate formulation might be that there were regional networks among Jews in North Africa, entailing the movement of people, ideas, and practices, so that through a combination of local 'invention' and intermittent diffusion, practices bearing a resemblance to one another might appear (and wane) in different areas. Patterns of diffusion notwithstanding, we would expect such practices to absorb specific local significances as well, which would need to be deciphered in each case.

More generally, these scattered materials suggest an approach of viewing such curious rituals as windows onto ongoing processes in which symbolic elements nurtured in Jewish tradition are grafted onto and 'sprout up' within defined local conditions that are initially either neutral in relation to Jewish content or may even be in tension with them. From the point of view of cultural content made up of a repertoire of 'building blocks' or symbolic kernels, ceremonies that have gestures or language features in common may appear as the same tradition, while a closer look at the local circumstances that inject significance into ritual expression shows them to vary in their forms, meanings, and purported impact.

A relevant example of such blocks or kernels may be found in a brief reference to a Yitro celebration in Algeria alluded to above, which supplies specific, albeit sparse, information:

In Algiers, they celebrate *ḥag siyum* on the Thursday preceding *seder* [the *parashah* of] 'Yitro'; they make it a holiday and do not recite Tahanun,[12] even during the *minḥah* [afternoon] prayer preceding it. On that day, the merchants, pedlars and artisans scattered among the Arabs in the villages come to hear the Ten Commandments. (Eisenstein 1909: 176)

As noted above, there is no indication in this source that the occasion is special for children. It does evoke a widespread economic pattern in North Africa of Jewish merchants and artisans scattered around the countryside, sometimes staying away from home for a whole week or even for weeks at a time (see Goldberg 1990a: 68–81). It is clear that such a manner of economic existence cannot easily be reconciled with routine synagogue attendance or regular hours for studying Torah. In addition, historical evidence exists from the sixteenth century onward, in the southern reaches of both Algeria and Tunisia, of 'Jews living among nomads or semi-nomads . . . who had forgotten almost all about their religion and only remembered that they were of Jewish origin' (Hirschberg 1963: 335). Established Jewish communities in Algeria and Tunisia adjacent to these regions assigned the term *baḥutsim* ('those who are outside') to these Jews (Hirschberg 1963: 328, 334–5; Slouschz 1927: 295–305), and in a study of Setif in eastern Algeria, Bahloul (1996: 111) briefly mentions a Yitro celebration and indicates that it was especially associated with those of *baḥutsi* origin. In these two contexts, of itinerant merchants and small groups who have almost lost their connection to Jewish life, the Yitro event may have served as a periodic re-initiation into Torah for those whose way of life kept them far from regular communal occasions of study or even from exposure to the *parashah* on a weekly basis.

The above interpretation is conjectural, but it adds to the picture of a possible 'Yitro culture complex' or, better, a 'Yitro kernel' in North Africa. There is not enough information to posit the existence of a commonly held and widespread tradition of a well-defined celebration. Rather, such a kernel may be one element of a set of cultural building blocks found among some Jews in North Africa, which may or may not be elaborated depending on local circumstances. Such elaboration depends not only on the existence of appropriate cultural materials, but also on interpretative initiatives and on forms of communal and Torah-oriented leadership and authority. Added to these would be factors stemming from local social and historical conditions relating to both Jews and Muslims in the region. With this model in mind, we now turn to some specific historical events and developments affecting nineteenth-century Tunisia and the Jews within it.

Se'udat Yitro and the History of Tunis

Both the main published accounts we have cited, and the explanations received from many informants, stress a disease that ravaged Jewish children in Tunis in the nineteenth century as the background to the Yitro celebration. To what extent may this be seen as historical? On the one hand, it is known that diseases such as cholera and the plague were important factors in economic and social developments during the nineteenth and early twentieth centuries in North Africa. On the other hand, the claim that the disease stopped miraculously, and particularly the implication that it affected only little boys, raises historians' eyebrows. Equivocation in this regard may be reflected in Malakhi's compromise description in which she states: 'The epidemic left many dead, particularly among the boys' (2002: 25). Our own position is that there is no reason to force a choice between the attempt to provide a historically grounded account of the ritual and analysing the perceptions, understandings, and valuations arising from the narratives we have collected. It is precisely the intertwining of these levels, in which there appear both correspondences and gaps, that makes the story of Se'udat Yitro intriguing.

Fortunately, a deeper insight into the historical background of the festival is provided by Nancy Gallagher's *Medicine and Power in Tunisia, 1780–1900* (1983). There is no mention of Se'udat Yitro in this study, but Jews figure in the investigation in several ways. First, there was a significant Jewish population in Tunis, concentrated in a Jewish quarter (the *ḥara*). Second, an important source for the study is the records kept by Abraham Lumbroso, a physician to the Bey of Tunisia and member of a prominent Jewish family from Livorno in the city. Lumbroso not only treated the Bey, but kept extensive records in order to better understand the spread of epidemics, and he meticulously included information on Jews along with other groups in the city. One instance was the rapid spread of cholera in the Jewish quarter in late 1849 and early 1850.

Lumbroso describes how a travelling merchant in the *ḥara* fell ill and died two days later, and then the disease began to move throughout the quarter. Gallagher (1983: 49) cites Lumbroso's written remarks that the disease 'spread to nearby houses, all inhabited by Jews, as if that germ had had some sort of knowledge and avoided all other sects except the Jews'. A Muslim scholar close to the Bey also noted that 'when the disease descended upon the capital, it first fell among poor Jews'. Gallagher adds: 'The peculiar spread of the disease by ethnic group was noted by the residents of the city, who made it the basis of a tale about the origin of the disease' (1983: 50). This tale puts the Jews at a disadvantage in relation to the Muslims and Christians of Tunis, who were portrayed as having been successfully protected by patron saints, while we are left without direct evidence of how the devastating events were then perceived by Jews.

While the pattern of the spread of that epidemic baffled both medical and popular understanding, Gallagher indicates that with our current knowledge of the mode of transmission of cholera the development is not puzzling.[13] The *ḥara* was impoverished and unsanitary, water supplies were localized in the different quarters of the city, and social practices relating to illness, dying, and mourning brought people together, increasing the likelihood of contagion. She nevertheless finds it important to document religious interpretations and ritual responses to the disease that arose among Tunisian Muslims.

Gallagher's account concerns two cases of cholera in 1849 and 1850: the one just cited and a second outbreak in the spring and summer of 1850. Both involved ritual events which are seen as part of the story from the perspective of Muslims. We mention both briefly in order to suggest that they may constitute some of the background to Se'udat Yitro among the Jews. It is useful to begin with the latter case.

At the end of June, when the second epidemic was rampant, Ahmad Bey ordered a *qadi* (judge) to arrange an invocation. Forty descendants of the Prophet (*sharifs*), all named Muhammad, were to convene daily at the Great Mosque from morning till noon and read a *sura* (chapter) of the Quran forty times. Soon after the invocation the disease abated and disappeared, and this auspicious turn of events meant that the men who had participated in the reading no longer needed proof of their holy descent (Gallagher 1983: 55–6). We have no doubt that this dramatic end to the disease impressed not only the Muslims of the city, but also the Jews. In an atmosphere of interreligious rivalry, it was a major triumph for Islam (see Awret 1984: 39–41 for a sense of rivalry among Jews and Muslims in Tunisia with regard to prayers in a year of drought).

The earlier epidemic involved a different twist regarding the various religious groups. As news of cholera began to reach Tunis from the countryside, Ahmad Bey moved to a residence in Carthage, outside the city. As noted, the disease first wreaked havoc in the Jewish quarter, and during the first few weeks of January only a few cases appeared among Muslims. In that year, the celebration of Mohammad's birthday—*mawlid al-nabiy*—fell on 27 January, and there was a debate as to whether the traditional public celebration should take place with the Bey absent. The Bey sent a letter saying that the rituals should be conducted as usual, and following the ceremonies the disease spread rapidly in Muslim quarters. Gallagher suggests that the large gatherings associated with the *mawlid* might have hastened its transmission. Major celebrations like this attracted the attention of the Jews, too, even though this is not mentioned explicitly in the account. From the point of view of the Jewish calendar, 28 January 1850 was the minor festival of Tu Bishvat (beginning 27 January at night), and on the sabbath that followed—2 February—*parashat* 'Yitro' with the Ten Commandments was read in the synagogues.

This constellation of events, we believe, may very well constitute the background for the crystallization of Se'udat Yitro in the form that it took in Tunis. We do need to employ some guesswork regarding the documented events to reach this conclusion, but this conjecture is based on a comparative perspective of popular religious interactions between Jews and their neighbours, and also an appreciation of the range of parallels, oppositions, and reversals familiar from structuralist analysis that might have played a role in the religious imagination of Jews.[14] This approach incorporated some of the existing facts selectively, placing them in a configuration that made sense and was appealing to Jewish audiences.

In the case of the second epidemic, history does provide us with an account of its dramatic end following religious intervention. True, it was a Muslim invocation, not Jewish prayer,[15] but with regard to that epidemic there is no mention of a special ethnic pattern of spread of the disease so the relief then might have been sensed by all the residents of the city. The two episodes of cholera were separated by only a few months, so the events could quickly have been merged in popular and also ritual memory. The celebration of Muhammad's *mawlid* followed by the reading of the Decalogue among Jews must have appeared retrospectively as a turning point with regard to the first outbreak. From a Muslim perspective, it is ironic that cholera began to spread precisely at this point, but for the Jews this might have provided at least some relief as they no longer remained the only victims of the disease—a fact that had received both learned and popular attention.

The whole concatenation of developments was highly charged with emotion, both at the personal-familial level (according to a man from Nabeul in Tunisia, 'more than half of our children would never see their second birthday'—see Awret 1984: 16), and on the intertwined ethnic-theological plane which distinguished Jews from the Muslim majority. In such a setting, for the Jews to draft in the reading of the Ten Commandments (in contradistinction to the Quran), and the name of Yitro that has long been associated with that liturgical act, as a redeeming moment, is not surprising. If it is correct that such a cultural kernel involving a festive celebration preceding 'Yitro's *parashah*' already existed in the region, and if we add to this historical dates that were prominent in relation to the first epidemic, then the rapid institutionalization of Se'udat Yitro among Tunis's Jews is easy to grasp. The influences that led to the emergence of this form of the ritual may have been so strong that it became part of local life even as precise explanations and interpretations faded over time.

Our suggested interpretation, in addition to containing conjectural elements, is also partial. It offers no explanation of why male children are central to the event, or of the significance of the special foods, or of the religious standardization that is expressed in the printing of instructional 'Yitro pages' (see below) that include blessings appropriate to the festive occasion. It does, however, satisfactorily illustrate, in our eyes, how rituals like this can arise through a linking of available cultural materials with specific events and structures that have great significance within communal life. Once embedded within the ritual repertoire of a community, such practices become available not only for further interpretation and growing systematization, but also for additional reworking as they affect other communities in shifting circumstances.

Regional Variation: Voices from Tunis, Jerba, and Gafsa

The literature cited thus far, including references to both Algeria and Tunisia, shows important variation under the general heading of a Yitro event. The interviews carried out among people from Tunisia reinforce this point. First, it appears that in recent times there were locales in Tunisia in which Se'udat Yitro was not celebrated or recognized at all. We have no basis of speculating whether a ritual with that name had once been more widespread and later disappeared in these places, or simply never existed.

Beyond that, as intimated above, there emerged fairly distinct emphases in the form of celebration, and to some extent in the meanings attached to it, in the descriptions from Tunis and the communities of the north as compared to those from Jerba and the south. This is not surprising in light of the cultural differences in Jewish life between these regions in recent times, as extensively discussed by Shlomo Deshen (2005).[16] Even though the data contain examples that contradict this simple bipolar portrait, the contrast in the matters stressed by the different groups is consistent, and a number of our interlocutors pointed out the variations in expression between the north and the south. We thus describe this difference in emphasis in terms of 'Tunis' as opposed to 'Jerba'.

In Tunis the explanation concerning the 'plague' is more salient than in Jerba. There were both general assertions about the epidemic and its cessation and also specific accounts featuring powerful rabbis who fasted and prayed in order to stop its spread. Other interviewees sought to make links between the epidemic and the custom of serving squab to the children. One interpretation was that pigeon meat was helpful in curing or preventing the spread of disease. Another is that the slaughter of a dove represented an act of atonement, implicitly paralleling some of the sacrifices in the Bible or the practice of *kaparot* before the Day of Atonement in which a chicken is slaughtered for each member of the family, roosters corresponding to males and hens to females.[17] The link between doves and propitiation may be reinforced by the description we received of pink ribbons being tied around the necks of the birds. The ribbon is perhaps to disguise the male child and represent him as a little girl, thereby protecting him from potential harm. Slaughtering and serving doves was so important that interviewees described how Muslims, aware of the importance of dove meat to the Jews, seized the opportunity to raise the price of pigeons. The fact that the narratives linked to the ritual have diversified while the custom itself has remained relatively invariable highlights the primacy of the behavioural patterns as enshrined in group practice and habitus,[18] with the rationales as secondary expressions.

A second emphasis in the Tunis description was on smallness. Not only was a squab smaller than a chicken (which the adults might eat on the same occasion; and some accounts said children might eat a young chicken), but everything else connected to the event was miniature: the table and chairs, the utensils in which the food was prepared and served, and the portions themselves. This was stressed by various interviewees, even as it was given different interpretations by them. Some saw the occasion as one that should be fun for the children, while others explained that serving on small plates conveyed a message of moderation in consumption.

In all of the above cases, the emphasis was on male children as the focus of a family home celebration. In this, there was a bold contrast with the form of the celebration in Jerba where the synagogue was a central venue of the Yitro event, as discussed below. The descriptions from Tunis seem to resonate with the interpretation of the local *kittab* ritual in Ghardaia cited above: the significance of the stage of early childhood, and the transition out of it, were culturally encoded into the practices of smallness.

Regarding Jerba, several sources, both oral and written, imply that the regular practice of Se'udat Yitro emerged more recently there. Given the scarce documentation, the process cannot be traced in detail, but the custom's adoption apparently involved conscious intervention and structuring by local rabbis. In the material available, we can see the efforts of Jerban (and other) rabbis to link the practice, which may have been perceived as foreign in its origin, to Torah literature.[19]

This process may be illustrated by the way the *se'udah* for the young boys was organized in Jerba, in contrast to Tunis. In the southern community, it took place in the synagogue and was prepared by the wife of the rabbi. Each boy was expected to bring a hard-boiled egg from home. The cooked birds were stuffed with these eggs, but before that, the rabbi would write the name of each child on the egg he brought along with a blessing having to do with the study of Torah.

The organization of this event in the synagogue underlines the role of rabbinic authority in the celebration and is complemented by the fact that the dominant explanation given for it in Jerba is the connection to the world of Torah and the reading of the Decalogue. One interviewee from Jerba described in detail how his rabbi-teacher used to challenge the pupils by demanding that they find new interpretations (*ḥidushim*) for the biblical phrase, 'And Yitro heard . . .' (Exod. 18: 1). The children of the *kuttab* had to answer the question posed by the rabbi: *Mah she-mu'ah shama yitro*—what were the tidings Yitro heard that brought him to visit Moses and share his new understanding of God's power? This question was taken from a midrashic passage,[20] and the children were thus prodded to recall the details of the Exodus narrative and supply their own answers to explain Yitro's recognition of the might of God and his relation to Israel. All this reflected the claim of the midrash that Yitro, originally a pagan priest, accepted the truth of the Jewish religion (further aspects of the midrash will be discussed below). His acknowledgement of God appeared as taken for granted in many of our interviews, and some people viewed Se'udat Yitro as commemorating the festive meal that had taken place on the occasion of Yitro's conversion to Judaism.

Another expression of rabbinic engagement with the celebration in Jerba is the convention that Tahanun—the penitentiary portions of the daily prayers—is not recited on the day of Se'udat Yitro.[21] Considering the event's vague historical background, the omission of Tahanun is indicative of a desire to bring the celebration within the framework of tradition, irrespective of what might be a questionable origin.

A further sign of rabbinic approbation and appropriation of the ritual is the preparation of a decorated 'Yitro page'—*warqat yitro*. This is a single printed page in which an explanation is given for the ritual along with texts—such as blessings over specific foods—that are fitting for the occasion.[22] This printed genre is not unique to the Yitro event, but was found in North Africa in connection with other customs that were part of a wider liturgical tradition but highly specific in their local forms, in particular foods and blessings that were part of the evening meal that initiated the New Year—Rosh Hashanah.[23] In this latter instance, the practice may be traced back to the Talmud (Goldberg 1990b), which highlights the cultural assertiveness of the Jerban rabbis in producing a formal document for Se'udat Yitro where textual roots were flimsy in the extreme. These pages were produced in Tunis as well, and in that instance became part of family ritual, like the Rosh Hashanah page. One way of viewing these initiatives is as steps that might eventually contribute to overriding problematic aspects of the celebration, even though those who acquired and used the sheets may have attributed talismanic properties to them. The erasure of such popular magical elements does not take place overnight: they often coexist in a non-polemical atmosphere with seemingly authoritative rabbinic and text-oriented inputs for a considerable time.

The puzzling and unanswered (or partially answered) aspects of Se'udat Yitro lead us to stress its dynamism. The interviews, placed in juxtaposition to the somewhat older historical sources at our disposal, seem to yield a snapshot of what was a fluid and evolving situation—one that continues today in Israel and in France. Thus, rather than seeking to objectify the two models of the Yitro event, one based on Tunis and the other on Jerba, we conclude by discussing data from the region of Gafsa in south-eastern Tunisia which do not fit neatly into either category. Material gathered from that region returns us to an issue we have already touched upon above, seemingly different from, but perhaps complementary to, the picture from Jerba, namely, the extensive exposure of Jews to the wider Muslim society.

Gafsa lies in a region considered the 'pre-Sahara', distant from larger Jewish communities. It was a site of Jewish settlement in the Middle Ages, but there is no way of assessing possible continuity from those days to recent centuries when the Jews living there numbered in the hundreds. In any event, our Gafsa-born interviewee distinguished between the way Se'udat Yitro was celebrated by old-time inhabitants of the town and the form it took among Jews from Tunis residing in the oasis. The latter account was in tune with our description of Tunis, provided above. With regard to local practice, a discussion of the Ten Commandments read during *parashat* 'Yitro' led our interlocutor to describe a different custom, practised during the other occasion in the ritual year on which the Decalogue is read—the festival of Shavuot.

He depicted how, after the morning prayers on Shavuot, local Muslim officials would come to the synagogue and listen to a reading of the Ten Commandments not during the formal reading of the Torah, but from a book in which the commandments were translated and elaborated into a Judaeo-Arabic version that the visitors were able to grasp.[24] Not only were these Muslims aware when Shavuot was approaching each year, but they appeared in the synagogue on both days of the holiday, with the reading of the first day being devoted to the first five commandments and the second to the latter five. According to our interviewee, what appealed to the Muslims was the mention of God—Allah—and of Moses—Musa—who is considered a prophet, even though the main prophet of Islam—Muhammad—nowhere appears in the text.

This situation conjures up settings cited above (Hirschberg 1963) in reference to earlier periods, and mentioned by Bahloul regarding the interior of eastern Algeria (which had population links with Gafsa) in the twentieth century, where the lives of some Jews and Muslims heavily intertwined. To our enquiry about a parallel phenomenon, of Muslims attending the reading of the Decalogue in less peripheral areas, an interviewee from the southern Tunisian coastal town of Gabes stated that ordinary Muslims, some of them with their herds, would gather near the synagogue to listen to the Ten Commandments, but insisted that they would stand outside and would never be allowed to enter.[25] When asked for further details, our informant from Gafsa produced the actual book he used in the Shavuot ritual.

This practice is not directly linked to Se'udat Yitro, but the Judaeo-Arabic text, which is more than a translation of the Decalogue and consists of an elaborate translation and commentary, appears to allude to the understanding that Yitro converted to Judaism. This reinforces his image as someone who 'was drawn close' to Moses and the God of Israel while also remaining somewhat apart.[26] The seemingly extraordinary coalescence of a Jewish–Muslim 'congregation' on Shavuot serves to highlight the dynamics of ceremonial practice, texts, and context that we seek to underline.

Group structural relations constitute the important point here, rather than any historical accuracy. One of our informants suggested that Yitro was a 'Christian', thus defining him as different from the Jews, but also not identical to the most salient and challenging 'others' in his environment, namely Muslims. It may be worth noting that in Islam, the Yitro figure is named Shu'eib, and the Quran sees him as a prophet to the Midianite people. Among the Druze, Shu'eib is a founding figure. Historically, the Druze religion developed out of Islam, but Druze today mostly distinguish themselves from Muslims. We thus suggest that, irrespective of whatever historical coincidence linked the week of reading *parashat* 'Yitro' to the spread or cessation of an epidemic, and the acts commemorating those events, the name Yitro itself has the function of marking boundaries between Jews and others, implying both separation and connection.

The data regarding Gafsa reinforce our assumption that the varying pictures of Se'udat Yitro emerging from Tunis and Jerba must not be separated from one another, even while ethnographic differences are acknowledged. Our search for a historical explanation regarding Tunis revealed the importance of the wider Muslim society in terms of group boundaries that became salient during a cholera epidemic, while our interviews focusing on Jerba stressed the activities of rabbis seeking to pour textually based content into the ritual. But these different portraits may be seen as complementary moments as well as contrastive emphases.

One common way of looking at the relations between Jews and their majority neighbours has been to distinguish cultural features reflecting written rabbinic tradition from what is absorbed from the wider society, and at times the significance of the latter is underestimated in the study of customs and rituals (see Valensi 1989 on Jerba). It has recently been noted by Shlomo Deshen (2005) that rabbinic authorities in Jerba also took into account some overlap between Jewish and Muslim practices within their writings. Thus, it is often precisely their deep involvement with the majority culture and religion that has stimulated Jews, both as rabbis and laypeople, to delve more deeply into their own past and sources, often reconfiguring them in ways that leave few traces of the steps taken. While there are many missing pieces to our puzzle, the ethnography stimulated by the Se'udat Yitro ritual presents a society that at once fits standard notions of being traditional while also exhibiting an active and innovative ritual habitus that responds to both its non-Jewish environment and time-honoured texts within Jewish life.[27] These thrusts, while seemingly pointing in opposite directions, are, in fact, intimately linked.

Concluding Thoughts

In this essay we have documented and analysed a puzzling ritual familiar only among the Jews of Tunisia. While the celebration was organized primarily around young male children, the cultural associations we uncovered, in both written accounts and field interviews, opened up various avenues of interpretation. This fluidity and lack of definiteness was as much a characteristic of our interviewees' approach as it was of our own piecemeal discoveries. The cultural materials we gathered did not organize themselves into a coherent picture, but remained loosely connected, often cryptic, constantly generating new associations. We concluded that it was important to relate to this situation as inherent to grasping Se'udat Yitro, rather than to try to tease out its stable essence. For this reason, this concluding section will be less of a summary of our findings, and more of a rumination that opens for consideration further implications of our approach.

A good place to begin is Marcus's historical-anthropological study of the initiation of young boys into the world of Torah in medieval Europe (1996). In this study, he takes threads from antiquity, including the deployment of classic rabbinic texts, and shows how they crystallized in a given region and at a defined period into a form that was socially and culturally meaningful within the communal life of Jews in Ashkenaz. Even while homing in on what may be seen as a single ceremony, Marcus points to variations in the form of the ritual in northern

France as compared to the Rhineland (1996: 25–6). In the first case, the ceremony was organized when a boy reached the proper age or level of maturity, while in the second it became accepted to carry it out close to the festival of Shavuot. On the basis of the above examples, it is possible to get some sense of dynamic and evolving practice, and of the push to create new cultural links.

Marcus also traces the waning of the ceremony, as another pedagogically oriented ritual—bar mitzvah—began to become prominent in the late Middle Ages. The elements of the earlier public event, however, did not disappear but continued to be part of a storehouse of ritual kernels that were available for use and reconfiguration in new circumstances. This may be seen clearly in the rituals of childhood among strictly Orthodox Jews today, analysed by Yoram Bilu (2000), in which some of the classic ceremonies of entering the *ḥeder* have become linked with a pilgrimage to the cenotaph of Rabbi Shimon bar Yohai in Meron, where 3-year-old boys are given their first haircut. This typically takes place on Lag Ba'omer—between Passover and Shavuot—and the whole development, from our perspective, illustrates a creative ritual 'urge', working within a fluid field of cultural symbols and associations, that we have encountered in trying to follow the path of Se'udat Yitro.

While there is a standard time for Se'udat Yitro within the liturgical calendar, some of our interviewees spontaneously linked it with other celebrations and narratives embedded in the ritual year. Some of these connections may stem from the desire to have the celebration make sense within the network of more solidly established holidays, but while doing so they also evoke meanings that enrich the cultural baggage of the Yitro event. Some of these interpretations have expressions in written texts, and others do not (except for appearing in the ethnographer's notes and publications), and there may be a variety of reasons for certain practices not making their way into the writings of rabbis (Goldberg 2003: 150–3). Our claim is that processes of local ritual variation, innovation, and reinterpretation in specific settings, which we have been able to tap in the case of Se'udat Yitro, have long accompanied the negotiation between local influences on the one hand and established Jewish practice and textual traditions on the other, and have characterized Jewish life from ancient times up until the present. The modern period may have provided new contexts for such mutual accommodation, but we suggest that the cultural mechanisms at work in which 'laypeople' as well as scholarly elites partake, bear resemblance across epochs.

We have already cited the connection with Shavuot that was made by the interviewee from Gafsa. Other people, particularly from Tunis, mentioned Purim, associating the two celebrations because of their shared merry atmosphere. Another association appears to have gained salience due to current sensibilities in Israel which couples Se'udat Yitro, focusing on males, with *rosh ḥodesh habanot* (the New Moon festival of girls) celebrated by Jewish women in North Africa in the middle of Hanukah six weeks earlier.[28] The most salient comparative comments that we heard, however, involved Passover and the story of the Exodus.

The *parashah* called 'Yitro' begins by stating that he 'heard of all that God had done for Moses, and for Israel his people, and that the Lord had brought Israel out of Egypt'. The foundational story referred to here is suffused with elements that clearly resonate with different aspects of Se'udat Yitro and its interpretations. The miraculous rescue of Moses as an infant ensconced in a miniature 'ark' foreshadows the eventual rescue of Israel. In addition, the story of the plague smiting the first-born Egyptians includes a public marking of the Israelites, through the blood placed on doorposts, as a prelude to God's choice of them as recipients of his covenant. All these events are implicitly invoked in the story about the epidemic in Tunis that particularly affected boys. The Exodus story entails a turning of tables, and if our reconstruction of Jewish perceptions of the 1850 Tunisian cholera epidemic is correct, the creation of Se'udat Yitro also involved an inversion of historical events in the Jews' memory.

These collective images may provide another route to appreciating a connection between the Tunis and the Jerba models of the celebration. The Exodus tells of God's providence for the Israelites at the level of basic survival, but reaches a high point in the covenant of the Decalogue, the revelation in written form that creates the Jewish people and its texts. Yitro, who provided refuge for Moses when he was forced to flee from Egypt, meets him again on the eve of this momentous cultural drama. As a witness who is both linked to the process and also provides outside validation, the image of Yitro epitomizes the initial steps of commitment to what the Decalogue entails.

We, too, in following various routes to discover 'what Yitro meant', found him to be a faithful if ever-moving guide. Just as young boys were challenged to figure out what it was that Yitro heard as an entrance point to the 'tent of Torah', so the puzzle of Se'udat Yitro provided us with an appropriate framework to encompass a series of ongoing tensions and ambiguities that we have sought to share: between explicit and latent symbolic links, tradition and innovation, reality and its representation, and—especially—between a cultural riddle and its deciphering.

Acknowledgements

We are indebted to many interviewees from Tunisia now living in Israel who generously shared their memories and insights, and particularly acknowledge the help of Eliahu Shimoni and of Shoshana and Gad Haddad. This essay benefited from both the professional and cultural input of Robert (Avraham) Attal, Esther Schely-Newman, and Zivia Tobi. Huguette Demri contributed additional perspectives and Judy Goldberg provided feedback on a draft of this essay.

Notes

1   On the Saharaneh see Halper and Abramovitch 1984, on the Sigd see Ben-Dor 1985, and on the Mimuna see Goldberg 1977. In modern-day Israel, these holidays have been intro-

duced by immigrants, and while at first labelled 'ethnic', have gradually entered the annual cycle of Jewish holidays marked on the Israeli calendar.

2   This reflects the fact that the conventional names of weekly readings stem from the first (or one of the first) word(s) in the *parashah*, and not its thematic content.

3   Without disputing this level of meaning (or, to be precise, lack of meaning), the hermeneutic imagination does not leave such names alone. *Parashat* 'Yitro' invites interpretative intervention because of a puzzle: if one chooses to seek significant content in the label, why should such a central portion of the Torah, in which God reveals himself to Moses, be named after Yitro, a Midianite priest? Another enigma stems directly from the text of the Torah and the rest of the Bible. Both in Exodus and other books, the man described as Moses' wife's father appears with different names, such as Reuel or Hovav. An ancient midrash states that Yitro had seven names (see *Mekhilta derabi yishma'el*, 'Yitro', section Amalek, *parashah alef*). What is salient in most of the biblical episodes in which Yitro appears is a close association with Moses on the one hand, along with a delineation separating him (and the group he represents) from the children of Israel on the other. Midian, the founding ancestor of Yitro's people, appears in Genesis as one of Abraham's sons by Keturah, whom he took as a wife after Sarah's death.

4   *Kuttab* is the term in Tunisia (and elsewhere) for the setting in which young boys receive their basic literacy and Torah education, similar to the Ashkenazi ḥeder. It is also the term used by local Muslims to describe basic quranic education.

5   See e.g. the website of AMIT—Association Mondiale des Israélites de Tunisie, accessed 19 September 2008, and its explanation of Se'udat Yitro presented as a question-and-answer conversation: <http://www.amit4u.net/home/nartdetails.aspx?mCatID=9812&nartID= 15811>.

6   See also the account of Tunisian-born Claude Sitbon (1979).

7   See Goldberg 2003: 87–8, 294 n. 52, and 304 n. 45.

8   The celebration of the completion of a study cycle; see Goldberg 2003: 108–9.

9   One example is her mention of a single rabbinic source, cited on a 'Yitro page' (see pp. 58–9 above), claiming that the practice was found in Yemen and the Caucasus as well. We have found no additional information to corroborate this.

10   See Evans-Pritchard 1961 and Geertz 1968.

11   This probably refers to the decorative image above the holy ark, the cabinet in which Torah scrolls were housed.

12   Tahanun is a set of penitential prayers and supplications that have become part of the weekday morning and afternoon service, placed after the Amidah prayer. It is not recited on sabbaths and festivals or in the afternoon prayer on the eve of the sabbath. Tahanun may be suspended situationally, for example when a circumcision is celebrated in a certain synagogue or even a town. In various places, where communities have developed local celebrations to mark deliverance from a persecutor, phrasing the event as a version of the Purim salvation described in the book of Esther (Goodman 1949), it is also common to suspend Tahanun on that day.

13   Some differential spread of diseases among different groups and quarters was probably not uncommon, at least for a time, in North African cities (Schroeter 1988: 198), but this case seems to have been particularly dramatic.

14   See e.g. Goldberg 1990a and Salamon 1999.

15   It is quite possible that Jews conducted their own special prayers to ward off the epidemic,
      even though this is not documented. It was common for Jews in North Africa to pray for
      rain at the time of drought; this was sometimes done after a request made by local Mus-
      lims. See Awret 1984: 39–41 for a Tunisian example, and also the picture on p. 199 of
      Schroeter 1988.

16   In addition to differences between Tunis and Jerba that are clearly attributable to longer
      and more intense European influence in the capital and the north of the country as com-
      pared to the south, there also have been historical ties between Jerba and Tripoli to the
      east, partly evident in the existence of overlapping liturgical traditions that were not
      shared with Tunis (Goldberg 1994).

17   On *kaparot* see *Encyclopaedia Judaica*, x. 756.

18   The notion of 'habitus', elaborated by Bourdieu (1977), provides a systematized and more
      refined perspective on the assumption of classic writers on ritual and custom that the
      practice of rituals takes precedence over the explanations given for them, even (or espe-
      cially) by those engaged in their performance (see Goldberg 2003: 6)

19   In his *Berit kehunah*, which might be considered the '*Shulḥan arukh*—Code of Jewish
      Law'—of Jerban Jewry, Rabbi Khalfon Moshe Hakohen (1874–1921) has one paragraph on
      Se'udat Yitro. He describes it as a practice that exists 'in some places', and indicates that
      'for some time the custom has been newly practised here on the Island of Jerba' (see the
      4th, revised, edn. (1941), 129). His authoritative voice stresses the celebration as honour-
      ing the Torah, making the figure of Yitro incidental.

20   In BT *Zev.* 116a, the question is asked, *Mah shemu'ah shama uva venitgayer?*—'What were
      the tidings he [Yitro] heard that he came and converted?' This question (without the last
      word concerning conversion) was incorporated by Rashi, the eleventh-century sage whose
      commentary became basic to Torah education for children in subsequent generations.

21   See n. 12 above.

22   A sample, reproduced in Israel, is provided by Malakhi (2002: 34).

23   See Udovitch and Valensi 1984: 71–2, and Bahloul 1989: 92–4.

24   The practice of reading the Ten Commandments in Arabic is described by Avraham Hai
      Addadi (1800–74) regarding Algiers, Tunis, and Tripoli. He indicates that the basis of the
      Arabic translation is attributed to Sa'adiah Gaon (882–942), while the specific translation
      was adopted to the spoken Judaeo-Arabic of each locale. Appearing in Hai Addadi's book
      Hashomer emet (Livorno, 1849), the description of the custom is also included in Ha-
      Cohen (1978: 207). Tobi (1996: 216–17) cites the publication of such a translation in 1737
      in Amsterdam, for use in Tunis. The custom apparently waned considerably in the twenti-
      eth century.

25   Discussing Se'udat Yitro, an interviewee from Sfax, further to the north, did not remem-
      ber Muslims listening to the Ten Commandments, but readily recognized that Muslims
      were familiar with aspects of Jewish liturgy (she gave the example of kiddush on Friday
      night) in instances when Muslims and Jews co-resided in the same Mediterranean-style
      house (see Bahloul 1996).

26   In elaborating upon the qualities of God, the translation attributes to him the power to
      'distance he who is near and bring close he who is far'. This echoes the midrash on

parashat 'Yitro' (see n. 3 above) that uses the language of 'bringing close' vs. 'distancing' with regard to Yitro, and to potential proselytes in general.

27   Life in contemporary Israel has provided some very new contexts, and Se'udat Yitro has evolved there in varied ways, with only some of them closely reminiscent of the specific forms in Tunisia. This situation is also fluid, so any consideration of these developments is beyond the scope of the present essay.

28   This was a celebration for women and girls on the New Moon of Tevet that was widespread in North Africa. For the Tunisian version see Malakhi (2002: 23–4). For Tunisian Jewish young girls' and brides' food regime see Salamon and Juhasz (forthcoming).

References

AWRET, IRENE. 1984. *Days of Honey: The Tunisian Boyhood of Rafael Uzan*. New York.

BAHLOUL, JOËLLE. 1989. 'From a Muslim Banquet to a Jewish Seder: Foodways and Ethnicity Among North African Jews', in M. R. Cohen and A. L. Udovitch, eds., *Jews Among Arabs: Contacts and Boundaries*, 85–96. Princeton, NJ.

——1996. *The Architecture of Memory: A Jewish–Muslim Household in Colonial Algeria, 1937–1962*. New York.

BEN-DOR, SHOSHANA. 1985. 'The Sigd of the Beta-Israel: A Holiday of Covenant Renewal' [Hasigd shel beta yisra'el: ḥag ḥidush haberit]. MA thesis, Hebrew University of Jerusalem.

BILU, YORAM. 2000. 'Circumcision, the First Haircut and the Torah: Ritual and Male Identity in the Ultraorthodox Community of Israel', in M. Ghoussoub and E. Sinclair-Webb, eds., *Imagined Masculinities: Male Identity and Culture in the Modern Middle East*, 33–64. London.

BOURDIEU, PIERRE. 1977. *Outline of a Theory of Practice*. Cambridge.

BRIGGS, LLOYD C., and NORINA L. GUÈDE. 1964. *No More For Ever: A Saharan Jewish Town*. Papers of the Peabody Museum of Archaeology and Ethnology at Harvard University, vol. 55, no. 1. Cambridge, Mass.

COHEN, DAVID. 1964. *Le Parler arabe des Juifs de Tunis*. Paris.

DESHEN, SHLOMO. 2005. 'Southern Tunisian Jewry in the Early Twentieth Century: Elements of French, Arab and Jewish Culture', *Journal of North African Studies*, 10: 183–99.

EISENSTEIN, Y. D. 1909. *Otsar yisra'el*, vol. vii. New York.

EVANS-PRITCHARD, E. E. 1961. *Anthropology and History*. Manchester.

GALLAGHER, NANCY E. 1983. *Medicine and Power in Tunisia: 1780–1900*. Cambridge.

GEERTZ, CLIFFORD. 1968. *Islam Observed*. New Haven.

GOLDBERG, HARVEY E. 1977. 'Introduction: Culture and Ethnicity in the Study of Israeli Society', *Ethnic Groups*, 1: 163–86.

——1987a. *Judaism Viewed from Within and from Without: Anthropological Studies*. Albany, NY.

——1987b. 'Torah and Children: Symbolic Aspects of the Reproduction of Jews and Judaism'. In id., *Judaism Viewed from Within and from Without: Anthropological Studies*, 113–14, 125. Albany, NY.

——1990a. *Jewish Life in Muslim Libya: Rivals and Relatives*. Chicago.

——1990b. 'Anthropology and the Study of Traditional Jewish Societies', *AJS Review*, 15: 1–22.

——1994.'Religious Responses to Modernity among the Jews of Jerba and of Tripoli: A Comparative Study', *Journal of Mediterranean Studies*, 4: 278–99.

——2003. *Jewish Passages: Cycles of Jewish Life*. Berkeley.

GOODMAN, PHILIP. 1949. *The Purim Anthology*. Philadelphia.

HA-COHEN, MORDECAÏ. 1978. *Higid Mordekhai: History of Libya and its Jews, their Settlements and Customs* [Higid mordekhai: korot luv viyehudeiha, yishuveihem uminhageihem], ed. and annotated by Harvey E. Goldberg. Jerusalem.

HALPER, JEFF, and HENRY ABRAMOVITCH. 1984. 'The Saharane as a Mediator of Kurdish-Jewish Ethnicity'. In Shlomo Deshen and Moshe Shokeid, eds., *The Jews of the Middle East* [Yehudei hamizraḥ], 260–70. Jerusalem.

HIRSCHBERG, H. Z. 1963. 'The Problem of the Judaized Berbers', *Journal of African History*, 4: 313–39.

MALAKHI (SARAF), MIKHAL. 2002. *Mikhal's Treasures: Studies in the Culture and Literature of the Jews of Tunisia and North Africa* [Ginzei mikhal: meḥkarim betarbut uvesifrut shel yehudei tuniziyah utsefon afrikah], ed. Zvi Malakhi. Lod.

MARCUS, IVAN. 1996. *Rituals of Childhood: Jewish Culture and Acculturation in the Middle Ages*. New Haven.

SALAMON, HAGAR. 1999. *The Hyena People: Ethiopian Jews in Christian Ethiopia*. Berkeley.

—— and ESTHER JUHASZ. Forthcoming. '"Goddesses of Flesh and Metal": Gazes on the Tradition of Fattening Jewish Brides in Tunisia', *Journal of Middle Eastern Women's Studies*.

SCHROETER, DANIEL J. 1988. *Merchants of Essaouira: Urban Society and Imperialism in Southwestern Morocco, 1844–1886*. Cambridge.

SITBON, CLAUDE. 1979. 'Seoudat Yitro'. In R. Attal and C. Sitbon, eds., *Regards sur les Juifs de Tunisie*, 133–5. Paris.

SLOUSCHZ, NAHUM. 1927. *Travels in North Africa*. Philadelphia.

TOBI, YOSEF. 1996. 'The Flowering of Judeo-Arabic Literature in North Africa, 1850–1950'. In Harvey E. Goldberg, ed., *Sephardi and Middle Eastern Jewries: History and Culture in the Modern Era*, 213–25. Bloomington, Ind.

TURNER, VICTOR. 1964. 'Symbols in Ndembu Ritual'. In Max Gluckman, ed., *Closed Systems and Open Minds: The Limits of Naïvety in Social Anthropology*, 20–51. Chicago.

UDOVITCH, ABRAHAM, and LUCETTE VALENSI. 1984. *The Last Arab Jews: The Communities of Jerba, Tunisia*. New York.

VALENSI, LUCETTE. 1989. 'Religious Orthodoxy or Local Tradition: Marriage Celebration in Southern Tunisia'. In M. R. Cohen and A. L. Udovitch, eds., *Jews Among Arabs: Contacts and Boundaries*, 65–84. Princeton, NJ.

TWO

Ritual and History: The Order of Prayers for Israel Independence Day (Yom Ha'atsma'ut)

SETH WARD

HOW DOES AN AGE-OLD WORSHIP TRADITION react to history? The period from the Second World War to 1967 saw the destruction of six million Jews, the establishment of the State of Israel in 1948, and the reunification of Jerusalem. How should these pivotal events be commemorated? Are 'civil' rituals enough, or do the events of the middle of the twentieth century create a need for revisioning religious ritual to reflect the new reality? How are such decisions reached?

Israel has instituted four dates, Yom Hasho'ah Vehagevurah (Holocaust and Heroism Memorial Day), Yom Hazikaron (Israel's Memorial Day for fallen soldiers), Yom Ha'atsma'ut (Israel Independence Day), and Yom Yerushalayim (Jerusalem Day),[1] to mark the establishment of the Jewish state so soon after the destruction of the Holocaust and the extension of Jewish sovereignty to Judaism's ancient capital.[2] These dates reflect the great significance of what is for many Jews in Israel and around the world a breathtaking history of great redemption arising after great destruction. They have been the occasion for a flowering of liturgical expressions, a modern-day procession of observances: the week after Passover marks the memorial to the Holocaust; the same day in the following week is Memorial Day, Yom Hazikaron, followed immediately by the celebrations of the founding of the state. The anniversary of the redemption of Jerusalem comes about three weeks later.

This ritual calendar itself tells a story: Passover marks the Exodus and the escape from the Egyptians at the Red Sea, paradigmatic, in Jewish prayer, of divine redemption and salvation. The story of the liberation from slavery in Egypt is matched in modern times, as the destruction in the Holocaust was followed by the sacrifices of Israel's defenders, redeemed, as it were, by the establishment of the state and the return to Jerusalem. Jerusalem Day is exactly one week before Shavuot, a festival considered to mark the giving of the Torah. Thus the ritual calendar fills the *omer* period from Passover to Shavuot, traditionally a time of mourning most probably linked with the last Jewish attempt to reinstate sovereignty in Roman times,[3] with events marking the rebirth of the Jewish state.

These dates both have a programmatic theme and are affirmed by Israeli legislation and practice, considerations missing from dates that are often recalled by Zionists (and anti-Zionists), such as the anniversaries of Lord Balfour's letter announcing the British government's 'favour' for a Jewish National Home in Palestine (2 November) and the United Nations' vote to recommend the establishment of an independent Jewish state in Palestine (29 November). They have remained entirely secular in nature and have developed no religious ritual.[4]

The legislated enactment of public holidays such as Israel Independence Day led to the development of synagogue rituals and raises questions about the types of liturgical innovation adopted for these holidays, primarily in the statutory *shaharit*, *minhah*, and *ma'ariv* (morning, afternoon, and evening) prayers, and other elements of the prayer book. Israel Independence Day supplies an especially good case study of such innovation. The most popular rituals for this day are events and ceremonies organized by the state, army, and other institutions in Israel; by federations and Jewish community centres and synagogues in the diaspora; and by families and individuals everywhere. They include state memorials, fireworks, and the award ceremony for the Israel Prize in Israel, as well as parades, fairs, cultural events, and barbecues. At the same time, the significance of the establishment of the state is also reflected in the traditional liturgy. As I will show, prayer books authorized by each of the major Jewish denominations in the United States have come to integrate substantive innovations into the basic prayer service to affirm through religious ritual the continuity between the founding of the modern State of Israel and ancient Jewish tradition.

Jewish ritual has often been conservative, but rarely has it been fixed. It is not uncommon for old prayers to be invested with new meanings and usages and, as Stefan Reif has shown, although most prayer books may appear to follow tradition slavishly, nearly all make choices and modifications to suit the spiritual needs of their audiences (Reif 1993). Thus they are both conservative and flexible: in this study, even those which depart in major ways from their predecessors were found to reflect the basic traditional elements of Jewish prayer, enabling comparison with more traditional liturgies, while the smallest changes, such as directions regarding what to say next in the service, can reflect important modifications. Even very traditional prayer books have ritual adaptations to fit the situation after the Holocaust, the rise of the State of Israel, and the return to the Old City of Jerusalem. Such adaptations reflect varying attitudes to the questions of what ritual innovation is allowed and whether a secular reality can be religiously meaningful.

The wide variety of these rituals demonstrates the breadth of liturgical creativity in marking the founding of the State of Israel. New rituals speak loudly about the priorities of those drafting and updating them, putting them into prayer books, and buying or deciding to use them. In this essay, I mainly consider prayer books compiled in Israel, those used by the three largest movements in the United States, and one British example (Sacks 2006). Participant-observation in synagogue services on Yom Ha'atsma'ut provided a context for how these rituals are observed in several congregations.

The most common revision of traditional synagogue practice on Yom Ha'atsma'ut is the addition of Hallel (Psalms 113–18, recited on biblical festivals and Hanukah) to the morning service, and the omission of Tahanun, petitionary prayers also cancelled on Jewish holidays, festive occasions, and many other days. Since 1967 the latter has often been extended to Yom Yerushalayim as well. This revision has been adopted in prayer books used by the national religious camp, such as *Rinat yisra'el* (1973) and the *Sidur tefilah* published by Koren (1985), and by Masorati (Conservative) Jews in Israel and Conservative Jews in the United States. In the past few years it has also appeared in the prayer book edited and translated by Rabbi Jonathan Sacks for British Jews (2006) and its US version, the Koren-Sacks Siddur (2009), approved by the Orthodox Union (OU) and published in Israel. In the introduction to the latter siddur, the discussion about Yom Ha'atsma'ut found in the Artscroll-sponsored *Kol Ya'akov* prayer book (standard in American Modern Orthodox congregations) seems to have been muted. The casual reader might not realize that many of the Israeli innovations for Yom Ha'atsma'ut are reflected in the Koren-Sacks prayer book, while none of them can be found in *Kol Ya'akov*, which only includes the Prayer for the State of Israel but no other ritual recognition of the state. There is only a brief mention of this rather radical departure in the Koren-Sacks siddur, and no detailed explanation is given for the modifications other than that they have become fairly common in Modern Orthodox congregations. Possibly the muted description of change satisfies both those who embrace the new rituals and those uncomfortable with any ritual change at all.

Many Orthodox rabbis have, however, rejected any emendation of the liturgy, even those who rejoiced in the establishment of the state. One commonly circulating story in Orthodox circles tells of Rabbi Joseph Cahanaman, founder and head of the Ponevezh yeshiva in Benei Berak, who explained that his practice 'was to follow the custom of Ben-Gurion', the secularist first prime minister of Israel: 'Ben-Gurion does not recite Hallel on Yom Ha'atsma'ut, and neither do I.' Of course Ben-Gurion, being a secular Jew, would not have recited Hallel on Hanukah or Passover, either, when this ritual was recited in the yeshiva.[5]

Although no ritual changes were made at Ponevezh, Rabbi Cahanaman established a 'secular' ritual: displaying the Israeli flag at the yeshiva on Independence Day (Arend 1998a).[6] This recognition was not merely political, as Rabbi Cahanaman saw the divine plan in the wars and deliverance of the Jews that had taken place in the Holy Land in his generation: 'Stricken and brought low, a generation of trials and tribulations' had merited witnessing 'the great abundance of evident and so very wondrous miracles', the greatness of which even those who had participated in them found hard to fully fathom (Neriah 1978: 189). Nevertheless, in many yeshivas and Orthodox circles outside the national religious camp, there is

no discussion of any liturgical change for Yom Ha'atsma'ut, even though traditional prayer books have several additions indicating that the editors are well
aware of the needs of those living in the Land of Israel in modern times. There is a
prayer to be recited at the Western Wall; directions are included for separating out
terumah and tithes (agricultural offerings relevant only to Land of Israel); and a
special version of Tefilat Haderekh, the traveller's prayer, is included for those
travelling by air (*Sidur hashalem kolbo*: 788, 798, 800).

During the early years of the state, Israel's Chief Rabbinate and Ministry of
Religious Affairs, Hakibuts Hadati (the religious kibbutz movement), and others
developed special rituals and liturgies going far beyond reciting Hallel and cancelling Tahanun, and circulated them on informal sheets, in booklets, or in other
publications for use within Israel. These rituals have since been incorporated in
various ways into the general prayer books and liturgical directives produced in
the national religious camp, into Conservative siddurs in Israel and America, and
into Rabbi Sacks's new prayer books.

Prayer books have also been published specifically for Yom Ha'atsma'ut which
include the entire text of the evening and morning prayers, as would be the case
in a *maḥzor* (festive prayer book) for the High Holy Days or festivals. Perhaps the
best known are *Tikun yom ha'atsma'ut* (1955/6) and *Seder hatefilot leyom ha'atsma'ut* (1978),[7] organized and arranged by the late Rabbi Moshe Tsevi Neriah, a fol-
lower of Rabbi Avraham Yitshak Kook, known for his role in founding the yeshiva
high school system as part of his work with the youth movements Benei Akiva
and Hapo'el Hamizrachi.[8] Others include siddurs for Yom Ha'atsma'ut published by Hakibuts Hadati in 1952, 1968, and 1992, and *Seder ha'avodah leyom
ha'atsma'ut*, the ritual introduced in the Italian synagogue in Jerusalem in 1956.[9]
Rabbi Neriah's *Seder* has notes and a few extracts from rabbinic works; in 1998,
on the fiftieth anniversary of Israeli independence, it was republished in a large
volume called *Go'el yisra'el* (Ariel 1998), together with a multitude of readings,
many from the works of Rabbi Avraham Yitshak Kook and his son Rabbi Tsevi
Yehudah Kook.[10] These hardly exhaust the list of such compilations found, for
example, in the Jewish National and University Library catalogue, many of which
have been described by Arend (1998a, 1998b).[11]

A surprising theme emerging from examining Israeli prayer books specifically prepared for Yom Ha'atsma'ut is that, for the first three decades or so, the
diaspora loomed large as a justification for these publications, as noted in their
introductions and title pages, or in letters of approbation published in them. This
is so even though most of them were clearly developed by and for Israelis. For
example, the introduction to the 1978 edition of Rabbi Neriah's *Seder* notes that
'the need [for this prayer book] was especially felt in the diaspora, amongst the
communities of Israel who help and assist the State of Israel . . . The form of celebrating Yom Ha'atsma'ut has not yet become set there, and an edited and annotated prayer book may contribute to determining the character and contents of

the day' (*Seder*, 1978: introduction by Moshe Kroneh). Similar sentiments had been mentioned by Rabbi Isaac Herzog, the Ashkenazi chief rabbi of the State of Israel, in a letter dated 1956 (published in *Seder*, 1978: 7). Both the 1956 and 1978 editions were published by the Division of Diaspora Torah Education and Culture of the World Zionist Organization, and most of the text was taken from *Rinat yisra'el* 'for those outside of Israel' (1978: copyright page). But the edition I examined was not particularly suited for diaspora use (for example, there was no translation, not even of the title page). The diaspora orientation appears to be absent from, or less important in, the more recent Israeli publications I examined, for example, *Go'el yisra'el*.

Differences between the diaspora and Israel extend to the date on which Yom Ha'atsma'ut is marked. The observance commemorates the reading of the Scroll of Independence by Ben-Gurion on 14 May 1948, corresponding with 5 Iyar 5708 in the Jewish calendar. But Israeli practice was to adjust the date to minimize sabbath desecration. Thus if 5 Iyar falls on Friday or Saturday, Yom Ha'atsma'ut is moved up to Thursday. In 2004 the law was amended to postpone Yom Ha'atsma'ut to Tuesday if 5 Iyar is a Monday, to prevent sabbath desecration in preparation for Yom Hazikaron when it begins Saturday night.[12] The Jewish calendar is constructed in such a way that 5 Iyar can only fall on a Monday, Wednesday, Friday, or Saturday, and yet Yom Ha'atsma'ut now can be celebrated only on a Tuesday, Wednesday, or Thursday—and on 5 Iyar itself only when it falls on a Wednesday. Nevertheless, some American Jewish calendars always note Yom Ha'atsma'ut on 5 Iyar; Microsoft Office Outlook 2003 even postpones it from the sabbath to Sunday, 6 Iyar.[13]

The 2004 revision may originally have been intended as a temporary one, based on the need for heightened security prior to the memorial service. The decision to postpone festivities was first made by the Council of the Chief Rabbinate and then unanimously adopted by the government.[14] The letter announcing this decision was accompanied by a ruling by Chief Rabbi Y. Metzger reviewing the main arguments for the recitation of Hallel with a blessing,[15] as well as for the 'Sheheheyanu' blessing and other special prayers, and for adjusting the date to avoid profanation of the sabbath, although he noted that such adjustments had been in place since the founding of the state (Metzger 2004: 4). According to an email memorandum sent to the (Orthodox) Rabbinical Council of America (RCA) by Rabbi Gedalyah Dov Schwartz (12 March 2004), Schwartz's original opinion had been that the sabbath desecration issues do not apply in America (much less security is required for synagogues than for the Israeli head of state), but he was asked by the Chief Rabbinate to rule in favour of uniformity of practice between Israel and the diaspora, and recommended that members of the RCA 'make every effort to schedule' celebrations and events in line with the Israeli decision.

When Yom Ha'atsma'ut is celebrated on a Tuesday or a Thursday, 5 Iyar itself receives no ritual or civil recognition in Israel. The Israeli prayer books examined are careful to refer to the festival without giving the date and mention no practices for 5 Iyar when Yom Ha'atsma'ut is commemorated on a different day. This concurs with the opinion of Rabbi Metzger, but Rabbi Ariel, editor of *Go'el yisra'el*, has written an article about Yom Ha'atsma'ut falling on the sabbath (*Sidur* Sharki 1999), suggesting that when the date is moved, at least some recognition of 5 Iyar ought to be preserved, such as cancelling Tahanun. In the United States many Reform congregations commemorate Yom Ha'atsma'ut only on 5 Iyar, or only on the sabbath regardless of when 5 Iyar occurs. As will be noted below, the Central Conference of American Rabbis (CCAR; the Reform rabbinical association) has objected to this latter practice—but has also recognized it in its prayer book.

Theological and halakhic questions underlying the approval of ritual changes derive from the principle of 'recognition of the day', requiring the precise day to be recognized. In America, the issue can complicate relationships between Israelis and local community members, and affects policies in many synagogues and Jewish communities which prohibit weddings, concerts, and certain other celebrations during most days of counting the *omer* (*sefirat ha'omer*), the period between Passover and Shavuot. These problems and how they are resolved reflect conflicts over who controls the ritual calendar—the Israeli rabbinate, the Israeli government, or American federations and JCCs, individual synagogues, or American Israelis—and for that matter whether it is capable of being controlled.

Thus both in early Israeli ritual publications and in recent discussions about date revisions, conflicts have arisen about the management of ritual, and about how and whether Israeli rituals can and should be reflected in diaspora (or specifically American) practice. Overall, Conservative/Masorati practice seems most successful at the management of ritual revision on a movement level, independent of Chief Rabbinate decisions but informed by Israeli practices (including date management), and maintaining a consistent line of development over time. I cannot say whether this is the case in actual practice: the American Conservative rabbis interviewed for this study made comments which suggest that their liturgical practice is not fully consistent with the Conservative prayer book. In the Reform movement, the liturgical implementations in *Shaarei Tefilah* (1975) and *Mishkan T'fila* (Frishman 2007) are quite different from each other and from the typical Israeli ritual; this has extended even to directions as to the date on which to recite them. *Shaarei Tefilah* does not incorporate any Israeli ritual practices at all, but rather uses ones developed for a CCAR meeting in Jerusalem. *Mishkan T'fila* has a *hoda'ah* (thanksgiving) inserted in the same portion of the Amidah where the 'Al hanisim' prayer is normally added, but this insertion is an innovative text, not at all like the traditional 'Al hanisim'.[16]

Even though Yom Ha'atsma'ut is often celebrated on a different date, it is linked to 5 Iyar in one respect that is sometimes seen as a miraculous 'sign': it always falls on the same day of the week as the seventh day of Passover. A well-known correspondence between the days of Passover and various other dates in the Jewish calendar had—up to 1948—lacked a match for the final day; Yom Ha'atsma'ut therefore completed this scheme (Ariel 1998; cf. e.g. *Sidur* Eshkol n.d.: 263 for traditional version without Yom Ha'atsma'ut).[17] Yom Yerushalayim has a similar correspondence: it never moves from 28 Iyar, and thus falls on the same day of the week as Shavuot.

The National Religious Ritual for Yom Ha'atsma'ut

The detailed description of Yom Ha'atsma'ut practices that follows is based on the *Rinat yisra'el* and Koren siddurs except when noted. *Rinat yisra'el* follows the directives of 'the Chief Rabbis of the Land of Israel, Rabbi Isaac Halevi Herzog and Rabbi Ben Zion Meir Hai Uzziel, after the War of Independence', who ruled that Hallel should be recited with a blessing and published a liturgy for the day, and 'the practices for Yom Ḥerut Yerushalayim on 28 Iyar . . . established by Rabbi Isser Yehudah Unterman after the Six Day War' (*Rinat yisra'el*, Sephardi edn. 1973: Introduction dated 5730 (1969–70)).[18] The recitation of full Hallel with blessings is also often supported by reference to a 1952 responsum by Rabbi Meshullam Rath (1875–1963).[19] In practice, recitation of Hallel is probably the most widespread of the synagogue rituals for Yom Ha'atsma'ut. According to Rath's responsum, addressed to Rabbi Judah Leib Fishman Maimon (1875–1962), Hallel should undoubtedly be recited on 5 Iyar, with the blessing. There is no mention of moving the date but, invoking the concept of *lo titgodedu* (Deut. 14: 1: 'you shall not cut yourselves', which can be interpreted as making sects), the avoidance of having differing traditions in the same community,[20] he wrote that the decision to impose the blessing would require the agreement of all the major rabbinic authorities of a generation. Rath supports saying Hallel, with the blessing, on account of miracles that happened to the entire people of Israel, not merely to a single community or family. The miracles represent the transition from servitude to freedom (as in Passover and Hanukah), and beyond that, going from death to life: the deliverance of the Jews from their enemies both in the War of Independence and in the diaspora when they emigrated to Israel. This in turn leads to the third miracle, the ingathering of exiles.

Rath also recommends but does not impose the recitation of 'Sheheḥeyanu', the blessing said at the beginning of biblical festivals and before the first observance of annual events. For one who wants to recite it, 'there is no question of *berakhah levatalah* [making a blessing including God's name in vain], and the recitation of the blessing is not optional but required for one who knows that he benefits from and rejoices in the event of the rise of the state on the day determined for the festival' (Rath 1952).

Thus the Neriah editions print the blessings in parentheses, but the directions indicate that some say the complete Hallel with the blessing—which is the practice of most of the prayer books. As a rule Hallel is only said in the morning, but Hakibuts Hadati prayer book has it—with the blessing—in the evening as well. The sources examined were careful to cite rabbinic rulings to justify reciting Hallel and blessings, but made only general statements concerning the other liturgical components.

Rinat yisra'el begins its description of the evening service for Yom Ha'atsma'ut by noting that 'Wearing festival clothing, people come to the synagogue in multitudes' (*Rinat yisra'el* 1973, 1992). Before the evening service, Psalms 107, 97, and 98 are recited. Koren generally gives more choice than *Rinat yisra'el*, suggesting here 'all or a selection' of these psalms, and often adding 'some say' or 'it is a tradition to say' (Koren 1985). Then, the fifth, sixth, and eighth stanzas of the sabbath-eve hymn 'Lekhah dodi' are recited (those beginning *hitoreri*, *lo tevoshi*, and *yamin usmol*), which may be read as referring to the rebirth of Jerusalem and the Land of Israel: 'The afflicted of my people will be strengthened within you, the city shall be rebuilt on its ancient site . . . You shall extend to the right and the left . . . Through the advent of a descendant of Perez [i.e. the Davidic messiah] we shall rejoice and exult' (translation follows Birnbaum 1949). The line 'this is the day the Lord has made, let us be joyful and glad on it' (Ps. 118: 24) is substituted for the 'Lekhah dodi' refrain; *Rinat yisra'el* says it is to be recited 'verse by verse' (*pasuk befasuk*). The use of this terminology rather than *shurah beshurah* (line by line) suggests that 'Lekhah dodi', as emended for Yom Ha'atsma'ut, is in a sense elevated to scriptural status, since in traditional parlance, *pasuk* is reserved for verses of the Bible. Rabbi Neriah's ritual includes additionally the third stanza of 'Lekhah dodi' (beginning *mikdash melekh*) and concludes this portion by reciting additional verses from the same psalm, Psalm 118: 15–16, *Kol rinah viyeshu'ah* (Neriah 1978: 31; Ariel 1998: 43).

The evening prayer is usually the weekday one, but it is chanted using the festival melody.[21] After the recitation of full Kaddish, the Ark is opened and—similar to the closing prayers on Yom Kippur—the service leader says the Shema, repeated by the congregation, followed by 'The Lord is God' three times; Neriah adds additional verses here. Then the service leader says:

May he who performed miracles for our ancestors and for us, and redeemed us from slavery to freedom, may he speedily redeem us with a full redemption, and gather our dispersed people from the four corners of the world. All Israel are knit together, and let us say, Amen.

This is recited as in the Blessing of the New Month, with some adjustments, and the congregation repeats it. Then Numbers 10: 9–10 is read:

When you come to war in your land upon your enemy who attacks you, you shall sound the trumpets, and you shall be remembered before the Lord your God and you shall be saved from your enemies. And in the day of your joy, on your festivals and the beginnings of your months, you shall blow the trumpets on your burnt offerings, and on your peace offerings, and they shall be a memorial for you before your God. I am the Lord your God.

These verses are quoted in order to justify celebrating a victory or miracle with trumpet blasts, Hallel, and the establishment of a day of rejoicing,[22] and are reproduced in the prayer books with the cantillation marks for the public recitation of Torah. The shofar is sounded with a single long blast (as on Yom Kippur), and everyone says 'Next year in the rebuilt Jerusalem.'

On Yom Kippur, this is the end of the service, but here the congregation then says: 'May it be thy will, O Lord our God, and God of our fathers, that just as we have merited witnessing the beginning of redemption, may we merit hearing the sound of the shofar of the messiah, speedily and in our days.'

This is followed by singing Psalm 126 (*Shir hama'alot beshuv hashem*), with its reference to the return to Zion, to the melody of 'Hatikvah', the Israeli national anthem. The service continues with the counting of the *omer* and 'Aleinu', the closing prayer, and concludes with the singing of 'Ani ma'amin', 'I believe with perfect faith in the coming of the messiah, and even though he may tarry I will daily wait for him.' 'Ani ma'amin' was sung in the European death camps; although there is no explicit reference to this here, its inclusion underscores the significance of the establishment of the state, seen as a necessary and sacred step in the progression from destruction to redemption.

The new festival required a new greeting, *mo'adim lesimḥah* (a joyous festival), to which the response is *lige'ulah shelemah* (for a full redemption) (*Rinat yisra'el*; Neriah 1978: 32 has 'for an immediate redemption'). Then 'a festive meal [*se'udat mitsvah ḥagigit*] is eaten with songs and praises, at which lights are lit' (*Rinat yisra'el*). The Hakibuts Hadati prayer book begins it with a kiddush based on the 'Blessing of Redemption' normally recited as part of the Passover Haggadah, which incidentally provides an occasion for saying the 'Sheheḥeyanu' benediction, otherwise missing in many of the rituals surveyed here.

The morning service includes the expanded morning psalms such as are said on Hoshana Rabba. The 'Song of the Sea' (Exod. 15) is read verse by verse. Rabbi Neriah explains this by noting that Yom Ha'atsma'ut falls on the same day of the week as the seventh day of Passover, the day associated with the crossing of the Red Sea. Similarly, according to him, one sings songs associated with the crossing of the sea at the evening meal, and recites at the daytime feast Judah Halevi's poem 'Yom leyabashah', written as a poetical insertion for the 'Ge'ulah' section of the morning service on the seventh day of Passover (Ariel 1998: 31; *Hilkhot hayom* chapter of Neriah 1978: 20). The regular daily service then continues, with full Hallel after the repetition of the Amidah. The prayer books indicate that, on Mondays and Thursdays, the regular weekday Torah portion is read, followed by the *haftarah* (reading from the prophets) *Od hayom benov la'amod* (Isa. 10: 32–12: 6).

This is the *haftarah* for the eighth day of Passover outside Israel; according to *Rinat yisra'el* and Koren, it is read without blessings; others say the blessings up to 'Magen david', the third of the four blessings recited after the *haftarah* on the sabbath and festivals. On Wednesdays there is no Torah reading and one proceeds directly to the *haftarah*. The 2004 revision postponing Monday to Tuesday meant there would be no Torah reading except on Thursdays, but some versions of the ritual have a special reading for Yom Ha'atsma'ut; for example, the Hakibuts Hadati prayer book (1968: 84–9) prescribes Deuteronomy 7: 12–8: 18 divided into three sections, as is customary for Torah readings during the week; others have sections of Deuteronomy chapter 30 or selections from the weekly Torah portion of 'Va'ethanan' (Deut. 3: 23–7: 11). In the *Rinat yisra'el* and Koren prayer books, the *haftarah* is followed by the Prayer for the State of Israel. The service continues with 'Ashrei' (Ps. 145) as on a regular weekday, and at the end, 'Ani ma'amin' may again be sung.

A formal announcement on Yom Ha'atsma'ut of the number of years since the founding of the State of Israel is included in the notes to Neriah (1978: 48, Ariel 1998: 63) and the Hakibuts Hadati prayer book (1968: 101). Patterned after a similar Sephardi tradition announcing the years since the destruction of the Second Temple on 9 Av, this small textual emendation of a well-known liturgy suggests time is reconceptualized to reflect not the destruction but the institution of Jewish independence.

A version of the 'Al hanisim' prayer taken from the Amidah on Hanukah and Purim was suggested by E. Z. Melamed in 1957 and adopted by Hakibuts Hadati (1968: 101) as an optional text on the page following the end of services.[23] Rabbi Shelomoh Goren had reservations about this practice, objecting to changes or additions to the traditional text of the Amidah (Goren 1964; Arend 1998a; Rackover 1984), and Hakibuts Hadati removed it from its 1992 edition. In contrast, a new 'Al hanisim' was introduced in *Go'el yisra'el* (Ariel 1998: 165), also as an optional text; there was no such prayer in the 1978 edition of Rabbi Neriah's *Seder hatefilot* on which it is based.

Many collections of rituals introduced for Yom Ha'atsma'ut call for holding a second festive meal. *Rinat yisra'el* notes that at the feast of the day there is much singing and thanksgiving for the miracles accomplished for the Jewish people on this day. The Hakibuts Hadati prayer book again includes a kiddush; Rabbi Neriah provides remembrances of Jerusalem, a hymn about Jerusalem by Moses Hayim Luzzatto, and a generous selection of *zemirot* (table songs) based on biblical passages for which there are familiar hasidic or Israeli tunes. The *Shaarei Simcha birkon* (booklet containing blessings and songs for the sabbath; 2007) suggests that the festive meal should include reciting Psalm 114 from Hallel, the lighting of five candles (symbolizing the fifth day of Iyar), a simple kiddush, the blessing of children, the benedictions 'Hamotsi' (on eating bread), 'Peri ha'ets' (on eating fruits that grow on trees), and 'Sheheheyanu', the prayer for the state, and 'Mi sheberakh', a blessing for the success of the Israeli army; after Birkat Hamazon (grace after meals) it recommends singing 'Next year in Jerusalem' and 'Hatikvah'. The Hakibuts Hadati and Neriah prayer books also prescribe elaborate ceremonies which place prominent elements usually considered part of the 'civil' ritual, such as unfurling the flag and singing 'Hatikvah', within the context of the religious liturgy for the day.

Most prayer books surveyed give no directives about special foods or rituals, other than kiddush and *zemirot*. Arend notes that Rabbi Neriah used to light eight candles on a Hanukah menorah at his Yom Ha'atsma'ut feast, and describes the tradition of beginning the festive meal with matzah and bread together in remembrance of the thanksgiving offering (Lev. 7: 11–18), which included leavened and unleavened bread. Rituals such as singing 'Hatikvah' and popular Israeli tunes (including songs based on biblical texts), displaying the flag, and eating a special meal with one's family might be typical of the 'secular' observance; but in these liturgies they are placed in the context of a festive meal similar to those held on religious occasions such as the sabbath and festivals or the performance of commandments such as circumcision.

Israelis like to take advantage of Yom Ha'atsma'ut to go out to national parks, the beach, or army bases. This may be in fulfilment of the biblical directive to 'rise and walk about the land' (Gen. 13: 17), and the Hakibuts Hadati prayer book provides appropriate blessings for those who pass by an important battle site, as well as for those who are not able to go out into the fields (1968: 11). Many Israelis use the occasion to enjoy a barbecue (*mangal* in Israeli slang, after the Turkish word for charcoal). Possibly this could be contrasted with the celebration of Passover only a few weeks earlier. Roast lamb was central to the Passover dinner in Temple times, whereas today most Jews customarily refrain from any roast meat on the Seder night.[24] While few if any are thinking in these terms as they are enjoying the fresh air and a delicious picnic on Israel Independence Day, it seems that perhaps the consumption of grilled meat, avoided on the Seder night, could be considered a sign of the beginning of the flowering of redemption.[25]

Rabbi Neriah's directives for the day also include studying matter pertaining to the sanctity of the land, the agricultural laws particular to the land, and 'Laws of Kings and their Wars' from Maimonides' *Mishneh torah*. As this is the first of the thirty days leading up to Shavuot, texts discussing the giving of the Torah and the first fruits, two major themes of Shavuot, should also be studied. Moreover, Rabbi Neriah notes that, to hasten full redemption, charity should be distributed to the poor, citing passages from the Talmud and Maimonides that Israel cannot be redeemed or stand firm without charity (1978: 20–1; Ariel 1998: 31–2).

In considering the rituals grouped together here under the rubric of 'national religious', one is struck by the liturgical creativity channelled into highly traditional words and structures. There are only minor adjustments to words within the individual components; the new rituals have wordings largely adopted from traditional prayer books. The only exceptions are the Prayer for the State of Israel and texts for a new 'Al hanisim'—and, as we have seen, Hakibuts Hadati withdrew the latter. The words of 'Hatikvah' and other compositions not included in traditional prayer books are part of the celebration—perhaps recited at the festive meal—but not the synagogue service. Perhaps even the choice of *haftarah*—a familiar text recited as a *haftarah* outside Israel—reflects this conservatism

Yet otherwise the prayer ritual creates a new and unique holiday, incorporating motifs from the sabbath, festivals, and High Holy Days. Verses from 'Lekhah dodi' perhaps allude to the establishment of the state as a modern equivalent of the sabbath: the selections chosen clearly suggest that just as the sabbath is a foretaste of the world to come, the state is a harbinger of messianic times. The role of the founding of the state is made even clearer at the end of the evening service, similar to the end of *ne'ilah*, the last service on Yom Kippur: as the hope for redemption comes at the end of a day of soul-searching atonement, so too does it come as a result of the establishment of the state. One difference, though, is that the messianic theme is far more explicit in this ritual than it is on Yom Kippur. The morning service directive to recite the 'Song of the Sea' (Exod. 15) line by line ties Yom Ha'atsma'ut closely to the paradigmatic example of divine redemption, the exodus from Egypt, suggesting that the birth of the state was a miracle of the same magnitude. The *haftarah* selection from Isaiah returns to the themes of messianic deliverance and the ingathering of exiles. Yet the rituals, texts, and words are all traditional.

The Israeli Masorati congregations, affiliated to the Conservative movement, have published a prayer book, *Va'ani tefilati* (2000), in which there is a greater degree of liturgical innovation in the actual ritual. It appends the reading of two paragraphs from the Israeli Scroll of Independence to the Hallel and includes the announcement of the number of years since independence; the 'Sheheheyanu' blessing is recited before the shofar blast, and rather than singing Psalm 126 to the melody of 'Hatikvah', this service concludes with the singing of 'Hatikvah' itself.

The basic synagogue ritual observances for Yom Yerushalayim, as given in *Rinat yisra'el* and Koren, are somewhat similar to those of Yom Ha'atsma'ut. The evening service is the regular weekday service, except chanted in the festival melody. After the counting of the *omer*, 'psalms of thanksgiving' are recited, which are not specified in either prayer book (*Go'el yisra'el* suggests Psalms 122 and 132). The morning service again features the extended morning psalms (without the verse-by-verse reading of the 'Song of the Sea') and full Hallel, followed by half Kaddish and the Prayer for the State of Israel. 28 Iyar can only be a Sunday, Monday, Wednesday, or Friday; on Mondays the Torah is read but I have found no reference to a special Torah reading or *haftarah*. Tahanun is cancelled on Yom Yerushalayim and at *minhah* the day before (as is the 'Tsidkatekha' prayer at the sabbath *minhah*). Otherwise the prayer continues as on a regular weekday.

For the memorial days, *Rinat yisra'el* calls for the lighting of candles and for the bereaved to say Kaddish on Yom Hazikaron; Koren has a special variation of the Memorial Prayer. Neither of these prayer books has a special synagogue ritual for Yom Hasho'ah, nor do the Neriah editions. Instead, the memorials are given ritual space within the celebration of Israeli independence, with memorial prayers for both the Holocaust and the soldiers of the Israel Defence Forces following the *haftarah* on Yom Ha'atsma'ut, similar to where they would be in a sabbath service (Neriah 1978: 139; Ariel 1998: 148); the Hakibuts Hadati siddur also includes a memorial in its Yom Ha'atsma'ut ritual.

In the United States both the Conservative and Reform prayer books have recognized Yom Ha'atsma'ut and some or all of the other days. Most Orthodox and traditional ones, however, do not include any special directives for these days. Regarding streams usually called 'modern' or 'centrist' Orthodoxy, this may be due to a traditionalist approach and concern about changing the formulas of prayer, and to the traditionalizing pressures described by Heilman in *Sliding to the Right* (2006), rather than to hesitancy about the State of Israel. For example, the popular prayer book *Kol Ya'akov*, approved by the Orthodox Union, includes the texts of the Prayer for the State of Israel and the 'Mi Sheberakh' blessing for the soldiers of the Israel Defence Forces. A survey of synagogues shows that many modern Orthodox congregations cancel Tahanun and recite Hallel with, or sometimes without, the blessing. Sometimes some of the other practices are also tried out in such congregations, or in schools or university campuses—including Yeshiva University, the rabbinical training institute of this movement. The late Rabbi Joseph Soloveitchik (1903–93), *rosh yeshivah* of the Rabbi Isaac Elhanan Theological Seminary at Yeshiva University and the leading figure of Modern Orthodox Judaism in America for a generation, is said to have walked out of services at Yeshiva University once when the Torah was read on Yom Ha'atsma'ut—presumably a sign of disagreement with the practice—although the story does not indicate that his action prevented the practice on that occasion. Indeed, as early as 1953, Rabbi Soloveitchik objected to an Israeli religious Zionist liturgy for Yom Ha'atsma'ut about to be circulated by the Orthodox rabbinical body, the RCA (Soloveitchik 2005: 123 ff.), and is said to have called a Yom Ha'atsma'ut service conducted in 1978 an 'acute halachic retardation' (Meiselman 2005: 93). Victor Geller includes Yom Ha'atsma'ut among a list of issues Soloveitchik 'considered for the RCA, and provided rulings', recalling that 'he said no, that ad hoc, non-halachic services were wrong' (2003: 261). These reports seem to suggest significant interest in these ritual innovations among rabbinical students and rabbis working in communities, but Soloveitchik's opposition to 'non-halachic services' was at least one major reason such innovations were not adopted by the RCA or the Orthodox Union.

Jonathan Sacks's new prayer book, published by Koren (2009), carries Orthodox Union approval; it has many of the elements of the national religious ritual including Hallel and the *haftarah*, largely following the Koren rituals. The introduction by OU executive vice president Rabbi Tzvi Hirsch Weinreb does not address whether the OU has moved away from Rabbi Soloveitchik's position on such rituals, suggesting only that it is 'especially valuable that this Siddur connects those who use it to the land of Israel in very contemporary ways . . . reflect[ing] our celebration of Israel's independence and our sorrow for those who have fallen in its defense' (Sacks 2009: p. xiv).

The Conservative Ritual on Yom Ha'atsma'ut

In the Conservative Movement, in accordance with the Rabbinical Assembly Law Committee's decisions (Klein 1979: 22, 27, and 143–5), Hallel and the 'Al hanisim' for Yom Ha'atsma'ut are an intrinsic component of *Siddur Sim Shalom* published in 1985; one does not need to turn to the back for directions or text. Conservative Judaism first introduced an 'Al hanisim' in the weekday siddur edited by Gershon Hadas and Jules Harlow in 1961. Interestingly, the *Shaarei Simcha birkon* includes a different 'Al hanisim' in the Grace after Meals, as well as a complete 'Seder for Yom Ha'atsma'ut' (pp. 126 ff.) with a passage based on the 'Modim derabanan', the paragraph recited just before 'Al hanisim' in the traditional Amidah. In *Sim Shalom*, Yom Ha'atsma'ut is called 'Israel's Independence Day'; its newest edition is the weekday prayer book (2002), which shows considerable further liturgical development marking Yom Ha'atsma'ut, Yom Yerushalayim, and Yom Hasho'ah.

In *Sim Shalom*, the 'Al hanisim' for Yom Ha'atsma'ut is found in all weekday services—morning, afternoon, and evening—but not on the sabbath, indicating that it follows the Israeli date, despite an occasional reference to 5 Iyar. This differs from the Reform prayer book *Shaarei Tefilah*, as we shall see. The English version of 'Al hanisim' (*Sim Shalom* 1985: 119) is as follows:

In the days when Your children were returning to their borders, at the time of a people revived in its land as in days of old, the gates to the land of our ancestors were closed before those who were fleeing the sword. When enemies from within the land together with seven neighboring nations sought to annihilate Your people, You, in your great mercy, stood by them in time of trouble. You defended them and vindicated them. You gave them courage to meet their foes, to open the gates to those seeking refuge, and to free the land of its armed invaders. You delivered the many into the hands of the few, the guilty into the hands of the innocent. You have wrought great victories and miraculous deliverance for Your people Israel to this day, revealing Your glory and Your holiness to the world.

Differences exist between the Hebrew and the English version. 'Land of our ancestors' is *erets avot* (not *erets avoteinu ve'imoteinu*), and 'those who were fleeing' are specifically called *aheinu* (our brethren) in Hebrew. Perhaps these differences reflect greater avoidance of gender-specific terms in English than in Hebrew.

Whereas the English reads 'to free the land of its armed invaders', the Hebrew text is *legaresh et tsivot ha'oyev min ha'arets*, which might have been translated 'to drive out the enemy hosts from the land'. Given the heated discourse about Palestinian Arabs today, one wonders whether the Hebrew text might reflect greater awareness that some of the 'enemy hosts' of 1948 were Arab irregulars rather than regular armies invading from surrounding countries. Perhaps most interesting, the English version switches the order of the final thoughts: the paragraph ends with a note on the revelation of divine holiness throughout the world, rather than, as in the Hebrew, a reference to the great victories and salvation of the people of Israel.

Hallel is recited on Yom Yerushalayim but 'Al hanisim' is not. As in a number of Israeli rituals, the Torah reading for Independence Day is Deuteronomy 7: 12–8: 12, and the *haftarah* is from the eighth day of Passover: Isaiah 10: 32–12: 6. *Sim Shalom* does not have the shofar blast and other features of the Israeli prayer books which appear in the Masorati *Va'ani tefilati*.

Sim Shalom recommends marking Yom Hasho'ah in the synagogue, but does not provide a specific ritual. Congregations may select from a few pages of readings. These include the 'Camps Kaddish', in which the names of the death camps are read as the traditional Kaddish is intoned, from the Martyrology section of the Conservative movement's Yom Kippur *musaf* (Harlow 1975: 566–9) and credited to Jules Harlow (weekday *Sim Shalom* 2002, credits). Yom Hazikaron is not represented.

The new weekday *Sim Shalom* (2002) has several amendments: the order of the end of the English translation now conforms to the Hebrew, and the day is now called Israel Independence Day, with Yom Ha'atsma'ut in Hebrew characters on the Hebrew pages. Most significantly, 'newly created liturgies' for Yom Ha'atsma'ut and Yom Yerushalayim, with psalms and readings, are printed, like the readings for Yom Hasho'ah, towards the end of the book. These may be used in conjunction with regular services or as stand-alone liturgies. Perhaps this practice suggests a need for rituals that exist outside the framework of evening or morning synagogue services. The Yom Ha'atsma'ut liturgy includes the announcement of the number of years since independence and the singing of 'Hatikvah'. The Yom Hasho'ah readings are fuller; there is a more complete introduction and no suggestion that congregations make a selection from the material. The new siddur may reflect a rediscovered urgency of Israel issues within the Conservative movement, and especially the influence of the Israeli Masorati movement; portions of the Hebrew were translated by Reuven Hammer, a leading exponent of the Conservative movement in Israel, or were taken from *Va'ani tefilati*.

The *Sim Shalom*, not specific to Yom Ha'atsma'ut, has a shortened version of the Prayer for the State of Israel. The Hebrew text retains *reshit tsemihat ge'ulatenu*, literally 'the beginning of the flowering of our redemption'. But the translation modifies this actualized commencement of redemption to a potential one in the future, rendering 'with its promise of redemption' (1985: 417). This version omits, in both Hebrew and English, the hope for the ingathering of all exiles and other passages which might raise some questions for American audiences. The end of the prayer retains the hope for peace for the inhabitants of the land. Without the strong language of the original, the text suggests a much more universal concept than that intended by the authors of the prayer.

The Reform Liturgy on Yom Ha'atsma'ut

In the Reform movement, the Central Conference of American Rabbis recognized Yom Ha'atsma'ut as a festival in 1969; accordingly, services for the day were included in its prayer book *Shaarei Tefilah* (1975: 590 ff.). These do not include the Hallel, shofar blast, or special greetings of the typical Israeli services, nor is there any passage reminiscent of the 'Al hanisim' prayer. However, a 'sanctification of the day' is recited, including a formula adapted from the 'Ya'aleh veyavo' blessing recited on biblical festivals. *Shaarei Tefilah* also contains lines from midrash and Talmud, Chaim Weizmann, Hannah Senesh, and Theodor Herzl. Other readings are based on a service at the CCAR Jerusalem convention in 1970, including passages from Ibn Gabirol's 'Keter malkhut' and Avigdor Hameiri's 'Yerushalayim' (*Me'al pisgat har hatsofim*). 'Hatikvah' is not included in this liturgy, which continues instead with the song 'Am yisra'el ḥai' (The People of Israel Lives). Part of 'Yerushalayim' having been sung early in the programme (1975: 593), its concluding lines are now quoted towards the end of the service, with their messianic note: 'Jerusalem, Jerusalem, I will not move from here. Come, O let the messiah come!' 'Yerushalayim' and 'Am yisra'el ḥai' explicitly link the observances to messianic hopes allowed by the fulfilment of age-old yearning for a return to Jerusalem; contrast this with 'Ani ma'amin' in many of the other rituals, which implicitly connects the same ideas with overcoming the horrors of the destruction of European Jewry only a few years before the establishment of the state—and looks forward to messianic times without explicit reference to Jerusalem. The service is followed by the Torah reading and concluding prayers.

This liturgy is somewhat disconnected from the exact date of Israeli observance of Yom Ha'atsma'ut in that it includes passages to be said if the festival falls on the sabbath, whereas according to the Israeli enactment, as discussed earlier, this can never happen. *Shaarei Tefilah* also has additions to the service for the sabbath before Yom Ha'atsma'ut (pp. 412 ff.). Its practice may reflect the realities of North American synagogues (Reform and non-Reform): many would have the liturgical celebration of Yom Ha'atsma'ut during their regular sabbath services regardless of the day on which 5 Iyar falls. This was not the intention of the CCAR, as it called for the observance of these days 'on the exact Hebrew dates on which they occur' in a resolution in 1988, but said nothing about synchronizing the observance with Israeli practice.

The CCAR called for observance of Yom Hasho'ah with various rituals, including memorial prayers and the lighting of six *yahrzeit* candles. They also recommended fasting or eating only a very light meal. Nevertheless, the section of the
Shaarei Tefilah siddur entitled 'In Remembrance of Jewish Suffering' does not
appear to be a ritual specifically developed for Yom Hasho'ah. Yom Hazikaron is
not represented.

The CCAR's new prayer book *Mishkan T'fila* (Frishman 2007) has new
thanksgiving inserts in the Amidah for Yom Ha'atsma'ut and Yom Hasho'ah, that
is, in the same place as its 'Al hanisim' inserts for Hanukah and Purim, although
without the latter formula. Hallel is not indicated on Yom Ha'atsma'ut. The
special service for the day is completely reworked to include the recommended
lighting of a seven-branched candelabrum, one candle at a time, interspersed
with readings of passages from Israel's Scroll of Independence—given in Hebrew
—songs by Naomi Shemer and others, and 'Hatikvah' (Hameiri's song is no
longer part of this ritual). There is a service for Yom Hasho'ah; one of its components is a Kaddish similar to that of *Sim Shalom*.

Despite all the changes and variations in prayer formulas, there has been considerable convergence between the mainstream of the national religious tradition
and the Masorati/Conservative rituals. Perhaps the most important differences
are the inclusion of new texts in the Conservative movements, primarily an 'Al
hanisim' and modifications in the wording and translations of some of the
Hebrew texts which at times tend to downplay the meaning of the state as the
inception of messianic redemption and a place for the ingathering of all Jews.

The Reform ritual, on the other hand, has had numerous changes and little or
no convergence with the other liturgies. There is ongoing innovation, including
the composition of specific prayers, but also significant incorporation of contemporary materials written for non-liturgical contexts. Unlike Hallel and 'Al
hanisim', firmly anchored in traditional Jewish liturgy, these new ceremonies rely
on secular texts: 'Hatikvah', the Scroll of Independence, and songs by Hameiri
and Naomi Shemer. It would seem that the Reform ritual is still closer in conceptualization to the ceremony established by the CCAR Jerusalem convention and
to the ceremonies created in synagogues, as well as to the 'civil' observance, than
to the Israeli national religious liturgical tradition, and that the movement has
retained a very fluid approach to liturgical innovation, crafting a totally new insertion for *hoda'ah* (thanksgiving) rather than marking the establishment of the state
as it does previous holidays by a rewritten traditional text.

A survey conducted in Denver, Colorado, provides a further perspective on
synagogue practices.[26] Modern or centrist Orthodox synagogues recited Hallel
on Yom Ha'atsma'ut, some with, some without a blessing. Some had a very modest festive meal; none reported that congregants made special efforts to attend
synagogue services to mark Yom Ha'atsma'ut. More traditional Orthodox synagogues had no special rituals. One of the Conservative synagogues followed the

Sim Shalom liturgy for morning services. Another did not hold morning services that day; the rabbi told me he marks Yom Ha'atsma'ut on the closest sabbath, primarily in his sermon. Somewhat surprisingly, he also told me he would not do all the rituals in the *Sim Shalom* if he had morning services that day. Although there were various events in other synagogues to mark Yom Ha'atsma'ut, they neither involved the *shaharit* or *ma'ariv* services available in the prayer books used by those congregations, nor had any other liturgical structure. This may be contrasted with Yom Hasho'ah, for which a number of synagogues had special services or special addenda to regular services, held mostly on the day, not on the nearest sabbath or Sunday. While they typically did not follow a traditional synagogue service format they all had standard liturgical elements, repeated without fail each year.

Yom Ha'atsma'ut Liturgies: Underlying Meanings and Contexts

These observations suggest that in practice, liturgical celebrations of these new holidays in America emphasize the emergence of the state against the background of fighting its many enemies, express hope for peace there, and memorialize the Holocaust and fallen soldiers. Those elements which define the state in terms of redemption or look forward to messianic times are downplayed. Perhaps it is the urgency of remembering the Holocaust while there are still survivors left that drives the need to establish a special time for this memorialization, rather than including it with themes of destruction, struggle, and redemption in the Israeli context. In contrast, the sense of urgency for noting the importance of Israel in the diaspora tends to arise in response to contemporary crises, and these occur on a regular basis. Like the planned memorial services, gatherings organized in times of crisis have a standardized liturgical component—perhaps more standardized than synagogue services marking Yom Ha'atsma'ut. In other words, the rituals studied here do not have as much visibility as the rituals adopted in mass meetings during crises, and in the recitation of psalms and prayers in synagogues in times of war. In practice, the message that wins out is that the State of Israel is a means of the continuity of the Jewish people. The sense of wonderment that drove the liturgies created in Israel has vanished, even as those liturgies themselves have come to the American synagogue.

The rituals connected with the rise of the state and the recollection of the tragedy of the Holocaust—still evolving—present a religious narrative about the meaning and importance of these events. The various rituals have manifold emphases, stressing themes of memorialization of the dead, the sanctity of the land, the unity of all Israel, miraculous salvation, and at least the partial fulfilment of ancient hopes that permeate the classic liturgy. Some new practices look back with memorial and thanksgiving; others evoke a forward-looking faith that the rise of the state marks the beginning of the flowering of redemption, or even suggest a reordering of traditional priorities. Liturgical innovation often reworks pre-existing texts from the sabbath and biblical or rabbinic holidays to suggest how the establishment of the state fits into the grand sweep of Jewish history and into everyday life.

Ongoing development also provides a contemporary example of continuing interactions between the popular need to recognize these historic events and the various stakeholders shaping Jewish rituals. The secular state, the Chief Rabbinate, various movements in the United States and Israel, prominent rabbis, and individual practices of synagogues and communities are active in the formation of new ritual, shaped by and in turn reshaping the theological framework for understanding the significance of events. Senior rabbinical leaders can object to various practices of congregations, or rabbis, or movements, or they can adopt (or adapt) innovations which have already become popular. Israeli civil practice, grounded in Knesset legislation, seems to be a major determinant of which days undergo the most ritual innovation and why, for example, Holocaust Memorial Day is so often marked a week after Passover rather than associated with the liberation of Auschwitz (27 January) or linked with pre-existing fast days. We have also seen that some of the ritual innovations suggest that the establishment of the state is too significant in a religious sense to be left to civil observance alone, and incorporate practices and texts such as the Israeli national anthem or its melody, or Israeli songs, taken from secular contexts and celebrations outside the sphere of regular religious services, into published prayer books for formal rituals, such as the evening or morning service or festive meals. (This is the reverse of a more common occurrence, the incorporation of religious rituals—such as the prayer for the state or the 'Sheheḥeyanu' blessing—into an otherwise secular event).

Despite the messianic and redemptive meaning given to the rise of the state, the national religious tradition, exemplified by Rabbi Goren, appears to be very uncomfortable about creating new liturgical texts emending the traditional halakhic prayer service (as was Rabbi Soloveitchik in the United States). Nevertheless, saying Hallel with the blessing puts the establishment of the state on a par with the redemption from Egypt (mentioned in the Hallel) and the rededication of the Temple by the Hasmoneans. The addition of 'Al hanisim' in some rituals also follows the model of *halel vehoda'ah* (praise and thanksgiving) associated with Hanukah. 'Al hanisim' texts can place the narrative in the past, recounting the victory of the few against the many and the rise of the state, interpreting exactly what is important about this process in a religious context, in a way that is more explicitly articulated than almost all of the other rituals examined. The symmetry of these rituals with traditional observances provides a symbolic expression of the deep significance of what may be seen as a renewed cycle of destruction, struggle, and national rebirth of the Jewish people in the twentieth century.

The liturgical innovations for Yom Ha'atsma'ut are dramatic markers of the importance of the State of Israel in modern Judaism. Many of the rituals reinterpret some of the most familiar elements of Judaism to emphasize motifs of nationalism, of homeland, and of redemption. Practices involving the shofar blast and the addition of readings from Torah, Prophets, and modern compositions go far beyond the themes and practices associated simply with saving Jews from persecution and danger. Some communities unfurl the flag in a formal ceremony incorporating biblical verses—seemingly putting the state on the same footing as the Torah, which is revered in a similar manner when removed from the Ark. We have seen that Numbers 10 is cited in the festive service for the eve of Yom Ha'atsma'ut found in many Israeli prayer books. This passage does not merely emphasize the dedication of the sanctuary, as in its original context, nor simply argue for the 'sounding of trumpets' on Yom Ha'atsma'ut. It also represents victory over enemies and coming into the Land, and speaks to the equalization of the sanctity of Torah with that of the Land, and of ancient past with contemporary reality. Some Yom Ha'atsma'ut rituals replace the sabbath bride as the focus of verses taken from 'Lekhah dodi', recited weekly in the *kabalat shabat* service, by using the same verses to represent redemptive and messianic hopes addressed to Jerusalem and the Land of Israel itself—and, quite obviously, using the sanctity of the sabbath (sanctity in time) to underscore the sanctity of the state (sanctity of land). In its rituals, the Chief Rabbinate has been reluctant to simply insert an 'Al hanisim' addition to the prayer recalling the miracles that have transpired; instead, we have seen a passage adopted from the Blessing of the New Month that looks forward rather than back, calling for the completion of the process of ingathering and redemption; similar themes are found in the *haftarah* and the Prayer for the State of Israel. Greetings emphasize the coming of the rebuilt Jerusalem and the completion of redemption. This ritual, with its choices of biblical texts and the blowing of the shofar, makes a strong statement about the place of the State of Israel in the overall history of Jewish—and human— redemption.

Several early Israeli publications of Yom Ha'atsma'ut rituals had an explicit diaspora orientation—to provide spiritual guidance to diaspora communities by creating a ritual clarifying the meaning of the state for all Jews. This may be a function of the sources available at North American libraries, which were more likely to collect books designed for diaspora use than pamphlets or booklets circulated for special occasions in Israeli synagogues. Nevertheless, it illustrates the importance the national religious camp attached to promoting the recognition of the religious value of the state in a revisioned ritual. At the same time, the rituals adopted in diaspora Conservative and Reform siddurs, and informally in some Orthodox synagogues, mesh only partially with those of the Chief Rabbinate. Indeed, the resolutions of the American Reform movement for the establishment of Yom Ha'atsma'ut and Yom Hasho'ah did not call for observance of rituals for these days as much as the need for links between the Jewish communities inside Israel and in the dispersion. Rather than stressing the theme of 'Al hanisim': miracles, or of the role of the state in the drama of redemption, they underscore the context of Jewish unity and mutual support.

In a study of the rituals and myths of Canadian Jewish civil religion, J. N. Lightstone has observed that 'the State of Israel today occupies a supreme place in the selfconsciousness of North American Jewry, despite the lack of a shared, coherent Zionist way of thinking or even familiarity with classical Zionist thinking' (1996: 60). In the twenty-first century, there may indeed be some convergence towards a shared coherent Zionist sense of religious ritual, especially among the Israeli national religious camp, Modern Orthodoxy in America, and the Conservative movement, and between Israel and the diaspora, as the new edition of *Sim Shalom* for weekdays and the prayer books of Rabbi Sacks have adopted many of the Israeli rituals. This convergence may reflect the slow but steady acceptance of the main features of Israeli practice, the interests of individual congregations or leaders, and the ease of travel, communication, and commerce linking Israel and the diaspora. But it is not clear that many within these movements actually practise these liturgies, or that they represent convergent thinking about their meanings. One is left with the impression that even though the conceptualization behind much of the liturgical creativity was to highlight a religious and redemptive interpretation of the historical events of the middle of the twentieth century, as a practical matter the themes of unity, continuity, memorialization, and peace have been in the fore. With the fading of the generation that witnessed the Holocaust and the establishment of Israeli independence—and made these innovations in the prayer book—it remains to be seen whether or how liturgies embedded into traditional ritual will reshape Jewish understanding of the significance of these events.

Acknowledgements

Thanks to Rabbis Bernard Gerson, Nancy Kasten, Fred Greenspahn, and Lawrence Hoffman for advice and perspectives in the earliest stages of this project, especially with Conservative and Reform prayer books. Thanks also to the editor of this volume for his enthusiasm and recommendations, and to the anonymous referees whose suggestions improved this article considerably.

Notes

1   Sometimes given as Yom Shiḥrur Yerushalayim or Yom Ḥerut Yerushalayim (Jerusalem Liberation or Freedom Day). The term *yom yerushalayim* occurs in Psalm 137, where it is a reference to the destruction of Jerusalem.

2   The Knesset established Independence Day in 1949 and Holocaust Memorial Day in 1951. The other two days were first set by the Ministry of Defence (Memorial Day) or the govern-

ment of Israel (Jerusalem Day), and were only anchored in Israeli law much later by Acts of the Knesset. Following its adoption, the 'Independence Day Law' was amended by the Knesset in 1950, 1951, and frequently thereafter. The current text of the law as amended is published on the Knesset website: <http://www.knesset.gov.il/laws/special/heb/chok_ yom_haatzmaut.htm>.

Israel's Memorial Day for fallen soldiers began by memorializing soldiers on Yom Ha'atsma'ut, a practice found in some of the prayer books examined for this essay. In 1950, Independence Day fell on a Saturday and was postponed to Sunday, but the Ministry of Defence decided to hold memorial services on the preceding Thursday. The following year David Ben-Gurion, as Defence Minister, convened a public committee which recommended that Memorial Day services would be held the day before Independence Day, a proposal adopted by the government of Israel. This practice was only enacted into Israeli law with an act of the Knesset on 28 March 1963. See <http://www.knesset.gov.il/laws/special/heb/chok_yom_hazikaron.htm>.

Holocaust and Heroism Day was originally called Yom Hasho'ah Umered Hagita'ot (Holocaust and Ghetto Uprising Day). Its name was changed with the enactment of the Yad Vashem Law in 1953. The current Yom Hasho'ah Law dates from 1959. <http:// www.knesset.gov.il/sho'ah/heb/sho'ah_intro.htm>, <http://www.knesset.gov.il/sho'ah/ heb/ memorial_law.htm>.

Jerusalem Day was established by a decision of the government of Israel dated 12 May 1968, two weeks before the first anniversary of the entry of Israeli soldiers into the Old City of Jerusalem. The observance was legislated by the Jerusalem Day Law passed by the Knesset in 1998. <http://www.knesset.gov.il/laws/special/heb/jerusalem_day_law. htm 1998>; <http://www.knesset.gov.il/holidays/heb/jer.htm>.

3   Traditionally the proscriptions of the *omer* period recall the deaths of Rabbi Akiva's students. Although tradition ascribes this to a plague brought about by their unethical behaviour, Akiva is of course strongly associated with the second Jewish revolt under Bar Kokhba and it is therefore possible that the deaths were military casualties.

4   A broader study of ritual revisioned in the light of the establishment of the State of Israel and the return of Jewish sovereignty to Jerusalem should also address additions and modifications to existing festival observances. Among these are Hamishah Asar Bishvat (15 Shevat), revisioned as Tu Bishvat to celebrate Jewish rebirth in Israel and ecological commitments; Tisha Be'av, with reworked liturgy in some quarters to reflect both the Holocaust and the reunification of Jerusalem; and practices such as reciting the Prayer for the State of Israel, or drinking a fifth cup of wine on the Seder night.

5   I have heard this story many times in many variations, not always ascribed to Rabbi Cahanaman; it is often found in postings to the internet, such as <http://haemtza. blogspot.com/2005/12/hakaras-hatov-to-state-of-israel.html>, <http://www. theyeshiva-world.com/article.php?p=6296> (with a photograph of the flag referred to in the next paragraph). In some versions of this story, Cahanaman's statement was 'no Hallel and no Tahanun'—including Israel Independence Day in a list of days in which Tahanun is cancelled, a minor ritual change. Even this change was resisted by some of the leaders of the yeshiva; Rabbi Shach is said to have recited Tahanun regardless. I have no information about the actual practice at Ponevezh.

6   According to Arend 1998a, the yeshiva still flies the flag on Yom Ha'atsma'ut. This work was available to me only at a very late stage in writing this essay. Other major halakhic treatments of Yom Ha'atsma'ut include Rackover 1984, Azari 1991, and Goren 1964.

7   I have had access to the *Seder* from 1978, published in honour of the thirtieth anniversary of Israeli independence. It notes the *Tikun* was originally published in 1955/6, with a second edition in 1961/2. Both the *Tikun* and the *Seder* were published by the World Zionist Organization's Division of Diaspora Torah Education and Culture.

8   See *Encyclopaedia Judaica* s.v. 'Ha-Po'el Ha-Mizrahi'.

9   Ed. E.S. Hartom et al. and published by the Italian Synagogue in Jerusalem in 1961. It is cited, for example, in the prayer book of Hakibuts Hadati, introd., p. 11, and in Arend 1998a. I have not been able to see this prayer book.

10   The copy I examined is *nusaḥ sefarad* (i.e. liturgy of the Ari); the edition of the *Seder* (1978) I had access to was Ashkenazi. Most prayer books note the liturgy on the cover or title page, but neither of these did.

11   Beyond the scope of this study are religious rituals in other formats, such as a 'haggadah' following the Passover model (for example the recent *Veshinantam levanekha*, described in Lichtman 2002); or directions for a Yom Ha'atsma'ut ritual feast in a booklet designed for Grace after Meals.

12   State of Israel, Law of Yom Ha'atsma'ut, 1949; Laws of the State of Israel p. 2384; cited in the prayer book of Hakibuts Hadati (1968). This rule is also given in the appendix on ritual practices arranged in the order in which they occur throughout the year (*devar yom beyomo*), at the back of the various versions of *Rinat yisra'el*. The *devar yom beyomo* section is nearly identical in all editions I consulted except for the page numbers. The law was further revised in 2004 to add the postponement of Monday.

13   This includes, for example, the popular *Jewish Home Calendar* for 5761 (2000–1), distributed by many synagogues, kosher restaurants, and other community organizations, which indicated Thursday 26 April 2001 as the day on which Yom Ha'atsma'ut is observed, but the following sabbath, 5 Iyar, was still indicated as Israel Independence Day.

14   Based on a letter dated 17 March to 'the rabbis of all locations' from Rabbi Meir Rosental, aide to the chief rabbi. My thanks to Rabbi Daniel Alter, who received this via email and brought the letters of Rosental, Schwartz, and Metzger to my attention. He also provided me with Rabbi Rath's responsum and was the first to mention reports 'circulating at Yeshiva University' about Rabbi Soloveitchik walking out of services in which Yom Ha'atsma'ut rituals were observed—mentioned later in my essay.

15   Hallel (Psalms 113–18) is traditionally recited on Hanukah and biblical festivals; the Hebrew term means 'praise'. Some verses are omitted on the seventh day of Passover (and the eighth day in traditional practice outside the Land of Israel), the usual explanation being that this day commemorates the Israelites' crossing of the Red Sea and rejoicing is reduced in deference to the death of Pharaoh's army there. The reduced Hallel is also recited on the intermediate days of Passover and at the beginnings of the Hebrew months (Rosh Hodesh), considered minor holidays. A blessing for the recitation of Hallel is said on all these occasions. Reciting the full Hallel with a blessing may suggest to some that Yom Ha'atsma'ut is as important as Hanukah or the first day of Passover. Reciting the Hallel with omissions may suggest that the occasion is no more important than Rosh Hodesh. Omitting the blessing might indicate joy and praise without religious or ritual significance. In practice, rabbinical deliberations about reciting Hallel on Yom Ha'atsma'ut have focused on whether the conditions for ritual revision have been met, as indicated in my discussion of e.g. Rabbi Rath's responsum.

16 The 'Al hanisim' prayer is a narrative composition recalling the specific historical events which led to the miraculous deliverance or military victories of the Jewish people. It is recited on Purim, Hanukah, and, according to some liturgies, on Yom Ha'atsma'ut.

17 Source: *Shulḥan arukh*, 'Oraḥ ḥayim', 428: 3.

18 In the Ashkenazi edition I consulted (1992: 7), the introduction is dated 1973 and apparently does not need to cite the rabbis; it simply refers to 'prayers which have been introduced in our land since we gained independence and since the liberation of Jerusalem'.

19 Rath (1952), cited, for example, in Neriah 1978: 8, and Ariel 1998: 13, 132–3; *Encyclopaedia Judaica*, s.v. 'Rath, Meshullam' (sometimes his name is romanized as Ratta or Roth. The Hebrew is *resh-alef-tet-heh*—we follow the *EJ*).

20 BT *Yev.* 13b; Gumbiner: *Magen avraham* and Isserles' *Mapah* on *Shulḥan arukh*, 'Oraḥ Ḥayim' 493: 3.

21 *Rinat yisra'el: ne'imah ḥagigit*; Koren has the more specific *bemanginah shel yom tov*, and Neriah *binimat ḥag*. Neriah's ritual, despite the festive melody, includes 'Vehu raḥum' and 'Shomer amo yisra'el la'ad' as in the weekday service. The Hakibuts Hadati prayer book, however, has the festival version of the prayer, omitting 'Vehu raḥum', and completing 'Hashkivenu' with *hapores sukat shalom alenu*. Similarly, in the morning, Psalm 100 is recited, as on weekdays which are not festivals, but unlike the others, the Hakibuts Hadati prayer book uses the longer form of the final blessing of the Pesukei Dezimrah section (beginning with 'Nishmat'), and the cantor begins at 'Ha'el beta'atsumot uzekha', as on festivals.

22 Neriah includes three traditional comments on this verse, from Rabenu Yonah on Mishnah *Berakhot* 2, Ibn Ezra ad loc., and Judah Halevi, *Kuzari* 5: 27. Rabenu Yonah, citing Rabenu Tam, and Ibn Ezra conclude from these verses that when a miracle is performed enabling Israel to overcome its enemies, a festival with Hallel or day of gladness is proclaimed.

23 Melamed's text appeared in *De'ot*, 1 (1957), 10.

24 See *Shulḥan arukh*, 'Oraḥ Ḥayim' 476, with *Mishnah berurah* and other commentaries.

25 Food practices are reviewed in Arend (1998b) and discussed in Keinon (1998). Arend points out that the *mangal* has 'no historic or culinary connection with Israel or the Jewish people'; instead, it reflects the natural tendency 'to tour the country that day, and by this [people] express their connection to the land and their sovereignty over it' (translations by Keinon).

26 The survey, conducted in spring 2009, consisted of a questionnaire emailed to lists of synagogues and rabbis, follow-up calls where possible, and the examination of website newsletters and calendars.

References

Prayer Books

ARIEL, YA'AKOV, ed. 1998. *Go'el yisra'el*. Special edn. for the fiftieth anniversary of the founding of the State of Israel. Ramat Gan.

Artscroll 1990. *Siddur Kol Ya'akov / The Artscroll Siddur*. Rabbi Saul Berman's introduction is dated 5746 (1985–6). New York.

BERKOWITZ, ADINA K., and RIVKA HAUT, eds. 2007. *Shaarei Simcha Gates of Joy: Traditional Prayers, Songs and Modern Inclusive Rituals.* Jersey City.

BIRNBAUM, P, ed. 1949. *Daily Prayer Book: Ha-Siddur Ha-Shalem.* New York,

FRISHMAN, ELYSE D., ed. 2007. *Mishkan T'fila—a Reform Siddur: Weekdays, Shabbat, Festivals, and Other Occasions of Public Worship.* New York.

HAKIBUTS HADATI. 1952. *Seder hatefilot uminhagim leyom ha'atsma'ut.* Tel Aviv.

——1968. *Seder tefilot leyom ha'atsma'ut keminhag kehilot hakibuts hadati ve'od kehilot bey-isra'el,* edited according to the opinion of the late Rabbi Elimelekh Bar Shaul and with the approval of Rabbi Shlomo Goren, Chief Rabbi of the IDF. Tel Aviv.

——1992. *Seder hatefilot uminhagim leyom ha'atsma'ut veyom yerushalayim.* Tel Aviv.

HARLOW, J, ed. 1975. *Mahzor for Rosh Hashanah and Yom Kippur.* New York.

KOREN, ELIYAHU. 1985. *Sidur tefilah.* Ashkenazi edn. Jerusalem.

NERIAH, M. Z. *Seder hatefilot leyom ha'atsma'ut.* Jerusalem: World Zionist Organization, Division of Diaspora Torah Education and Culture, 1978.

REISNER, AVRAM ISRAEL, ed. 2002. *Siddur Sim Shalom Le-hol.* Siddur Sim Shalom for Weekdays. New York.

SACKS, JONATHAN. 2006. *Hebrew Daily Prayer Book.* London.

——2009. *The Koren–Sacks Siddur.* Jerusalem.

Shaarei Tefilah, Gates of Prayer. New York: Central Conference of American Rabbis, 1975.

SHARKI, URI AMOS, ed. 1999. *Sidur beit melukhah.* Jerusalem.

Siddur Sim Shalom: A Prayer book for Shabbat, Festivals and Weekdays. New York: Rabbinical Assembly and United Synagogue of Conservative Judaism, 1985.

Sidur hashalem kolbo ashkenaz. Jerusalem: Eshkol, n.d.

Sidur tefilot lehayal, nusah yahid. Tel Aviv: Ministry of Defence, 1980.

Sidur va'ani tefilati: seder hatefilot limei hol, shabat umo'ed. Jerusalem: Rabbinical Assembly in Israel (Conservative), 2000; <http://www.masorti.org/mason/have/siddur/prayers_atzmaut.html>; <http://www.masorti.org/mason/have/siddur/prayers_sho'ah.html>.

TAL, SHLOMO, ed. 1973. *Rinat yisra'el,* Sephardi edn. Ashkenazi edn.: 1992. Jerusalem. The editions are identical except as noted.

Tikun yom ha'atsma'ut: seder tefilah, tikunei se'udah ushe'ar halikhot hayom. Jerusalem: Division of Torah Education in the Diaspora of the World Zionist Organization, 5715–16 (1955–6).

Other Sources

AREND, AHARON. 1998a. 'Yom Ha'atzmaut in Halakhah, Custom, and Story'; lecture for Yom Ha'atsma'ut—Israel Independence Day 1998/5758, <http://www.biu.ac.il/JH/Eparasha/yomatz/are.html>.

——1998b. *Research Chapters on Yom Ha'atsma'ut* [Pirkei mehkar leyom ha'atsma'ut], Ramat Gan: Bar-Ilan University.

AZARI, M. 1991. *Independence Day and its Development in Israel* [Hag ha'atsma'ut vehit-pathuto beyisra'el]. Jerusalem.

Encyclopedia Judaica, ed. Cecil Roth et al. Jerusalem, 1972.

GELLER, V. B. 2003. *Orthodoxy Awakens: The Belkin Era and Yeshiva University*. Jerusalem.

GOREN, S. 1964. 'Yom Ha'atsma'ut in the Light of the Halakhah' (Heb.), in id., *The Laws of Festivals* [Torat hamo'adim], 568 ff. Tel Aviv.

HEILMAN, S. C. 2006. *Sliding to the Right: The Contest for the Future of American Jewish Orthodoxy*. Berkeley, Calif.

HOFFMAN, L. 1978. *Shaarei Bina, Gates of Understanding: Notes to Shaarei Tefilah*. New York.

KEINON, H. 1998. *Jerusalem Post*, 30 Apr. <http://info.jpost.com/1998/Supplements/Jubilee/5.html >, accessed 27 June 2001.

KLEIN, ISAAC. 1979. *Guide to Jewish Religious Practice*. New York.

LICHTMAN, GAIL. 2002. *The Jewish Agency for Israel Magazine*, 5/4. <http://www.jafi.org.il/ arts/2002/april/haggadah.rtf>.

LIGHTSTONE, J. N. 1995. 'The Religion of Jewish Peoplehood: The Myth Ritual and Institutions of Civil Religion of Canadian Jewry'. In J. N. Lightstone and F. B. Bird, eds., *Ritual and Ethnic Identity: A Comparative Study of the Social Meaning of Liturgical Ritual in Synagogues*, 53–62. Waterloo, Ont.

MEISELMAN, M. 2005. Review of J. Soloveitchik, *Community, Covenant and Commitment*, ed. N. Helfgot. *Jewish Action* (Fall 5766), 89, 92–4.

METZGER, Y. 2004. *Pesak halakhah*. 12 Feb. (circulated electronically).

RACKOVER, NAHUM. 1984. *The Laws of Yom Ha'atsma'ut and Yom Yerushalayim* [Hilkhot yom ha'atsma'ut veyom yerushalayim]. Tel Aviv. Reprint of Ministry of Religions (1973).

RATH, MESHULLAM. 1952. *She'elot uteshuvot kol mevaser (1955–62)* [Responsa], pt. I, no. 21, 24 Adar 5712 (21 Mar. 1952), Jerusalem (from Bar-Ilan Teshuvah database).

REIF, S. 1993. *Judaism and Hebrew Prayer: New Perspectives on Jewish Liturgical History*. New York.

SOLOVEITCHIK, J. 2005. *Community, Covenant and Commitment*, ed. N. Helfgot. Newark, NJ.

THREE

The Masquerade of Ideas: The *Purimshpil* as Theatre of Conflict

JEAN R. FREEDMAN

'Man thinks, and God laughs.'

YIDDISH PROVERB

'Nothing is funnier than unhappiness.'

SAMUEL BECKETT, *Endgame*

ON 3 MARCH 2007, a relatively warm night in Washington, DC, a crowd of costumed celebrants gathered in a modest redbrick synagogue in the city's north-west quadrant. Dressed as construction workers, baseball players, animals, and kings, they milled around the lobby, exchanging greetings, laughing at each other's costumes, and waiting for the service to begin. A teenage boy in a pirate hat and fake moustache chatted with his friends, while girls in silk and velvet finery practised songs and tried on outrageous hats. As the congregation moved into the sanctuary, children found places on the floor or sat with grown-ups on folding chairs, but all faced north that evening, not east (as usual) towards Jerusalem. The rabbis sat among the congregation that night, while fifteen lay congregants took their places on a makeshift wooden stage or moved (with hushed laughter) behind movable wings on either side. Most congregants had brought a device—a metal toy, a box of dry pasta—with which to make a noise. Nothing was as usual that night, and this oddity meant that everything was in order. It was Purim, and the synagogue's Purim play was about to begin.

Of all the holidays in the Jewish calendar, Purim is both the jolliest and the strangest. It is a time when the ordinary Jewish emphasis on moderation and self-discipline is abandoned, when laughing at the sacred is permissible and drunkenness is actively encouraged. Purim commemorates the biblical book of Esther, which chronicles a thwarted attempt to annihilate the Jews of ancient Persia. In the story, the Jewish Queen Esther pleads for the life of her people, and her success is the *raison d'être* of the Purim celebration. Because it celebrates the triumph of life over the threat of death, Purim is a joyous holiday, characterized by feasting, the giving of gifts, and general merriment. Because it focuses on the reversal of expectations, Purim has become a classic holiday of inversion, its leitmotif taken from a verse in the ninth chapter of the book of Esther, which proclaims 'the reverse happened' or 'it was turned upside down'. The topsy-turvy world of Purim, in which the underdog emerges as the victor, gives licence to a range of behaviours not normally condoned in traditional Judaism: cross-dressing, poking fun at rabbis and sacred texts, excessive drinking, and theatre (see Baumgarten 1992; Belkin 1999; Rozik 1996).

Rabbinic objections to theatre focused on its pagan origins and on the assumption that theatre was a waste of time, an occupation for fools and impious ne'er-do-wells (Belkin 1985, 1996; Free 1999). Yet since the late Renaissance, and possibly even earlier, Jewish communities have staged plays on Purim (Belkin 1999). These plays shared many of the attributes of the Christian pre-Lenten festivities and, like them, were filled with irreverent and anti-authoritarian exuberance, expressed by physical comedy, vulgar jokes, and mockery of those in power. Like much folk theatre, Purim plays serve a dual function: they maintain a community's traditions while simultaneously altering them. Purim plays enact and present community values, yet they may also introduce new elements and can suggest new ideas to performers and audience. Anthropologist Victor Turner argues that such forms are far more than harmless entertainment. Nor do they simply, as Shakespeare suggested, hold the mirror up to nature: 'Cultural performances are not simple reflectors or expressions of culture or even changing culture but may themselves be active agencies of change, representing the eye by which culture sees itself and the drawing board on which creative actors sketch out what they believe to be more apt or interesting "designs for living"' (Turner 1986: 22). The Purim play (or *purimshpil* to use the Yiddish word) becomes a kind of lens through which the past is refracted and visions of the future might be glimpsed.

Purimshpiln flourished in Europe and, to some extent, the United States until the end of the Second World War. With the destruction of their traditional milieu in Europe, Purim plays suffered a decline in the United States as well. In the past few decades, however, together with a general revival of interest in Yiddish culture, *purimshpiln* have sprung to life in the United States, Canada, Australia, South Africa, Europe, and former Soviet Asia.[1] What do these contemporary *purimshpiln* share with their traditional ancestors? Do modern Purim plays present contemporary conflicts and, if so, what are they? How do present-day Jewish communities revise and reinterpret *purimshpiln* in the light of contemporary issues? How does this revisioning and re-envisioning illuminate the text of Esther, even while changing it from sacred narrative to quotidian performance? The meanings that arise from these 'cultural performances', to use Turner's phrase, emerge from three major themes: the use of humour as a tool of social criticism, the construction of gender and sexuality, and the use of Purim as a model for the diaspora Jew. These themes are common throughout the history of *purimshpiln*, yet their articulation by specific communities varies enormously.

The Text of Esther

Because many *purimshpiln* dramatize the book of Esther, it is useful to provide a synopsis of the plot. The story takes place in ancient Persia, where the Jewish community seems to suffer no legal disability, though antisemitism eventually erupts with deadly force. The story begins with the Persian king Ahasuerus who, at the end of a 180-day feast, decides that another party is in order. Meanwhile his wife, Queen Vashti, is holding a feast for the women in another part of the palace. After seven days of drinking, Ahasuerus commands Vashti to come to his party and show her beauty to the men gathered there. Vashti refuses. The king is extremely angry and asks his advisers what he should do. The advisers are perplexed by the wider significance of Vashti's act; if this behaviour is tolerated, then women throughout the kingdom may think it acceptable to disobey their husbands. In order to avoid this possibility, the advisers suggest that Vashti be dethroned and that fair young virgins from throughout the kingdom be gathered in the palace so that the king can choose from among them. This seems a good idea to Ahasuerus, who practically never makes a decision on his own, and he decrees that it shall be done.

At this point, the narrative shifts and introduces the two main Jewish characters, Mordechai and Esther. Technically they are cousins, but Esther had no parents, so Mordechai adopted and reared her as his daughter. Since Esther is beautiful she is taken with the other virgins to the king's palace. For some reason, Mordechai tells her not to reveal that she is a Jew, and she obeys.

Before the maidens are presented to the king, they undergo a year-long beauty makeover. Then they go, one by one, to spend the night with him. When they return the following morning, they are incorporated into the harem, the house of the king's concubines. When it is Esther's turn to spend the night with the king he is so smitten that he makes her his queen—one of the few decisions he makes without the help of advisers. So it is Esther's sexuality as well as her beauty that delights him.

Why Esther enters the palace in the first place is never explained. After all, this is decidedly odd behaviour for a nice Jewish girl: joining the harem of a non-Jewish king, spending the night with a man who is not her husband (even if she does get the crown in the end), concealing her heritage, and breaking Jewish law by eating non-kosher food. Mordechai is concerned for her welfare in this non-Jewish world, and walks every day by the women's house in order to find out how she is doing. One day, while keeping his vigil outside the palace, he overhears two of the king's chamberlains plotting to harm the king. He communicates this information to Esther, and she in turn tells the king. The chamberlains are caught, found guilty, and hanged, and the incident is recorded in the king's chronicles, with Mordechai named as the hero.

Here the narrative shifts once again and introduces Haman, the king's chief minister. The king decrees that all shall bow down before Haman, and most do so, but Mordechai does not. When asked why he refuses to bow, Mordechai only replies that he is a Jew. This behaviour infuriates Haman, and he suggests that the Jews be destroyed, since they dare to disobey the king's law. Ahasuerus, once again showing blind faith in his advisers, agrees to Haman's plan and issues a decree for destruction of the Jews.

When Mordechai hears the decree, he realizes that Esther, the Jewish queen, is in an ideal position to save her people. He charges her to go to the king, reveal her heritage, and plead for their lives. Esther is reluctant at first, for the king has not called for her in thirty days. She knows that anyone who approaches him uninvited is put to death—unless he holds out his golden sceptre. Mordechai reminds her that she cannot hope to escape the decree herself, so she agrees to the plan and prepares for her ordeal with a three-day fast. On the third day, she dresses beautifully and stands in the king's courtyard awaiting his decision. The king likes what he sees and holds out his golden sceptre, telling Esther that he will grant her request even if it is for half his kingdom. But Esther bides her time and requests only that the king and Haman come to a banquet that evening. At the end of the banquet, the king again asks Esther for her petition, and she requests that the king and Haman come to another banquet the following evening. Haman is proud of his favoured status with the queen, but he is still obsessed with Mordechai's intransigence and commands that a gallows be built for him.

The next night, Ahasuerus and Haman go to Esther's second banquet, and once again Ahasuerus promises to grant Esther's petition. At this point, Esther pleads for the lives of her people and names Haman as the man bent on destroying them. The king is furious and wanders into the garden, possibly looking for advisers to tell him what to do next. Haman is terrified and falls at Esther's feet, begging for his life. The king returns and becomes even angrier when he sees Haman prostrate before Esther; he misinterprets Haman's humble posture for a rape attempt. By this time, advisers are on the scene; they suggest that Haman should be hanged on the gallows he has created. Ahasuerus agrees.

Many *purimshpiln* end with the death of the villain. The book of Esther does not. It describes the complications of ancient law, by which a king's decree cannot be reversed even by the king himself. Thus the only way for the Jews to survive Haman's decree is by killing those who attempt to kill them. This the king encourages, with Mordechai at the helm, and a bloody battle ensues. The Jews emerge victorious militarily and politically; Mordechai is placed at the head of the House of Haman and becomes the king's right-hand man. Mordechai and Esther decree that the days of victory shall henceforth be celebrated as the holiday of Purim.

It is reasonable to wonder where God figures in this narrative. The theme of threat and salvation is common in the Bible, and usually God overcomes the former and accomplishes the latter. In the book of Exodus, for example, the Israelites are oppressed and enslaved by the Egyptian pharaohs. Moses cries out to God, who responds with a plethora of miracles and very specific instructions regarding what to do next. But God never makes an appearance in the book of Esther. No one prays or hopes for divine intervention; the closest anyone gets to a religious act is Esther fasting before the banquet. Moses cries out to God for salvation; Mordechai, on the other hand, cries out to Esther.

What are we to make of this godless sacred text, this ancient narrative in which a woman stands in for the deity? The rabbis were clearly perplexed by the oddity of the book of Esther, and its inclusion in the canon was late (Fisch 1994: 70). The rabbis were still debating its canonical status in the third century CE, and Christian clerics did not accept it as holy writ until even later (White 1989: 161). Even after the book was securely within the biblical canon, midrashim (rabbinic commentaries) took pains to explain Esther's seemingly un-Jewish behaviour. Many midrashim declared that Esther prayed to God, observed the sabbath, and ate only kosher food, which was specially brought to her (see Bronner 2004). The Zohar, a medieval mystical work, even suggests that Esther never actually slept with her uncircumcised husband, because God sent a spirit to Ahasuerus in her place (Bronner 2004: 185). Additions to the book of Esther that supply the spiritual element lacking in the original appear in the Apocrypha and the Septuagint, but they (like the commentaries cited above) are known only to a small group of scholars and specialists. It is the book of Esther itself, and the attendant raucous joy of Purim, that remain widely known and loved.

Historical Background

Though religious authorities continued to voice discomfort with the book of Esther, the holiday of Purim has been popular in Jewish communities since talmudic times. Even before formal plays were produced, performance held a central place in Purim ritual. By medieval times, European Purim celebrations shared much with the pre-Lenten festivities of Fastnacht and Mardi Gras, festivals of inversion in which a fool was crowned Pope (or rabbi) and beggars could freely demand money from the rich. At Purim, ritual inversions were played out by members of the community: children stole food with impunity, effigies of Haman were burned in the streets and in the synagogue, and throngs of costumed revellers roamed the streets, mocking the sober pieties of those in authority, both within the Jewish community and in the dominant culture.

Within the synagogue, the main activity of the holiday is the reading of the book of Esther (often referred to as the Megillah, or scroll), and all Jews are expected to hear it. This reading requires a special degree of audience participation: congregants must listen for Haman's name and then make enough noise to drown it out. Congregants hiss, stamp their feet, and use special noisemakers to temporarily bring the reading to a halt. Again, this is an example of the reversible world of Purim: at no other time is it acceptable to interrupt the person who reads the holy texts. But at Purim, the voice of the people becomes louder than the voice of their leaders, and the leaders must wait until the merrymaking of the people has died down.

Though there are references to Purim plays during medieval times, no actual scripts appear before the late Renaissance. Purim plays can be found throughout the Jewish world; they exist in Hebrew, Yiddish, Ladino, German, Russian, English, and other languages. Most *purimshpiln* were in the vernacular of the community involved. Before the twentieth century, most Jews lived in small towns in eastern Europe, where Yiddish was the language of everyday life. Significantly, a large number of extant Purim play scripts are in Yiddish. A language that combines warmth with irony, and uproarious humour with unending pathos, Yiddish is the ideal vehicle for a humorous production about the threat of annihilation.

I shall concentrate primarily on the Purim plays of European Jews and their descendants in the United States. Originally, Purim plays were performed by itinerant players who went from house to house, asking for a few coins (often to pay for the expenses of Passover) in exchange for their entertainment. Purim plays were also performed in private homes, in houses of study, and finally within the synagogue itself. Scripts were informal and allowed performers to add jokes, topical commentary, music, and other items of popular culture, many of them borrowed from the dominant society in which the Jews lived. Since Orthodox Judaism forbids women to perform in public, all the players were men, and the sight of a bearded man disguised as a woman added to the merriment. Occasionally, rabbis and other leaders of the Jewish community were involved in the production of Purim plays, but more commonly, the plays were produced by those on the lower rungs of Jewish society (Belkin 2003). In keeping with the Purim tradition of inversion, the players took the opportunity to satirize the sacred and insult the powerful. On this one day, students could make fun of their teachers, congregants were free to lampoon their rabbis; any person and anything that was stuffy or self-righteous got a metaphorical kick in the pants.

Although many Purim plays dramatize the book of Esther, other stories have also been performed, generally those that share the Purim theme of victory over the threat of annihilation. Some of these narratives are drawn from the Bible (such as the book of Daniel), others from history (such as tsarist Russia and Nazi Germany), while still others are purely the product of fantasy. What is most striking about virtually all Purim plays is the fact that they tell these stories of near-disaster in a comic, even boisterous, way. *Purimshpiln* turn the sacred text of Esther into a profane, sometimes even vulgar, parody, filled with irreverent jokes, sexual innuendo, and utterly secular popular culture. The Bible states that Esther is beautiful, but many Purim plays describe her appearance as grotesque, calling attention to the fact that she was traditionally played by a man inadequately disguised in women's clothes. Male characters also suffer degradation from their biblical status. Mordechai, dignified and heroic in the Bible, becomes a clownish buffoon who greets the king with a volley of insults, in much the same way that Purim players must have wanted to speak to authority figures. Scatological humour, in which Mordechai tells Ahasuerus to lick his backside or instructs Haman to eat his dung, destroys any possibility of keeping the sacred story sacrosanct (Belkin 1996, 2003).

In looking at *purimshpiln* historically, we can see how they varied according to the kind and intensity of local conflict. Theatre studies scholar Ahuva Belkin cites Purim plays from the sixteenth, seventeenth, and eighteenth centuries whose primary function was to let off steam and to express resentment of those in authority—both within the Jewish community and in the dominant culture (Belkin 1996, 2003). Bawdy and scatological humour, the irreverent treatment of sacred texts and community leaders, and the mocking of serious subjects such as sex and matchmaking were all part of the Purim players' toolkit. They could attack the arbitrary authority of the non-Jewish culture around them by insulting non-Jewish characters such as the evil Haman or the foolish Ahasuerus. They could also attack leaders of their own community by representing the Jewish characters (Esther and Mordechai) as clowns and buffoons.

Sometimes authority figures accepted such effrontery as part of Purim hijinks, an exercise in reversal that would last no longer than the holiday itself. At other times, the revolutionary potential of Purim rites became too much for both Jewish and Christian authorities, and Purim festivities were restricted or even banned. In 1639 the ruling authorities of the Sephardi community of Amsterdam (which had a long tradition of performing Purim plays in Hebrew, Spanish, and Portuguese) banned the production of Purim plays in the synagogue, though they continued to be produced in private homes and theatres (Belkin 1995: 42). In the early eighteenth century, the leaders of the Frankfurt Jewish community ordered the script of their *purimshpil* to be burned, its licence and vulgarity finally becoming too much to be associated with a religious holiday (Belkin 1996: 56). Jewish leaders also sometimes sought to restrain Purim revelry in order to ingratiate themselves with the Christian community. Particularly during the eighteenth and nineteenth centuries, when Jewish integration into mainstream European and American society was beginning but was not yet solidified, Jewish communities in locales such as London, Charleston, and the German states prohibited Purim rituals that seemed vulgar and unrefined, such as the use of noisemakers to drown out Haman's name during the Megillah reading (Horowitz 1994).

Whereas Jewish leaders objected to the profanation of a sacred text or sought to remake their rituals in ways that would not give offence to outsiders, Christian leaders sensed in Purim revelry a suppressed resentment of their own authority. In 408 the Roman emperor Theodosius II forbade the burning of Haman in effigy, seeing in this symbolic exercise a mockery of the crucifixion of Christ. (In the Hebrew original, Haman is hanged. However, in both the Septuagint and the Vulgate, the method of his execution is listed as crucifixion—an example of the dangers of translation.) In 1750 Frederick the Great granted privileges to the Jews in his realm, conditional upon their not praying in ways that might give offence to Christians, with particular stress laid upon the 'improper excesses' of Purim (Horowitz 1994). In 1941 Hitler ordered all synagogues to be closed on Purim and prohibited the reading of the book of Esther.

In Nazi Germany Purim took on a particularly powerful and terrifying reson-ance. Jews who had never considered themselves religious flocked to the syn-agogue on Purim, shouting down the name of Haman, cheering wildly at his death (Horowitz 1994). *Purimshpiln* in Nazi Germany took on a heightened sig-nificance, as German Jews faced their own Haman and waited for an Esther who never came. They even offered a beacon of hope in the concentration camps. Solly Ganor describes a *purimshpil* in Dachau in 1945, organized by a fellow prisoner known as 'Chaim the Rabbi'. Wearing a paper crown, clad in a blanket decorated with paper stars, he began his call for a *purimshpil* by shouting, 'Haman to the gal-lows! And when I say, "Haman to the gallows", we all know which Haman we're talking about!' Ganor played Mordechai in the production, and recalls that 'we all ended up dancing in the snow'. By enacting a story of triumph over incredible odds, Chaim the Rabbi was able to infuse a moment of hope into a particularly bleak situation (Ganor 2005).

The Holocaust dealt a mortal blow to the traditional European *purimshpil*. In the decades after the war, there were some attempts to revive the genre, but these were hampered by the loss of its practitioners and its milieu, as well as by the hideous irony that the story brought to mind. The world had just watched an annihilation attempt that had very nearly succeeded, a Haman who had ruled unchecked for twelve horrific years. The Purim story, with its victorious happy ending, seemed perhaps a bitter mockery, the *purimshpil* the tattered remains of a dying culture. But the culture stubbornly refused to die. In the past few decades, as those who remember pre-war Jewish life slip away, there has been a world-wide revival of interest in its culture.[2]

Keeping pace with this renewed interest is a widespread revival of the *purim-shpil*. Research on the genre is likewise burgeoning, in English, Hebrew, French, German, Spanish, and other languages. Much of this research is historical in nature (Baumgarten 1992; Belkin 1985, 1995, 2003; Kirshenblatt-Gimblett 1980) or focuses on the Purim plays of the Bobover hasidim, who retain many features of pre-war practice (Epstein 1987, 1995; Kirshenblatt-Gimblett 1990; Troy 1995). Yet little research has been done on contemporary Purim plays produced by non-hasidic congregations, or on plays that deliberately introduce new practices in order to shed light on contemporary concerns. I turn now to an examination of a Purim play produced in 2007 by a Reform congregation in Washington, DC. Though it shared much with its historical antecedents, it introduced many new elements as well, some of them common to contemporary American Jewish cul-ture, others specific to this congregation. I studied as well as participated in this

Purim play, and thus had the opportunity to watch it develop and to interview the participants about their ideas and interpretations.

A Modern American *Purimshpil*

A close examination of this contemporary American *purimshpil* reveals both similarities to and differences from its European ancestors. It was only the second full-fledged *purimshpil* that this Reform congregation had produced, although for several years before 2007 they had put on a small-scale Purim play as a Sunday school project, organized by middle-school students and their teachers. In 2006 the synagogue's staff chose to mount a larger production that would involve more congregants. Several factors influenced this decision: the desire to involve adults as well as children, the growing popularity of similar plays in the area, and the ease with which *purimshpil* scripts and other materials can now be acquired from the internet. Rehearsals for the 2007 production began in November 2006 and were open to any congregant interested in participating. All participants were volunteers, with the exception of the synagogue's music director, who served as music director of the *purimshpil*. Since rehearsals were held on Sunday afternoons directly after Sunday school, the majority of the participants were Sunday school children and their parents. Several congregants who had some experience with theatre also joined the cast. In all, the volunteers numbered fourteen actors and two directors.

Some contemporary congregations write their own *purimshpiln*, while others choose from the many internet sites that allow one to download or purchase ready-made scripts. In the United States, many *purimshpiln* are parodies of Broadway musicals, but plays based on popular music, film, and television are also common. In this instance, the synagogue's music director, in consultation with the cantor, chose the script from the internet. After viewing several potential Purim plays (all of which were musicals), he chose one based on Beatles' songs, a common choice in the English-speaking world, perhaps because of the broad appeal of this music across nations and generations. The Beatles' tunes were used unchanged, while the Lennon and McCartney lyrics were altered to fit the story. Yiddish and Hebrew words were added, and the audience took special delight in puns, such as 'Hey Jews' and 'Estherday'. Just as traditional European Purim plays took their inspiration from the secular music around them, so do contemporary American Purim plays. In this case, the middle-aged players took a nostalgic pleasure in teaching their children the popular culture of their youth. A surprising number of the children knew the Beatles' tunes already, from YouTube and iPod downloads, from CDs and films and radio, as well as from the fragile vinyl records carefully stored at home.

The play was presented in the synagogue's sanctuary as part of the evening celebration of Purim. Scenes from the play were interspersed with the reading of

Figure 3.1 The 'Purim Fab Four': synagogue staff in Sergeant Pepper's Lonely Hearts Club Band costumes at a *purimshpil* in a Reform congregation, Washington, DC, 2007. *Photo: Jodi Enda*

the Megillah; several times during the evening the play stopped, and members of the congregation (both clergy and laypeople) chanted portions from the book of Esther. The play also stopped at one point to allow synagogue staff to perform a song—tacitly showing their approval and acceptance of the rowdy entertainment in the sanctuary. The synagogue's cantor, associate rabbi, education director, and music director dressed for their performance in elaborate replicas of the Beatles' Sergeant Pepper outfits, complete with golden trim, epaulets, Beatles wigs, and fake moustaches. Since three of the four 'Beatles' were women, this masquerade supplied a layer of gender reversal that was both reminiscent of and in opposition to the traditional *purimshpil* custom of men playing women.

Unlike the splendid Sergeant Pepper outfits of the synagogue staff's entr'acte, most Purim players' costumes were simple and came from the participants' own wardrobes. The younger girls and women (who played Esther, Vashti, the narrator, and an array of smaller roles) wore attractive, feminine clothing in rich fabrics: velvet skirts and dresses, silken tunics and jackets, costume jewellery, and shiny silver belts. Bits and pieces were added as needed: Vashti carried a handbag in the first scene (indicating wealth and position); Esther wore a crown after winning the beauty contest; and the narrator donned a deerstalker hat and carried a pipe for a memorable imitation of broadcaster Alistair Cooke. The older women and the male characters dressed in simple clothing (predominantly black) but added costumes and props as needed. Ahasuerus wore a royal blue robe and a purple and gold crown, though his golden sceptre was an unimpressive piece of wood with a few shiny embellishments. Mordechai wore a *kipah* (skullcap) throughout the performance, while another cast member donned hasidic head-gear and sidelocks for one scene. Haman wore a pirate hat, a fake moustache, and a fake police badge, thus capturing the perfect combination of lawful authoritarian control and lawless cruel abandon.

There was no scenery, but the sanctuary was completely reorganized. This synagogue's sanctuary is shaped like a long rectangle, with the short end at the *bimah*. During most of the year, congregants sit in relatively short rows facing east, towards Jerusalem. However, the *purimshpil* is an event in which spectacle, rather than prayer and contemplation, is emphasized. In order to allow more people to have a good view, the sanctuary was reoriented so that the front row was on the long end of the rectangle, and the audience faced north. A temporary wooden stage was constructed, and movable screens created wings at either side. The music director sat upstage right with his electronic keyboard and provided accompaniment to the songs, sometimes playing along, sometimes playing pre-recorded music.

Purim play scripts have traditionally been fluid, and this one was no exception; it was essentially a guideline, with additions and deletions continuing until the night of the performance. Yet the fact that the play was presented in the sanctuary as part of a religious service affected what could be said. So too did the presence of

Figure 3.2 The 'Purim king and queen', Ahasuerus and Vashti at a *purimshpil* in a Reform congregation, Washington, DC, 2007. *Photo: Jodi Enda*

Figure 3.3 Haman figure with pirate hat, moustache, and police badge at a *purimshpil* in a Reform congregation, Washington, DC, 2007. *Photo: Jodi Enda*

children in the audience. The rich sexual and scatological humour common in European Purim plays was deemed inappropriate for a religious celebration that children would watch. The play retained the traditional forms of *purimshpil* humour—physical comedy, puns, topical jokes, and free adaptations of non-Jewish culture—while deleting some of the traditional content. Political controversies were avoided, but the intensely political atmosphere of Washington was invoked by naming the queen's confidantes 'Hillary' and 'Liddy' after two current women senators. Partisanship was avoided by choosing one senator from each of the two major political parties. (Like many professional political operatives, Hillary and Liddy switched their loyalty from Vashti to Esther with the change of administration.) As befits a religious ritual in the synagogue, this Purim play mentioned God three times, making it a more overtly religious piece than the book of Esther itself.

Like most contemporary American Purim plays, this production was in English, the vernacular of the community.[3] Yet the influence of Yiddish remained, since most American Jews are descendants of Yiddish speakers. The play was peppered with Yiddish words, and participants consistently referred to it as a *purimshpil*, not a Purim play.

Traditional European Purim plays frequently lampooned their rabbis, and this American congregation did the same, though in a gentler fashion than their European forebears. There were no direct insults or veiled complaints. Instead, the play targeted the senior rabbi's love of baseball: the directors wrote and performed a parody of Abbott and Costello's 'Who's on first?' routine, in which a Hebrew teacher attempts to instruct Ahasuerus in the rudiments of the language.[4] The humour comes from the confusion caused by Hebrew words that sound the same as English ones but mean something quite different: the Hebrew word that means 'he' sounds like 'who', the Hebrew word for 'she' sounds like 'he', and the Hebrew word for 'who' sounds like 'me'. As in many traditional Purim plays, the king is presented as a fool, and the clever Jew is able to confound him:

King. I'm very excited about this Esther girl. So, tell me: Who is she?

Teacher. Your highness, it's a pleasure to see you and I'm glad to work with you on this. It's simple: Who is me.

King. What?

Teacher. Who is me.

King. Let's see here, what I'm asking is indeed rather simple: who is she?

Teacher. No, my lord, I'm afraid not. Who is me.

King. My dear friend, I don't really care about your identity problems—all I want to know is who she is.

Teacher. Yes, your highness, and I'm here to tell you: She is he.

(*Pause*)

King. I beg your pardon? She is [a] he?

Teacher. That's right, sir, you've got it!

King. No!

Teacher. Yes, and we're very proud of it!

King. She?

Teacher. He!

King. Who?

Teacher. Me!

King. But who is she?

Teacher. No, who is me. He is she. (*To audience*) He's a little slow.

In this production, Esther and Mordechai were neither the stately, untouchable characters of the Bible nor the vulgar buffoons of many Yiddish *purimshpiln*. Instead, both were portrayed as decent people with amusing human foibles. The character of Esther showed both the political satire and the physical comedy typical of *purimshpiln*. Though she held the exalted position of queen, Esther could not make an entrance without tripping over her own feet. Her political sophistication was demonstrated as she prepared to tell Ahasuerus about her Jewish heritage. She wrote a speech and rehearsed it, with tearful delivery, for Hillary and Liddy. Her rhetorical strategies were familiar to anyone who has heard American politicians apologizing for embezzling funds or having illicit sex: 'I have given a false impression, though legally accurate. I did not volunteer information. I misled people, including even my own husband. I made a bad mistake. It's indefensible and I'm sorry about it.' Her tears vanished as she finished her speech, and she turned to her advisers with a bright smile: 'So what do you think of my speech?' (They reject it as 'awful'.)

Even Shakespeare was adapted for this modest theatrical production. One of the boys in the play was named Henry, and he recited part of Henry V's 'we few, we happy few' speech to rally the Jews. To make the speech appropriate for a Jewish festival, references to 'St Crispian' were omitted.

The *purimshpil* is a popular event at the synagogue, and the audience is a large and indulgent one. Many synagogue members attend this family-friendly evening, and it is also common to invite friends and neighbours to view the performance. The *purimshpil* lacks the solemnity of much Jewish ritual, and the fact that it is in English makes it easy for most Americans to understand. Any mistakes are overlooked or treated as further opportunities for comedy. Because the cast has to be assembled from those willing to participate, casting produces some amusing anomalies: in the 2007 production Ahasuerus was played by a boy preparing for his bar mitzvah, while the role of Esther was taken by a young teacher preparing for her wedding. The sight of a pubescent boy playing the lordly ruler while a grown woman played the innocent ingénue was another sign of the topsy-turvy world of Purim. The woman playing Esther had briefly been a professional actress, and both she and the man who played Mordechai were trained singers, but no one objected to younger or less experienced performers who showed, by their enthusiasm, that they were 'doing their best'. The performers' willingness to extend themselves for the pleasure of the congregation was considered far more important than any roughness in the execution.

Did our Beatles *purimshpil* reflect conflicts within the community, as did the Yiddish *purimshpiln* of eastern Europe? The story is filled with clashes between Jews and non-Jews, and the Beatles music recalls the eloquent iconoclasts of the 1960s. Yet when I asked participants for their thoughts on this, no one suggested that the play was an avenue of subversion or a means of venting suppressed rage. To the contrary, most saw it as a means of strengthening the community and having a good time into the bargain. One of the play's directors saw his role as an opportunity to 'feel like a contributing member of the community'. He also stressed the joyous nature of Purim: 'The goal here is to have fun.' Robin, who acted in the play with her first-grade son, echoed this theme: 'So many of our holidays are "They tried to kill us, we lived, let's eat". This has the same theme, but it's happy.' Lisa, who played Esther, appreciated 'the utter joy that Purim is and the utter abandonment of rules'. Laurel saw the *purimshpil* as 'a good family activity' for herself and her children. The echoes of Yiddish humour are apparent in her words: 'People get dressed up, people make lots of noise, people eat sweets, what's not to like?' Her daughter Miriam, who played the narrator, likewise appreciated the 'chance to perform for the community' and found the *purimshpil* 'a lot of fun'. Despite a story filled with strife, most participants interpreted their *purimshpil* as a chance for the community to come together rather than to stress dissent.

Do these findings suggest that Purim plays are no longer expressions of conflict? Or do they reflect the degree to which conflict has been muted and in some sense overcome by a middle-class Jewish community in twenty-first-century America? The congregation is filled with highly educated and successful people who feel completely integrated into mainstream American life. Many congregants have non-Jewish spouses, and all have non-Jewish friends. In our play, when Esther revealed her Jewish heritage, Ahasuerus assured her that this revelation changed nothing in his feelings for her; his use of several Yiddish words added a comic touch yet also affirmed his acceptance of Jewish culture. Just as Esther and Mordechai remained loyal Persians, American Jews have long mitigated the conflicts between their American and Jewish identities by becoming as American as possible. American Jews—like other Americans—read Shakespeare, listen to the Beatles, love baseball, and hang out with the local Persians. In a country that has guaranteed religious freedom for more than 200 years, at a time when Haman seems powerless or at least very far away, congregants' relationship with the dominant culture seems so effortless that any tension therein is small, almost invisible. Antisemitism still exists, of course, but respectable people do not express it in public.[5]

Thus the congregation's relationship to the dominant culture is generally one of harmony rather than overt conflict. The congregants' relationship with one another likewise stresses unity rather than divisiveness. This is a congregation in which the notion of 'community' is crucial; the word is frequently invoked when congregants describe what they value about the synagogue. Yet this sense of community must be carefully built and maintained, for it has no obvious basis beyond that of religion. Geographically, it is not really a community; some members live in the Washington neighbourhood where the synagogue stands, while others live in distant parts of the city or in the Maryland and Virginia suburbs. Synagogue members differ in terms of age, race, marital status, political views, philosophical outlook, and sexual orientation. Events such as the *purimshpil* can bring this diverse group of individuals together and allow them to identify with one another. By focusing on shared knowledge—whether of the Purim story or of the Beatles songs—the *purimshpil* can help them become a community. Rabbi Toby

Manewith, who was then associate rabbi of the congregation, commented: 'As the American Jewish community grows more diffuse, we're looking for things to bring people back in and to bring community together . . . Fifty years ago the community lived on top of each other, so they needed less of this sort of thing.' The very success of the Americanization process meant the attenuating of the Jewish community: instead of the tight-knit communities of the past, in which members could argue passionately because unity was taken for granted, today's Jews frequently inhabit 'imagined communities', in which unity must be actively proclaimed and disagreement held somewhat in abeyance. Rather than presenting conflicts within the Jewish community or with the dominant culture, the congregation's *purimshpil* became an active vehicle for muting conflict and overcoming difference.

Thus, in common with its European antecedents, this modern play enacted the Purim story in humorous fashion, with jokes ranging from puns to physical pratfalls. It adapted the music and popular culture of the dominant society, poked fun at members of the community, and made reference to topical political personalities. The fluidity of the script, looseness of performance practice, and use of the vernacular indicated an informal spectacle meant for all members of the community, not a ritual reserved for the learned or the powerful. The use of disguises, for both performers and audience, showed that Purim is a holiday in which things are not always what they seem.

Yet this modern adaptation differed in telling ways from its forebears. The play was not performed by members of the community who wished to air grievances; instead, it was performed by those who wished to bring the community together. Nor did it exhibit marked criticism of the Christian majority, with whom American Jews live on terms of legal equality and social amity. The traditional Purim licence to offend was not invoked; sexual and scatological materials were not included, out of respect for the place of performance and the nature of the audience. As the American Jewish community grows more middle-class, perhaps it also becomes more respectable, its rituals more in accordance with generalized American standards of politesse. We have noted a similar phenomenon in eighteenth- and nineteenth-century Europe and America, when Jews sought to restrain the excesses and vulgarity of Purim rites in order to conform to—and belong to—mainstream Western societies. In twenty-first-century America, the *purimshpil*, formerly a fierce tool of social criticism, can become a means of overcoming conflict and asserting the importance of community, goals that are not peculiar to Jewish Americans.

I do not wish to suggest, however, that the American Jewish community exists entirely without conflict and that the *purimshpil* has become a theatre of complacency. In the first place, division must exist before it can be overcome. The synagogue studied here has other forums, such as intellectual debates, committee meetings, and informal conversation, in which differences among synagogue members become apparent and can be expressed. The *purimshpil* does not pretend that such differences do not exist; it simply highlights the greater good of community solidarity. Secondly, the social and economic success of American Jews has engendered a certain anxiety about 'assimilation', a fear that, as Karl Kautsky predicted, Judaism would disappear once Jews were firmly integrated into mainstream Western societies (Kautsky 1926). In Reform congregations where intermarriage is common and where Jews dress, eat, and live like mainstream Americans, certain rituals and forms of folk culture may be revived as conscious ethnic markers, a hedge against the possibility of disappearance. The *purimshpil*, then, can exist primarily as a sign of ethnicity, an index of Yiddishkeit; not a means of exploring conflict, but a means of asserting difference. Third, the Purim story seems to resonate with American Jews in ways that other portions of the Bible do not. It is the most homely and human of biblical stories, a tale in which people, at their most heroic and at their most frail, control all of the action. We may admire Moses or Aaron or Isaiah, but it is hard to relate to them; their shadows are too long, their lives too unlike the ones we know. But Esther seems like one of us: an urban diaspora Jew with a non-Jewish spouse, a woman who negotiates--with difficulty and yet with success--both the public world of power and the private world of family. Who among us would dare play Moses? Yet who among us would not know how to play Esther or Mordechai?

Finally, American *purimshpiln* are not monolithic: they can and do highlight specific political or social conflicts, and some of these plays are discussed below. The critical eye can find conflicts even when participants assert that none exists. As Victor Turner notes:

Even when, in certain kinds of theatre, in different cultures, conflict may appear to be muted or deflected or rendered as a playful or joyous struggle, it is not hard to detect threads of connection between elements of the play and sources of conflict in sociocultural milieus. The very mufflings and evasions of scenes of discord in some theatrical and natural traditions speak eloquently to their real presence in society, and may perhaps be regarded as a cultural defense-mechanism against conflict rather than a metacommentary upon it. (Turner 1982: 105–6)

The conflicts between Jews and non-Jews and between men and women are a fundamental part of the Purim story and must be present, in some sense, in the *purimshpil*. Antisemitism is both text and subtext of the Purim story. The play shows that antisemitism can be laughed at and overcome, but it cannot be forgotten or ignored; it can spring to life even at times when the Jewish community seems secure, such as in ancient Persia or present-day America. Gender conflicts are also an inescapable part of the Purim story and of the contemporary political landscape, and these conflicts are beginning to find their way into *purimshpiln*. As we look at the diversity of contemporary *purimshpiln*, we can see how different communities interpret the story in ways that are meaningful to the participants and audiences involved.

Purimshpiln in the Modern World

Though it is difficult to get an accurate count of how many *purimshpiln* are currently being produced, it is clear that their number is substantial. A Google search for '*purimshpil*' yields 4,300 hits, while a search for 'Purim spiel' shows ten times that many. Many of these are reports of plays that have recently been produced by synagogues, community centres, and colleges; others provide scripts for sale or downloading; still others delve into the history of *purimshpiln* or their meanings for contemporary Jews. *Purimshpiln* appear to be particularly abundant in the United States, but one finds them throughout the English-speaking world, in Europe, and in former Soviet Asia. In the United States, many *purimshpiln* appear similar to the one in which I participated: light-hearted productions whose primary function is to bring the community together and for participants to have a good time. Synagogues in the north, south, east, and west show a remarkable consistency in citing these two functions—fun and community-building—as essential reasons for producing *purimshpiln*. Within these general objectives, however, there is variation that indicates the specific values, preferences, and talents of the community involved.

Debbie and John Orenstein wrote an original play for their Minneapolis synagogue entitled *Vashti Was Right or The Book of Zeresh (A Purim Spiel)*.[6] As Debbie Orenstein explained in an email message:

We wrote the song 'Vashti Was Right' before we even thought about doing a whole spiel. A friend of ours was wearing a button that said, 'Vashti Was Right', and we thought it would make a good song. We sang it in our synagogue at Purim and it was a huge hit. At that time, our synagogue was purchasing parody spiels from another synagogue and we thought we could do as good a job, if not better, doing one of our own.

The Orensteins' production of *Vashti Was Right* was extremely successful at their synagogue. In 2007, 800 people attended, including members of other synagogues, 'the biggest turnout to any religious event in our synagogue except for the high holidays' (Orenstein email). Several other synagogues have purchased the script, and the music (particularly the title song) has proved even more popular. The Orensteins have sold hundreds of CDs of their original songs and have discovered that people throughout the country are singing 'Vashti Was Right'.

In the first scene of the play, the audience is asked to consider a midrash that is fairly sympathetic to Vashti's act of rebellion. The midrash states that Vashti refused Ahasuerus's request out of modesty: the king had demanded that she appear naked before his party guests. The play also foregrounds the other woman in the book of Esther: Zeresh, Haman's wife, an enigmatic but powerful character, who instructs Haman to build the gallows for Mordechai and later prophesies Mordechai's ultimate victory over Haman. The prominence and power of women in the book of Esther have long been of interest to feminists, and many have questioned Ahasuerus's summary dismissal of Vashti. *Purimshpiln* have often explored and aired conflicts, and gender conflicts are hotly debated in contemporary Western societies. The *purimshpil*—a form that upholds tradition even while it expresses new ideas—could be the ideal vehicle for exploring new solutions to gender conflicts. Yet when I asked Debbie Orenstein about the gender politics of *Vashti Was Right*, she wrote:

Gender politics was not really the issue. We did what we thought was funny and we wrote songs that would suit the people we had chosen for the cast . . . What we have really tried to do is be as faithful to the text as we could. And we feel there's a heart to the original story and we tried to capture that, too. (Orenstein email)

Even in a *purimshpil* that highlights the problems of gender, the ultimate goal may be the muting, rather than the exploration, of conflict. Debbie Orenstein's thoughts on the purpose of *purimshpiln* are remarkably similar to the ideas expressed in my own congregation: 'We just think it's great fun and an opportunity for a congregation to come together' (Orenstein email).

A similar point of view is expressed by Wendy Damoulakis, whose Massachusetts congregation has been performing *purimshpiln* for about fifteen years. They began with simple productions, 'like a talent show', then moved on to plays that are approximately thirty-five to forty minutes in length. Some productions were written by the congregants, including the rabbi, while others were purchased, such as their 2008 offering, *Oy-klahoma*. Adults and children collaborate as actors, musicians, and technical crew, and the *purimshpil* always draws a large crowd. Damoulakis cites several reasons for doing *purimshpiln* at her synagogue:

It gives our choir members and others a congregational 'performance' venue, it is definitely part of the fun around Purim (lots of congregants come in costume to the Megillah reading beforehand), and it crosses the line between a 'social' event and a religious one. But mostly, it is the fun and silliness which we all need more of in our lives—a place where children, their parents and grandparents can come and laugh with jokes and have a really good time. (Damoulakis email)

As Damoulakis notes, the *purimshpil* has both religious and secular functions: it draws congregants to the synagogue, provokes laughter, and builds community.

In Tracy Rice's Marin County (suburban San Francisco) congregation, *purimshpiln* are a recent innovation, dating only from 2003. Congregants and synagogue staff, 'from the maintenance staff to the rabbis', collaborate on the *purimshpil*, and synagogue employees write the scripts. Rice echoes the themes of fun and community-building and sees a serious purpose in this holiday of laughter:

I think that Purim spiels are very important. It's a way to show that Judaism isn't all about synagogue and ritual. That there is an element of fun and laughter to be had. For our congregation it is a great way to join together people who may not know each other outside of our walls. Any opportunity to build community is vital to the future of Judaism. (Rice email)

Yet Rice provides an interesting variation on this theme, one that reflects the needs of her congregation. *Purimshpiln* have often commented on relations between the Jewish community and the dominant culture, but in Rice's synagogue they also provide a means of building bridges between the two. Rice writes:

In Marin there are a lot of interfaith couples and Purim is a great example of a celebration that can be welcoming and not intimidating to some one who is not Jewish. I think that one of the kids in the cast said it best when she asked, 'Do you have to be Jewish to come to the show?' It's really important for her to share this with the people in her life and not all of them are Jewish. Purim can be a great way to reach out to those who may not normally come to the Synagogue, and the Spiel is even more accessible. (Rice email)

Though *purimshpiln* have traditionally been a folk and hence amateur form of theatre, there is a growing number of professionally written scripts and professionally produced *purimshpiln*. Several organizations have found that the homely, familiar *purimshpil* can be a successful fundraising tool. In 2008 the fourth annual Broadway *purimshpil* was produced at the Hudson Theatre in New York City. Publicity information states, 'For one night only, stars from Broadway's biggest hit shows join together for the Broadway Purim Shpiel, a hilarious retelling of the Purim story. All proceeds from the . . . event will benefit Taglit-Birthright Israel, an organization dedicated to sending young Jews from across the world to Israel.'[7] Broadway actors also performed in a 2006 fundraiser for Congregation Beth Simchat Torah, New York City's gay synagogue.[8] On a smaller scale, Gail Foorman of Atlanta has been writing *purimshpiln* since the mid-1990s. Though she primarily writes *purimshpiln* for her own congregation, she also writes and sells them for other communities, specifically tailoring scripts to the congregation involved. As such, she sees the *purimshpil*'s function as varying according to the community in question. She also comments on the difference between writing professional and amateur *purimshpiln*:

There are two ways to go about creating a spiel. One is as a moneymaker (more lucrative), the other is as a community building experience (very rewarding in other ways). The function of the spiel really depends on the nature of the community for which it is being written. Is it aimed at children? Is it aimed at a knowledgeable community? Is it aimed at an egalitarian community? Is it aimed at an intermarried community? Is its purpose educational or didactic, is its purpose community building? (Foorman email)

The Shushan Channel *purimshpiln*, which began in 2003, show that professionalism and community-building can go hand in hand. Initially performed in New York as fundraisers for the Jewish environmental organization Hazon, these plays make liberal use of American television, in part because they are created by television professionals. Originally organized by Rob Kutner, a writer for Jon Stewart's *The Daily Show*, the plays consist of sketches written by professional writers and then put together by producers and editors. Kutner initially became interested in *purimshpiln* while studying at a yeshiva in Israel, where:

they have a tradition of putting on an old-fashioned, everything but the kitchen sink, multi-hour spiel—and with my burgeoning interest in writing comedy . . . I took it to heart, coordinating, directing, and writing much of our extravaganza. My favorite was a spoof of Star Trek wherein we used what we'd learned in Halacha class to do a sketch about the Enterprise coming upon a treyfe space vessel, and what they had to do to kasher it . . . I ran the spiel at the minyan I attended in LA for a few years, then, when I moved to New York, I found myself without a Jewish community per se. So, in effect, I created one around this fake TV network called the Shushan Channel, which showed all familiar TV shows, but each of them told a piece of the Purim story or riffed off a contemporary Jewish theme. (Kutner email)

These *purimshpiln* proved highly successful, garnering rave reviews and playing to sold-out audiences in New York. The link to American television remained consistent and deliberate: the plays have titles such as *Desperate Matriarchs* (instead of *Desperate Housewives*), *Persia's Next Top Monarch* (instead of *America's Next Top Model*), and *Curb Your Antisemitism* (instead of *Curb Your Enthusiasm*) (Hecker 2005).[9] Kutner writes:

I want to tell the story in a fun, accessible way, so I always look for connections between current shows/trends and the issues raised in the story. For example, the megillah begins with an objectifying pageant where women are paraded before a powerful man who controls their fate. This is all but the template of so many reality shows, and has been the easiest (sadly) to find a modern equivalent to each year . . . Another recurring theme is of Esther having to hide her Jewishness from the world—also, again, a contemporary theme. (Kutner email)

The 2007 production added Stephen Colbert (who, with Jon Stewart, is one of Comedy Central's most successful political humorists) in a video prepared specially for the performance in which he attacks Mordechai and defends Haman.[10] Just as medieval and Renaissance Jews borrowed from the Christian rites of Fastnacht and Mardi Gras, contemporary Jews find that *purimshpiln* can incorporate the political humour of Comedy Central.

The success of the Shushan Channel *purimshpiln* led to the decision, in 2007, to offer them for sale on the internet. The Shushan Channel website declares, 'Jewish people are the funniest people in the world. So why are most *purimshpiln* so lame? We're not sure, but we decided to fix the problem. Enter "The Shushan Channel".'[11] The introduction of payment creates a crucial distinction between these plays and the home-grown productions created by volunteers in synagogues and on college campuses. The Shushan Channel website is targeted at organizations that can spend $500 on a script, and who hope to recoup the expense by charging admission, but in many synagogues the *purimshpil* is entwined with the Megillah reading and is seen as a religious ritual open to all, not a professional production charging an entrance fee. Thus, as Gail Foorman has remarked, the purpose of the *purimshpil* must be clear: is it primarily for religious sentiment, the building of community, the display of artistic virtuosity, or some other reason? If the primary function is to invoke religious feeling or build community, then any factor that mitigates against maximum inclusion might work against the *purimshpil*'s purpose. Congregants who do not wish to pay for a religious ritual may choose to stay at home or seek out a congregation in which the Purim celebrations are free. Folklorist Barbara Kirshenblatt-Gimblett, in her study of the *purimshpiln* of the Bobover hasidim, discusses Robert Plant Armstrong's distinction between an aesthetic of invocation and an aesthetic of virtuosity, the difference between art for art's sake and art for the sake of something else. The Bobover plays are designed to please the *rebbe* and the community, and they succeed mightily, despite a performance that may seem amateurish to outsiders. Kirshenblatt-Gimblett explains that 'Sincerity, enthusiasm, and depth of feeling are more important than artistic excellence' (1990: 117). Thus, the aesthetic of invocation highlights specific community values rather than generalized artistic ones.

On the other hand, there is no inherent conflict between artistic excellence and religious expression. The Shushan Channel creators realize that, for many people, a professionally crafted *purimshpil* can increase enjoyment of the holiday and induce more celebrants to attend. Joel Levinson, one of the writers of these *purimshpiln*, explains:

I spent years traveling around the country working as a BBYO [B'nai B'rith Youth Organization] songleader and music educator . . . Jews across America were dying for something watchable to be performed in their Temples, and it only made sense to make the stuff available to them.

In particular, when I was working with a Temple in LA as a music teacher, I was forced to be in a Purim spiel that was, I kid you not, called 'Shmaustin Shmowers' and was basically a terrible retelling of Purim + Austin Powers, but longer and without the jokes. It was an awful experience, and I told Rob [Kutner] we just couldn't stand by knowing cantors and rabbis across the country were going through the same painful things. (Levinson email)

Thus, an aesthetic of virtuosity may foster community by providing enjoyable entertainment that entices congregants to attend.

Other American Purim plays focus on specific conflicts and highlight specific issues important to the community involved. The Workmen's Circle (Arbeter Ring) of New York has been involved in several productions that focus on and raise money for political causes. Founded by Yiddish-speaking workers in the early twentieth century, the Workmen's Circle has long been active in progressive politics. In 2002 the New York organization teamed up with Amnesty International USA and the theatre company Great Small Works to produce a puppet *purimshpil* against the death penalty. The Purim story was read in English and Yiddish while giant puppets acted it out. In their play, Haman was the villain who supported the death penalty, while Esther was the heroine who fought against it. On the website for the 2002 production, Louis Shipman declares:

The traditions represented by this Purim carnival called on the traditional religious culture of the Jewish people, but perhaps more importantly, the more recent past when the
Jewish community in New York City was the bedrock of progressive politics. By using
Yiddish and focusing on the politics of opposing the death penalty, this event was truly
faithful to those traditions. (Shipman 2002)

In 2007 the Workmen's Circle teamed up with Jews for Racial and Economic Justice, Domestic Workers United, and Great Small Works to produce *Roti and
Homentashn*, a fundraiser for domestic workers, many of whom are from the
West Indies. This play 'takes a progressive twist on the book of Esther, telling it
from the perspective of the palace workers'.[12] By highlighting the salient strands
of Jewish and American political tradition, the Workmen's Circle is able to create
vibrant and timely theatre from an ancient text.

While the *purimshpil* remains a distinctly Jewish art form, awareness of it is
starting to reach non-Jewish Americans. In a 2002 article in the conservative
National Review, Jay Nordlinger asserts that, 'At a major Washington, DC synagogue, [Attorney General John] Ashcroft figured in a "Purim spiel": He was
equated with Haman, a figure of extreme danger—of mass murder—to Jews'
(Nordlinger 2002: 2). Nordlinger makes this assertion without attribution or further detail, but what is particularly interesting is his offhand mention of a *purimshpil*, with very little explanation, in a predominantly non-Jewish publication.

The apparently limitless ability of the *purimshpil* to serve as a political touch-
stone is highlighted in a speech given by Speaker of the House Nancy Pelosi on
13 March 2007 for the American Israel Public Affairs Committee (AIPAC), a
pro-Israel lobbying organization. Her speech, predictably enough, stresses her
personal commitment and the commitment of the United States to the state of
Israel. But her opening remarks are far from typical; she describes how her
grandchildren celebrated Purim this year with a Beatles *purimshpil*. Though not
Jewish herself, Pelosi is able to establish herself as a grandmother with Jewish relatives and then discusses the political implications of her personal remarks:
'amidst the fun, they once again recalled the history of a Persian leader threatening the Jewish people, and the heroine Esther who had the courage to speak out
and save them. Today, the Israeli people have and need that same courage to
meet that same challenge.'[13] In her discussion of the threats that Israel faces, she
lays particular emphasis upon Iran, site of the original Purim story, and casts
Ahmadinejad as a modern-day Haman.

Purimshpiln in Canada, Australia, and western Europe show many of the
tendencies one finds in the United States: a general sense of ease with the dominant culture, a light-hearted playfulness, and conflicts that are muted but not necessarily absent. The internet has created a virtual community of *purimshpil* actors
in the English-speaking world; scripts move effortlessly from Sydney to Toronto
to New York to London.[14] In 2007, Temple Emanuel of Woollahra in Australia
presented *Pirates of Purim*, a *purimshpil* using Beatles tunes, that pays homage to

pirates.[15] A Jewish community centre in Ottawa presented a *purimshpil* based on Beach Boys songs to a sold-out house, while an Anglophone synagogue in Montreal produced a Motown *purimshpil*—both plays purchased from a synagogue in Boca Raton, Florida.[16] But the *purimshpil* revival is not just an Anglophone phenomenon. *Purimshpiln* are becoming popular in Sweden, while an international *purimshpil* competition was recently held in Belarus.[17]

In England, the Movement for Reform Judaism sponsors a competition for young people, entitled 'Purim Spiel-Off'.[18] Teams from synagogues across the country create and perform short Purim plays or films, which are presented at a weekend-long event. Adults act as judges and may help with writing or play minor roles, but the bulk of the work must be done by young people (aged 16 and under). Prizes are awarded for best spiel, best costume, best acting, best direction, best music, and best team spirit. The rules state that the *purimshpil* 'should reflect the story of Purim or any issues raised by the story' and that the content 'must be appropriate for the age ranges involved in the production, and for the audience that will view the Purim spiel competition' (Littman email). Like their American counterparts, English *purimshpil* actors frequently adapt television and other forms of popular culture (*High Spiel Musical* was a recent offering), while adding their own music and political references (Littman email). However, the winning spiel of the 2008 competition was based on the gold standard of English high culture: it was an adaptation of Shakespeare, written by the young people involved, with only a small amount of music at the beginning (Miller email). Though humour is the primary component of the *purimshpiln*, serious issues occasionally surface. Jon Littman, a youth worker for the Movement for Reform Judaism, writes:

We did have a film a couple of years ago that set the story in a school and dealt with bullying. The same group also dealt with anti-Semitism in a much stronger way the next year. Some issues do come up, but only really as a tool for comedy. Certainly I would like to see more education and development of particular issues, or even for the spiels to be dramas or dramatic, rather than always concentrate on humour. (Littman email)

Littman's thoughts on the purpose of *purimshpiln*, while similar to those of his American counterparts, are somewhat more serious: 'This competition is about bringing reform communities together, celebrating the achievement of the youth, celebrating and giving authenticity to reform expressions of Judaism' (Littman email). Arieh Miller, a youth worker for the Sinai Synagogue in Leeds (which produced the winning team for the 2008 competition), stresses the educational and entertainment values of *purimshpiln*: 'Purim spiels serve multiple functions. On a simple level, they are an easy way to tell the Purim story to younger (and older) kids. On a more adult level, they provide entertainment, and can often bring out some of the more hidden messages of megilat Esther' (Miller email). Both Littman and Miller show a sophisticated understanding of the multi-layered Purim story, how serious messages may lurk beneath the surface humour.

In central and eastern Europe, *purimshpiln* have a longer and darker history. At present, there is a particularly intriguing interest in *purimshpiln* (and in Yiddish culture in general) in Germany. In 1999 advanced students of Yiddish performed Itzik Manger's Yiddish Purim play *Megile-Lieder* (Songs of the Megillah) at the University of Trier.[19] In 2002 Berlin filmmaker Ulrike Ottinger produced *Ester: A Purim Play in Berlin*. Performed in German, the actors were Jewish immigrants from central and eastern Europe. Publicity information states that this version is 'a parable about [having] the courage to arrive in a foreign country and a funny masquerade about blessing in disguise' (Ottinger 2002). In 2007 a *purimshpil* was produced in Ratingen by the Jewish cultural organization Shalom, which was founded by Jewish immigrants from Russia and the Ukraine. Publicity information explains that a goal of the organization is to share its Purim celebration with the local Christian and Muslim communities.[20] Despite the humour inherent in the *purimshpiln*, descriptive information about the German productions tends to be relatively sombre, stressing serious themes, scholarly rigour, and religious co-operation. The self-deprecating humour so common in descriptions of American *purimshpiln* is completely absent. In Germany, the licence to offend, to laugh at Jewish culture, can go only so far.

Poland is another site where the theme of Jewish annihilation has a particularly resonant and harrowing history. In 2000 Polish filmmaker Izabella Cywinska presented *Purim Spiel* (also called *The Miracle of Purim*), a comedy about contemporary antisemitism in Poland. The film was critically acclaimed and was particularly well received in Germany (Steinberg 2002). The main character, Jan Kochanowski, is a middle-aged Polish worker who blames everything—including the loss of his job—on the Jews. While struggling to make ends meet he receives word from an American lawyer that a wealthy relative has died, leaving Jan a considerable amount of money. But the wealth comes with a revelation: Jan's relative, and Jan himself, are Jewish. (The family name was originally Cohen.) When Jan confesses his Jewish identity to his wife, it turns out she is Jewish as well, but had been hiding this fact (like Esther) in order to escape antisemitism. All ends well as the family ultimately embrace their Jewish heritage and concomitant wealth. Cywinska uses a familiar antisemitic stereotype (the rich Jew) with a more recent European stereotype (the rich American) in order to make fun of antisemites and denounce antisemitism. The film has received several awards, and Cywinska got a warm reception when she presented it at the Auschwitz Jewish Centre.[21] Like the German *purimshpiln*, this Polish *purimshpil* uses humour for the most serious of purposes, as it walks the minefield of Jewish–Polish relations.

These modern *purimshpiln* differ from their ancestors in many ways: the languages and texts are different; the music and topical references vary with the circumstances of the Purim players; and even who may act and what may be said have changed. Yet certain themes remain tenaciously embedded within the tradition, consistent and perhaps essential components of the *purimshpil* as a genre. As we have seen, three of these themes are the construction of gender, the importance of humour, and the use of Purim as a model for the diaspora. As we examine these themes, we can see how their expression differs within different communities and how the rites of Purim have changed with the changing conditions of Jewish communities.

Gender and the *Purimshpil*

Gender plays an unusually important role in the holiday of Purim, which highlights a biblical book named after a woman and gives us a heroine who succeeds by prototypically feminine means. The issue of gender also accounts for some of the most interesting and far-reaching differences between historical and modern Purim plays. Though women are crucial to the story, only men acted in traditional European Purim plays, and this tradition continues amongst the hasidic communities of Brooklyn. In many contemporary American congregations, however, women are active participants in all aspects of synagogue life, including *purimshpiln*. The Reform congregation discussed above boasts a woman rabbi and a woman cantor, and women are often called up to read the Torah during services. In this production, women and girls played the women's parts, while men and boys played the men's parts, and the role of the narrator (who ties the entire story together) was played by a 15-year-old girl. This gender equality so reflected the congregation's ethos that it was no more controversial than having the play in English. Yet the use of female Purim players ruled out certain kinds of humour used in traditional European Purim plays. If Esther is played by a cross-dressing man, then it is amusing and completely appropriate to describe 'her' appearance as grotesque. But if such descriptions are directed at a real woman they become hurtful and vicious, not in keeping with the desire to forge community. Other means must be found to make the character of Esther funny: in this congregation, Esther was presented as consistently clumsy, her entrance accompanied by the rattle of pots and pans. To make fun of her behaviour was acceptable, because she was obviously 'acting'.

The contemporary American Purim play has sanded down the rough edges of its European ancestors in other ways, too. The assumption that children should not hear sexual or scatological material probably accounts for some of this bowdlerization. In the Washington, DC congregation's play, no mention was made of Esther spending the night with Ahasuerus before she became queen, and the selection process for the virgins turned into a simple beauty contest with a real crown at the end. Whereas the congregation easily accepted the gender equality that European Purim plays had lacked, it could not accept the rough street humour of an earlier age.

The fact that a woman emerges as the saviour of her people is another example of the topsy-turvy world of Purim. Though Mordechai has wisdom, he lacks power; only Esther is in a position to save the Jews. Her potential as a feminist heroine has been the subject of lively debate. Bea Wyler calls Esther's emancipation 'incomplete' since it addresses only her Jewishness and not her womanhood: she fights valiantly for herself as a Jew but wastes the opportunity to fight for herself as a woman (Wyler 1995: 132). Mary Gendler laments the fact that the image of a pious, obedient Esther has been held up as a model for Jewish women (Gendler 1976). Gendler prefers the straightforward assertiveness of Vashti, who refuses to obey the king's command when it seems unreasonable. Interpretations of Esther as weak and pious were fostered by rabbinic commentaries that sought to discover God's hidden place in the godless book of Esther. Whereas the Bible shows Esther acting independently and making important decisions on her own (albeit with Mordechai's guidance), various midrashim depict angels providing her with assistance and helping her to do what she was too weak and frightened to do by herself. As Leila Leah Bronner says, 'Rabbinic literature, by emphasizing God's constant assistance, in a way diminishes Esther's personal strength and independence of action; but it also increases her spirituality, which was, after all, where rabbinic interest really lay' (Bronner 2004: 197).

If we return to the biblical original, however, other interpretations of Esther are equally possible. Her real art lies in getting what she wants while presenting herself as submissive and obedient. She knows that the direct approach as practised by Vashti does not work. When Mordechai hears Haman's decree he dresses in sackcloth and ashes, but Esther knows better than to appear before Ahasuerus in such a state. She carefully presents herself at her most beautiful and sexually alluring, and she softens the king up by providing a sumptuous meal and two nights of drinking. Celina Spiegel sees Esther as a representation of the power of female sexuality:

Inborn and natural, Esther's sexuality is presented as the embodiment of Jewish virtues. In this sense the story is truly utopian for its world remade—through Esther's intervention—hearkens back to an unself-conscious, unfallen female sexuality. It also demonstrates that the subtle, indirect workings of a woman can be more effective than the brash carryings-on of a man. (Spiegel 1994: 202)

Esther's beauty and sexuality caused Ahasuerus to choose her as queen; they continue to hold his interest when he sees her standing uninvited in the courtyard, and he is quick to hold out his golden sceptre to her waiting hand. Esther uses her beauty and sexuality as tools to gain power—not for personal profit, but to save the lives of her people.

Contemporary *purimshpiln* have begun to investigate the gender politics in the book of Esther. In the Washington, DC congregation's play, Vashti's advisers, Hillary and Liddy, agreed with her proto-feminist stance and suggested that she 'hit that king for a healthy alimony and hit the road' (a reversal of the biblical account, in which Ahasuerus rejects Vashti). Cast members had a wide variety of opinions on the Purim story and its relationship to feminism. In my interviews with the players, Robin saw Esther as an admirable figure, someone who uses a position of power for good: 'Esther is chosen for her beauty, but she succeeds by bravery and cleverness.' Laurel thought the story had 'mixed signals as far as women's rights go ... Vashti is punished for standing up for her rights, but Esther stands up and she's a heroine'. On the other hand, Laurel pointed out that the story highlights strong women, while the men in the story, with the exception of Mordechai, are portrayed as evil or weak. Miriam, who played the narrator and had played Esther the previous year, found Purim 'a politically incorrect holiday' in some ways: Vashti is punished for refusing to show off her beauty and Esther gains power by doing so. Lisa, who played Esther and had played Vashti the year before, found feminist messages in Vashti's straightforwardness and in Esther's subtlety: 'I grew up in a very feminist household, and when I was growing up, Vashti was always who I wanted to be—I never wanted to be Esther. This year being Esther was interesting because I sort of feel a kinship with her now ... As feminism has evolved, we've all recognized that there's nothing wrong with being powerful in your femininity, in your sexuality, and wanting to please your partner ... that doesn't take away from your innate power as a woman.'

I suggest that the book of Esther gives us the two faces of feminism in the characters of Esther and Vashti. Though Vashti certainly makes an important stand for personal dignity, her refusal to compromise removes her from any position of power and from the story. Esther never overtly speaks out for women's rights, but her ability to play the political game provides a model of a powerful woman who uses courage and intelligence to successfully defend an oppressed group. Karen Offen defines two types of feminism that emerged in the late nineteenth century: relational feminism and individualist feminism. Relational feminists 'emphasized the complementary and interdependent relationship between women and men, women's distinctive nature and contributions to society as a sex ... and their responsibilities to a broader collectivity—in some cases the nation and in others the working class' (Offen 1998: 331). Individualist feminists 'focused more exclusively on philosophical demands for women's "natural" rights, for freedom from social restraint and opportunities for personal development' (Offen 1998: 332). We can see Esther as the prototype of the relational feminist, who places community responsibility on a par with women's rights. Though she never protests women's subordination to men, she gains power in uniquely feminine ways and then uses this power on behalf of the Jewish community. Vashti, on the other hand, is the prototypical individualist feminist, one who seeks personal freedom and refuses to submit to arbitrary male demands. Whereas Vashti speaks primarily—or only--for herself, Esther is an inescapable part of the Jewish community. Together, they make a feminist statement that, like much in the book of Esther, remains somewhat hidden. I suspect that feminist Purim plays, those that actively investigate gender politics and explore the gender conflicts in contemporary Western societies, may soon appear. When one considers how cleverly other political causes have been incorporated into *purimshpiln* (anti-Nazism, workers' rights) and when one considers how many important feminist writers are Jewish (Marge Piercy, Judy Chicago, Gloria Steinem, Naomi Wolf, Susan Brownmiller, Adrienne Rich), we should not have to wait long.

Purim as a Model for Diaspora

Only two biblical books—Ruth and Esther—are named after women. The story of Ruth is fairly conventional: Ruth is a non-Jewish woman who marries a Jewish man and is incorporated into the Jewish community. The story of Esther is pretty much the opposite: Esther is a Jewish woman, married to a non-Jew, living in a diaspora community. Her Hebrew name, Hadassah, appears only once, and many scholars have commented on the similarity between the non-Jewish name 'Esther' and the Middle Eastern goddess Ishtar, who was famed, like Esther, for love and beauty (Rozik 1996). The book of Esther presents the essential condition of the diaspora Jew, who lives in a predominantly non-Jewish world but remains on guard against the potentially deadly force of antisemitism. Daniel Boyarin (whose work combines philosophy, religious history, and Jewish cultural studies) calls Purim 'the holiday of Diaspora. It is the only Jewish holiday that celebrates an event which took place in Diaspora, and, as such, it is a key symbol of Jewish culture, for Diaspora has been the primary cultural feature of Jewish existence for *more than* two thousand years . . . this is the founding text not only of Purim, but of Diaspora' (Boyarin 1994: 4; emphasis in original).

As a woman in a diaspora community, Esther's marginality is twofold: as a Jew, she is the Other in Persian society; as a woman, she is the Other within the Jewish community itself. Although this position as the Other Other makes Esther especially vulnerable, I suggest that it has advantages as well. As someone who has dealt with marginal status all her life, Esther has a unique understanding of how to succeed in this position. Unlike Vashti (the normative woman) or Mordechai (the normative Jew), Esther eschews direct confrontation in favour of oblique requests, and she succeeds while they fail. In a way, her double otherness mutes her marginal status. As a woman, Esther cannot be the quintessential Jew, for, as Simone de Beauvoir reminds us, the quintessential human being is always a man. Because she is a woman, Esther's place in Jewish society is less central than that of men, but this anchorlessness allows her to move easily within Persian society. Historian and biblical scholar Leila Leah Bronner cites several midrashim that attest to a universal admiration for Esther's beauty: 'every man took her for a member of his own people' (Bronner 2004: 181). As a woman, she is judged and deemed worthy to be the wife of a king. On the other hand, Esther cannot be seen only as a woman, for her Jewish identity threatens her very life. Thus, unlike normative women, who are defined entirely by their bodies, Esther is also defined by her soul, which is Jewish.

Like Esther, the Purim players of eastern Europe often represented the Other Other (see Belkin 1999). As Jews, they were the Other within European society; as poor and powerless individuals, they were the Other within the Jewish community itself. As such, their targets were both the oppressors of the dominant society and the authorities within the Jewish community. We have already seen how Purim festivities were restricted or banned when they became an embarrassment to Jewish authorities or when they were perceived as a threat to the dominant culture. What is equally interesting is the way that relations with the dominant culture are played out in the *purimshpiln* themselves. As previously mentioned, the Yiddish plays of central and eastern Europe expressed hostility toward the Other by mocking and insulting non-Jewish characters such as Haman and Ahasuerus. One of the most famous examples is the *Akhashveyros-shpil,* a Yiddish play from eighteenth-century Germany. The *Akhashveyros-shpil* uses insults, bawdy jokes, and references to bodily functions in order to make all authority figures look ridiculous and, hence, non-threatening (Belkin 2003; Pollack 1971). Barbara Kirshenblatt-Gimblett notes another significant phenomenon in Yiddish Purim plays: the popularity of productions about robbers and smugglers in nineteenth- and early twentieth-century Europe. By focusing on clever criminals and incompetent lawmen, these plays 'suggest that justice resides outside the official system, that law enforcement is often ineffectual, and that nonviolent breaches of the law . . . may be necessary for survival in an unjust and capricious world—themes found in the original Purim story' (Kirshenblatt-Gimblett 1980: 9). For the Yiddish-speaking Jews of eastern Europe, who were hemmed in by antisemitic laws restricting their residence, occupation, and education, the clever lawbreaker who successfully circumvents the system had a definite appeal. In a world where the dominant culture asserts authority through vicious and capricious laws, praising the scofflaw is an act of resistance.

Ahuva Belkin describes a very different example in *Simḥat purim,* a Hebrew Purim play that was published in Amsterdam in 1650 (Belkin 1995). Although the play is anonymous, Belkin deduces that it was a product of the Sephardi community, which by this time was firmly established in Amsterdam and was prospering in the relatively tolerant atmosphere of the Netherlands. Thanks to its prosperity, this community was able to devote considerable time to education, with particular attention to the study of Hebrew. As a result, Hebrew literature flourished, and the output included several plays. Like other Purim plays, *Simḥat purim* is amusing and has as its climax the defeat of Haman. However, it presents a far more middle-class mentality than the Yiddish Purim plays of central and eastern Europe. It is in the learned and sacred language of Hebrew, not the vernacular of the community, and takes its inspiration from several midrashim that would have been known only to advanced students of Torah and Talmud. Like traditional Yiddish *purimshpiln*, *Simḥat purim* is filled with jokes, stylized insults, and references to bodily functions; however, unlike their Yiddish counterparts, these references are neither vulgar nor obscene. The play does not insult biblical characters, nor does it present subversive or controversial ideas. It is, instead, a fairly light-hearted production of a community that knew Hebrew and rabbinic literature well enough to be able to play with them. In a way, *Simḥat purim* is similar to the Washington, DC congregation's Beatles Purim play, the product of an educated middle-class community at peace with its non-Jewish neighbours. Lacking the fierce tensions that created the far more barbed humour of eastern Europe, endowed with the education that allows one to easily play with high culture, these middle-class Purim plays are either blander or more refined (depending on one's point of view) than their working-class equivalents.

The diaspora could be haven or horror for the Jewish community, and a Yiddish *purimshpil* from 1948 captures both possibilities. Shifra Epstein's splendid reconstruction of the Bobover hasidim's *Tzayt in farnumen poyland* (Times in Occupied Poland) captures a remarkable example of the will to overcome human tragedy by creating dramatic comedy. Produced in New York in 1948, the play was performed by Holocaust survivors for an audience composed primarily of Holocaust survivors. In keeping with the Purim theme of inversion, 'the Bobover believe that at certain troubled times, God can endow the actors of the *piremshpiyl* [*purimshpil*] with power to change the course of disastrous events by enacting a reversal of them in the course of the play' (Epstein 1995: 240). In the first scene of the play a woman watches her child being dragged from a Polish ghetto by the SS. In the next scene, which occurs several years later, an SS officer presents her with a bag of ashes, the remains of the son who was taken away. Yet the SS officer does not have the final word. In the last act, American soldiers liberate Poland and help this woman rebuild her shattered life. In the final scene, the woman's son arrives at her door, having escaped the SS and hidden with the partisans (once again, hiddenness emerges as a survival tactic in a Purim story). The triumph of life in the midst of so much death proclaims the continued existence of the Jewish community, of miracles, of God, and of an ultimate happy (if heart-wrenching) ending. Two very different non-Jewish worlds affect the same people: the cruel SS officers are contrasted with the liberating American soldiers. In this way, Holocaust survivors could confront the terrors of their European experience from the safety of American soil. Despite its theme of ultimate survival, the play was too raw, too close to the bone to be repeated. The Bobover hasidim continued to perform *purimshpiln*, but most did not confront the experience of the Holocaust directly.

Purim has always been about the position of the Jew in the diaspora, the dangers and the possibilities that this condition embodies. In the post-Holocaust world, even the most raucous Purim laughter is not without a touch of bitterness. *Purimshpiln* rarely address the Holocaust directly; even Elie Wiesel's searing *The*

Trial of God, which Wiesel calls 'a *Purimschpiel* within a *Purimschpiel*' and is based on an incident he witnessed at Auschwitz, is set in a different historical time (Wiesel 1979: 1). Yet the Holocaust remains an unavoidable subtext. The American Jewish community may be the most secure in history, but it lives in the shadow of Jewish history's most horrific era, which took place during the lifetime of many of its members. The Holocaust forces a re-envisioning of Purim as more than a good story that may have happened long ago. It is a comment on diaspora status in a world where Haman lurks and where Mordechai and Esther are still needed. The Purim story may serve for many contemporary Jews as the first step in Holocaust education. Parents who might be squeamish about explaining the Holocaust to 7-year-olds can introduce the parallel story of long ago—a story of laughter and success. The Purim story teaches that even the most terrible threats can be fought with courage, ethnic solidarity, and unconventional acts, and it teaches this lesson with laughter. Humour, then, emerges as a form of courage—a way of focusing the mind on action and not on fear. There will be time enough for children to learn that such battles are not always won.

The *Purimshpil* as a Weapon of Humour

Laughter is the *sine qua non* of Purim; it is a holiday that actually requires one to be joyful. Humour is a tool of disorder, for the thing that is funny is the thing that is out of place, yet it is also a tool of creativity, for it allows us to take the sacred narratives of the past and to revise them in ways that are startling, irreverent, or even profane. The *purimshpil* descends from medieval rituals that inverted official hierarchies and overturned normal standards of behaviour. These inversion rites showed the possibility of a brave new world, of an alternative way of being. At times a blueprint for destroying the old world, at times a sop that temporarily appeased communal longing, these inversion rites showed life not as it was but as it might be. The *purimshpil* shares much with its medieval ancestors, but it is also more stylized, less spontaneous, both more orderly and, at times, more overtly critical. In analysing the *purimshpil*, it is useful to consider Victor Turner's distinction between the liminal rites of tribal and pre-industrial societies and the liminoid genres of industrial society. Turner builds on van Gennep's description of the transitional phase of ritual, when one leaves one group to become part of another, but is temporarily free of both. This transitional or liminal phase takes place in a space and time that is designated as special, set apart from the quotidian world. This special world is both sacred and playful, a world of heightened concentration, a place of uncertainty but also of possibility and unwonted freedom. According to Turner, liminal phenomena (such as religious rituals) predominate in agrarian and pre-industrial societies, tend to be collective in nature, and ultimately serve the function of making society work smoothly. Liminoid phenomena (such as plays and concerts) predominate in industrial societies, are primarily created by individuals (though they may be enacted by groups), and are frequently critical of the status quo. Participation is often required in liminal activities, while liminoid activities are felt to be freely chosen. Turner says: 'The *liminoid* is more like a commodity—indeed, often *is* a commodity, which one selects and pays for—than the *liminal*, which elicits loyalty and is bound up with one's membership or desired membership in some highly corporate group. One *works* at the liminal, one *plays* with the liminoid' (1982: 55, emphasis in original). In Turner's formulation, both liminal and liminoid genres partake of the freedom of ambiguity, though in different ways. Liminal rites allow freedom only under carefully controlled conditions; they ultimately serve to keep things as they are. But liminoid genres have the capacity to suggest major structural change and ultimately to subvert the status quo (Turner 1982).

As Ahuva Belkin notes, the *purimshpil* embodies qualities of both the liminal and the liminoid; one might say it occupies a liminal place between the two: 'The temporary overthrow of the social order sends out two messages: one is Utopian, allowing the individual to identify with the community; the other is subversive' (Belkin 1996: 56). Tied to the communal celebration of a religious ritual, the *purimshpil* is nonetheless an opportunity for social criticism by disaffected members of that community. Though the *purimshpil* may present a brave new world, it can also be a tool for maintaining the status quo (see Niditch 1995). Purim festivities, such as the *purimshpil*, keep disorder strictly bounded within day-long, ritually prescribed events; in this sense, the *purimshpil* acts as a liminal event. But it also provides an opportunity for individual creativity and social criticism, and to present alternative visions of reality that may indeed be *turned into* reality. In this sense, the *purimshpil* is a liminoid genre. Turner cites the Industrial Revolution as the dividing line between the world of the liminal and the world of the liminoid; thus it is appropriate that the *purimshpil*, which is both pre-industrial and post-industrial, should partake of both. It holds in its heart the medieval culture of communal laughter, even while it is overlaid with modern critical thought. The ways in which these qualities are made manifest in the *purimshpil* depend on the Jewish community in question and on factors such as the community's relationship to the dominant culture, the position of women within the community, and the class position of the Purim players. In looking at different communities and different historical eras, we have seen that *purimshpiln* vary according to the needs of the community involved and the conflicts that it faces. The *purimshpil* can become a means of resolution, a way of affirming identity, a call to action, a suggestion of possibility, or a pleasant escape. But always, it makes its point with laughter.

What, then, is the legacy of the *purimshpil* in the modern world? Many scholars see it as the seedbed of Jewish, particularly Yiddish, theatre, and of a particular brand of Jewish comedy that emphasizes social criticism, self-mockery, and the constant interplay of humour and sadness (see Oring 1983). It is the comedy of uncertainty, of marginality and accommodation: the comedy of diaspora. Adam Gopnik, who was asked to be the Purim player at a New York fundraiser before he knew what a *purimshpil* was, sees the story of Esther as 'a comedy in which worldly people took risks and did unworldly things ... I saw now that there was a connection between a certain kind of comedy, the comedy of assimilation, and a certain kind of courage, the courage to use your proximity to power, bought at the price of losing your "identity", to save your kinsmen' (Gopnik 2006: 71). Jewish humour is forged in the fire of Otherness, through constant contact with the dominant culture, contact that bruises and enriches, enlightens and condemns. Jewish humour is a response to this contradictory insider/outsider status, with its richness and its danger: one can cry or one can laugh or one can do both at the same time.

Sigmund Freud, a celebrated raconteur of Jewish jokes, contrasts Jewish jokes made by non-Jews, which are often brutal and cruel, with jokes that Jews make about themselves. The former divide people by making a sharp distinction between the joker and the object of the joke; the latter unite people by providing a common basis of laughter. The former destroy the dignity of the joker's targets by making them into the Other; the latter create a world in which there are no Others, where all have dignity but none are immune to criticism. In his work on carnival and festival, Mikhail Bakhtin makes a similar distinction between the utopian and regenerative power of carnival laughter and the smug mockery of modern laughter: 'The satirist whose laughter is negative places himself above the object of his mockery, he is opposed to it ... The people's ambivalent laughter, on the other hand, expresses the point of view of the whole world; he who is laughing also belongs to it' (Bakhtin 1968: 12). The *purimshpil* still retains the inclusive humour of the pre-modern era. Though its point of view may be specific to the community that produces it, and hence not of 'the whole world', no one is excluded from the circle of its laughter. It is an invitation to dialogue, not the building of a wall.

Like all art forms, *purimshpiln* vary according to the historical conditions in which they exist and in accordance with the values and desires of the community involved. Frequently, *purimshpiln* have served as means of articulating, negotiating, and overcoming conflicts, both within the Jewish community and between the Jewish community and the dominant culture. By presenting these conflicts in the fictionalized guise of theatre, Purim players can freely express social resentment or lodge protest (see Belkin 1999). Historically, Purim players were often from the lower end of the social stratum, and the Purim play allowed subaltern members of Jewish society to criticize leaders of the Great Tradition of rabbinic Judaism without actually abandoning that tradition. The Purim play could also examine relations with the dominant culture and suggest ideas for change. Presenting these ideas in disguise made them palatable and relatively safe; disguise

is also a central theme in the holiday of Purim. Queen Esther hid her Jewish identity until the time when it had to be revealed; her very name may be derived from
the Hebrew root meaning 'hidden' or 'concealed' (see Bronner 2004). Wearing
masks and costumes has been common on Purim since at least the fourteenth
century. In the Purim play, performers disguise both themselves and those ideas
that may be controversial or subversive. The Purim play, then, emerges as a
masquerade of ideas; it presents ideas that speak to us in disguise.

The revitalization of the *purimshpil* in the late twentieth century is probably
best explained by a growing interest in preserving Yiddish culture. But the popularity of the genre goes beyond those interested in Yiddish or in preservation.
More and more people are turning to this comic genre for serious purposes: to
build community, to combat despair, to express ethnic pride, even to sort out the
intricacies of current political conflicts. In the modern age, as societies become
increasingly multicultural and the myths of racial purity sound increasingly
threadbare, this story of ethnic conflict has a host of new meanings.

Freud reminds us that jokes work in much the same way that dreams do: they
present ideas to us in disguise. This disguise can make the ideas more difficult to
understand, but it can also make them more palatable, just as the masked speaker
can talk freely because his or her face is not seen. Purim is a holiday that has long
been associated with masquerade and disguise: Esther hides her Jewish identity;
Purim celebrants hide their faces behind masks and disguise their bodies with
costumes; and rabbinic commentaries suggest that God's presence is hidden
throughout the book of Esther, though God's name is never mentioned. At its
best, the *purimshpil* can present difficult ideas disguised as light-hearted entertainment. At their best, contemporary Purim players follow in the footsteps of
Aristophanes, Molière, Chekhov, and Oscar Wilde, who knew that great comedy
is deadly serious.

Notes

1   An internet search for *purimshpiln* revealed an astonishing number and variety throughout the Jewish world. Many *purimshpiln* were home-grown productions in synagogues,
colleges, and community centres. Others were scholarly re-creations: attempts to assert
Jewish identity or revive a moribund art, while still others attempted to forge understanding with non-Jews.

2   The YIVO Institute for Jewish Research (founded in Vilna in 1925; moved to New York in
1940) maintains a steadily growing centre for the study of Yiddish and Jewish culture.
YIVO holds one of the world's pre-eminent archives of Jewish scholarship, and it pub-
lishes books, sponsors exhibitions, and offers classes in Yiddish language and culture.
Klezmer music and other forms of Yiddish folk culture are celebrated at festivals such as
the Yiddish Folk Arts Program (KlezKamp), which was founded in 1985 and takes place
each summer in the Catskill Mountains of New York State, and Montreal's KlezKanada,
founded in 1996. Classes in Yiddish language and culture are offered by organizations

such as the Stichting Jiddisj (Yiddish Foundation), founded in Amsterdam in 1999, and the Vilnius Yiddish Institute, founded in Vilnius (Vilna) in 2001. Festivals of Yiddish culture are found throughout Europe, in North America, and in Israel.

3   The hasidim of Brooklyn still speak Yiddish and produce Purim plays in Yiddish, and other attempts are made to preserve the rich tradition of Yiddish Purim plays. In 2007 the National Yiddish Theater-Folksbiene presented an original Yiddish production entitled *Purim in Khelm* in New York City.

4   In the 1930s comedians Bud Abbott and Lou Costello developed a routine based on the premise that Costello was a baseball player on a team where Abbott was the coach. Costello wants to learn the names of all the players, and Abbott tries to teach him, despite the fact that 'they give ballplayers nowadays very peculiar names . . . Who's on first, What's on second, I Don't Know is on third' ('Who's on First?' <http://www.phoenix5.org/humor/WhoOnFirstTEXT.html>, accessed 26 July 2009).

5   American Jews, probably the most assimilated in the world, were shocked in June 2009 when a guard at the United States Holocaust Memorial Museum was killed by a rabid antisemite. Organizations such as the Southern Poverty Law Center, which track hate groups, remind us that antisemitism is alive and well in the United States. But it is an increasingly marginalized stance and has no place in mainstream political discourse.

6   *Vashti Was Right or The Book of Zeresh (A Purim Spiel)*. 2005. <http://www.purimspiel.com/index.html>, accessed 9 Aug. 2007.

7   'About Fourth Annual Broadway Purim Spiel'. <http://www.broadwaybox.com/shows/4th_annual_broadway_purim_spiel_nyc_tickets.aspx>, accessed 12 March 2008.

8   BWW News Desk. 7 Mar. 2006. 'Seth Rudetsky's Purim Cabaret Features Felciano, Orfeh, Marx, Lopz, Price, Skinner on March 12'. <http://www.broadwayworld.com/viewcolumn.cfm?colid=8064>, accessed 19 June 2008.

9   See also 'The Shushan Channel Purim Spiel with The Daily Show's Dan Bakkedahl and Stephen Colbert'. *Jew School* (16 Feb.), posted by Kung Fu Jew. <http://jewschool.com/2007/02/16/the-shushan-channel-2007/>, accessed 24 July 2007.

10   Jon Stewart and Stephen Colbert are political comedians on the American cable channel Comedy Central. Stewart's *The Daily Show* and Colbert's *The Colbert Report* are presented as fake news programmes, in which accurate news stories and biting political satire come together, the kind of thing that might have happened if newscaster Edward R. Murrow had collaborated with Jonathan Swift.

11   'Why isn't your Purim spiel funny?' <http://www.shushanchannel.com/>, accessed 11 June 2008.

12   'Jews and West Indians Create Purim Spectacle for Workers Rights'. 28 Feb. 2007. <http://www.jfrej.org/purim2007pr.htm >, accessed 13 July 2007. See also Ryzik, 'Roti and Homentaschn'.

13   'Pelosi Delivers Remarks at AIPAC Policy Conference'. 13 Mar. 2007. <http://speaker.gov/newsroom/speeches?id=0023>, accessed 14 July 2007.

14   See for example 'Testimonials'. Congregation B'nai Israel. <http://www.purimshpiels.com/testimonials.htm>, accessed 24 May 2008.

15   See *Pirates of Purim*. <http://www.emanuel.org.au/Purim% 20Spiel.pdf >, accessed 14 July 2007.

16   'Testimonials'. Congregation B'nai Israel. <http://www.purimshpiels.com/testimonials.htm>, accessed 24 May 2008.

17   'Vilken kul fest det var!' <http://www.judstud.se/purim2006.html>, accessed 15 July 2007.

18   'Purim Spiel-Off'. 2007. *The Movement for Reform Judaism.* <http://www.reformjudaism.org.uk/component/option, com_eventcal/Itemid,109/task, event/>, accessed 13 July 2007.

19   'Purim-Spiel: Megile-Lieder von Itzik Manger'. 24 Feb. 1999. <http://www.uni-protokolle.de/nachrichten/id/47606/>, accessed 10 Aug. 2007.

20   'Purim-Feier mit Musik und Purim-Spiel'. 2007. <http://www.service-ecom.de/cgi-bin/jkt2007/search_detail.pl?id= 20060928131546>, accessed 14 July 2007.

21   'Meeting with Izabella Cywinska'. 2002 (30 Sept.). <http://www.ajcf.pl/de/eventcywinska.htm >, accessed 22 July 2007.

Interviews

LAUREL, 11 Feb. 2007

LISA, 16 May 2007

MIRIAM, 4 Mar. 2007

PLAY'S DIRECTOR, 28 Jan. 2007

ROBIN, 29 Apr. 2007

TOBY MANEWITH, 6 May 2007

References

Emails

WENDY DAMOULAKIS, 21 Mar. 2008

GAIL FOORMAN, 19 Mar. 2008

ROB KUTNER, 12 May 2008

JOEL LEVINSON, 31 Mar. 2008

JON LITTMAN, 13 Mar. 2008

ARIEH MILLER, 15 May 2008

DEBBIE ORENSTEIN, 22 Mar. 2008

TRACY RICE, 12 Mar. 2008

Other Sources

BAKHTIN, MIKHAIL. 1968. *Rabelais and his World.* Cambridge.

——1981. *The Dialogic Imagination.* Austin, Tex.

BAUMGARTEN, JEAN. 1992. 'Le *Purim shpil* et la tradition carnavalesque juive'. *Pardès,* 15: 37–62.

BELKIN, AHUVA. 1985. '"Habit de fou" In Purim Spiel?' *Assaph,* C2: 40–55.

——1995. 'Joyous Disputation Around the Gallows: A Rediscovered Purim Play from Amsterdam'. *JTD: Haifa University Studies in Jewish Theater and Drama,* 1 (Autumn): 31–59.

——1996. 'Citing Scripture for a Purpose—The Jewish *Purimspiel* as a Parody'. *Assaph*, C12: 45–59.

——1999. 'Masks and Disguises as an Expression of Anarchy in the Jewish Festival Theatre'. In Shimon Levy, ed., *Theatre and Holy Script*, 203–12. Brighton.

——2003. 'The "Low" Culture of the Purimshpil'. In Joel Berkowitz, ed., *Yiddish Theatre: New Approaches*, 29–43. Oxford.

BOYARIN, DANIEL. 1994. 'Introduction: Purim and the Cultural Poetics of Judaism—Theorizing Diaspora'. *Poetics Today*, 15(1): 1–8.

BRONNER, LEILA LEAH. 2004. 'Esther Revisited: An Aggadic Approach'. In Athalya Brenner, ed., *A Feminist Companion to Esther, Judith and Susanna*, 176–97. London.

DE BEAUVOIR, SIMONE. 1952. *The Second Sex*. New York.

EPSTEIN, SHIFRA. 1987. 'Drama on a Table: The Bobover Hasidim *Piremshpiyl*'. In Harvey Goldberg, ed., *Judaism Viewed from Within and from Without*, 195–217. Albany, NY.

——1995. 'The Bobover Hasidim Piremshpiyl: From Folk Drama for Purim to a Ritual of Transcending the Holocaust'. In Janet S. Belcove-Shalin, ed., *New World Hasidim: Ethnographic Studies of Hasidic Jews in America*, 237–55. Albany, NY.

FISCH, HAROLD. 1994. 'Reading and Carnival: On the Semiotics of Purim'. *Poetics Today*, 15(1): 55–74.

FREE, KATHARINE B. 1999. 'Thespis and Moses: The Jews and the Ancient Greek Theatre'. In Shimon Levy, ed., *Theatre and Holy Script*, 149–58. Brighton.

FREUD, SIGMUND. 1960. *Jokes and their Relation to the Unconscious*. New York.

GANOR, SOLLY. 2005. 'Bearing Witness: A Purim Story from the Holocaust'. 18 Mar. <http://www.chgs.umn.edu/histories/documentary/ganorBearingWitness.pdf>, accessed 3 Aug. 2010.

GENDLER, MARY. 1976. 'The Restoration of Vashti'. In Elizabeth Koltun, ed., *The Jewish Woman: New Perspectives*, 241–7. New York.

GOPNIK, ADAM. 2006. *Through the Children's Gate: A Home in New York*. New York.

HECKER, RAQUEL. 2005. 'Purim Poseurs'. *New York Observer*, 30 Mar. <http://www.joi.org/bloglinks/nyobserver-corddry.htm >, accessed 14 July 2007.

HOROWITZ, ELLIOTT. 1994. 'The Rite to Be Reckless: On the Perpetration and Interpretation of Purim Violence'. *Poetics Today*, 15(1): 9–54.

KAUTSKY, KARL. 1926. *Are the Jews a Race?* <http://www2.cddc.vt.edu/marxists/archive/kautsky/1914/jewsrace/index.htm>, accessed 9 June 2008.

KIRSHENBLATT-GIMBLETT, BARBARA. 1980. 'Contraband: Performance, Text and Analysis of a Purim-shpil'. *The Drama Review*, 24(3): 5–11.

——1990. 'Performance of Precepts/Precepts of Performance: Hasidic Celebrations of Purim in Brooklyn'. In R. Schechner and W. Appel, eds., *By Means of Performance*, 109–17. Cambridge, Mass.

NIDITCH, SUSAN. 1995. 'Esther: Folklore, Wisdom, Feminism and Authority'. In Athalya Brenner, ed., *A Feminist Companion to Esther, Judith and Susanna*, 26–46. London.

NORDLINGER, JAY. 2002. 'Ashcroft with Horns: This Is Dedicated to the One They Hate—Attorney General John Ashcroft's Public Relations'. *National Review* (25 Mar.).

<http://findarticles.com/p/articles/mi_m1282/is_5_54/ai_83,591,409>, accessed 15 July 2007.

OFFEN, KAREN. 1998. 'Contextualizing the Theory and Practice of Feminism in Nineteenth-Century Europe (1789–1914)'. In Renate Bridenthal, Susan Mosher Stuard, and Merry E. Wiesner, eds., *Becoming Visible: Women in European History*, 3rd edn., 327–55. Boston.

ORING, ELLIOTT. 1983. 'The People of the Joke: On the Conceptualization of a Jewish Humor'. *Western Folklore*, 42: 261–71.

OTTINGER, ULRIKE. 2002. 'Ester: A Purim Play in Berlin'. <http://www.ulrikeottinger. com/en/fest-pp.html >, accessed 24 Jan. 2007.

POLLACK, HERMAN. 1971. *Jewish Folkways in Germanic Lands (1648–1806)*. Cambridge.

ROSTEN, LEO. 2001. *The New Joys of Yiddish*. New York.

ROZIK, ELI. 1996. 'The Adoption of Theater by Judaism Despite Ritual: A Study in the Purim-shpil'. *The European Legacy*, 1(3): 1231–5.

RYZIK, MELENA. 2007. 'Roti and Homentaschn'. *New York Times*, 2 Mar.

SHIPMAN, LOUIS. 2002. 'Celebration Condemns Death Penalty'. *People's Weekly World Newspaper*, 23 Mar. <http://www.pww.org/index.php/article/articleprint/858/>, accessed 13 July 2007.

SPIEGEL, CELINA. 1994. 'The World Remade: The Book of Esther'. In Christina Büchmann and Celina Spiegel, eds., *Out of the Garden: Women Writers on the Bible*, 191–203. New York.

STEINBERG, STEFAN. 2002. '12th Cottbus Festival of East European Cinema'. *World Socialist Web Site*, 15 Nov. <http://www.wsws.org/articles/2002/nov2002/cott-n15.shtml >, accessed 14 July 2007.

TROY, SHARI. 1995. 'On Smiting Borders and Staging Bedlam: The Live Frog as Prop in the Purim Play of the Bobover Hasidim'. *Assaph*, CII: 65–74.

TURNER, VICTOR. 1982. *From Ritual to Theatre*. New York.

——1986. *The Anthropology of Performance*. New York.

WHITE, SIDNIE ANN. 1989. 'Esther: A Feminine Model for Jewish Diaspora'. In Peggy L. Day, ed., *Gender and Difference in Ancient Israel*, 161–77. Minneapolis.

WIESEL, ELIE. 1979. *The Trial of God*. New York.

WYLER, BEA. 1995. 'Esther: The Incomplete Emancipation of a Queen'. In Athalya Brenner, ed., *A Feminist Companion to Esther, Judith and Susanna*, 111–35. London.

FOUR

Be Worthy of Your Heritage: Jews and Tradition at Two New England Boarding Schools

MICHAEL HOBERMAN

FOR AMERICAN JEWS secularization has been the key to a large-scale social and economic transformation, in which increasingly assimilated Jews have surmounted not only cultural but class and even racial barriers in their collective climb up the ladder of American success. With the exception of the Orthodox, whose day-to-day existence continues to be shaped by religious practice, linguistic continuity, and cultural tradition, the plurality of contemporary American Jews who deviate from the national mainstream do so because they are, in the words of sociologist Paul Ritterband writing on American Jewish identity, 'politically liberal, resolutely secular in values, well-educated and prosperous, patrons of the arts . . . [and] devotees of the various forms of psychotherapy' (Ritterband 1995: 390). If complete assimilation were a fait accompli, however, Jewishness as a cultural attribute and traditional practice would have vanished from the American scene several decades ago. A new generation of Jewish Americans born in the late twentieth century has inherited Jewish secular values in education, liberal politics, and patronage of the arts but at the same time become more concerned than their parents were with exhibiting a distinctive cultural identity. Members of this generation have developed adaptive strategies for transforming and thereby re-envisioning Jewish traditions and rituals in expansive, albeit controversial, ways within the framework of contemporary American life. This essay explores the oral testimony of one such group in one such new context that would have been unheard of in an older generation: Jewish students who attend predominantly white Protestant New England boarding schools.

Among contemporary non-Orthodox American Jews, challenges to conventional ways of defining Jewishness come in myriad forms. The exceptionally large number of mixed marriages—nearly a third of all current Jewish marriages, according to one estimate—has resulted in a redefinition for some of the traditionally matrilineal basis of Jewish identity, to include as Jews those who can identify a single, distant ancestor as Jewish or, for that matter, those individuals who wish to be or who will themselves to be Jews. Increased acceptance of gays and lesbians, as well as of other diverse constituencies within the Jewish community, has led to the reshaping of rituals in the interest of broader inclusion. Environmental concerns, among others, have spurred the refashioning of ancient dietary laws and *mitsvot*. Reinventions of Jewish tradition and identity occur not only on the political and social margins of American society but at its core as well, where fully assimilated, prosperous, and decidedly privileged young people who might otherwise choose to dispense entirely with any Jewish legacy cultivate a Jewish identity and a reinvented ritual practice.

Like the elite Ivy League universities to which they were once considered the natural gateway institutions, New England boarding schools have long stood as a world apart, an ivory tower of extreme privilege, wealth, and social status. The majority of the schools, including several of the 'select sixteen' highlighted in Peter Cookson and Caroline Hodges Persell's 1985 book *Preparing for Power: America's Elite Boarding Schools*, were founded in the latter half of the nineteenth century, when rising industrialization, urbanization, and immigrant flow inspired a white Protestant retreat to a largely invented version of New England cultural purity and, to use one catchphrase for the phenomenon, a Roosevelt-era 'muscular Christianity'. This anti-modernist trend—which was significantly complicated by the fact that it had been the large-scale capitalism of the industrialists themselves that had drawn the immigrant masses and underlay the poverty and squalor in which they lived—saw many manifestations.[1] Though New England boarding schools have evolved considerably since their earliest days, the mantle of exclusivity has been a long-standing element of their existence, at least in the American imagination.

From the latter half of the nineteenth century onward, many of the schools borrowed liberally and quite deliberately from the models closest to hand—the famous 'public schools' of England, including such institutions as Eton, Harrow, and Rugby. Hence, even today, student officers are referred to as 'prefects', and grades at the more Anglophilic schools are designated 'forms'. Sporting practices, including rowing, also derive from the legacy of the English schools. Popular culture renderings of American 'prep' (short for preparatory, as in preparation for admission to elite universities) schools have portrayed them as insular bastions of unearned privilege, petty cruelties, and flawed heritage—from Salinger's *Catcher in the Rye* (1951) to no less troubled novels by such prep-school survivors as John Knowles (*A Separate Peace*, 1959), John Irving (*The World According to Garp*, 1978), and, most recently, Curtis Sittenfeld (*Prep*, 2005). Film depictions have been no less fraught: *Dead Poets Society* offers a powerful lesson in how inspiring an individual teacher can be, but the example provided by the Robin Williams character is all the more pronounced for the context of hyperconformity and dysfunctionality in which his and his students' actions take place. Similarly, the Farrelly brothers' *Outside Providence* posits the New England prep school as a font of psychological and social maladjustment, not to mention drug and alcohol dependence. On the topic of Jews in such places, the film *School Ties* represents the trials of a Jewish football quarterback who is recruited and financially sponsored by a prep school in the 1950s and must face and transcend all manner of large-scale and petty antisemitic acts on the part of his fellow students, as well as the school's faculty members and administrators.

Among the myriad ironies of boarding-school life is the fact that, unlike state schools, which have long been proscribed from collecting information pertaining to, much less observing, their students' religious practices, private boarding schools, purporting as they do to support religious life, must allow for a certain amount of diversity in practice. Add to this the fact that Jews who attend boarding schools, as a rule, tend to be among the most secularized. More deliberately Jewishly affiliated families, for understandable reasons, will be reluctant to send their children to such remote outposts of Jewish life when so many possibilities for Jewish practice and communal life abound, not only in their own urban and suburban communities but in Jewish day schools and—most recently—at the American Hebrew Academy, in Greensboro, North Carolina, the nation's first and only 'pluralistic' Jewish boarding school, which was founded in 1996 and opened its doors in 2001.[2]

As any number of scholars have pointed out in recent decades, the movement towards a secularized identity among American Jews has exacted a price. In a national culture within which religious practice has, for better or worse, represented a precious means of asserting difference, Jews who do not seriously practise Judaism may have a difficult time convincing their non-Jewish neighbours (and themselves) that they are, in fact, different. In the Old World, Jews did not need to attend synagogue services in order to be known or to know themselves as Jews. From living quarters to economic livelihood to social context, the world of the shtetl Jews was built around palpable, physical separation from non-Jews. In the United States, on the other hand, and especially among the generations of American Jews born since the Second World War, religiosity has been one of the few recognizable means of marking difference. Even religiously affiliated Jews, however, are not necessarily retaining the high level of cultural distinction that their predecessors knew; indeed, if their only identifiably Jewish allegiance is manifest in their religious practice, they may, in fact, be unwitting participants in the undoing of a collectivity which once knew no distinction between secularity and religiosity. As a recent article by Laura Levitt suggests, a deliberately secularized Jewishness is considerably more difficult to finesse if one wishes not to relinquish one's separate identity as a Jew. In the contemporary American context, Levitt writes, 'the containment of Jewish difference within such narrow categories as required by liberal pluralism is no longer viable' as a means of Jewish participation (Levitt 2007: 809). Mere affiliation with a synagogue, in other words, is hardly equivalent to an assertion of difference; to some, it simply suggests, in the American formulation, that Jews 'go to another "church"' (Levitt 2007: 808). The inherent difficulty of asserting Jewish difference is nowhere more manifest than at the elite margins of American society, where by their actual presence, at least as individuals, Jews show that they have, indeed, 'made it'. In the rarefied but dutifully pluralistic atmosphere of the two New England boarding schools where I conducted my research, Deerfield Academy and Groton School, Judaism is quite acceptable and, indeed, encouraged, as a form of alternative churchgoing.

Ritualizing Jewish Social Space at Elite Boarding Schools

Well into the latter half of the twentieth century, New England boarding schools were among the least likely places for any kind of Jewish presence to be known, let alone felt. With the exception of a handful of schools whose founding dated back to one or another evangelical Protestant movement of the nineteenth century (Northfield Mount Hermon, for instance), the majority of these elite institutions were historically exclusively WASP havens, places where one sent one's children in order to avoid the influences of a burgeoning multi-ethnic culture. In the aftermath of the Second World War, however, and particularly from the 1960s onward, such schools faced increasing pressure to admit students of varying backgrounds. In part owing to the schools' professed high regard for their own and their students' religious heritage, some form of Jewish life began to take shape. Jewish practice is hardly a headline feature in New England boarding schools, but it is a reliable and quite visible constant that assumes many forms, none of which conform by any stretch of the imagination to anything approaching Orthodoxy. All the same, today's on-campus rituals are lively and celebratory on the whole and, as such, contrast quite sharply with the rather staid practices of the recent past, when Jewish religion and culture were, at best, tolerated forms of deviance from the white Protestant norm.

As a graduate of one of these schools, I could not help but be struck, upon my visits to Groton and Deerfield, by how Jewish life has evolved. From 1978 to 1982, I attended the Episcopal Kent School, founded in 1907 in Kent, Connecticut. Jewish life there was, quite literally, relegated to a basement where once a week some half-dozen of us gathered on Friday nights in the student common room. Our faculty adviser—a German teacher who was the one Jew on the school's payroll at that time—delegated the various responsibilities to us and presided over a fairly traditional service that was based on an outdated Conservative siddur. After the formalities had been seen to, the group of us tore into the freshly baked challah that 'George the baker' had made for us. Typically, we would also be given a case or two of warm soft drinks and some bags of chips—commodities that were in quite high demand on that campus. If we chatted over our challah and treats, it would usually be about all manner of common school concerns and interests. The stories that I remember the most clearly, however, are the ones that either the older students or our faculty adviser would tell about some of the more outstanding Jewish students who, thanks to their prominence, often did not last long at the school. One guy, famously, had punctuated his time at the school with a sequence of fistfights, each occasioned by antisemitic comments that had come his way. The lesson of his tenure at the school was clear enough to those of us who wished to survive the experience of being Jewish there. To last at Kent, we would have to master the art of being unobtrusive and resist any temptation to fight too hard against the antisemitism we were sure to encounter.

Jewish students at boarding schools today would appear to inhabit a different universe. My alma mater now has a chapter of the Hillel Society.[3] The Friday night services that I attended at Groton had a far less fraught feeling to them than those I remembered from my boarding-school days. As folklorist Barbara Kirshenblatt-Gimblett puts it, such a change marks an evident shift from 'anxiety about one's otherness to a celebration of it' (Kirshenblatt-Gimblett 1987: 89). Students were happy to be there, eager to engage in a Jewish ritual together before schmoozing and returning to their active boarding-school lives and busy evening schedules. The chatter was mostly about how much homework they faced that weekend. A few students got into a heated debate in which they compared the intellects of the school's mathematics teachers. The service itself was quite short and placed greater emphasis on interaction than on adhering tightly to any set liturgy. At Deerfield, where I was able to attend a Passover Seder in the enormous wood-panelled study of the administration building, students made their way through a fairly traditional Haggadah, searched for the *afikoman* among the room's plush furnishings,[4] and dined on sumptuously prepared matzoh ball soup, roast chicken, and potatoes provided for them by the school's caterers. The Jewish faculty adviser presided over the service, and the school's (non-Jewish) head chaplain was an enthusiastic participant.

Notwithstanding the current climate of acceptance in which students are encouraged to celebrate all manner of diverse religious and cultural differences, boarding school can still hardly be said to be a natural environment for any kind of thriving Jewish practice. In this respect, the Jewish students' arrival at New England boarding schools mimics the broader societal pattern in which Jews—as individuals, if not as members of a collective polity—have 'arrived' as mainstream Americans. The New England prep school, like the United States itself, is a predominantly Christian entity in which arrival is posited upon and necessitates endless compromises, adaptations, and transitional acts. On the one hand, the presence and visibility of Jewish students in the elite context of such schools reminds us that arrival is entrenched. On the other hand, if Jews throughout the United States are already compromising by subscribing to an American worldview and participating in the rituals of American life, those privileged few of them well situated enough to be attending boarding schools cannot but be understood as compromisers in the extreme. My own choice to focus my ethnography on Jews in boarding schools follows from my sense that the phenomenon offers a useful metaphor for the broader implications of Jewish arrival in American culture.

In visiting and interviewing Jewish students who attend two of the nation's most esteemed New England boarding schools—places which may very well constitute the outermost fringe of contemporary Jewish life in America—I have found that, while transition is not equivalent to erasure, it does bear the markings of a cultural identity in crisis. In this context, accommodation far outweighs any fastidious regard for the strictures of 'proper' Judaic practice. On the other hand, while their engagement of heritage and practice may appear to fail the test of what constitutes Jewish tradition in the typical non-Orthodox synagogue, their achievement in the context of the boarding school is a singular one. My fieldwork on Jewish life in the two schools in question points to three discrete means by which these students have managed to insinuate a deliberately Jewish presence on campuses which, until recently, had hardly known such a thing. First, they express a new and markedly positive interest in developing and sustaining rituals that allow them insight into what it means to be Jewish in the world and in the United States today. Second, they interpret their recent experiences in boarding school as leading them to feel more Jewish and, in some cases, more consciously committed to Jewish practice, than they felt before attending these schools. Finally, they speak consistently to a shared interest not only in participating in Jewish services and Jewish activities on their campuses but in ensuring their groups' long-term survival through the passing on of old traditions and the development of new ones within the framework of their schools' extracurricular club systems and informal protocols.

For each of the above scenarios, some pre-existing element of prep-school tradition or practice stands as both an enabling component and a stumbling block. Jewish students' increased appreciation for the meaning of Jewish heritage appears to derive from their schools' long-standing policies of inculcating broad participation in a social dynamic that, in effect, is intended to erase or at least level signs of outward difference (i.e. through uniform dress codes, for instance, or participation in team sports) and replace them with some version of independent thought that, in turn, fuels true self-awareness. Naturally, this same set of factors can and often does inhibit Jewish expression in so far as it demands of students that they minimize the role within their lives of any cultural practices perceived as deviant. Although it may also be a function of the students' feeling outnumbered in these predominantly non-Jewish environments, their developing sense of Jewish identity and experience of having become more Jewish by virtue of attending boarding school proceeds at least in part from their schools' official endorsement and promotion of diverse spiritual practices, including—on one of the two campuses—mandatory religious services. Of course, this atmosphere of choice can also be seen as a watering-down factor in any attempts on the students' part to craft an integrally Jewish life on campus. Finally, their efforts to pass on some sort of Jewish legacy at these schools would appear to follow, at least in part, from the considerable emphasis on traditional preparatory school rituals and practices, such as the naming of prefects at the end of the school year or the informal means by which younger students learn 'how things are done' by witnessing their older classmates exercising various privileges and responsibilities. In other words, the schools' own high regard for traditions, even where these are largely invented or are adaptations of those employed at famous English public schools such as Eton and Harrow, provides the very means by which Jewish students attempt, at least, to bring about a Jewish future on their campuses. Unfortunately, such traditions are also a significant factor in the stifling of Jewish participation—perhaps, indeed, the most significant factor of all in maintaining a powerful check on Jewish agency.

As a folklorist and ethnographer, I proceed from the notion that, as Henry Glassie and others describe it, tradition is 'culture's dynamic' (Glassie 2003: 181) —a fluid force by which 'out of the past' we bring about the 'creation of the future' (2003: 176). If tradition plays a shaping role in determining future practices and affinities, then continuity hardly implies fixity. But when and how does tradition in transition—the reinvention of an old set of practices in the context of new circumstances—evolve into an actual break with tradition? Where is the line that separates reinvention from recession? The Jewish boarding-school students I met are the undeniable beneficiaries of American plenitude—indeed, all the attendees of such illustrious schools are, arguably, experiencing the finest secondary education available in America today. Even as they have gained full access to the corridors of power, these students have resisted the temptation to relinquish their origins. Yet their adherence to Jewishness is certainly nuanced, manifested largely through what sociologist Herbert Gans refers to as 'symbolic ethnicity' (Gans 2000: 1217–37), as opposed to a more liturgically determined, prayer-based practice of Judaism or, for that matter, a fully committed and public assertion of Jewish cultural difference. However, since the ethnic or religious belonging of individuals is almost entirely overshadowed by the social practices, cultural traditions, and, indeed, elegant physical surroundings of the prep schools, Jewish participation becomes a conscious act of deviance from the prep-school norm, at least as defined at these two elite institutions, setting these students apart from their schoolmates.

My object in studying this particular group of young Jews was to learn as much as I could about 'the lessons from privilege' (Powell 1996), and how those lessons may relate to the present and future conditions of Jewish life in the United States. It is worth noting that some of American Jewry's most vocal prognosticators make fairly dire predictions on this account. The perpetual tension 'between the gain of freedom and the loss of identity', as Earl Raab writes (1991: 2), has been a constant in Jewish American life. The standard argument is that Jews' unprecedented success as individuals, in combination with a large-scale erosion of both institutional and casual antisemitism, has 'rewarded' them with the endlessly cushioning and narcotic effects of assimilation. One would hardly wish to witness or experience any resurgence of antisemitism in America, but the argument is a powerful one: if antisemitism *were* to rear its ugly head, Jews would—by necessity and in pursuit of their greater dignity—become Jews again. In the absence of such a traumatizing experience, then, how do Jews who enjoy full acceptance not only as Americans but as elites among Americans, mark their differences, and why do they choose to do so in the first place, with all the opportunities they have had to turn their back upon, or at least not emphasize, their differences?

Given the shared socio-economic status of so many Jews and white elite Protestants, can the religious and cultural practices of these two groups as encountered at New England boarding schools even be distinguishable? Factor in as well the endlessly transitional nature of adolescence itself, and the study of Jewish life in prep schools offers still more possibilities for insight into shifting traditions. Boarding school is itself a font of tradition and change. Deerfield Academy long ago adopted the motto, 'Be worthy of your heritage.' In many ways, such schools maintain their status—nationally and internationally—by inculcating adherence to tradition through ritualized practices—the sit-down meal, the dress code, a classical curriculum, and so forth. At the same time, the continued viability of these schools has been, in large part, a function of their adaptability, like that of the Jews, to changing times. As it turns out, the convergence of Jewish customs—albeit in an often severely truncated form—and prep-school regard for long-standing, hallowed traditions is exactly what makes it possible, at least on occasion, for Jews at these schools to 'create the future'.

Writers and researchers who have undertaken studies of boarding-school life in modern-day America reach one consensus: such an environment, perhaps to a greater extent than any other context in which one finds adolescents, is defined by both a facade and what one author refers to as an 'underside' (Cookson and Persell 1985: 157).[5] 'What you see in any boarding school's catalogue will be nice', writes 'Hibberd Melville'.[6] Those same catalogues will not, as Melville puts it, 'show students smoking dope, snorting coke or doing shots'. The same author continues: 'The prep subculture places a premium on deception' (1991: 9). I do not, by any means, believe myself to have been deceived by the students I interviewed for this project, but I do take it as a given that their accounts and stories of being Jewish in such places are hardly transparent. The mere fact of their being teenagers and my being an adult who had no previous contact with them stipulated a gap in communication. Moreover, I was reluctant to ask potentially awkward questions such as 'Have you experienced antisemitism in boarding school?' Instead, I assumed a less leading approach. I asked students to describe their family background and Jewish education. I asked them about how they came to prep school in the first place. Finally, in the interest of hearing more about revised rituals as evidence of tradition in transition, I asked them to tell me about boarding-school traditions and about specifically Jewish activities on campus. I also spent some time as a participant observer, attending sabbath services at Groton School and a Passover Seder at Deerfield Academy.

Two Types of New England Boarding Schools

A 1985 study of prep schools in the United States, *Preparing for Power*, classifies such schools into several categories. Historically speaking, the earliest ones to have been founded are the 'academies', which number among them such elite institutions as Phillips Academy (Andover; founded in 1778), Phillips Exeter Academy (1781), and Deerfield (1797). Though not affiliated to any particular religious denomination, the academies, from their founding as early as the late eighteenth century until perhaps two decades ago, were more or less exclusive bastions of WASP culture. Their founders, writes Barbara Bernache-Baker, a former faculty member at the Northfield Mt. Hermon School, 'viewed higher education as linked closely with Protestant Christianity as a means to enhance . . . respectability and to provide entry into the world of financial success' (Bernache-Baker 2001: 52). While visiting Deerfield, I did hear from both students and faculty that the school's historical lack of any formal religious affiliation had made it possible, at least going back to the post-Second World War period, for Jews to attend, albeit in small numbers. As Bernache-Baker puts it, notwithstanding their formal charters, all of the most prestigious New England boarding schools were, at their founding, 'mainline, reflecting an upper-class, socially acceptable version of Christianity' (2001: 56). Hard-core religiosity, on the other hand, even at New England boarding schools that once had or still retain an official connection to one Protestant denomination or another, has always been alien to such environments.

Deerfield is certainly one of the better-known boarding schools in the United States. Among its several unique features, its location in the centre of Old Deerfield, Massachusetts which, prior to the Revolutionary War formed the outer frontier of the New England settlements, gives it a symbolic historical status that even its greatest rivals in the heritage and prestige categories cannot approach. In the middle years of the twentieth century, Frank Boyden, the academy's illustrious headmaster, distinguished himself as a model of old-fashioned leadership and inspiration, and was profiled in John McPhee's successful and critically acclaimed book, *The Headmaster* (1966). In recent years, Boyden's legacy has still been felt and frequently invoked. A *New Yorker* article published in 2006 describes the affinity formed for Deerfield by Jordan's present-day King Abdullah, who was a student there in the 1970s. Abdullah and a council of Deerfield faculty, administrators, and alumni have recently created a Jordanian version of the Academy, in which the combination of a classical curriculum, a competitive athletic programme, and veneration for tradition and old-fashioned leadership will make generations of Middle Eastern (including, quite notably, Israeli Jewish) students 'worthy of their heritage'.

In addition to the academies, Cookson and Persell enumerate a few other categories into which the 'select sixteen' New England boarding schools fit—among them the 'entrepreneurial' schools.[7] In connection with my own research, however, the other important category is that of the Episcopal schools. Besides the fact that my own alma mater, Kent School, falls into this category, I was quite intrigued by the prospect of visiting a school in which, unlike the academies, not only would Jewish students be a numerical minority but also, at least on the level of religious observance, actual outsiders to the school's official practice and history. Groton School (founded in 1884 in Groton, Massachusetts), which I visited three times, is a stalwart in this category, along with St Paul's (1856), located in Concord, New Hampshire.

Groton was founded by a member of the Episcopal clergy who sought, among other things, to replicate in New England the best of the English public schools. As Bernache-Baker writes, religion—and, more particularly, the practice of mainstream Protestant Christianity—has always been at the centre of Groton School's existence. The school's catalogue 'restates its founder Endicott Peabody's intent that religion not only be an important part of the official life of the Groton School, but also make a claim on the entirety of life' (Bernache-Baker 2001: 56). Indeed, visitors and insiders to Groton alike cannot help but be impressed by the stunning architecture of its chapel, whose profile quite deliberately dominates the already spectacular scene. It was pointed out to me, in fact, that when Peabody founded the school, he insisted upon this one feature. On the school's central quad, or—more properly—circle, the one building that is always clearly visible from every other building is the chapel. Endicott Peabody could hardly have known, of course, that his school's deep commitment to religious life might one day result not only in its steadfast adherence to its Episcopal tradition but also in its recent efforts to build and support small non-Christian student groups, including the Jewish group I studied.

Episcopal schools might appear to be less than natural choices for deeply committed Jewish students, but the history of Jews vying for admission to Harvard and Yale, among other Ivy League schools whose founding occurred under deliberately Protestant auspices, offers a useful parallel for such a phenomenon. Beginning in the 1960s, as the national culture evolved in the direction of greater tolerance for and fuller recognition of cultural and ethnic minorities and as increasing numbers of New England boarding schools began to expand their student base by accepting minority students, these bastions of WASP power and privilege also grew away from exclusivity. Schools that had, until that point, taught boys only became co-educational. 'Shaken from isolation', as Pearl Rock Kane and Christopher Lauricella write in *The Encyclopedia of New England*, 'many of the New England preparatory schools began to adopt some of the social advancements of public education, including the commitment to a more diverse population and a multicultural curriculum' (Kane and Lauricella 2004: 311). Prep schools today, in fact, especially the ones with the largest endowments, boast significantly larger minority populations than many leading suburban public schools. Where they had once operated as exclusive clubs 'to whom Catholics, black and Jews need not apply', the post-civil rights era ushered in considerable change. One spur in this new direction was a report by a United States commissioner of education, who argued that prep-school students would be 'culturally deprived unless their schools contained significant numbers of urban disadvantaged' (Powell 1996: 89).

Boarding-school underlife, of course, like any other folk phenomenon, changes at a different rate. As 'Moxie B. Benevolent', another of the pseudonymous authors of *Casualties of Privilege*, explains, the schools themselves deserve at least part of the blame for whatever harassment or maladjustment problems their students encounter at the hands of prejudiced schoolmates. 'You can't bring minorities in', she writes, 'and say: "Mix in; I'll see you at graduation in three years"' (Benevolent 1991: 45). Where sociological research into boarding-school life has been conducted, however, the suggestion is that, at least until very recently, such a stance was exactly the one taken. Cookson and Persell write that, of all the students they surveyed, the highest marks for 'authenticity' (that is, the degree to which a school measures up to its vaunted greatness) came from white students with the highest socio-economic status and academic achievement. Black students, on the other hand, were the least likely to return a positive verdict (Cookson and Persell 1985). The underlife of the school, which could well expose such students to the stubborn prejudices and snobberies of the old days, may offer at least a partial explanation for minority isolation and dissatisfaction, much as it would have at the English public schools whose *de facto* policies may have discouraged hazing practices but whose *de jure* treatment of these infractions might have turned a blind eye to such long-standing informal traditions.

Jews in Boarding Schools

As mentioned above, Jews with strong religious and ethnic affiliations will tend not to self-select into New England boarding schools in the first place. The students who do choose such schools, on the other hand, might be said to reify the optimistic arguments of the so-called transformationalist school of Jewish American prognostication. Their re-inventions and improvisatory insinuations of Jewish culture in non-Jewish settings may help, according to the transformationalist view, to keep Judaism and Jewish culture alive for future generations. With the noteworthy exception of schools such as Andover and Exeter, whose unaffiliated status, large size, and supreme academic standing offer the same sort of attraction that the Ivy League universities have long had for Jews (and whose administrations, owing to the significant percentages of Jewish students they enrol, hire rabbis to serve that student population), boarding schools simply do not offer what deeply committed Jewish students and their families are seeking. For this reason, we must take it as a given that those who attend boarding schools are by and large, to borrow Charles Liebman's term, 'private Jews' (Liebman 1995: 443). This is not to say that such students conceal their Jewishness or are in the least bit ashamed of their background. If 'public' Judaism is defined as being based on a conception of 'the Jew as a part of a collective entity', it is, by necessity, an endeavour that can only make sense within the context of a larger Jewish demographic, which one is unlikely to find in the context of a New England boarding school. 'Private Judaism', on the other hand—'more concerned with the self', as Liebman explains—'is more compatible with the style of modernity in general and American life in particular' (1995: 443).

Put differently, the arrival of Jewish students at exclusive boarding schools has hardly been an achievement of the Jewish community; it has come about as a result of the many individual Jewish American success stories that have, in the years since before the Second World War, catapulted Jews, by virtue of their academic achievement and entrepreneurial spirit, from the status of ghettoized, religiously observant working-class immigrants to that of naturalized members of the suburbanized upper middle class. Indeed, at the earliest stages of this transformation, boarding schools represented perhaps the most entrenched opposition to Jewish assimilation, and Jews were well aware of this fact. In the 1940s, when Jews had grown to compose a startling 5 per cent of Andover students, the school's headmaster, on the assumption that their presence would tarnish the school's elite status, fought to reduce their influence (Powell 1996: 85). On a comic note, and on the subject of Jewish influence, Richard Dorson, himself a quietly Jewish graduate of Phillips Exeter Academy (1933), recounts the story of a Jewish businessman who, 'trying to get somewhere socially', and seeking in particular to rid his family of its characteristic east European Jewish accent, enrols his son at a 'little school in New England which was highly recommended' (Dorson 1960: 167). When the son comes home still speaking as Jewishly as ever, the father manages to pull enough strings to get him into Eton itself. As the English headmaster tells him, 'It may be that your American schools have not been able to teach your son to speak properly, but here in addition to the most modern technical methods, we have the tradition of centuries to reinforce our pedagogical techniques' (Dorson 1960: 168). When the father comes to fetch his son after a year at Eton, he asks the headmaster, 'Vell . . . how ju make out? Mine Jake he's speaking de King's English, nu?' The headmaster's reply brings on the comic tale's punch line and its ironic and mock-triumphalist message about how, in an imaginary world, Jews would instigate assimilative practices on the part of the English: 'Netchally . . . vat else?' (Dorson 1960: 168).

In the 1960s, as racial barriers, at least in the north-eastern United States, began to be breached, notwithstanding Dorson's burlesque tale, Jews were not pursued by most boarding schools as potential students. They had up until then presented a singular threat to the cultural uniformity of boarding schools because they could not be refused entry on the basis of the natural barriers of economic class or academic achievement. In actuality, the exact values promoted by many of the leading prep schools—my own school's Latin motto, 'Temperantia, Constantia, Fiducia' translates as 'simplicity of life, directness of purpose, self-reliance'— are virtually identical with American Jewish values, especially the so-called 'achievement drive'. As sociologists Seymour Lipset and Earl Raab write, Jewish success in the United States has come about because many of the salient American Jewish traits embodied in this drive for achievement 'strongly resemble the modal national pattern set by New England Protestant sectarians' (Lipset and Raab 1995: 5). This is evidently the same force that, generations earlier, propelled Jews into the Ivy League universities, whose severe quotas had kept them out, or at least at bay, for decades preceding the Second World War.

Cookson and Persell show that the walls of exclusion began to give way in the wake of the civil rights movement. In 1985, Jews composed 11 per cent of boarding-school attendees in the United States—three times higher than the percentage of Jews in the population as a whole. Within the sample of 2,475 boarding-school students that they studied, Jews came from families with the highest level of educational achievement. They shared with blacks, however, the lowest status in terms of 'legacies', being unlikely to represent a second or third generation of preparatory school attendance within their families. This distinction from other prep-school pupils seems, in itself, to sum up the singular and tenuous place that Jewish students occupy not only in boarding schools but as some of the newest members of the American elite. As individuals, their credentials for inclusion are unimpeachable; where family connections are a consideration, membership is problematic.

If actual religiosity and belief were central factors in prep-school life, Jews might, on that basis too, be outsiders. But even at the Episcopal schools, with their mandatory chapel attendance, religious faith is not necessarily widespread among students. Many of the non-denominational schools gave up on mandatory religious services long ago. A 1990 survey indicated that one-third of prep-school sophomores—a much higher number than was found in state-funded schools— asserted that they held no religious belief. Barbara Bernache-Baker notes the apparent discrepancy between the schools' official touting of religious values and practices and the students' own beliefs. Of the students she surveyed, 80 per cent—all of whom were at one time enrolled in religion courses at their respective prep schools, checked 'false' in answer to the assertion, 'God is interested in my sexual behaviour.' Among their state-funded school counterparts, for whom a religious curriculum is not even an option, that number was 70 per cent

(Bernache-Baker 2001: 52–3). The consensus among scholars who have studied prep-school students is that religious values and practices, for all of their inclusion in the schools' official representations of themselves, have long been of dwindling importance. As one Deerfield student put it, Judaism can gain a foothold at his school in part because religion itself 'is not prevalent . . . it's not like Christianity takes over at all'.

'What it really means to be Jewish': Revising the Sabbath as Ritual

Judaism and Jewishness, at least among the students whom I met at Deerfield and at Groton, take shape in the face of this larger context of religious looseness. Jewish students who attend these schools express themselves as Jews by choice. Their participation in their school's Jewish life seems to be an enhancement of their personal lives and an exploration of their identity. Like many other assimilated American Jews, they regard the enactment of Jewish rituals as considerably less important than their sense of a collective ethnic heritage. Theirs, in political scientist Charles Liebman's words, may be 'a Judaism focused upon the legitimization of self and the kind of lives American Jews have chosen to lead' (Liebman 1995: 447–8). It is not, as Liebman would no doubt lament, '[in order] to stand before God the King' that these Jews attend services but, rather, 'to join [their] peers in some shared enterprise' (1995: 447). All the same, attendance at boarding school has enhanced these students' sense of their own Jewish identity and, as a consequence, motivated them to participate in creative reinventions of Jewish ritual. Though their Jewish affiliation may seem marginal by conventional standards, their sense of what it means to be Jewish and their engagement with that heritage is magnified by their minority status in prep school. Their school's attempted equalization of cultural differences subsumes such differences under the rubric of a generalized sense of school-specific heritage and by means of the classical tradition, but these policies make possible, at least, the rediscovery of collective heritage or the insight that one's past does, in fact, matter. The students' own words give voice to this sense of increased awareness. While the outward markers of their participation may be less than obvious, their expressions speak to a deeper level of commitment.

Ed, whose Jewish background is as firm as or firmer than that of any of my interviewees, tried to explain the transformational effect of his years at Deerfield. He described taking courses on Holocaust history with the academy's only Jewish teacher (who also serves as faculty adviser to the Jewish student group). The class had been discussing

what it really means to be Jewish and Jewish history, and also discussing other religions. Right now, I kind of find myself questioning Judaism a bit, not [questioning] being a

Jew, but the interactions between Jews and Christians and Muslims, the similarities between all of our religions, and why we can't get along and stuff like that. So I think that . . . boarding school [is] shaking the foundations of being Jewish. It's not just a given anymore, but it's also made me want to be Jewish. Now it's more of a conscious choice, which is a good thing.

The deepening of students' Jewish affiliation occurs in the context of the larger educational experience of being at boarding school. Classroom discussions certainly constitute one area in which such awareness may be enhanced, but more deliberately Jewish activities provide room for still more obvious engagement. Within the context of these endeavours, which include Friday night sabbath services, Jewish discussion groups, and, occasionally, Jewish-themed outings and special guests on campus, Jewish identity is strengthened, even as students appear to be merely adhering to accepted ways of cultural expression. Besides promoting a form of Jewish participation that is more than perfunctory, the activities cultivate an active sense of what it means to be a Jew in the context of contemporary American life and, indeed, world politics.

In telling me about their participation in and co-creation of the Friday night service and Jewish gatherings in general, the students at Groton described a warmth and pleasing intimacy—a feeling that suggests a casual and welcoming solidarity that exists not in opposition to the school's unforgiving mainstream but, rather, as a confirmation of how their Jewish heritage enhances Groton's many strands of tradition. The group is led by a French teacher who—as at Deerfield—appears to be the sole Jewish member of the faculty. Dave described the Friday night service as 'a highlight of my Groton experience', even as his description gave voice to the challenges faced by students in a school where ordinary activities take place, sometimes, at the expense of the minority.

They are held in Madame's apartment, who is the only Jewish faculty member on campus. So she has become sort of my surrogate Jewish mother on campus, [and] that has been nice, and she plays the role really well. I think there are about ten [who come], officially, but you usually end up with about eight, because the school is really bad with scheduling things right during Friday night service, because the Shabbat service is really not on the radar of the people who make the schedules, because this is an Episcopalian school.

Dave's description of the actual service offers insight into its broad appeal and suitability to a group of students whose connection to Judaism is occurring in exile, so to speak, from mainstream observance.

The service is short. It's done from The Gates of Prayer, which is a Reform siddur, so we mostly read the English version because most of the kids are not as observant as I have been in the past, but I love it. It's homey, it's nice, it's basically just a half hour out of the week to cool your jets and sit for a little, and I guess try to understand what it means to be Jewish on this campus. So I guess one of the things I like most is [that] each week, each student gives a two- or three-minute presentation on anything Jewish. Some kids present a situation in Israel. Also kids talk about their Jewish community back home, like their temple in their town, so that's interesting to me. Then they light their candles, and we have wine and stuff.

As Dave suggests, the Friday night service at Groton, which I observed twice, proceeds according to a predetermined structure but, at the same time, is sufficiently loose as to foment and incorporate more 'social affiliation', to borrow anthropologist Jack Kugelmass's term, than adherence to any set liturgy (Kugelmass 1988: 5).

Over the last several years at Groton, as the faculty adviser has presided over the Jewish group, the setting for the services has usually been in the living room of her apartment, which is located in one of the school dormitories. Casual and spirited chatter defined the experience the first time I attended, as well as a feast of Korean takeout food. At the second service, which was held in a student common room just outside the faculty adviser's apartment, students who had nothing to do with the service came and went and even had brief and unobtrusive interactions with the participating students. Officially, the talk that night was on the stand-off in the occupied territories between Hamas and Fatah. It bears mentioning that, in all of my conversations with Jewish students at the two schools, and unprompted by my own questions, they consistently mentioned the situation in Israel and the conflict between Jews and Arabs in the Middle East as a factor in their own grappling with Jewish identity. 'What it really means to be Jewish', in other words, is clearly more than a matter of what spiritual practice, or option, one chooses in the context of boarding-school extracurricular life.

At Deerfield Academy, religiously oriented Jewish activity is downplayed in favour of a more secular approach that, at its best, stresses Jewish history, politics, and cultural identity. This may be the result of the current Jewish adviser's role as a history teacher on campus. 'We always used to go to his house', says Fred, 'maybe once or twice every other week, for cookies, and other refreshments, and then we would talk. We never did prayers or anything. We talked about current events, what it means to be Jewish in modern society, and stuff like that.' Ed's elaboration draws an important distinction: 'Strictly, rather than a religious group', he explains, 'it is more of a support group, so there's no chanting or services.' He continues, and in his description, gives voice to the Jewish group's apparent interest in promoting dialogue about Jewishness rather than rote adherence to a set practice:

A typical meeting would be like, probably ten kids in his apartment . . . talking about current events: [the faculty advisor] was very on top of that. We also had someone come down from UMASS [Deerfield is located less than ten miles away from the University of Massachusetts at Amherst, which supports a large Hillel group and a number of Jewish groups and activities] at the time, and it was a group of ten of us and we'd probably meet for forty-five minutes. I think we'd mostly talk about current events.

As the Deerfield students describe the Jewish group at their school, they emphasize its outlets for social interaction and their own participation in fairly open-ended activities that stress discourse as opposed to liturgy.

The students' Jewish identity, to the extent that it is at least partly formulated in such a context, is itself the result of a conversation, rather than a fixed sense of lineage, liturgy, or even ideological affinity with Israel. Nonetheless, the meetings combine elements from two pre-existing ritualized practices, one of which is drawn from Jewish tradition while the other derives from the prep-school milieu. In meeting regularly on Friday nights, engaging in exclusively Jewish subject matter, and sharing food, the students are replicating the sabbath experience, or at least a secularized version of it that they may have known at home. Their small-group dialogue, on the other hand, notwithstanding the structuring presence and participation of a faculty adviser, bears a significant resemblance to the prep-school 'bull session'—a time-tested ritual practice in its own right—as well as to the sort of conference-style class discussion through which Deerfield Academy seeks to prepare its students for entry into the nation's most selective colleges and universities. A direct engagement with the outside world is a primary means for this conversation, and Deerfield's own apparent commitment to encouraging students to explore citizenship and history through the ritualized practice of informed discussion and debate provides at least part of the context.

When the Jewish faculty adviser first came to the school, according to Ed,

There was nothing [Jewish] going on campus, [so] one of the things he brought up [is that] we're affiliated with the group the Curriculum Initiative, which is based out of New York, and they support Jewish values in prep schools. So they sent a lady from UMass [University of Massachusetts], Rachel or Sophie, or something like that, a really fun college girl who was Jewish, and she would facilitate things.

The Curriculum Initiative, as the students describe it, sponsors an annual event for boarding-school students called Jewbilee, which both Ed and Adam have attended. 'We've been the only students to do it from Deerfield that I know of', said Adam. 'Some schools bring twenty students', he added, further reflecting,

So we're really in the minority when we go to that. We have a Friday service . . . We break off into little groups and we have different events that go on. Sometimes, I don't know how they relate to being Jewish, but it's just great to get to know Jewish students from all the other prep schools around and to know you have other Jewish students who are going through the same stuff.

The support of outside organizations suggests that Jewish boarding-school students have hardly been disregarded as worthwhile constituents within the American Jewish world. That these students' primary mode of engagement is one of conversation, as opposed to merely passive reception of religious services, suggests that Jewish identity in the boarding-school context is most readily sought through an inquisitive pursuit of meaning that fits the mould of the schools' academic and social curricula. Even at Groton, where more emphasis is placed on religious services, students seem most convincingly Jewish as they articulate an active understanding of the significance of Jewish tradition. As Dave put it, his had not been 'a really observant Jewish life, but [it had been] enough to understand what's going on and further [his] appreciation for prayer and speech to God'.

'I don't feel like I am forced to do this': Making Jewish Choices

If anything, the experience of being in prep school and thus set apart from any larger Jewish community has revived and, in some cases, actually kindled an interest in being Jewish, students told me. Home life, perhaps in keeping with a more general trend among Jewish Americans to view their heritage through the lens of American individualism, seems in most of their experience to have presented them with Jewishness as one of several options. Their schools, at the same time, placing emphasis as they do on the importance of some kind of spiritual life, reinforce the idea that Jewish adherence is something that one chooses. The palpable sense of some sort of inevitable Jewish inheritance, in other words, seems as remote as ever in such a context. Again, the influence of so many mixed marriages is an underlying aspect of such an open-ended view. On the other hand, if students are freely choosing a Jewish identity when they might just as easily be ignoring their heritage entirely, they can also be said to be bringing about the exact sort of potentially expansive changes for which the transformationalist (or 'glass half full') school of contemporary Jewish American thought argues. Former affiliations, in this view, are less important than the choices one makes in the present. Adam, who came to Deerfield Academy from Austin, Texas, described his Jewish background in such terms:

We are very reformed. I did have a bar mitzvah, [but] didn't really go to service or temple at all except the year before my bar mitzvah because I had to start learning Hebrew. I'm Jewish, but I don't practise very often. I go to major, high ceremonies, and Passover, but the bar mitzvah is probably the high point of my Jewish life. I'm proud to be Jewish, proud to be part of the group.

All three of the students I interviewed at Groton described similarly assimilated backgrounds. Indeed—and here, the intrinsic Episcopalianism of the school may be seen as a factor that would make it less attractive to more 'fully' Jewish families—these students all happen to have grown up in households with one Jewish parent.

Dave explained: 'My father is Jewish, my mother is Christian, and we were raised Jewish [by] my father's choice.' Jeff described his background in more detail, highlighting the Jewish lines and emphasizing the historical narrative that, perhaps, makes that lineage all the more intriguing:

My Judaism comes from my mom's side. My dad is Christian and comes from Tampa and a Wall Street background. But my grandpa on my mom's side is from Lithuania, and during World War II was drafted into the Russian army, and then met my grandma, who comes from a New York Jewish family.

Jeff continued by describing how his cousins recently 'turned more Orthodox, since there's a new rabbi in town, so they are a lot more serious about it now'. For his part, Jeff indicated that his family 'basically live out our Judaism in terms of major holidays and services'. He himself did not undergo a bar mitzvah. He explained that, as a regular attendee of Friday night services at Groton, he was 'the only one in [his] family who does this every Friday night'. He added, 'If I were at home and not at boarding school, I don't think I would be able to do this. I don't feel like I am forced to do this. I think just being here helps make me more Jewish than I was before.'

Even students whose Jewish backgrounds might appear to be more firm, like two of the three boys I met at Deerfield Academy, tended to describe their families' histories and their own Jewish practice as having been more a matter of choice and self-direction than an incontrovertible inheritance. Ed, who is a day student and commutes to Deerfield from nearby Northampton, Massachusetts, described a Judaism that takes shape within a surrounding context of non-Jewish cultural life:

We're pretty practising, as far as our faith, but the area I live in really doesn't have that many Jews, so . . . I was conscious of the difference between myself and my surroundings . . . When I was younger we would go to a lot of services and I would participate and I had my bar mitzvah there. And once I came to Deerfield Academy, I kind of stopped going to a lot of minor services and only go to the high services.

Ed's Jewish participation has grown since he first came to Deerfield and became involved—by choice—in the school's small Jewish group. He knows, however, how starkly his experience stands out from that of an earlier generation, whose Jewish practice and identification was less a volitional matter than one of inheritance and group solidarity in the face of at least minor oppression. His father grew up in the town of Athol, Massachusetts, and 'was probably one of three Jews in his whole school. So for him, he had to deal with a lot of antisemitism growing up, so he was very clear about his faith [and] being different.'

Even in attending Hebrew school before he came to Deerfield, Ed described a feeling of being 'less religious', or believing himself to be so, than his schoolmates. 'I actually felt more separated at Hebrew school', he said, 'just because I felt like when I went there, I wasn't religious enough.' Beyond the realm of religious expression, his family's commitment to Jewishness felt, in the context of Northampton's tight-knit Jewish community, weak. 'I have relatives in Israel,' said Ed, 'but some of these kids wanted to go to Israel, join the army, become a citizen and stuff like that. My family wasn't like that.' Jeff at Groton, whose dual heritage might otherwise have caused him to doubt his Jewish identity, described his re-engagement with the Jewish community. 'You know, in middle school', he said, 'I never came up with Jewish heritage.' In the context of his Episcopal boarding school, however, the connection he felt to his Jewish identity was deeper. 'Now I find myself saying sometimes, "Yeah, I'm Jewish," so it is out there and clarified.'

For these students, then, boarding school has brought about a strange convergence of clarification and a measure of ambivalence. As Adam explained, they walk a fine line between wishing to express their Jewishness and being reluctant to broadcast it too loudly. Whether their ambivalence springs from typical adolescent self-consciousness or from an inherited sense that being Jewish, at least in the context of a bastion of white elite Protestant heritage, may not be in one's best interests, one thing is clear: any appearance of deep commitment, especially as manifested through Orthodox religiosity, is far from what they wish to project. Their participation in Jewish life is quiet. I had asked the group if they faced any challenges as Jewish students attending a boarding school: 'I guess for us', explained Adam from Deerfield, 'it's not really a setback if we don't go to Shabbat or don't practise.' He continued: 'I don't think there is any difficulty that we face, other than the fact that we're proud to be Jewish and it's OK that we're not vocal or publicize and throw ourselves out there.' The boarding-school experience seems to have both magnified and diluted these students' Jewishness. But where a previous generation of students in such schools—if such a generation can be said to have existed—would appear to have shrunken its expression of Judaism in the face of social pressures to conform to a white elite Protestant standard, today's Jewish students seem to be motivated by opposite concerns. In a general atmosphere of openness and a spirit of at least officially promoted tolerance, minority status seems almost to have become a boon. The transformation of tradition, in this regard, takes shape as an expression of autonomous selves. The students' decision as to whether to participate in Jewish life follows, in part, from the current smorgasbord approach to organizing spiritual life in these schools. At Groton and at other places where attendance at religious services of some kind is required, Friday night Jewish services constitute an option—a single item on a menu that also includes the Episcopal service held in the campus chapel, Catholic Mass, and, most recently, Muslim and Hindu prayers. Naturally, 'God the King' occupies considerably less space in such a formulation than we might expect in even the most 'reformed' of synagogues.

'The many forms that came before us': Traditions, Invented and Otherwise

Even as their observance of Jewish tradition is compromised at nearly every turn by the overarching and determining factors of American assimilation, as well as boarding-school protocols and, for that matter, cultural biases, the students I interviewed make an effort to build and sustain a Jewish life on campus. In this endeavour, their most formidable stumbling block *and* aid appears to be the schools' own predilection for tradition. On the one hand, boarding schools leave comparatively little room in their schedules, curricula, and policies for much in the way of variation from the norm. They are controlled by powerful and moneyed interests—for the most part, alumni—whose primary wish quite frequently is to see their own particular, and historically situated, visions of the schools perpetuated. On the other hand, to the extent that these schools' traditions, by design, rely on the continued participation of their current students, they must allow for intermittent acts of adaptation and change. Where Jewish students have succeeded in creating an active Jewish life on campus, they have done so by making the most of their schools' pre-existing channels for extracurricular and spiritual activity. Moreover, their success is predicated on their ability, from one cohort to the next, to pass on some sort of Jewish legacy. Where they fall short, through no fault of their own, is in their inability to transcend or overrule the 'ancient' legacies of prep-school tradition that might just as soon keep such incursions of Jewishness at bay.

Student organizations and officers constitute an integral part of this formula. In order to ensure continuity and coherence, Groton appoints two Jewish prefects each year; Dave served in that capacity in the 2006/7 year when I conducted my research. At Deerfield, as we have seen, the activities have varied, but have taken shape less around liturgy than around ritualized social interactions and affiliations that the Jewish students seek to sustain consistently and pass on to newcomers. Their efforts occur in accordance with what folklorist Jack Santino might describe as a 'ritualesque' pattern not only of repetition but of public display within the larger context of the school community itself, most of whose members comprise an outside audience 'domain' (Santino 2004: 365) within which Jewish activities take place.

As my three interviewees described the ebb and flow of energy that has marked the school's Jewish life, their explanation goes far towards showing how, put simply, boarding school often ends up being too hectic for any spiritual life to take root. All the same, their efforts to keep something going suggest an interest on their part in—to return to Glassie's formulation—'creating the future'. As Fred put it,

Junior year, when it was time to elect new presidents, [Adam] and I showed up for the elections. We were the only people that showed up, and it came down to basically which one of us would vote for which one of us, so we became co-presidents. That was probably the lowest point in JSC [Jewish Student Council] history. So, Ed, you were here last year. I don't know—[he addresses Ed], you can try really hard to bring JSC back into its former glory, or former whatever it had. We've tried doing a lot of meetings with Jewish students, but it's really hard at a boarding school, with all the sports going on and very intense curriculum, there isn't really a lot of people. Not to mention that there are not a lot of Jewish students on campus, but there are actually a very small amount that have the time and have the will to come to these meetings, and we've been trying to plan dances, and tee shirts to sell, and all these events that haven't come to fruition.

Jewish life, as pointed out above, assumes the form of one among many extra-curricular activities in boarding school. As such, it transforms religious ritual into an opportunity for a set of pleasant interactions, and exists as a respite from the intense pressures exerted by academic and athletic demands. Identifying with other Jews on a campus where Jews are scarce seems to be the central motivating factor behind the students' steady and faithful attendance. The practice and its continuation are fuelled by the high value placed on tradition within these schools.

Brief and casual as the Friday night service at Groton is, it has its devotees. In their regular affirmations of Jewish affiliation and—I would argue—in the spirit of prep-school ceremonialism, the students I met there seem to have created a few small transformationalist traditions of their own. At the beginning of the service, the portion of the Reform siddur that they use includes a line saying that the glow of the sabbath candles is meant 'to cast love, freedom, [and] justice'. After that line was read I noticed that three of the students, in rotation, and without having to look at each other for guidance, ad-libbed the words, 'freedom', 'justice', and 'peace'. Later that evening, in an interview I conducted with a handful of the students, I asked how that little improvised quirk in the service had come about. Evidently, one or another recent graduate had originated the practice on a whim; the others have carried it forward with thought and care to its proper execution. What seemed to matter most to them, as their conversation afterwards indicated, was the question of who had instigated the tradition. In keeping perhaps with Groton's culture of apparently quirky and often untraceable traditions carried forward into the present, these students had developed their own variation on the practice. A bit later, as the service ended with the breaking and sharing of the challah and the recitation of the 'Hamotsi' blessing, I noticed that students used the tradition of salting the challah as an opportunity for grafting a new ritual onto an old one. After looking around the room in order to assess whether it was his or someone else's turn to perform the task, one student got up from the table, entered their teacher's apartment, and emerged with a salt shaker. Although the salting of the bread, they assured me, was performed because 'it just tastes good', the students clearly had a strong sense of their ritual obligation not only to salt their bread but to create a routine around the simple act of fetching the shaker from its ordinary place on their teacher's dining room table.

Boarding schools are distinct for their frequent invocation, in all sorts of circumstances, of traditional practices. From unique school cheers to ceremonies for the naming of new prefects to legends of the schools' founding and stories about the illustrious behaviour of long-departed students, prep schools abound in rituals and esoteric practices. Although hazing has been eliminated on most campuses, benign school traditions continue to exist in order to initiate new members of the group and as markers of belonging. Some repeated practices, like the sabbath services on Friday nights or, for that matter, chapel on Sunday mornings, pale in comparison, from an esoteric standpoint, to the more arcane traditions that mark boarding school as a world apart from life off campus. When I sat at sabbath services at Groton and at the Deerfield Passover Seder, I had no difficulty whatsoever in adjusting, as a casually observant American Jew myself, to the celebration of these rituals as the students and their faculty advisers marked them. My lack of familiarity with the Reform siddur used at Groton or with the fairly traditional Haggadah used by the Deerfield students was hardly a stumbling block. Like the students, I knew the bare bones—the covering of the eyes during the candle-lighting, the blessing over the wine. Where I came up short and instantly knew my status as an outsider was in witnessing the students as they casually referred in conversation to the tight traditional structures that govern their daily life in boarding school—their verbal shorthand. I did not know their nicknames, or the nicknames they used for other students or faculty or classes. I did not know the names of their buildings, nor could I follow the many references they made—in casual conversation with one another—to the daily patterns formed from one year to the next, by school practices and traditions.

The transformation of Jewish tradition and practice taking place at New England boarding schools comes about in the context of the already existing and much stronger traditions that separate these schools and their students from the denizens of the 'real world'. Judaic practice must be moulded to fit into this context; it needs to conform to the scheduling needs, spatial patterns, social templates, and speech practices that are intrinsic to prep-school life. The question then arises: if it is so fully and fundamentally shaped by the above needs and demands, can it still be seen as meaningfully Jewish? Needless to say, Friday night services at the boarding schools I visited do not begin anywhere near sunset. What is more important, however, is the fact that they are held on Friday nights and not on Saturday mornings in the first place in order not to interfere with most prep schools' practice of devoting Saturday mornings to classes and afternoons to sports competitions. The appointment or election of Jewish prefects or officers results not from this or that student's deeper familiarity with the Torah but from their level of interest and commitment to the school's model of excellence. Boarding school itself shapes the need for opportunities for students to enjoy some quiet time to be with other Jews and explore what it means to be a Jew, as they put it, 'in the modern world' and at boarding school. Its rigorous routines, often out of character with those imposed on teenagers in the 'real' world, appear to inspire a need and appreciation, on the part of these Jewish students, to imbibe, if only for a brief interval on a Friday night, the spirit of the sabbath.

It is this exact point that has been levelled at American Judaism across the board—that, to borrow from Jack Kugelmass's critique, it expends a greater effort in adjusting itself to its American context than it does in observance of halakhic principle. A closer look at some of these boarding-school traditions offers additional insight. In my interviews at Groton and Deerfield, I was eager to ask the students not only about their participation in practices that derived from their Jewish background but also about some of the traditions that made their schools distinct places from a cultural standpoint. When the students' efforts to carve out a Jewish niche can be made to converge with these indigenous school practices, 'tradition in transition' avoids being synonymous with 'tradition in recession'. On the subject of school traditions at Groton, 'the first thing that comes to mind', Dave told me,

is the song we sing at sit-down dinner. It's really old actually. Three times in the fall and the spring, we gather as grades in the dining hall and it's sit-down dress and it's very formal and everything. But there was one dinner [at which there] was this song that was called *Many Forms that Came before Us*, and the junior class sings it to the sixth form, which is the senior class. I'm not going to sing it because I can't sing, but it just talks about how this school is so old and how many forms have come before you, like you are one more, and many forms will come after you, and do the same things people have done that have come before to make themselves great. That song is sung on the school's birthday. I think the school is 123 years old, which is pretty old. [It] basically emphasizes the past, the present, and the future coming together—the forms marching on in the past, the present, and the future, the ones that come and the things that are happening right now.

The feeling of reverence for the past that Dave describes is certainly a palpable part of the experience of attending a school like Groton. The architecture exudes just such a feeling. Throughout the campus, and especially in the buildings that house classrooms and offices, one cannot help but stumble upon room after room that has been lavishly furnished with pieces of the past. 'When I walked through the main hall over there', Dave told me as he described how he chose Groton in the first place, 'I felt this sense of oldness and sense of academic tradition that really captivated me.' It takes a large and wilful effort on the part of students like Dave to create lasting traditions that can avoid being overshadowed by the school's entirely non-Jewish legacy.

Indeed, the hallowed and almost mystical traditions of such places must naturally have an intimidating effect. The two other Groton students I interviewed told me about how, before the tenure of the current Jewish faculty adviser, the Jewish group at Groton had used to meet in a place that they referred to as 'the garden room'. The place was, as they described it, 'really old and dark—it's where the disciplinary meetings take place'. Few settings can evoke more awe, particularly on the part of students, for whom the school disciplinary committee would naturally represent a maximum concentration of official school power. Ben told me he had once, when this space was being used for Jewish services, formed the habit of sitting on one particular chest. 'It was', he was told later, 'worth a couple . . . maybe tens of thousands'. Surrounded by relics of past forms and by reminders of their school's long tradition of excellence, and on the exact site where generations of errant students had been humbled by school authority, the Jewish group at Groton must have been made to feel quite small. Their presence in such a place, may have felt somewhat incongruous. What, we might ask, would the bygone forms have made of all of their Jewish talk in the midst of so much white elite Protestant splendour?

Deerfield students, whose school can boast nearly a hundred years' more 'heritage' than tradition-rich Groton, are not only surrounded by the relics of the forms, or classes, who have gone before but are also affected by the school's immediate proximity to the village of Deerfield, whose history as a frontier outpost and a target for French and Indian raids in the eighteenth century has long been enshrined in the national memory. 'The American history of Deerfield itself', said Fred, was 'probably the biggest story around' at his school. When I first asked the students to tell me about school traditions, they mentioned quite a long list—sit-down meals, formal dress, all-school meetings. This discussion occasioned their telling me about the school motto: 'Be worthy of your heritage.' Fred elaborated:

I guess people come in here, and I guess the school itself does not change that much. It's probably been like this for a hundred years, but it takes a lot of work to change anything at the school. I guess [it means] 'Be aware of your heritage when you come in here.' I guess Deerfield really wants you to learn a lot. I guess people get out feeling like they have a lot of pride in where they come from and the school itself. Everyone who graduates is usually extremely happy to have come from Deerfield Academy, to have been here. To have experienced it. Most students are like, 'Yeah I went to high school, it's time to go to college now,' but from here, when you go to college, it's like, 'I went to Deerfield Academy,' and . . . it's nice to be a part of that.

Students at Deerfield and Groton or at any other boarding school who wish to nurture a Jewish presence in such places meet with success in so far as they are able to create and articulate traditions in the mould of already existing ones, not only for other Jews but for the school community as a whole.

'It demands something from you': The Limits of Transformation

The schools adapt as necessary—slowly, to be sure, and always in keeping with their own long-standing and stated interests in maintaining some vital link to what they perceive as the incontrovertible legacy of past worthiness and heritage. In recent years, a pluralistic view has held sway, and Deerfield and Groton appear to be prepared to educate their students about diverse traditions, as long as they can avoid any disruption to their orderly routines or undue challenges to the general atmosphere of cultural uniformity that they seek to maintain. Jewish students mark the High Holidays by departing from their campuses and attending services either at a local synagogue or with their families at home. Hanukah, conveniently enough, often coincides with Christmas and poses no inconvenience to boarding schools. Catering to religiously observant Jewish students would be unthinkable. During Passover, a holiday that many secular Jews mark by participating in a single ritualized dinner, on the other hand,

the dining hall puts some matzoh out, and more non-Jewish kids than Jewish kids take advantage of those type of things. They know the story behind where the matzoh comes from, so it's good for them to learn about another religion. For Jewish events, sort of the entire school knows about them. It doesn't mean they participate in them, but it means they do know, 'Well this week's Passover,' and they sort of know what's going on.

Regardless of how much knowledge their non-Jewish schoolmates may or may not have of Judaism, the establishment of a campus precedent for any kind of Jewish tradition, especially within such a context where precedent is essentially equivalent to endorsement, may help to ensure a Jewish future in prep schools that, until recently, lacked a Jewish past. A key element is the limited but increasing agency of students for whom drastically revised Jewish traditions are the only possible means of perpetuating such a future.

In the same way that the transformationalist view of Jewish American life cannot fully encompass or explain the challenges posed by a general loosening of Jewish bonds in the United States, such a view also has its limits in the context of Jewish life in boarding schools. In this regard, the lessons of privilege are difficult and chastening lessons indeed. Prospects for Jewish life in these schools have clearly improved in recent years, but no amount of benevolently pluralistic and tolerant effort can bring about the total shift that would be a necessary prerequisite for a truly vibrant Jewish life on campus. For their part, the students may wish for such an occurrence, but they too know quite well what they are up against. A sad irony—perhaps indicative of a similar irony in American Jewish life—is that so many of these students are more than willing to go halfway towards affecting a compromise. I offer a final illustrative story as evidence of this.

All of the students I met at Deerfield and Groton expressed an acute appreciation for their schools' deep commitment to historical precedent. One of them had recent occasion to articulate that appreciation: at Groton School, graduating seniors are given the opportunity to give a talk in the chapel and Dave, who was due to graduate the day after I interviewed him, told me about his speech, which was, as he put it, about how his time at Groton had given him 'a profound connection with the past'. The subject of his chapel talk reminded him, he told me, of the school's many illustrious and accomplished graduates. On my first visit to Groton, I had noticed that the main hallway of the Schoolhouse building was decorated by, among other things, a collection of framed letters from over a dozen American presidents congratulating the various headmasters of the school on their steady achievement of excellence. Indeed, as Dave told me,

They have all the names of the graduates etched in wood in the Schoolhouse, so when you sit in a room, you get to see those who came before. You have Franklin D. Roosevelt's name, 1900; all of these really good people who have come to this school, so it instils a sense of pride in where you go. But at the same time, it demands something from you; you know you have to live up to those standards, in some ways. You know, I'm probably not going to be the president like FDR, but I can still embody the same principles that he lived by in my own life, so I think that the sense of oldness and tradition and excellence to the school has really inspired me and captivated me for four years.

A scant few of the names etched on the walls are those of Jews, but it is easy to see how and why Jewish students, whose own heritage has long been advanced not by unthinking reverence for the past but by an eagerness, inspired perhaps by the models of excellence that both precede and surround them, to make something of themselves in the future, have been moved by the notion of prep-school tradition.

Blind allegiance to such notions, however, would only result in the relinquishment of an actual Jewish difference. The central and perhaps quite ironic twist that underlies these students' ability to build meaningful Jewish traditions at prep school is that their expressions of Judaism are intrinsically secular. Just like the achievement drive that helped raise their great-grandparents and grandparents out of the ghetto without forcing them to sacrifice their Jewishness, the efforts made by younger Jews in prep school today to gain success and implant tradition derive from their elevation of Judaism's strong intellectual component. If Jews are still outsiders in today's prep schools, it is because their cultural and religious identities are fused and because their most salient contribution to the surrounding discourse is one of questioning and problematizing overly simplistic spiritual formulas. In this regard, secularity has been the source of both their acceptance and their exclusion. The 'deep-structure affinity of Calvinist Puritanism for Judaism' (Lipset and Raab 1995: 5) that has made America—and prep school, perhaps—such an appealing place from a Jewish perspective has not always led to the embrace of actual outspoken Jews.

Dave found this out at a campus forum he attended at Groton to which parents, alumni, current students, and faculty had been invited to discuss the school's religious legacy, and more specifically its policy of mandatory chapel services for all students. Several people spoke out in ways that he had not anticipated: 'Everyone there . . . was voicing this pretty unilateral position that the school has forgotten its Episcopalian tradition, the Christian life, the muscular Christianity that they thought they were sending their kids to.' Making the best of a fairly tense situation, and speaking candidly about his own experience of faithfully attending the school's required 'non-denominational' services for four years running, when his turn came he said he 'thought chapel was a [valuable] intellectual experience'. He met with 'faces contorted in anger'. All the same, he persevered to press his point: 'If we aim for diversity', he said, 'of not only colour and socio-economic background, but also religion, we need to do our best to make everyone feel equal on this campus, and not marginalize, [by] only doing a Christian service in the morning.' Only once their own rituals have helped to bring about a larger transformation of prep-school tradition, a newer and older heritage of which all students might aspire to be worthy, will Jews in places like Groton know that they have made their mark.

Notes

1   Henry James's *American Notebooks*, as well as Henry Adams's *Autobiography*, is often cited as a primary source on the growing antimodernism of American Anglos at the turn of the twentieth century. Contemporary cultural historians explore the phenomenon as well: a detailed study of, among other themes, the rise of a 'countercultural' spiritualism in the face of the nation's modernizing trends, T. J. Jackson Lears's *No Place of Grace: Antimodernism and the Transformation of American Culture, 1880–1920* (1981) comes to mind. So too does Dona Brown's *Inventing New England: Regional Tourism in the Nineteenth Century* (1995).

2   'Modeled after the best boarding schools in the nation', the American Hebrew Academy provides a non-Orthodox but deeply observant Jewish religious and cultural atmosphere to students from over twenty states and several foreign countries. A significant number of its faculty members received at least some of their education and training in Israel.

3   The Hillel Society, founded in Illinois in 1923, sponsors Jewish religious and cultural life on campuses throughout the United States, as well as elsewhere in the English-speaking world.

4   The *afikoman* is a portion of the ceremonial matzah that is hidden during the Passover Seder. Traditionally, the children in attendance search for this piece and are offered a reward for its recovery.

5   If nothing else, and notwithstanding the quite dulled edges of my own memories of adolescent experience, I knew ahead of time that ethnographic research among boarding-school students would have to be conducted with sensitivity and with an assumption that, by not actually being an adolescent attendee of one of these schools, I would be an outsider. My efforts could only scratch the surface of prep-school life, despite the common

background I shared with these students. The inherence of a generational gap was one factor that would inevitably have the effect of keeping me outside. Boarding schools are also notoriously sensitive to enquiries from outsiders (or insiders, for that matter) regarding such controversial topics as the status of religious or ethnic minorities. One school, in fact, turned down my request to interview its chaplain and some of its Jewish students on this exact basis. I also had to take into consideration the legal status of the students, a few of whom were minors at the time of the interviews. Accordingly, and for the sake of consistency, I have changed the names of all the students I interviewed.

6   All seventeen contributors to Louis Crosier's essay anthology, *Casualties of Privilege*, write under pseudonyms.

7   These schools have in common the fact that they were all founded by wealthy benefactors and closely tied, on that basis and others, to the world of finance; among the more noteworthy are Choate and Hotchkiss, both in Connecticut. This category of school has the highest percentage of Jewish students enrolled.

Interviews

I visited both Deerfield Academy and Groton School twice, and on each occasion was fortunate to meet with several of the Jewish students there. My first visit to Groton coincided with a regular Friday evening sabbath service, which I was able to attend. One of my two visits at Deerfield took place during that school's elaborate, if scantily attended, Passover Seder. These four visits also resulted in my having conducted formal, audiotaped interviews with five individual students. Because the students were minors at the time, I have chosen to change their names in this essay. These students are listed below.

ADAM, interviewed at Deerfield Academy, 16 Apr. 2007

DAVE, interviewed at Groton School, 17 May and 1 June 2007

ED, interviewed at Deerfield Academy, 16 Apr. 2007

FRED, interviewed at Deerfield Academy, 16 Apr. 2007

JEFF, interviewed at Groton School, 17 May 2007

References

ADAMS, HENRY. 1918. *The Education of Henry Adams*. Boston, Mass.

BENEVOLENT, MOXIE B. 1991. 'That Confusing Wall of Color'. In Louis Crosier, ed., *Casualties of Privilege: Essays on Prep School Culture*, 39–46. Washington, DC.

BERNACHE-BAKER, BARBARA. 2001. *Whose Values? Reflections of a New England Prep School Teacher*. Bloomington, Ind.

BROWN, DONA. 1995. *The Invention of New England: Regional Tourism in the Nineteenth Century*. Washington, DC.

COOKSON, PETER, and CAROLINE HODGES PERSELL. 1985. *Preparing for Power: America's Elite Boarding Schools*. New York.

DORSON, RICHARD. 1960. 'Jewish Dialect Stories on Tape'. In Raphael Patai, Francis Lee Utley, and Dov Noy, eds., *Studies in Biblical and Jewish Folklore*, 111–74. Bloomington, Ind.

GANS, HERBERT. 2000. 'Symbolic Ethnicity: The Future of Ethnic Groups and Cultures in America'. In John Hutchinson and Anthony Smith, eds., *Nationalism: Critical Concepts in Political Science*, vol. iv, pp. 1217–37. New York.

GLASSIE, HENRY. 2003. 'Tradition'. In Burt Feintuch, ed., *Eight Words for the Study of Expressive Culture*, 176–97. Champaign, Ill.

JACKSON LEARS, T. J. 1981. *No Place of Grace: Antimodernism and the Transformation of American Culture, 1880–1920*. New York.

JAMES, HENRY. 1907. *The American Scene*. London.

KANE, PEARL ROCK, and CHRISTOPHER LAURICELLA. 2005. 'Preparatory Schools'. In Burt Feintuch and David Watters, eds., *The Encyclopedia of New England*, 306–11. New Haven.

KIRSHENBLATT-GIMBLETT, BARBARA. 1987. 'The Folk Culture of Jewish Immigrant Communities: Research Paradigms and Directions'. In Moses Rischin, ed., *The Jews of North America*, 79–94. Detroit.

KUGELMASS, JACK. 1988. Introduction to *Between Two Worlds: Ethnographic Essays on American Jews*, 1–29. Ithaca, NY.

LEVITT, LAURA. 2007. 'Impossible Assimilations, American Liberalism, and Jewish Difference: Revisiting Jewish Secularism', *American Quarterly*, 3, 807–32.

LIEBMAN, CHARLES. 1995. 'Jewish Survival, Antisemitism, and Negotiation with the Tradition'. In Robert Seltzer and Norman Cohen, eds., *The Americanization of the Jews*, 436–50. New York.

LIPSET, SEYMOUR, and EARL RAAB. 1995. *Jews and the New American Scene*. Cambridge, Mass.

MELVILLE, HIBBERD. 1991. 'Living Inside the Prep Culture'. In Louis Crosier, ed., *Casualties of Privilege: Essays on Prep School Culture*, 9–28. Washington, DC.

POWELL, ARTHUR. 1996. *Lessons from Privilege: The American Prep School Tradition*. Cambridge, Mass.

RAAB, EARL, ed. 1991. *American Jews into the 21st Century: A Leadership Challenge*. Atlanta.

RITTERBAND, PAUL. 1995. 'Modern Times and Jewish Assimilation'. In Robert Seltzer and Norman Cohen, eds., *The Americanization of the Jews*, 377–94. New York.

SANTINO, JACK. 2004. 'Performative Commemoratives, the Personal, and the Public: Spontaneous Shrines, Emergent Ritual, and the Field of Folklore', *Journal of American Folklore*, 466(3), 364–75.

PART II

Revisioning Weddings and Marriage

Engendering Halakhah: Rachel Adler's *Berit Ahuvim* and the Quest to Create a Feminist Halakhic Praxis

GAIL LABOVITZ

HALAKHAH, the classical body of rules and directives for Jewish life and practice, has often been the focus of attention in Jewish feminist writings. Until recently, and in some communities to this day, women have not been direct participants in the process by which halakhah is studied, debated, and decided. They have functioned, in Rachel Adler's phrase, as 'peripheral Jews', both in the sense of their exclusion from setting the terms of the system, and also in the actual rulings of the system regarding women and gender relations (Adler 1983a). At the early stages of the current wave of feminism, thinkers such as Cynthia Ozick, Judith Plaskow, and Adler debated whether women's disadvantages within traditional halakhic legislation—such as their exclusion from large parts of Jewish ritual, or the inequality of rights and responsibilities between husbands and wives—constituted a sociological problem which could be resolved through the existing rules and methods of halakhic enquiry, or whether there were underlying theological issues to be addressed. In her book *Standing Again at Sinai*, Plaskow broached the question of a feminist approach to halakhah 'as baldly and badly as possible: Is law a female form?' (Plaskow 1983: 65). Other writers, with a variety of perspectives both denominational and not, have argued that halakhah should remain a vital aspect of Jewish thinking, practice, and spirituality, and even that it defines what makes Judaism 'Jewish'. As Adler has written, 'If Judaism cannot be engendered without solving the problem of women, it is equally true that it cannot be engendered without solving the problem of halakhah . . . Without concrete, sensuous, substantial experiences that bind us to live out our Judaisms together, there is nothing real to engender' (1998: 25).

As the debate continues, for those who seek to integrate halakhah into a feminist Judaism and feminism into halakhic Judaism, there are a number of challenges to address. The first of these is to define—both for those who profess a commitment to halakhah and those who do not—what the term 'halakhah' means, or could mean, in a feminist context. As Mark Washofsky has observed, advocates of a 'liberal' halakhah confront the problem that both 'Jewish religious liberals . . . who have little use for halakhic thinking' and 'those in the Orthodox camp' are often

at one in their definition of Jewish law . . . This core and content, it turns out, are identical with the understanding of Jewish law presented in contemporary Orthodox *pesikah* [decision-making] so that, according to both groups, 'the' *halakhah* is whatever today's Orthodox rabbinate says it is . . . There is no *halakhah* other than the current existing body of substantive rulings, interpretations, and behaviors that bear the name. (Washofsky 2004: 18)

Adler, however, refuses to cede the term in favour of some other name: 'We need to reclaim this term because it is the authentic Jewish language for articulating the system of obligations that constitute the content of the covenant' (1998: 25). Therefore, together with other liberal streams of Jewish thinking, feminist halakhists must begin from a non-fundamentalist, historically minded outlook (which is not to suggest that all traditional approaches to halakhah should be facilely categorized as fundamentalist). If the Written Law of Scripture is an exact record of direct communication between the Divine and man (and I choose that word deliberately, since the recipient of this divine communication is first and foremost Moses[1]), and the Oral Law of rabbinic tradition is no more than the development of what was already implicit in it, then there is little if anything to discuss. The vision of gender and gender relations found therein would be the very word of God, and how could the word of God be challenged or changed? Rather, as Adler writes,

The crucial difference between traditional halakhists and modernists is that modernists accept the premises of modern historiography: that societies are human constructions that exist in time and change over time, that ideas and institutions inhabit specific historical and cultural contexts, and that they cannot be adequately understood without reference to context. These premises are incompatible with the belief that halakhah was divinely revealed in a single event and reflects an eternal and immutable divine will.[2] (1998: 27)

On this point, Adler is in agreement with nearly all non-Orthodox—as well as some Orthodox—interpreters of halakhah. Numerous writers professing a variety of denominational affiliations have provided cogent arguments that in practice, halakhah has historically allowed for significant flexibility and adaptability.

A fundamental criterion of a re-envisioned feminist halakhah is that it must incorporate gender as a tool for critical analysis, and that the experiences and voices of people of all genders must play an essential part in any conversation. At a minimum, the many traditional laws and practices that have materially disadvantaged women or excluded them from equal participation in religious expression and leadership would have to be reconsidered, and rectified. This, however, has opened the question of whether even liberal approaches to halakhah can in fact accommodate such proposals or formulate viable solutions if they attempt to do so by applying the classical methods and categories of traditional halakhah. Many have come to the position that traditional, so-called formalist or positivist methods of adjudicating issues in Jewish law are not sufficient to create a halakhic praxis that may legitimately be called feminist. While specific issues and problematic laws can sometimes be addressed, reinterpreted, or ameliorated by classical methods, even in such cases the underlying inequality that generated the problem is often built into the system and its basic categories in a way that is far more difficult to uproot. In Adler's words,

> The presumptions set the questions. The categories shape them. Adjudication creates precedents that reinforce the form future questions must take . . . Hence, when women advance topics that do not affect preestablished legal concerns, the system either rejects them because it has no information on them or attempts to restate them in distortive androcentric terms that would allow it to apply its own categories and advance its own goals.[3] (1998: 29)

As will be seen below, the halakhah of marriage, the focus of this essay, provides a strong example of this difficulty.

Feminist halakhists have thus begun to seek new methods and theoretical frameworks by which to think about what a reconstructed halakhic system might look like, strive for, and set as its operating procedures. Here I want to explore how feminist halakhah is beginning to move in this direction, that is, how Jewish feminist thinkers have been developing their critiques of classical (and liberal) halakhic methodology as well as their advocacy for new methods and theories into a vision of a functioning engendered halakhic praxis. What happens when the feminist legal thinker becomes a halakhic decisor, a *poseket* (if *poseket* is indeed the role to which she aspires)? What topics and questions will her analyses address, and what methodologies will she use to articulate her visions and decisions? To begin answering these questions, I will analyse Adler's revisioned wedding ceremony, *berit ahuvim* (lovers' covenant), as an example of an attempt at creating such an engendered halakhah.[4] I will explore the details of the ceremony itself, Adler's reflections on her vision of the ceremony and how it is meant to function, how it relates to the traditional form of Jewish weddings and to classical halakhic sources, some preliminary evidence of how it is being received and used, critiques that may be raised against Adler's ceremony or overall approach, and some questions about the way forward.

Marriage is, in fact, an excellent example through which to consider the place that feminist halakhic thinking currently finds itself in. The traditional wedding ceremony, as it is usually performed today, consists of two parts: *kidushin* (betrothal), and *nisuin* (nuptials). It is the first of these that creates a legal bond between the couple, a form of inchoate marriage, while the latter blesses and seals the union so that cohabitation becomes permissible and the full rights and responsibilities of marriage become active. To effect *kidushin*, the man gives the woman an item of at least minimal value—a ring in standard practice—and declares, 'Behold you are betrothed to me with this ring according to the law of Moses and Israel.' The woman signals her acceptance silently, by allowing the man to place the ring on her finger. In numerous places in rabbinic literature, this act is designated as *kinyan*, acquisition (Mishnah *Kid.* 1:1). Thus it is inaccurate to say that *kidushin* creates a *mutual* legal bond; rather, through *kidushin* the man unilaterally acquires the woman as his wife, and particularly the right to exclusive sexual access to her.[5] Since marital halakhah in the Bible and rabbinic literature allows polygyny (and even up until the modern period in countries that permit polygyny under Islamic law), the woman has no legal right to sexual exclusivity from her husband. Although few Jewish communities, if any, still formally practise polygyny (Ashkenazim have considered it forbidden since the eleventh century and it is generally prohibited to all in Israeli law), this history continues to manifest itself in halakhah in several ways; most notably, a man is forbidden to remain with his wife if it is known that she had sexual contact with another man during the marriage, but there is no such requirement to dissolve the marriage if the husband engages in extramarital sex. This lack of equality and mutuality is itself sufficient to make *kidushin* highly problematic from a feminist perspective. It may also be noted that the traditional ceremony, which assigns roles based on gender, is not (easily) adaptable for solemnizing a commitment between two people of the same gender.[6]

Another hint that marriage is not an equal relationship can be found in the *ketubah*, the marriage contract that traditionally accompanies Jewish weddings. The contents of this document include responsibilities that the husband takes on towards his wife—to provide maintenance, clothing, and sexual intercourse—and a monetary pledge which she may collect from his property should he divorce or predecease her.[7] As Adler notes, the *ketubah* does not establish marriage, but is rather given to the woman after *kidushin* takes place, 'for its function is to moderate the husband's power over his acquisition' (1998: 196). The *ketubah* is thus often framed as advantageous for women, but this can only be so if one starts from the presumption that the woman is the weaker party and in need of protection—as is in fact the case under the provisions of classical halakhah governing the marital relationship (economically and otherwise): 'the *ketubah* . . . presumes that most economic power and resources belong to the male' (Adler 1998: 192).

Moreover, although the *ketubah* is given to the woman during the wedding ceremony and is legally hers thereafter, Laura Levitt has raised some important questions as to whether the woman should be considered a party to this contract. The *ketubah* is not signed by either the bride or the groom, but rather by two, traditionally male, witnesses. One of the things the witnesses attest to is that the groom has performed an act of *kinyan*, acquisition of the *ketubah* (usually signified by the groom taking hold of an item, such as a handkerchief, handed to him by the witnesses): 'Once he does so, it becomes his property, signifying that an exchange has taken place and, through this exchange, that he has taken on all of the obligations and privileges spelled out in the ketubah.' This leads Levitt to the question: from whom has he acquired these rights and responsibilities? She answers, 'I believe that the groom contracts not so much with the bride but more with the community. This means that the witnesses act on behalf of the community. Through them the groom obligates himself to the community as opposed to the bride . . . She is not important to this legal procedure' (Levitt 1997: 41–2). Finally, it may be noted that rabbinic law regularly invokes the threat of depriving a woman of her *ketubah* as a means of controlling or punishing women's social and sexual behaviour (see, as just a few examples, Mishnah *Ketubot* 5: 7, 7: 6, and *Sotah* 1: 5).

In the modern era, a *ketubah* is generally a formality of a traditional wedding, and is not usually considered to be an enforceable contract. Nonetheless, the model of marriage as *kidushin* remains materially dangerous for women. Like *kidushin*, a halakhic divorce is, indeed must be, a unilateral act of male agency. In contrast to the procedure in many modern Western legal systems, where a marriage is terminated by the decree of a civil court or judge—and particularly in locations where 'no-fault' divorce laws hold, even at the individual petition of either spouse—halakhic divorce is an act of the husband; to the extent that a court is involved, it is in a supervisory role only, to ensure that proper procedure is fully followed, but the divorce is not effected by the court. The husband commissions the writing of a *get* (divorce document) and gives it, or has it delivered, to the woman. Just as the essence of *kidushin* is the acquisition of the woman, so too the core of the divorce procedure and the *get* is a statement in which the husband relinquishes his ownership of, and sexual claim to, his wife: 'Behold you are permitted to any man' (Mishnah *Gitin* 9: 3). The latter reverses and undoes the former. This means that although there are grounds for a woman to seek a divorce, and a *beit din* (Jewish court) may find merit in her petition, a divorce cannot happen without the husband's consent and participation (whereas in rabbinic law, albeit not in modern practice, the husband may divorce the wife without her consent; see Mishnah *Yev.* 14: 1). It further means that the husband may use the threat of withholding the divorce as a form of blackmail to extract money or favourable terms in the divorce settlement, or he may refuse to give it altogether. The woman who wishes to abide by halakhah is then legally unable to remarry or even have a relationship with another man. She is 'anchored' to her original husband, and is known as an *agunah*. A woman who does enter a new relationship without a *get* has, legally speaking, committed adultery, and her children by this latter man will be deemed *mamzerim*, unable (in Orthodox circles in particular) to marry other Jews of 'unblemished' lineage.[8]

Liberal halakhic solutions to the problem of the *agunah* have been proposed and put into use, both within the Conservative movement and some segments of Orthodoxy.[9] These include: forms of prenuptial agreement that bind the couple to appear before a *beit din* if summoned and to abide by its dictates, or that allow the *beit din* to place sanctions on a man who does not fulfil a ruling to give his wife a divorce;[10] conditional marriages; and even annulment of marriages.[11] The authors of these strategies work valiantly to find sources within the classical legal canon that can serve as grounds for procedures and as means to compel the husband to give the divorce or to turn over power to the court to declare the marriage void altogether. What none consider is undoing the one-sided nature of marriage and divorce.

An intriguing aspect of Adler's thinking is that, as a scholar convinced of the necessity of halakhah to Jewish living, she accepts that *kidushin* is a legal ritual and that it creates a legally binding relationship. It cannot be reinterpreted, reconstructed, mutualized, or otherwise retained so long as its fundamental act of unilateral acquisition can be understood as having taken effect—which almost certainly will be the case if the man gives the woman an item of value and says, 'You are betrothed to me.'[12] Highly relevant here is Jonah Steinberg's analysis of Adler's work in yet another area of Jewish law that affects women, and men with whom they are in a sexual relationship, that is, the regulations surrounding the *nidah*, the menstruating woman. Adler has addressed this topic in two articles, published almost twenty years apart: in the first, in 1973, she attempted to formulate a theology of purity and impurity based on women's spirituality and bodily experiences, but then in a second piece in 1992 she detailed reasons why she could no longer stand by the views expressed in her earlier work. Steinberg documents how Adler's earlier ideas became part of the discourse of *nidah* (both among those who observe these laws and those who hope to influence others to do so), in such a way that 'a set of rules and practices . . . has remained remarkably constant, while the recorded thought and propaganda generated to support this body of Jewish law have undergone a near-complete reversal' (Steinberg 1997: 6). He observes, however, that this 'change of ideology, when the change is not expressed in praxis, allows multiple frameworks of theorization to exist superimposed'. He then delineates a highly problematic result:

That may not initially sound foreboding to pluralistic ears; but Adler's branding of her own attempt at purely intellectual redemption of *hilkhot niddah* as the creation of 'a theology for the despised' highlights the problem of such multivalence when one already extant framework is so detrimental. No matter in what different ways the details of *hilkhot niddah* may be understood by certain women or couples, the differences can have only limited effect if the practices themselves are still entirely amenable to a former, harmful justification that abides conspicuously in canonical sources. (1997: 24–5)

In our context this means that so long as the basic form and content of *kidushin* remain fundamentally intact, reinterpretation of its meaning does not dislodge earlier models, and it thus retains its potentially deleterious effects on women's lives.

One option, then, might have been to simply forgo *kidushin*, and to allow relationships to fall into a 'halakhic vacuum', a space in which there are no halakhic data to legitimate them (Adler 2007). Along these lines, Adler notes the existence of (relatively undeveloped) halakhic categories for relationships that are non-marital, but also not considered to be *zenut* (illicit sexual activity)—particularly *pilageshut* (concubinage). While these still do not provide a model of a mutual, egalitarian relationship (let alone one that can accommodate same-sex partners), they nonetheless do suggest to Adler that 'concubinage may be valuable as a placeholder for relationships differentiated from *kidushin*', thus serving as a possible precedent for a sanctioned form of commitment that does not constitute *kidushin* (1998: 205). However, fundamental to Adler's outlook, and quite possibly to any halakhically oriented perspective, is the strong conviction that, by virtue of its performative function, ritual is indispensable for effecting a change in reality, in status and obligation. What is needed, therefore, is not simply the lack of *kidushin*, the vacuum, but 'a wedding ceremony that embodies the partners' intentions to sustain and strive with each other all their lives . . . The marriage agreement must specify the obligations that will form the fabric of the marriage' (Adler 1998: 192).

What are the means by which a feminist halakhah might confront this situation and develop a new ceremony and mechanism to create a binding relationship between two people? A key influence on Adler—and on a number of others working in this field—are the writings of legal theorist Robert Cover, most notably (though hardly exclusively) his essay 'Nomos and Narrative' (1983). In the widely quoted opening to this law review article, Cover lays out the fundamental insight of his theory:

No set of legal institutions or prescriptions exists apart from the narratives that locate it and give it meaning . . . Once understood in the context of the narratives that give it meaning, law becomes not merely a system of rules to be observed, but a world in which we live.

In this normative world, law and narrative are inseparably related. Every prescription is insistent in its demand to be located in discourse—to be supplied with history and destiny, beginning and end, explanation and purpose. And every narrative is insistent in its demand for its prescriptive point, its moral. (1983: 4–5)

Cover further characterizes law and law-making as a bridge, strung between the current reality of our existing *nomos* or normative world and another *nomos* we might imagine or desire: 'Law may be viewed as a system of tension or a bridge linking a concept of reality to an imagined alternative—that is, as a connective between two states of affairs, both of which can be represented in their normative significance only through the devices of narrative' (1983: 9). Reflecting on this image, Adler writes: 'we must discover within ourselves the competence and good faith through which to repair and renew the Torah within time. We must *extend* Torah as we extend ourselves by reaching ahead. The aptest metaphor for that task is that of the bridge we build from the present to possible futures' (1998: 37). For Adler, then, the feminist halakhic bridge must take us to a place in which unilateral ownership (or indeed any form of ownership; see below) is no longer a tenable basis for creating a legal and binding bond between two people, and moreover to a place in which any two loving Jewish partners who so desire can make a binding and mutual commitment to each other, irrespective of their gender.[13]

Moreover, when this Coverian emphasis on narrative is translated into a feminist halakhic enquiry, it manifests itself in (at least) two ways, both of which can be seen in the creation and form of *berit ahuvim*. First is the introduction of personal stories into legal discourse. These may be the stories of individuals living, or attempting (sometimes against resistance) to create a life, within a legal community and system, and they may describe the (often harmful) material effects of a law or legal interpretation. As Thomas Ross observes, 'The last, and most controversial, of the feminist methods is the telling of stories—the use of narrative . . . Thus, feminist legal scholarship is replete with stories about the author's experiences, the experiences of other individual women, and the lives of women in general.' Further on, he explains the importance of these narratives to feminist jurisprudence:

The legal feminist tells stories aloud partly because she must overcome the other stories that are already powerfully present . . . Feminist practical reasoning is not merely rhetorically useful, it is an essential response to the abstract talk of the State's apologists . . . to get the initial premises right, legal feminists displace the culture's stories with their own stories.[14] (1993: 106, 115)

In another context, that is, the Orthodox rabbinic response to the development of women's prayer groups, Adler notes the effects of failing to bring these voices into the conversation:

The male elite who claim responsa literature as their domain continue to converse only with one another to render anonymous the outsiders whose acts provide the context for the elite conversation . . . There is a 'gentlemen's agreement' to converse *about* rather than *with* these mothers of invention so that their accomplishments may be reframed for the purposes of the responsa literature as problems detected by one rabbi and referred to another for a solution . . . Suppressing the social history of the prayer group, then, is a distortion designed to reinforce a rabbinic monopoly on authority. (Adler 2001: 5)

In an interview I conducted with Adler in November 2007, she described the role of several personal narratives as they impacted on her process of creating *berit ahuvim*. In her first marriage, as the wife of an Orthodox rabbi, she was witness to her husband's (unsuccessful) attempts to help a woman who had been physically abused in her marriage obtain a *get* from her recalcitrant husband after a civil divorce. Also obviously significant was her own experience of going through the process of Jewish divorce and receiving a *get*, and then later her search for a different means by which to effect and celebrate her commitment with a new partner. Indeed, Adler notes that the creation of the *berit ahuvim* ceremony and the development of her thinking on feminist halakhah that would form the basis of her writings in *Engendering Judaism* occurred together and were mutually reinforcing experiences (Adler 2007).[15]

Secondly, Cover's insights mean that the narratives already extant within the Jewish tradition, and not just the body of legal rulings and precedents, can become the ground in which to root and grow new halakhic visions and practices. Adler frames her chapter on halakhah with a story of her own, a Yiddish folk tale about the character Skotsl, who is delegated by the other women of her community to present their grievances with the traditional halakhic system directly to heaven. In the story, Skotsl disappears as the women attempt to lift her up to heaven, but Adler asks: what will Skotsl have to do and say if and when she arrives before those who will hear her plea? Imagining what Cover might have advised, she suggests, 'His advice to Skotsl would be to tell stories about the law . . . she must bring revelations to heaven, disclosing stories unknown to the tradition, the stories of its female claimants. It is equally important, however, that Skotsl tell the tradition its own stories in a new way' (1998: 51). That is, Skotsl must have access to the full resources of the Jewish tradition, the ability to use and adapt existing legal models to new purposes and meanings. More significantly, however, she must have the freedom to bring to the conversation sources from the Jewish canon that have until now been partitioned off from legal discourse, that is, aggadah: biblical narratives and their midrashic expansions, rabbinic stories, ritual practices, and rediscovered or reconstructed narratives of Jewish social practices of other times and places.[16]

In her revisioning of marriage Adler therefore invokes the complex and difficult stories found in prophetic texts, notably the book of Hosea, of the metaphorical marriage between God and Israel (1998: 156–67). This is a model of a marriage that starts from patriarchal premises, and which entails images of extreme violence and abuse against the wife—Israel. Yet, Adler observes, the divine impulse to punish can be seen to derive from the fact that God is injured and hurt by Israel's behaviour: 'It acknowledges that God is dependent on the other partner for what God wants . . . God's desire for sincere and unconstrained recognition from the other renders God vulnerable to disappointment and abandonment' (1998: 161). What is more, despite divine anger, and despite biblical law that demands capital punishment for a woman (and her partner) if she has sexual contact with a man other than her husband (Lev. 20: 10, Deut. 22: 22) and prohibits a man from taking back a wife whom he has divorced if she subsequently married another man (Deut. 24: 1–4), the prophetic text proposes a chance at reconciliation between God and the adulterous (that is, idolatrous) Israelite people. This is marriage not as a contract (wherein a breach by one side frees the other of any further obligations), but rather as a renewable covenant between the parties. In these aspects of the prophetic marriage metaphor, then, we begin to see hints (if only hints) towards a usable model 'based not upon ownership, but upon mutual responsiveness' (Adler 1998: 164).[17] Adler draws a further link to narratives found in the wedding ceremony itself, in the *sheva berakhot*, the seven blessings that traditionally constitute the ritual core of *nisuin*. These blessings, which first appear in the Babylonian Talmud in *Ketubot 7b–8a*, intertwine themes of creation, the future redemption and restoration of Israel (both the land and the people), and the joy of marriage (again, both the joy of the couple themselves and of the community that celebrates their union). Adler thus observes: 'What the blessings celebrate is not "taking" but "wedding," a cojoining that, according to the prophets supersedes the rules of acquisition-marriage' (Adler 1998: 181). That is, while the *sheva berakhot* are usually paired with *kidushin* in current practice, the narratives interlaced through and underlying them stand in contrast to, and thus can support the challenge to, the unilateral and acquisitional transaction of *kidushin*. This latter part of the wedding is, in fact, left intact in Adler's revisioned ceremony.

Similarly, when Adler seeks another form of binding commitment instead of unilateral acquisition that the couple could make to each other and to their relationship, she finds it within the existing Jewish legal tradition. First, she makes reference to the research of Mordecai Friedman, which has documented a variant text in early medieval Palestinian *ketubot* (marriage contracts)—one different from the Babylonian version that has become the dominant norm—that referred to marriage through the language of covenant and partnership (Friedman 1980–1).[18] This latter concept further inspired Adler to turn to classical rabbinic laws regarding the creation of a business partnership as a model out of which she could shape the legal core of an egalitarian ceremony (1998: 179–80, 192–3, 195–6). Rabbinic law originally concretized the concept of 'pooling resources' through the image of people putting money into a common pouch. Adler revives and enacts this gesture in her ceremony: each partner places an item of personal emotional significance to them—alternatively or in addition they may use their wedding rings—into a bag that they then lift together as the concrete act by which they each acquire responsibility for their partnership.[19]

The other essential element of Adler's proposal is the partnership deed, or *berit* (covenantal) document. She explicitly differentiates this from the traditional *ketubah*; unlike the *ketubah*, the *berit* document is part of the process of effectuating the marriage, and is made between both parties to the marriage, as equals. At its core are contractual commitments that the couple make to each other. Adler's recommendations include sexual exclusivity, joint responsibility for children, and a commitment to care for one another towards the end of life, but she also encourages couples to add or vary the stipulations in accordance with their individual circumstances; for example, they might include understandings regarding the care of children from a previous relationship or of an elderly parent. It is important, however, that Adler names this document a *berit*, a covenant, and explicitly distinguishes it from a contract (or *shetar* in Hebrew legal language). This distinction gains significance first in regard to the actual provisions to which the couple agree: 'The stipulations must be flexible enough to accommodate changes either in external conditions or in the two parties themselves' (1998: 194). More broadly, the *berit* document, too, partakes of the covenantal marital metaphor of the prophets. Adler writes, 'as in classical covenants, the partners are committed ultimately to one another and not merely to the terms they have promised to fulfil. To the extent that this covenantal commitment is realized in the relationship, it can survive breaches in contractual obligations' (1998: 193–4). To this effect, her draft document opens by 'rooting *b'rit ahuvim* in biblical covenant stories and identifying the relationship with the rabbinic ideal of holy companionship' (1998: 194).

Adler's distinction between contract and covenant suggests that she is responding, albeit somewhat indirectly, to a feminist critique of the liberal marriage contract (and social contract theory more generally), particularly as articulated by Carole Pateman (1988). Pateman observes that marriage is often framed in social contract theory as a form of contract between husband and wife, but that upon closer examination its contractual nature proves to be highly ambiguous. This is reflected, for example, in the fact that the marriage contract is not actually a negotiable agreement between the parties, adaptable to their particular needs and desires; indeed, there is no written agreement that the parties can review and sign to, and what they bind themselves to is rather the civil laws and common understanding of marriage in whatever location they undertake to marry. As Pateman writes, 'There is not even a choice available between several different contracts, there is only *the* marriage contract . . . A married couple cannot contract to change the "essentials of marriage". . . . The general parameters are set by the law governing marriage' (1988: 164–5).[20] Pateman goes further, however, to argue against other feminists who suggest that the solution is to transform marriage into a genuine contract between equal parties, and claims instead that this cannot be the basis for a marital relationship in which the woman is not subordinate. For women to participate equally in contracts, they must do so as 'individuals', but Pateman contends that the concept of the individual in social contract theory is a patriarchal category, that the individual is inherently masculine: 'Odd things happen to women when the assumption is made that the only alternative to the patriarchal construction of sexual difference is the ostensibly sex-neutral "individual" . . . When contract and the individual hold full sway under the flag of civil freedom, women are left with no alternative but to (try to) become replicas of men' (1988: 187).

One possible understanding of Adler's move to the model of covenant is that it aims to go beyond contract as the basis of marriage. As she writes, 'Relationships expose our nakedness. To seek anything from another is tacitly to acknowledge that we cannot attain our desire alone . . . Modern contracts hide this nakedness by presenting the fulfillment of needs as a reciprocal arrangement between equals, even though in actuality both parties may not benefit equally' (1998: 156). If we read Adler this way, however, there are questions to be asked as to whether covenants can in fact serve as a new and different model. Notably, Laura Levitt's reading and critique of Eugene B. Borowitz's covenantal theology—as articulated in his book *Renewing the Covenant*—raise some important potential challenges to Adler's work as well (Borowitz 1991; Levitt 1997). Levitt asks whether a covenant, particularly when derived from the biblical model of the God–Israel relationship as one of covenant (and the understanding of that covenant being moreover developed through marital metaphors), is really significantly different from a contract. Like the liberal marriage contract, it is a binding arrangement between parties of unequal standing: 'Despite his reluctance to speak about covenant as contract, Borowitz acknowledges its legal/contractual roots and affirms them . . . Even in Borowitz' resistance to the language of contract, there is an uncanny resemblance between his covenant and the sexual contract' (Levitt 1997: 80–1). On the one hand, Adler's discussion of the vulnerability of God in the prophetic marital metaphor, as well as her observation that the God–Israel 'marriage' can (and does) survive violations of the strict standards of either contract or Jewish marriage law, may be seen as an answer to a critique of this sort. On the other hand, her language moves ambiguously between contract and covenant, invoking both terms repeatedly as part of her discussion of the *berit ahuvim* ceremony and document and her process of creating them.

Another possibility, however, is to read Adler's work as a critique of some of the assumptions underlying Pateman's contention that contract cannot provide a sufficient feminist resolution to the problem of patriarchal marriage. It is notable in this context that Adler's ceremony can be used by any two unrelated Jewish adults who wish to make a long-term commitment to each other—precisely what Pateman states must be the outcome of making marriage a 'genuine' contract: 'Freedom of contract (proper contract) demands that no account is taken of substantive attributes—such as sex. If marriage is to be truly contractual, sexual difference must become irrelevant to the marriage contract; "husband" and "wife" must no longer be sexually determined' (Pateman 1988: 167). As noted above, Pateman finds this problematic because she believes that the 'sexless' individual is not actually sexless (but, rather, masculine), and thus this result does not allow for the equality of women *as women*.[21] Some reviewers of Pateman's book have challenged this assumption, however: 'her claim that all theories built around the notion of freely contracting individuals must necessarily assume the subjection of women is less convincing' (Okin 1990: 659). Several contend, among other concerns, that Pateman presents a particular way of understanding contracts and contract theory as representative of contract theory more generally, when in fact a variety of views and interpretations on the nature of contracts and the people entering into them exist within the field. More specifically, as Elizabeth S. Anderson writes, Pateman's model 'is flawed by two confusions: (1) between particular contracts and contractarian theory; and (2) between possessive contractarian theory and the general form of contractarian theory' (Anderson 1990: 1804). In the possessive model of contract theory, the individual who participates in a contract is considered to be 'related to his body as an owner is to a piece of property' (Anderson 1990: 1801), from which should follow the conclusion that 'If all freedoms are necessarily embodied in property rights, and people own their bodies as property, they are only completely free if they can completely alienate their bodies for anything they please' (Anderson 1990: 1802, n. 25)—including, paradoxically, selling or giving oneself into slavery or gender-based subordination in marriage. If contracts and the individuals (using this term as Pateman does) who make them are understood in this way, then contracts indeed may 'constitute a powerful tool for creating relations of domination' (Anderson 1990: 1801). This is not, however, the only possible way by which contract theorists could, or do, understand the nature or evaluate the legitimacy of what occurs in a given contract. Again, Anderson writes that contract 'can take forms besides a possessive one. It can, for instance, be constituted by a mutual commitment to construct a common life based upon gifts whose value for one party depends on their being shared rather than offered up for exclusive possession' (1990: 1808). In a similar vein, Susan Moller Okin proposes that 'there are other criteria for evaluating their [contracts'] legitimacy . . . and that the inequality of the parties and the potential for exploitation are high on the list' (1990: 667). It may be telling, then, that Adler refers to *berit ahuvim* as a 'marriage between subjects', if not between 'individuals' (1998: 169).[22] Similar attention may be paid to the language Adler uses to discuss a mutualized *kidushin*: although she endorses the view that a ceremony of this sort does not create legally binding *kidushin*, she nonetheless does not find it sufficient to meet her criteria for an appropriately reworked basis on which to create a marriage because the concept of the acquisition of another person remains embedded within it:

From an ethical perspective, the double-ring ceremony is a dubious amelioration. The problem with marital *kinyan* is not simply that it is unilateral, but that it commodifies human beings. The groom's commodification and acquisition of the bride is not rectified by the bride's retaliation in kind . . . The vocabulary and constitutive assumptions of *kidushin* cannot be made to reflect a partnership of equals.[23] (1998: 191)

She further writes that classical Jewish partnership law, her model for *berit ahuvim*, 'mediates between the partners' need for autonomy and their needs for interdependence'; each remains an independent person and 'individually accountable' to the terms of their agreement. Acquisition does not mark the relationship of these two subjects to each other. Instead, both have a stake in the partnership, and it is the partnership rather than the participants themselves that 'is regarded as a kind of property in which the partners have invested' (Adler 1998: 192).

Finally, another recurring critique of Pateman's work is that she proposes no alternative models to supplant social contract theory and thereby create the grounds for a relationship that a man and woman (or any two people) could enter as true equals. It may be noted that Pateman herself writes towards the end of her book, 'To retrieve the story of the sexual contract does not, in itself, provide a political programme or offer any short cuts in the hard task of deciding what, in any given circumstances, are the best courses of action and policies for feminists to follow' (1988: 223). Given that Levitt's analysis relies heavily on Pateman's thought, she too becomes open to this concern. Indeed, David Blumenthal makes this very point, referring to Adler's work: 'I think that *Engendering Judaism* raises some questions for Levitt: What is your view of praxis? How do you pray? How do you marry? . . . What do you do to be Jewish?' (1999: 118). Thus, while the particular details of Adler's halakhic innovation in *berit ahuvim* may be open to critique and question from a variety of angles (a point Adler herself freely acknowledges; see below), I would suggest that this discussion ultimately affirms Adler's argument for the necessity of the attempt to create such a halakhah. The act of pooling resources and the ratification of the *berit* document together serve important purposes in a feminist halakhah. Most significantly, they fulfil what a halakhically oriented thinker would deem a requirement, namely, that there be a *legal* act or acts to bind the marriage. Presumably, even a clearly non-contractual form of marriage would need to provide an alternative means to achieve this end.

When Adler claims that 'a halakhah is a communal praxis grounded in Jewish stories', and that 'if we claim it [the story] as our own, we commit ourselves to be the kind of people that the story demands, to translate its norms and values into a living praxis', it should be further observed that invoked here are not just stories that ground a praxis, but ones that a collective claims 'as our own', leading to 'a *communal* praxis' (1999: 25–6). It is not only the story, but the community in which it is told that is necessary for the creation of a feminist halakhic praxis. In one sense, this leads back to the point made above about the importance of personal narratives of community members (or would-be members) in the creation of this revisioned halakhah. These narratives become significantly more difficult for community leaders or the interpreters of the halakhah already in place to resist when they come from those who profess their commitment to the community and to its values. Gordon Tucker observes how this applies in the case of gay and lesbian (Conservative) Jews who 'have not sought to separate themselves from the Jewish community', who 'agree that halakhah has a valid moral claim to obedience by the community', and thus 'force all official interpreters of halakhah . . . to choose between reaffirming the official interpretation, and thus criminalizing and isolating this committed community, or . . . to extend the delicate but vital area of family structure' (2006: 20–1). He goes on to note that it is precisely this process that has lead to expanding gender egalitarianism in the Conservative movement and elsewhere:

Before there were any legal arguments for the full equalization of women and men in the synagogue and house of study, there were communities that had formed themselves with a vision of such equalization. They were committed to Judaism in a way that included ritual and liturgical traditionalism, but their own narrative, their own under-standing of our texts, led them to the conviction that the tradition was wrong in exclud-ing women from any public roles . . . The received halakhic tradition, governed by precedent, was failing to account for a reality that would not go away: here were egalitar-ian communities that were preserving, not dismantling, Jewish tradition. (2006: 20–1)

In another sense, the halakhah that will be created when these narratives enter the process must be community-based. A marriage—to return to our central example—concretizes a relationship between two people, but it takes place with the community's sanction and entails commitments to the community as well as to each other: 'A Jewish wedding is not a private arrangement, but a commitment to establish a *bayit b'Yisrael*, a household among the people Israel, to contribute to its continuity and to engage in the task of *tikkun olam*, repairing the world' (Adler 1998: 170).[24]

This commitment to community also manifests itself in Adler's work as a concern for the relationship between adherents of a progressive feminist halak-hah and other Jewish communities, including those that continue to observe clas-sical forms of Jewish law; the citation above continues, 'Consequently, we have a responsibility to consider how *b'rit ahuvim* may affect the difficult enterprise of maintaining a pluralistic Jewish peoplehood' (1998: 170). It is partly for this rea-son that Adler makes it her goal to create a ceremony that should not be inter-pretable as a deviant yet binding form of *kidushin*. It must be possible for all to accept that the *berit ahuvim* can be dissolved without a *get* being necessary. This is important so that the children of a woman's subsequent relationships need not be deemed *mamzerim*, making them unable to marry readily in some segments of Jewish society, and thus making the boundaries between Jewish communities that degree more difficult to cross. Those who nonetheless choose to define the relationship as *kidushin* and demand a *get* in order to dissolve it must be the ones to bear the responsibility of their choice.[25]

This focus on community, however, is also central to what I see as a primary challenge that stands in the path of the development of a feminist halakhah in general and as the key as yet unresolved tension in Adler's model in particular —the issue with which I would like to conclude. Robert Cover distinguishes between two modes of legal development, the paideic and the imperial, or the world-creating and the world-maintaining. The paideic mode is generative: it is the mode of creating or re-creating a *nomos* (law). The maintenance of that *nomos*, however, needs the imperial mode. In this mode, standards are set, universalized, and enforced. The expansive jurisgenesis (law-creating) of the paideic mode is met by the necessary jurispathic activity of the imperial mode: [26] *these* are tolerable interpretations of the law, and *those* are not. Cover asserts that 'No normative world has ever been created or maintained wholly in either the paideic or the imperial mode' (1983: 14).[27] Applying this idea to the Jewish context, Adler writes that 'Our modern problem with halakhah is reflected in the failure of this equilibrium, in the unmediated gap between the impoverished imperial world we inhabit and the richer and more vital worlds that could be' (1998: 35). Feminist halakhah is at this time still functioning largely in a paideic mode; can its praxis evolve to a point where the paideic and imperial modes exist in a workable balance?

Once more, I turn to *berit ahuvim*, this time to illustrate this ongoing challenge. By now, there is readily available empirical evidence for the ways in which *berit ahuvim* is penetrating into and being used by the Jewish community. In published articles and on internet pages such as blogs and chat sites, individuals and couples have recorded their personal struggles over their dissatisfaction with the traditional form of the Jewish wedding ceremony, and their thoughts about the alternative forms such as *berit ahuvim* by which they might, or did, restructure their ceremonies. Some couples have adopted *berit ahuvim* as Adler designed it, while others have created their own alternatives to *kidushin*. Adler fully accepts that her ceremony need not be the only possible feminist halakhic alternative to *kidushin*. She acknowledges that mistakes will be made in the course of trying to bring a feminist halakhah into being and that some proposed innovations will be rejected (2007).[28] On the other hand, there are examples of couples who have incorporated some aspects of *berit ahuvim* into their ceremonies while also retaining more traditional forms that they do not feel ready to relinquish, particularly the statement of acquisition with the giving of a ring or rings.[29] Responding to this in an email, Adler admitted to being 'frustrated by people who don't understand the legal ramifications of the wedding ceremony'. Yet it may be the case that some women (and men) continue to choose to participate in traditional forms and rituals for reasons that are complex and personal. In a jointly authored consideration of their respective weddings, for example, Heather Altman (a Conservative rabbi) and Susan Sapiro (who worked at the time for Ma'yan, a Jewish feminist organization in New York City), explain their choices as follows:

Both of us decided to go ahead with the partnership ceremony in addition to the traditional kidushin. The partnership would come first, so in our eyes, it would be the marriage ceremony. The kidushin that would follow would be our homage to tradition ... In the eyes of halacha, however, the kidushin under the chuppah was the main event. In the end, while we both incorporated and made central the partnership aspect of our wedding ceremonies, through our adaptations of the B'rit Ahuvim, we still both decided to be acquired through kidushin/kinyan as part of the wedding. We allowed ourselves to be 'co-opted by the system' for a complex set of personal, historical, and halachic reasons. Sometimes the weight of tradition, as distasteful as it can be, is too difficult to abandon. (2005)

There is no mechanism by which a 'rigorous' form of *berit ahuvim* can, nor perhaps should, be enforced even among those who are attracted to its underlying narratives.

How, then, might we determine if *berit ahuvim* has succeeded as a workable alternative to *kidushin* and as a credible model of a revisioned halakhic process? Thomas Ross suggests that much depends on the criteria we use to make such a determination:

When feminist scholarship is measured by its converts and its connection to formal law reform, it is easy to dismiss the work as a failure. The converts seem few; the law is mostly unchanged. When feminist legal scholarship is seen as part of the maintenance of a normative community, the bases for judgment are more complex . . . By this work, feminist legal scholars have . . . altered the dominant discourse about women in today's culture and, thus, contributed to the surest form of meaningful legal reform. (1993: 119)

Ultimately, however, more than a change in discourse is demanded: 'The sympathetic outsider cannot simply see this as a rhetorical battle between the feminist and the State's apologists in which the sympathizer's explicit support for the feminist position is a full discharge of his responsibilities . . . The realization of a harder and more demanding choice begins to appear' (1993: 120). Further on he spells out the full import of this point:

Law is executed through commitment. Knowing this puts one in an uncomfortable position. It is difficult to imagine that one can profess an interpretive position and be free of the necessity to act on it. Interpretation without a willingness to act on that interpretation may be the derivation of meaning but it is not *legal* meaning. No law can exist without commitment. (1993: 131)

The question, then, is: if *berit ahuvim* cannot be enforced, what will ensure that it (or a credible alternative) will be observed? It is most fundamentally the community, in Adler's vision, that invests the halakhah with its authority. Yet it is far from a new or original insight that Jewish communities today generally have limited coercive—imperial—powers over their members. Individual rabbis or communities may be able to dictate which rituals and acts are acceptable or not within their own 'four *amot* (cubits)', but congregants who are dissatisfied with the options and restrictions presented to them can often readily choose to go elsewhere or to disaffiliate altogether. Certainly, for a feminist halakhah to exist and grow there must also exist a self-selecting community with a commitment to the (engendered) halakhah, the halakhic process, and to living halakhically.

The open question I would conclude with, then, is that of how this community will grow and develop, and how it will choose a convincing source or sources of authority in which to ground its practices and decision-making processes.[30]

In my interview with her, Rachel Adler stressed the importance of an educated community, a community whose members will have sufficient 'expertise' and a willingness to commit themselves to ongoing learning, so that they will be able to take responsibility for their religious lives, choices, and acts. Through her work, both in laying the theoretical ground for a feminist halakhah and in moving towards applied halakhah such as *berit ahuvim*, she suggests that it is the mutually reinforcing growth of both the halakhah and the community that would observe it, together, that will build the bridge to a well-established feminist halakhic praxis.

Notes

1   The tradition is then handed down to a series of men who transmit and elaborate the law in the homosocial environment of the rabbinic court and study house; see the rabbinic account of the transmission of revelation in Mishnah *Avot* 1: 1–12.

2   Moshe Zemer, too, makes this the first of his 'Principles and Criteria of Liberal Halakhah': 'The *halakhah* is a developmental and changing phenomenon' (1991: 12). It should also be noted that this modernist outlook can continue to incorporate the theological premise that Torah/halakhah is of divine origin, through the claim that divine revelation itself occurred in such a way as to make possible or even demand its ongoing development, as in the following from Alana Suskin: 'God deliberately gave us the Torah written ambiguously enough that we would need to interpret it . . . God wishes of us to move as a nation toward partnership, toward a more holy understanding of ourselves and the world, and so God created the language of the Torah in such a way that we would have to re-examine the precedents we have set as we developed' (2005: 376).

3   It may be for this reason that Shaul Magid suggests that the incorporation of egalitarianism into halakhic discourse is in fact a 'hypernomian', 'heretical' process, one that 'involves taking a step outside the halakhah in order to fulfill it'. He further writes, 'I propose that we view egalitarianism as a new dogma—that is . . . a foundation upon which halakhah can function. The underlying principle here is not halakhic and therefore cannot be justified solely by halakhic means. Rather, it is a redrawing of the boundaries of halakhic discourse on the basis of an ethical principle, one that I recognize as incompatible with the ethical world constructed by the rabbis' (2004: 190, 200). In a similar vein, the law professor Thomas Ross has written, 'Feminist legal scholars are engaged in the struggle to create an entirely new legal meaning . . . Their disagreement with the State is a disagreement of the most destabilizing sort. Feminist legal scholars deny the State's most basic assumptions about the law' (1993: 102).

4   Although Adler's ceremony will be my primary focus here, I will cite other examples as relevant. In particular, because it is the only other halakhic piece of writing I am currently aware of that explicitly employs the work of Robert Cover which also crucially informs Adler's approach (see below), I refer extensively to Gordon Tucker's 'Halakhic and Meta-halakhic Arguments Concerning Judaism and Homosexuality' (2006), originally submitted to (but not adopted by) the Committee on Jewish Law and Standards of the Rabbinic Assembly, the rabbinic organization of the Conservative/Masorti movement. My use of this particular responsum is not meant to suggest that a Coverian and feminist halakhah

could not come out of, or is not relevant to, other denominational or non-denominational perspectives; indeed, Adler herself identifies as Reform at the time of this writing.

5   In rabbinic law, the marital acquisition also gives the husband significant control over the wife's economic resources, including items she brings to the marriage, and what she acquires (for example through inheritance), earns, or produces during the marriage. In the modern era, civil law generally supersedes the provisions of halakhah in this area.

6   Indeed, variations of this latter point have figured in recent discussions in both the Reform and the Conservative movements regarding the permissibility and form of same-sex marriage. In 1997 the majority of the CCAR (Central Conference of American Rabbis) Responsa Committee ruled that 'a Reform rabbi should not officiate at a ceremony of marriage between two persons of the same gender, whether or not this ceremony is called by the name *qiddushin*', while a minority held that 'a Reform rabbi may officiate at a wedding or "commitment" ceremony for two homosexuals, although for important historical and theological reasons, that ceremony should perhaps not be called *qiddushin*' (1998: 5). Writing on behalf of the committee, Mark Washofsky explained,

> We do not understand Jewish marriage apart from the concept of *qiddushin*, and our interpretation of rabbinic authority does not embrace the power to 'sanctify' any relationship that cannot be *qiddushin* as its functional equivalent. For this reason, although a minority of us disagree, our majority believes that Reform rabbis should not officiate at ceremonies of marriage or 'commitment' for same-sex couples. (1998: 29)

> The Conservative Movement adopted a responsum in 2006 by Elliot N. Dorff, Daniel S. Nevins, and Avram I. Reisner (a counter-responsum by Joel Roth was adopted as well), sanctioning commitment ceremonies for same-sex partners, but here too the authors concluded:

> 'We are not prepared at this juncture to rule upon the halakhic status of gay and lesbian relationships. To do so would require establishing an entirely new institution in Jewish law that treats not only the ceremonies and legal instruments appropriate for creating homosexual unions but also the norms for the dissolution of such unions. This responsum does not provide *kidushin* for same-sex couples.' (Dorff et al. 2006)

> Note: all websites cited in this essay were accessible as of Sept. 2010.

7   Should she predecease him, he inherits her entire estate (although the rabbinic *ketubah* also includes provisions to pass property that she brought into the marriage to her sons, and not to any sons the husband might have from another woman).

Nearly all scholars who have written on this pledge, including Adler (1998: 175), take it as a form of deferred or transformed bride price. It may also be noted that bridal virginity is privileged in the *ketubah*; such a bride is pledged double the amount guaranteed to a widow or a woman otherwise presumed to be a non-virgin (see *Ket.* 1: 2 and 4); to this day, a *ketubah* typically records, with appropriate monetary arrangements, if the bride is previously unmarried, widowed, divorced, or a convert.

8   The Conservative movement, reacting to the ethical dilemma of punishing the child for an act of the parent, has an official position allowing a rabbi to ignore or suppress evidence of *mamzerut* when a Jewish couple seek to marry (Nevins 2002; Spitz 2002).

9   The Reform movement generally considers civil divorce sufficient to end the Jewish aspect of marriage as well, thereby obviating (within Reform communities) concerns of women becoming *agunot* or their children *mamzerim*. That being said, some Reform

rabbis do encourage couples to undergo the process of giving and receiving a *get*, and there have been proposed versions of a Reform divorce document.

10   The Conservative movement has been using a form of this method since the 1950s. More recently, variants have been accepted in some Orthodox communities as well.

11   These latter two are both accepted within the Conservative movement, and annulment in particular is regularly used by its Joint Bet Din. While proposals to use forms of annulment have also been made in Orthodox circles, these have been extremely controversial.

12   This quite possibly includes a ceremony in which the woman also presents a ring to the man and says the betrothal formula (with the gender changed accordingly) to him; there is more than one way within halakhic precedents to understand the status of the *kidushin* after the fact if such a formula is recited. One possibility is that the acquisition is cancelled, as it has rather become an exchange in which the woman has not actually gained anything of value in the transaction with which she could be acquired (some Orthodox authorities prohibit *any* giving of a ring by her to him in conjunction with the *kidushin*—some permit it at other points in the ceremony—for this reason or because of the possibility that onlookers will be misled as to the unilateral nature of *kidushin*). Alternatively, the significant act is his acquisition of her, while anything she says or does afterwards is legally irrelevant, and thus *kidushin* is established: 'Once the traditional formula has been recited the betrothal is binding, and whatever is added is of no legal significance (BT *Ned.* 87a).' (Klein 1979: 396).

13   This, it seems to me, is apart from the question of whether marriage or long-term monogamous partnerships (in whatever form) should be held out as the ideal (or even the only fully sanctioned) avenue for sexual expression and relationship, whether hetero- or homosexual, a challenge that has been raised (in the Jewish context) particularly by Levitt (1997: 98–103).

14   Tucker also provides an example of this process as he discusses the role and status of homosexuals in the halakhic Jewish community: 'hearing their stories is the analogue to the moment when Einstein got confirmation from his eclipse measurements that the venerated laws of Newton could not adequately explain all of the world. They are the proof that halakhah and its precedents, as they are presently constituted, are inadequate to account for the reality of committed Jews who know deeply in their hearts that they are not sinning when they love those whom they are capable of loving' (2006: 18).

15   David R. Blumenthal cogently intuits in his review what Adler confirmed in our interview—namely, that the processes of articulating the theological and halakhic underpinnings for the ceremony and the ceremony itself were inextricably entwined: 'In Chapter 5 [where *berit ahuvim* is discussed], Adler sets about *what she intended all along*' (1999: 116, emphasis added).

16   Tucker advocates and applies this process as well:

> So the narrative, the *aggadah*, must be looked to carefully, and it must be connected to genuine Jewish narrative. I have detailed above the personal and compelling stories of Jewish gays and lesbians, and they are in and of themselves an 'aggadic' source that can claim status within a Halakhic method. But there is still much value in being able to root these stories in the soil of classical *aggadah*. (2006: 28)

This, then, is one of the places in which Adler parts company with many other advocates of a liberal halakhah, who retain a more limited conception of what materials may legitimately be brought into halakhic discourse. Note, for example, the way in which Mark Washofsky privileges a very particular kind of precedent even in the liberal context: 'If we describe what we are doing as *halakhah*, then the way we do it must fit the contours of that centuries-old rabbinical practice. If there is no law—or *halakhah*—without precedent, then liberal *halakhah*, too, must take precedent seriously' (Washofsky 2002: 50). Along these lines, Tamar Ross expresses the concern that 'Cover's image of law as a bridge applies not only to where the law is going, but also to where it is coming from . . . Adler's contrasting emphasis . . . disregards the fact that these standards and rules do control . . . the nature of the bridge that is to be formed' (2004: 156).

17   This move is one of the more controversial aspects of Adler's work on this topic. As Blumenthal writes,

> Adler asserts the value of the stormy, indeed abusive, image of covenanted marriage of Hosea, denying thereby the affirmation of God as the Abuser . . . It seems to me that if God is depicted as wishing, or encouraging, the gang-rape of his bride, Israel, then God has a problem. One must admit the problem and confront the abusiveness of God as directly as tradition and spiritual courage allow—especially if one is to assert the value of this metaphor. (1999: 117)

However, see also Susannah Heschel's review, in which she observes: 'Labeling the texts as pornography or calling God an abuser, as others have done, does not explain why the prophetic literature has inspired so many powerful movements of social justice' (1999: 475).

18   As both Adler and Levitt remark, the Palestinian documents are also notable in that they give the bride or her appointed representatives a voice in the documentary language (Adler 1998: 179–80; Levitt 1997: 178).

19   In this way, Adler's ceremony also realizes one of Ochs's suggestions in her 'Characteristics of the New Rituals of Jewish Women', namely, 'allowing for improvisation and personalization'. Perhaps, however, Adler's ceremony also somewhat counters Ochs's claim that this characteristic has developed because 'most new women's rituals are not meant to change or challenge laws or be legally binding' (Ochs 2007: 49).

20   At first glance, then, the *ketubah* might seem like a counter-model; however, Levitt's observation that the bride is not a direct party to it, discussed above, might be telling in this regard, as would be the fact that the *ketubah* has developed a single standardized form in Jewish practice.

21   In addition to the critique about to be discussed, one may also note here the questions raised by Susan Moller Okin (1990: 665): 'Is Pateman using "women" and "men" as defined by patriarchy? Surely she must be, but then what does she mean by suggesting that it cannot "be otherwise"? . . . Or can changes be made in the structure and expectations of both the workplace and the family such that men and women can become equal as spouses, as parents, and as workers?'

22   Indeed, this phrase is incorporated into the title of the chapter that outlines *berit ahuvim*.

23   One additional possibility that Adler does not address is a ceremony in which the participants 'invert' the standard formula into a personal statement of change in one's own status, that is, some variant of 'I consecrate myself to you with this ring' (a form that has been deemed explicitly to be ineffective for creating *kidushin* in the rabbinic and halakhic

tradition: Tosefta *Kid.* 1: 1; BT *Kid.* 5*b*; *Mishneh torah*, 'Laws of Marriage' 3: 1–2, 6). See Greenstein (2009).

24   A similar sentiment is also expressed on p. 193. A question that arises in this context is that of romantic commitments between people coming from within the Jewish community, and thus potentially bound by its values and practices, and those who do not—that is, intermarriages—and whether the community and halakhah can accommodate them. Adler herself has participated in the adaptation of *berit ahuvim* for such a ceremony (2004).

25   Washofsky describes how already existing precedents in halakhic sources equally allow for a decisor to either invalidate or accept a marriage ceremony that does not conform to standard *kidushin*:

> One approach denies any validity whatsoever to these wedding ceremonies, on the grounds that they do not conform to the rules that define the contracting of Jewish marriage (*kidushin*). A conflicting approach recognizes these ceremonies as halakhically valid . . . because the rule of common-knowledge testimony . . . establishes the evident desire of the Jewish couple to live together legally as husband and wife, and that desire is sufficient evidence to the intent to form a valid Jewish marriage. (2004: 37)

Thus, I believe Blumenthal's critique of Adler on this point somewhat misses the mark. He writes:

> It seems to me more than naive for Adler to think that the rabbinic halakhic culture will accept her proposal as a non-halakhic form of marriage for the sake of saving the collective Israel. The men who dominate that culture, be they modern Orthodox or *haredi*, are, by Adler's own analysis, more likely to opt for stubborn resistance than to yield power to women on the issue of the role and place of women in the patriarchal household. (1999: 117)

I do not think that Adler necessarily expects that 'rabbinic halakhic culture will accept her proposal as a non-halakhic form of marriage' (she, of course, would consider it to be fully halakhic within her revisioned system); rather, she recognizes that it is possible within their own system for them to evaluate it as something other than *kidushin*, and therefore insists that *they* bear the responsibility for the choice to instead impose the definition of *kidushin* (and hence the requirement for a *get*) on the relationship.

26   Law-killing, i.e. activity that limits what will be considered viable interpretative possibilities in a given legal debate going forward.

27   It is worth noting, though, that slightly further on Cover writes of the paideic mode that 'its primary psychological motif is attachment', and of the imperial that 'its primary psychological motif is separation' (1983: 16). He thus remarks in note 43, 'I am tempted at least to invite comparison between the psychological dimension of the paideic/imperial distinction and the differences some scholars have suggested exist between male and female psychologies of moral development', referencing in particular Carol Gilligan (1982). Marie Ashe observes that Cover 'does not yield to the temptation' and ponders 'What if he had done so? Is Cover suggesting that his paideic/imperial distinction corresponds to a male/female distinction? Or is he suggesting the opposite? Would further inquiry into Gilligan's work have perhaps disturbed *N&N*'s model of jurisgenesis?' (2006: 28).

28   Note also Ochs's comments on ritual innovations: 'I needed to recognize that even clumsy or misguided efforts held redemptive possibility—if only for the innovator. Less successful ritual practices would fade away. Even the innovations that were misguided, even crude or tasteless, would not destroy "the whole thing". Neither the endurance of a new ritual nor rabbinic approval defined its success' (2007: 13).

29   See the example in Ochs 2007: 243–4.

30   Thus, one final avenue by which some have critiqued Adler's approach to reconstructing halakhah has been to point to the relative absence of a role for the Divine that it entails. Tamar Ross, for example, makes the claim that 'A halakhic narrative that completely dispenses with transcendence (mythic or otherwise) and leaves all its interpretation's claims to authority up to contemporary communal life and its interpretive ingenuity will inevitably lose its fervor and passion—and the reason for its existence' (Ross 2004: 161). It is indeed worth noting that the words 'command', 'commandment', or 'commandedness' do not appear in Adler's index to *Engendering Judaism*, nor does 'mitzvah'.

      One can continue to experience a commanding God within the framework of a feminist, progressive halakhah. A not uncommon approach is to assert that the growth and development of halakhah is itself part of God's will, built into the nature of God's revelation.

References

ADLER, RACHEL. 1973. 'Tumah and Tahara-Mikveh'. In Richard Seigel, Michael Strassfeld, and Sharon Strassfeld, eds., *The Jewish Catalog*, 167–71. Philadelphia.

——1983a. 'The Jew Who Wasn't There: Halakha and the Jewish Woman'. In Susannah Heschel, ed., *On Being a Jewish Feminist*, 12–18. New York.

——1983b. 'I've Had Nothing Yet, So I Can't Take More', *Moment*, 8(8) (Sept.): 22–6.

——1993. 'In Your Blood, Live: Re-Visions of a Theology of Purity'. *Tikkun*, 8(1) (Jan.–Feb.): 38–41.

——1998. *Engendering Judaism: An Inclusive Theology and Ethics*. Philadelphia.

——2001. 'Innovation and Authority: A Feminist Reading of the "Women's Minyan" Responsum'. In Walter Jacob and Moshe Zemer, eds., *Gender Issues in Jewish Law: Essays and Responsa*, vol. v, pp. 3–32. New York.

——2004. '"To Live Outside the Law, You Must Be Honest"—Boundaries, Borderlands and the Ethics of Cultural Negotiation'. *The Reconstructionist*, 68(2): 4–15.

——2007. Interview with Gail Labovitz, 12 Nov. 2007. Los Angeles.

ALTMAN, HEATHER, and SUSAN SAPIRO. 2005. 'Acquiring Equality'. <http://www.ritualwell.org/lifecycles/intimacypartnering/Jewishweddingscommitmentceremonies/sitefolder.2005-06-07.5921979856/AcquiringEquality.xml>, accessed 16 Nov. 2008.

ANDERSON, ELIZABETH S. 1990. 'Women and Contracts: No New Deal'. *Michigan Law Review*, 88 (May): 1792–1810.

ASHE, MARIE. 2006. 'Beyond "Nomos and Narrative": Unconverted Antinomianism in the Work of Susan Howe'. *Yale Journal of Law and Feminism*, 18(1): 1–59.

BLUMENTHAL, DAVID R. 1999. 'Constructive Feminist Theology and Reflective Self-Critique: A Male Reading of Rachel Adler and Laura Levitt'. *AJS Review*, 24(1): 111–19.

BOROWITZ, EUGENE B. 1991. *Renewing the Covenant: A Theology for the Postmodern Jew*. Philadelphia.

CCAR Responsa Committee. 1998. 'On Homosexual Marriage'. *CCAR Journal: A Reform Jewish Quarterly*, 45(1): 5–35; also available at <http://data.ccarnet.org/cgi-bin/resp disp.pl?file=8&year=5756>.

COVER, ROBERT. 1983. 'The Supreme Court 1982 Term—Foreword: Nomos and Narrative'. *Harvard Law Review*, 97(4): 4–68.

DORFF, ELLIOT N., DANIEL S. NEVINS, and AVRAM I. REISNER. 2006. 'Homosexuality, Human Dignity and Halakhah: A Combined Responsum for the Committee on Jewish Law and Standards'. <http://www.rabbinicalassembly.org/docs/Dorff_Nevins_Reisner_Final.pdf>, accessed 16 Nov. 2008.

FRIEDMAN, MORDECHAI AKIVA. 1980–1. *Jewish Marriage in Palestine: A Cairo Geniza Study*, 2 vols. Tel Aviv.

FRYMER-KENSKY, TIKVA. 2006. 'The Feminist Challenge to Halakhah'. *Studies in Bible and Feminist Criticism*, 263–81. Philadelphia.

GILLIGAN, CAROL. 1982. *In a Different Voice*. Cambridge, Mass.

GREENSTEIN, DAVID. 2009. 'Equality and Sanctity: Rethinking Jewish Marriage in Theory and in Ceremony', *G'vanim*, 5/1: 1–35.

HESCHEL, SUSANNAH. 1999. Untitled review. *Journal of the American Academy of Religion*, 67(2): 473–6.

KLEIN, ISAAC. 1979. *Guide to Jewish Religious Practice*. New York.

LEVITT, LAURA. 1997. *Jews and Feminism: The Ambivalent Search for Home*. New York.

MAGID, SHAUL. 2004. 'Is Egalitarianism Heresy? Rethinking Gender on Margins of Judaism'. *Nashim*, 8 (Fall): 189–229.

NEVINS, DANIEL S. 2002. 'A Concurring Opinion Regarding Mamzerut'. In Kassel Abelson and David J. Fine, eds., *Responsa 1991–2000: The Committee on Jewish Law and Standards of the Conservative Movement*, 587–92. New York.

OCHS, VANESSA. 2007. *Inventing Jewish Ritual*. Philadelphia.

OKIN, SUSAN MOLLER. 1990. 'Feminism, the Individual, and Contract Theory'. *Ethics*, 100(3): 658–69.

OZICK, CYNTHIA. 1983. 'Notes Towards Finding the Right Question'. In Susannah Heschel, ed., *On Being a Jewish Feminist*, 120–51. New York.

PATEMAN, CAROLE. 1988. *The Sexual Contract*. Stanford.

PLASKOW, JUDITH. 1983. 'The Right Question Is Theological'. In Susannah Heschel, ed., *On Being a Jewish Feminist*, 223–33. New York.

ROSS, TAMAR. 2004. *Expanding the Palace of Torah: Orthodoxy and Feminism*. Lebanon, NH.

ROSS, THOMAS. 1993. 'Despair and Redemption in the Feminist Nomos'. *Indiana Law Journal*, 69(102), 101–36.

SPITZ, ELIE. 2002. 'Mamzerut'. In Kassel Abelson and David J. Fine, eds., *Responsa 1991–2000: The Committee on Jewish Law and Standards of the Conservative Movement*, 558–86. New York.

STEINBERG, JONAH. 1997. 'From a "Pot of Filth" to a "Hedge of Roses" (and Back): Changing Theorizations of Menstruation in Judaism'. *Journal of Feminist Studies in Religion*, 13(2): 5–26.

SUSKIN, ALANA. 2005. 'A Feminist Theory of Halakhah'. In Elliot N. Dorff, ed., *The Unfolding Tradition: Jewish Law After Sinai*. 368–89. New York.

TUCKER, GORDON. 2006. 'Halakhic and Metahalakhic Arguments Concerning Judaism and Homosexuality'; available at <http://www.rabbinicalassembly.org/docs/Tucker_paper.pdf>.

WASHOFSKY, MARK. 2002. 'Taking Precedent Seriously: On Halakhah as a Rhetorical Practice'. In Walter Jacob and Moshe Zemer, eds., *Re-Examining Progressive Halakhah*, 1–70. New York.

——2004. 'Against Method: Liberal *Halakhah* between Theory and Practice'. In Walter Jacob, ed., *Beyond the Letter of the Law: Essays on Diversity in the Halakhah in Honor of Moshe Zemer*, 17–77. Pittsburgh.

ZEMER, MOSHE. 1991. 'Authority and Criteria in Liberal *Halakhah*'. In Walter Jacob and Moshe Zemer, eds., *Progressive Halakhah: Essence and Application*, 9–23. Tel Aviv.

Same-Sex Marriage Ceremonies in a Time of Coalescence

VANESSA L. OCHS

JEWISH CEREMONIES[1] uniting same-sex couples in marriage have been going on fairly quietly, almost beneath the radar of public awareness, for about forty years. Until recently, the majority of couples used the term 'commitment cere-mony' to describe the celebration of their partnership, 'an appellation', accord-ing to Rabbi Elizabeth Tikvah Sarah, that has 'entered into public discourse to describe a new phenomenon in the lives of lesbian and gay people: the public declaration of a couple's commitment to one another' (2000: 125). The cere-monies have also been referred to less frequently with the terms 'union service', 'covenant of love' (*berit ahavah*), 'sanctification of love' (*kidush ahavah*), or 'coven-ant of friendship' (*berit re'ut*). All of these terms point to a distinction, made either by the couple or by their community, between same-sex and traditional heterosex-ual Jewish weddings. Of late, in those places where the former have been accorded equal or similar status to the latter in civil law, and in a period when this practice is becoming more socially familiar, same-sex couples have been likely to refer to their ceremonies as weddings, announcing, 'We're getting married!'

This changing nomenclature, with its multiple variations, suggests a cere-mony still in flux, and reflects significant interfamilial, personal, cultural, reli-gious, and legal negotiations taking place behind the scenes. The name chosen might reflect the particular way in which a couple wish their ceremony to present their personal situation to the public: their own positive or negative associations with the institution of marriage, whether it sanctifies an enduring relationship of many years, whether their families endorse their union, or whether the couple plan to raise a family. It may reflect how they, their rabbi, and their Jewish com-munity perceive a same-sex wedding: whether they see it as analogous to other Jewish weddings or distinct from them. Finally, the name may depend upon who in the wedding party is speaking, reflecting their level of comfort, from a social or religious perspective, with the proceedings. Douglas Wythe and Andre Merling chronicle the discussion they had when they met Rabbi Liz Bolton, who would perform their 1996 ceremony, when she asked them what term they would be using:

'It depends on who you ask,' I answered enigmatically.

'You each call it something different?'

'No—not us! My parents. Sometimes my mother calls it a wedding. Lately she calls it a commitment ceremony . . . My father has always called it a commitment ceremony. For Doug and me, it's a wedding.' (Wythe et al. 2004: 134)

Whatever they are called, such ceremonies bring to the minds of the couple, the officiant, the guests, and even the hired staff that the rights of same-sex couples to engage in legal partnerships and to enjoy the same privileges and benefits as heterosexual couples have been and remain a matter of often-vociferous debate. This debate is taking place in state and national courts of law, among clerics, in the public square, and, no need to mention, as intimate and often wrenching conversations within families. There remains an awareness that even when same-sex marriages *can* be conducted as religious rituals, they 'rarely', as Mark D. Jordan claims, 'bring automatic civil entitlements' (2006: 17) such as health care benefits, inheritance benefits, parental rights, pensions, tax benefits, health care proxies, hospital visitation, and family leave policies.

In this transitional period, such ceremonies may be perceived as radical and transformative gestures with a potential to challenge the status quo on a governmental level and to continue to expand the rights and dignities of Jews who are gay within Jewish communities. This remains the case even when a ceremony's novelty is consciously and strategically suppressed, when its continuity with tradition is highlighted, and when it is presided over by clergy who have been fully endorsed by their denominations to do so.

My goal here is to depict emerging same-sex wedding ceremonies in the United States, noting the legal and religious contexts where they are relevant. While I distinguish between two models of ceremony, traditional and reconstructed, it will quickly become apparent that they are hard to keep apart at this moment when coalescence, or the development of a stable format, is still underway. Indeed, such blurring and overlapping between distinct approaches and the ideologies they may represent is precisely characteristic of rituals in a phase of coalescence. For a guest at a wedding, the distinctions may be hard to detect; possibly the only way one knows if the ceremony is traditional or reconstructed is by reading the wedding booklet the couple has prepared, which offers clues, explaining the *kavanah* (intention) behind texts, acts, and objects. I conclude my analysis by noting a fairly recent innovation, one in which heterosexual couples create ritualized ways in their wedding ceremonies to express their dismay at, and offer protest against, the fact that in the majority of places, same-sex couples do not enjoy full rights to marry in either the civil or religious sphere.

A New Script Reflecting Political Change

A Jewish same-sex ceremony resembles a heterosexual wedding in that it is a ritual with witnesses, based upon a script that allows for personalization. The script includes set and improvised Hebrew and English texts to be spoken and sung, as well as actions that are to be carried out by various participants, involving simple or elaborate choreographies. Finally, it features certain Jewish wedding-related objects that have become iconic: there will probably be a *ḥupah* (wedding canopy), a *ketubah* (wedding contract), wedding rings, wine for drinking, a glass to be broken, and a concluding feast that is likely to include music and dancing. Unscripted, but anticipated, are the feelings and energies brought by all who have assembled on that day. Consistent with other Jewish ceremonies, the wedding invokes diverse moods, highlights Jewish values and responsibilities, links the present to memories of the past, and connects the couple to other Jewish couples. Its script establishes responsibilities for the officiant, the couple, and the witnesses that extend into the future, and certifies that a sacred rite of passage is being performed: the two people who enter the ceremony as single individuals will leave as being bound to each other, their love for each other will be celebrated and acknowledged, and their commitment to create a Jewish home for themselves and any children they may have is made public.

Any wedding ceremony only seems to begin once the guests have arrived and the couple are walking down the aisle; it only seems to end when the last guests leave after the reception. In reality, the ceremony begins with all the preparations beforehand and winds down only after the couple has gathered and assembled the photographs and videos that will be their keepsakes and have found places for all the gifts they have received. Same-sex arrangements are furthermore likely to include assessing the viability of the available wedding script, fashioning a new one, evaluating its success, and passing it on to other couples (usually over the internet) who might adapt it as their own. Since it is a relatively new practice that has yet to become standardized, the celebrants (along with their officiant, who may be clergy or a lay ritual expert) often find themselves actively fashioning and selecting the ritual components of their ceremony, using sources gay and straight, religious and secular, Jewish and non-Jewish.

Thus, a distinguishing feature of Jewish same-sex ceremonies is that the script is so new that it is possible that the officiant, the couple, and the guests at a given ceremony are all encountering or performing such a script for the first time. Novelty in a familiar life-cycle ritual can be refreshing, breaking down the dulling effects of routinization, but it can also be jarring, distracting, or unnerving, and sage officiants devise ways, often through words of introduction and side comments, to prepare those who have assembled, thereby reducing their discomfort.

Keys to understanding the personal meanings behind the ritual choices woven into the script are often found in the couple's wedding booklet, which is distributed as guests enter so that they have time to peruse it. For both straight and gay Jewish couples, carefully written, lovingly crafted, and hotly debated wedding booklets often serve not just as a 'playbill' for the event, but also as a liturgical script and as a primer for guests unfamiliar with Jewish weddings of any kind at all. They will also demonstrate, either overtly or between the lines, how the couple, straight or gay, liberal or Orthodox, has wrestled with older Jewish wedding practices and revised them so that they reflect contemporary sensibilities, political convictions, and the desire to have one's ceremony express one's individuality.

No Jewish couple is likely to invent the contents of their wedding booklet *de novo*. Typically they will consult booklets from other people's weddings or commitment ceremonies and they will select those parts they find appealing, touching, and appropriate. They will also turn to websites such as www.ritualwell.org and consult guides to popular creative or new Jewish weddings, the most ubiquitous being Anita Diamant's *The New Jewish Wedding*. The borrowings usually come without attribution, suggesting that appealing and successful new Jewish ritual innovations enter the cultural vocabulary as items of tradition belonging freely to all.

The booklets of same-sex weddings can persuade those present that the new ceremony has sufficient authoritative power to render it viable. In other words, the booklets serve to convince guests, who cannot rely upon their own cultural memory, that what they are about to see and hear is a legitimate, authentic Jewish ceremony. As I have explained in my book, *Inventing Jewish Ritual*, this provides a possibility for forming a temporarily cohesive witnessing community that stands in harmonious relationship to Jewish practices of the past.

The 2004 wedding booklet of Mara Benjamin and Miryam Kabakov announces in its note of welcome: 'Many of you have never participated in a lesbian or gay wedding, and we suspect that even fewer have ever been to a Jewish lesbian wedding. Today is an opportunity for us all to participate in a new ritual based on customs going back two thousand years' (2004).

References to a still unfolding backdrop of both civic and religious change can be quite overt, as in the case of the 1996 wedding of Katherine Simon and Inbal Kashtan, which Kashtan has chronicled. As one of the guests wrote to the couple after the wedding, 'I get it now . . . It wasn't just a wedding; it was a political rally' (2003: 149). The political backdrop was also made explicit in Benjamin and Kabakov's booklet: 'As our wedding takes place on the thirty-fifth anniversary of the gay pride movement, we acknowledge our gratitude for the many brave souls who have . . . given us the courage to declare publicly our commitment to each other' (2004). They wanted to be sure their guests understood that even though they would be married, they were vulnerable in this time of political flux: 'Recognizing that there have been important gains in equal recognition of same-sex couples, these have not yet resulted in widespread or uniform protection. We have thus worked with an attorney to draw up wills and healthcare proxies to make each other our legal next-of-kin' (2004).

Messages concerning equal rights under the law, both civil and religious, can be detected even when many couples claim that they have not made 'any conscious effort to inject political meanings into their ritual', as Kathleen Hull, author of the interview-based contemporary study *Same-Sex Marriage: The Cultural Politics of Love and Law*, explains (Hull 2006: 56).

Against the Backdrop of Other Rituals Reflecting Change

Same-sex ceremonies are not the only Jewish innovation of the contemporary period reflecting a complex political backdrop. Innovative rituals that have concerned women in particular, such as holding naming ceremonies for baby girls or drawing up *ketubot* with clauses that protect women in the event of a divorce, have all been influenced by the Women's Movement and the consequent legal protections that were achieved for women and girls, such as the right to have an abortion or provisions for maternity leave. But with the exception of feminist Passover Seders, which are generally overt in declaring their political agenda, the new rituals addressing the history of women's exclusion do *not* tend to draw attention to this underlying content. If anything, as they become established, they are presented as being timelessly traditional and are, hence, experienced thus; a conscious strategy that augments their capacity to evoke the desirable aura of what is often experienced as 'authenticity'. A young person who grew up with, say, baby-naming ceremonies for girls and bat mitzvahs might well assume that these (along with female rabbis and cantors) had been Jewish practices all along.

By contrast, Jewish same-sex ceremonies *do* typically disclose the political struggles to achieve legal, social, and spiritual legitimacy. As I have suggested, some do it overtly and pointedly; some simply by virtue of being held and celebrated. And they often go a step beyond by being calls to communal action—either a gentle nudge towards awareness or a clarion call to organize. They reflect the dramatic social change that is taking place outside and inside the Jewish community, as Mark D. Jordan points out: even in the absence, in a given ritual, of naming past injustices or offering rebuke, same-sex ceremonies are 'acts of social reform' because they 'protest against the assumption that queer couples need to be *given* equality as a liberal concession or to be *welcomed* as if for the first time' (2006: 153).

Coalescence

Despite the struggles of same-sex couples ongoing in the civic and religious realms, and despite the continued existence of settings in which they do not enjoy social acceptance, full legal (civic or religious) equality, or the experience that their human dignity is being fully honoured, there is, as I have suggested, evidence that at this moment, same-sex Jewish commitment ceremonies are achieving a state of coalescence. Whether the ceremonies are judged negatively (as jarring, clumsy, dangerous, blasphemous, or disrespectful of tradition) or positively (as daring, seemingly natural, of a piece with tradition, holy, or authentic), they are certainly no longer perceived as experiments or nonce rituals. Like other new practices of the contemporary period that have gained a following and that exhibit signs of achieving some permanence, they have been 'collected, published (and) promulgated' (Goldstein 2009: 89) by laypeople and community professionals (rabbis, cantors, educators, and freelance ritual experts). The question remains: if we can imagine a future time when same-sex Jewish couples that choose to wed do not face discrimination, what will their ceremonies look like? Will they contain vestiges of the creative struggle with the marriage ritual now going on, or will signs of such engagement fall away?

Same-sex Jewish couples creating their own ceremonies today know there is effort involved in arriving at one that feels authentic to them (although many heterosexual Jewish couples, particularly those coming from different religious or ethnic backgrounds, would say the same—see Ochs 2007: 215–49). While same-sex Jewish couples may feel that they are 'reinventing the wheel', this is no longer necessary, for there are now more resources, more experts (even wedding planners), and more memories of what did and did not work at other ceremonies. As Melanie Kohler Levav and Hope Berger Levav described the process of planning their August 2000 wedding:

We had a great deal of work to do in order to get to that day, as Jewish tradition doesn't offer many models for a marriage between two women. With the guidance of our rabbi, the support of friends, a thick binder filled with copies of ceremonies we'd collected, and knowledge gained from our attendance at about a dozen gay and straight weddings in the previous years, we embarked on a wonderful journey that culminated in our wedding day. (2001: 11)

While the scripts for these ceremonies are still mainly available as copied pages passed around among friends, as forwarded electronic files, or as collections accessible at centres and websites for ritual innovation,[2] they are beginning to acquire a more stable format. They are being prepared for inclusion in rabbinic manuals, a clear indication of their acceptance as conventional vehicles of tradition, worthy of being part of the canon. One such preliminary document is the Reform movement's 500-page publication entitled *Kulanu: All of Us. A Program for Implementing Gay and Lesbian Inclusion*, which contains services for same-sex commitment, marriage ceremonies, and a prayer for the transitioning of genders (Address et al. 2007).

Soon, when a couple asks, 'What is the official Jewish same-sex wedding ceremony?' there may well be a far more limited range of answers, particularly as scripts are now integrating within them aspects of the two different models available, which I discuss below. Stability, of course, does not mean rigidity: there is still much latitude for individualization, a characteristic of wedding ceremonies in general and of new and refashioned contemporary rituals.

Historical Context

Same-sex Jewish ceremonies have been performed since the 1970s. With the publication of compilations of commitment ceremonies such as Elizabeth Resnick Levine's 1991 *A Ceremony Sampler: New Rites, Celebrations and Observances of Jewish Women*, they were still far from commonplace, but many American Jews could at least say, regardless of their approval from the perspective of Jewish law or their own comfort level, that they were aware that such new ceremonies were taking place.

If Jewish ceremonies for same-sex couples initially provoked shock, disbelief, anger, or disgust, the growing response in the current period appears to be curiosity, interest, and acceptance. For the sake of comparison, it might be useful to recall other Jewish ritual practices that have recently undergone similar processes of coalescence before achieving greater acceptance. In order of their emergence, these include: bat mitzvahs, Rosh Hodesh celebrations for women, ceremonies of welcome for baby girls, rabbinic ordination for women, prayer groups for Orthodox women, Miriam's cup at the Passover Seder, and shared liturgical leadership for women and men in Orthodox settings.

When studying same-sex ceremonies, we must recognize that the traditional heterosexual Jewish wedding has also been undergoing transformation during the very same period of time, roughly since the 1970s to the present, with a political backdrop of its own.[3] If more gay couples are open to Jewish commitment ceremonies now, it is not just because early debates among gay activists which opposed the heterosexual marriage model as a desirable social structure have been resolved in favour of the feasibility of marriage. It is also because the Jewish heterosexual marriage ceremony has itself been challenged and transformed, and is consequently more appealing. Certainly in America, there are few heterosexual Jewish couples, aside from the strictly Orthodox, who tend to allow their rabbis to stipulate how a 'traditional' Jewish wedding ought to be done without some conversation and input. With or without rabbinic guidance, with wisdom gleaned from their own Jewish study or from Anita Diamant's guide, and with the booklets saved from weddings they have attended, they make decisions. How will they enact elements of the ceremony stipulated by Jewish law? Where is there latitude so they can emphasize ritual practices that feel ethical and moving to them or omit or de-emphasize those practices that might be annoying?[4] How can they add a personal touch? I have observed that most couples, entering into the debate buoyed by the spirit of invention, do not fret that their custom designs will endanger the continuity of Jewish wedding traditions or render their own ritual illegitimate. This new Jewish wedding, while still evolving, has become a commonplace alternative. In fact, a guest who is not well-learned in Jewish practice may just assume that there is a tradition, for instance, for *both* members of the couple to circle around the other one under the *ḥupah* and to break a glass. These two new practices that have become more established are examples of ways in which, as Rabbi Elizabeth Tikvah Sarah explains, outward forms of tradition are kept while the early model of the man's acquisition of his bride is replaced by a contemporary Western model of 'marriage as a loving partnership formed in the presence of God' (2000: 141).

Before embarking on my exposition and analysis, I offer a brief synopsis of the relevant aspects of the simultaneously unfolding political and religious backdrops, in so far as they may illuminate the emerging ceremonies.

The Legal Backdrop

Today several countries acknowledge same-sex unions to differing extents. At the time of writing, these include Argentina, Belgium, Canada, Iceland, Norway, Sweden, the Netherlands, and Spain. Countries endorsing some form of same-sex civil partnership include Australia, Britain, Denmark, France, Finland, Germany, Hungary, Liechtenstein, New Zealand, Portugal, South Africa, and Sweden. In Israel the Supreme Court, in a majority ruling in November 2006, ordered the government to recognize same-sex marriages performed abroad, just as it recognized unions of Jews and non-Jews outside Israel. Such same-sex households have, thus, been acknowledged as legal entities in Israel, meaning that couples are accorded certain tax benefits and the right to adopt. This decision has raised the ire of Israeli Orthodox religious parties.

In the United States same-sex marriages are at present legal in Massachusetts (the first, in 2003), Connecticut, Iowa, Maine, Vermont, and New Hampshire (as of January 2010). They were briefly performed in California (between June and November 2008); since Proposition 8 was upheld in 2008 in a contentious vote, they have no longer been possible. Legal unions (alternatively called civil unions) of same-sex couples are currently allowed in Colorado, Hawaii, Maryland, Nevada, New Jersey, Oregon, Washington, Wisconsin, and the District of Columbia.

The countries and states listed above are few and exceptional, and, while their number will surely increase in the near future, generally the legitimacy of same-sex unions is still denied or vigorously opposed, most often by those who claim that the only form of marriage that is legitimate, natural, or deserving social sanction is that between one man and one woman. In 2008 in America, citizens in over twenty-six states proposed constitutional amendments that would restrict marriage to a union between a man and a woman and assert that all other arrangements are not only aberrations, but also threaten the legitimacy of marriage as an institution. Even where same-sex unions have been successfully established by law, the rights and protections that should theoretically be provided for couples have not been uniformly ensured. In New Jersey, for instance, where the State Supreme Court has mandated that gay couples in civil unions are to receive the same rights and benefits as heterosexual couples, many companies were still refusing, in 2007, to extend health benefits to same-sex partners, according to a report in the *New York Times*.[5] While civil unions may ensure rights and protections, they do not, as gay rights advocates have noted, offer the same social sanction as marriage does.

The Religious Backdrop

Interest in investigating how gay and lesbian couples can proclaim and sanctify their partnerships in a Jewish context has been expressed by individual rabbis, the movements to which they belong, members of such movements, unaffiliated Jews, and Jews in interfaith relationships. This widespread interest parallels that among Christian communities. Laurie Goodstein reported in the *New York Times* on 30 January 2004 that Christian churches currently permitting commitment ceremonies for gay couples include the Unitarian Universalists, the Disciples of Christ, the United Church of Christ, and the Metropolitan Community of Churches. The Episcopal Church allows individual dioceses to perform commitment ceremonies and the Presbyterian Church allows the ceremonies provided they are not called marriage.

The most recent debates within American Jewish communities, while rancorous and long lasting, have ultimately yielded outcomes reflecting a desire to treat homosexual relationships with respect and on an equal par with heterosexual ones. This is currently the attitude of all denominations, with the exception of Orthodoxy. According to Rabbi Steven Greenberg, himself a gay Orthodox rabbi, Orthodox Judaism is 'essentially unequivocal in its condemnation of same-sexual expression . . . and representative bodies have vehemently protested the adaptation of same-sex marriages' (2006: 82). Greenberg believes that while halakhah clearly identifies same-sex marriages as a forbidden practice, Orthodox rabbis may eventually reconsider their policies, for one, because there is now greater gay visibility within the Orthodox community, and secondly, because Orthodox mental-health professionals are no longer treating homosexuality as a mental illness that can be cured. In certain Orthodox communities, an increase in educational programmes and in the public discussion of homosexuality in a compassionate light as a biological fact and not a personal social choice has led to greater awareness and, with it, understanding, if not acceptance. The widely shown and discussed film *Trembling Before G-d*, which features Rabbi Greenberg, has been one such educational vehicle for much reflection in Orthodox communities. This documentary tells the personal stories of gay and lesbian Jews, both open and closeted, who are struggling to reconcile their strong attachment to Orthodox Judaism and their sexual identities. According to the film's website,[6] in the five years since Rabbi Greenberg and the film's director, Sandi Simcha DuBowski, started touring with the film around the world, it has reached more than 8 million people who have attended screening parties, debates, and discussion groups and have been exposed to a campaign that would foster a greater welcome to gays in Jewish life.

Deliberations within the Reform and Conservative movements have eventually generated support for same-sex unions, either as a mandate or an option. Thus, on 29 March 2000, the Central Conference of American Rabbis (CCAR) adopted a resolution that the relationships of Jewish same-sex couples not only could, but also should be affirmed by Reform clergy in a Jewish ritual along these lines (at that point, no specific practice was suggested or mandated). Their president, Rabbi Eric Yoffie, asserted that he, as an individual, supported the resolution

because of my belief that our gay and lesbian children, relatives, and friends are in great need of spiritual support; that the Torah's prohibition of homosexuality can reasonably be understood as a general condemnation of ancient cultic practice; that loving, permanent homosexual relationships, once difficult to conceive, are now recognized as an indisputable reality; and that in these relationships, whether or not we see them as 'marriages', it is surely true that God and holiness can be present. I know that many disagree. But whatever one thinks on the commitment ceremony question, I assume that we will respect those who believe otherwise, and remember what unites us in this debate: our responsibility to welcome gays and lesbians into our synagogues. Because this I know: if there is anything at all that Reform Jews do, it is to create an inclusive spiritual home for all those who seek the solace of our sanctuaries. And if this Movement does not extend support to all who have been victims of discrimination, including gays and lesbians, then we have no right to call ourselves Reform Jews. (Yoffie 2000)

While Conservative Judaism has had an official policy of welcoming gay members as congregants, the movement has only recently permitted, and demonstrated enthusiasm for, same-sex marriage, claiming that they should not just be permitted but encouraged, as they have, in the words of Rabbi Samuel Barth, 'the potential to increase loyal households among the Jewish community, to raise the sanctity of relationships within our Congregation and bring more Jews close to Torah' (2004). Before, many Conservative rabbis were performing religious ceremonies for same-sex couples without the sanction of their movement. In 2005 Keshet Rabbis, an organization of Conservative rabbis championing the religious rights of gay Jews, was created. More than one hundred Conservative rabbis worldwide, including prominent leaders, signed on, proclaiming, 'Through our understanding of Jewish sources and Jewish values, we affirm that gay, lesbian, bisexual, and transgender Jews may fully participate in community life and achieve positions of professional and lay leadership.'[7] The movement's Committee on Jewish Law and Standards had been re-examining its approach to homosexuality and, in December 2006, determined that if Conservative rabbis wished to do so, they could perform same-sex commitment ceremonies (and simultaneously ruled that openly gay students could enrol in the movement's seminaries and be ordained as rabbis).

In response to the 2008 decision of the California Supreme Court that ended the state's ban on gay marriage, ruling that same-sex couples had a constitutional right to marry and raise children together as a family, Jewish clergy joined those who had already stepped forward to sign a petition supporting gay marriage, circulated by Keshet, entitled 'Jews for Marriage Equality'.[8]

Internationally, rabbis of Britain's Liberal Judaism movement had already prepared a liturgy called 'Covenant of Love' to meet the needs of Jewish gay and lesbian couples who would be able to marry when a Civil Partnership Act took effect in 2005. They were hailed in the British press as 'the first mainstream religious organization to create and authorize a gay marriage service'. In 2007 the South African Union of Progressive Judaism voted to allow its rabbis and lay marriage officers to marry same-sex couples in a full Jewish ceremony. According to the SAUPJ website, 'At the National Assembly of the SAUPJ held in Durban on 6 May (2007), it was agreed that there should be no distinction in the status of religious marriages of same-sex partners and heterosexual couples.'[9]

In America and abroad, previous to declarations of official sanction, individual rabbis in the liberal movements were quietly performing ceremonies, based on liturgies that were already circulating. Except for the many cases in which the rabbis were themselves gay or lesbian, in good measure the impetus for the development of ceremonies came from couples who wanted their relationship to be blessed, honoured, and acknowledged by their religious tradition. They were insistent and persistent, and mustered championing energies for social change within their denominations. Reporting for the *New York Times*, Laurie Goodstein noted that clergy in various faiths were seeing 'religiously observant gay couples who are sidestepping the debate over legal rights and seeking to consecrate their unions in churches and synagogues', even if these ceremonies bestowed no legal or civil rights as heterosexual marriages would (2004). She added that 'ministers and rabbis are responding to the demand' for relationships that could be 'blessed not by the government, but by God', and that such ceremonies were becoming more and more common (2004). The same point is made in a Christian context by Mark D. Jordan, who has observed, 'Requests to bless unions are not coming from outside the churches. They are made by Christians of their own leaders', members of good standing who are often learned, devout, and active in congregational life (2006: 13).

There is, Rabbi Rebecca Alpert maintains, a connection between the same-sex ceremonies performed by religious denominations and the public policy debate. The religious support of same-sex marriage influences public policy 'by demanding the right to perform same-sex marriages that have legal authority based on religious liberty' (2001).

The Emerging Ceremonies: Traditional and Reconstructed

Having demonstrated the extent to which changes in governmental and religious policies have made Jewish same-sex ceremonies overall legally and socially significantly more feasible than before, I want now to look at the two broad types of ceremony that have emerged. I begin with the distinctions made by cultural critic Johanna Drucker in my interview with her:

There is the split between those who feel that gay marriage allows homosexuals to approach norms, absorb themselves into the structures and conventions of society, and thus not be stigmatized or distinguished by their gayness. They are saying, 'Why should we be condemned to being outside the comfortable institutions of bourgeois life?'

There are those who think that being gay by definition challenges those norms and that gay behaviours should help undo the conventions and their oppressive qualities (basic models of domesticating sexuality, eros, autonomy, etc. through the conventions of property-driven marriage patterns). Like radicals in other groups, they are saying, 'Changing and challenging normative values is essential to what gayness is.' (2007)

Christian same-sex ceremonies that have emerged at the same time demonstrate similar variations. Describing them, Jordan writes, 'some barely depart from established forms used by male-female couples. Others are almost wholly invented—though these too are not so different from the more experimental rites used occasionally to marry women to men in church' (2006: 144). When Jordan studies Christian same-sex wedding liturgies, he is interested in noting 'what displacements of meaning or agency happen when same-sex unions are performed using "traditional" materials' (2006: 144). Apologetic in tone, the rituals he sees want to demonstrate that they are authentically Christian. 'At the same time', he explains, 'they appeal to tradition without claiming to retrieve a lost liturgical genealogy. They show, in other words, the persistence of tradition through invention' (2006: 145–6).

Couples desiring to embrace the pattern of the heterosexual Jewish wedding as their model prefer a more traditional Jewish ceremony. They find it a compelling way of claiming authenticity, stating that theirs too is a 'real' Jewish wedding—being gay should not condemn them to standing outside the Jewish institution of marriage. They want their commitment to one another to be expressed through culturally familiar Jewish terms. There are many rationales for this approach, trumping its obvious problems. One is a simple matter of personal style. Torie Osborn, a recent Jewish bride (who married her partner of thirty years only when urged to do so by her mother), chose a traditional form, offering a rationale that seemed obvious to her: 'I guess I'm just a traditional girl.' She realized only after her ceremony (not a Jewish one) why the conventional wedding had compelling power for her:

The astonishing outpouring of support from our straight friends taught me a profound lesson: getting married is a rite of passage into a wide circle of shared humanity. With a real wedding—not a commitment ceremony, not a domestic partnership registry—we were initiated into a crowded circle of people who automatically affirmed our very beings. It was a club we never even knew existed until we joined. (Osborn 2008)

'Choosing any framework other than traditional Judaism for our wedding was unthinkable for us', wrote Inbal Kashtan about her wedding, 'because the particular rituals of our tradition are the ones we find most meaningful' (2003: 149). The traditional model appealed to Kashtan and her partner because they wanted their wedding to have a Jewish resonance for themselves and their guests, almost as an antidote to its novelty. They would highlight the centrality of Judaism and queerness to their lives by 'taking a traditional Orthodox wedding and wrestling with every ritual and text that we could uncover'. Their guests' responses confirmed that their 'attempt to create a recognizably "normal" Eastern European Jewish wedding had succeeded; these people were able to resonate with the sacredness and power of the day' (2003: 149).

Traditional rituals intentionally highlight the ways in which commitment ceremonies are the same as heterosexual marriages, with obvious linguistic changes reflecting the fact that the bride and groom are replaced by two brides or two grooms. Reform rabbis feel most at ease using the traditional format with reasonable adaptation, and decide whether they consider a same-sex union to have the status of *kidushin*, the sanctified marriage of a man and woman. Given the Reform movement's flexible attitude towards halakhah (Jewish law), this is not a fraught process. Anecdotal evidence from Reform women rabbis in Virginia who have performed same-sex ceremonies suggests that the advantage of a traditional, near-analogous approach is that it affirms a gay partnership as a real Jewish marriage, with the same rules and regulations for entrance and, if necessary, for exit in the case of divorce. As one Reform rabbi said to me in a private conversation (emphasizing her own agency as much as the agency of the tradition), 'When I tell the couple to repeat after me, *harei at mekudeshet li* or *harei atah mekudash li* ('Behold you are sanctified unto me', spoken to a woman or to a man), they are married' (2006). I understood her to be saying that when she, as a rabbi, invoked this traditional Hebrew formula (even when adapted to suit the same-sex couple), then the ceremony was authentically Jewish, and created an authentic

Jewish marriage, despite the fact that their ceremony was not recognized as a legitimate marriage by their state.

The second type of ceremony, which I call reconstructed, reflects the impulse to reject, or rebel against, the heterosexual wedding. Here Rabbi Elizabeth Tikva Sarah writes about her own wedding: 'marriage was and has remained to this day an institution for regulating heterosexual unions. So what has it got to do with lesbian and gay people? From a Jewish perspective, the institution of marriage emerged in a context in which there was no concept of same-sex relationships' (2008: 128). The reconstructed ceremony challenges heterosexual social paradigms implicit in much of Jewish practice, as well as contesting the patriarchal heritage of the Jewish wedding in particular, which includes the assumption that male and female alone constitute a normal model and the only hope, as they create a home and procreate, for Jewish continuity. As Kabakov explains, 'When we were going through our process we thought it was quite fascinating, the way we were forced to deconstruct the rituals, taking them out of their hetero-normative context, re-think them and if necessary re-work them if they still had meaning for us' (2008).

Reconstructed ceremonies highlight the fact that there are important distinctions between same-sex partnerships and the traditional heterosexual Jewish marriage. Not bound by traditional models, the former may allow for a freer, more creative bricolage as the couple make their plans. Here, Nora Klimist describes the ceremonial choices she and Nina Kaiser made:

We wrote our own ceremony with our rabbi. We had six meetings with him over four months in which we would sit and talk about who we are and what we wanted. He gave us three different ceremonies to choose from. One was a very religious ceremony, one was sort of interfaith, and one was Reform. We took all three, pulled out what we wanted, and created our own ceremony. (Sherman 1992: 114)

The reconstructed wedding ceremony that Rabbi Elizabeth Tikvah Sarah and her partner Cathy created allowed them to merge their experience of being lesbians and their experience of being Jews.[10] In their wedding booklet they wrote: 'So, our wedding ceremony is both like and unlike a traditional wedding! . . . The framework is identical, the content is quite similar in places, but the emphasis it places on equality, mutuality and reciprocity make it radically different' (Elizabeth Tikva Sarah 2000: 135). Thus, in their *ketubah* (based on others they had seen) they pledged to care for each other and themselves; this differs from the traditional *ketubah* in which one partner cares economically for the other and neither pledges self-care. Their *ketubah* also declared that both partners had taken a shared middle name, a gesture inspired by another couple. In lieu of a *bedekn* ceremony, in which the groom unveils the bride, they looked deeply into each other's eyes. They also wrote their own betrothal formula for the exchange of rings: 'By this ring you are consecrated to me in the spirit of the people and the traditions of Israel' (1998: 141). Each broke a glass at the end of the ceremony.

Their wedding booklet explained that this act reflected their very particular personal sorrows and expressed a communal one, too: 'Cathy and Elli grieve together for the intrusion of homophobia into their lives and pray that, as the glass shatters beneath their feet, so may the yoke of bigotry be broken . . . speedily in our own days' (1998: 145).

Couples wishing to separate themselves proactively from the templates of heterosexual or traditional Jewish marriage are not the only ones preferring a reconstructed ceremony. Such innovative rituals are also created when the couple or clergy do not feel that an accurate interpretation of Jewish law would allow them to apply heterosexual ceremonies to homosexuals. Most rabbis in the Conservative movement prefer the reconstructed model for same-sex couples, maintaining that the halakhic format and language of heterosexual Jewish marriage which includes *kidushin* between a man and a woman is not extendable to same-sex unions. Consequently, the reconstructed ceremonies adapt certain aspects of the traditional service and introduce some new elements. Rabbi Samuel Barth, for instance, commended that the *ḥupah* as the symbol of a home could be used in commitment ceremonies, and some document other than a *ketubah* (historically created to oblige men to offer women economic protection) could be drawn up to formalize the couple's relationship and stipulate mutual obligations to one another. In lieu of the *sheva berakhot*, the seven blessings, which Barth noted should be 'reserved for a heterosexual union', new blessings and praises could be invented.

While some same-sex couples may find this approach unyielding and even offensive, an act of hypocrisy in the context of congregations that claim to welcome gay Jews, there are same-sex couples that embrace halakhah, acknowledging it is a constant struggle. Susan Sapiro chronicled the choices made by one such Conservative couple whom she calls Michelle and Aimée as they planned their 1995 union (1997: 17). In their wedding booklet, they explained that they did not see their ceremony as *kidushin*, but hoped their guests would experience its authenticity nonetheless. Sapiro writes, 'They decided to call their ceremony a *kiddush ahava* (sanctification of love), a term that retained the *k'dusha* (sanctification) aspect of *kiddushin* . . . (They) relished the freedom they felt in making changes compared with the relative constraints on a heterosexual couple. "But again, that didn't make us feel that we had total carte blanche"' (1997: 17).

What changes did they make? Using the betrothal formula traditionally recited by the groom to the bride seemed too radical for them. They would not say, 'Behold you are consecrated to me by this ring according to the Law of Moses and Israel', when in fact the Law did not apply to their situation. They chose instead words associated with the donning of *tefilin* as they were fond of its imagery, and since its language uses the technical term *erusin* (betrothal), 'it sounds legal', they claimed (Sapiro 1997: 17). For the *sheva berakhot*, they kept the form of seven different blessings they would receive from others but, so as not to tinker with the traditional content, they found alternative sacred texts from a variety of biblical and liturgical sources that expressed significant relevant themes in their lives, including their relationship, family, home, social ethics, community, God, and new beginnings.

Consequences Rippling Out

The consequences of grappling with same-sex marriages as a legal reality and ritual form have been rippling out for over a decade, enabling new practices linked to the rights of homosexual couples that appear in both gay and straight weddings. Progressive heterosexual Jews (typically those acquainted with same-sex couples who have experienced discrimination) apply liturgical strategies intended to raise awareness and instigate change, while simultaneously acknowledging their own privileged status. To that end, for instance, the Progressive Jewish Alliance, founded in 1999 in California, has created a programme called 'Bringing the Orange Under the Chuppah' so that heterosexual Jews can demonstrate their support at their weddings for same-sex couples wishing to marry. Rituals of solidarity include a second cup of wine under the *ḥupah* that is not drunk from, bringing an orange under the *ḥupah*, and breaking a second glass.[11] Rabbi Deborah Eisenbach-Budner explains the genesis of a blessing she and her husband Steven offered at their wedding, recognizing the privileged status enjoyed by heterosexual couples:

In the course of planning our wedding . . . (we) came face to face with a painful contradiction between our love for our gay and lesbian friends and relatives, and our attachment to Jewish wedding liturgy—which is blatantly heterosexist . . . We feel that we can only drink a full cup of joy when the union of all lovers is celebrated . . . We have therefore added an eighth blessing . . . Akin to taking ten drops out of our glasses during the Passover seder . . . we diminish one full cup of joy in recognition that the world is not complete. (Eisenbach-Budner 1995)

This liturgical addition, which suggests that empathy should lead to protest and social action, is to be added as a blessing to follow the seven traditional ones:

You are blessed, Adonai our God, Source of Life,
who enables us to strive toward the devotion of Jonathan and David,
the life-sharing of Ruth and Naomi,
and the commitment of Jacob and Rachel.
May the time come soon when the voices of all lovers,
the music of all friendships, will rise up to be heard and
celebrated in the gates of our cities.
May the time come soon when we can all drink a full cup of joy.
Blessed are You, Source of Love.

(Eisenbach-Budner 1995)

This liturgy is obviously in conversation with the one offered in the 'Union Service for Same-Gender Couples' the Reform movement's sourcebook *Kulanu*, first made available in 2004 by the CCAR's Working Group on Same-Gender Officiation, whose text is to be recited before the breaking of one or two glasses:

> The Jewish people have a partnership with God in the task of *tikkun olam*, the healing and repair of the world . . . Because so many gays and lesbians sadly still know the oppression and pain of hiding, because so many gays and lesbians still lack equality of civil rights in our world, we break a glass/glasses on this day of celebration to remind us that even in this hour of great joy, our world is still incomplete and in need of healing . . . May the shattering of these glasses by _____ and _____ remind them and us to work towards this time of wholeness, this *tikkun*, for ourselves and our world. Amen. (Address et al. 2007: 219)

When such empathetic rituals are performed at heterosexual weddings, according to my observations, some guests are touched by Judaism's capacity to be sensitive to current ethical concerns. Precedent exists of wistful notes being given space in Jewish weddings: there is the absence of a deceased parent which is acknowledged at the beginning of the ceremony (or by a visit beforehand to the cemetery), or the memory of the destruction of the Temple, recalled when the glass is broken. The new supplemental rituals were preceded by other contemporary innovations, ones that cut briefly into spaces of joy, without destroying them, for the sake of justice. There was the fifth cup of wine or the fourth matzah at the Passover Seder which both brought attention to the plight of Soviet Jewry. More currently, there is Miriam's cup and the orange on the Seder plate, placed there initially to raise consciousness of the ways Jewish lesbian women have experienced exclusion, and then to reflect upon all Jewish women who have been excluded from certain aspects of Jewish life. While some wedding guests have found the new, empathetic rituals intrusive and agenda-driven, politically correct gestures that impinge on their joy for the couple and take attention away from the celebration of the day, my intuition is that in the current period, as advocacy or compassion for the right of same-sex couples to marry in the civil sphere intensifies among the most politically engaged liberal American Jews, such supplemental rituals will become more widespread, fading away only when gay civil weddings become legal in more states.

Conclusion

Looking towards the future, we might wonder what the scripts for ceremonies of Jewish same-sex couples will look like in ten or twenty years from now. Granting that it is foolhardy to make predictions about ritual, I can say that the ultimate form will be shaped by two primary factors. The first concerns the extent to which changes in heterosexual Jewish weddings that flatten gender difference and delimit male-centred hierarchies will continue to grow and catch on in liberal and

Orthodox communities. If the movement in this direction continues, and evidence suggests that it will, we can anticipate that a straight wedding ceremony denuded of patriarchal trappings—particularly as it acquires its own patina of tradition—will be appealing enough to the broadest range of gay couples who will use it with only minor adaptations. The second factor concerns how long it will take until same-sex marriages are legalized permanently in more states and countries. If the process is fairly rapid (that is, in the greater scheme of social change) and if, along the way, more people actually attend the Jewish and non-Jewish same-sex unions of their friends, relatives, and colleagues, the rituals in gay and straight ceremonies concerning empathy and the need for social action will fall away. If the process seems not just endless but unendurable, on the other hand, such calls for ethical attentiveness and activism are likely not only to persist, but also to expand and find even more dramatic modes of expression.[12]

Notes

1   I use the word 'ceremony' to refer to the whole complex of rituals, and 'ritual' to refer to particular practices, both customs (such as encircling one's partner under the ḥupah) and legal acts (such as giving and receiving a ketubah). In this essay, I am considering ceremonies that the participants themselves describe as being 'religiously' Jewish.

2   For example, those generated by Ma'yan, a feminist organization at the Jewish Community Center of New York. Websites of ritual innovation include www.ritualwell.org or www.keshetrabbis.org, where various versions of same-sex commitment rituals can be freely accessed.

3   Ours is not the only era that has seen the radical transformation of Jewish wedding practices. See Michael Satlow (2001).

4   One such element is the bride's lack of agency and voice in various aspects of the ceremony and its documentation in the ketubah, which is sometimes resolved by shifting the central act of the wedding from kinyan (acquisition) to a covenantal partnership (berit ahuvim).

5   See Fahim 2007.

6   See <www.tremblingbeforeg-d.com>.

7   See <http://www.keshetrabbis org>.

8   Because of the significance of this document, I quote it in full:

The most fundamental human right, after the necessities of food, clothing and shelter, is the right to affection and the supportive love of other human beings. Just like their heterosexual counterparts, gay and lesbian couples form loving bonds, establish shared households, and raise children together—all contributions to social stability and collective welfare. All credible scientific studies find that sexual orientation is irrelevant to raising a happy, healthy child. What matters in any family is the security and quality of the relationship children have with their parents. Indeed, what puts children of gay and lesbian parents at risk is the lack of permanence, stability, serenity and safety that other children of legally recognized families enjoy. And for children who are gay and lesbian, the denial of the precious right to marry when they become adults undermines their sense of self-worth and their dreams of a life together with a cherished partner. Society is strengthened by allowing gay and lesbian couples to legally formalize both their bond with one another and their mutual responsibility for their household and children. Society should not only permit but also encourage civil marriage for such couples. Efforts to prevent civil marriage for gays and lesbians through legal means, such as state or federal Constitutional amendments that deprive them of the benefits and dreams others enjoy, are unjust and discriminatory. Denial of the status of marriage to those who accept its rights and responsibilities creates legal and economic inequities in addition to social injustice. Although California's domestic partnership law (now in jeopardy by upcoming ballot initiatives) provides limited protections, it does not provide equality.

We as rabbis, cantors and community leaders committed to Jewish tradition urge all Jews to remember our heritage of justice and to recommit ourselves to not wavering on this holy principle. We take heed of our historic mission to bring all Jews into the community and to bring peace to all persons. We join together as brothers and sisters in faith and call for an end to the shameful and hurtful idea that some families are less worthy and less human than others. All are created *b'tzelem elohim*, in the image of God. We acknowledge that gays and lesbians have too often been excluded, and we pledge to correct this inequality—both by fighting any and all legislative efforts to deprive gays and lesbians of their human and civil rights, including the right to marry—and by continuing to redouble our efforts to make every gay and lesbian family member, friend, colleague and congregant feel welcome in our synagogues and community as equals to their heterosexual neighbors.

We oppose appeals to sacred texts and religious tradition for the purpose of denying legal equity to same-gender couples. As concerned citizens, we affirm the liberty of adults of the same gender to love and marry. We insist that no one, especially the state, may either coerce people into marriage, or bar two consenting adults of the same gender from forming the family unit that lets them be more fully loving and thus more fully human. We respect the fact that debate and discussion continue in many of our religious communities as to the theological and liturgical issues involved. However, we draw on our tradition to arrive at a common conviction: we are resolved that the state should not interfere with same-gender couples who choose to marry and share fully and equally in the rights, responsibilities, and commitments of civil marriage. Further we are resolved that the state should not interfere with any adult couple, same-sex or heterosexual, who choose to create a domestic partnership. We affirm the right to freedom of conscience in this matter: we recognize that the state may not require religious groups to officiate at, or bless, same-gender marriages. By the same token, a denial of civil recognition dishonors the religious convictions of those communities and clergy who do officiate at, and bless, same-gender marriages. The state may not favor the convictions of one religious group over another to deny individuals their fundamental right to marry and have those marriages recognized by civil law. As Jewish leaders, we commit ourselves to public action, visibility, education, and mutual support of the right and freedom to marry. (www.jewsformarriageequality.org; accessed 15 May 2008)

9   <http://www.saupj.org.za/articles/gaymarriages.html>, accessed 2 Aug. 2010.

10   This was a British ceremony performed by an American rabbi. The couple chose to call it 'a *Brit Ahava*, "Covenant of Love," to emphasize its difference, and to . . . demonstrate that

what is the same can be completely different too' (Elizabeth Tikva Sarah 1998: 136).

11   See <http://www.pjalliance.org/UserFiles/File/Marriage%20Equality%20Packet%20PDF
      .pdf>. Here, a glass-breaking ritual written by Rachel Biale is also included.

12   My research on Jewish same-sex marriages is part of a more extensive project that has
      been made possible by a Brandeis–Hadassah Institute Senior Research Award and a
      research grant from the College of Arts and Sciences of the University of Virginia.

Interviews

ANONYMOUS REFORM RABBI, 2 Nov. 2006

JOHANNA DRUCKER, 6 Dec. 2007

MIRYAM KABAKOV, 20 May 2008

References

ADDRESS, RICHARD, JOEL L. KUSHNER, and GEOFFREY MITELMAN, eds. 2007.
Kulanu: All of Us. A Program for Implementing Gay and Lesbian Inclusion. New York.

ALPERT, REBECCA. 2001. 'Same Sex Marriage and the Law'. The Shalom Center website,
<http://www.shalomctr.org/node/3>, accessed 25 Apr. 2008.

BARTH, SAMUEL. 2004. 'Gay/Lesbian Ceremonies of Commitment'. A discussion
paper/responsum sent to members of Congregation Agudas Achim. Austin, Tex.

BENJAMIN, MARA, and MIRYAM KABAKOV. 2004. Wedding booklet, courtesy of
authors.

DIAMANT, ANITA. 2001. *The New Jewish Wedding*. New York.

EISENBACH-BUDNER, DEBORAH. 1995. 'Spilling out Wine: A New Wedding Blessing', *Lilith* (Winter); also at <http://www.ritualwell.org/lifecycles/intimacy partner
ing/Jewishweddingscommitmentceremonies/sitefolder.2005-06-07.6188218104/
primaryobject.2005-09-14.8227785097>.

ELIZABETH TIKVA SARAH. 2000. '"Marriage" by Any Other Name: Lesbian and Gay
"Commitment Ceremonies" and "Our Jewish Wedding"'. In Sylvia Rothschild and
Sybil Sheridan, eds., *Taking Up the Timbrel*, 134–46. London.

FAHIM, KAREEM. 2007. 'United Parcel Service Agrees to Benefits in Civil Unions',
New York Times, 31 July.

GOLDSTEIN, ELYSE. 2009. 'The Pink Tallit'. In Elyse Goldstein, ed., *New Jewish Feminism: Probing the Past, Forging the Future*. Woodstock, Vt.

GOODSTEIN, LAURIE. 2004. 'Gay Couples Seek Unions in the Eyes of God', *New York
Times*, 30 Jan.

GREENBERG, STEVEN. 2006. 'Contemplating a Jewish Ritual of Same-Sex Union'. In
Mark D. Jordan, ed., *Authorizing Marriage*, 81–101. Princeton.

HULL, KATHLEEN. 2006. *Same-Sex Marriage: The Cultural Politics of Love and Law*. Cambridge.

JORDAN, MARK D. 2006. *Blessing Same-Sex Unions*. Chicago.

KASHTAN, INBAL. 2003. 'Breaking Ground: A Traditional Jewish Lesbian Wedding'. In
David Shneer and Caryn Aviv, eds., *Queer Jews*. New York.

KOHLER LEVAV, MELANIE, and HOPE BERGER LEVAV. 2001. 'Transforming the Covenant', *Ma'yan Journey* (Spring): 11–14.

OCHS, VANESSA L. 2007. *Inventing Jewish Ritual*. Philadelphia.

OSBORN, TORIE. 2008. 'The Joy of Marriage Was Ours, for a While', *New York Times*, 20 Apr.

RESNICK LEVINE, ELIZABETH. 1991. *A Ceremony Sampler: New Rites, Celebrations and Observances of Jewish Women*. San Diego.

SAPIRO, SUSAN. 1997. 'Two Lesbian Women and their Pretty Straight Wedding', *Lilith* (Winter): 16–18.

SATLOW, MICHAEL. 2001. *Jewish Marriage in Antiquity*. Princeton.

SHERMAN, SUZANNE, ed. 1992. *Lesbian and Gay Marriage: Private Commitments, Public Ceremonies*. Philadelphia.

WYTHE, DOUGLAS, ANDREW MERLING, ROSLYN MERLING, and SHELDON MERLING. 2004. *The Wedding: A Family's Coming Out Story*. New York.

YOFFIE, ERIC. 2000. 'Same Gender Officiation'. Union for Reform Judaism website. <http://urj.org/about/union/leadership/yoffie/archive/gender/>.

The Power of Discourse: Negotiating Modernity and Tradition in the Jewish Wedding

IRIT KOREN

IN THIS ESSAY I interpret in terms of discourse a recent phenomenon among young religious Jewish women that reflects a significant shift the modern Orthodox community in Israel has begun to undergo as it grapples with feminist ideas and values. For women who regard themselves as feminists, or are at least conscious of the principles advocating gender equality,[1] the traditional wedding ritual, which is at its core a ritualized transfer of ownership of the woman's sexuality to her husband, creates a troubling dissonance. It forces such women to confront the tension between modernity and tradition and more specifically between their feminism and their religiosity, and this necessity has pushed them to come up with a variety of coping strategies.

The dispute over the wedding ritual has taken shape both in legal resistance to its problematic construction as well as in actual performance. My interviews with Modern Orthodox women have revealed four distinct strategies of action:

1. creating a female ritual act parallel to the male one;

2. introducing variations of the traditional ritual acts;

3. avoiding a particular ritual; and

4. employing legal resistance.

Below, I explore the implications of these different strategies for the participants and for the ritual itself.

The Jewish wedding is a significant cultural icon, which can explain why it is experienced by these women as a crucial moment in their lives in which they publicly proclaim who they are as religious women, as well as their loving relationship with their future husband. It is important for them to challenge the religious system specifically at this point of their lives in order to relieve the tension between their Orthodox conviction and modern feminist principles. This conflict underlying the call for changing the wedding ceremony has been addressed in theories which view the performance of ritual as embodying the tensions and paradoxes in any given society, and measure its success by its ability to resolve, at least to some extent, these tensions.[2] The Modern Orthodox wedding ritual is a case in point as it reflects the tensions and paradoxes of Modern Orthodox society: a society that tries, on the one hand, to follow halakhah and customs and on the other hand to address modern sensibilities and notions. The new, innovative acts that the brides perform in their wedding ritual enable them and their grooms to resolve, at least to some extent, precisely this tension. By introducing ritual acts that do not contradict halakhah but create a new visual experience that represents equality and mutuality between the partners, the brides feel they can come to terms with the wedding ritual.

Although the women I interviewed acted individually, they were influenced by watching other women challenge traditional ritual acts in their wedding, and they in turn incorporated similar or identical elements into their own ceremony; thus this trend can be referred to as a social rather than an individual phenomenon.

I focus on the discourse between the brides and those in their social environment (for example the grooms, their mothers, their fathers, and the rabbis) about the wedding ritual and, specifically, about the act of *kidushin*. The discourse and views of my interviewees reflect, as I demonstrate below, the ways in which these women express and interpret themselves in relation to the wedding ritual. I include a summary of the interaction between the different groups, and particularly focus on the dialogue between the brides and the rabbis since I see them as the most influential participants in this scenario. By comparing each group's narratives about the wedding ritual, I wish to expose the meaning and the social significance their discourse carries. In other words, I wish to show how spoken language has the power to maintain the continuity of tradition on the one hand, and to transform tradition on the other.

Tradition versus Modernity—What Is at Stake?

In researching the above phenomenon, I have interviewed twenty-five women, each of whom sought to challenge the traditional expectations regarding her own wedding by producing alternative practices which aimed at creating change in the religious system at large. In order to better understand the social context in which these acts of challenge occurred, I have also interviewed their relatives (mothers, fathers, and husbands) and some of the rabbis who performed the weddings. In addition, I was a participant-observer in many such wedding rituals.

The women in my study compose a fairly homogeneous group.[3] All were in their mid-twenties to mid-thirties at the start of their marriage. For women in Orthodox society this is significant as they are expected to marry in their early twenties, preferably soon after finishing their army service or *sherut le'umi* (special civil service for religious women). My interviewees lived in Jerusalem while single, specifically in the neighbourhoods of Rehavia, Katamon, and Baka.[4] They all got married within the past decade and are well educated.[5] As they expressed

in the interviews, the years they had spent as single women in these neighbourhoods had had an impact on their identity and religious perspective. Living in
this specific context had exposed them, through synagogues, friends, and political movements, to feminist ideas that they had not encountered beforehand.
Therefore, they had some years to redefine their religious outlook prior to their
marriages.

Using the wedding ritual as a case study has enabled me to demonstrate how
women negotiate between modernity and tradition in relation to their own identity as feminist and religious women. Additionally, a negotiation is apparent on a
broader scale between themselves and their tradition-centred group, often viewing feminism with suspicion and even contempt. Jewish theologian Tamar Ross
explains this hostility towards women's critical engagement with the religious
system, and specifically with religious rituals, by observing that 'even the slightest
symbolic change in ritual creates a dissonance with primeval memories, associations, and traditional patterns of worship that have nurtured the spiritual self-
image of Jewish women for centuries' (Ross 2004: p. xiv). The clearly defined,
rigid boundaries of the religious system and a social context which discourages
change combine to make attempts at transforming the wedding ritual much
more difficult for these women than for those who do not see themselves as
bound by Orthodox halakhah (religious law). The latter group is able to freely
choose the elements they like and to 'play' with the different parts of the ceremony without threatening their own identity or their social environment.[6]

The typical Orthodox ritual comprises a series of steps. Although the blessings and the general structure of the wedding are uniform, there are a variety of
customs that change from community to community. The ritual I describe henceforth is typical of the Modern Orthodox Ashkenazi (European Jewish) community in Israel.[7] First, before the wedding ceremony itself, the groom signs the
ketubah—a contract delineating his financial and sexual obligations towards his
wife. Then he is led, with loud singing and dancing, to his bride who is sitting on a
throne-like chair, awaiting him. Upon reaching her, he covers her face with a veil,
an act which is called *bedekn*. The groom then turns and walks to the *ḥupah* (wedding canopy), still accompanied by the wedding guests, and awaits the bride
there. She is similarly escorted to the *ḥupah* by relatives and guests, amidst loud
singing and dancing. In most cases the guests will remain standing throughout the *ḥupah* ceremony. Upon reaching the wedding canopy, the bride circles
around the groom seven times, accompanied by her mother and mother-in-
law-to-be. Then she stands beside the groom and they both face the crowd. The
officiant (generally a rabbi) stands near the couple, also facing the guests.

Only now does the formal two-part ritual begin. The first part is the *kidushin*
(sanctification) ceremony, in which, following the rabbi's recitation of the
betrothal blessing and the benediction over wine, the man performs the active
role of betrothing the woman by addressing to her the Hebrew words *harei at*

mekudeshet li (you are hereby consecrated unto me) while giving her a ring. After this, the *ketubah* is read out by a male participant, separating the two parts of the ritual. Now the second part, *nisuin* (marriage), begins and the *sheva berakhot*, the traditional seven wedding blessings,[8] are recited by the rabbi or by men who are close to the family and have been given this honour. At the end of the ritual the groom shatters a glass wrapped in a cloth by stamping on it. Finally the bride and groom seclude themselves in a private room for a short while, symbolizing the consummation of the marriage, and then join the rest of the crowd in celebrating.

Special attention must be given to *kidushin*, the main element of this ritual without which the couple is not married according to Orthodox halakhah. The *kidushin* act is based on the ruling of the Mishnah, which states: 'A woman is acquired [in marriage] in three ways and acquires her freedom in two. She is acquired by money, by a document (the *ketubah*), or by intercourse' (*Kid.* 1: 1). The ritual described above includes all these three modes: the ring given to the bride symbolizes her acquisition by money, the *ketubah* that by a document, and stand-ing under the *ḥupah* and the couple's seclusion in a private room after the cere-mony symbolize her acquisition by intercourse. Many rabbis and religious leaders have argued that the acquisition established through this act does not mean the man's ownership of his wife. This argument is echoed by Rabbi Mau-rice Lamm, a prominent contemporary Orthodox rabbi, who claims that *kidushin* is not an act of acquisition, but rather implies exclusivity: 'When a man "takes" a wife, he chooses one woman and, with her consent, makes her his life-long part-ner. She has no other husband' (Lamm 1980: 151). However, what is markedly absent from this analysis is the fact that the bride does not perform a reciprocal act of *kidushin*. It is exactly this point that has produced numerous feminist critiques of the traditional wedding ritual, specifically targeting *kidushin* as an act of acquisition and, therefore, one of oppression (e.g. Aranoff 2000; Okin 2000).

Jewish legal scholar Judith Wegner points out that the framers of the Mishnah viewed marriage first and foremost as the transfer of the ownership of a woman's sexuality from her father to her husband.[9] Wegner states that in the mishnaic cat-alogue of various types of chattel and the legal procedures for acquiring them, wives head the list. She suggests that the redactors of the Mishnah listed the dif-ferent types of property along with the wife so as to indicate both a formal and a substantive analogy between the acquisition of a woman's sexuality and the acquisition of chattel. The traditional view of the woman's sexuality as chattel is further expressed in the unilateral nature of the espousal ceremony, whereby the man recites a formula to the woman, who does not give any verbal reply. Even if she were to speak, her words would have no effect, since she is not legally capable of acquiring the groom's sexuality in the way that he is capable of acquiring hers. In fact, it is specifically forbidden by halakhah for the woman to 'acquire' her hus-band in a mutual act (Wegner 1988: 66–72). Moreover, some rabbis rule that not only do her words lack such power, but they also cancel the man's act of acquisition and, therefore, she must be silent in response to this ritual act.

There are some harsh implications to this legal arrangement—the transformation of the woman's sexuality into a possession of her husband's—especially since it is still followed in the rabbinical courts of Israel as well as in the rest of the Orthodox Jewish world. Most significantly, a Jewish woman wed by the laws of the Torah can be divorced only by her husband's act of giving her a traditional *get* (bill of divorce). Should her husband stubbornly refuse or be unable to release her in this way, she will remain a *mesurevet get* or an *agunah*,[10] that is, someone who is unable to remarry according to Jewish law. In this matter, halakhah discriminates again between men and women.[11] A *mesurevet get* or *agunah* who chooses to live with another man pays a heavy price. Her children by that man are considered *mamzerim* (bastards) and neither they nor their offspring are allowed to marry Jews. Because all marriages between Jews in Israel are governed by Orthodox religious law, such children and their descendants are unable to marry in the State of Israel. In contrast, a married man can have children by another woman without legal sanction (Kamir 2002: 142–6).

The women in my study have confronted the wedding ritual by performing its various elements in novel ways which undermined their traditional function. Examples include a mutual *bedekn*, in which, parallel to the groom covering the bride's face with her veil, the bride in turn covers the groom with a *talit* (prayer shawl); the groom and the bride circling around each other at the beginning of the ceremony instead of the bride alone circling around the groom; adding an eighth blessing to the traditional seven blessings which are read at the end and allowing a woman to read the last one; and the bride giving a ring to the groom parallel to his giving a ring to her (although without the bride reciting the same formula of *kidushin*, which is forbidden by Orthodox law).[12]

Another way the traditional wedding ritual has been challenged is by employing legal innovation. This strategy typically does not involve a public ceremony under the *ḥupah*; rather, it has to do with drafting and signing documents in the presence of an attorney before the wedding. The intention of such documents is to diminish the legal status of *kidushin* as an act of acquisition, and is still considered socially as a radical act, at least in Israel. The core legal document in this strategy is the prenuptial agreement,[13] which purports not to replace the *ketubah* but rather to supplement it by stipulating the exercise of economic pressure, in the form of increased alimony payments, if a man refuses to give his wife her *get* (or if she refuses to take it).[14] The prenuptial document deals with what happens at the time of divorce; however, it needs to be understood that the imbalance that exists between the couple at the time of divorce (where only the man can initiate and give a *get* to the woman and not vice versa) is directly linked to the construction of the *kidushin* in which the man acquires the woman's sexuality and thus he alone can release her from this bond. Therefore by creating a prenuptial document at the time of the wedding, the acquisitional nature of the *kidushin*, which gives unlimited power to the husband, is challenged. Another solution that has been suggested by the brides is to create a condition in the *kidushin* act in which the bride and groom state that she is willing to be acquired by him only on the condition that he will never refuse to give her a *get* if she wishes to divorce. Eventually this was never employed because of the rabbis' refusal to work with the couples on such a solution.

The prenuptial agreement thus represents an attempt to balance the unequal power relations between the couple and to change the halakhic reality in which only a husband has the legal right to decide whether to grant a *get*. These legal agreements have come about because of the difficulties and harsh confrontations that *agunot* and *mesuravot get* have faced in the rabbinical courts.[15]

The Competing Discourses

The term 'discourse' refers to various forms of communication (for example, conversation, performative acts, art, media, and literature) that produce a social reality and an understanding of any given social phenomenon. In this essay I have limited the term to refer to spoken language alone, following Teun van Dijk's definition: 'The emphasis on the interactional and practical nature of discourse is naturally associated with a focus on language use as spoken interaction' (1997: 4). The way people talk about their present and past experiences reveals their outlook and the meaning they assign to their own behaviour. Therefore, understanding the discourse between individuals or within a group helps to illuminate their motives as well as their perception of any given social phenomenon. Comparing the discourses that different social groups produce helps to ascertain how certain ways of talking and perceiving become dominant while others become subordinate, and thus sheds light on the ways social realities are shaped and explained.

When asked about their understanding of the wedding ritual and, specifically, of the *kidushin* act, the young women invoked the language of halakhah and of traditional texts, relying on their religious knowledge. For example, Shira, a lawyer by profession, opposed *kidushin*, and yet expressed this resistance by using a language that reflected her knowledge of religious law and text:

The rituals assume that from the moment that the man gives the ring to the woman and says to her whatever he says to her, then what he really does by this act is he stakes an exclusive claim on her sexuality. Now this whole concept is not acceptable. It is a feeling that if he betrays me so it is bad! But if I betray him it is horrible! This concept is amazing. In all the matters that relate to my sexuality I am consecrated to one man, but he, on the other hand, can fool around and even if he is a pimp, they [the religious court] don't obligate him to give a *get* [in a case where the woman wants a divorce].

Shira clearly communicated her own interpretation of the legal meaning of *kidushin*. Although she did not cite the Talmud or the Mishnah, it is clear that her understanding stemmed from her knowledge of Jewish legal texts—a knowledge that she continually conveyed throughout her interview. Her stance was also informed by her profession as a lawyer as she repeatedly referred to civil legal terms in addition to Jewish ones. Other women also made the connection between the act of *kidushin* and the acquisition of a woman's sexuality, couching it in halakhic and textual terms. For example, Miri, who studies Torah in the *beit midrash* (religious house of study) at the Hebrew University, asked: 'What does *kidushin* mean? From a halakhic point of view it is an act of acquisition.' Shelomit, a talmudic scholar and teacher, also expressed her discomfort with the act of *kidushin* and stated: 'I couldn't ignore the rule of the Mishnah, which states that the "woman is acquired in three ways".' By using the language of religious knowledge, these brides entered into a realm which had, until recently, belonged only to men.

Some of the brides went beyond merely using halakhic language and reappropriated it for their own purposes. For example, Rivki demonstrated a non-literal understanding: 'It was clear to me that halakhically *kidushin* is not an actual acquisition and it is only symbolic.' Anat, who, similar to Shira, used specific terms related to religious laws, gave them her own interpretation:

The whole meaning of the ritual wasn't easy for me. That is, the fact that he consecrates me. So I gave my own interpretation. *Kidushin* (to consecrate) means also to single someone out (*leyaḥed*). That means that he singles me out from the rest of the women in the world and I also single him out from the rest of the men in the world. But at the same time it was clear to me that although I single him out, I am still not consecrating him to me.

Some of the women, throughout their interviews, expressed their initial belief that this knowledge would put them on an equal footing with the rabbis. That is to say, they had thought they would be perceived as partners in the halakhic discussion about the boundaries of the wedding ritual; yet, this was not the case. For some of the rabbis the brides' ability to justify changes based on religious knowledge did not make a difference. Knowledgeable or not, they were not viewed as equal partners in discussions on halakhic matters, precisely because of their gender. Thus, instead of concentrating on the brides' actual legal argument, the rabbis often shifted the focus and questioned their motivation for changing the ritual. This attitude towards women's knowledge and towards their desire to change tradition has not been restricted to the wedding ritual. Rather, women's attempts to increase their participation in any ritual or public role have been, as the religious feminist scholar Tova Hartman explains, 'overall adamantly resisted . . . It is neither women's knowledge that is questioned nor the halakhic validity of what they propose. Rather, it is their motivation—that is, their *use* of knowledge— that is scrutinized, suspected, and impugned' (2007: 18).

The grooms on the other hand expressed indifference to, or only minimal concern for, the way the wedding ritual and, specifically, the act of *kidushin* was conducted. Articulating their excitement over beginning a new life together, they did not focus on the wedding or on the ritual itself but rather on their relationship and on their love for their spouse-to-be. Yossi, one of the grooms, expressed this point of view when he said:

I could tell you today that it bothered me very much [the whole issue of acquisition in the ritual], but that would be a lie, because I did not ascribe any importance to the ritual itself. What was significant for me was finding my spouse, the relationship that was established between me and Anat . . . I was like a teenager in love who discovers it every day anew and that's what amazed me.

A similar attitude was expressed by Nir, another groom, who said: 'the meaning of getting married was very, very important to me. Did the actual ritual have the same significance? No.' Some spouses did articulate their increasing awareness of the problematic elements of the ritual, but this usually occurred only after their wives had pointed these out to them. Even those who came to this conversation with more understanding of the issues emphasized the gap between their feelings about the ritual and their feelings for their future wives.

The grooms supplied various explanations to account for their stance and, specifically, for their indifference to, or little interest in, the wedding ritual and *kidushin*. For example, one of them stated that as a man he was not so much concerned with the feminist issues engendered by *kidushin*; another groom emphasized that his relationship with his spouse was based on equality and mutuality, which contradicted the idea of acquisition. Another asserted that in case of a divorce, he would never use his advantage as a man within the religious system.

Although the language these grooms invoked reflected their total or partial indifference towards the wedding ritual, they did not generate an insensitive discourse. Rather, they empathized with their spouses in their distress over the instances of blatant inequality in the wedding ritual (for example, only men can say the seven blessings at the end of the ceremony and the *ketubah* uses patriarchal language), as well as over its problematic legal construction manifested in the unilateral act of the groom giving his bride a wedding ring and saying to her the phrase of *kidushin* with all its legal ramifications. Thus the grooms tried, in the name of their love, mutual respect, and equality to reach some compromises, such as changing the language of the *ketubah*, or having the bride give a ring as well, which would soothe her anxiety and tone down the patriarchal elements of the ritual.

The mothers of the brides generated a complex discourse that reflected, on the one hand, their identification with their daughter's unhappiness with certain aspects of the wedding ritual, and, on the other hand, their commitment to the Jewish tradition. Compared to their daughters, these mothers articulated a more conservative approach to tradition and ritual, and were less enthusiastic about initiating changes in the religious system, especially ones relating to women's equality. On the contrary, they felt they needed to place a fence around the tradition to protect it from radical, or even moderate, changes.[16]

The mothers described how they had first learned about feminism from their daughters and how, as a result, they had begun to empathize with them and to understand their difficulties with the tradition, particularly the wedding ritual. Their language revealed a perception of themselves as integrally connected to their daughters, which meant that they saw their own experience of things as closely intertwined with their daughters' experiences.[17]

Although the mothers found this connection to their daughters important, they also emphasized the gap that existed between their viewpoints. While they admitted that some changes were necessary, such as preventing situations in which a woman could suffer disadvantages as a result of her husband's refusal to give her a *get*, they also stressed that these changes needed to be introduced gradually and with rabbinic approval. Overall, they underscored the need for continuity and the importance of the community, fearing radical reforms, which they saw as leading to a break with the community and to a distortion of the familiar face of tradition. They viewed themselves as agents of socialization and, thus, as guardians of the tradition,[18] including the Jewish wedding. By supporting the wedding ritual as it is performed today, they were able to retroactively confirm the choices they had made about their own weddings and to communicate the idea that they and their daughters were links in a long chain worthy of reverence. This emphasis on the chain of tradition also influenced the tone of their discourse: while the daughters used a religious terminology that reflected their knowledge, the mothers spoke the language of emotions when describing their relation to the tradition. This emotional attachment was one of the reasons they were unwilling to give full support to the changes that their daughters had envisioned.

Regarding changes to the wedding ritual and, specifically, to the act of *kidushin*, the fathers, much like the grooms, were unconcerned with this question and were, in general, indifferent to the ritual elements of the wedding. Instead, they emphasized the importance of the relationship of the couple. Yet, there was a difference between their discourse and that of the grooms in that the fathers focused on the maintenance of three main institutional structures: the legal, the social, and the religious. Avi and Shmuel voiced their position accordingly:

I would say to my daughter, 'Do whatever you want to do in another place, but [here] do a ritual that will be accepted. So that you will be married according to what is accepted through the rabbinic institution in Israel' . . . I am not saying that I wouldn't want to change what is accepted in Israel, but first one needs to do what is acceptable, so no one will question if the marriage is according to the halakhic law and the Israeli law . . . There is the ritual, there is the legal issue, and there is the relationship between the husband and the wife and that's what is important. And I think that the relationship between the husband and the wife is not affected by the fact that the ritual is not mutual.

From a pragmatic point of view I would not suggest to any one of my daughters to get married in a Conservative wedding because, unfortunately, it is not acceptable to the rabbinate in Israel . . . there is no civil marriage in Israel and Jewish religious marriage is defined as only Orthodox, and I am not in favour of my daughters fighting for principles. There is no use in it . . . Let's assume they solve the legal problem regarding the Conservative wedding, so I would have no problem if they married that way, or even in a Reform wedding, but not in the Israel of today, or [at least] not in my social circle.

The fathers all insisted on keeping the traditional format intact, but they were motivated by different considerations. Both Avi and Shmuel highlighted the importance of performing the ritual according to the laws of Israel. Shmuel's position was especially interesting. Although he was, in principle, in favour of separating religion and state, he emphasized that until this happened his daughters had to remain within the traditional framework for political reasons. He accentuated the social implications in addition to the legal ones. He related what he had said to his daughters: 'Why don't you do your wars on other people? Instead, you embarrass the parents who have put down all the money for the wedding and invited all their friends, and in the end your [feminist] principles blow everything up.'

It is worth noting that in their statements, and throughout the interviews, Avi and Shmuel, as well as the other fathers, frequently used some form of the word 'acceptable', indicating their internalized concern for established institutions. To sum it up, the fathers spoke about the importance of maintaining the different structures from a practical and utilitarian point of view.

The rabbis' discourse can be divided into two parts. One relied on the language of law and on religious terminology, similar to the discourse of the brides. The other part, which was greater and therefore more significant, was their use of mythical and transcendental imagery to talk about the wedding ritual. Such language was applied, for example, by Rabbi Zvi:

I see a lot of wisdom in the fact that a man marries a woman. I see something mythical about it . . . I still think that a certain definition of masculinity is that the man can marry (*laset*) a woman, meaning in the simplest way that he can carry her (*nose*), and I think a woman wishes to be carried (*niset*). I think that there is something beautiful in the image of Boaz and Ruth,[19] and in the mythical scenes in the Bible when a man goes to a well and lifts up the stone [when he meets his beloved].[20] Yes, all these mythical images are powerful pictures in my mind. They are stronger than the postmodernist language which we live by, and according to which apart from some physical differences everything is completely equal.

After describing his ideas about gender relations through the play on the Hebrew word *laset*, which means both to marry and to carry, Rabbi Zvi continued to delineate how this idea was embodied in the act of *kidushin*:

From this concept [the mythical view of male and female] I think comes the idea of *kidushin*, of this ability to carry. And you wrap this idea in the language of *kidushin*, when in the ancient Jewish language, *kidushin* were done through acquisition. The acquisition is not the centre. The acquisition is the objectification through which this whole idea [of manhood and femininity] came into the world.

Rabbi Zvi recognized the element of acquisition as the essence of *kidushin*, yet he wished to interpret it in a different way. In an effort to use language to construct reality, he viewed *kidushin* as embodying a deep universal, romantic, and mythological truth, which relates to the basic relationship that is created between a man and a woman—the man who carries and the woman who wishes to be carried. It is precisely this notion that is reflected in the fact that only the man can consecrate (*lekadesh*) the woman, while the woman can only be consecrated. He, therefore, transformed the meaning of the *kidushin* act from one that has legal and halakhic bearings to one that expresses a romantic and mythical relationship. Ironically, his discourse, which sought to negate postmodern language, relied on a modern and western terminology and emphasized romantic love, which is in itself a modern concept in the context of marital relationships.

The rabbis all used terms that pointed beyond the halakhic meaning of the *kidushin* act. For example, Rabbi Shelomoh compared the bride to the Shekhinah through the use of metaphorical language.[21] By doing so he replaced the physical nature of the bride with metaphysical and spiritual dimensions. The other rabbis I interviewed expressed a similar perspective, claiming that the act of *kidushin* reflected the true reality of gender relations as they ought to be in this world: a dynamic of carrying versus being carried, activeness versus passiveness, and centrality versus marginality. Yet, the relationship between the couple stems not from the man's public activeness, but precisely from the centrality of the woman, from her sexual strength, from her silence, and from the fact that the wedding ritual is non-reciprocal. Therefore, *kidushin* is tied not only to a cosmological truth, but also to a deep psychological and sociological need to view the different genders as having innate and essential differences between them which make them unequal. Thus a clear division is made in which the male is the active one who needs to protect his bride, while she is inherently passive and needs his protection, defence, and declared devotion.

While the rabbis tend to present their reasons for forbidding innovations in the wedding ritual as rooted in halakhah, a deeper analysis of their discourse demonstrates that halakhah is not the only factor that guides their decisions and the boundaries that they set for these brides. The fact that different Orthodox rabbis allow different innovations (e.g. one rabbi will allow the bride to give a ring to the groom, while another rabbi will say this is forbidden; one will allow a woman to read the *ketubah* while another will say that this is not allowed) shows the political, psychological, and social considerations that are in play in their decision-making. Some rabbis explained why they drew the limits where they did by their emotional, rather than halakhic, connection to the tradition. That is, they forbade a change not because it was not allowed according to halakhah but rather because emotionally it felt wrong and strange to them. Some referred to the social pressure they were under from their own community, knowing that if they allowed some changes the community would disregard their authority. Others talked about their need to follow the strict rules of the rabbinate which forbade any radical changes in the legal construction of the wedding or any acts which exhibited gender equality, as this would go against their political and philosophical convictions about gender relations, regardless of what halakhah allows or does not allow. These rabbis claimed that although halakhah allowed for a certain degree of change, they did not wish to capitalize on this because they were worried about losing their authority to perform marriages in the State of Israel if the rabbinate found out. They were especially careful to make sure that their ceremonies should be distinguished from Conservative or Reform weddings, which are considered odious in Orthodox society.

In summary, the political, psychological, and social factors that influence the rabbis' decisions can explain why their discourse was uniquely marked by the use of metaphorical rather than halakhic language. Furthermore, although their authority was unquestionable, they were also aware of the limitations placed on their power by social, political, halakhic, and emotional considerations.

Social Position and Hierarchical Axes: Gender, Religious Knowledge, and Authority

On the basis of my observations, I contend that a direct correlation exists between the social position of each group and their discourse. I have identified three hierarchical axes that are instrumental in establishing the social position of each of the five interviewed groups in this context: gender, religious knowledge, and authority.[22] These axes were not chosen randomly, but because they represent two significant cultural concepts: power and control. That is, they reveal who has more power and control throughout the negotiations regarding the wedding ritual. These two concepts are present in each of the hierarchal axes and have enabled me to determine if a given group is dominant or subordinate on a particular axis.

The Gender Axis

In Judaism, men are considered more powerful than women and thus have control over them.[23] This patriarchal power, implied in giving the bride a ring and in pronouncing to her the *kidushin* phrase, is also evident in the man's legal status and the power he holds over his wife in the case of divorce. Although from a ritual point of view the woman seems to be at the centre of the ceremony with her elaborate dress and with actions revolving around her, in the legal sense it is the man who dominates in the wedding. Therefore, gender plays an important role from the outset in establishing power and control within the marital relationship, and, as we have seen, men are dominant on this axis in the Orthodox context.

The Knowledge Axis

Amos Funkenstein and Rabbi Adin Steinsaltz, authorities on Jewish literacy and history, explain why women were forbidden to take part in Torah study until recently. In their view, the Jewish world has always perceived the acquisition of religious knowledge as one of its highest and worthiest goals. In spite of this ideal, there have been marginal groups who could not participate in such an endeavour due to their social status or lack of means. As a result of their subordinate position, women historically constituted one of these groups. The widespread assumption was that they would naturally misunderstand religious texts or would use their knowledge in the wrong way since they were considered 'light-headed' and sexual beings. Therefore, women were not encouraged to study Jewish texts and were even forbidden from doing so; as a result, they largely remained ignorant in most halakhic matters (Funkenstein and Steinsaltz 1987: 75–6). Summing up the phenomenon of Torah literacy in Jewish religious society, anthropologist Tamar El-Or claims:

Religious-halachic knowledge forms the primary power centre in the organization of the daily life of religious Jewish individuals and communities. It is the material from which the imperative conceptual, moral, political, and ideological fabric is woven. This knowledge lies in the hands of 'knowing' men. (El-Or 2002: 29–30)

Thus, in strictly Orthodox and even in modern religious society, men are still considered to be more knowledgeable and, therefore, more powerful than women. Since they are the 'knowing ones', they have the tools to interpret and to develop religious laws and hence have more control than women within the religious system.

The Authority Axis

The concept of authority in our case can be divided into two parts: authority within the family—that of the parents over their children—and within society—that of the rabbis and, specifically, the rabbinic establishment which governs all the participants of the ritual. Within the family, the parents are more authoritative than their children: the brides and the grooms negotiated with their parents about the changes they wished to make to the ritual, and often ended up relinquishing their desires to meet the demands of their parents. They explained their submission by saying that they wished to show them respect, so as to avoid conflict and to maintain their good relationship. For example, Michal, who got married at the age of 30, described how she had wanted to get married in a traditional ceremony but with a Conservative rabbi. Yet she gave up on this idea since her parents insisted on having an Orthodox rabbi. It seems that even though most of these brides were in their thirties when they got married, they still relinquished many of their plans in favour of their parents' and in-laws' desires regarding their wedding ritual. This dynamic testifies to the fact that the parents were more powerful and had more control over their children than vice versa.

Viewing the concept of authority from a broader social perspective, the rabbis, and especially the rabbinate, are more authoritative than the rest of the participants in any wedding ritual, since they are the ones who dictate the rules of the traditional wedding. This authority, moreover, is not without its own inner hierarchy. On the one hand, the interviewed rabbis referred to their limited ability to change certain aspects of the wedding ritual. On the other hand, they had the authority to forbid the changes requested by the brides and grooms, a point of emphasis in my interviews with the couples. Since marriages are only acknowledged in Israel if sanctioned by the rabbinate, and since ultimately the rabbis have to be willing to perform the ceremony, people are forced to accept the rabbis' decisions (unless, of course, they choose to marry outside Israel or in a ritual that the state does not acknowledge). The rabbis, therefore, acted as delegates of the rabbinate; they were more powerful and had more control than the rest of the interviewed groups, but the ultimate authority was held by the Israeli rabbinic institution.

Between Discourse, Social Position, and Power

The way each group is positioned on the above hierarchical axes can explain their distinctive discourses. The brides were subordinate on the gender and authority axes, but dominant on the knowledge axis: they were unique among Jewish women in their ability to attain religious knowledge. They have been part of the 'literacy revolution' within Orthodox religious education which started in the 1990s and which, according to Tamar El-Or, 'has proceeded in parallel with the general progress of feminism in Israel' (2002: 28). A sign of this revolution is women learning in different *batei midrash* (religious study houses) and yeshivas for an extended period of time. These women, for the first time in history, have engaged in the study of Talmud. By entering this world of knowledge, they have also come closer to the centre of religious power (El-Or 2002: 29).

The brides' knowledge enabled them to access the religious laws and their interpretations by studying the Talmud and other complicated religious texts, and thereby to see the limits of these laws. This in turn encouraged them to enter into negotiations with their husbands, parents, and rabbis regarding certain changes they wished to make to their wedding ritual. Not only did they feel that they possessed sufficient halakhic knowledge, but also that they could use this knowledge as a source of empowerment to try and introduce new ideas. However, this ambition was crushed when confronted with the will of the others who were involved in the negotiations, especially that of the rabbis, who acted as mediators between the brides, halakhah, and the rabbinate at large.

The position of the brides on the three hierarchical axes can explain why they emphasized law and halakhic language in their discourse: it strengthened their dominant position and therefore had an empowering effect. Their knowledge enabled them first to interpret the different ritual acts, then to negotiate for the desired changes, and finally, to act, within limits, to effect change, ultimately reclaiming and reconstructing their wedding ritual.

The grooms were dominant on the axes of religious knowledge and gender, and subordinate on that of authority. Their dominance in knowledge resulted from their yeshiva education, which made it seem logical that they would produce a similar discourse to that of the brides, using the language of Jewish text and law. In fact, although some of them did refer to halakhah, it was not their main concern, as we have seen before. This can be explained by the fact that for these men dominance on the knowledge axis was taken for granted: having been born into this privilege, they had no need to use their knowledge in order to feel more empowered.

Rather, the discourse of the grooms can be characterized by the separation of the halakhic and the personal realms. They mostly demonstrated indifference to the wedding ritual and to the act of *kidushin*. This can be explained by their dominance on the axis of gender, which meant that they did not feel threatened by this ceremony: in the case of divorce, they would be in a more favourable legal position than their spouses. Therefore, they could afford to separate the halakhic construct—a hierarchical ritual—from their feelings concerning their marriage and their future wives. Hence, they stressed the personal realm, invoking the language of love and romance, and claiming that their shared life together was more significant to them than the wedding ritual.

The mothers were dominant on the authority axis as parents, yet subordinate on the gender and religious knowledge axes. Their discourse, as seen above, concentrated on the need to maintain the traditional boundaries of the wedding ritual and, in general, the Jewish tradition. They perceived themselves as socialization agents responsible for cultural and religious continuity within the family, having internalized the long-existing social message that mothers were the guardians of Jewish life. Historian Paula Hyman describes the origins of this message:

When life in the modern Western world led most assimilating Jewish men to abandon traditional Jewish culture and limit their religious expression to periodic appearances at synagogue and the performance of some communal service, their wives absorbed the dominant societal expectations of women as the guardians of religion. (Hyman 1995: 25–6)

This process accounts for the mothers' domination in the religious sphere of their home and for their insistence on preserving Jewish tradition. In comparison with the men and even with their daughters, they were subordinate on the religious knowledge axis, not having engaged in the extensive study of Jewish texts. This can explain the absence of religious and legal terminology from their discourse, and the proliferation of emotional language involving tradition. Finally, the fact that they, like their daughters, were subordinate on the axis of gender meant that they identified, at least to some degree, with the girls' aspirations and frustrations in confronting the religious system.

The fathers were dominant in all three axes: gender, religious knowledge, and authority. Their dominance on the gender axis explains their general lack of sympathy for their daughters' efforts to change the wedding ritual. Moreover, this position can also explain their indifference to the wedding ritual, or at least their choice to downplay the significance of the element of acquisition in the act of *kidushin*. Instead, like the grooms, they emphasized the importance of couplehood and of maintaining a loving relationship. The fathers and grooms were also similar in their avoidance of references to law and text. Like the grooms, the fathers viewed their knowledgeable status as a given within their social system.

Besides similarities with the grooms, the fathers also shared a dominant position with the mothers on the authority axis. However, their dominance here had an additional dimension that was absent from the mothers' authority. The fathers' authority was not restricted to the small family unit, but extended to the larger society. The power they had as men resulted from the religious authority bestowed upon them by both society and religious law. Therefore, their identification with the different institutional systems (for example, social, religious, or political) was stronger than that of the mothers and was hence articulated more loudly in their discourse. They emphasized the importance of remaining within the different institutional frameworks and the need for social and legal approval of the wedding ritual. Their discourse served, albeit indirectly, to preserve their status in the religious and social systems.

The rabbis were dominant on all three axes and consequently produced, as I explain below, a mythical and metahalakhic discourse. Although they seemed to be located on the three hierarchal axes at positions similar to the fathers', their actual status was higher on the authority axis, because their power to make religious decisions was absolute.

Since the rabbis' discourse was informed by their absolute dominance on the authority axis, it is not accidental that their language was ideologically based. Ideology is often produced by the elite precisely to justify and maintain the social order without using physical force. Moreover, it is not surprising to discover that gender ideology—an ideology of difference which, according to sociologist Susan Sered, 'elaborates and legitimates the attribution of a range of traits, roles, and statuses to men *or* women' (2001: 154)—is intertwined with the discourse about the wedding ritual. In this context ideology is a powerful tool used to persuade the unconvinced about the importance of leaving Jewish ritual unchanged.

In the specific case of Jewish marriages, rabbinic ideology finds its expression in a mythical discourse that perpetuates an outlook centred on gender power and relations, pointing to broader considerations than the halakhic construction of the wedding ritual. Using a transcendental-spiritual-mythical language in this context stabilizes and reinforces the power of the religious authority and maintains the status quo of gender roles. The rabbis' discourse portrayed men and women as essentially different and construed gender roles not as culturally derived, but as natural. Although part of this discourse placed women in the centre of the ritual, it did not really subvert the established gender roles and power relations. Rather, it strengthened them, because the final result was the justification and preservation of *kidushin* as a non-reciprocal act with all its legal implications. This perception left almost no room for fluidity and mobility in gender roles. Thus, the power of the rabbis' discourse strengthened social stereotypes regarding masculinity and femininity and presented them as inherent truths. The use of mythical images and transcendental language (for example, Jacob and Rachel, Ruth and Boaz, the Shekhinah) gave added weight to the narratives of the rabbis, because myth uses a symbolic language that evokes essential social archetypes and images, thus investing the rabbis' ideas with greater influence (Bar-Itzhak 2005: 34). When a couple speak to their rabbi and hear this language, it evinces many layers of meaning for them and touches a deep core where nationality, history, and belief converge, reminding them of the connection between the present and the past.

The mythical and transcendental language employed by the rabbis is not unique to them. Susan Sered states that many cultures use language which is grounded in biological and transcendental notions in order to create gender hierarchy. The idea that the sexes are essentially different from each other is deeply ingrained in society; therefore, the use of this concept, as well as of supernatural language, serves the social elite as a powerful tool to idealize and reinforce gender differences, which in turn establishes gender hierarchy. That is, men are perceived as having superior characteristics to women; accordingly, they should be the ones who rule and who are in control of women (Sered 2001: 115).

In describing the *kidushin* ceremony as reflecting an ultimate truth about the psychological needs and the essence of men and women, the rabbis created two different types of being: the man, who needs to be the carrier and hence, the one who consecrates, and the woman, who needs to be carried and hence, to be consecrated. These explanations illuminate why the rabbis shifted so naturally from a halakhic language to one that was mythical and transcendental (for example, referring to the bride as Shekhinah).

The ideology that the rabbis created became an interpretative tool for them, which strove to downplay the hierarchical and oppressive elements in the wedding ritual and to ease the distress of the brides concerning these elements. Their language, then, tried to compensate the brides for the absence of any essential changes in the wedding ritual. By using romantic imagery they tried to convince the brides that the inequality that existed in the ritual was not merely an unchangeable halakhic must; rather, it served the social and psychological needs of society. They thus tried to reconcile the halakhic and the modern feminist stance by romanticizing the patriarchal elements of the wedding.

Undoubtedly, the rabbis' discourse has been powerful enough to be able to maintain the social order and the notion of male authority perpetuated by the act of *kidushin*. By ascribing to this ritual act a cosmic significance, they have legitimized and sanctified it, leaving almost no room for criticizing or changing the legal construction of the wedding.

Conclusion

The different discourses examined above convey the tension that exists between the participants' subordination to the authorities and their search for autonomy and self-expression. Each group of interviewees was situated differently on the three hierarchical axes and, therefore, the discourses they produced were also positioned differently within the social pyramid. As writers on media and cultural studies Rosalind Coward and John Ellis argue, understanding language as a symbolic system, one cannot comprehend the revolutionary potential of the individual, regardless of their location in the social construct. They contend that discourse has the power to make social change, even if this change might be minor, being limited by other social forces.

The power of the brides' discourse lies in its criticism of the power of halakhah, the religious institutions, and society to determine the wedding ritual. It has the ability to create a new way of thinking about the traditional Jewish wedding. Moreover, it demythicizes the act of *kidushin* and, consequently, the hegemonic ideology surrounding it. In this sense, the brides' discourse can be defined as feminist discourse which allows women to redefine themselves in a way that undermines cultural conventions.

Yet more than just empowering these young women to reinterpret the different ritual acts, this discourse has motivated them (and their grooms) to create some significant changes, especially in the way the wedding ritual is performed (for example, the couple circling around each other instead of the bride alone circling around the groom; the bride giving a ring to the groom; allowing women to participate at the ceremony; and walking to the *ḥupah* without a veil). However, it has not had the strength to bring about a fundamental transformation in the legal construction of the wedding as expressed in the *kidushin* act and, therefore, has not been able to change significantly the legal status of women or the imbalance of gender power relations that results from this act.

The rabbis' discourse and its tendency to mythicize the *kidushin* ceremony, on the other hand, has the power to shape the boundaries of the wedding ritual. Here the identification of *kidushin* as an act of acquisition does not merely reflect the demands of halakhah, but rather creates a new gender ideology. The rabbis are able, as sociologist Pierre Bourdieu puts it, to 'constitute the given by stating it, to create appearances and belief, to confirm or transform the vision of the world and thereby action in the world, and therefore the world itself' (1977: 117). In other words, beyond affirming social power, their discourse creates reality, and since it receives its legitimacy from different institutions (religious, social, and political) as well as from the people themselves, its power to 'constitute the given' is greater than that of the other discourses, which do not enjoy such legitimacy. In general, the discourse of the social elite has much more power compared to the other discourses and thus acts as a dominant force in society and in the construction of power relations (Bar-Itzhak 2005: 48). At times it even silences other discourses and any of their efforts to resist and to change the social order. In this way, one ideological discourse becomes sacred while the others are marginalized.

The brides (and husbands) who wish to transform the religious system find themselves in an ironic situation. The women who choose to press for change while recognizing the limits are, consciously or not, contributing to the perception of the monopoly of halakhic power, and, in turn, of the rabbis' authority.

Folklorist Haya Bar-Itzhak demonstrates how the stories that mythicize and demythicize the society of the kibbutz reflect the tension between preservation and contemporary complexities in that society (2005), and I have found a similar situation in the case of the wedding ritual. The existence of two linguistic tendencies, mythicization—expressed in the rabbis' discourse—and demythicization—expressed in the brides' discourse—reflects a social tension. On the one side there is the struggle to defend and maintain the tradition, with its ancient roots, and on the other side exists the desire to expose the tradition with all its imperfections and complexities.

As for the discourse of the grooms, mothers, and fathers, it has the ability either to increase or to diminish the power of the brides' discourse. If they choose to offer support, the brides have more leverage to stretch the boundaries of the wedding ritual. Women who had the support of those around them were able to create more significant changes compared to brides who had no social support for their wishes. That is, these discourses can create additional pressure on the rabbis and the rabbinate.

Women are not only passive objects within given patriarchal constructs. Rather, they can choose to be active subjects who work within those same constructs to bring about change by creating an alternative discourse followed by action. The brides in my research, being dominant on the axis of religious knowledge, demonstrated their ability to be agents of social and cultural change. Discourse is the first critical step for women to initiate change in a religious system by articulating, and protesting against, its problematic elements; this step must take place before actual change can occur. Thus, the power of discourse is not abstract, but rather has concrete influence on reality.

In closing, I refer to the words of anthropologist Clifford Geertz who wrote, 'seeing heaven in a grain of sand is not a trick only poets can accomplish' (1973: 44). Geertz sought out of these grains of sand the heaven of a much broader phenomenon. Similarly, although I have focused here on one religious ritual, I believe that these women's discourse represents a larger struggle faced by citizens of a modern, increasingly transnational world to remain at home with their religious traditions and to reconcile their modern identities with pre-modern ritual practice. Thus while this essay discusses a specific ritual phenomenon, it addresses more broadly the tension between religion and modernity that is apparent in a whole range of contexts, both within and outside the Jewish world.

Notes

1   The fear of being identified as a feminist and, thus, the hesitancy to define oneself as one has been discussed elsewhere. For example, see Goldhor Lerner 1985.

2   To learn more about the role of ritual in society, see Myerhoff 1982; Bell 1992, 1997.

3   I was looking for women who defined themselves as religious and as feminists and for whom the wedding ritual was a point of contention. Since these women had similar characteristics in other respects, too, the group came out fairly homogeneous.

4   These neighbourhoods are home to several progressive Jewish study centres and various types of social, religious, and spiritual activity, and have a high concentration of immigrants from English-speaking countries.

5   Most of these women had a graduate degree and some had a Ph.D. or were in the process of getting one. In addition, most of them had spent a considerable amount of time after high school at women's yeshivas, where they learned material that is traditionally only studied by men in their yeshivas, such as Talmud.

6   To learn more about the ways in which rituals are modified and invented, see Ochs 2007.

7   I have chosen to focus on the Ashkenazi ritual since most of the brides I interviewed were Ashkenazi and had been married according to Ashkenazi customs. To learn more about the customs of the Sephardi community, see Goldberg 2003; Ochs 2007.

8   The seven blessings, which come from different religious texts, were added at the time of the Sages (the mishnaic period, c.200 BCE–200 CE) to strengthen the religious component of the Jewish wedding ritual. Its importance is exemplified by the requirement to have ten Jewish men in attendance to be able to say these blessings. See Rubin 2004.

9   There is a certain age past which the woman does not need her father's consent, but even then she transfers her sexual rights to her husband's ownership through this act. In the wedding ritual this transformation is not expressed in any visible way.

10   An *agunah* is a woman whose husband has disappeared or is otherwise unable to give his wife a *get* (bill of divorce). A *mesurevet get* is a woman whose husband abuses the power

bestowed on him by the halakhah and refuses to grant her a *get*. For more information on *agunot* and *mesuravot get*, see <http://www.agunot.org>.

11   At the turn of the 10th and 11th centuries Rabenu Tam (Gershom ben Yehudah) issued a ruling in Ashkenazi Europe, stating that a man's *get* was not valid unless the woman agreed to accept it. This rule was supposed to balance the power relations between men and women in cases of divorce. Nevertheless, the gap between the sexes in this context was still significant, since in the case of her refusal he could get permission to divorce her as long as he got a hundred rabbis to agree.

12   For a discussion of the changes made by the brides through action, see Koren 2005.

13   The Hebrew text of the prenuptial agreement worked out by Kolech: Religious Women's Forum for use in Israel can be found at <http://www.kolech.com>.

14   According to the halakhah, for a Jewish couple to get divorced, the man must give the woman a *get* of his own free will, and she must accept it.

15   According to the Israel Women's Network and the women's organization Mavoi Satum, there are several thousand *mesuravot get* in Israel, in addition to some twenty *agunot*.

16   This approach does not contradict their acknowledgement that tradition has evolved throughout time and that some changes are needed in different aspects of Jewish law. On the ways Jewish tradition has evolved see Webber's comments in Webber 1994.

17   On mother–daughter relationships and attachment, see Chodorow 1978; Gilligan 1993.

18   On the relationship of Jewish and Christian mothers to their religion, see Halbertal 2002.

19   Boaz and Ruth are figures in the biblical book of Ruth.

20   This is a reference to the story of Jacob who was enabled to remove a heavy stone blocking a well by himself when he saw Rachel, his future wife, for the first time (Gen. 29: 10).

21   The Shekinah is held by many to represent the feminine attributes of the presence of God (*shekhinah* being feminine in Hebrew), based especially on readings of the Talmud and later on the mystical trend in Judaism called kabbalah.

22   A similar study was conducted by Susan Sered, Romi Kaplan, and Samuel Cooper, who compare the discourses of different groups based on a different set of social hierarchical axes and in the context of a different religious ritual. See Sered et al. 1999.

23   See e.g. Biale 1984.

References

ARANOFF, SUSAN. 2000. 'Two Views of Marriage—Two Views of Women: Reconsidering *Tav Lemetav Tan Du Milemetav Armelu*', *Nashim*, 3: 199–227.

BAR-ITZHAK, HAYA. 2005. *Israeli Folk Narratives: Settlement, Immigration, Ethnicity*. Detroit.

BAUMAN, RICHARD. 1992. 'Performance'. In id., ed., *Folklore, Cultural Performances, and Popular Entertainments: A Communications-Centered Handbook*, 41–9. New York.

BELL, CATHERINE. 1992. *Ritual Theory, Ritual Practice*. New York.

——1997. *Ritual, Perspectives and Dimensions*. New York.

BIALE, RACHEL. 1984. *Women and Jewish Law*. New York.

BOURDIEU, PIERRE. 1977. 'Symbolic Power', trans. Colin Wringe. In Denis Gleeson, ed., *Issues in the Sociology of Education*, 112–19. Nafferton, Driffield.

CHODOROW, NANCY. 1978. *The Reproduction of Mothering: Psychoanalysis and the Sociology of Gender*. Berkeley.

COWARD, ROSALIND, and JOHN ELLIS. 1977. *Language and Materialism: Developments in Semiology and the Theory of the Subject*. London.

DAVIDMAN, LYNN, and SHELLY TENENBAUM, eds. 1994. *Feminist Perspectives on Jewish Studies*. New Haven.

EL-OR, TAMAR. 2002. *Next Year I Will Know More: Literacy and Identity among Young Orthodox Women in Israel*, trans. Haim Watzman. Detroit.

FAIRCLOUGH, NORMAN. 1992. *Discourse and Social Change*. Cambridge.

FUNKENSTEIN, AMOS, and ADIN STEINSALTZ. 1987. *The Sociology of Ignorance* [Hasotsiologiyah shel haba'arut]. Tel Aviv.

GEERTZ, CLIFFORD. 1973. *The Interpretation of Culture*. New York.

GILLIGAN, CAROL. 1993. *In a Different Voice: Psychological Theory and Women's Development*. Cambridge, Mass.

GOLDBERG, HARVEY E. 2003. *Jewish Passages: Cycles of Jewish Life*. Berkeley, Calif.

GOLDHOR LERNER, HARRIET. 1985. *The Dance of Anger: A Woman's Guide to Changing the Patterns of Intimate Relationships*. New York.

GORDIS, DANIEL H. 1993. 'Marriage: Judaism's "Other" Covenantal Relationship'. In Rela Geffen, ed., *Celebration and Renewal: Rites of Passage in Judaism*, 90–131. Philadelphia.

HALBERTAL, TOVA. 2002. *Appropriately Subversive: Modern Mothers in Traditional Religions*. Cambridge, Mass.

HARTMAN, TOVA. 2007. *Feminism Encounters Traditional Judaism*. Waltham, Mass.

HAUPTMAN, JUDITH. 1998. *Rereading the Rabbis: A Woman's Voice*. Boulder, Colo.

HYMAN, PAULA E. 1995. *Gender and Assimilation in Modern Jewish History: The Roles and Representation of Women*. Seattle.

KAMIR, ORIT. 2002. *Feminism, Rights, and Law* [Feminizm, zekhuyot umishpat]. Tel Aviv.

KOREN, IRIT. 2005. 'The Bride's Voice: Religious Women Challenge the Wedding Ritual', *Nashim*, 10: 29–52.

LAMM, MAURICE. 1980. *The Jewish Way in Love and Marriage*. San Francisco.

MANNING, CHRISTEL J. 1999. *God Gave Us the Right: Conservative Catholic, Evangelical Protestant, and Orthodox Jewish Women Grapple with Feminism*. New Brunswick, NJ.

MIRSKY, YEHUDA. 2007. 'Modernizing Orthodoxies: The Case of Feminism'. In Tova Cohen, ed., *To Be a Jewish Woman* [Lihyot ishah yehudiyah], 37–51. Jerusalem.

MYERHOFF, BARBARA. 1982. 'Rites of Passage: Process and Paradox'. In Victor Turner, ed., *Celebration: Studies in Festivity and Ritual*, 109–35. Washington, DC.

OCHS, VANESSA. 2007. *Inventing Jewish Ritual*. Philadelphia.

OKIN, SUSAN. 2000. 'Marriage, Divorce, and the Politics of Family Life' (Heb.). In Tova Cohen, ed., *Marriage, Liberty and Equality: Shall the Three Walk Together?* [Nisuin, ḥerut veshivyon: hayelkhu sheloshtam yaḥdav?], 7–26. Ramat Gan.

ROSS, TAMAR. 2004. *Expanding the Palace of Torah: Orthodoxy and Feminism*. Waltham, Mass.

RUBIN, NISSAN. 2004. *The Joy of Life: Rites of Betrothal and Marriage in the Talmud and Midrash* [Simḥat haḥayim: tiksei eirusim venisuim bimekorot ḥazal]. Tel Aviv.

SERED, SUSAN S. 2001. 'Religiously Doing Gender: The Good Woman and the Bad Woman in Israeli Ritual Discourse', *Method and Theory in the Study of Religion*, 13(2): 153–76.

——ROMI KAPLAN, and SAMUEL COOPER. 1999. 'Talking about Miqveh Parties, or Discourses of Gender, Hierarchy and Social Control'. In Rahell Wasserfall, ed., *Women and Water: Menstruation in Jewish Life and Law*, 139–65. Hanover, NH.

SHERZER, JOEL. 1992. 'Ethnography of Speaking'. In Richard Bauman, ed., *Folklore, Cultural Performances, and Popular Entertainments: A Communications-Centered Handbook*, 76–80. New York.

VAN DIJK, TEUN A. 1997. 'Discourse as Interaction in Society'. In id., ed., *Discourse as Social Interaction: Discourse Studies: A Multidisciplinary Introduction*, ii. 1–37. London.

WEBBER, JONATHAN, ed. 1994. *Jewish Identities in the New Europe*. London.

WEGNER, JUDITH. 1988. *Chattel or Person? The Status of Women in the Mishnah*. New York.

EIGHT

Tradition in Intercultural Transition: Marriage Rituals in Ethiopia and Israel

RACHEL SHARABY

TRADITIONALLY, ETHIOPIAN JEWS have perceived the act of marriage as a series of rituals taking place over many months. This long process of institution-alizing the bond between spouses and of forging a new family unit can be seen as reflecting the basic norms of Ethiopian Jewish society since, in accordance with Haim Hazan's definition, it mirrors the local social relationships and hierarchies as well as the beliefs and ideologies of the participating individuals (Hazan 1992). Israeli sociologist Nissan Rubin's thesis (1995: 12), according to which ritual changes take place in parallel with changes in the social structure, is also applic-able to the case of marriage rituals among Ethiopian Jews. In this essay, I examine the connection between marriage ritual and social structure among Ethiopian Jews as they underwent a major cultural shift following their move from Ethiopia to Israel. Together with other elements of their tradition, the wedding cere-mony was significantly revised and the meaning of Ethiopian Jewish identity sub-sequently reconceptualized. These developments have led me to ask what role changes in marriage rituals play in facilitating the transition from a non-Jewish to a Jewish social environment.

My research is based on interviews with twenty-five men and women bet-ween the ages of 35 and 70 who had married in Ethiopia and emigrated to Israel as part of the Israeli government initiatives known as Operation Moses (1984) and Operation Solomon (1991).[1] I also interviewed five young couples in their twenties who had married in Israel, as well as four men who were *kessoch* (plural; singular *kes*), the priests of the community. The interviews were conducted in Hebrew in the informants' homes, and younger members of the family served as interpreters in cases where the interviewees only spoke an Ethiopian lan-guage (Amharic or Tigrinya). However, my main focus was on older members of the community who could offer a comparative perspective on ritual conduct in Ethiopia and Israel.

Informants fondly and vividly recalled the marriage-related customs of Ethiopia. However, women often avoided (for reasons of modesty) speaking ex-plicitly about intimate matters; for example, instead of using the word virginity, they spoke of the bride's purity. Most of the interviewees seemed to have accepted the ritual changes they had experienced in Israel, such as people marrying at an older age, fewer celebrations, and the way young people chose their partners, which appeared to them to be only minor changes. The older generation understood that immigration had necessitated social change, and they deferred to the wishes of their children.

The idea for this research first came to me when in 2005 I interviewed a *kes* for another study I was involved in, relating to the menstruation huts (*margam gojo*) of Ethiopian immigrants in Israel (Cicurel and Sharaby 2007). It was through him that I came into contact with the first of the older interviewees, who belonged to his community. The number of interviews then quickly snowballed as these people referred me to additional men and women from other settlements where immigrants from Ethiopia were concentrated. Younger couples who had married in Israel provided valuable narratives on Ethiopian Jewish rituals as they are practised in Israel today. However, the description that follows is based mainly on video recordings that they shared with me. I also participated in weddings that took place in various banqueting halls in Israel. After learning about Ethiopian ritual activity from written descriptions and from interviews, these personal observations enriched my knowledge of how marriage rituals are conducted today, and enhanced my understanding of the differences between the past and the present.

Jewish Social Structure and Village Life in Ethiopia

In Ethiopia the Jews, also known as Beta Israel, were concentrated mostly in the north of the country. They typically lived in rural communities and earned their living from agriculture (Ben-Ezer 1992; Corinaldi 2005), residing in Jewish villages or in enclaves within predominantly Christian villages. They chose to live near rivers as they needed access to fresh water for purification purposes (Kaplan and Rosen 1993). Beta Israel has sub-groups which are defined according to their district of origin in Ethiopia. The main district is Tigray province in the northern highlands, whose Tigrinya-speaking inhabitants are called 'Tigrinya people'. Another large segment of Ethiopian Jewry is from the Amhara region in the north-western part of the country, including the area around the city of Gondar, the old imperial capital of the emperors of Ethiopia who claimed descent from King Solomon and the Queen of Sheba. Ethiopian Jews from this region are called Gondars or Amharis (Kacen and Bakshy 2004).

An important aspect of Ethiopian Jewish social structure was the leadership of the *kessoch*. The *kessoch* had authority in a number of fields including matters pertaining to religion and custom, setting the dates of holidays, and officiating at marriage, divorce, and burial ceremonies, as well as placing sanctions on anyone who deviated from religious and social conventions (Banai and Bachar 1988;

Kacen et al. 2005). The priests encouraged separation from Christian society to preserve tradition and to curb intermarriage and assimilation (Bodowski et al. 1994).

Informants recalled Jewish villages in Ethiopia as consisting of an array of huts (*tokols*) within fenced lots. Each *tokol* was home to an extended family (*seb*) of up to four generations. Bound by marital ties, several extended families lived in each village (Minuchin et al. 1997: 73–4); solidarity and mutual help were highly rated both within the families (Shabtai 1999: 57) and in the larger community (Bodowski et al. 1989). The extended Jewish family in Ethiopia was patriarchal and patrilocal. One of the interviewees, who had been born in the village of Seramle, said that after getting married, he and his wife went to live in a hut that was set up on his father's land in the village, and so did his married brothers. This was typical of multigenerational extended families headed by the father, where married sons lived in huts near the father's hut on a piece of land owned by the father, and households were managed jointly, so as to avoid breaking up the family property. This social structure further facilitated mutual aid and collective activity.

Ethiopian Jews maintained social boundaries through customs of purification. A prime example is the way they differentiated themselves from Christians in purification rituals related to unclean blood. Women stayed in a special hut (*margam gojo*) on the outskirts of their village during menstruation or after childbirth (Anteby-Yemini 1997; Weil 2004). Residents erected a stone fence around the hut to mark the impure space, and female members of the impure woman's family left food for her next to the fence, avoiding any contact with her (Alpert 1958: 10–13; Cicurel and Sharaby 2007). This strict observance of purity was one expression of the commitment of the Jewish community in Ethiopia to maintaining a separate Jewish identity within a multi-ethnic society (Salamon 1993).

Custom also required the Ethiopian Jewish woman to submit to her husband; if she did not obey him, he was permitted to divorce her. Nonetheless, in cases of separation or conflict, arrangements existed to preserve a woman's rights, including equal division of the property and child support from the husband (Shabtai 1999). The extended family which the woman joined after her marriage constituted her primary support system, but she could always obtain help from her family of origin in case of trouble or a conflict with her husband, even after her marriage. In extreme cases she could even return to her parents' home (Bodowski et al. 1994).

A clear distinction existed between the 'private sphere' (the woman's realm) and the 'public sphere' (accessible only to men). As the heads and spokesmen of their families, men worked in agriculture, shepherding, and different crafts. The women were responsible for running the household and for raising the children. In certain regions they worked in pottery, embroidery, or weaving baskets, and sometimes helped the men in agricultural work, thereby contributing to the family income (Weil 1991). However, since women's work was often interrupted for reasons of childbirth and childcare, in practice it was secondary as a source of livelihood for the family, and the husband was the main provider. Reserved for the men, the public sphere was the venue for making communal decisions; since women were not granted access to this space, they were excluded not only from holding economic power but also from exercising political influence (Leitman and Weinbaum 1999).

Immigration and Absorption in Israel

How did the immigration and absorption process affect the transition of traditions from Ethiopia to Israel? In 1975, the chief rabbis of Israel formally recognized Beta Israel as Jews, thus enabling their immigration in accordance with the Law of Return. They first started fleeing via Sudan in 1977 and, following a civil war and famine that endangered the entire country, the ethnic exodus of a few individuals turned into mass migration in 1982. Ethiopian Jews often walked hundreds of kilometres, enduring hunger and thirst, attacks by bandits, and threats of rape (Yilma 1995). Once in Sudan, refugees faced harsh conditions in the camps and many observers were concerned that camp life would undermine the support systems of community and family (Corinaldi 1988).

Following numerous deaths in the camps, the need arose to support those who had been widowed, and many men and women quickly married. Arranged by the *kessoch*, these new family bonds, which were called 'Sudan marriages', often broke up soon after the couples arrived in Israel: either it was discovered that the first husband or wife was still alive,[2] or the relationship was not stable enough to survive life in a new country (Weil 1991). Another immigration issue arose with 30,000 refugees called Falashmura (Jews who had converted to Christianity), who were pressured to reconvert to Judaism upon arrival in Israel (Weil 2004).

Unlike other immigrants to Israel, most Ethiopian Jews were integrated in a process of 'mediated absorption' (absorption centres), rather than 'direct absorption', where émigrés could choose their place of residence and settle independently (Sever 2000: 165–84). The existence of a separate immigration policy towards the Ethiopians reflected the view of the Israeli government that they needed close supervision by absorption centre workers in order to successfully integrate into Israeli society. This paternalistic attitude led to feelings of alienation and dependence among the immigrants from Ethiopia, and hindered their integration (Halper 1985; Newman 1985[3]).

The fact that the absorption centres were organized around the concept of the nuclear family characteristic of Western society, without taking into account the traditional structure of the extended Ethiopian family, presented a further problem. The officials interfered not only in the immigrants' social connections but also in their customs: no synagogues or community centres were established for those living in the absorption centres, and they were not encouraged to practise their rituals. Moreover, immigration officials rarely studied the history and traditions of the new arrivals beforehand and did not regard Ethiopian culture as playing a major role in their absorption (Halper 1985).

The immigrants from Ethiopia posed a new challenge for Israeli society, which had to cope with a difference that was expressed in external appearance, skin colour, and a cultural distance which Israel had not experienced previously (Yossi and Shenhav 2005: 62–3). The ethnocentric goal of the officials was to use the absorption centres to enable the adjustment of the new immigrants to Israeli culture (Newman 1985; Shechory 2006). In order to register as Jews in the population census, the Ethiopians were first required to undergo circumcision and ritual immersion as part of a 'conversion' to Judaism. Some of the immigrants objected and viewed the demand to convert as humiliating or racist. In response, the Israeli rabbinate retracted in 1985, recognizing Ethiopian circumcision and giving authority to a national marriage registrar to determine marriage registration on a case-by-case basis (Kaplan and Salamon 2004: 131–2; Kimmerling 2004: 442).

The debate regarding the authenticity of the Ethiopians' Judaism also harmed the status of the community's priests (Weil 1997) who, not being recognized by the religious establishment, lost their authority both among the Ethiopians and in Israel at large to handle religious matters and customs of the Jews of Ethiopia (Corinaldi 1988: 191). Additionally, Ethiopian youths who underwent accelerated processes of modernization and secularization did not seek out the *kessoch* any more (Minuchin et al. 1997: 27; Shabtai 1999). After a struggle by activists from the Ethiopian community in the early 1990s, some of the *kessoch* were integrated into the rabbinical establishment (Kaplan and Salamon 2004): they officially became recognized as rabbis and received a salary from the state. These *kessoch* handled issues of religion, including marriage, divorce, and burial rituals.

Family life also underwent a significant change following immigration to Israel. The women and children adjusted to Israeli society with greater ease than the men, whose status had been significantly weakened in the transition. Opportunities stemming from the new society's egalitarian ethos opened for female immigrants and they were learning to be independent in making decisions and in managing their lives (Leitman and Weinbaum 1999). For the first time, women had access to higher education; national insurance payments became available to them, and they were encouraged to work outside the home and to collect a social security pension. This economic support turned the Ethiopian woman into a provider separate from her husband, and promoted her economic and emotional independence. Furthermore, women were afforded the possibility of controlling their fertility by using contraceptives, which led to a decline in the birth rate following their immigration to Israel (Phillips 1999). Another consequence was an increase in the number of women who were single parents. These were mainly divorcees, but there were also some who had babies out of wedlock (Weil 1991). As the above changes indicate, immigration can serve as a lever for new opportunities for female immigrants and as a source for their empowerment (see e.g. Gilad 1989; Yung 1995).

Marriage Rituals in Ethiopia

To assess the cultural changes triggered by the shift from a hierarchical social structure in Ethiopia to an egalitarian system in Israel, I turn now to the marriage ritual as it was practised in Ethiopia. Marriages comprised several stages: match-making, engagement, and henna and wedding ceremonies in the villages of the bride and the groom, with each ritual having a discrete function. They took place in parallel or alternately, at the home of the bride or the groom, with the participation of the community elders, who had been involved in making the connection between the families from the onset. As will be demonstrated, the entire ritual system depended on the distance between the villages of the marrying families and their economic status.

The Marriage Period and Matchmaking

In Ethiopian custom, the pre-wedding period of several months contains a series of rituals to help the bride and groom disengage from their former social status and adjust to the new one. During this period the young couple are in a liminal state, which has been characterized by Turner as betwixt and between (1967: 93–110). In other words, the participants are 'no longer' (single) and 'not yet' (married). This is a moratorium period in which the bride and groom become 'invisible'. Their first names are taken from them and they are called 'bride' and 'groom' by their families and community members. The 'liminal' couple accept the authority of the adults who represent the common good of the community and enter into a phase of passive learning of the values represented by this good.

Interviewees emphasized that in Ethiopia the bride and groom were not permitted to work outside or in the home in the month before their marriage. They did not leave the house unescorted, and were under supervision and control at all times. A folk rationale for these and other pre-wedding restrictions is that the bride and groom are considered vulnerable and need ritual protection.

It was customary for parents to make arrangements for their children (especially the daughters) to marry. Girls usually married around the age of 12, when they reached puberty. However, the girl's physical and emotional maturity was not always taken into account when choosing the time for the marriage, and some women told me that they had been matched as young as 9 or 10 years old. They explained that the reason for marrying early stemmed from the need to preserve their honour (code for virginity) and their family's reputation as well as to avoid intermarriage with Christians. The parents did not regard their daughter's marriage before her sexual maturity as a problem; their main concern was to ensure she was married.

Boys usually married between the ages of 15 and 18, when they began to work with their fathers (Corinaldi 1988: 78; Shabtai 1999: 54). The practice of marrying young was made possible, as in other traditional societies, by a socioeconomic structure in which the young couple became part of the extended household of the husband's family (Rubin 2004: 40). Furthermore, in a traditional agricultural society young people could be considered adults socially and could marry even before puberty since by that point they had already learned most of the skills that adults in their society needed to have (Rubin 2005: 143).

The matchmaking stage began with the search for a bride by the groom's parents (Corinaldi 1988: 78; Waldman 1990: 26, 41). Together with the village elders, they carried out an in-depth enquiry into the intended bride's genealogy. They first examined whether any kinship existed between the two families (both on the mothers' and the fathers' sides) as far back as the last seven generations; if kinship did exist, the marriage was forbidden (Corinaldi 1988: 78). According to some field studies, in practice families accepted a distance of only three or four generations rather than strictly adhering to the limit of seven (Bodowski et al. 1994: 41; Sabar 2006: 187). The interviewees related that in the Tigray region of Ethiopia the tradition allowed for fewer generations to be counted, whereas other communities followed the more stringent rule. The interviewees explained that this restriction was observed for medical reasons: the fear that any offspring would have genetic diseases. They also said that the Jews of Ethiopia regarded a relative within the range of seven generations as a brother or sister, and therefore marriage between them would constitute incest.

These concerns about possible kinship meant that parents preferred to look for a bride in distant villages. An informant related, for example, that 'my parents went and found a Jewish girl in a distant village, which was a day's walk away, and made a match for me. She was 9 at the time and I was 15. A year after the match we were married.' The groom's parents also made enquiries about the girl's behaviour and her ability to run a household, as well as her family's economic status.

When the enquiries were over, the groom's father sent elders from his village to the bride's parents to ask for her hand. This process of mediation was important for preserving the family's honour in case of a refusal. According to the interviewees, this custom originated with the patriarch Abraham, who had sent his servant to Rebecca's family to ask for her hand in marriage for his son Isaac (Gen. 24). They added that in some communities it was customary to send three envoys to the bride's home, in imitation of the three angels who informed Abraham of the coming birth of Isaac (Gen. 18). Another explanation was that two of the emissaries were to serve as witnesses as the third one transmitted the message to the bride's family.

The bride's father usually did not give an immediate answer, since this would have indicated that he was eager to part with his daughter, but asked for time to think. During this time he consulted with his relatives and, using envoys, enquired about the lineage of the intended groom. They too checked back seven generations to ensure that there was no kinship, and scrutinized additional details of the boy's behaviour, his health, and his family's economic and social status. Any antagonism between the relatives of the bride and groom was also a reason for rejecting a match.

A few weeks later the envoys paid a second visit to the bride's home, this time with the groom's father. If the answer was negative, they returned to their village; if the girl's family answered in the affirmative, the groom's father handed a sum of money (*iag minshia*) to the bride's father in the presence of witnesses from both sides to seal the agreement (Corinaldi 1988: 78; Waldman 1990: 41).

The payment symbolized that the girl now 'belonged' to the boy, and upon its acceptance the girl's father made a commitment to give his daughter to no other man except the intended groom. If he broke his promise, the village elders could make him pay a steep fine to the groom's family. The money could also be regarded as part of the dowry payments, which were customary among other traditional Jewish societies as well (Sabar 2006: 196–7). Since it was the wife who joined her husband's clan, the dowry constituted a compensation to her extended family for the loss of her work power and the children that she was to bear for her husband's household (Rubin 1972: 118–19).

The Engagement Ritual

When the matchmaking took place between nearby villages, the families set a date for the engagement at the time of handing over the money. However, when the villages were far apart, or when the economic status of the families allowed, an engagement ritual (*kal-kidan*) took place on the spot. The entire matchmaking and engagement process was negotiated by the fathers of the families; the future bride and groom were uninvolved. The families did not ask them whether they wanted to get married or whether they liked each other, and the couple did not meet until the wedding day.

According to the interviewees, the engagement ceremony was a great feast held by the bride's family, to which the groom's parents were invited, as well as relatives, neighbours, and the elders of the villages (see also Corinaldi 1988: 78; Waldman 1990: 5, 41). The bride's family slaughtered a sheep or goat, prepared traditional dishes and served home-made beer (*tela*). The engagement ritual symbolized the beginning of the bond between the two young people and their families as well as of the bride's disengagement from her parental home and passage to her husband's house (Rubin 2004).

During the ceremony, the groom's father presented the bride's father with shoes, clothes, and jewellery—earrings, gold bracelets for the hands and feet, and a long necklace composed of three silver chains—for the bride. The girl also received a medallion of a silver coin, which she had to wear around her neck until her marriage as a statement that she was betrothed. Wearing the jewellery symbolized the transition to married life, since according to the women I interviewed, in Ethiopia unmarried women did not wear any jewellery, which made it easier to know who was single and who was married. Simultaneously, the groom's parents received clothes along with sheep and cattle for the groom from the bride's parents, so that the couple would have some assets and a source of income.

The exchange of gifts between the parties was a prominent expression of bonding between the families and symbolized their betrothal pact. During the engagement ceremony they agreed on the conditions and date of the marriage which could take place within a few months, a year, or sometimes several years later. Typically, the wedding could not be held before the bride's first menstruation (see Shabtai 1999: 54). As mentioned above, cases of early marriage did arise with girls marrying as young as 9 or 10 years old and leaving their parents' home to live with the groom's family. This, however, could only happen if the groom's parents promised the bride's father that they would take the girl under their patronage and would make sure that the wedding would not be consummated until she matured physically. She also had to be able to manage a household, a role which she learned under the supervision of her mother and her future mother-in-law. When the two women concluded that the bride was ready for marriage, the families agreed on a date.

While the community was still based in Ethiopia, there were additional factors the two families had to take into consideration when setting the date for the marriage (Shabtai 1999: 54). In winter, attention turned to agricultural work, and the frequent rains during these months could hamper the wedding, which was customarily performed in a hut. Another reason why the marriage had to take place in summer was the economic consideration that it was only after collecting and selling the crops that there would be sufficient money to buy provisions and to prepare the meals and the beer from wheat, barley, or other grains.

Choosing the date of the wedding was a major decision informed by a number of conditions. The wedding night had to be a full moon, since there was no electricity in the villages and the guests had to return home late. The groom and his men also had to reach the hut in the bride's village and were to return to the groom's hut late at night aided only by moonlight. Another condition was that the bride could not be menstruating because Ethiopian Jews strictly followed the biblically derived laws of purity. The responsibility for choosing the wedding date fell on the parents; the couple had no say.

After the two families had set a date for the wedding, preparations were begun. One of the difficulties in planning the wedding was the physical distance between the villages: travel was hampered by a lack of automobile transportation and dangers encountered on the way. The problem was solved by each family constructing a wedding hut next to its home, covered with branches and straw or olive leaves that symbolized love and peace. The two families would then celebrate separately, each with its own guests. Preparations for the wedding thus proceeded, with the investment of much thought, time, and money (Shabtai 1999: 54; Waldman 1990: 41).

The preparations reached their peak during the week of the wedding, and this final stage included building a house for the couple (undertaken by the groom's family), getting new utensils, sewing new clothes for the bride and groom, buying bulls or sheep and slaughtering them two days before the wedding, collecting wood, preparing a mixture of spices as well as traditional dishes, kneading the dough for the Ethiopian thin bread (*injera*) and baking it, cooking meat sauce to accompany the bread, and making beer and other alcoholic beverages.

Thus, as in other traditional societies, the engagement period in Ethiopia was a liminal state between being single and being married. The passage from one state to the other was a long process, which required an intermediate period for the families to make economic preparations (especially on the groom's side) and for the couple to adjust to the idea of married life.

The Henna Ritual

On the evening before the wedding, the bride (*mushera*) went to the river with a married woman to purify herself. That night a henna ceremony took place in the bride's home, marking the last ritual phase before the wedding (Corinaldi 1988: 78; Waldman 1990: 42). It was held only for the bride and not the groom, because marriage constituted a more significant rite of passage for her than for him: she was undergoing what Ethiopians viewed as a major transition from young girl to wife. Additionally, she became separated from her parents and went to live in her husband's home. Before the henna ceremony, the bride's girlfriends gathered around her and entertained her with traditional songs and dances. At the conclusion of the ritual, the bride's family slaughtered a goat or sheep and prepared a meal for the relatives, neighbours, and acquaintances.

In Ethiopia the henna paste was made from the red, potato-like root of a local plant called *gurshit*, which was peeled and washed. There were two ways of preparing the henna paste (*insusilei*). Some Ethiopian Jews cut the roots into small pieces and cooked them in a bowl until a thick red paste was obtained, in which the bride dipped her fingernails and toenails. Others recalled rubbing the root on a tool similar to a grater. They then placed the paste in a bowl and dried it in the sun; it thus acquired a deep red colour and remained warm until the ceremony. Afterwards the paste was mixed with lemon juice to give it a smooth texture, and the girlfriends or women neighbours spread it over the bride's hands and feet. They then applied the paste on their own hands and feet. The interviewees explained that the red colour was intended to dye the skin. Henna was also attributed healing properties and was considered good for the skin.

The *Keshra* Ritual

At noon on the wedding day a festive event took place in the groom's village, which was called the *keshra* ritual (Corinaldi 1988: 78–9; Waldman 1990: 42–3). The priest slaughtered a goat or sheep in the morning and the women prepared a festive meal. As noon approached, the groom put on a white shirt and trousers (as symbols of purity), and went with his groomsmen to the large wedding hut, where they ate with the guests.

At the end of the meal the groom's relatives brought a chair into the centre of the hut and placed it on a stage. Escorted by his family, the groom walked up to the chair and sat down. Upon the sounding of drums and cymbals the priests blessed the groom for success in his marriage and for economic prosperity. In the meantime one of the priests prepared a red-and-white ribbon (or two ribbons, one red and one white) called *keshra* to be tied around the groom's forehead. Interviewees said that the white colour symbolized the purity of the groom and red the purity of the bride (the blood of virginity).

According to another explanation by people from the Tigray region, the colours of the ribbon were a reference to the rainbow that had appeared after the flood (Gen. 9). Like the rainbow, it was a reminder of the eternal covenant between God and Noah, and of the promise that there would never again be a flood. Similarly, the covenant between the bride and groom should also exist forever. In folklorist Arnold van Gennep's structural model of rites of passage, the ribbon ritual represents the unification of the couple and hence it constitutes, following the stages of separation and transition, the incorporation stage which, in his description, celebrates the entry to a new, higher status (1960: 9–10).

After the ribbon was ready, the priest placed it at the groom's feet. The groom's sister, sister-in-law, or married female relative painted the young man's eyes with black eyeliner (*kool*) representing beauty and health. She also spread perfumed butter on his head as a blessing for economic affluence. She then painted the eyes of his best man to show that they were like brothers. The priest made a short blessing in which he wished the groom fertility, prosperity, and success in his marriage. Afterwards he placed the ribbon on the groom's chest and repeated the blessing, then placed it on his forehead reciting the blessing again, and finally tied the ribbon.

The interviewees explained that this movement of the ribbon along the groom's body meant that the blessing should apply to the groom's entire body. He would continue to wear it on his head until the end of the seven days of festivities. While tying the ribbon, the priests sang and recited a special prayer. The woman who had spread butter on the groom's head danced in front of him to the accompaniment of drums and cymbals, and the entire audience joined in the singing and dancing.

According to folklorist Shalom Sabar, acts of tying as part of marriage rituals were also common in other Jewish communities, which typically attributed a magical significance to it (2006: 231–2). Since, according to folk belief, the bride and groom were in a transitional state in their lives, they were vulnerable to the evil eye and other harmful forces. They were in danger of 'being bound': the hidden world could prevent them from having intercourse on the wedding night. The people close to the bride and groom therefore stepped in and 'tied' them (or the groom) with a symbolic bond before the marriage ritual, in order to protect them and prevent their 'binding' by external forces.

The priest tied another, thinner, ribbon around the head of the best man (*beker-mezei*), then blessed the groomsmen and ritually demanded their loyalty to the groom. The best man accompanied the groom everywhere and was the oldest of the groom's entourage, which normally consisted of ten to twenty-five men. These groomsmen were appointed by the groom's family to guard him and his bride and to serve as witnesses at the wedding. The fact that the bride and groom were constantly accompanied by the groomsmen again emphasized their liminal state, which forced them to depend on others for protection.

At the end of the ritual the groomsmen and the *kes* bowed to the congregation. The groom's parents thanked them, blessed them, and paid the *kes*. The congregation then sang in honour of the groom, who came out of the hut and got on a horse or mule that had been prepared for him. The second most senior man in his entourage picked up the gifts intended for the bride, which were wrapped in a white bag: an embroidered dress, jewellery, shoes, and a jar filled with perfumed butter. The groom's entourage left for the bride's village, and his companions sang, danced, and drummed all the way, until they reached the bride's village.

Reception and Marriage Ritual in the Bride's Village

On the morning of the wedding day, coinciding with the tying ritual in the groom's community, wedding preparations were underway in the bride's village (Corinaldi 1988: 79–80; Waldman 1990: 12, 35–45). Her family set up a hut (*das*) next to their house for the marriage ritual; it served as a type of canopy opposite which they built another hut for the numerous guests awaiting the arrival of the groom and his entourage. The openings of the two huts faced each other, so that the guests could watch the ceremony. According to another account, only one large hut was built for the wedding, which also had room for the guests. A separate small hut served as a storeroom for the celebration. The bride's family also prepared traditional food and drink according to its economic capabilities.

The bride waited for the groom in one of the rooms in her parents' house together with her girlfriends. Women from the village and other female guests sang and danced in front of her. According to the descriptions of the women I interviewed, the bride was prepared for the ritual by her girlfriends or female neighbours. However, there were places where this function was given to older married women or the wives of the priests, which symbolically reflected the bride's protected, dependent, and passive state. She had to have complete faith in the older women who were knowledgeable and were responsible for passing on the cultural and social traditions, since she was in a liminal state, was symbolically confused, and had to learn the new rules and forms of behaviour from people of authority.

The women spread bread dough (*buho*) on the bride's body so that her skin would be shiny and beautiful, and after about half an hour they washed her body. Differences in the social status of brides were apparent already at this stage. A bride from a rich family was bathed in milk, which symbolized wealth and was good for the skin, or she was covered in honey so that she would be radiant. The preparations also included braiding the bride's hair and painting her eyes with black eyeliner (*kool*).

The bride's clothing and jewellery were supplied by both families, reflecting their social status. The gifts that she received from her father and father-in-law symbolized the dominance of these two men in her life, and the numerous new changes that were about to take place for her: a change of home, of social surroundings, of status, and of responsibilities. The groom's gifts further symbolized the traditional gender-based division of labour, where the wife was dependent on her husband even for her basic needs.

The bride wore a traditional white wedding dress (*keimis*) with colourful floral embroidery on its hem. The interviewees mentioned that while women in Ethiopia did not normally wear trousers under their dress, the bride had white trousers for the sake of modesty, since during the ritual she was carried on the groomsman's back and later also on a horse. The white colour of the trousers and the dress symbolized her purity. Her head was covered with a thin white scarf (*netela*), which was part of the traditional garb of Ethiopian women. However, uniquely to the bride, her face was also covered with this scarf, which served as a kind of veil, so that the groom could not see her properly. She was also adorned with gold chains, earrings, rings, and bracelets.

As the groom was approaching the bride's village with his entourage, he sent a groomsman to announce his arrival, while the others blew a shofar to herald his approach. My interviewees explained that a shofar was used because it was very loud, and thus all the people in the village would know that the groom and his men were coming. As they approached the wedding hut they were greeted by the priests with songs and blessings. One of the men I interviewed recalled that when he had got married, a playful competition took place, enacted through singing and dancing, between members of his family who wanted to enter the hut and perform the marriage ritual, and the bride's family who were trying to prevent it. The symbolic significance of this ritual was to show the family's difficulty in separating from the daughter who was about to leave home.

Finally the groom and his entourage entered the hut and the ceremony began with a series of questions and answers between the fathers and the marrying priest. The questions pertained to the names of the participants and their families, and the names of their villages, as well as whether the parents agreed that the marriage should take place. After the fathers confirmed their consent to the marriage of their children, the ritual began, with the families sealing the agreement of marriage conditions (*wol*). This document included the date, the names of the bride and groom, and a declaration that the wedding was being performed with the consent of their parents. The agreement recorded the bride's dowry, the property given by the groom, and their mutual commitment (Waldman 1990: 16, 44). The *wol* was written in three copies and was signed by the two fathers, the groom, the marrying priest, and three witnesses. The signatories and the groomsmen left the hut and took the agreement to be signed by the bride, who was still in her parents' home.

After the signing, the bride's father gave his daughter to the groom and the groom's father accepted her as a wife for his son. The bride and her father-in-law exchanged gifts. The entire course of the ritual, performed by the fathers and without any involvement by the young couple, was a reflection of the patriarchal structure of the Jewish family in Ethiopia. Therefore, the physical presence of the bride, at least at this stage of the ritual, was not necessary. A festive meal was then held, and the celebrations continued until dawn.

Marking the second stage of the wedding, the next day a festive lunch was held with songs and dancing. The bride was brought to the hut on the back of the groom's best man, with her face covered. The men I interviewed explained that the carrying of the bride was an expression of honour. In my opinion, however, this act also symbolized ownership, the bride's passivity, and her passage into the patronage of her husband. The young couple bowed to the bride's parents and received their blessing. To end the ritual, the priest gave a sermon on marriage and its sanctity and blessed the newlyweds.

When the ceremony ended, the groom's family prepared to return to their village together with the bride. As the bride's parents said goodbye to the couple, they gave blessings and showered them with gifts. Women recalled that their mothers had also bestowed on them a large colourful straw basket that contained jewellery, a mirror, *kool*, and sewing accessories. These items symbolized, according to the interviewees, that the girl had reached maturity and was establishing a household of her own. The basket was presented to the bride by the person closest to her, so that she should remember her family when she was far away from her parents. The interviewees could not explain the significance of the mirror. However, in marriage rituals in other communities it symbolized the bride's life, which should be as shiny and filled with light as a mirror (Sabar 2006: 236).

When she left her father's home, a representative of the family went with her, so that he could receive the confirmation of her virginity. The second groomsman helped the bride carry the basket filled with the clothes and the gifts she had received from her girlfriends and her relatives. The couple and their escorts rode on horses or mules towards the groom's village, singing all the way. The bride's passage from her parental home to the groom's parents' home brought her child-hood to an end and marked the beginning of her new life as a wife, which also meant the end of the close protection of her parents and family and the develop-ment of new personal relations in her new surroundings.

Reception in the Groom's Village

When the bride and groom's entourage was approaching the village, a shofar was sounded to announce their safe return from the bride's village. They were received with singing, dancing, and a festive meal in a hut (*das*) which the groom's family had constructed. The couple sat in one of the corners of the hut, under a decorated *ḥupah* (traditional Jewish marriage canopy), encircled by many guests (Waldman 1990: 45–6; Corinaldi 1988: 80–1).

They then entered a special hut, where they were alone for the first time and had sexual intercourse. If the bride was not a virgin, the groom informed the groomsmen waiting outside. Then he took off the *keshra* ribbon that was tied around his forehead and left the bride. The ribbon, which was, as described above, a typical element of marriage rituals in Ethiopia, thus illustrates the sym-bolic importance of the couple's dress and jewellery. If the bride was indeed a virgin, the groom similarly told the groomsmen and they informed the guests in the hut, who in their turn cheered with joy and praised her for preserving her and her family's honour. After the bride had passed this 'test', the wedding celebra-tions continued for seven days, with guests arriving every day. During this time, the couple stayed in the hut, and they were not permitted to enter the groom's parents' house. The hut thus served as their temporary home, a kind of transit station between the parental homes.

The bride and the groom were served by members of the groom's family and the best men, and interviewees emphasized that they were treated as a king and queen. The girls of the village spent time with the bride, and served as a replace-ment for the family she had left behind. Meanwhile the groom socialized with his friends and best men. In many villages it was customary to play a humorous game, in which the groomsmen demanded or 'stole' food and bread from fami-lies in the village. These games typically took place on Fridays and Saturdays when people did not work and had more time to celebrate.

On the seventh day (*haftat*), the groom's parents invited the couple into their home and a festive meal was held for them. The *kes* blessed the groom, removed the ribbon from his forehead and tied it to the central pillar in the house as a sou-venir that the wedding had taken place. The act of removing the ribbon by the priest at the end of the rituals expressed the closure of a symbolic cycle, since once the ribbon had fulfilled its function of protecting against harmful external forces and the marriage had taken place according to plan, it was no longer needed.

When the bride entered her husband's house formally for the first time, the groom's parents asked her to sit and hold a pitcher from which nobody had drunk before and which was filled with beer. The interviewees explained that the pitcher symbolized femininity. The *kes* blessed her and everyone present playfully suggested a new first name for the bride. Her mother-in-law then came and chose a name for her, which superseded her original name. Her childhood name held no meaning any more, except for her family and for the people who had grown up with her.

Marriage Rituals in Israel

According to interviewees who moved to Israel during the 1980s, immigrants maintained most of the marriage practices they remembered from Ethiopia for several years. As I have explained above in detail, in the Ethiopian tradition the groom's father searched for an appropriate match for his son: a girl from a good family who had not been related to them for seven generations. Having found a suitable woman he asked the father for her hand in marriage and gave him a nominal sum. The payment symbolized that the woman was promised to his son and they then set a date for the wedding.

At 27 for men and 25 for women, the average age of marriage for all couples in Israel was higher than was customary in Ethiopia; accordingly, Ethiopian Jews adjusted their marital age to around 18 years old. A legal factor in this rise was the minimum marriage age of 17 in Israel. This age limit implied a definition of maturity that carried a different meaning to that accepted by Ethiopian Jews. In Israel, young people are considered adults socially only from the age of 17, regardless of their physical maturity (see Rubin 2005: 143).

The preparations for the wedding were carried out by each family separately, as in Ethiopia, informants told me. These included looking for a banquet hall, slaughtering a cow on the wedding day, cooking that continued until the afternoon hours, and neighbours and relatives helping in the preparations. The groom prepared for the wedding ritual in his home, accompanied by groomsmen from among his friends and relatives. Instead of the traditional white shirt and trousers, he wore a Western suit during the wedding ceremony, as is customary in Israel. The bride wore the traditional Ethiopian white dress with flowered embroidery and a thin white scarf. However, some rented a modern bridal gown. The bride got ready in her parents' home, accompanied by her girlfriends. They organized a bridal shower for her, applied make-up using the traditional *kool*, and adorned her with jewellery bought by the groom.

Some of the weddings of my interviewees took place in the more remote settlements where the majority of Ethiopian immigrants lived. However, most were held in Tel Aviv because of its central location. Choosing a venue in the city still involved challenges, such as long drives, arranging places for the guests to stay, and higher expenses. However, the location of the event reflected the wish of the immigrants to have all their scattered relatives participate and to try and preserve their traditional community structure, even in the new society.

Notwithstanding efforts to maintain the traditional structure, several marriage patterns have emerged in the Ethiopian community in Israel; one is the marriage of immigrants who have agreed to the conversion process by the Chief Rabbinate of Israel; a second pattern, which was common among the immigrants from Ethiopia during the 1980s, was civil marriage by a *kes* (who is not recognized by the rabbinate in Israel), following the custom in Ethiopia.

Transplanting to Israel the many rituals that in Ethiopia traditionally took place over a period of several months interfered with the work schedules of the immigrants. A further deterrent was the expense of reproducing the elaborate events in the new country. As a result, the number of days devoted to the marriage celebration was reduced and several rituals that had formerly been spread out in discrete events over several months were unified. In the years immediately after their immigration, for example, there was a tendency to omit henna rituals. Of the Ethiopian marriage ceremonies, the *keshra* persisted the longest, since it was perceived as an important marker of the start of a wedding. Ethiopian Jews in Israel did not perform the *keshra* at noon on the wedding day as they had in Ethiopia, but integrated it into the wedding ceremony. Before the groom entered the place where the wedding was held, the *kes* blessed him and tied the ribbon on his forehead. The groom then entered the hall and a wedding ceremony was performed, followed by music and traditional dancing accompanied by Ethiopian singers.

While the guests were celebrating, the new couple retired to a separate room, as is customary in Israel, to symbolize the consummation of the marriage. Unlike the norm in Israel, at the weddings of Ethiopian immigrants the couple actually had sexual intercourse for the first time and the bride's virginity was tested. If she was found not to be a virgin, she was sent away and she and her family were dishonoured. If her virginity was confirmed, the celebration increased. Immigrants from Ethiopia were thus strict in observing the custom of examining the bride's purity and honour even in Israel, but the location of the custom and its timing had changed.

After the marriage ritual the celebrations continued as they would have done back in Ethiopia, but they were reduced due to the new circumstances. They were also held alternately in the homes of the bride and of the groom, taking place first in the home of the groom; from Saturday night until Monday or Tuesday the celebration was hosted by the bride's parents. The fact that the bride returned to her parents' home immediately after her wedding and participated in ritual activity there indicates the significant change that had taken place in the marriage ritual as a rite of passage. The changes taking effect in the wedding patterns of Ethiopian immigrants indicated not only an adjustment of tradition within the community, but also a shift in the role of the ritual as an expression of patriarchal authority.

Changes in the Pre-Marriage Rituals

Sociologist Nissan Rubin has provided an explanation for the changes in marriage age following the move to a new location such as Israel: in a traditional agricultural society, such as the one in Ethiopia, a person can be socially viewed as an adult in parallel to being physically mature and can marry young around the time of puberty since, as explained above, he or she has already learned most of the skills that an adult in his or her society must master (Rubin 2005: 143). In contrast, in a Westernized society such as Israel, where youth devote many years to studies, including higher education, the average age of marriage has been rising. The Ethiopian community has adopted the social norm that is common among young people in Israel, and many marry at an older age: men in their late- and women in their mid-twenties.

Another new trend that is becoming prevalent in Israel among the immigrants from Ethiopia is marriage with members of other ethnic communities. Most of the interviewees said that they preferred their children to marry members of their own community, who were familiar with its customs and traditions. They expressed fear that mixed couples would not get along because of a different cultural mindset. However, there were other interviewees who said they had no particular preference, and only wanted their children to be happy. For some, the most important consideration was that the mate would honour and provide for his family. This attitude may be sincere, but may also reflect, at least among some of the interviewees, their fatalistic acceptance of the assimilation process in Israel.

One of the major changes in the pre-marriage rituals is the transformation of the traditional matchmaking customs. The entire process of the groom's father looking for a bride has disappeared, due to the emphasis Israeli society places on the choice being made by the couple on the basis of romantic love. Young Ethiopians have adopted the modern Western world-view of the individual's freedom in love as well as in occupational choices. They meet at school, in the army, at places of work, and at family events, and go out on their own in the Israeli style. Therefore, a pattern of friendship-acquaintance has evolved, which replaces the traditional approach of matchmaking. This pattern of socialization independent from parents has undoubtedly been possible due to the fact that in Israel women fulfil a more active role in the public sphere than in Ethiopia. One of the women I interviewed underscored this contrast as central to the changes that followed the immigration to Israel: 'My daughter met her husband at work, but I was matched to my husband without having known him.'

After a period of dating, if the couple decide to get married, only then do they inform their parents of their decision. At this stage the parents still feel obliged to check for kinship going back seven generations. If none is found, then the parents accept the couple's decision. However, if blood relations do exist, some parents are not willing to compromise. The consequence is often severance between the families and the couple unless, afraid of being ostracized, the bride and groom break off their engagement. However, many interviewees predicted that objections by parents and the *kes* would with time mean less and less because young people do not recognize their authority any more.

However, it is clear from the interviews that both older and younger immigrants still attribute importance to determining whether kinship exists through several generations. They refuse to abandon this traditional element, which they perceive as an essential part of the marriage ritual, but the former stringent standard has been subject to negotiation in Israel. The community elders regard the counting of seven generations as crucial to Ethiopian ethics, whereas most young people today will marry someone with whom they have kinship ties extending back five or six generations, and immigrants from the Tigray region will wed someone with whom they have kinship ties four generations removed.

Although it is the couple who make the decision to marry, symbolic remnants of matchmaking have remained, and young interviewees claimed that they do this to honour their parents. It is still customary for the groom's father to go to the bride's parents to ask for her hand. The groom's parents give a sum of money to the bride's parents, as in Ethiopia. This creates an agreement and legitimizes the couple's union. A shift in the tradition from the elders to the young is evident in the initiation of the event by the couple rather than the parents, as can be inferred from the statement of one of the women I interviewed: 'My partner sent his parents to my parents' home in order to ask for my hand on the day that we set, and at the same time I told my parents that the groom's parents were coming to ask for my hand. My family prepared a meal in honour of the guests.'

Several months later the bride's parents, in co-ordination with the couple, hold an engagement celebration in their home. Among immigrants from the Gondar region, almost the entire ritual process has been preserved as it was in Ethiopia, whereas a change has occurred among immigrants from other regions. The intended groom plays a part in the ritual today: unlike in Ethiopia, he brings the intended bride clothes, shoes, and jewellery. The gifts are usually chosen by the bride and not by the groom's family. The bride's parents invite a *kes* to bless the couple. Subsequently, traditional food is served, musicians sing in Amharic, and guests perform Ethiopian dances.

The engagement ritual today is a symbolic event that serves mainly to acquaint the families. It is also a public statement by the bride's family that their daughter has found a husband. Interviewees even admitted that the engagement served as a sanction for the couple to do as they wish: to live together and to buy things together from then on. The bride-to-be becoming pregnant before the wedding does not shock the community or shame the family, because the legal status of the couple has already been determined and publicized with the engagement ritual.

The interviewees also indicated that breaking off the engagement was not viewed as seriously as it had been in Ethiopia, where families considered the rift to be especially humiliating to the woman and demanded compensation. In Israel, the break was simply accepted as a sign that the couple was unfit for marriage.

In Israel only a few families have maintained the ritual of tying a red and white ribbon around the groom's forehead. Interviewees explained that this custom had not been preserved for two reasons. First, the ritual presupposes the girl to be a virgin, and premarital sex is more common in today's Israel than it was in Ethiopia. Second, Ethiopian youths do not attribute great symbolic importance to the tying as a marker of ethnic identity or a rite of passage any more. Greater significance is attached to the henna ritual, especially by couples from the Tigray region, but its timing has been altered: in Ethiopia it used to be held on the day preceding the wedding, whereas in Israel it takes place two days earlier so as to enable the families to rest before the wedding. The ritual is not unique to the bride, as it was in Ethiopia; rather, the bride and the groom participate in it together, which again reflects the influence of the Israeli egalitarian ethos.

Another reason for the occurrence of changes in the henna ritual has been the contact with ethnic cultures from Morocco and Yemen in Israel maintaining different versions of henna application. Ethiopians have replaced the original henna paste from the roots of the *gurshit* plant with lawsone drawn from the leaves of the flowering plant *lawsonia inermis* (called henna in Arabic). A further change, as mentioned above, is that the groom also takes part in the ritual together with his family. Nonetheless, the food, the dress, and the music at the event are traditional and so is the *kes*'s blessing of the bride and groom and their guests.

Unlike the tying of the coloured ribbon, the henna rite has continued to serve as an ethnic marker possibly due to its persistent use by other ethnic groups from Africa. Interviewees observed that the Westernized Israeli format of the wedding is more practical in the new surroundings but less enjoyable and symbolically less significant. They avow that the survival of the henna ritual represents a form of continuity with the past that is nevertheless compatible with the new environment. Interviewees predicted, in fact, that it was likely to grow in importance in weddings among young Ethiopians as a result.

The expansion of the henna ritual among Ethiopian immigrants may be viewed as part of the broader process of the renewal of ethnic customs among the children of immigrants from different countries (Bilu 2004; Sharaby 2006; Shokeid 1984). The general population treats henna decoration as an art form, and young members of ethnic groups have adopted it to mark sub-cultural belonging in response to assimilation. Allowing for ethnic difference in weddings has also received approval in the post-Zionist ideology of pluralism in Israeli society, which has especially sought to elevate the status of formerly marginalized groups from North Africa and Islamic countries (Eisenstadt 2004; Sabar 2009; Weingrod 1998; Yaar and Shavit 2003).

The preparations for the wedding are similar to those undertaken by any Israeli couple, and although the bride and groom typically take full responsibility in organizing the event, one area that the parents do get involved in is the compilation of the guest list, since the younger generation does not know all the distant relatives. Ethiopian couples have adopted the Israeli practice of the bride's girlfriends throwing her a wedding shower. Some couples also follow the custom of taking an extended trip together in Israel before their marriage.

Changes in the Wedding

In Ethiopia Jews determined the time and place of the wedding by relying on custom; the couple (or their parents) could not freely choose. Today, the schedule is decided upon by the bride and groom alone. Summer is the preferred season, as it is for all couples in Israel (Abuab 1998: 577), partly because of favourable weather and the timing of the vacation period in educational institutions. Additionally, since the Jews of Ethiopia customarily celebrate from the evening before the wedding until the next morning, almost all their events take place on Thursdays, as people usually do not work on Fridays. The weddings are typically held in large and splendiferous banquet halls that can seat many guests, including the couple's friends, as is customary among Israelis.

A key change has taken place in dress: unlike in Ethiopia, most of the young couples choose their wedding clothes themselves and dress in private. On the wedding day, the bride will have her hair done in a bridal salon. She wears a white Israeli bridal gown, modern jewellery, and commercial make-up applied by a professional. The groom picks her up from the bridal salon in a decorated car, they drive to the designated site where they are to be photographed and from there they go to the wedding hall.

In Ethiopia the wedding party comprised men only, whereas today in Israel the bride is also accompanied by two to four bridesmaids on the wedding day and until after the days of celebration following the wedding. They wear clothes that match the colour of the groomsmen's clothes, whose number is identical to theirs. The groom usually gets dressed at home and is helped by his groomsmen on the wedding day and on the following days. The Ethiopian wedding is thus organized today according to the Israeli model, but the traditional component of having several groomsmen is still common.

At the reception preceding the ceremony, the parents and grandparents from both sides as well as other relatives stand at the entrance and receive the guests. Although the format of the wedding follows the Israeli custom, ethnic markers will be evident in the dress and jewellery of the older guests. Women wear a white Ethiopian dress (*telef*) with colourful embroidery on the sleeves and over it they wear a white scarf (*netela*) which is decorated in the same colours as the embroi-dery on the dress. Men over 60 hold a wooden cane in their hands in accordance with Ethiopian tradition, which symbolizes their being adults who must be respected.

Participants will also wear a combination of Western and ethnic dress. For example, at one of the events I observed, the bride's mother wore a traditional dress and scarf and Ethiopian jewellery but also covered her head with a hat. At another event the bride wore an Israeli evening gown but had an Ethiopian hairdo, with braided hair. The bride's father wore a regular Israeli evening suit and a skullcap. The groom's father, who was older, wore a regular Israeli suit, but over it he had a white scarf (*netela*) decorated in different colours and on his head he had a brimmed hat. In his hand, he held the above-mentioned cane symboliz-ing respectability.

The groomsmen enter the hall first and together with the guests they receive the bride and groom, clapping hands and singing in Amharic. The groom signs the *ketubah*, whose formulation differs from the Ethiopian marriage agreement (*wol*), and then covers the bride's face with a veil. They walk up to the *ḥupah* separately, accompanied by their parents and grandparents, to the sounds of Ethiopian music. The bridesmaids and groomsmen also escort them until they step under the *ḥupah*, together with their parents. The canopy is typical of con-temporary Jewish-Israeli weddings: a sheet of fabric stretched between four tall poles, under which the bride and groom and their parents stand with the rabbi performing the ritual.

In Ethiopia the *kes* had religious authority to conduct the wedding ceremony, whereas in Israel only a rabbi or *kes* who has been certified by the rabbinate is allowed to marry people. A *kes* whom I interviewed complained of the harm done to his authority and said, 'Although most of the community invites me to special events such as engagements, I feel that my honour was damaged after immigrat-ing to Israel because the rabbinate does not recognize the *kessoch* as rabbis who have the authority to marry or slaughter according to Jewish law. Thus, we as *kessoch* have lost our authority.'

Although the Ethiopian *kessoch* who are not recognized by the Israeli rab-binate are not permitted to perform the marriage ritual itself, it is important for the family to have them included in the ceremony and they join in the prayers and blessings. Interviewees said that even today there was a minority of immigrants from Ethiopia who were married only by a *kes* even though he is not accepted by the religious establishment, and the state does not recognize these marriages. They also observed that today some couples lived together and had children with-out getting married, although this contradicted the religious norms of Ethiopian Jews.

Some prominent elements of the traditional Ethiopian ceremony have given way to Israeli practices. The ritual is performed in Hebrew, and the groom marries the bride with a ring. The immigrants have also adopted the custom of saying a blessing over wine and breaking a glass, which is customary in most Jewish communities worldwide as a remembrance of the destruction of the Temples in Jerusalem (Goldberg 1998; Sabar 2006: 244). After the ceremony Ethiopian music is played by a live band or a disc jockey, and the guests dance traditional dances. Later the musicians also play Israeli and foreign songs and Israeli friends join in the modern dancing.

Ethiopian food such as the sour bread (*injera*) with a dressing or beer is no longer on the menu in many weddings, and today Israeli food, such as humus, tehina, and salads are served. The couple sometimes go to the seclusion room (which in Israel is called the yiḥud room), but, as mentioned above, they do not have sexual intercourse. Rather, they eat and rest. Most of the celebrations of the immigrants from Ethiopia last, as customary, until morning, with the guests staying with relatives who live in the area. The families continue celebrating for several more days, as they used to in the original custom. The interviewees explained that the purpose of the celebrations after the wedding (in the groom's and the bride's respective homes) was to welcome the young couple. The fact that the interviewees called these 'receptions' expresses their nostalgia and need to continue the 'reception' rituals that were held in the villages of the bride and the groom in Ethiopia.

The couple usually do not oppose the families' desire to hold celebrations after the wedding. The customary division of labour is that the couple are responsible for the wedding and its funding, whereas the parents take care of the hospitality for the relatives and guests during the days after the wedding, according to their economic capabilities.

On Friday, with the beginning of the sabbath, celebrations are held in a marquee that is positioned in the garden of the bride's parents or at the neighbourhood community centre. The guests sing and dance to the sounds of Amharic music and traditional food is served. Guests who could not come to the wedding stay at the home of the groom's parents on Friday and Saturday to rejoice with the young couple. The custom of the 'groom's sabbath'—as the sabbath after the wedding is called, when the groom's family hosts the bride's family along with the young couple, and the groom reads the Torah in the synagogue—has been adopted by the Ethiopian immigrants from religious Israeli society. On Saturday night all the relatives gather to eat, drink, exchange stories, and to give the couple presents. People from the Tigray region have copied another Israeli custom, namely, that the bride's family stays at the groom's parental home on this sabbath.

From Saturday night until Monday, they continue to celebrate in the home of the bride's family. This ritual pattern enacts familial and community ties, largely disrupted during the absorption process. As one of the interviewees said, the celebration takes on the function of a reunion, a reference to the past: 'Everyone stays, and this is a kind of family reunion. We see all the relatives whom we have not seen for a long time, and this enables us to maintain the unity that we had in Ethiopia.' When the festivities end, the guests disperse to their homes and the couple go on a honeymoon abroad or for a weekend to a hotel in Israel.

Conclusion

Analysis of the marriage ritual systems in Ethiopia and Israel reinforces the claim that marriage is a means of preserving social order, but also constitutes a mechanism for adjustment to a new social and cultural reality (Hazan 1992). Comparison of the different traditions in Ethiopia and Israel shows a connection between social structure and ritual change (Rubin 1995: 12). In traditional society, as explained above, the passage between being single and marriage is a long process, which requires an intermediate period for preparations and adjustment. Weddings in Ethiopia were significant rites of passage for the groom and especially for the bride, since they prepared her for her new life in which she turned from a young girl into a wife, was separated from her parents, and went to live in the home of her husband's family. The marriage ritual was thus a strategy for forming a new family unit and integrating it into the social structure.

The transition of the Ethiopian immigrants from a traditional patriarchal system into a modern Western society with an egalitarian ethos has forced them to adjust their rituals to the new economic and social conditions. Since Israel prohibits the marriage of minors, and young people devote their adolescent years to studies, the age of marriage for immigrants from Ethiopia has sharply risen, but it is still lower than the average age of marriage of the general Israeli population.

Traditional matchmaking by parents is no longer practised due to a decrease in their authority and the influence of modern education. Young Ethiopians today meet, choose their mates, and decide to marry independently. The impression that I gained from the extensive ethnographic material was that in spite of their patriarchal background, young Ethiopians in Israel have accepted the values of both equality and feminism, since the education and socialization processes in Israel are similar for both genders.

In the past, the engagement symbolized the first stage in the creation of a bond between the two mates and their families as well as the beginning of the bride's disengagement from her father's house and her passage to her husband's home (Rubin 2004). However, in Israel it has lost its original significance, because secular couples live together before the wedding (Prashizky 2006: 31). The symbolic significance of the henna ritual as a rite of passage has also decreased, although it has taken on a new function, as mentioned above, as an ethnic marker, placing it in line with the rituals of other ethnic communities in Israel. Much of the wedding ceremony has taken on an Israeli character and traditional Ethiopian elements have been replaced by new customs. For example, in

Israel today the *ḥupah* fulfils the function formerly served by the two huts in which receptions took place for the bride and groom in Ethiopia.

However, it can also be seen that the families try to celebrate as in Ethiopia, and the younger generation is aware of the interaction between tradition and their new society. Although Ethiopian couples in Israel usually decide to marry without parental intervention, they still assign a special role to their elders: the groom often dispatches his parents to the home of the bride's parents to ask for her hand in marriage. Whereas the insistence on genealogical separation for seven generations has weakened, the value placed on familial distinction is still apparent in the tracing of four to five generations being generally accepted. Some continue to practise the *keshra* ritual of the groom, but because of time constraints typical of modern capitalist society, it has undergone transformation and is today done before the wedding.

After the rabbi performs the marriage ritual, the families customarily invite the *kes* to bless the couple. The older adults wear traditional clothes, the number of groomsmen is large, as was customary in Ethiopia, and many songs in Amharic are played. The bride's virginity is today a private and intimate matter, but the immigrants still regard it as important. As in Ethiopia, the families continue to celebrate alternately in their homes for several days after the wedding, and these celebrations are characterized by traditional motifs. A hierarchy of meaning can be discerned in the cultural elements that have been preserved: for example, the status of the *kes*, virginity, and the celebrations after the wedding remain important, while others, such as the *keshra* ritual, have lost some of their significance.

This process of reproducing traditional customs through selection and adaptation to time, place, and new economic conditions is an instance of syncretism—a mixing of traditions and the creation of a new cultural pattern (Sharaby 2002: 17–22; Stewart and Shaw 1994: 1–26). Thus, in situations of immigration old customs do not necessarily disintegrate, but are rather integrated into new forms; the result is hybrid forms of tradition in response to modernity (Gusfield 1973: 333–41; Shils 1981: 12–21).

To be sure, the observation of marriage rituals among the Israeli-born offspring of Ethiopian immigrants clearly reflects a decline in the influence of Ethiopian tradition on the new generations. Nonetheless, it shows some degree of identification with that tradition, often expressed in symbolic ways, and a desire to preserve the cohesion of the family and the community. In one way, Ethiopians are different from other immigrant groups undergoing change in Israeli society. For them, since their Jewishness has been brought into question, marriage rituals play a critical role in ethnic preservation and create a new social space in which the family and society are joined together. The members of the community are aware of their responsibility for imparting their values to the coming generations, and the ritual activities are thus intended to pass on to the young couple the essential social and cultural elements of the society.

Analysis of the wedding rituals of the Ethiopian Jews in Israel is especially important since it shows the level of Israeli culture adopted by these immigrants and the changes they have implemented in their social structure while preserving an ethnic difference, even if in a symbolic intergenerational manner. The attitude of Ethiopian immigrants towards marriage customs highlights their social and cultural position within Israeli society as Jews but also their racial and cultural apartness (Holt 1997). To be sure, the challenges that face the traditional culture of Ethiopian Jewry are similar, in some respects, to those of other immigrant groups who arrived after the establishment of the State of Israel and accepted Hebrew as their language and Zionism as their ideology (Goldberg 1973; Weingrod 1995). However, the immigrants from Ethiopia have encountered prejudice because of suspicions concerning their brand of Judaism, and bias as a result of the entrenchment in Israel of whiteness as a social standard.

Nonetheless, the Ethiopian presence has also forced a change in Israeli society. They, along with other immigrant groups from non-European countries that started arriving in the 1970s, have influenced ethnic strengthening among other communities in Israel (Goldberg 1984; Shokeid 1984). Thus, although sociologists expect assimilation to eradicate the ethnic components of public performances, there are signs of revival in symbolic enactments which fulfil new functions. These functions are often an attempt at negotiation in post-Zionist Israeli society for a positive ethnic status while achieving integration into the national culture.

Acknowledgements

This research was supported by the Schnitzer Foundation for Research on Israeli Economy and Society and the Research Committee of the Ashkelon Academic College.

Notes

1   By most estimates, more than 130,000 Ethiopian Jews, or 85 per cent of the community, emigrated to Israel under its Law of Return in these two waves of immigration.

2   Because of the perilous journey, families often did not travel together. Furthermore, sometimes robbers attacked them on the way and members of the family fled and did not know what happened to the others—sometimes assuming they were killed.

3   See also the French film *Live and Become* (*Va, Vis et Deviens*, 2005) about an Ethiopian Christian boy who disguises himself as an Ethiopian Jew in order to escape famine and emigrates to Israel. It was directed by Romanian-born Radu Mihaileanu and won the category of Most Popular International Film at the 2005 Vancouver International Film Festival.

References

ABUAB, ORIT. 1998. 'A Wedding of Money: Material and Monetary Gifts at Israeli Weddings' (Heb.). In Orit Abuav, Esther Herzog, Harvey Goldberg, and Immanuel Marx, eds., *Israel: Local Anthropology* [Yisra'el: antropologiyah mekomit], 571–93. Tel Aviv.

ALPERT, HAVA. 1958. *The History and Customs of Ethiopian Jews* [Toledoteihem uminhageihem shel yehudei etyopiyah]. Jerusalem.

ANTEBY-YEMINI, LISA. 1997. 'Rituals of Birth and Death: Meanings of Identity among Ethiopian Jews' (Heb.). In Shalva Weil, ed., *In the Spotlight: The Jews of Ethiopia* [Yehudei etyopiyah be'or hazarkorim], 49–60. Jerusalem.

BANAI, NURIT, and DORON BACHAR. 1988. *The Absorption of the Ethiopians: The Hidden Challenge* [Kelitat ha'etyopiyim: ha'etgar hanistar]. Jerusalem.

BEN-EZER, GADI. 1992. *Like Light in a Jar* [Kemo or bakad]. Jerusalem.

BILU, YORAM. 2004. *Best Men* [Shoshvinei kidushim]. Haifa.

BODOWSKI, DANNY, JOSEPH DAVID, E. YECHIEL, and H. ROSEN. 1989. *Issues on Family Matters of the Jews of Ethiopia* [Sugyot benosei mishpaḥah shel yehudei etyopiyah]. Jerusalem.

BODOWSKI, DANNY, JOSEPH DAVID, AKIVA BARUCH, and ERAN YECHIEL. 1994. *The Jews of Ethiopia in Inter-Cultural Transition: The Family and the Cycle of Life* [Yehudei etiopiyah bama'avar habein-tarbuti: hamishpaḥah uma'agal haḥayim]. Jerusalem.

CICUREL, INBAL, and RACHEL SHARABY. 2007. 'Nida houses (*Margam Gojo*) among Ethiopian Immigrant Women in Israel: Sectoral, Religious, and Ethnic Protest' (Heb.). *Sotsiologiyah yisra'elit*, 8(2): 323–47.

CORINALDI, MICHAEL. 1988. *The Jews of Ethiopia: Identity and Tradition* [Yahadut etyopiyah: zehut umasoret]. Jerusalem.

——2005. *The Jews of Ethiopia* [Yahadut etyopiyah]. Jerusalem.

EISENSTADT, SHMUEL NOAH. 2004. *Changes in Israeli Society* [Temurot baḥevrah hayisra'elit]. Tel Aviv.

GILAD, LISA. 1989. *Ginger and Salt: Yemeni Jewish Women in an Israeli Town*. Boulder, Colo.

GOLDBERG, HARVEY E. 1973. 'Culture Change in an Israeli Immigrant Village: How the Twist Came to Even Yosef'. *Middle Eastern Studies*, 9: 73–80.

——1998. 'Breaking a Glass at the Wedding: An Anthropological-Analytical Perspective' (Heb.). In Orit Abuav, Esther Herzog, Harvey Goldberg, and Immanuel Marx, eds., *Israel: Local Anthropology* [Yisra'el: antropologiyah mekomit], 595–607. Tel Aviv.

GUSFIELD, JOSEPH. 1973. 'Tradition and Modernity: Misplaced Polarities in the Study of Social Change'. In Eva Etzioni-Halevi and Amitai Etzioni, eds., *Social Change*, 333–41. New York.

HALPER, JEFF. 1985. 'The Absorption of Ethiopian Immigrants: A Return to the Fifties'. *Israel Social Science Research*, 3(1–2): 112–39.

HAZAN, HAIM. 1992. *The Anthropological Discourse* [Hasiaḥ ha'antropologi]. Tel Aviv.

HOLT, DAVID. 1997. 'Cultural Coalescence: A Comparative Look at the Problems of Ethiopian Jews in Israel' (Heb.). In Shalva Weil, ed., *In the Spotlight: The Jews of Ethiopia* [Yehudei etyopiyah be'or hazarkorim], 99–116. Jerusalem.

KACEN, LEA, and IRIS BAKSHY. 2004. *Educational Authority in Ethiopian Immigrant Families in Israel* [Hasamḥut haḥinukhit bemishpaḥot yotse'ot etyopiyah beyisra'el]. Beer Sheva.

——GITA SOFER, and LIAT KEIDAR. 2005. 'Domestic Violence among Ethiopian Immigrants in Israel' (Heb.). In Malka Shabtai and Lea Kacen, eds., *Moloalam: Ethiopian Emigrant Women and Girls* [Moloalam: nashim une'arot yotse'ot etyopiyah], 111–35. Tel Aviv.

KAPLAN, STEVEN, and CHAIM ROSEN. 1993. 'Ethiopian Immigrants in Israel: Between Preservation of Culture and Invention of Tradition'. *Jewish Journal of Sociology*, 35: 35–48.

——and HAGAR SALAMON. 2004. 'Ethiopian Jews in Israel: A Part of the People or Apart from the People?' In Uzi Rebhun and Chaim Waxman, eds., *Jews in Israel: Contemporary Social and Cultural Patterns*, 118–50. Hanover, NH.

KIMMERLING, BARUCH. 2004. *Immigrants, Settlers, Natives* [Mehagrim, mityashvim, yelidim]. Tel Aviv.

LEITMAN, EVA, and ELISABETH WEINBAUM. 1999. 'Israeli Women of Ethiopian Descent: The Strengths, Conflicts and Successes'. In Tudor Parfitt and Emanuela Trevisan, eds., *The Beta Israel in Ethiopia and Israel*, 128–36. London.

MINUCHIN-ITZYKSON, SARA, RINA HIRSCHFELD, RIVKA HANEGBI, and DAVID KARSILOVSKI. 1997. 'Family Roles among Ethiopian Immigrants: Tackling Change' (Heb.). In Eli Amir, Alex Zehavi and Ruth Pargai, eds., *One Root, Many Branches* [Shoresh eḥad ve'anafim rabim]. Jerusalem.

NEWMAN, STANLEY. 1985. 'Ethiopian Jewish Absorption and the Israeli Response: A Two-Way Process'. *Israel Social Science Research*, 3(1–2): 104–11.

PHILLIPS, DAVIS. 1999. 'Fertility Decline and Changes in the Life Course among Ethiopian Jewish Women'. In Tudor Parfitt and Emanuela Trevisan, eds., *The Beta Israel in Ethiopia and Israel: Studies on the Ethiopian Jews*, 137–59. London.

PRASHIZKY, ANA. 2006. 'Wedding Rituals in Israeli Society: A Comparative Study of Ritualization and Performativity' [Tiksei ḥatunah baḥevrah hayisra'elit: meḥkar hashva'ati shel ritualizatsiyah uperformativiyut]. Ph.D. diss., Bar Ilan University.

RUBIN, NISSAN. 1972. 'He Mourns over Him: A Sociological Explanation of Talmudic Sources on the Extent of Binding Kinship' (Heb.). *Bar-Ilan*, 10: 111–22.

——1995. *The Beginning of Life* [Reshit haḥayim]. Tel Aviv.

——2004. *The Joy of Life* [Simḥat haḥayim]. Tel Aviv.

——2005. 'Marriageable Age in the Rabbinical Sources: An Anthropological Analysis' (Heb.). In Yehuda Friedlander, Uzi Shavit, and Avi Sagi, eds., *The Old Shall Be Renewed and the New Shall Be Sanctified* [Hayashan yitḥadesh vehaḥadash yitkadesh]. Tel Aviv.

SABAR, SHALOM. 2006. *The Cycle of Life* [Ma'agal haḥayim]. Jerusalem.

——2009. 'From Sacred Symbol To Key Ring: The *Ḥamsa* in Jewish and Israeli Societies'. In Simon J. Bronner, ed., *Jewish Cultural Studies, 2: Jews at Home: The Domestication of Identity*, 140–62. Oxford.

SALAMON, HAGAR. 1993. 'Blood among the Beta Yisra'el and their Christian Neighbours'. *Jerusalem Researches into Jewish Folklore*, 15: 117–34.

SEVER, RITA. 2000. 'And I Will Gather You from the Nations: Aliyah and Absorption Procedures' (Heb.). In Jacob Kop, ed., *Pluralism in Israel* [Pluralizm beyisra'el], 165–84. Jerusalem.

SHABTAI, MALKA. 1999. *My Closest Brother* [Hakhi aḥi]. Tel Aviv.

SHARABY, RACHEL. 2002. *Syncretism and Adaptation: The Encounter between the Traditional Community and Socialist Society* [Sinkretizm vehistaglut: hamifgash bein kehilah masoratit uvein ḥevrah sotsialistit]. Tel Aviv.

——2006. 'The Bride's Henna Ritual: Symbols, Meanings, and Changes'. *Nashim*, 11: 11–42.

SHECHORY, MALLY. 2006. 'Ethnic Stereotypes and Social Gaps in Israeli Society' (Heb.). *Sugyot ḥevratiyot beyisra'el*, 1: 64–88.

SHILS, EDWARD. 1981. *Tradition*. Chicago.

SHOKEID, MOSHE. 1984. 'Cultural Ethnicity in Israel: The Case of Middle Eastern Jews' Religiosity'. *AJS Review*, 9: 247–71.

STEWART, CHARLES, and ROSALIND SHAW, eds. 1994. *Syncretism/Anti-Syncretism*. London.

TURNER, VICTOR. 1967. *The Forest of Symbols: Aspects of Ndembu Ritual*. New York.

VAN GENNEP, ARNOLD. 1960. *The Rites of Passage*. London.

WALDMAN, MENACHEM. 1990. *Marriage and Divorce among Ethiopian Jews in the Light of Halakhah* [Nisu'in vegerushin etsel yehudei etyopiyah le'or hahalakhah]. Nir Etzion.

WEIL, SHALVA. 1991. *Single-Parent Families among Ethiopian Immigrants* [Mishpaḥot ḥad-horiyot bekerev olei etyopiyah]. Jerusalem.

—— 1997. 'Changing of the Guards: Leadership among Ethiopian Jews in Israel', *Journal of Social Studies*, 1(4): 301–7.

——2004. 'Ethiopian Jewish Women: Trends and Transformations in the Context of Transnational Change', *Nashim*, 8: 73–86.

——2008. 'Zionism and Immigration to Israel'. In Hagar Salamon, ed., *Ethiopia*, 187–200. Jerusalem.

WEINGROD, ALEX. 1995. 'Patterns of Adaptation of Ethiopian Jews within Israeli Society.' In Steven Kaplan, Tudor Parfitt, and Emanuela Trevisan-Semi, eds., *Between Africa and Zion: Proceedings of the First International Congress of the Society for the Study of Ethiopian Jewry*, 252–7. Jerusalem.

——1998. 'The Righteous are Galloping Forwards' (Heb.). In Orit Abuav, Esther Herzog, Harvey E. Goldberg, and Immanuel Marx, eds., *Israel: Local Anthropology* [Yisra'el: antropologiyah mekomit], 625–40. Tel Aviv.

YAAR, EPHRAIM, and ZEEV SHAVIT. 2003. 'Processes and Trends in Collective Identity' (Heb.). In Ephraim Yaar and Zeev Shavit, eds., *Trends in Israeli Society* [Megamot baḥevrah hayisra'elit], vol. ii, pp. 1197–269. Tel Aviv.

YILMA, SHMUEL. 1995. *The Road to Jerusalem* [Haderekh liyerushalayim]. Tel Aviv.

YOSSI, YONAH, and YEHOUDA SHENHAV. 2005. *What Is Multiculturalism?* [Rav-tarbutiyut mahi?]. Tel Aviv.

YUNG, JUDY. 1995. *Unbound Feet: A Social History of Chinese Women in San Francisco*. Berkeley, Calif.

PART III

Revisioning Mourning and Death

Kaddish for Angels: Revisioning Funerary Rituals and Cemeteries in Nineteenth-Century Jewish Warsaw

AGNIESZKA JAGODZIŃSKA

'WHAT AN AGE OF PROGRESS IT IS', British philosopher John Ruskin exclaimed in 1872, and his sense of admiration resonated through much of Europe in the nineteenth century (1907 [1872]: 820). An important component of the spirit of the age was a sceptical attitude towards tradition and a preference for modern science and rationalism following the spread of Enlightenment ideas in the eighteenth century. For many advocates of progress, east European Jews epitomized the opposite of modernity: superstitious, self-isolating, and focusing on the past. Well aware of the post-Enlightenment challenges of modernity, Jews entered into a lively debate, both among themselves and with non-Jews, about the meaning of tradition, while material development was affecting their community at an accelerating pace. The emergence of key ideas such as emancipation, acculturation, and integration,[1] or, broadly speaking, increasing interaction with the non-Jewish world, led to questions about the future of Jewish identity. Those Jews who responded to the Enlightenment's call to modernize their religious tradition and cultural identity often began their reform project by labelling some Jewish rituals as backward and those who held on to them as irrational. But many Jews who saw their religion as based on fidelity to precedent, and who wanted to maintain the element of piety in their lifestyle, felt that such changes needed to be resisted.

In this essay I analyse the particularly heated controversy in the Warsaw Jewish community over funerary rituals and cemetery practices during the nineteenth-century 'age of progress', when a number of Polish Jews drew attention from Jews and non-Jews alike in their call for modernization. The pace of integration and acculturation intensified particularly in the second half of the nineteenth century. Because funerary and burial traditions are typically more resistant to change than other customs, they provided a special challenge for the modernization movement among Polish Jews. To investigate this problem, I have focused on the Jews in Warsaw because, besides being the country's capital and largest city, it was widely known for being a place where substantial populations of strictly Orthodox and modernizing Jews met, and sometimes clashed. Warsaw was also a crossroads in other ways. For many observers of European affairs, it stood at the dividing point of western and eastern Europe, the west representing a rising cosmopolitanism associated with modernity and the east a pre-industrial world immersed in the past. The main focus of my analysis is Warsaw's large Jewish cemetery in Okopowa Street, and I follow the debates over the revision of funerary and burial traditions there that took place in the newspapers of the period. As I demonstrate below, the funerary controversy was one of the key developments that ultimately led to a split in the traditional model of ethno-religious Jewish identity, replacing it with one in which the religious and ethnic components were separable. One could thus be Polish by nationality and Jewish by confession, which gave rise to the concept of 'Poles of the Mosaic persuasion'.

Warsaw Jews at the Crossroads of Tradition and Modernity

Jews living in the Polish lands constituted the largest Jewish population in the world before the Holocaust. As a centre of Jewish settlement, Poland had an active Jewish press catering for a variety of ideological groups. In Warsaw, the cultural and political capital of the Kingdom of Poland, Jews were the largest minority group, accounting for a third of the overall population. To be sure, during the nineteenth century the Warsaw Jewish community was avowedly more conservative in adopting ritual change than others in western cities, and those that actively supported Jewish integration into Polish society were viewed as a splinter group —although a vocal and politically important one—collectively called 'integrationists', 'Poles of the Mosaic persuasion', 'progressives', or 'enlightened Jews'.[2] The enlightened Jews were followers of the Haskalah, or Jewish Enlightenment, a movement promoting the abandonment of Jewish cultural and social distinctiveness and adaptation to the non-Jewish majority. Although it is usually associated with western Europe, the Haskalah had a profound effect on Jews in Poland, too.[3]

The integrationists came from the intelligentsia and a newly emerging social class, the bourgeoisie.[4] The primary outlets for propagating their views were the Polish-language Jewish periodicals *Jutrzenka* (1861–3) and *Izraelita* (1866–1915), and a number of other, smaller publications. Ideologically, progressive Jews were inheritors of the Haskalah, but their stance was also influenced by the social, economic, and political changes of the period. Their aims included the promotion of education and progress, legal emancipation for the Jews, the modernization of various aspects of Jewish life (including the religious sphere), acculturation (understood as the abandonment of distinctive clothing, language, names, and customs), and integration into appropriate groups of the host society. In matters of religion, progressive Jews advocated a continued devotion to Judaism, although they frequently called for religious reform.[5] Their aim was to become Poles in a cultural and national sense while preserving their Jewish religious identity. However, the meaning and scope of the 'Jewish' component in their Polish Jewish identity was open to interpretation, and the group was far from being ideologically homogeneous.

Integrationists frequently commented on the tension created by 'living in-between', balancing affiliation with a Christian-dominated Polish society and the maintenance of a public Jewish identity.[6] As they aspired culturally and socially to the middle and upper classes, they were expected to change some of their cultural observances in order to be accepted by the Poles. On the one hand, they embraced the emancipatory opportunities of modernity and its promise of progress as freedom; on the other hand, they were attached to Judaism by an emotional bond that provided communal belonging and a sense of heritage.[7]

The reforms desired by the integrationists (and by the Poles, or so the progressives thought) could be achieved without much effort in cases when there was a chance of physical separation from the rest of the community, as, for example, in establishing private prayer houses.[8] With funeral rituals and cemetery space, however, such separation was difficult or even impossible to accomplish because in nineteenth-century Warsaw the same burial place and funeral service were used by all members of the Jewish community. The fight over the standard form of rituals ensuing between the advocates of progress and the advocates of tradition became a struggle for the right to express one's identity according to one's individual conscience. Emotions over this issue ran high because the presentation of one's identity in a tombstone was believed to be final and ultimate. Moreover, taking leadership in the sphere of funeral rituals and the cemetery also meant exerting influence on the world of the living.

Politics Enter the Realm of Death: Progressive Jews versus the Ḥevra Kadisha

At the beginning of the nineteenth century funeral ritual in Warsaw was controlled by the burial society or ḥevra kadisha (lit. 'holy society'). According to Ignacy Schiper of Warsaw, the society consisted of a few

fathers of local families, who are thought to have, apart from religious piety, a detailed knowledge of ritual law, and who out of religious devotion have taken on the responsibility of visiting the poor and the bedridden, to watch over them in need. They attend to the deceased in the final hours of their life; they say prayers and conduct religious rituals at the deathbed, and if the dying person is of some significance, they accompany the body to the grave and perform the assigned ceremonies for giving last respects to the deceased.[9] (Schiper 1938: 9)

The three main areas of the society's activities were thus hospital service, the performance of the burial rituals, and assistance to the poor, the ill, the elderly, and the crippled.[10] The people chosen for this service were men considered to be of high moral character who were greatly esteemed by the community. The sewing of garments for the dead (*takhrikhim* or *takhrikhin*) and the washing of dead bodies was sometimes performed by women. The *ḥevra kadisha* could also be joined by members of the priestly caste (*kohanim*), but they were not allowed to attend to the dead bodies.

The *ḥevra kadisha* functioned within the *kahal* structure,[11] but a special Polish government instruction in 1806 guaranteed the society independence from *kahal* authority. However, when the government (supported by enlightened Jews) started to introduce plans for restructuring the Jewish communities, aiming to end Jewish class separateness[12] and its representation in the form of *kahals*, the situation changed. After the abolition of *kahals* in 1823, the burial society was put under the supervision of the Dozór Bóżniczy (Jewish Community Board), which replaced the previous authorities. However, because the Community Board was not able to assume all powers and obligations, including those of the burial society, the latter continued to operate unofficially, although its make-up changed. After 1855 the former *ḥevra kadisha* functioned, according to Schiper, as 'a committee for the maintenance of the cemetery' and apart from *mitnagedim*,[13] its members also included integrationists (Schiper 1938: 81–2).

Progressive Jews who were trying to gain control over the communal institutions referred to keeping pace with the Enlightenment, both Jewish and non-Jewish, as a justification for introducing reforms. A goal of the Enlightenment was to promote an organization of public life that was based on reason and science, and to eliminate irrational superstitions and what progressives considered backward behaviour from everyday life. The semantic range of the word 'backwardness', though, was wide, and the term could describe many phenomena, from old superstitions to religious mysticism, and even some *halakhot* (laws). It could refer, for example, to the wearing of traditional Jewish costume, preserving customs that had grown around some Jewish rituals, or even speaking Yiddish. In the nineteenth century anything labelled by Poles as backward immediately drew the attention of the Jewish reformers, who used the 'anti-backward' propaganda to battle their political and ideological opponents. Their criticism was directed at the activities of many traditional organizations and communal institutions (for example, the *kahals*, the *ḥevra kadisha*, or Jewish elementary schools, called *ḥeders*). It also targeted the hasidim, a part of the Jewish community perceived by the intelligentsia to be particularly backward and superstitious.[14] This criticism was reflected in government actions and contributed to the transformation of many aspects of Jewish life (and death).

Enlightened Jews accused the *ḥevra kadisha* members of backwardness, fanaticism, vindictiveness, and even embezzlement. Such accusations could in some cases have a more political than cultural basis, for example when ḥevra kadisha members were criticized for the high charges they imposed for the burial of more affluent members of the community or of opponents of burial societies. For instance, Pinkus Eliasz Lipszyc, a wealthy Jewish merchant from Opoczno, published a tract in 1820 in which he presented the ḥevra kadisha as one of the reasons (in addition to kahal taxes and excommunication) for Jewish poverty in the Polish lands in general, and in the Warsaw community in particular. In this tract, which became popular in government circles and quickened the decision to abolish kahals, Lipszyc claimed that if the burial society could not break its opponents with taxes or censure, 'then the elders of the society note down [the name of] such an opponent in the so-called black book and patiently wait for his death'; later 'his successors, if they are of age, must give away a significant part of the assets, and sometimes even more than half of it in cash, to the above elders. On the other hand, if the successors are underage, they are completely robbed by the elders who use the pretext of taking assets under their care' (Lipszyc 1820: 8).

Similar accusations were made by Stanisław (Ezechiel) Hoge, a maskil, who later converted to Christianity and finally converted back to Judaism. He claimed that the ḥevra kadisha could 'either ban, postpone, or carry out in an insulting manner the funeral of such a Jew, who educated himself and lived sensibly, in order to wreak revenge on him posthumously if it was not possible during his life'.[15] These claims seem to be supported by the testimony of Mordko Frei, a progressive Warsaw Jew who claimed to have suffered ill-treatment by the society. Frei testified that in 1823, when his son Juliusz died, his body was dressed in such improper garments that it had to be exhumed and the shroud changed. Additionally, in 1826, when his daughter Anna died, the hearse that was to take her body to the cemetery had to wait for an hour and a half for the cemetery workers to arrive. When they finally appeared, they apparently told the bereaved family in a disrespectful manner that 'it would not matter if such a kiełbaśniczka ('sausage-eater') lay there another ninety minutes' (Schiper 1938: 100–1). This scornful reference to Anna Frei as a 'sausage-eater' (or 'pork-eater') is a revealing testimony of the animosity felt by the conservatives for the integrationists who allegedly did not observe kashrut (Jewish dietary laws).

The prevalence of such accusations of excessive charging for burials and cemetery plots (as well as its widespread practice) is evident in an anecdote quoted in 1908 in Izraelita. According to the story, an examiner in a ḥeder decided to test an allegedly brilliant pupil and asked him if Moses was rich. The pupil proved his intelligence by answering that he must have been poor because no one knew where his grave was and 'after all, if he had been rich, then the ḥevra kadisha would have demanded a large payment for his burial and we would know where his grave was'. This anecdote was quoted by the examiner, a correspondent for Izraelita, as a commentary on the widely known incident in 1908, when burial societies hindered the interment of a rich man. The family had been approached by the societies of three different towns—Węgrów, Kałuszyn, and Jadów—but they all demanded an exorbitant sum for the burial and the plot. The scandal erupted with the disclosure that the house of the deceased was surrounded by guards around the clock to make sure the body was not stolen by the competing societies. Orthodox Jews were shocked that the funeral only took place on the sixth day after the death, when the heirs had finally managed to collect the amount demanded by the *ḥevra kadisha* in Węgrów (Ln.Lm. 1908). Jewish law requires that burial occur as soon as possible, preferably within twenty-four hours of death.

Another controversy in 1908 was of even greater importance as far as the connection between funeral rituals and Jewish identity was concerned. Probably no one expected that the funeral of the 10-month-old son of Helena and Herman Grynszpan that year would become one of the most widely discussed moral scandals in the capital, stirring up a media storm and giving rise to divisive questions about Jewish identity in the new century. The child's parents counted themselves among the progressive Warsaw Jews, who decided not to follow what they called the barbarian tradition of *berit milah* (circumcision).[16] The boy's uncircumcised state, which was discovered during the ritual washing of the body, sparked a rancorous response from the traditional Jewish community. The Community Board, when notified of the incident, told the child's father to take away the body and bury it outside the Jewish cemetery, but he refused. The final decision on the matter was made by the rabbinate, who ordered a posthumous circumcision of the infant and its burial in the Jewish cemetery (see Bacon 2001). This event precipitated a fierce debate in the press and in the streets, pitting the progressives against the traditionalists over whether some Jewish rituals were inviolable and sacred.

In the debate, the progressives perceived and pictured the ritual of *berit milah* as an 'absurd idolatrous relic, one of the many anachronisms of ancient times which should be abandoned once and for all' (Lichtenbaum 1908c: 402). Others who were also against circumcision pointed out that the mark of the covenant with God should be made in the heart and not in the body, echoing a Christian concept. Others calling for Jews to modernize in the new century urged an advancement of Judaism above 'the level of some fetishes and cults worth of cannibal Botokuds or Papuans'. They believed that 'the covenant of a corpse with God becomes the mockery of a lofty religious idea, a repulsive and disgusting act, which causes a cultured and truly religious man to shudder' (Lichtenbaum 1908c: 402–3). The controversy that broke out around the question of circumcision revealed ritual to be at the heart of the debate over Jewish identity. The criticism of progressive Jews focused on the irrationality and anachronism of Jewish practices in general (and not only on funerary rituals), while its defenders insisted that fidelity to the tradition on the basis of ancient scriptural precedent was essential to the maintenance of Judaism (see e.g. Lichtenbaum 1908c).

Similar debates over the problem of ritual burial for uncircumcised Jews erupted elsewhere during a later period, for example, in Russia. Writing on Jewish burial customs and cemeteries in the Soviet Union in the interwar period, Mordechai Altshuler states:

Since the Jewish cemeteries were managed by the Hevra Kadisha societies, disagreements between various sectors of the Jewish population tended to erupt over this issue. The Hevra Kadisha often refused to let uncircumcised children be buried in Jewish cemeteries, while the parents of those children categorically refused to bury them in Christian cemeteries. (Altshuler 2002)

Altshuler interestingly notes that the *ḥevra kadisha* could (and did) also refuse to perform funeral rituals for people who did not observe halakhah, were anti-religious, or were communists (Altshuler 2002: 97).

What was the significance of being buried in a Jewish cemetery for those Jews who were loosely (if at all) connected to the Jewish tradition? This can be well explained by the case of the English burial controversy. In Victorian England, a controversy followed the campaign of the MP Sir David Salomons, known as a leading figure in the nineteenth-century struggle for Jewish emancipation in the United Kingdom, to protect Jewish burial traditions against government interference in the 1840s and 1850s. What gained public notice for his argument was that he 'belonged to the Anglo-Jewish patriciate that felt comfortable in Victorian England despite the existence of civil and political disabilities. Handsome, well-built, well-mannered, and highly anglicized, he had no trouble being socially accepted in non-Jewish circles' (Gilam 1983: 148). Yet, despite the extent of his integration and secularization, Salomons did not hesitate to fight for the preservation of the autonomy of the Jewish burial tradition against the government's plans for the nationalization of cemeteries that could violate Jewish burial law. According to historian Abraham Gilam, Salomons's stance was based on the identity-forming function of ritual: 'Apparently, even for a radical secularist there was a certain minimum of tradition that had to be preserved. Certainly, his adjustment to circumstances did not lead to a total repudiation of Judaism. Salomons confined his Jewishness to minimal observance of the rites of passage' (Gilam 1983: 155). For David Salomons and for the burial authorities in Poland and Russia, being buried in a Jewish cemetery was the ultimate way of confirming Jewish identity.

Science Enters the Realm of Death: Revisions and New Visions

Influenced by the scientific outlook of the Enlightenment, many progressives held the view that burial practices should be based on a common-sense approach to interring or destroying the corpse rather than on the so-called superstitious beliefs of ancient times. For example, historian Falk Wiesemann chronicles the impact of the Enlightenment on German burials: 'When it came to explaining natural phenomena, modern thinkers were no longer prepared to accept the binding validity of religion, tradition and inherited wisdom' (Wiesemann 1992: 18). The German approach to this problem was quite similar to that of the progressive Jews of Warsaw. Whenever government orders based on medical research (especially concerning hygienic and sanitary principles) were incompatible with tradition, 'Poles of the Mosaic persuasion' tended to favour rational scientific laws over religious rules and customary practice.[17]

A prime example of introducing Enlightenment rationalism into funerary practice was the issue of prompt burial required by Jewish law.[18] That this custom was familiar to Poles is suggested by a folk saying of the period, 'as quick as a Jewish burial' ('prędki jak żydowski pogrzeb'), and the practice prompted much speculation in the Polish community. According to a commonly held Christian belief, Jews were ready to 'help' a dying person when a quick burial was needed, for example on the eve of the sabbath (Wiesemann 1992: 20). Accepting the non-Jewish point of view, progressive Jews adopted a critical approach, viewing quick burials as irrational and improper: 'We are talking here about the custom of the premature, one could say abrupt, burial of the deceased, which has, incidentally, only survived here, but has completely vanished in countries where Israelites have access to better education', wrote the author of an anonymous letter to the editor of the *Izraelita* (Anon. 1872). The main legal and hygienic concern about a quick burial was that authorities often did not have a chance to examine the body to check for signs of violent death or of the presence of an epidemic disease that had to be reported. Another argument brought against this practice was the fear of burying someone while they were still alive, for example in a comatose state.

The concern about misdiagnosing death was an *idée fixe* in Enlightenment calls for the reform of traditional Jewish funerary practices. As Falk Wiesemann points out,

Around 1750, non-Jews, and Jews who had been influenced by the Enlightenment, began to question the Jewish way of death and to seek to change it. Among the enlightened circles of the day the belief had taken hold that many people were buried alive . . . The Enlightenment spokesman therefore warned against burying the dead too rapidly. Instead, the interval between death (or apparent death) and burial should be extended as long as possible in order to rule out any possibility of error. (1992: 18)

The fear of being buried alive was also fuelled by the popular literature of romantic Gothicism which frequently used the horror theme of being buried alive (Ariès 1989: 387–97), although a few cases of burial of people in a coma do appear in the historical records of the period. Such occurrences turned public attention to Jewish law that insisted on quick burial after death. The idea of the dead coming back to life could also have been linked to a quite different Jewish popular belief. In the early twentieth century Regina Lilientalowa, a famous

Polish Jewish ethnographer, while researching the subject of Jewish funeral practices, reported that Jews believed that a dead body should be guarded until its burial and constantly watched at least by two people, so that if one falls asleep, the other still keeps guard. In case there is only one guard and he or she falls asleep, the body—animated by evil spirits—may come back to life in a zombie-like state. In another version of this superstition, unguarded bodies could rise up and spew blood from their mouths.[19]

Progressive Jews were sceptical not only about such beliefs, which they derisively labelled bizarre superstitions, but also, as noted above, about the desirability of quick burials as required by religious law. It is evident that the author of the letter to *Izraelita* complaining about 'abrupt burial' among the Jews was aware of the rarity of cases of misdiagnosed death, but warned that 'nevertheless all precautions must be taken not to commit a terrifying, dreadful murder' (Anon. 1872). In his opinion such actions would also help to improve the public perception of Judaism and its followers: 'This service would benefit our religion, which would be cleared of the charge of supporting harmful vestiges of the age of ignorance; it would benefit mankind, in whose interest such laws were established; and it would benefit law, which would gain in respect and reputation' (Anon. 1872). He also pointed out that the situation was still better in Warsaw than in the provinces because in the capital, as a result of the supervision of the authorities, people were more likely to keep to the state-regulated minimum time between the pronouncement of death and the inhumation (in theory at least forty-eight hours, and in practice three days). However, the enforcement of this regulation was generally lax: it was only periodically that the police cracked down on violators, as was the case for example in 1881.[20] Another way around the regulation that was commonly practised was to report an earlier death date to the authorities. If someone died on 16 October 1887, for example, on the same day the representatives of the Jewish community or family members reported that he or she had passed away on 13 or 14 October. This way both parties were satisfied: the authorities believed that the legal requirements had been fulfilled, and Jews who wished to observe the halakhah could bury the deceased on the day of their death.[21]

A further example of applying a scientific approach to the conduct of funerary ritual was the insistence on autopsy. Whether performed for criminal investigation or for scientific reasons, it always caused a considerable uproar among observant Jews, who claimed that it violated the prohibition against *nibul haguf* ('defilement of the body'). A controversy erupted in 1888 when the Warsaw Jewish Hospital performed an autopsy on a Jewish *duchowny* ('clergyman', probably referring to a *dayan*) from the province, who had died of brain tumour. Despite the protests held by Orthodox Jews in front of the hospital, the autopsy was successfully carried out and 'science achieved its aim', according to a report in *Izraelita*.[22] Progressive Jews admitted in this case that the 'dissection of a dead human body with a knife undoubtedly hurts in some way the feelings of the living'—especially of the family members. However, they were convinced that for the sake of science such sentiments had to be overcome:

The issue of one's feelings should completely be put aside for the benefit that can be derived by medical science from the examination of dead bodies. Here at stake is the development of science with new clues on how to restore health in patients, and quite a few deceased may have provided the greatest service to others not with all their deeds during their lifetime, but by the dissection of their remains that led to knowledge useful in the treatment of the living.[23]

Modernization of the Cemetery and the Revisioning of Funeral Rituals

In the nineteenth century the managers of the Warsaw Jewish cemetery in Okopowa Street wanted to modernize the increasingly crowded site. They devised a plan to clean and organize the cemetery, ensure the safety of visitors, and improve the efficiency of cemetery services. Yet several alterations divided the Jewish community along ideological lines. Some of the modernization work, ostensibly carried out for the benefit of the whole community, such as the reorganization of the cemetery site, the planting of trees, the levelling of footpaths, and the maintenance of burial plots, was ideologically motivated. The so-called reorganization or beautification of the cemetery was strongly supported by Polish as well as Jewish reformers.[24] In fact, the new aesthetics of the burial space were imposed on the community in a somewhat dictatorial way. Acculturated Jews accepting Polish or broader European cultural and social standards were concerned that, in the eyes of the Christian society, the image of the Jewish cemetery was unsightly or repulsive. A characteristic expression of such feelings can be found in the short story 'Na grobach ojców' ('At the Fathers' Graves') by Feliks Kohn, in which a progressive Jew visits a Jewish cemetery in the company of a Christian and confesses with a sigh that he would rather not be a Jew so that he would not have to be buried in such a shabby place (1870: 286–8). This ought to be understood as an aesthetic rather than a religious declaration by the Jew, who was embarrassed in front of his Christian companion because of the disorder of the cemetery. *Izraelita*'s editor, Samuel Henryk Peltyn, wrote with emotion of the shame the cemetery brought on Jews in the eyes of the non-Jews:

The disorder and neglect prevalent at our cemetery are so glaring that each Israelite of even moderate aesthetic disposition will feel ashamed when visiting this place out of sad necessity or to take a walk. What can we say about the *ḥilul hashem* [desecration of God's name] that the sight of this neglect arouses in gentiles, who traditionally show reverence to the ashes of their close ones and use tokens of serious beauty more disposing towards recollection than chaotic disorder and filth?[25] (Peltyn 1870: 166)

Figure 9.1 Traditional plots at the Jewish cemetery in Warsaw. *Photo: Marzena Szugiero, 2009*

In the eyes of acculturated Jews, Christian burial places were characterized by their linear order and serene tranquillity.

A Christian perception of the Warsaw Jewish cemetery is given in a report by Teodor Andrault, the mayor of Warsaw, who visited the site in 1850:

As I have personally learned, there is absolutely no order at the Jewish cemetery—neither spatial, nor administrative. The tombstones are in a state of disarray. There are no plots. They [the Jews] observe the separation of sexes on the burial ground, but the places [designated for each sex] are not clearly measured and marked. One cannot guess where the border should be, especially on plots which do not contain any graves yet. And the places where some tombstones of all odd shapes can be found constitute something that is difficult to name—something that the eye would not expect to meet in the present progressive time.[26]

Reading this, the progressive leadership decided to improve the general condition of the cemetery, and to have a section for enlightened Jews so as to separate themselves from the non-progressive members of the community. The new physical layout also led to a separation of ritual. Ignacy Schiper, a historian of the Warsaw Jewish community, described this phenomenon as a 'two-track funeral custom' (1938: 180–9).

The main feature of this phenomenon is the separation of burial plots for integrationists, and the application of different rules to their plots. Traditionally there were separate plots for men and women, and for children of both sexes who died before the age of 7. According to further traditional divisions, inside the men's section the married men were supposed to be buried separately from bachelors and in the women's section there were subdivisions for unmarried women, married women, and women who had died during childbirth (Schiper 1938: 96). In 1856 Adam Epstein, a prominent representative of the integrationist camp and at that time a vice-chairman of the Warsaw Jewish community, proposed the introduction of family graves. The chief rabbi of Warsaw, Dov Ber Meisels, approved this innovation, noting, however, that such graves had to be located in a separate place within the cemetery, so as not to offend the conservative majority of the community.

In the burial plots designated for progressive Jews the traditional stratification had changed—women, men, and children were buried not only side by side but sometimes also in a common family grave. The traditional simple *matsevah* (headstone) often gave way to elaborate gravestones that expressed the new aesthetic and the new cultural identity; prominent sculptors—Jewish and non-Jewish—were commissioned to create the designs for 'progressive' stones in materials such as marble, considered to be fancy or ostentatious. Sculptors were asked to include allegorical and symbolic ornaments referring mostly to mourning and the passing of time, such as broken columns, broken trees and flowers, funeral wreaths, torches, and urns. These designs were probably borrowed from

Figure 9.2 Contemporary flower decoration on one of the gravestones in the Warsaw Jewish cemetery. *Photo: Agnieszka Jagodzińska, 2008*

the nearby Christian Powązki cemetery. A new custom, also adopted from Christians, was the decoration of graves with flowers and wreaths (Schiper 1938: 207). In the traditional section, a piece of stone on the grave was the primary symbol of lasting memory; flowers, which belonged to the world of living, were not to be brought to the world of death.

The two-track custom was also evident in burial celebrations known as *pompa funebris*. The integrationists introduced innovative customs to reflect their new aesthetics and social ambitions, but the traditional part of the community boycotted them. Such innovations included the use of a ceremonial hearse and the modernization of the uniforms of officials performing the funeral service. Previously Jews had transported dead bodies on a converted coal wagon. By 1851 there were three classes of hearse in use: 'ceremonial', 'medium', and 'ordinary' (Schiper 1938: 110). However, acculturated Jews were not able to implement the modern custom of the driver sitting in the coachman's seat and steering the horses from the top of the carriage as this was considered disrespectful by the traditionalists. Observers noted that scuffles over this sight frequently broke out. In some cases the mourners participating in the funeral procession forced the driver to the ground and made him walk next to the horses.[27]

Another custom that was adopted only by acculturated families was the display of the body of the deceased on the catafalque. This viewing violated Jewish ritual law, which prohibited the public exposure of the body, insisting rather on its natural return into the ground based on Genesis 3: 19 ('You return to the soil, for from it you were taken. For you are dust and to dust you shall return'). Decorating the room where the body was displayed with black drapery also complied with the non-Jewish aesthetics of mourning, which dictated restraint and quiet dignity. This was in stark contrast to the often loud expression of grief in traditional Jewish funerals, based on Ben Sira's directive to 'Weep bitterly, and make great moan, and use lamentation' (Ecclus. 38: 17).[28]

Although progressive Jews often invoked the rationality of the Enlightenment as a justification, there was another, often unstated, social factor underlying their rejection of such customs: as aspirants to the intellectual and financial elite of Warsaw, they wanted to adopt more of the demeanour as well as of the custom of the established Christian classes. The introduction of the catafalque into the Jewish funeral ritual, for example, resulted from the attendance of socially well-connected Jews at Polish Christian funerals. Aspiring to integrate into Polish society often resulted in fascination with its practices, which were considered more dignified, refined, and socially respected. This attraction of progressive Jews to the aesthetic standards of the dominant Christian society often resulted from the fear that adherence to traditional Jewish rituals and their public display would hold them back from rising socially.

The new aesthetics gave rise to ideas for more drastic changes, such as burial in coffins and cremation, which initially aroused controversy even within the pro-

Figure 9.3 View of the Christian Powązki cemetery, neighbouring the Jewish one. *From Wojcicki 1856, reproduced by courtesy of the Ossolineum Library, Wrocław*

gressive camp. Christians considered burial in an elaborate, lined coffin a sign of the elevated social and financial status of a family. In 1872 one of the respected progressive families wished to bury their dead in secular clothing and in a coffin, and had already made the necessary preparations, but at the last moment the Jewish Community Board denied consent and, as a result, 'the body was put between the four grave boards in an ordinary white garment, as demanded by tradition' (Peltyn 1872). Still, the issue of burial in a coffin was regularly discussed in the Jewish press and the voices in favour of its acceptance became louder and louder. In this case, too, it was the so-called aesthetic reasons that mattered, as shown by the following quote from an editorial, reprinted in *Izraelita* in 1886: 'The deceased probably do not care at all that their remains will be handed over to worms; however, for the living the sight of the almost naked body put into the ground is most unpleasant and repulsive.'[29]

Figure 9.4 View of the 'progressive' plots in the Jewish cemetery, Warsaw. *Photo: Agnieszka Jagodzińska, 2008*

As to the cremation of bodies, the views of acculturating Jews evolved over the course of several decades. In 1874 *Izraelita* still claimed that bodies could not be cremated from the standpoint of Judaism and burial was a higher and more civilized form of funeral, similar to prayer, which was a higher stage of worship than sacrifice (Anon. 1874).[30] However, several decades later the same organ expressed the opinion that the only opponents of the more sanitary and civilized ritual of cremation were the members of the backward *ḥevra kadisha* societies. Writing in 1908, Henryk Lichtenbaum, *Izraelita*'s editor, claimed that a body should turn into dust so that it could resurrect, and that it was logical that cremation would achieve this more quickly than decomposition inside a grave (1908a). In his opinion, from the point of view of the Jewish religion there were no obstacles to the incineration of dead bodies.

Controversy was also raised by the practice of 'funeral services' held in synagogues and houses of prayer. The problem started with how to name and understand such rituals: were they traditionally allowed as remembrance of the deceased (*hazkarat neshamot*) or were they an actual religious service conducted for the soul of the deceased, modelled after similar Catholic customs? Whereas Catholic dogma permitted and even recommended communal prayers in church for the dead as a method of shortening their suffering in the afterworld, Judaism developed a different perspective (Cohn 1888). Although the concept of good deeds or charitable acts performed for the sake of the elevation of a dead person's soul (*le'iluy nishmoteihem*) had existed in Judaism before, the nineteenth-century Jewish 'funeral services' held in synagogues sounded too Christian for some Jews and were condemned by these more traditional members of the community as a breach of the ban in Leviticus 18: 3, *uveḥukoteihem lo telekhu* ('and you shall not follow their [the non-Jews'] laws').[31] However, the discussion of this problem touched upon deeper levels of the transformation of Jewish life, as described uncompromisingly by one of the progressives:

> In the face of our actual life, shutting out embellishments in God's service and religious practices, following the ancient ban of *uveḥukat hagoyim lo telekhu*, is deceitful and ridiculous . . . We try to Europeanize ourselves in every possible way and we adopt in our life all aesthetic forms used by the civilized world . . . but when it comes to the introduction of harmless funeral services, the tradition that causes no offence and has been long practised by the whole western Judaic world, our *mukerim* yell: *ḥukat goyim!* (S.W. 1888)

In this case, the *mukerim* (members of the burial society) who tried to prevent violations of the Jewish tradition were right to be more concerned than they were about other attempts at beautification of funeral customs, as this innovation was much more radical than simply decorating a gravestone with flowers.

The Language and Rhetoric of Epitaphs

The introduction of Polish inscriptions on Jewish gravestones became one of the most significant manifestations of the modernization of Jewish life and had a significant impact on some funeral customs. The way to this innovation was paved by the introduction of grave inscriptions in German written in Hebrew characters, which was first done in 1836 in the Warsaw Jewish cemetery. The first Polish inscription on a Jewish stone in all of the Polish lands appeared in 1855 on the Warsaw gravestone of Antoni Eisenbaum, a prominent integrationist and a director of the pro-Polish Rabbinical School. His students and friends wished to commemorate his merits and his attachment to Polish culture with an epitaph in Polish (in Latin characters). However, this project stoked a furious debate, called by Schiper a *Kulturkampf* (culture war), that lasted three years until the reform was accepted in an official governmental decision.[32] With this innovation as precedent, after 1855 Polish became the dominant language in the specially separated burial plots for progressive Jews in the Warsaw cemetery.

The Polish-language epitaph, in addition to providing vital information, such as first name, last name, and the date of death, also included additional facts that helped to identify the deceased. There were references to the ancestry, place of birth, marital status, surviving family, occupations, positions, accomplishments, and merits of the deceased. While some of the above followed previous practice (for example, the listing of virtues in the form of a eulogy or the statement of marital status) and were already present in traditional Hebrew inscriptions, others, such as occupational attainment, were innovative.

Polish inscriptions became a means of conveying knowledge about the social profile of progressive Jews. Characteristically, most professions, social status, and merits were not mentioned on traditional headstones. The separation between the sacred and profane spheres in Jewish life translated into the choice of languages in the epitaph. For the cemetery's purposes a special protocol was developed: religious content was expressed in Hebrew, whereas that which belonged to the profane sphere was presented in Polish. According to tradition, professions unrelated to religious or social functions fulfilled on behalf of the community could not be included in the Hebrew inscription, whose aim was the religious, and not secular, commemoration of the deceased. The introduction of Polish in epitaphs therefore provided an opportunity to express the secular aspects of the life of Warsaw Jews, similar to Christian epitaphs. Over time epitaphs in the cemetery in Okopowa Street started to include descriptions of completely secular functions and professions (for example, 'a citizen and a factory owner', 'Master of Mathematics', 'sworn agent of the Warsaw Stock Exchange', 'painter and archaeologist'), and sometimes even referred to a specific event in Polish and Jewish history, such as the inscription on the grave of Michał Landy (20/XI/5),[33] martyr hero of the Polish–Jewish brotherhood ('participant in a patriotic demonstration').[34] Integrationists especially drew attention in their inscriptions to occupations which held stature in the non-Jewish world. Most of these were in the men's world. If Jewish women did not have a professional profile as a result of cultural and legal limitations in the second half of the nineteenth century, they did frequently have their social functions listed: being a wife and mother, raising children, administering children's education, and charitable work.

Polish inscriptions on gravestones signalled a distinctive cultural rhetoric accessible to a Christian as well as to a Jewish audience. They showed the secular involvement of 'Poles of the Mosaic persuasion', and their concern as Polish citizens for national matters and social integration into Polish society. Being in Polish, the inscriptions—more than their Hebrew counterparts—could make mention of accolades that mattered to Christian Poles, such as being awarded with medals of the Virtuti Militari, of the Legion of Honour, or of St Helen. The Polish epitaphs at the cemetery in Okopowa Street were influenced by the texts used in the nearby Christian Powązki cemetery. Identified as Jewish, the individuals buried in Okopowa Street conveyed in their inscriptions their negotiation between traditional and modern culture on the one hand, and between the Jewish community and Christian-dominated Polish society on the other.

A key rhetorical element of the Polish inscriptions is information about the surviving family and their emotional attachment to the deceased. However, it should be noted that mention of surviving relatives and loved ones had appeared even before the introduction of Polish in the inscriptions. This occurred for the first time in the above-mentioned German epitaphs in Hebrew characters, which were inscribed on the graves of progressive Warsaw Jews coming from a German background.

According to Jewish tradition whoever erected a gravestone for a deceased family member was not supposed to mention him- or herself in the inscription. This was rooted in the conviction that erecting a *matsevah* on the grave of a loved one was the obligation of every religious Jew and that self-praise in the text of the epitaph was inappropriate. An exception to the above was the installation of the so-called 'second tombstone', replacing the original one if it was destroyed. Then, and only then, the executor of such a gravestone could be mentioned in the inscription (Woronczak 1989: 71–3). In the case of Polish Jewish tombstones it was not uncommon to mention the executor even on the first gravestone. However, erecting the tombstone was not just about recognition for the executor; it primarily served to express feelings towards the deceased and emotional states connected with his or her demise, sometimes accompanied by the delineation of his or her virtues and accomplishments. Thus the epitaph needed a special author who could express sentiments beyond relating the person's vital statistics. The emotions written in stone connected to the loss of a loved one included grief, sorrow, despair, and longing. Mention was also made of love, gratitude, attachment, yearning, loneliness, and pain caused by the death of a family member or friend. The surviving family was described as 'inconsolable', 'desolate', and 'bereaved'. The public expression of these feelings in inscriptions was an innovative step whose significance lay in the fact that it reconstructed the emotional space that had once existed between the deceased (presently symbolized by the tombstone, their substitute in the material world) and the living. This is also reflected in the landscape of the progressive section of the cemetery, where bonds between the dead were emphasized by the introduction of family memorials and plots, where the members of one family could be buried close to each other.

The progressive tendency for expressing emotions in the epitaphs spread into the traditional section. In the epitaph on the *matsevah* of Shemuel Tsevi Shtaynloyf, a Gerer hasid who died in 1894 and was buried in Warsaw, we read, for example, *tsar lanu al avinu hayakar* (we are anguished over our dear father) and *evel kaved nafal lemishpaḥto shtaynloyf/ le'ishto gam lebanav he'ashir aḥarav* (heavy grief fell on the Shtaynloyf family, on his wife and his sons whom he left behind).[35] This personalized, emotional bond to the deceased father and husband goes far beyond the pattern of a traditional Jewish epitaph. It is quite probable that the custom of expressing personal feelings in the inscription was first adopted by progressive Jews from Christian cemeteries, and then, once it had found its way into the Jewish cemetery, it circulated quite freely within its borders.

The close connection of the living to the world of the dead could be reflected, among others, by an appeal on the gravestone asking passers-by to pray to God for the dead person's soul, which was also a significant innovation. An example of such an attempt to introduce an element of interaction between the two worlds is the following passage from the inscription on the grave of Władysław Rosenfeld, who died in 1910: 'Passer-by, walking past this grave/ Say a few words of prayer to God for this righteous soul/ Amen!' (33/VIII/11) This cemetery poem derives from the Christian theological concept of continually praying for the dead in order to ease their suffering in the afterlife, and is alien to customary Hebrew inscriptions. According to Jewish tradition, Kaddish, the prayer for the deceased, has to be said every day for eleven months after death, but later it is recited only once a year. Placing on the *matsevah* an inscription in which the deceased asks for a prayer transferred his or her plea from a periodic, yearly perspective to an eternal one. Consequently, epitaphs such as the one on the gravestone of Władysław Rosenfeld violated Jewish tradition. Some Jews criticized such continuous prayers, or even giving alms on behalf of the deceased, as a pagan custom (Rabin 1869).

It should be remembered that the introduction of Polish as a language of Jewish inscriptions generated a demand for new standards in epitaphs, which were most easily found in Christian cemeteries. Often the established formulas of the Polish inscriptions that were borrowed also transported encoded references to the Christian religion. An example of how eschatological content depended on the language and the conventions used to express it can be found on the tombstone of Bernard (Dov) Landau from the Kromołów cemetery, who died in 1893 (Woronczak 1999: i. 225–6, ii. 123–4). Here, on the same stone there are two inscriptions, in Hebrew at the top and in Polish at the bottom. The first one includes a reference to the virtues of the deceased and the message: *zekhuto ya'amod lanu ulezarenu* ('May his merits help us and our descendants'). In the second inscription not a single word is said about his virtues but there is a request by the surviving family . . . to pray for him. There is an incongruity here: the same person is presented as a righteous man with considerable merits and impeccable deeds in the Hebrew inscription, whereas the Polish text suggests he was less than righteous and even required prayers on his behalf. This case is a fascinating example of conflicting cultural codes in separate epitaphs.

In some inscriptions on the gravestones of small children buried in the plots of progressive Jews, another Christian concept, adopted together with the text of the Polish epitaph, can be discerned. According to Christian tradition, small baptized children, who depart from this world without any guilt or sins, sing to God in heaven together with angels and are consequently frequently identified with them. An expression of this belief can be found in the final words of the epitaph popular on Christian children's gravestones: '[he/she] has joined the group of little angels in heaven'. In the section of progressive Jews, epitaphs such as that of Henio Rozencweig (33/IV-V/61) take the form of a euphemism replacing the word 'died':

(of blessed memory)
Henio Rozencweig
son of Maurycy and Kazimiera of Steuermark
born on 12 September 1890
joined the group of little angels
on 18 August 1898

In the grave inscriptions of progressive Jews at the cemetery in Okopowa Street, the deceased children had become angels and the dead asked people to pray for their soul. The linguistic image of the world drawn up in the epitaphs had changed due to the change of language. Although progressive Jews could attempt to preserve the traditional aspects of Jewish epitaphs in the Polish inscriptions, their rhetoric gradually became a culturally autonomous creation, combining the elements of two worlds and two religious systems. Intentionally or not, the integrationists transferred to the cemetery Polish norms rooted in Christian tradition, thus producing a new, hybridized sepulchral practice.

Conclusion

On a practical level, gravestones marked the spot where a given person was buried. Apart from this function, in the context of sepulchral practice, they were a sign referring to someone who had departed from the world of the living. The tombstone was believed to be a visible symbol of the invisible reality, or rather, of two realities—one physical, hidden underneath it, and the other eschatological and spiritual, hidden beyond the scope of the physical world.

But on a symbolic level, the tombstone was more than a mere representation: it became a substitute for the deceased, a physically detectable trace of his or her presence in the realm of the living. Although a given person was dead and thus absent from the collective reality of those who still dwelt in this world, the gravestone made the ones left behind remember him or her. A French scholar called this cultural phenomenon 'prothèse de la mémoire', literally translated as 'prosthesis of memory' (Dansel 1970: 13, as quoted in Urbain 1978b: 319). The gravestone reflected a human desire to be remembered, or even to be immortalized.[36] Of course, its ability to replace the dead person was significantly limited. Its ambiguous ontological status destined it from the very beginning to fail as a human substitute, as it could never express someone's presence without also announcing the opposite—his or her real absence.

Nevertheless, in the understanding of nineteenth-century European culture, both Jewish and Christian, there was a close, even intimate, relation between the dead and their gravestones. Taking into consideration the belief that a stone erected on someone's grave was supposed to be a reflection of their personality and identity, the ferocity of various Jewish debates concerning 'the dead issue', as *Izraelita* called the complex of controversies revolving around funerary practice in modern times, comes as no surprise. By being buried in a Jewish cemetery, progressive Jews wanted to convey an important message: no matter to what extent they supported modernization, acculturation, and integration into Polish society, they still identified themselves as Jews. However, by choosing a certain form of burial ritual, plot, and gravestone, they wanted to specify what kind of Jews they were: 'progressive' Jews, 'enlightened' Jews, 'Poles of Mosaic persuasion', and so on. The first part of each of these terms was as important to them as the second. Therefore to retain this element of their identity, they were ready to use all their cultural influence and political power to win 'the cemetery wars'. They insisted that the ideological choices made during one's life should continue after death. A Jew who had abandoned traditional Jewish dress, spoke Polish, used a non-Jewish name, and participated in the cultural, social, and even political life of Polish society would lose all his worth or stature if he were deprived of a proper form of burial and a proper gravestone.

With the creation of a cultural space where progressive Jews could follow a hybridized funerary practice based on Christian and Jewish traditions, Jewish modernity in Poland saw the decline of a pre-modern Jewish identity that combined both religious and ethnic (pre-national) aspects. The erosion of Jewish tradition regulating practically all aspects of Jewish life and death was coupled with the rise of a more flexible identity framework into which various forms of Jewish responses to modernity would fit. With the introduction of the possibility of separating religious observance from ethnic or national participation, one could compose one's identity from individually picked elements, rather than from an inherited tradition imposed by the community. Practices that were once obligatory under the halakhah, such as *kashrut* or sabbath observance, became optional in this new setup. The question of identity became largely a question of self-identification, and for some progressive Polish Jews it was only their burial in the Jewish cemetery that still reflected their Jewishness.

Acknowledgements

I would like to thank Simon Bronner, Michael Steinlauf, and an anonymous reviewer for sharing with me their comments on an earlier draft of this essay. Their remarks helped me to clarify some issues and to eliminate some inaccuracies.

Notes

1 Emancipation, acculturation, and integration are understood here according to Todd Endelman's definition: emancipation is 'the acquisition of rights and privileges enjoyed by non-Jewish citizens/subjects of similar socioeconomic rank'; acculturation is 'the acquisition of social and cultural habits of the dominant non-Jewish group', and integration is 'the entry of Jews to non-Jewish social circles and spheres of activities' (Endelman 2008).

2   A distinction has to be made between the scholarly terminology describing the groups under discussion (integrationists, acculturated Jews, etc.) and the language used by those participating in the nineteenth-century discourse. 'Progressive' and 'enlightened' are words that the modernizers used to describe themselves, whereas 'backward' or 'orthodox' reflect how they saw their opponents. I adopt these loaded terms to expose the ideology hidden behind them. It should also be noted that the term 'progressive' is used in its nineteenth-century sense, describing a supporter of general modernization and reforms, and has no connection to Progressive Judaism.

3   For more on the Polish Haskalah, see Wodziński 2005.

4   On the development of the Warsaw bourgeoisie, see Siennicka 1998: 25–9.

5   The question of Jewish religious reform in the Kingdom of Poland has not been sufficiently researched. Although it is certain that in the Polish lands there was no Reform movement comparable to the German one, there were some local initiatives that aimed at reorganizing the synagogue space, modifying some of the rituals, and revising the role and form of Jewish worship and the language of the prayers. For a case study of religious reform in Germany and Poland, see the biography of Marcus Jastrow (Galas 2007). For a more general overview (unfortunately not free from oversimplifications), see Meyer 2001 and Corrsin 2000.

6   For more on this problem see Jagodzińska 2008.

7   I follow the cultural history of this group in my book (Jagodzińska 2008). As I argue there, although Poles of the Mosaic persuasion managed to achieve a high degree of acculturation and national identification with the Poles, they did not became fully integrated into Polish society, and in fact constituted a 'nation in-between'.

8   For more information on Jewish prayer houses in Warsaw see Bergman 2007.

9   Despite Schiper's biased attitude towards 'orthodox' parts of the Jewish community, and despite some inaccuracies or even mistakes that he made as a historian, his book is a source of great importance as he had access to the archives of the Warsaw Jewish Community which have not been preserved; this is the main reason why I quote him in this article.

10   More on the character and functions of burial societies in the Kingdom of Poland can be found in Guesnet 1998: 357–86; for more about the Warsaw case, see ibid. 370–81.

11   *Kahal* is a Polish Jewish term adopted from the Hebrew word *kehilah* meaning 'community'; it was a governing board of elders that made important decisions in Jewish municipal affairs.

12   In the pre-modern period Jews functioned practically as a separate estate (or social class) within the framework of Polish society, next to the nobility, clergy, townsmen, and serfs.

13   *Mitnagedim* literally means 'opponents' in Hebrew; the term was used to refer to Jewish opposition to hasidism that had emerged both on the religious and on the political level.

14   For more on the relation between *maskilim* and hasidim in the Kingdom of Poland, see Wodziński 2005.

15   In AGAD, CWW rec. no. 1723: 30.

16   An interesting insight into the problem of the contested rituals of *berit milah* and *sheḥitah* (ritual slaughter) in the context of Jewish political life in Germany between 1843 and 1933 can be found in Judd 2007.

17   For a discussion of Jewish customs relating to death, burial, and mourning, and their rabbinical sources, see Sperber 2008: 359–609.

18   An interesting debate from 1823 concerning this problem can be found in AGAD, CWW 1448: 9–12.

19   See LR, section 'Przesądy, wierzenia, zwyczaje' subsection 2: Obrzędy pogrzebowe', 107, 114.

20   *Izraelita*, 1881, 24: 198.

21   I am grateful for this information to Paweł Woronczak, who compared the cemetery and archival records of the Kromołów community. For more on his detailed research, see Woronczak 1999.

22   *Izraelita*, 1888, 29: 247.

23   Ibid. An interesting study on the autopsy of Christian and Jewish corpses in the context of the racial discourse and social segregation in Poland in the 1920s and 1930s was presented in Natalia Aleksiun's lecture 'Segregating Beyond Death: Anti-Semitism, Corpses and the Training of Medical Doctors in Poland of the 1930s', delivered at the Eleventh Biennial Lessons and Legacies Conference on the Holocaust: Expanding Perspectives on the Holocaust in a Changing World, Florida Atlantic University, 4–7 November 2010. I thank Natalia Aleksiun for sharing with me the unpublished draft of this paper.

24   For more on the nature and significance of various cemetery reforms, see Guesnet 1998: 303–25.

25   *Ḥilul hashem* means the danger of offending God and discrediting Judaism in the eyes of non-Jews by giving them reason for ridicule and contempt of Judaism.

26   See AGAD, CWW rec. no. 1727: 397–8.

27   AGAD, CWW rec. no. 1729: 494–500, 501–3, 506–9; Schiper 1938: 111.

28   For a discussion of Ben Sira and Jewish funeral tradition, see Kraemer 2000: 15–16.

29   *Izraelita* (1872), 42: 93.

30   This text articulates the belief, characteristic of the Enlightenment, that the history of humankind is the history of progress and that earlier stages are always less developed than the ones to come.

31   See the polemics between Mojżesz Cohn and 'S.W.' in *Izraelita*, 1888, 22: 194; 24: 209; 26: 225–6, and 28: 239–40.

32   For more on the course and significance of this *Kulturkampf*, see Schiper 1938: 126–47.

33   References to the location of gravestones at the Jewish cemetery in Okopowa street use a tripartite numbering system (e.g. 20/IV/14), where the first figure represents the number of a cemetery section, the second, the number of a row within a section, and the third, the number of a gravestone within a section.

34   The Polish–Jewish brotherhood of 1861 was a unique expression of the widespread solidarity of Poles and Jews united in the face of a common enemy (tsarist Russia). Its most vivid and also dramatic manifestation could be found in Warsaw. For more on the character, course, and fate of the brotherhood see Bartal and Opalski 1992.

35   I am grateful to Michael Steinlauf for drawing my attention to this interesting phenomenon and for providing me with the photograph of the *matsevah* as well as with information on its location (54/ XVII/23).

36   For more on the role and significance of the tombstone as funeral object, see Urbain
      1978a, 1978b.

References

Primary Sources

AGAD, CWW. The Main Archive of Old Records, Central Religious Authorities. Rec. No.
   1448, 1723, 1727, 1729.

Epitaphs at the Jewish Cemetery in Okopowa Street, Warsaw (Sections 1, 20, 26, 33).

Izraelita, a weekly published in Warsaw, 1866–1908.

LR. The Private Ethnographical Archive of Lilientalowa Regina, in the collection of the
   Public Library of the City of Warsaw, Manuscripts and Old Prints Section, Rec. No.
   2377.

Other Sources

ALTSHULER, MORDECHAI. 2002. 'Jewish Burial Rites and Cemeteries in the USSR in
   the Interwar Period'. *Jews in Eastern Europe*, 1–2: 85–104.

ANON. 1872. 'O potrzebie rozciągnięcią przepisów pogrzebowych i na gminy prowin-
   cjonalne', *Izraelita*, 46: 375.

ANON. 1874. 'Palenie ciał zmarłych ze stanowiska judaistycznego', *Izraelita*, 16: 128–9.

ARIÈS, PHILIPPE. 1989. *Człowiek i śmierć*. Warsaw.

BACON, GERSHON. 2001. 'Religious Coercion, Freedom of Expression, and Modern
   Identity in Poland: J. L. Peretz, Shalom Ash, and the Scandal of *Berit Milah* in
   Warsaw, 1908' (Heb.). In David Asaf et al., eds., *From Vilna to Jerusalem: Studies in the
   History and Culture of the Jews of Eastern Europe. Presented to Professor Shmuel Verses*.
   [Mivilna liyerushalayim: meḥkarim betoledoteihem uvetarbutam shel yehudei
   mizraḥ eiropah mugashim lifrofesor shemuel verses], 167–85. Jerusalem.

BARTAL, ISRAEL, and MAGDALENA OPALSKI. 1992. *Poles and Jews: A Failed Brotherhood*. Hanover, NH.

BERGMAN, ELEONORA. 2007. *Nie masz bóżnicy powszechnej. Synagogi i domy modlitwy w
   Warszawie od końca XVIII do początku XXI wieku*. Warsaw.

COHN, MOJŻESZ. 1888. 'Jeszcze jedno słówko o żałobnych nabożeństwach', *Izraelita*,
   24: 209.

CORRSIN, STEPHEN D. 2000. 'Progressive Judaism in Poland: Dilemmas of Modernity
   and Identity'. In Zvi Gitelman et al., eds., *Cultures and Nations of Central and Eastern
   Europe. Essays in Honor of Roman Szproluk*, 89–99. Cambridge.

DANSEL, MICHEL. 1970. *Au Père Lachaise*. Paris.

ENDELMAN, TODD M. 2008. 'Assimilation'. In G. D. Hundert, ed., *The YIVO Encyclopedia of Jews in Eastern Europe*, i. 81–7. New Haven.

GALAS, MICHAŁ. 2007. *Rabin Markus Jastrow i jego wizja reformy judaizmu. Studium z
   dziejów judaizmu w XIX wieku*. Kraków.

GILAM, ABRAHAM. 1983. 'The Burial Ground Controversy between Anglo-Jewry and the
   Victorian Board of Health, 1850', *Jewish Social Studies*, 2: 147–56.

GUESNET, FRANÇOIS. 1998. *Polnische Juden in 19. Jahrhundert. Lebensbedingungen, Rechtsnormen und Organisation im Wandel*. Cologne.

JAGODZIŃSKA, AGNIESZKA. 2008. *Pomiędzy. Akulturacja Żydów Warszawy w drugiej połowie XIX wieku*. Wrocław.

JUDD, ROBIN. 2007. *Circumcision, Kosher Butchering, and Jewish Political Life in Germany, 1843–1933*. Ithaca.

KOHN, FELIKS. 1870. 'Na grobach ojców', *Izraelita*, 36: 286–8.

KRAEMER, DAVID. 2000. *The Meanings of Death in Rabbinic Judaism*. New York.

LICHTENBAUM, L. 1908a. 'Palenie zwłok', *Izraelita*, 35: 344–5; 36: 354–5.

——1908b. 'Przymierze . . . z kim?', *Izraelita*, 41: 402.

——1908c. 'Na dobie', *Izraelita*, 42: 406–7.

LIPSZYC, PINKUS ELIASZ. 1820. *Prośba, czyli usprawiedliwienie się ludu wyznania Starego Testamentu w Królestwie Polskim zamieszkałego*. Warsaw.

LN.LM. 1908. 'Odgłosy', *Izraelita*, 24: 234.

MEYER, MICHAEL A. 2001. 'The German Model of Religious Reform and Russian Jewry'. In id., ed., *Judaism within Modernity: Essays on Jewish History and Religion*, 278–303. Detroit.

PELTYN, S. H. 1870. 'Rzut oka na sprawy gminy warszawskiej', *Izraelita*, 21: 166.

——1872. 'Pogadanki', *Izraelita*, 42: 338.

RABIN, S. R. 1869. *Izraelita*, 40: 335–6.

RUSKIN, JOHN. 1907 [1872]. 'Letter 19: Rain on the Rock'. In E. T. Cook and A. Wedderburn, eds., *The Works of John Ruskin*, 820–3. London.

SCHIPER, IGNACY. 1938. *Cmentarze żydowskie w Warszawie*. Warsaw.

SIENNICKA, MARIOLA. 1998. *Rodzina burżuazji warszawskiej i jej obyczaj*. Warsaw.

SPERBER, DANIEL. 2008. *The Jewish Life Cycle. Customs, Lore and Iconography: Jewish Customs from the Cradle to the Grave*. Jerusalem.

S.W. 1888. 'Kronika z miast i z prowincji', *Izraelita*, 22: 194.

URBAIN, JEAN-DIDIER. 1978a. 'Rzeźba/Grób: przedmiot graniczny', trans. from the French by Marian Leon Kalinowski. In S. Rosiek, ed., *Wymiary śmierci*, 309–15. Warsaw.

——1978b. 'W stronę historii Przedmiotu Funeralnego', trans. from the French by Marian Leon Kalinowski. In S. Rosiek, ed., *Wymiary śmierci*, 317–27. Warsaw.

WIESEMANN, FALK. 1992. 'Jewish Burials in Germany—Between Tradition, the Enlightenment and the Authorities', *Leo Baeck Institute Year Book*, 37: 17–31.

WODZIŃSKI, MARCIN. 2005. *Haskalah and Hasidism in the Kingdom of Poland: A History of Conflict*. Oxford.

WOJCICKI, KAZIMIERZ WŁADYSŁAW. 1856. *Cmentarz Powązkowski pod Warszawą*, ii. Warsaw.

WORONCZAK, JAN PAWEŁ. 1999. *Cmentarz żydowski w Kromołowie jako tekst kultury*. Ph.D. diss., 2 vols. University of Wrocław.

WORONCZAK, JERZY. 1989. 'Inskrypcje nagrobne z cmentarza żydowskiego w Białej Prudnickiej', *Annales Silesiae*, 19: 71–3.

TEN

Rituals of Mourning among Central Asia's Bukharan Jews: Remembering the Past and Addressing the Present

ALANNA E. COOPER

LATE ONE AFTERNOON IN DECEMBER 1993, a few days after arriving in Uzbekistan, my travelling companions and I ventured into Tashkent's Jewish quarter.[1] Meandering through the narrow, maze-like streets, searching for signs of Jewish life, we stopped passers-by to ask if they could direct us to a synagogue. One man seemed to know and tried to help, but others gave us puzzled looks and walked away.

Built 150 years before, the neighbourhood could hardly be characterized as Jewish any longer. Over the years, the residents had migrated into the city's newer, more urban areas, and since the dissolution of the Soviet Union most others had emigrated to the United States and to Israel. Uzbeks and Tajiks (local Muslims) had moved in, and little trace of the area's Jewish character had been preserved.

After much wandering, we found someone to guide us through a narrow alley to a small synagogue tucked away behind other structures. As we made our way into the building through an obscure entrance, I imagined the scene behind the doorway: a few old men, sitting around, waiting in vain for a quorum of ten to begin their evening prayer service.

Much to my surprise, we were ushered into a warm room that was bustling with activity, noise, and excitement. Far more than a quorum of ten, the men sat together towards the front of the sanctuary praying loudly, as the women in the back chatted with one another while preparing an elaborate meal. At the conclusion of the prayers, tables were set, food was served, and we were invited to join the group for dinner, toasting, and speech-making in honour of a deceased woman who had been related to many of those present.

Having just begun ethnographic research among Bukharan Jews,[2] I was unable to determine the connections of people in the room to one another and to the deceased, or what they said in their toasts and speeches. I was, however, able

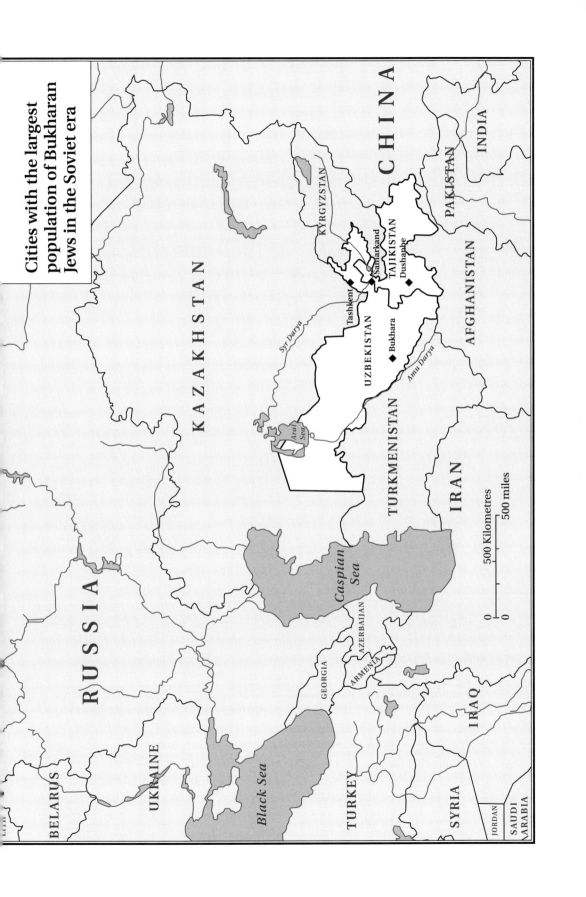

Cities with the largest population of Bukharan Jews in the Soviet era

to ascertain that the event was called a *yushva* (a Judaeo-Tajik term derived from the Hebrew *yeshivah*; see Fuzailov 1996: 231) and that it was in honour of a woman who had died on that day thirty-five years before.

I was struck by the fact that so many years had passed, yet a small crowd still gathered to publicly mark the day of this woman's death. But more than that, I was taken by the fact that in spite of their mass migration, the Jews of the quarter still convened and organized an elaborate religious and social gathering in her honour. Perhaps community disintegration was the very force that drew together those left behind, who sought camaraderie and spirituality in the face of loss. If so, the event was not only a vehicle for mourning and remembering, but also a tool to contend with social needs in the here-and-now. It is this intimate link between the act of remembering a life gone and the forming and reaffirming of social bonds in the present that forms the focus of this article.

This particular *yushva*, held in Tashkent's disintegrating Jewish neighbour-hood, was the first of many that I would attend during my years of research among Bukharan Jews who still remained in Uzbekistan, as well as among those who had emigrated to the United States and Israel. Although the study of rites of passage was not foremost on my research agenda, I quickly learned that the *yushva*—memorial service—was a ubiquitous aspect of Bukharan Jewish social life that could not be ignored easily. Whereas in the United States rituals of death and mourning are carried out as affairs that are relatively cut off from the every-day flow of life, among Bukharan Jews they are a common element of social life, tightly woven into the fabric of daily living. This meant that I received invitations to attend memorial services with great frequency, and, as a cultural anthropol-ogist, I welcomed them as an excellent opportunity to meet people. Those in attendance were generally open to talking to me, and many invited me to con-tinue our discussions in their homes. In addition to expanding my network of informants, I found that the events provided a window into the relationships between the people I was studying. Through careful attention to who was present at each *yushva* I attended, and to how these people reckoned their ties to one another, I gained tremendous insight into what sorts of relationship were con-sidered most salient, and into the ways in which these relationships were being reorganized in the face of dramatic social change.

Finally, I was drawn to memorial services by the riveting speeches that are so integral to the ritual. While I was unable to understand the words of the animated speaker at the first *yushva* I attended in Tashkent's old Jewish neighbourhood, as my language skills improved, I found that these mostly impromptu orations pro-vided valuable insight into the ways in which Bukharan Jews were working to make sense of the major changes they were facing. I learned that in the midst of massive communal rupture, the *yushva* served not only as an occasion to recollect the life of an individual, but also as a means to mark and reflect upon the passing of an era in communal life. In some ways, this reflection might be described as a nostalgic and mournful backward gaze. Remembering, however, is also present-oriented in that it is employed as a strategy to come to terms with the conditions of the here and now. By its very nature, then, the *yushva* is a ritual of continual revision. Yet, we will see that this revision is compelling and effective precisely because it is framed by stable and enduring forms transmitted from the past.

What is a *Yushva*?

Amongst Bukharan Jews, the treatment of the deceased and the rites of mourning surrounding the shiva (seven days of ritual mourning) and *sheloshim* (thirty days of ritual mourning) are carried out in much the same way as they are among most Jews around the world. The *yushva*, which is particular to this group, is added to these normative practices. Although little information is available regarding the development of this ritual, it seems to be largely an instance of adaptation to the local Central Asian cultural context.[3]

This essay offers ethnographic descriptions and analysis of three such events, with a focus on the ways in which memories of the deceased, and of an era gone by, both shape and are shaped by conditions in the present. First, however, I turn to a description of the ritual's basic features.

The most authoritative discussion of the *yushva* (also referred to as *pominki*, or *azkarah*, depending on the geographical and historical context of the speaker[4]) is provided by Giora Fuzailov.[5] His descriptions focus on those features of the ritual that remain relatively constant regardless of where and when the event takes place. The service, Fuzailov explains, is held each day during the shiva, then once a week during the first month, and once a month during the first year.[6] Finally, it is held on the first anniversary of the individual's death, and on the same date every subsequent year.

The event is structured around *minḥah* and *ma'ariv* (the afternoon and evening prayer services). In addition, it includes readings from the Zohar, the recitation of the Hashkavah prayer,[7] and speeches delivered in memory of the deceased. The *yushva* culminates in an elaborate meal, which begins with a variety of fruits and vegetables, and then proceeds to ritual hand-washing and partaking of bread inaugurating the main course. This course generally includes fried dough, fried fish, and a meat dish. The meal concludes with *kush-kilik*, a pastry dessert (also made from fried dough), which is served together with alcohol, and toasts are offered in honour of the deceased. The variety of food provides those present with the opportunity to make a great number of blessings (one for each type of food), which are understood to be *le'iluy neshamah* (for the uplifting of the soul of the deceased). Wishes for the well-being of the soul are also invoked with the toast *rachmat kuna* (Judaeo-Tajik for 'may God have mercy'). Finally, although Fuzailov does not address the prevalence of fried food at the memorial service, informants told me that that the rising smoke during food preparation is likewise intended to uplift the soul.

Fuzailov's description of the *yushva* appears in two works published in Israel in the 1990s, in the midst of the Bukharan Jews' great migration and massive communal upheaval (Fuzailov 1993; Varstil 1996: 189–242). Their demographic movement occurred against the backdrop of the break-up of the Soviet Union, a rise in Uzbek and Tajik nationalism, the creation of Central Asia's independent nation states, and the difficult shift from communism to capitalism, all of which had a major impact on Bukharan Jews' financial situation, social relationships, behaviour, beliefs, and world-views. So too did the break-up and reorganization of community and family units, and the process of resettlement and cultural adjustment. Yet, Fuzailov's texts, written in the enduring present,[8] suggest that the way the *yushva* is currently practised is identical to the way it has always been practised.[9] His writings also imply that no differences have arisen between the practice of those immigrants who resettled in New York, for example, and those who moved to Tel Aviv, Israel.

Fuzailov's choice of verb tense and his decision to depict ritual practice as uniform are probably related to the fact that he intended his work to serve as a printed collection of *minhagim* (customs) that had been transmitted orally and mimetically over generations. Jewish historian Bernard Cooperman proposes that there is a frequent causal link between community rupture (due to mass migration or expulsion) and the compilation and printing of *minhagim*. This, Cooperman suggests, is a 'form of memorialization': an attempt to remember and record how things used to be done, so that their practice might continue in spite of communal displacement and change (2006: 138 n. 76).

In this case, the texts are meant to be prescriptive: to convey a set of rules that Bukharan Jews should follow. Yet, the tone of the works suggests that they are also descriptive and are meant to provide an ethnographic portrayal of Bukharan Jewish practice. The result of this effort to write a text that is to pass both as prescriptive and as descriptive is that ritual practice is presented as frozen and utterly predictable, unfolding in catalogue fashion regardless of when or where it is enacted. Lacking variability, flexibility, and adaptability, rituals are reduced to a set of rules that individuals play no role in creating, maintaining, and altering as they respond to changing circumstances. In this sense, Fuzailov's depiction of the Bukharan Jewish *yushva* is not only about death and mourning in the most literal sense. It may also be read metaphorically as a text about the death of a community. Like a museum diorama, constructed behind a glass window for viewers to learn what life was like in the past, Fuzailov's book is not an ethnographic description about how life is unfolding in the here and now, but about how it once was, at some undefined point in time. Below, I offer another way to analyse and think about Bukharan Jews and their ritual. I focus on the *yushva* in particular because it is the ritual where one might least expect to find vibrancy, but where it is, in fact, strongly present.

During the course of anthropological fieldwork conducted in the 1990s, I attended nineteen memorial services, three of which I discuss in detail here: one held in Samarkand, Uzbekistan (1997), one in Tel Aviv (1996), and one in Boston (1994). My analysis concentrates on the variation between them, rather than on the features they shared. The prayers that were said and the dishes that were served, for example, varied little, but who chose to speak about the deceased, what they said, and the messages they conveyed differed dramatically. These flexible aspects of the event provide a view of ritual that is not only governed by static rules but is also subject to contingency and variation. In the stable framework of the *yushva*, people honour and remember the deceased and find comfort in the familiar rituals of the past. But in its open, dynamic junctures they have the opportunity to reflect on their fluid present, and to shape, renew, and create relationships with one another in the midst of ongoing change. This change is addressed below in a brief discussion of Bukharan Jewish history, which focuses on the upheavals that have taken place since the dissolution of the Soviet Union.

Historical and Cultural Overview

Before the advent of glasnost and perestroika in the late 1980s, over 100,000 Jews lived in Uzbekistan and Tajikistan, Central Asian republics of the former Soviet Union. More than half of them were Ashkenazi Jews of east European origin, most of whom had fled or were evacuated to Central Asia during the Second World War.[10] The Bukharan Jews, on the other hand, were old-timers in the region.

Little information is available about how and when Jews first appeared in Central Asia. While some claim that they were among the lost Israelite tribes, the data available suggest that the first to arrive were probably part of the group who were exiled—or whose ancestors were exiled—from the Land of Israel in 586 BCE at the hands of the Babylonians. When the land came under Persian rule seventy years later, and the Jews were permitted to return to their homes, the ancestors of those who later found their way to Central Asia chose not to do so. Instead, they began moving eastward, probably as merchants along trade routes (Zand 1990: 531), spreading out from Babylonia (contemporary Iraq) into the territory that is today Iran. They moved further east to Afghanistan and north-east to the fertile river valleys and oases of present-day Uzbekistan and Tajikistan. This area, classically called Transoxiana,[11] was controlled by various Persian empires for centuries.

Over time, the Jews came to have much in common with the non-Jewish, Persian-speaking, sedentary inhabitants of Transoxiana's urban centres who were their neighbours. Partaking of the local composite culture, the Jews' dress, cuisine, architecture, language, and customs took on many local qualities. Yet, in spite of these cultural similarities, with Islam's appearance and then rise to dominance in the region in the eighth century, Transoxiana's Jews came to be marked as outsiders. They were labelled *dhimmi*, a status which granted them—like Jews in all other territories under Muslim rule—a degree of tolerance and protection in return for their acceptance of certain prohibitions and discriminatory measures.[12]

In the fifteenth century Uzbek dynasts (settled people of Turkic lineage) conquered Transoxiana and divided it into loosely governed territories called khanates or emirates. The Jews of the region clustered primarily in the Bukharan Khanate, where the cosmopolitan silk-route cities of Samarkand and Bukhara were located. With the decline of overland trade, and with the Bukharan Khanate's severance of political relations with Afghanistan and Iran, the relationship between Bukhara's Jews and Jews outside the khanate became attenuated. Historians believe that this political and social isolation set in motion the formation of their separate identity as 'Bukharan Jews' with linguistic and cultural elements that distinguished them from other Jews (Zand 1975: 183–4).

In the latter half of the nineteenth century, the Russians took control of Central Asia, including large parts of the khanates' territories. Transportation and communication with the west improved, and the local Jews' ties with Jewish communities in Moscow, Europe, and Ottoman Palestine intensified. These new relationships led to the first wave of Jewish emigration from the Bukharan Khanate, which lasted from the 1890s to the 1920s.

Among those who relocated were merchants travelling back and forth between their Central Asian home towns and Europe. When the Soviets solidified their borders in the 1920s and made it difficult to travel in and out of their newly incorporated Central Asian territories, many of these merchants simply remained in Moscow, Paris, London, and the other urban centres where they found themselves. They probably numbered 1,000 at most and little information about them (or their descendants) is available. Others in this wave of migration moved to Palestine at the end of the nineteenth century and in the early twentieth century, drawn by a religious calling to settle in the Holy Land. This group of no more than 2,000 individuals was active in establishing and building the Bukharan Jewish residential quarter in Jerusalem.[13]

A second small wave of migration began in the 1920s, as a result of the economic depression Central Asia's inhabitants faced after the region's incorporation into the Soviet Union. In 1928 Stalin implemented his first five-year economic plan. Intended to spark commercial growth and productivity, industrialization and collectivization resulted instead in widespread poverty and famine. By 1932 an estimated 60,000 refugees had illegally crossed the border into Afghanistan to escape poverty (Koplik 2003: 356). Among them were a few thousand Jews, some of whom were fleeing from starvation, and others from the Soviets' religious restrictions (Kaganovitch 2008; Koplik 2008; for a personal refugee account, see Tilayov 1981). Many of these Jewish refugees appealed to the British government to acquire certificates of immigration to Mandate Palestine

(Asherov 1977; Koplik 2008). From among those who were not successful, some remained in Afghanistan until 1948 when the State of Israel was established and migration into the country became legal. At that point, the Jewish population of Afghanistan,[14] with very few exceptions, left the country for Israel—some 2,000 Bukharan Jews among them. Others moved to Iran or to India, and then on to Israel when the state was established (Koplik 2003 and 2008).

Throughout most of the Soviet period the authorities implemented policies that severely restricted emigration. In the 1970s, however, these restrictions were slightly relaxed, and many Soviet Jews took advantage of the opportunity to leave, including several thousand from Uzbekistan and Tajikistan,[15] most of whom settled in Israel.

In 1989, on the eve of the Soviet Union's dissolution, some 45,000 Bukharan Jews still lived in Uzbekistan and Tajikistan. They were urban dwellers settled primarily in Tashkent (Uzbekistan's capital), Samarkand, and Bukhara, in some of the towns of the Fergana valley (including Fergana, Kokand, Margilan, Andizhan), and in a few cities in north-western Tajikistan (including Dushanbe, the capital).

Today, the Bukharan Jews' presence in the region is rapidly drawing to a close. With the disintegration of the Soviet Union, the lifting of emigration restrictions, economic instability, and the project of Uzbek and Tajik nation-building from which Jews were largely excluded, Bukharan Jews have emigrated en masse. They have resettled primarily in the United States and in Israel, leaving behind a population that is less than one-tenth of its previous size and that continues to dwindle.[16]

Despite the fact that in their new homelands Bukharan Jews are largely concentrated in particular urban centres (such as New York and Tel Aviv), complex migration patterns have fractured the tightly knit communities and family groups that had historically been centred around specific locales in Central Asia. This is well illustrated by the case of the Bukharan Jewish population in Samarkand.

Throughout the Soviet era, the rate of Bukharan Jewish intermarriage with non-Jews was very low.[17] Furthermore, they tended to marry only Bukharan Jews from their own city or from surrounding towns.[18] Given the fact that their population in Samarkand was relatively small,[19] and given the high rate of endogamy in the domain of the city, cousin marriages were not unusual. Kin relationships within the Jewish community, then, became tightly woven, overlapping in many ways. This pattern was accentuated because ties to patrilineal relatives were given no preference to those of matrilineal relatives (Cooper 2000: 419–23). Accordingly, lineage groups, clans or moieties did not emerge, and Samarkand's Jewish population never divided into clearly demarcated subgroups. This kinship pattern translated into much confusion when mass migration began. Because a husband's kin ties did not take precedence over his wife's, and because people belonged to expansive kinship networks rather than to clan groups, Bukharan

Jews considering a departure were uncertain as to who should make migration decisions with whom.

Frida and Sasha, for example, had a hard time deciding if they should emigrate to the United States or to Israel. Their daughter Lena, who had moved to Israel with her husband and his parents, tried to persuade her own parents that they too should emigrate to Israel, and settle near her. Frida had visited Israel, liked it, and longed to be close to Lena. Lena's brother, Edik, however, was making the decision difficult for Frida and Sasha. He was planning to move to the United States, where his wife had strong ties. She wanted to join her sister and her parents who had emigrated to New York several years before. Edik was quite amenable to this idea because he believed his economic prospects were better there.

The plight of Frida and Sasha (and many others like them), who were suddenly forced to choose between scattering family members, is neatly illustrated in a cartoon that appeared in 1997 in *Shofar*, Samarkand's Jewish newspaper. An elderly woman and her husband stand side by side in the centre of the frame. Their son stands on their left, next to a suitcase marked 'To America', while their daughter stands on the right, next to a suitcase marked 'To Israel'. As the son tugs one way and the daughter tugs to the other, the elderly couple is pulled apart.

This fractured-family narrative is one that I have heard told and retold in many guises and forms. In 1994, for example, a teenage girl in Samarkand showed me her class photograph, which had been taken two years previously. As she moved her finger from portrait to portrait she explained, 'This one has moved to New York. This one has moved to Chicago. That one has moved to Ramleh.' Similarly, people often showed me videos of their wedding that had been held in Central Asia. Always, they would point to the people who appeared on the screen and tell me where each one now lived, and then reflect on the scattering of their friends and family. Likewise, I often walked with people through Jewish neighbourhoods and they would gesture towards the houses as we passed by, telling me who used to live in them and naming the various cities to which they had emigrated.

Perhaps it was the cemetery caretaker in Samarkand who most poignantly highlighted the fracturing of family and community. As I wandered with him from burial plot to burial plot, he identified the people marked on the gravestones, and then proceeded to tell their stories, which were not about the accomplishments, education, profession, or personal qualities of the deceased. They were, instead, stories about their family's migration: 'Here Rafael Abramov is buried. His son has moved to Phoenix and his daughter to Tel Aviv. His brother died here ten years ago and his sister moved with her family to New York. Everyone is gone now. There is no one left to visit his grave.' As we moved from gravestone to gravestone, the stories of splintering families bled together into a grander narrative about a fractured community.

As a result of these dramatic population shifts, the Bukharan Jewish homeland has not only been decentred, it has exploded and dissolved. In the midst of these demographic and social transformations, there is a pervasive sense that life as it used to be has been lost forever.

The *yushva* I describe below was held in Samarkand in 1997 in memory of Nerio Shalamayev. It provided a framework for Ilya—Nerio's son—to mourn for his father and to be comforted by those who attended the event. At the same time it created an opportunity for all those present to mourn the loss of the way things used to be in Samarkand in days gone by.

Samarkand, 1997: Memorial Service for Nerio Shalamayev (d. 1975)

Nerio was born in 1905 in Samarkand and died there in 1975, leaving behind two daughters, two sons, and many grandchildren. On the anniversary of his death, twenty-two years after his passing, a memorial service was held in his honour. The event took place in the home of Boris and Nina (Nerio's granddaughter), where I was living while conducting ethnographic research in Uzbekistan.

During the Soviet era, it would have been quite unusual for a memorial service to be held in the home of a deceased person's granddaughter (particularly his daughter's daughter). Instead, it would have been organized by the son or grandson (son's son) of the deceased, and held in his home. Most likely this would have also been the home where the deceased had lived, as homes were passed as inheritances from father to son. Since the USSR's dissolution, however, this has all changed. Now scattered, sons and grandsons are often no longer able to host memorial services in the homes where their parents and grandparents once lived, and various accommodations are made.

In Nerio's case, only his son Ilya remained in Samarkand. He had recently got divorced, and subsequently married a non-Jewish woman. Because she does not keep a kosher kitchen, he was unable to hold a memorial service for his father in his house. Nevertheless he felt it his responsibility to organize the event. With no children of his own left in Samarkand, Ilya turned to his niece, Nina (his sisters's daughter), who agreed to host it in her home.

On the day of the event, Nina and Boris's house bustled with activity: crates of soft drinks, vodka, fruits, vegetables, and meat were brought in, food was prepared, and tables were arranged. By the evening, Ilya's wife, Valerie, and Nina had completed setting the tables with small plates of raisins and sugar cubes, meant to 'sweeten the sadness of loss', as well as with trays of fruit, including apples, oranges, and grapes, and platters of radishes and pickled tomatoes. Finally, they placed teapots on the tables, which were arranged in a U shape, echoing the seating arrangement of the synagogue. Boris had removed the large picture of his own father from the dining room wall, and replaced it with a portrait of Nerio, which was hung just behind the base of the U, where the community dignitaries

Figure 10.1 Attendees pose for a portrait after a memorial service, Samarkand, Uzbekistan, 1993. *Photo: Gregory Maniouk; courtesy of Alanna E. Cooper*

who would preside over the service took their seats. Ilya stood at attention at the back of the room, hands clasped in front of him; facing the dignitaries, he would retain this pose throughout much of the evening. As guests arrived, they filed in along the perimeter, with the women sitting towards the back (which also echoed the synagogue's seating arrangement).

Although most of Ilya's family and friends had already left Samarkand, the living room filled up with people until all the seats at the table were occupied. Among them were all of Nerio's children, grandchildren, and great-grandchildren who still lived in Samarkand, as well as their spouses. However, this number had dwindled to a mere eight.[20] Aside from these family members, eleven other 'relatives' attended the event, many of whom were connected through distant ties: Gavriel, for example, who was Ilya's brother's wife's sister's husband,[21] identified himself as a 'cousin'. Gregory, who also called himself a 'cousin', was Ilya's sister's husband's first cousin.

Ten years before, when the pool of possible guests had been ten times as large, the cousin-through-marriage relationship to which both Gavriel and Gregory referred may not have been thought of as close enough to warrant the attendance of either of these guests. Yet, these ties were now being activated in a continuing effort to honour the memory of the dead and to gather together the living in the face of the rapid dwindling of Samarkand's Bukharan Jewish population.

In addition to those guests who regarded themselves as kin, five others explained that they were in attendance because of their friendship ties. Analysis of these friendship ties reveals another important dimension of the relationships between those in attendance at the memorial meal: Yonatan attended because he had been a friend of Nerio's for many years. David attended because he was a friend of Ilya, the host. Yasha attended because he was a friend of Ilya's deceased brother. Benyamin attended because he was a friend of Sasha's (who was Nerio's daughter's daughter's husband's mother's brother). The guests' ties of friendship were not limited to the deceased (Nerio) or to the host (Ilya). There were so many ways to reckon who belonged at such a meal that really anyone could in some way be construed as an appropriate guest.

A further interesting point regarding the guests is that for some of them it was not clear if they came because they were related or because they were friends. Rocheldu, for example, was said to have attended because he was a friend. However, I was also told that his wife's sister was the daughter-in-law of Ilya's brother. While it is unclear whether 'friend' or 'relative' is the more salient relationship in this case, it is significant that among the Bukharan Jews in Samarkand, many friendships often have a kinship dimension to them. Because their population has always been small and highly endogamous, and because the net of kinship reckoning is cast very wide, almost everyone can in some way be considered related to everyone else. Indeed, a response that I often received from Bukharan Jews when I asked, 'Are you related to each other?' was, 'We are all relatives.'

At the memorial service for Nerio, emphasis was placed on family ties, but family here did not refer to the descendants of a single ancestor. Rather, there was a sense of being from the same family because 'we are all from Samarkand'. As the Jews of Samarkand watch their friends and relatives leave, those who remain seek comfort by interacting with one another as family members would. Indeed, this is what they were at this memorial service for: to pray together, to eat together, and to reflect on their common loss. This sense of loss was powerfully articulated in the two main speeches that were made in the course of the evening.

Following *minḥah* and a reading from the Zohar, Isak, a religious teacher and community leader, delivered the first speech. A distant relative of the deceased, he spoke at length about Nerio's life and his character, and described him as an embodiment of the spirit of Samarkand's Bukharan Jewish community. The speech served not only to educate those present about Nerio's biography, but also to strengthen the guests' identification with one another and with Samarkand as their community home.

Isak opened with a description of Samarkand's Bukharan Jewish community as it used to be: 'Our Bukharan Jewish neighbourhood existed for 150 years as an autonomous district in Samarkand. Everyone was part of the community organization, and together we would solve our pressing problems, and participate in common endeavours.'

When Isak spoke of 'our Bukharan Jewish neighbourhood', he was referring to the Jewish *mahallah* (residential quarter) in Samarkand's old city, which was built prior to the colonial era. When the Russians arrived, they built up an urban infrastructure in the area that came to be known as the 'new city'. Although Jews continued to live in their *mahallah,* and the neighbourhood retained its Jewish character, many moved out to the new city, which is where Nina and Boris's house is situated. The areas are served by separate synagogues, and the residents of one often invoke stereotypes to refer to those living in the other (traditionalists versus modernists, for example). In the case of this particular memorial service, some of the attendees resided in the new city—like Nina and Boris—while others came from their homes in the nearby Jewish *mahallah.* Over the course of his speech, Isak drew them together into a single community who were all in some way attached to the Jewish neighbourhood, regardless of where they currently lived.

Isak then turned his attention to the deceased, focusing on his role as a generous community benefactor. Unlike most of the residents of Samarkand's Jewish neighbourhood, who received meagre salaries for their work as teachers or as factory employees, Nerio had managed a state-owned grocery store. Isak praised him for his generosity towards the community members who had frequented his store, many of whom were poor:

If you had a guest visiting your home, or if your daughter gave birth and many people came to visit you, whatever you would need—tea, sugar, spices—you could borrow from Nerio. He helped people, and he made sure that the people of the neighbourhood were provided for. Unlike most other businessmen of the time, who kept a careful account and who lent to the poor in order to make a profit from them, Nerio lent out of kindness.

Isak memorialized Nerio for his community spirit and his financial largesse:

During Stalin's reign, people were expected to inform against each other. In these complicated times, Nerio supported the Bukharan Jews. He never did such things. And then there was Simhat Torah. Under Stalin, we were forbidden to celebrate any religious holidays. But Nerio still brought rice and meat and carrots to the community club house to make *plov* [a Central Asian dish] on the holiday, and every Jew who came there was nourished.

In short, Isak's speech was about Nerio as a focal point of community and neighbourhood solidarity. While it memorialized life as it used to be, it also provided those who were in attendance—even if only for the fleeting present—with a sense of community as they shared together in the memory of Nerio as a local hero.

After completing his speech, Isak read another section of the Zohar, and then led the *ma'ariv* service. Upon conclusion of this first part of the evening, fried fish was served, and toasts to the deceased were made over vodka. Yan then arose from his seat at the front of the room to speak.

Unlike Isak, Yan was not a religious leader, nor a Bukharan Jew, and he did not trace kinship ties to anyone present. Indeed, his speech indicated that he may not have known anything about Nerio's life history at all. Although he was not asked by the family members to address the group, he took the task upon himself. After the dissolution of the Soviet Union, Yan had begun to take an active and public interest in his Jewish roots, and had become involved with the city's newly established Ashkenazi culture club. It was in this leadership capacity that he spoke at Nerio's memorial service about the palpable feeling of loss that permeated both the room and the city.

Yan's speech suggests that this loss was a communal one, which transcended the Bukharan–Ashkenazi ethnic divide. He begins:

These days, whenever I pass through the Jewish neighbourhood, I am upset. So many people used to live here! As I walk along the streets [I think to myself], 'This was the house of the Kohenov family, and this was the house of the Benyaminov family. On the opposite side of the street was the house of the Yitzhakov family, the house of the Aronbayev family, and the house of the Mullokandov family.' But now [they are all gone and] this is all history.

With these opening remarks, Yan converts the memorial service held in honour of Nerio into a memorial service for Samarkand's Jewish community. He then moves from his recollections about the community that once was to a description of the pain that has accompanied this loss:

The first time I encountered such pain was when I went to visit the [nearby] town of Navoi. I went to the synagogue where ten men had gathered for prayer services. After the service one of the men turned to me and asked, 'My dear brother, to whom shall we leave our ancient books? Our cemeteries? The graves of the ancestors of this synagogue?' Everyone else [listened and] tearfully agreed: 'How can we leave our history behind?' And yet, while we wring our hearts in our fists, we continue to emigrate.

With these few sentences, Yan poetically depicts the complex feeling of attachment to and estrangement from the place that was once home. He then turns his attention back to Ilya, skilfully blurring the distinction between personal and communal bereavement: 'Ilya, our brother, we have come here to share your bereavement. Although it was long ago [that your father passed away], the pain remains great in the heart of a son. No matter how much time passes, we always remember those who have passed away; those who will never be able to sit beside us at these tables.'

The people whom Yan characterizes as 'no longer sitting at the tables' are, of course, family members who are no longer among the living. But they also include those who could not participate in this meal of personal and communal remembrance because they have left Samarkand.

At this very sad and moving point in his speech, Yan offers comfort to Ilya and to anyone else who has lost a loved one:

A wise man once said, 'A man does not die when his heart stops or when he closes his eyelids. A man does not die when he is wrapped in a shroud or when he is put into the grave. He dies when his grave is [left untended and] grown over with grass.' So as long as we are alive, we must visit their graves and pay them respect.

In his metaphorical style, Yan extends this message of comfort to everyone who still lives in Samarkand: 'Wherever Samarkand Jews are going, wherever they are resettling, they will always remember Samarkand. And you here, although you may move to Israel, you must not forget to return to visit the graves.'

Here again, Yan blurs the distinction between the personal and communal through his reference to different sorts of graves. On the one hand, there are the graves of the deceased that are marked by tombstones in the cemetery, and on the other hand there are those that are marked by houses in the Jewish neighbourhood: houses that had once been occupied by the Kohenov family, the Benyaminov family, the Yitzhakov family, and all the others who had emigrated.

He warns those present to tend to both sorts of graves, not only physically by ensuring that they are not grown over by grass and weeds, but also by remembering. A man does not die, he tells those present, when he is buried. He dies when he is forgotten. And so, too, with Samarkand's Jewish community. For Yan this is an inclusive community that does not differentiate between the city's Bukharan Jews and Ashkenazi Jews. It may be dissolving because of migration, but it will not die as long as it is kept alive through the act of remembering.

This assertion is true in a metaphysical and cerebral way, but also in a very concrete and tangible sense. As long as those who remember gather together, eat together, pray together, and reflect with one another, they preserve the community. But more than preserving, they also create. These particular individuals with distant and tenuous kinship ties, who had come together and called themselves family, had generated a new community; one that was fleeting and unstable, but which offered comfort and a sense of belonging nevertheless.

Tel Aviv, 1996: Memorial Service for Bezalel Rafael (d. 1996)

Bezalel Rafael was born in Bukhara in the early 1900s, and he emigrated from there as a young man, among those who crossed into Afghanistan to flee harsh life under Soviet rule. Not much later, he was forced to move once again, this time to India. In 1949 he, his wife, and their eight children moved yet again, resettling in the newly established State of Israel, which is where they have all remained until today.

I never met Bezalel, who passed away in June 1996. I was, however, friendly with one of his grandsons, Dani, whom I had met through my field research among Bukharan Jewish immigrants in Tel Aviv. Dani told me that his cousins and aunts and uncles had been getting together each month since his grandfather's passing to hold memorial services in his honour, and he invited me to attend one.

The event, which took place six months after Bezalel's passing, was held in the apartment in Tel Aviv where he had been living just prior to his death. No one lived there any longer and it had been emptied of all decoration and furniture aside from a few folding tables and chairs. Ready to be sold as soon as the year of mourning was over, the home was not to be passed down as an inheritance to a son who would have traditionally become the new head of the house.

Just as the apartment belonged to the family, but to no one in particular, so too the event was organized by the family, but hosted by no one in particular. The food was bought ready-made and all of the family members chipped in to pay their part. No one assumed the role of host or hostess; rather, all took part in arranging the tables, serving the food, and cleaning up. Unlike memorial services held in Uzbekistan during the Soviet era, there was no daughter-in-law designated to prepare the meal and there was no son to gather the family together, to preside over the others, or to claim inheritance. Rather, the family as a whole took upon themselves the responsibility for the memory of their grandfather and for staying together as a unit.

Indeed, the event served as one important mechanism for maintaining family bonds. It was attended by all of Bezalel's eight children, thirteen of his grandchildren, and fourteen of his great-grandchildren. In addition, many spouses were present, bringing the total number of family members in attendance to some forty-five. Aside from myself, the only other non-family members were a few elderly men who had prayed in the same synagogue as Bezalel.

This memorial service qua family reunion was different from any that I had attended in Uzbekistan, where such a large gathering of close kin would not have been possible since the massive wave of migration had begun. The event was also different in that little about it seemed Central Asian. All of the family members in attendance had either been born in Israel or had lived there most of their lives, and those who addressed the group spoke in Hebrew (as opposed to Judaeo-Tajik and Russian).

Nevertheless, there was a familiarity about the event. The tables were arranged in a U shape, as they had been at the memorial services I had attended in Uzbekistan, with those who would preside and make speeches (in this case Bezalel's learned sons and grandsons) situated at the front. The event was structured around the *minḥah* and *ma'ariv* prayers, readings from the Zohar, speeches, and a multi-course meal. Finally, the food itself (with some adaptation to the Israeli take-out context) followed a very similar pattern, including sugar cubes and raisins placed on the table at the beginning of the event, so as to sweeten the sadness of loss.

This group loss, however, was discussed in very different terms from those invoked at Nerio's *yushva*. In Samarkand there prevailed a raw, palpable sense of mourning for the days when community, family, and place had been tightly interwoven; days that existed not so long ago. On the other hand, for Bezalel's children, whose life histories had involved much movement, the relationship of family to community and place had always been highly tenuous. And his grandchildren, who had been born in Israel and had grown up there, had no tangible sense of the rupture that accompanies migration.

Nevertheless, Bezalel's grandsons, who were the speechmakers at this *yushva*, did speak of a loss of community life as it used to be. For them, though, these 'days gone by' were in the distant past: a mythical time in which their parents' history bled into the history of the biblical forefathers. Yet, despite the remoteness of that past, they reflected upon it with sorrowful nostalgia. Avi, the first grandson to speak, began:

We are living in a time in which nothing is lacking. We are the golden generation. We are set up and not wanting for anything—not like our grandparents, who had hard lives when they came here [to Israel].

But do you know what the real difference is between our generation and the ones past? When people live in tents, they all know one another. They say good morning to each other. They ask one another, 'How are you doing?' They are concerned for one another's welfare.

Today [on the other hand] people don't even know their neighbours. I was in Ramat Gan, visiting someone who lives in a building with many floors. I asked him about someone who I thought might also live in that building. He said to me, 'I don't know anyone who lives here—not a single one of my neighbours.' That's how it is today.

In this section of his speech, Avi expresses a romantic longing for a time when people were organically bound together through their simple lifestyle and through the difficult times that they had confronted together.

It is unclear if the past that he is depicting—when people still lived in tents—was in biblical times, or in the days when his grandparents first arrived in Israel. He plays upon this ambiguity in later sections of his speech. Turning his attention to the weekly Torah portion, he tells the story of Abraham moving away from his father's house and the place of his own birth in response to God's command. Avi explains, 'Abraham had good neighbours and a house in [his home town] Haran, and he left it all. He left because of his love of the Land of Israel.'

At this point, he draws a parallel between Abraham and those who—like his grandfather, Bezalel—emigrated to Israel in the early days of statehood: 'They were people who were established [in their homes in the Old Country] and when they came here to Israel, there was no Joint [Distribution Committee] and there was no Ministry of Absorption [to offer social aid]. But they withstood the test. They came here because of their love of the land.'

Again, Avi speaks wistfully about the past when his grandparents—like Abraham—moved to Israel, motivated by a pure desire to live in the Holy Land. With this statement, he offers an implicit critique of the new immigrants from the former Soviet Union, whom Israelis popularly disparage, claiming that they move to Israel for pragmatic and economic reasons rather than out of a deep feeling of connection to the place. In Avi's narrative, the immigrants of the past, unlike those of today, withstood the trials of migration. They did so not by becoming dependent on impersonal bureaucratic systems, but rather by relying on one another and on their spirited love for Israel. Avi's nostalgia is for an imagined time when strong, organic ties bound people to one another and to their land.

He concludes by imploring all those present to reflect on his recollections of the past in a very personal manner: 'We all have to ask ourselves: are we the grandchildren of Abraham? Are we the grandchildren of Bezalel?' As though answering this question, Rafael—another one of Bezalel's grandchildren—delivers a speech in which he demonstrates that all of those gathered are, in fact, the grandchildren of both Abraham and Bezalel.

Rafael opens his speech with an expression of his pride, drawing attention to the large turnout of family members at this particular memorial service. He continues by pointing out that the number of attendees at Bezalel's memorial services had not dwindled over the course of the past six months.

He then goes on to speak about Abraham, explaining that the Torah portrays him as a man with two very different sides to his personality. On the one hand, he is depicted as welcoming and hospitable: he keeps his tent open on all sides as he watches for travellers to whom he can extend his warm hospitality. On the other hand, he banishes his concubine Hagar and her son from his home and into the desert.

Abraham welcomes and banishes; both of these character traits are contained within one man. Rafael continues, 'In our family, we have many different ideas', drawing a parallel between Abraham—one man who embodied two different approaches to dealing with others—and his own family in which many different opinions and viewpoints come together. He then alludes to the different approaches that various family members have to understanding Israel's complex political situation. Finally, he concludes, 'But we can stay together.' Just as two extremes could be contained within one man, so they could be contained within one family. In short, their qualities as a family mirror the personal qualities of Abraham. Bezalel's descendants are, in other words, also the children of Abraham.

Neither Avi nor Rafael offered much information about the life story of their grandfather who was being remembered; nor did Bezalel's other grandsons who spoke subsequently. They made references to a few of his qualities in passing, but did not go into much detail; for example, 'Grandfather honoured the land of Israel' and 'Grandfather highly valued the Torah' and 'He was always holding a religious book in his hand.'

This portrayal of Bezalel differed from the narrative told at Nerio's *yushva*. There, details of Nerio's life story were related to demonstrate the central role he had played in community and neighbourhood solidarity. At Bezalel's memorial service, on the other hand, the focus was less on his personal qualities and biography, and more on the links between his life story and the history of the biblical patriarch, Abraham.

Bezalel's children, grandchildren, and great-grandchildren came together to mourn the loss of their own patriarch. In tandem, they mourned for a romantic biblical past when simple, organic ties had bound people to one another and to the Land of Israel. They drew comfort by speaking words of Torah, by remembering together, and by strengthening the connections between their personal family narrative and the history of the Jewish people.

Boston, 1994: Memorial Service for Miriam Borokhova (d. 1994)

Rahamim Borokhov was born in Bukhara. In the 1970s, when there was an ease in emigration restrictions in the USSR, he, his wife, and their two young children moved to Israel. Around the same time, Rahamim's mother and two brothers moved to Israel as well. They and their families, however, remained there, whereas Rahamim and his family packed up about ten years later and moved once again.

Solomon, Rahamim's son, explained to me that this second move took place in 1985: it was only a couple of years before he was to turn 18, and his parents suggested that he leave Israel to avoid being drafted into the army. Rahamim's aunt, Tamar, who had emigrated to the United States several years previously, agreed to help Solomon settle in the Boston area, where she lived. Not long after Solomon arrived, his parents and sister followed. At the time, there were no other Bukharan Jewish families living in the area.

Since then, however, a small population has trickled in. By 1994, when I was doing research as a graduate student at Boston University, there were some twenty-five families scattered across the Boston area. These families found themselves in a kind of double (or perhaps triple) diaspora situation. First, they had left behind their homes in Bukhara and moved to Israel, and then to the United States. Second, by choosing to resettle in Boston, they had separated themselves from almost all other Bukharan Jews in the US, who have made their homes in Queens, New York. In contrast to these immigrants, who number some 30,000 and who have a strong network of ethnic institutions (including restaurants, synagogues, youth clubs, schools, and newspapers), those who settled in the Boston area have little social support. They are scattered across a sprawling metropolitan region, are very few in number, and have no communal institutions to bring them together. Memorial services, however, remain one forum for gathering through which they forge bonds that may not have existed in the past.

Miriam, Rahamim's mother, had passed away in Israel two months before the memorial service that I attended in Rahamim's home. Present at the event were the two women living with him (his wife, Riva, and his mother-in-law, Frida), as well as his aunt, Tamar (Miriam's sister) and her husband, his daughter Marina, his son Solomon, and his daughter-in-law.

Aside from this handful of individuals, Rahamim has few relatives in the United States, none of whom attended the memorial service. His wife Riva, however, has several kin members who did come to the event. Among them were her brother, Eddie, and her sister-in-law, Janet, who had emigrated from Bukhara to the Boston area in 1990 with Riva's help. Also in attendance were Janet's two brothers and parents, who had moved to the Boston area with Janet's help just a few months previously.

In addition to these kin members, eleven people who called themselves friends attended the event. These individuals all lived in the Boston area and were all Bukharan Jews. Most of them had not known Riva or Rahamim in Bukhara, but met them since their immigration.

In terms of the distances the attendees travelled, this memorial service was unlike the one for Nerio in Samarkand, where the guests lived in the nearby neighbourhoods, but similar to the one held for Bezalel in Tel Aviv, where people had travelled from various parts of the city and from other towns. In terms of the relationships between the individuals, this memorial service was unlike Bezalel's (where nearly all of the guests were direct descendants of the deceased), but similar to Nerio's (where relationships between those in attendance were loose).

In short, attendees at the Samarkand memorial service had a strong sense of belonging to a neighbourhood community, and the event served to reinforce and strengthen those bonds in the face of dramatic social change and community erosion. Those present at the Tel Aviv memorial service, on the other hand, had a strong sense of belonging to a common family group, and the event served to reinforce and strengthen their kinship bonds in the face of geographic distances separating the family members. The memorial service in Boston was strikingly different from both of these. Although the participants shared a common experience of being immigrants from the same home country, they did not form a common kinship group, they did not live in the same neighbourhood, and most of them had not known one another prior to their migration. Rahamim's mother did not represent a community hero for the guests in the way that Nerio did; nor did she represent a common matriarchal figure in the way that Bezalel was seen as a patriarch.

While the prayers, food, and room arrangement took on a predictable order, speeches reflected the fact that attendees had little sense of social cohesion. There was no religious or community leader to preside over the event. Rahamim's son, Solomon (grandson of the deceased), who is not a ritual expert, led the prayer service, fumbling through some of the sections. The speeches, which were made by anyone who was moved to speak regardless of how well he or she knew the family or the others present, were short and without much content. One woman, for example, spoke about Riva and Rahamim's family, praising them without any mention of the deceased:

I met the Borokhov family in Boston. Frida is a good friend of mine. She never says anything bad about anyone. And Rahamim is like a son to her. He is such a good person. And look at Solomon. I am so happy to see him leading the prayer service. And look at Eddie. He is such a great soccer player. This is a wonderful family and we can only say good things about them.

While the speaker was fond of her friend Frida, and of Frida's family, it was clear that this friendship was a new one and that they did not share a long history. Likewise, another man made a toast to Rahamim, with no mention at all of his mother or of a common past: 'I wish you and your family good health. You should live for many years.'

Rahamim's aunt Tamar spoke about her trip to Israel just a few months before Miriam passed away: 'When I was in Israel last year, I saw my sister Miriam for the last time. She told me that she longed to see Rahamim. I told her: "All is well with Rahamim. His work is fine. His wife and children are all doing well".' This short statement, which leaves so many details unsaid, calls attention to the difficulties of maintaining close relationships when they are stretched across oceans.

Only one speaker managed to find the words to draw together a community of shared memory. This elderly man, who had recently emigrated to the Boston area, addressed his remarks to Rahamim:

You and I do not know one another well. But I know that you came to this country several years ago, and I have heard how you have helped many of the Bukharan immigrants who arrived in Boston after you. I knew your parents in Bukhara and we all know that you can ascertain the good qualities of a mother by looking at her children.

With these brief comments, the speaker praises Rahamim for his loyalty to his fellow immigrants in the area, and alludes to the Bukharan Jewish community in Boston to which those present belong. Furthermore, by pointing out that he knew the deceased in Bukhara, he serves as a link that draws together the host, the deceased, and the guests into a community of shared memory.

While this link may be a weak one, it illustrates a desperate attempt to find a common discourse in the face of much anomie. And so it was with the memorial service itself: the guests in attendance shared little common history or memory. So tenuous were their bonds that they could not even join together in a discourse of mourning. Yet, in an effort to weather the social disorientation that had accompanied their move from Central Asia to Boston, they gathered to form a community of comfort to grapple with the past that they had each individually lost. Through the *yushva*, they created a common experience to help negotiate the present in which they all now found themselves.

Yushva as a Ritual of Stability and Revision

At its most basic level the memorial service might be characterized as a ritual that addresses the personal experience of death and mourning. The event marks the death anniversary of a single individual. Likewise, the primary mourner is singled out both for bearing the responsibility of organizing the event, and as the one to whom speeches are addressed throughout the evening. Although much time may have elapsed since a family member's passing, the memorial service offers comfort to those whose feelings of acute grieving may resurface at the anniversary of a death. Ilya's father passed away twenty-two years ago but, as in the case of Rahamim, whose mother had died only two months previously, the speechmakers acknowledged his personal loss as he stood facing them to receive their comfort.

In a more nuanced analysis it becomes clear that the *yushva*—which purports to be about the individual—is not only centred on the person whose death is being commemorated. Nor does it only serve the emotional needs of those who were closest to the deceased. The service also provides a forum for all those in attendance to mourn. In this communal mourning, remembering the deceased bleeds into a remembrance of the community as it once was (or as it is imagined to have been) in days gone by. The participants at Nerio's memorial service mourned Samarkand's Jewish neighbourhood and community as they imagined it to have existed prior to the dissolution of the Soviet Union. Those at Bezalel's memorial service in Tel Aviv mourned the close-knit sense of family and peoplehood they imagined to have existed in the Holy Land (either in the early days of statehood, or in the distant era of the patriarchs). And at Miriam's memorial service in Boston people alluded to feelings of group belonging that had existed before they left their respective hometowns.

A multi-layered analysis also reveals that the memorial service does not treat death as a closed ending. At the level of the individual, Nerio's *yushva* was a vehicle for Ilya to mourn the passing of his father. Yet, throughout the evening, Ilya was reminded that his father had not fully left. Although his corporeal form was gone, his spirit—or *neshamah*—was still present. Nerio's portrait was hung on the front wall, behind the table of dignitaries, in the same spot where the *aron kodesh* (holy ark) stands in the synagogue. As though presiding over the space, his image seemed to signify his active part in the service. Indeed, attendees engaged his hovering spirit throughout the evening, wishing it well, and hoping their words, blessing, toasts, and prayers would have an influence over its fate.

At the communal level, too, the event is not only a vehicle for coming to terms with a past era, now closed forever. Rather, the past and present intermingle in conversation with one another. In the same way that attendees at Nerio's memorial engaged his spirit (while recognizing the death of his corporal form), so too, they engaged the spirit of the past (different from the past itself).

At Nerio's *yushva*, circumstances in the present shaped the way the past was remembered. With so few Jews left in Samarkand, those who join together, in spite of the tenuous nature of their bonds, work to weather the disintegration of Jewish communal institutions and the loss of communal space as they watch friends, neighbours, and family pack their bags and leave. One vehicle for doing so is by recalling a past that reaches beyond the Bukharan–Ashkenazi and Old City–New City divides. This act of remembrance works to construct a past that addresses the needs of those present through the imagining of a common Jewish–Samarkandian experience.

Just as circumstances in the present shape the way the past is remembered, so too the past plays a powerful role in shaping the reality of the present. At Bezalel's memorial service, for example, children and grandchildren, who were scattered across the country, and who did not necessarily see eye to eye with one another, were provided with a framework to create a shared experience. Though deceased, it was the patriarchal figure of the past who brought them together to articulate common bonds in the present.

The ways in which ritual can serve as a vehicle for the past to shape present realities were perhaps most poignantly expressed at the memorial service held in Rahamim's home in Boston. Attendees at this event had not actually known one another before their migration, and had only met in the midst of the disorienting process of resettlement. Yet, they all knew what to expect at the memorial service. This ritual, then, with its stable, predictable elements, was the past that they had in common. Transmitted from generation to generation, the *yushva* provided them with a framework through which they could join together as a community, despite the absence of pre-existing social ties or institutional life.

Those who gathered at the memorial services for Nerio, Bezalel, and Miriam all call themselves Bukharan Jews, yet their experiences over the last century have varied greatly. Attendees at the service for Bezalel collectively remembered their grandparents' and parents' participation in the building of the newly formed State of Israel. Those at Nerio's *yushva* recalled what life had been like prior to the dissolution of the Soviet Union, before their friends and family left Samarkand. Guests at Miriam's memorial in Boston remembered the days when they themselves lived in Central Asia.

Regardless of these differences, the *yushva* plays a ubiquitous and important role among Bukharan Jews everywhere, with the basic framework remaining more or less the same: the room arrangement, the order of the meal, the prayers, and the speech-making. By providing the sense of a stable, shared past in each setting, this ritual creates the possibility of narrating a common history. While other rites of passage may fulfil similar functions, the *yushva*, which serves as a specific occasion for reflection through spontaneous public oration, engenders discussion and contemplation about lost eras in communal life. Such reflection is not simply a mournful backward gaze: it also provides a forum for coping with the imminence of change, both by reorganizing and affirming new social forms, and by imparting ideas about how to carry on in the face of hardship, mourning, and rupture. By offering the comfort of a common past, the *yushva* allows for renewed visions of a shared present.

Acknowledgements

I wish to thank Morton H. Meyerson, the Sino-Judaic Foundation, the Lady Davis Fellowship Trust, and Boston University for their financial support of the research conducted for this article.

Notes

1   Participants in this research trip, which was organized by the Jewish University of St Petersburg, Russia, included a handful of other graduate students and scholars.

2   A diaspora group whose ancestors arrived in Central Asia over 1,000 years ago. A discussion of their history and contemporary situation follows.

3   The Muslims and Christians of the region conduct similar rituals of mourning, which involve food, prayer, and remembering. However, they are held at different intervals, and each is structured around its own religious liturgy.

4   The use of multiple terms to refer to the same ritual is an indication of the many languages spoken by Bukharan Jews. It also reflects the various geographical settings in which this ritual has been carried out. *Yushva* is in Judaeo-Tajik (a dialect of Persian), which is the Bukharan Jews' native language. *Pominki* is the Russian term (meaning funeral repast), adopted during the colonial era. *Azkarah* is the Hebrew name (meaning remembrance or commemoration) widespread amongst immigrants in Israel. Occasionally, the Yiddish term *yahrzeit* is used, having been adopted from Ashkenazi Jews.

5   In his book *Bukharan Jews* (Heb., 1993), and in his chapter on Bukharan Jews, which appeared in Varstil 1996.

6   If someone dies on a Tuesday, for example, a memorial service will be held every Tuesday during the first month, and if they pass away on the tenth of the month, a service will take place on the tenth of each month during the first year.

7   A prayer for the peaceful rest of the deceased, popularly recited among Sephardi communities.

8   A verb tense that connotes an ahistorical state of being; one which is out of time. It is also referred to as the 'ethnographic present'. For further reading on this topic, see Johannes Fabian's *Time and the Other,* in particular the section 'Time and Tense: The Ethnographic Present' (pp. 80–7).

9   For example, 'When the comforters come to the home of the deceased, they fall on the shoulder of the mourners and cry', and 'They do not go to the home of a mourner empty-handed' (Fuzailov 1996: 231). In some sections, Fuzailov does indicate that certain details of the ritual were carried out differently in the past than in the present. The past, however, is framed as a distant, undefined time. Likewise, the geographical and temporal co-ordinates of 'the present' are undefined. For example, 'Before, the family in mourning would pay the sage [who presided over the service] . . . Today, they no longer do' (1996: 231).

10   Although some Ashkenazi Jews did arrive as far back as the 1870s, with the Russian conquest of the region.

11   Transoxiana was bounded in the south by the Persian province of Khorasan and by the Amu Darya (in ancient times called the Oxus River), and in the north by the Syr Darya (in ancient times called the Jaxartes River).

12   For a list of these see Ben-Zvi 1957: 86–7 and Becker 2004: 164.

13   According to Kaganovitch (2008: 111), some 1,500 Bukharan Jews lived in Ottoman Palestine in 1914. During the First World War, the Ottoman army requisitioned the buildings of the Bukharan neighbourhood for its own use, and many who lived there and had taken an active role in building it moved out (Wahrman 1991). As in the case of those Bukharan Jews who settled in Europe during this period, little information is available about what became of these individuals once they left their initial point of settlement and moved out of their ethnic enclave.

14   Numbering several thousand (Koplik 2008).

15   The number of émigrés from Soviet Central Asia in the 1970s was no more than 6,000 (Tolts 2008).

16   For an extended discussion of this mass migration, see Cooper, forthcoming.

17   Statistics for Jewish intermarriage in Samarkand are unavailable. However, in 1962 Mordechai Altshuler estimated that the rate of intermarriage among the Bukharan Jews of Tashkent, Central Asia's most populous and cosmopolitan city, was only 8 per cent (1970: 31). Presumably the rate in Samarkand was even lower.

18   For example, from among eighty-seven couples (born between 1940 and 1979) whom I surveyed in Samarkand in 1997, 74 per cent were endogamous within the domain of their city (Cooper 2000: 247–8, 409–10).

19   They numbered some 7,000 during the Soviet era (Zubin 1987).

20   Nerio's son Ilya and Ilya's wife; Nerio's granddaughter Nina (who hosted the event), her husband Boris, their three children, and their son-in-law. In addition, one great-nephew was in attendance.

21   For clarity in describing relationships I use expansive rather than collapsed terminology. So e.g. 'grandmother' is rendered as either 'mother's mother' or 'father's mother'.

References

ALTSHULER, MORDECHAI. 1970. 'Some Statistics on Mixed Marriages Among Soviet Jews', *Bulletin on Soviet and East European Jewish Affairs*, 6: 30–2.

ASHEROV, SHLOMO HAYIM. 1977. *From Samarkand to Petah Tikva: Memoirs of a Bukharan Immigrant* [Misamarkand ad petaḥ tikvah: zikhronot mapil bukhari]. Tel Aviv.

BECKER, SEYMOUR. 2004. *Russia's Protectorates in Central Asia: Bukhara and Khiva, 1865–1924*. New York.

BEN-ZVI, ITZHAK. 1957. *The Exiled and the Redeemed*. Philadelphia.

COOPER, ALANNA E. 2000. 'Negotiating Identity in the Context of Diaspora, Dispersion and Reunion: The Bukharan Jews and Jewish Peoplehood'. Ph.D. Diss., Boston University.

——Forthcoming. 'Where Have All the Jews Gone? Mass Migration and Uzbekistan's Independence'. In Michael Laskier and Yaakov Lev, eds., *The Divergence of Judaism and Islam: Interdependence, Modernity and Political Turmoil*. Gainesville, Fla.

COOPERMAN, BERNARD D. 2006. 'Ethnicity and Institution Building among Jews in Early Modern Rome', *AJS Review*, 30/1: 119–45.

FABIAN, JOHANNES. 2002. *Time and the Other*. New York.

FISCHEL, WALTER J. 1945. 'The Jews of Central Asia (Khorasan) in Medieval Hebrew and Islamic Literature', *Historia Judaica*, 7: 29–50.

——1964. 'The Leaders of the Jews of Bokhara'. In Leo Jung, ed., *Jewish Leaders: 1750–1940*, 535–47. Jerusalem.

FUZAILOV, GIORA. 1993. *Bukharan Jews: Their Leaders and their Customs* [Yahadut bukharah: gedoleiha uminhageiha]. Jerusalem.

——1996. 'From the Customs of the Bukharan Jews' (Heb.). In Asher Varstil, ed., *Anthology of Customs: From the Customs of the Tribes of Israel* [Yalkut minhagim: miminhageihem shel shivtei yisra'el], 189–242. Jerusalem.

KAGANOVITCH, ALBERT. 2008. 'The Bukharan Jewish Diaspora at the Beginning of the 21st Century'. In Ingeborg Baldauf, Moshe Gammer, and Thomas Loy, eds., *Bukharan Jews in the 20th Century: History, Experience and Narration*, 111–16. Wiesbaden.

KOPLIK, SARA. 2003. 'The Demise of Afghanistan's Jewish Community and the Soviet Refugee Crisis (1932–1936)', *Iranian Studies*, 36(3): 353–79.

——2008. 'The Experience of Bukharan Jews outside the Soviet Union in the 1930s and 1940s'. In Ingeborg Baldauf, Moshe Gammer, and Thomas Loy, eds., *Bukharan Jews in the 20th Century: History, Experience and Narration*, 91–110. Wiesbaden.

TAGGER, NISSIM. 1970. *The History of the Jews of Bukhara: In Bukhara and in Israel* [Toledot yehudei bukharah: bebukharah uveyisra'el]. Tel Aviv.

TILAYOV, SHULAMIT. 1981. *The Poetry of Shulamit* [Shirat shulamit]. Tel Aviv.

TOLTS, MARK. 2008. 'The Demographic Profile of the Bukharan Jews in the Late Soviet Period'. In Ingeborg Baldauf, Moshe Gammer, and Thomas Loy, eds., *Bukharan Jews in the 20th Century: History, Experience and Narration*, 77–90. Wiesbaden.

VARSTIL, ASHER. 1996. *Anthology of Customs: From the Customs of the Tribes of Israel* [Yalkut minhagim: miminhageihem shel shivtei yisra'el]. Jerusalem.

WAHRMAN, DROR. 1991. *The Bukharans and their Neighbourhood* [Habukharim ushe-khunatam biyerushalayim]. Jerusalem.

ZAND, MICHAEL. 1975. 'Bukhara'. In *Encyclopedia Judaica Yearbook*, 183–92. Jerusalem.

——1990. 'Bukharan Jews'. in Encyclopedia Iranica, iii. 30–545. Costa Mesa, Calif.

ZUBIN, M. 1987. 'The Jews of Samarkand in the Year 1979: A Statistical Survey' (Heb.). *Pe'amim: Studies in the Cultural Heritage of Oriental Jewry*, 35: 170–7.

ELEVEN

Shiva as Creative Ritual in an Institutional Home

JILLIAN GOULD

AT THE TERRACES OF BAYCREST, a Jewish retirement home in Toronto where residents are part of a new collective group, Jewish domestic customs that were once practised privately within single-family homes—for example, lighting sabbath and Hanukah candles—have been reinvented. While customary rituals provide comfort, meaning, and continuity throughout life, for many of the Terraces' elderly residents, entry into this new senior community and stage of life calls for variations on certain ritual themes. This essay highlights how an institution may foster creative rituals; in particular, I examine the Shiva Gathering, the Terraces' original response to the customary shiva (seven-day Jewish mourning period).

When a resident of the retirement home dies, the shiva typically takes place at the home of surviving family. While the other residents make a 'shiva call' to express their sympathy to the family members, for them the loss is double-layered: not only have they lost a member of their community, but also, as residents of the same 'home', a member of their collective family. While the traditional shiva may provide continuity and comfort, it does not fully meet the needs of this particular group, as I discuss below; on the other hand, the additional Shiva Gathering offers a flexible version of the mourning ritual that meets their specific needs. Consequently, Terraces residents observe two shivas: comforting family members at an off-site shiva house, and mourning one of their own at their own Shiva Gathering—a creative ritual facilitated by Terraces staff in the public space of the institutional home.

This essay derives from my research of the process by which elderly Jews create 'home' in an institution. While Jewish ethnography is a burgeoning field, ethnographic research about ageing Jews and institutional domestic culture is relatively untapped. There is no dispute that Barbara Myerhoff's *Number Our Days* (1978) paved the way for studies on the relation of Jews to ageing—it certainly inspired my own research—but other studies between then and now have been few and far between.[1] One general issue that pervades this literature is the ambivalent attitude of older Jewish adults living in communal and institutional settings towards the rule-bound observance of sickness and death rituals. In such institutions, where multigenerational families are not the norm, the elderly form a peer cohort in which discourses of life, health, identity, and mortality predominate. Ethnographers frequently seek to find a pattern or explanation for the way elderly Jews dealing with their own mortality negotiate between their expedient needs and the continuity of their values and culture as reflected in the following of strict halakhic guidelines for burial and mourning. This situation is of particular interest as life expectancy grows and an ever larger proportion of old people enter institutions where new social structures and cultural relationships arise in addition to the novel material surroundings of a group home. A question that frequently comes up is whether Jewish burial and mourning rituals, which purportedly give comfort to the living and ease of passage to the deceased, serve to increase or ease anxiety about impending death among older adults living in the close confines of institutions. I follow up this question by looking at the role of the ritual changes implemented by the residents of such institutions as a communal response to issues of mortality on the one hand and of maintaining their cultural identity on the other.

The Terraces of Baycrest is a Jewish institution, and yet for its diverse resident population, cultural identity continues to change as it reflects the nuances of Jewishness, the various understandings and experiences of home, and the cultural—and physical—realities of ageing. While to outsiders the Terraces may represent little more than a home where old Jewish people live, in reality to be old and Jewish is as complex and multi-faceted as the place itself, which incorporates many beliefs and values not unlike those in writer Vivian Gornick's recollections of the East Bronx of the 1920s and 1930s: 'The dominating characteristic of the streets on which I grew was Jewishness in all its rich variety. Down the street were Orthodox Jews, up the street were Zionists, in the middle of the street were shtetl Jews, get-rich-quick Jews, European humanist Jews' (quoted in Moore 1981: 63).

The Terraces is a single building that is first and foremost a retirement residence; nevertheless, it is a complex of spaces: at once a home and an institution, and a mixture of the sacred and the secular. Located near midtown, it is part of the Baycrest Centre for Geriatric Care. In addition to the eleven-storey residence, there is a senior adult day centre, a nursing home, and a hospital. That the retirement home is called the Terraces of Baycrest can be somewhat confusing, as people may imagine several buildings when there is only one. Baycrest's physical structures hold complex historical and contemporary meanings, many of which are connected to a large segment of the Jewish community in Toronto. Although the Terraces is a fairly new building (dating from 1976), its location tells the story of the northward and westward migration of so many Toronto Jews from their original downtown neighbourhoods; furthermore, the residents are the living social memory of Jewish life in the twentieth century.

Jews in Toronto

The first synagogue in Toronto was established in 1856, but it was not until half a century later that east European Jews—fleeing political turmoil and religious persecution—began to have a presence in the city. At this time, the main Jewish neighbourhood was called St John's Ward, also known simply as the Ward, or even St John's Shtetl (Tulchinsky 1993: 172). It was a very narrow area bordered by Yonge Street (east), University Avenue (west), Queen Street (south), and College Street (north). As Canadian Jewish historian Gerald Tulchinsky describes, it was 'a slum by early-twentieth-century standards, it attracted notoriety for its crowded conditions, filth, squalor, poverty, and lack of adequate sanitation' (1993: 172). By the next decade, Jews started moving westward, to the Spadina area. By this point, their immigration to the United States had slowed down due to restrictive quotas, but Toronto's Jewish population continued to grow as they fled persistent religious persecution in eastern Europe.

From the 1920s to the 1950s the area around Spadina Avenue and Kensington Market was the heart of the city's Jewish life and culture. Yiddish theatres, grand synagogues, and *shtiebls* (small storefront synagogues), *ḥeders* (Jewish elementary schools), fruit and vegetable stands, bookstores, and *landsmanshaftn* (mutual benefit societies), along with countless garment factories, created the Spadina streetscape. The predominant language was Yiddish. 'The immigrant neighborhood in downtown Toronto, even as late as the 1950s, was reminiscent of New York's Lower East Side decades earlier', recalls folklorist Barbara Kirshenblatt-Gimblett, who grew up there, 'amid a host of Jewish institutions' (Kirshenblatt-Gimblett 2007: 360)—including the forerunner to Baycrest: the Toronto Jewish Old Folks' Home (1918).

As the immigrant community became more comfortable and financially secure, families began to move away from the downtown core of Spadina and Kensington Market—continuing the northward and westward pattern—to neighbourhoods such as Downsview, Lawrence Manor, and Bathurst Manor. Jewish institutions were relocated as well, including the Toronto Jewish Old Folks' Home, which was renamed Baycrest Centre for Geriatric Care to reflect its new location on Baycrest Avenue in the Bathurst Manor area. Other Jewish institutions followed the move to Bathurst Manor, including the Jewish Immigrant Aid Services (JIAS), the Jewish Family and Child Services, the Ontario Jewish Archives, the Latner Jewish Library, and the Holocaust Centre of Toronto (all housed in the Lipa Green Building for Jewish Community Services). An uptown Jewish community centre also opened in the neighbourhood.

Today the community that surrounds Baycrest is home to many hasidic and Modern Orthodox Jews. On Saturday mornings, men in traditional hasidic garb—black hats, beards, and long coats—walk to *shul* (synagogue) with their families. Girls in long skirts and boys wearing dark trousers, yarmulkes (skull caps), and *peyos* (side curls) are seen on warm days riding their bicycles along the sidewalks. Jewish seniors—not necessarily religious—are also predominant in the district. In fact, as indicated on the United Jewish Appeal (UJA) Federation-sponsored website, Doing Jewish in Toronto, the neighbourhood where Baycrest is located, Bathurst Manor, was reported by the 2001 Statistics Canada census report as having the 'fifth-highest population density of Jews in the country . . . [and] the largest proportion of Jewish seniors in the city'. In addition to those at Baycrest, some live independently, while others are residents of various assisted-living facilities, nursing homes, and senior-friendly apartment buildings. As a large proportion of the senior population ages at home, it is becoming more and more common for them to require the assistance of personal caregivers, who often live locally. Since many of these carers are from the Philippines and the Caribbean, shops and restaurants that carry specialty items and products from these countries stand next to kosher shops and eateries, reflecting the subtle diversity of the area.

Many buildings and neighbourhoods of Toronto are associated with the Jewish experience in the eyes of Jews and non-Jews alike. Whereas the downtown area near Spadina and Kensington Market was once the hub of Jewish life, as mentioned above, today their residential quarters and institutions have relocated uptown. This is by no means a singular story. As Jonathan Boyarin points out about New York's Lower East Side, 'the living conditions, as in any immigrant ghetto, were terrible, and thus the usual sociological and popular valuation of the neighborhood's depopulation by Jews as upward mobility seems so transparently obvious as not to require explanation' (Boyarin 1992: 3). While nearly all the Jewish organizations are gone, many of the remaining original downtown buildings are public, material reminders of the everyday life and ritual observance of the Jewish community of the past. Some buildings, such as synagogues, tell a story on their own (through structure and cornerstones); others—a *ḥeder*, a kosher bakery—have been torn down and rebuilt, their former function living on only through narrative and public memory. Always serving new communities, buildings in urban neighbourhoods reveal the layers of successive waves of migration—if not physically, then through memory culture. Folklorist Elaine Eff gave walking tours of North Avenue in Baltimore, where Jewish, Irish, and African Americans lived. She says the missing cultural sites help residents recall what happened there (cited in Zeitlin 1994: 217); it becomes their social responsibility to document and share what they know. Like the buildings in the focus of walking tours, the Terraces also holds its own stories and prompts its own kind of events.

Fostering Creative Ritual in an Institutional Home

The Terraces of Baycrest houses a multi-denominational and multi-lingual community of approximately two hundred residents who range in age from their seventies to their nineties and beyond. In the main lobby you may hear kibitzing in various languages including English, Yiddish, and Hungarian, to name a few. While only a handful of residents are Orthodox, in order to meet the needs of the most observant Jews, the institution is run according to Orthodox standards.

In *The Power of Place*, Dolores Hayden refers to Rina Benmayor and John Kuo Wei's definition of 'cultural citizenship', which is defined as 'an identity that is formed not out of legal membership but out of a sense of cultural belonging' (Hayden 1995: 8). Being old and Jewish offers a sense of cultural belonging at the Terraces, but for the non-observant residents, the strict rules of kashrut or the institutional festival observances may impede personal choices. However, because residents choose to live in a Jewish institution, they mostly understand that, regardless of their own practices and beliefs, there is a price to pay—be it through food options or degrees of festival observance. Furthermore, even though the majority of residents are not observant, they accept traditional Jewish values as positive, while also seeking out flexible alternatives to formal religious events.

For many residents, the move to the Terraces not only redefined their understanding of expressions of Jewish identity, but also recast social relationships as new friendships quickly developed. The residents' negotiation between their relationships in the 'inside' and 'outside' worlds is underscored by life-cycle events and religious festivals: on the one hand, a wedding, a grandchild's bar mitzvah, or the birth of a great-grandchild are all celebrated with family outside Baycrest. On the other hand, Jewish festivals such as the sabbath, Passover, and Hanukah are observed inside, with other Terraces residents. These latter festivals may be celebrated twice: both at the Terraces home as well as at the homes of friends and relatives. This double observance practice is not unique to Terraces culture. Many people who work together celebrate calendar holidays or birthdays with colleagues, and also with family. In fact, it is increasingly common for people to have several support and/or social networks outside the home, and for these groups to celebrate festivals and life-cycle events together. Residents of the Terraces are unique, however, for at least two reasons. Firstly, their relationships with their peers are particularly multi-layered and complex: unlike other peer groups who get together on certain occasions, but who may return home for more intimate gatherings, Terraces residents share a roof, as well as meals and festivals with their peers. Secondly, in contrast to the more general experience of celebrating rites of passage at home, they leave their Terraces home to observe life cycle events such as birth and marriage with family members at an 'outside' home.

When a fellow resident dies, the traditional custom of 'sitting shiva' is complicated to observe. As I established earlier, the shiva generally takes place at the home of the adult children, but for Terraces residents this practice leaves a void. The Shiva Gathering, of which I present a case study below, uses aspects of the shiva to highlight the close connection, as well as the home space, that Terraces residents share with each other. Furthermore, it emphasizes the flexible nature of ritual, as well as the significance of ritual negotiation in an institutional home.

According to Terraces chaplain Ernie Gershon, it began when he and his wife Laurie realized that 'There was a gap that needed to be filled for the residents in terms of mourning.'[2] When they first became chaplains at the Terraces, the

Gershons met with residents and asked what they needed. Ernie recalls: 'The residents had three things: they wanted us to be around, so they could get to know us; they wanted educational programmes to learn; and finally, they wanted some way to mourn. Even then, about fifteen years ago [1993], they were much more mobile but still, they couldn't always get to the funerals and shivas.' As an early response to these needs, the Gershons designed and led a Memorial and Healing Service, which was held every three or four months to remember those who had passed away. While the service provided certain comfort, it was problematic for the residents. They felt there was too long a delay between the death and the time to mourn. They did not want to mourn a month—or several months—later; they wanted to follow Jewish custom, which has a prescribed schedule beginning shortly after death.

Death and Shiva in the Jewish Tradition

Like other life-cycle events, Jewish death and mourning has its particular customs. In the Ashkenazi tradition, the funeral generally takes place within twenty-four hours of death. Immediately following the funeral, mourners attend the shiva, which is customarily held at the home of the family of the deceased for the duration of seven days. This time frame may vary, as it has become common for Reform Jews to observe shiva for only three days. While the funeral customs focus on the deceased, shiva provides comfort to the living. As sociologist Samuel Heilman explains, 'many of the subsequent mourning rituals are an effort to compensate for the swift funeral and burial and to help rearrange the relationship between the dead and the living' (2001: 120). He lists the various stages of mourning that follow the funeral and the seven-day shiva: 'The first is shivah (seven days); the second, *shloshim* (thirty days); the third, *yudbeit chodesh* (twelve months); and the last, *yahrzeit* (yearly anniversary)' (2001: 120). These temporal markers assist the bereavement process, allowing mourners to reflect on death and life over time. As folklorists Steve Zeitlin and Ilana Harlow remark, 'These traditions tell us how to act and what to say at times when we otherwise might not know what to do or say' (2001: 7).

When Jews partake in these rituals, they step outside everyday life to acknowledge that something different or special is taking place. As defined by Van Gennep (1909), rites of passage can be divided into three stages: separation, transition, and incorporation. Funerary rites separate the dead from the living, and the Jewish custom of family members and friends shovelling earth into the grave helps incorporate the deceased into the world of the dead (Zeitlin and Harlow 2001: 108). The shiva and the various stages of mourning throughout the year separate the mourners from the rest of society. This not only provides comfort and meaning to the participants, but also engenders, as Myerhoff notes, an

'intense camaraderie'—which anthropologist Victor Turner calls 'communitas'—
between them (Myerhoff 1978: 225).

By performing and participating in these rituals throughout their lives, people
bring the past into the present. Both Myerhoff (1978) and Kirshenblatt-Gimblett
(1989) describe how reading the Kaddish (the mourner's prayer) may accomplish
this. Other rituals, such as lighting the sabbath candles or attending shiva achieve
the same outcome. As Myerhoff explains,

> Rituals . . . have the capacity to carry one back to earliest times and selves with nostalgia
> and great yearning . . . For the old people the Kaddish was associated with the Eastern
> European past, for the younger people it was part of their ethnic identification associ-
> ated with family and home. For all it was a moment of the kind of mythic timelessness
> that allows for an experience of the indestructible parts of self and tradition, parts
> beyond change and history, eternally valid. (Myerhoff 1978: 226)

For the residents of the Terraces, it was important to create a parallel mourning process in line with their own understanding of Jewish tradition. Moreover,
explains Laurie Gershon, 'the more religious residents felt [that the timing of the
original Memorial and Healing Service] was duplicating *yiskor*—some found it
disconcerting'. *Yizkor*, the memorial service for the dead, is recited in the synagogue four times a year, on the festivals of Passover, Shavuot, Sukkot, and Yom
Kippur. Nearly every resident—religious and secular, male and female—attends
these services. Taking into account their concerns, the chaplains gradually
phased out the Memorial Service, and the Shiva Gathering began to take shape.
They named it thus because residents knew what a shiva was, 'so they would have
somewhat of an idea of what to expect', explains Ernie. 'More importantly', adds
Laurie, 'for those who can't visit the shiva, they still needed to mourn.'

While it was important for the Shiva Gathering to take place shortly after an
individual's death, its scheduling was not as precise as that of the traditional
shiva. Rather, Shiva Gatherings could be held at any time: some within the actual
shiva period, some shortly thereafter. Scheduling a gathering during the seven
days of shiva was tricky, however, if it was to include the family of the deceased. 'It
all depends on the family and the situation', Ernie says. Since the mourning relatives are not supposed to leave their home for the duration of the shiva, 'participation of the family [during the shiva period] requires a less traditional family', he
explains. This may include Reform families, who observe a three-day shiva. In
any case, the Shiva Gathering is not meant to replicate the traditional ritual, and
although it shares some of the social and functional aspects of the latter, it does
not include the structural elements or specific customs associated with it.

As historian Jenna Weissman Joselit explains, 'A highly elaborated Jewish
code of behavior governed the shivah period, from personal expressions of
mourning and the conventions of the condolence call to the appearance of the
"shivah house"' (1994: 278). For the uninitiated, some explanation would be in

order before making a visit. At Baycrest, all staff receive the *Jewish Life at Baycrest* guide, which explains some of the more esoteric Jewish customs including those concerning death and dying. The section entitled 'Visiting a Shivah House' describes what a visitor may encounter when making a shiva call: 'mirrors may be covered (as one should not be concerned with personal looks at this time); a candle will be burning; and mourners may be sitting on low stools, shoeless—all indications of the bereaved state' (Baycrest Education Dept. 1994: 51). It is also traditional for mourners to rend their clothing upon hearing of the death and to wear the torn garment throughout the shiva period.

The writer Elizabeth Ehrlich recalls the funeral of her uncle, and her grief-stricken *bubbe* (grandmother) burying her son: 'Suddenly the small hands of our *bubbe* rose. Her crooked fingers grasped the collar of her blouse, on the right side, as was proper, having lost her child. Weeping, moaning, with the shocked strength of grief, she tore her garment, ripped the woven cloth. As mourners rent their clothes in Bible times' (1997: 318). Contemporary mourners may choose to wear a black ribbon instead, or a piece of torn black material (Marcus 2004: 206).

None of these customs is observed at the Shiva Gathering. Instead, it highlights the social and spiritual functions, such as sharing narratives about the deceased, the coming together of the community to offer hope and strength for the bereaved, and spiritual strength through prayer. Hufford, Hunt, and Zeitlin relay the experience of folklorist Kenneth Goldstein, who shared with the authors the stories that had been told during his father's shiva:

The tales . . . went through several stages. First, a period of speechless grief gave way to stories of his father as a saint; later they changed to stories of his father as an ordinary man; by the end, stories were told of his father as a trickster, a shrewd and funny man, good and bad by turns. These last entered the family repertoire as stories that maintain his father's spirit as a vital force in the life of the family. (Hufford et al. 1987: 24)

The narrative stages reflect the healing process, as layers of pain are peeled away to reveal some kind of comfortable truth. In *Giving a Voice to Sorrow*, the authors explain that telling stories is a way to bring 'the departed to life in words' (Zeitlin and Harlow 2001: 11). Furthermore, they suggest: 'The narrative impulse to tell the life stories of the dead, and thus to conjure up their essence, is a creative act that counters the destructiveness of death' (2001: 11).

In addition to sharing narratives about the deceased, the Shiva Gathering also meets a spiritual need through prayer. 'Congregation is the Jewish antidote to death's abandonment', suggests Heilman. 'The orderly schedule of prayer balances the disorderly schedule of dying' (2001: 130). At a traditional Ashkenazi shiva house (generally Conservative or Orthodox), prayer services are held twice daily. It is considered a *mitsvah* (a commandment or good deed) for Jewish community members to make a shiva call in order to ensure that there will be a *minyan* (quorum of ten people required for prayer) so that the mourner's Kaddish may be recited. Samuel Heilman recalls his father's shiva: 'Nothing was quite so jarring as the ubiquitous morning and evening *minyan*. Every afternoon at sunset and every morning at around six-thirty, people would walk into my house for services. The first morning I barely had time to jump out of bed before they came, so I learned to leave the front door unlocked' (2001: 132).

Certainly prayer and the opportunity to say Kaddish are important aspects of the shiva house, bringing formal religious structure into the home. Furthermore, the shiva not only turns the home into sacred space, but also the private into public: it is transformed by a new set of rules into a gathering place where community members may walk in as they would enter a synagogue (Heilman 2001: 130).

The shiva call is unlike any other house visit of sympathy; it has its own set of rules based on Jewish law and custom. Here, the order of a typical house visit, as well as of everyday home life, is disrupted by religious mourning customs, and thus, a form of symbolic inversion occurs. As folklorist Susan Stewart points out, many studies have focused on how 'symbolic inversions present the world upside down, the categories and hierarchical arrangement of culture in a recognizable disorder' (1993: 106). In this way, although the shiva has its own set of specific rules determined by religion, remarks Heilman, 'even when mourners observe shivah inside what is to all appearances a familiar place, that place suddenly ceases to be familiar' (2001: 129). Nevertheless, participants find comfort in the familiarity of the ritual.

Shiva Gathering in an Institutional Home

While certain aspects of the shiva are woven into the Shiva Gathering, purportedly providing residents with comfort through community and prayer, which prayers are recited and when varies from gathering to gathering. Ernie Gershon calls this tap dancing: 'Depending on how the flow is going we might wait until the end and do the prayers from the [*Afternoon Service for Memorial and Healing*] book. Sometimes the prayers would be at the middle. It all depends on the flow, you really have to tap dance to figure it out.' So while the ordered structure at a traditional shiva may comfort the bereaved family, the Shiva Gathering provides an opportunity for residents to take part in a creative ritual that meets their specific needs. On a very practical level, explains Ernie, the Shiva Gathering occurs within a set time frame: usually one hour. 'This is very important', he emphasizes, 'so residents don't get restless or wonder when it will end.' The fixed time frame of the Shiva Gathering presents a very different scenario from the traditional shiva, which is punctuated with visits throughout the day, in some cases to an extreme, 'transforming this doleful occasion into an exercise in conviviality', Weissman Joselit remarks (1994: 278). Since the more formal aspects of the shiva do not reflect the needs or the situation of Terraces residents, they wish to participate in a version that is physically convenient for them to attend and that highlights life and narrative, as well as their unique relationship to the deceased. Furthermore, at the actual shiva they might feel out of place, not quite certain how to fit in with the pre-Baycrest friends and family of the deceased. In this way, the Shiva Gathering is an alternative ritual that allows Terraces residents to mourn one of their own in their own space.

At the heart of the Shiva Gathering is the coming together of residents to remember a fellow resident in an intimate, personal setting. Nevertheless, although Shiva Gatherings fill a void, the frequency with which they may occur presents new challenges. 'Because they all live together, [the Shiva Gathering] casts a pall', Laurie explains. 'They don't want to focus all the time on people dying; but of course, people are dying', she says emphatically. In this light, the one-hour Gathering (as opposed to a seven-day shiva) seems not only tactful, but also necessary. 'At the same time', Ernie adds, 'residents are saying, "I don't want to die and be forgotten".'

Ernie's last point highlights a final difference between the Shiva Gathering and the traditional shiva. While both observances serve to comfort the living, the Shiva Gathering provides an extra cushion, some kind of reassurance that residents will not be forgotten by their peers. Those who attend the Shiva Gathering may anticipate how they will be remembered in the very same space.

Case Study: The Shiva Gathering for Esther Goldstein and Harvey Langer

The following notice caught my eye as I was waiting for the elevator to visit a resident. A regular 8½ by 11 sheet, typed in large bold lettering, was conspicuously displayed on the wall:

Coming together to Remember Esther Goldstein and Harvey Langer

Please join the Terraces' Chaplains and staff for an informal gathering to share thoughts and memories

Wednesday, June 1, 2005 Terraces/Wagman Lobby 4:00–5:00 pm

Esther Goldstein and Harvey Langer died within approximately one week of each other, so theirs was a joint Shiva Gathering. I knew them both; I always enjoyed casual conversations with Esther in the lobby, and I even visited her apartment once. She was bright and spunky, but she had few friends. She walked to the beat of her own drum, and was one of only two residents who owned a cat. My relationship with her did not go beyond our casual meetings. Harvey, on the other hand, I knew on a more personal level, as I had conducted several audio-recorded interviews with him. He was cheerful and optimistic, and well known around the Terraces since he had lived there for almost fifteen years. As a result, although he and Esther shared a Shiva Gathering, the residents had more to say and to recall about him. Harvey was born in Toronto on 11 March 1916. He was one of the six children of Yetta (Naiman) and Joel Langer, who had immigrated to Canada from Poland in the early 1900s. Joel worked in the garment business, first as an operator, then as a designer for Eaton's. 'He was so good at [his work]', recalled Harvey, 'that he wanted to go into business for himself.' It was not long before Joel opened a tailor shop of his own. Harvey had fond memories of his parents, his father's store on Avenue Road near Bloor Street, and his mother's baked goods. She had come from a long line of bakers and loved to make treats for her daughter and five sons. Harvey and two of his brothers went to university; they studied medicine, while Harvey studied pharmacy. He moved to the Terraces in 1991, shortly after his wife, Anna, died. He was encouraged to move by his youngest brother, Michael (Mike). 'A couple of weeks after my wife died he showed up with about ten brochures', remembered Harvey with a laugh. Mike told him he couldn't stay in the house alone, and suggested Baycrest as a top choice. Harvey was already familiar with Baycrest, having been a regular at the exercise programmes at the facility's senior community centre (the Wagman Centre) several times a week, so it was not a difficult decision. He was very happy with his life at the Terraces: 'I owe it all to Mike', he grinned. His bachelor apartment was full of old knick-knacks: from a 1970s-era toaster oven still in the box —'never been used!'—to a collection of well-read sports magazines and old newspapers, to a ukulele which had belonged to his wife. Harvey and Anna did not have children, so unlike other residents, whose adult children were frequently able to help them with their shopping, or who were generally around to look after them, Harvey was incredibly independent. He had been a widower for many years, cooked his own meals (his speciality was chickpea soup with crushed matzah crackers), and did his own laundry. He remained close with his surviving brothers, especially Bernie and his wife, Ryna, who made sure that he was taken care of as his health began to deteriorate. Sadly, Harvey spent his last months in palliative care at the Baycrest Hospital. Despite his ailing health, he was always up for a visit and a chat, stayed up to date on all the sports news, and always wore his trademark moustache, baseball cap, and a smile.

Just as when any resident dies, fellow residents learned of Harvey and Esther's deaths from a printed announcement, delivered by resident volunteers to individual mailboxes on each floor. While this system of notification is the most efficient way to relay the news, some residents, like Edith Kursbatt, find the notices unsettling. She believes it is a cold-hearted method to communicate the news that someone who was close to her—or who used to be in her circle—is gone. Furthermore, she views the notice as a reminder of her own imminent death. Informing residents of a death in a tactful manner is challenging, partly because it is important that they receive the information in a timely manner. Because Jewish funerals generally take place within twenty-four hours of the death, people need time to make arrangements if they are planning to attend.

On the afternoon of 1 June 2005 I joined twenty residents, along with Terraces director Sheila Smyth, social worker Heather Lisner-Kerbel, and chaplains Ernie and Laurie Gershon, in the Wagman Lobby for the Shiva Gathering of Harvey and Esther. Ryna, Harvey's sister-in-law, attended as well. We met in the back area of the lobby, near the Wagman entrance, and quickly settled into the couches and chairs that were set up in a circle so that we could all see each other. Sitting there—in the public 'living room' of the Terraces—it occurred to me that this was the most appropriate space for a Shiva Gathering: it was accessible and belonged to everyone (as opposed to the lobbies on the individual floors). It was spacious and comfortable. One drawback was that it happened to be very noisy that day. There had been a leak in one of the building's skylights, and workers were rolling carts with tools and equipment across the tiled floor. As people arrived and sat down, the surrounding noise was disruptive to the point of chaotic—I was worried that we would not be able to hear each other. The mood seemed somewhat awkward; there was a sense of uncertainty as to how the next hour might play out. Finally Laurie Gershon checked her watch and broke the ice: 'We are here today to remember Esther Goldstein and Harvey Langer.' Her tone was friendly, not too serious, warm and encouraging. She asked if everyone could hear her. Several people could not, so she turned on the microphone and the portable speaker. Although using a microphone impedes the intimacy a Shiva Gathering attempts to create, it is also a necessary—and expected—piece of equipment at mid- to large-sized gatherings at the Terraces. An outsider may find the amplified sound jarring, but it is par for the course. That day, especially, the microphone was needed because of the extra noise in the lobby. Blurring the lines between shiva and Shiva Gathering, and between neighbours and family, Laurie continued: 'While shiva is for family, both Harvey and Esther made the Terraces their family—it's your family whether you like it or not.' People sitting around nodded in agreement, and the notion that Terraces residents recreate themselves as family seemed more poignant just then. Both Harvey and Esther came from large families (five and seven siblings respectively), but neither had children—unusual for Terraces residents—so it was somewhat of a coincidence that they shared their Shiva Gathering.

With the microphone in her hand, Laurie explained that we heal through mourning, and that remembering our friends and loved ones helps this process. 'We all have memories of Harvey and Esther', she said. 'Let's go around the circle and share stories and memories.' While at a shiva storytelling is a natural event, rarely is it so staged. Nevertheless, the order of the gathering retained an air of improvisation; Ernie and Laurie 'tap danced' with the flow and according to the responses of the residents and staff. Mostly, the memories shared were about Harvey, as he was better known around the Terraces—partly because of his extroverted personality, partly because he had been there a long while, and partly because of his gender. As women outnumber the men by four to one at the home, it is difficult for male residents to go unnoticed. Laurie suggested they begin with memories of Esther. These were more general: 'She was friendly and sharp', said Edna Lester. 'She had a cat', Dorothy Moses offered. 'A good person', volunteered Ruth Hanff. 'She never said a bad word about anyone.' That comment received nods all around. Despite the fact that memories of Esther were vague and slightly superficial, she was remembered fondly and naturally. As we made our way around the circle, not everyone spoke, but even those who did not seemed engaged and responsive. Later I discussed with the Gershons what would happen if they went around the circle and no one had anything to say about a particular resident. 'If someone was not well known it can be pretty tough', said Laurie. 'Each gathering is different', added Ernie, 'and if there isn't a lot to say we end up relying more on the prayer book.' Of course it also helps if the gathering commemorates two people.

It did not take long before the microphone had made its way around the circle and was back in the hands of Ernie, who did not hesitate to offer his first memory of Harvey: 'When I think of Harvey, the first thing that comes to mind is his extensive collection of baseball caps.' People smiled at that, and it helped to have an image of the man they would be remembering. Although Ryna did not bring pictures of Harvey, Ernie said that sometimes family members bring pictures to Shiva Gatherings to help trigger memories. I imagine that is why his first memory was so visual. He passed the microphone to Riva London, one of Harvey's neighbours from the second floor, who began: 'Harvey was one of a kind.' She and Harvey had both grown up on Palmerston Avenue among many Jewish immigrant families in downtown Toronto. Although they did not know each other as children, they often shared stories and nostalgia for growing up both in that era and in that neighbourhood. Dorothy Moses took the microphone next to say that Harvey had had a knack for making people feel at ease with a joke or a smile. Eva Heffner agreed, recalling the time she had signed up to go on a fieldtrip to a Blue Jays baseball game. 'I didn't know from baseball', she said. 'But Harvey explained the game and made me feel comfortable', she added with a laugh. Another resident, Danny Gilbert, recalled Harvey's love for sports. 'He always knew the scores and who was playing. Baseball, hockey, tennis—didn't matter what—Harvey loved them all.' When it was Elsie Kay's turn, she remembered how, on the way down to lunch, Harvey always used to rush to the elevator when it opened on his floor. 'Hold it!' he would shout comically, making everyone laugh.

When it was my turn to speak, I told of my visits with Harvey, especially during his last months in palliative care. He was always happy for company, and even when he was not feeling well enough to talk, we sat together comfortably in silence. I also shared some of his stories about *shtefen*—the mysterious baked treat of his childhood. Some of his happiest memories were of this sweet, sticky beet strudel. I always wondered if it was a dish invented by Harvey's mother, but he insisted it was a fairly common Purim treat. I was not too surprised that no one had heard of it, but we all laughed at his enthusiasm for such an unusual recipe. The mood was sweet and upbeat. As the hour came to an end, the chaplains led the group in a traditional memorial prayer in Hebrew and English, 'El male raḥamim' (Lord of Many Mercies); it is described by Heilman as 'among the most common prayers at funerals, which asks to send the spirit of the dead on its way and appeals to God to accept it upon its arrival at its divine destiny' (2001: 95). There are variants, he explains, but what they all have in common 'is their insertion of the name of the deceased into the prayer, which thus personalized the request' (2001: 95).

Together we said, 'May they rest in peace. Amen.' The circle was quiet. Ernie said, 'Let us all have fond memories.' 'That's how they continue to live, we hold them in our hearts', added Dorothy Moses. Laurie announced that Dorothy's brother had died the previous weekend. Everyone around the circle expressed their sympathy. Dorothy, emotional, smiled and nodded. Ryna Langer had been silent throughout the gathering, but as it came to a close she looked around and gently said: 'You became his family, and I mean this in all sincerity. He did love you all.' The circle was quiet. 'Thank you for coming, for sharing', Ernie said. Elsie interrupted, 'You're not supposed to say that.' 'I stand corrected', Ernie replied, explaining that since attending a traditional shiva is a *mitsvah*, it is not customary to thank people for attending. In fact, according to tradition, the mourner does not acknowledge when visitors leave, but instead visitors bid farewell to the mourners with the traditional saying, 'May you be comforted among the mourners of Zion and Jerusalem', or the abbreviated version: 'May you be comforted' (Heilman 2001: 150–1).

Conclusion

The Shiva Gathering gives residents reassurance that they will not be forgotten. The fear of not being remembered is connected to 'a certain feeling of abandonment', which is familiar in retirement homes, explains Ernie Gershon. As Jenny Hockey points out, 'residential homes have traditionally accommodated large groups of people of the same age who are given care by professionals in exchange for pay rather than family members out of love or duty' (1999: 108). Upon entry, some residents may feel abandoned by their families and inevitably worry that they will be forgotten by family members—and everyone else. This became clear to me from Edith Kursbatt's reaction to the death of a close family friend. Joan was like a second daughter to Edith. She had been a dear friend to Edith's late daughter, Irene, who had died from lung cancer in 1996. After her death, Joan took on certain daughterly duties such as taking Edith on shopping trips and checking in with regular phone calls. It was a great shock when she died at a relatively young age, in her mid-60s, and in good health. Edith was devastated. 'No one's left who knew me *before*', she said softly. Joan was one of the few people who had a window onto her life before she moved to the Terraces. Since Edith came from England, and then Montreal, she did not have much of a social circle in Toronto. Her son lived in Northern Ontario, her grandchildren and their families in the United States. Joan was the last person in Edith's everyday world who held the link between her past and her present experiences. As such, her death represented a double loss.

In pondering the meaning of the past in our present lives, Yi-Fu Tuan writes: 'I am more than what the thin present defines' (2005: 186). This holds particular resonance for those who live at the Terraces. At a glance, there is little to distinguish residents from one another regarding their former lives. Although material items in the individual apartments—furniture, photographs, art works—offer clues about how people may have lived before they moved to the Terraces (see Csikszentmihalyi and Rochberg-Halton 1981; Halle 1996), for the most part, only close friends visit there. Their past (as well as private aspects of their present lives) can thus only be known either by people who knew them before, or from the narratives residents tell about themselves. In *Number Our Days*, Barbara Myerhoff writes of 'survivor's guilt'. The old people of her study 'were a distinctive breed, survivors all' (1978: 22). As she explains, her centre's members—like so many Terraces residents—'were survivors twice over, once due to their escape by emigration from the unnatural ravages of the Holocaust, and again later by living into extreme old age, surviving their peers, family, and often children' (1978: 23). While in Edith's case it was her parents who had made the decision to leave Russia for England, her survival into old age, outliving her family, friends, and even her daughter, has been a constant challenge. In the words of Myerhoff, 'That the more recent losses were the natural, inevitable results of the mere passage of time did not necessarily make them more bearable' (1978: 23). Joan's death was especially difficult for Edith to absorb because she was the last witness to her past life.

Outliving loved ones may be the harshest reality of living into old age. However, even as physical witnesses disappear, the narrative process of remembering and sharing the past with the present creates new witnesses, albeit through the transmission of memory only. As the authors of *The Grand Generation* explain, 'Self-integration is, of course, only one reason for recovering the past. Sharing it is another. These two functions work in tandem . . . Without witnesses the expressions are like one hand clapping' (Hufford et al. 1987: 64). These narrative memories create witnesses by proxy. Joan may have been the last one to know the details of Edith's past: the dinner parties she took such pride in hosting; her beautiful furniture; the company she kept. Joan knew first-hand that Edith's husband, Ivor, had been an engineer, that they began to raise their family first in Oxford (UK), and later in the prestigious Westmount neighbourhood of Montreal. As empty-nesters, Edith and Ivor moved to Toronto, where they lived in posh Forest Hill before moving to the Terraces. Because Edith did not have many friends at Baycrest, Joan's role as a witness was especially significant. Nevertheless, through life review, Edith creates a narrative to share with her peers. The term 'life review' was coined by psychiatrist Robert Butler in 1963 (Zeitlin and Harlow 2001: 61). As gerontologist Marc Kaminsky explains, '[life review] is the construction of the self they wish to be remembered by. And this bestows poise and intensity; it allows them to live more fully as they face the knowledge of their death' (1993: 88).

For Edith, because her family lives far away from her, these narratives are even more important since they serve as evidence of her individuality and of her life before moving to the Terraces. For other residents, past and present lives may be more intertwined, as regular visits from family members help to create a seamless narrative.

The need for witnesses and the ritual sharing of life narratives is especially meaningful for the collective Terraces community. Barbara Myerhoff maintains that such 're-membering' calls attention 'to the reaggregation of members, the figures who belong to one's life story, one's own prior selves, as well as significant others who are part of the story' (1992: 240). Life review ritually brings together various aspects of a person's life, and shapes it, 'extend[ing] back in the past and forward into the future . . . Without re-membering we lose our histories and our selves' (Myerhoff 1992: 240). Terraces social worker Shawn Fremeth facilitates a weekly session, 'A Bintel Brief'—named for the popular Yiddish advice column that had its heyday in the *Forward* newspaper in the early to mid-1900s. During the hour-long programme, residents discuss topics that range from personal love stories and work experiences to immigration and holiday memories. Usually he begins the session by reading a story or an excerpt from an essay on a particular theme. On 19 October 2003, I sat in on a session about grieving, healing, and mourning. What follows is based on my field notes from that day: 'I don't normally read material like this', Shawn warned. The story was about a woman who was battling cancer. 'It's sad, but hopeful', he added somewhat nervously. Nevertheless, he went ahead and read the story—it was sad because she died, and hopeful because facing death helped her to strengthen family and friendship bonds, and to ensure her legacy. The story led to a discussion about what it means to face death, as well as about how to cope with losing loved ones. One resident, Tillie Binder, wept softly. We sat in a circle in the Fireside Lounge so everyone could see each other.

'You never forget', said Tillie. 'That's why we go for *yizkor*—to remember', Lawrence Sandy remarked. I thought about the collective loss in the room. Fourteen residents were sitting in the circle. In addition to being a full-time social worker at the Terraces, Shawn also facilitated the Baycrest Bereavement Group, so this was a topic he was familiar with. 'We can get stuck in grief', he said, opening up the discussion to the residents. Mrs Rabovsky replied that it took longer than two years: 'That's how long it's been since my husband died, and it still hurts.' Nearly everyone agreed that it took years. And yet the group did not linger on any sad stories. They shared, they assessed, they moved on. Next they were discussing Jewish law and the mourning customs that eased the pain of loss. 'You have to go on living', offered Faye Fischler. Shawn pointed out that while there were prescribed customs for mourning, it was important to recognize that everyone heals at her own pace. One woman recalled finding comfort at her mother's shiva. 'It helps to grieve in a group', she said. Mina Lauterpacht, who was blind and took her knitting with her wherever she went, agreed: 'It helps to be with people.' Group members responded with nods. Ann Rosner mentioned that after her husband died, she became very ill. Shawn noted, 'I feel like the mood here is solemn.' To which Judy responded, 'We're all here now, let's live.' Yes, the group agreed. Fela said many of the Terraces residents had come as widows. 'We understand each other, we have all lost someone we love, but we continue to live and to make our lives meaningful', she explained. According to Barbara Myerhoff, 'The prospect of death for many of these elderly was often less fearsome than that of dying without having had an opportunity to unburden themselves of their memories' (1992: 241).

Like the elderly at Myerhoff's centre, who 'required witnesses to their past and present life' (Myerhoff 1978: 33), Terraces residents wish to remain 'visible' as they strengthen their bonds with one another, narrating and sharing aspects of their lives. In doing so, they not only imagine that their peers will understand their sorrow (and their joy), but also hope that they will be remembered when they are gone. The Shiva Gathering is a creative ritual that helps residents cope with death, mourning, and remembrance on both a personal and a collective level. In her working definition of ritual, Myerhoff suggests, 'Ritual is an act or actions intentionally conducted by a group of people employing one or more symbols in a repetitive, formal, precise, highly stylized fashion' (1992: 129). In the outside world, sitting shiva is a ritual in its own right; inside the Terraces, however, the Shiva Gathering reframes the elements of a traditional Jewish mourning custom to make it relevant to the lives of the residents, relying on individual and collective memory to bring meaning and energy into their present lives.

As anthropologist Harvey E. Goldberg explains, 'The concern for the perpetuation of memories reflects not only the individual facing his or her own demise, but the tremendous dislocations that have affected Jewish communities over the course of the past century and a half' (2003: 221). Terraces residents recreate a sense of family and community through their common Jewish history and culture, as well as through their shared experience of growing old; nevertheless, much remains that separates them, including religious beliefs, state of health, and background. By giving people an opportunity to speak about their individual experiences, Baycrest staff facilitate the affirmation of each person's self-worth and sense of unique identity.

Creative rituals like the Shiva Gathering help residents to face death and mourning and to remember in a supportive, familiar environment. This event contributes to the sense of family, culture, and community they share, and relies on a combination of spontaneity, creativity, and traditional Jewish culture. The Shiva Gathering came out of a need to acknowledge that residents have created a home and a family at the Terraces. The traditional shiva, which is observed in the private space of the home, does not allow them to mourn for one of their own. The Shiva Gathering, on the other hand, observed in the public space of the institutional home, fills that gap. In this way, it strengthens the bonds between residents, and also provides a unique opportunity for the family members of the deceased to take part in the community their loved ones had created. As such, the Shiva Gathering builds bridges between the larger community and the Terraces as well as between the Terraces and families, while also strengthening bonds within the Terraces community.

As a re-envisioned ritual based on the traditional shiva, the Shiva Gathering meets the needs of a particular group. The shiva inevitably takes place outside the institutional home, and it is not always practical (or possible) for residents to attend the ritual when a friend or neighbour dies. Moreover, while it provides comfort, continuity, and *communitas* for the general Jewish population, the unique living situation of elderly Jews in institutionalized homes calls for a re-imagining of the traditional shiva call. Even so, residents consider their gatherings a significant addition to the shiva, not a replacement for the customary practice. Some time after I had completed my fieldwork, they actually voted to change the name from Shiva Gathering to Memorial Gathering. As social worker Shawn Fremeth explained in an interview, the residents were no longer comfortable using the word 'shiva' since the gathering mostly took place after the seven-day mourning period, and it was decidedly *not* a shiva. Rather, as I have demonstrated, the Shiva Gathering borrows some of the functional elements of the latter, but the mourners do not follow its customary rituals, such as wearing a piece of black torn material, sitting on low stools, or covering mirrors. Instead, the Shiva Gathering is the distilled essence of the shiva: the gathering of friends and family, providing comfort for the mourners, and remembering the deceased. From a socio-psychological perspective, it can be compared, like the conventional shiva, to successful group psychotherapy—a thesis which has been explored by Irwin Kirdorf (1966).

The Shiva Gathering reinforces the notion that Terraces residents have re-created themselves as a family who share a home. By taking a close look at a creative ceremony in an institutionalized home, we can appreciate the significance—and flexibility—of ritual at various stages of the life cycle. Here, the performance of domestic rituals in public and private spaces shows how residents create and maintain home. Other acts, such as lighting candles on the sabbath or festivals, allow them to construct their present home space while connecting with their past. 'A Jewish home', resident Rebecca Hoch explained in an interview, 'means continuing Jewish customs. If you break away from these customs, it's no longer a Jewish home.' When I visited private apartments, although I expected to see Jewish ritual objects such as sabbath candles and kiddush cups, I was somewhat surprised that so many residents continued to use them. As Jenna Weissman Joselit suggests in her overview of Jewish domestic culture from 1880 to 1950, over time and through different physical settings 'the home played host to changing notions of Jewish domestic culture' (1990: 23). From a historical perspective, she attributes the shift in attitudes towards Jewish home-based rituals in part to patterns of immigration and assimilation. Her discussion of domestic matters also focuses on family solidarity and how home-based rituals may or may not be transmitted from generation to generation.

Because Terraces residents were now living on their own after having raised their families in their previous homes, initially I imagined that these Jewish ritual performances and objects were maintained or displayed for aesthetic and sentimental reasons. This was not the case. Not only were these old people eager to participate in certain ceremonies such as the Shiva Gathering or festival observances (for example, candle lighting) in the public spaces of the Terraces, but also, Rebecca and many of her peers continued to light sabbath candles alone in the privacy of their apartments. This was not for the next generation, but rather, for the sake of continuity in their own lives.

The Shiva Gathering highlights the flexible nature of ritual, but at the same time, as the residents insist, it is *not* a shiva. Their reaction and their suggestion to change its name to Memorial Gathering show that while they value and wish to continue the new custom, they do not want to compromise the original tradition. The Shiva or Memorial Gathering is thus seen as a re-envisioned ritual with threads of the shiva—but it is not a replacement for it. The significance of ritual, whether performed in private or in public, or whether traditional or re-envisioned, continues to have relevance, providing comfort, continuity, and beauty throughout the life cycle. Its dynamic nature allows participants to showcase their creativity, and to highlight what is significant and meaningful at all stages of life.

Acknowledgements

This essay is the revised version of a chapter from my Ph.D. dissertation, '*Heimish* and Home-ish: Aging, Jewishness, and the Creation of "Home" at a Toronto Assisted-Living Residence, the Terraces of Baycrest' (Memorial University of Newfoundland, 2009). I am most grateful to Simon Bronner for his encouragement and insightful comments, and would also like to thank Haya Bar-Itzhak and Steve Siporin, the committee readers of the

Raphael Patai Prize in Jewish Folklore and Ethnology, for their helpful reports and suggestions for future research.

Notes

1   On elderly Jews and place, see Bronner 2001; Francis 1984; Furman 1997; Hazan 1994; Kugelmass 1996. On elderly Jews and narrative, see Griff 1994 and Kirshenblatt-Gimblett 1972, 1989. On elderly Jews and ritual see Lévy and Zumwalt 2002; Starr Sered 1992.

2   On 25 April 2008 I conducted a telephone interview with both Ernie and Laurie Gershon. All subsequent quotations by them are from this interview.

Interviews

SHAWN FREMETH, telephone interview, 14 Sept. 2008

ERNIE GERSHON and LAURIE GERSHON, telephone interview, 25 Apr. 2008

REBECCA HOCH, personal interview, 7 May 2004

HARVEY LANGER, personal interview, 25 Feb. 2004

References

Baycrest Education Department. 1994. *Jewish Life at Baycrest*, 3rd edn. Toronto.

BOYARIN, JONATHAN. 1992. *Storm from Paradise: The Politics of Jewish Memory*. Minneapolis.

BRONNER, SIMON. 2001. 'From *Landsmanshaften* to *Vinkln*: Mediating Community among Yiddish Speakers in America', *Jewish History*, 15: 131–48.

CSIKSZENTMIHALYI, MIHALY, and EUGENE ROCHBERG-HALTON. 1981. *The Meaning of Things: Domestic Symbols and the Self*. Cambridge.

EHRLICH, ELIZABETH. 1997. *Miriam's Kitchen: A Memoir*. New York.

FRANCIS, DORIS. 1984. *Will You Still Need Me, Will You Still Feed Me, When I'm 84?* Bloomington, Ind.

FURMAN, FRIDA KERNER. 1997. *Facing the Mirror: Older Women and Beauty Shop Culture*. New York.

GOLDBERG, HARVEY E. 2003. *Jewish Passages: Cycles of Jewish Life*. Berkeley, Calif.

GRIFF, HANNA. 1994. 'A Life of Any Worth: Life Histories of Retired Brandeis University Faculty'. Ph.D. diss., Indiana University.

HALLE, DAVID. 1996. *Inside Culture: Art and Class in the American Home*. Chicago.

HAYDEN, DOLORES. 1995. *The Power of Place: Urban Landscapes as Public History*. Cambridge, Mass.

HAZAN, HAIM. 1994. *Old Age: Constructions and Deconstructions*. Cambridge.

HEILMAN, SAMUEL C. 2001. *When a Jew Dies: The Ethnography of a Bereaved Son*. Berkeley, Calif.

HOCKEY, JENNY. 1999. 'The Ideal of Home: Domesticating the Institutional Space of Old Age and Death'. In Tony Chapman and Jenny Hockey, eds., *Ideal Homes? Social Change and Domestic Life*, 108–18. London.

HUFFORD, MARY, MARJORIE HUNT, and STEVEN ZEITLIN, eds. 1987. *The Grand Generation: Memory, Mastery, Legacy*. Seattle.

KAMINSKY, MARC. 1993. 'A Table with People: Storytelling as Life Review and Cultural History', *YIVO Annual*, 21: 87–131.

KIRDORF, IRWIN W. 1966. 'The Shiva: A Form of Group Psychotherapy', *Journal of Religion and Health*, 5: 43–5.

KIRSHENBLATT-GIMBLETT, BARBARA. 1972. 'Traditional Storytelling in the Toronto Jewish Community: A Study in Performance and Creativity in an Immigrant Culture'. Ph.D. diss., Indiana University.

——1989. 'Objects of Memory: Material Culture as Life Review'. In Elliot Oring, ed., *Folk Groups and Folklore Genres: A Reader*, 329–38. Logan, Ut.

——2007. 'A Daughter's Afterword'. In Meyer Kirshenblatt and Barbara Kirshenblatt-Gimblett, *They Called Me Mayer July: Painted Memories of a Jewish Childhood in Poland before the Holocaust*, 359–85. Berkeley, Calif.

KUGELMASS, JACK. 1996. *The Miracle of Intervale Avenue: The Story of a Jewish Congregation in the South Bronx*, expanded edn. New York.

LÉVY, ISAAC JACK, and ROSEMARY LÉVY ZUMWALT. 2002. *Ritual Medical Lore of Sephardic Women: Sweetening the Spirits, Healing the Sick*. Chicago.

MARCUS, IVAN G. 2004. *The Jewish Life Cycle: Rites of Passage from Biblical to Modern Times*. Seattle.

MOORE, DEBORAH DASH. 1981. *At Home in America: Second Generation New York Jews*. New York.

MYERHOFF, BARBARA. 1978. *Number Our Days*. New York.

——1992. *Remembered Lives: The Work of Ritual, Storytelling, and Growing Older*, ed. Marc Kaminsky. Ann Arbor, Mich.

STARR SERED, SUSAN. 1992. *Women as Ritual Experts: The Religious Lives of Elderly Jewish Women in Jerusalem*. Oxford.

STEWART, SUSAN. 1993. *On Longing: Narratives of the Miniature, the Gigantic, the Souvenir, the Collection*. Durham, NC.

TUAN, YI-FU. 2005 [1977]. *Space and Place: The Perspective of Experience*. Minneapolis.

TULCHINSKY, GERALD. 1993. *Taking Root: The Origins of the Canadian Jewish Community*. Hanover, NH.

United Jewish Appeal (UJA) Federation. 2009. 'Doing Jewish in Toronto'. <www.jewishtorontoonline.net>. Accessed 4 May 2009.

VAN GENNEP, ARNOLD. 1909. *The Rites of Passage*. London.

WEISSMAN JOSELIT, JENNA. 1990. '"A Set Table": Jewish Domestic Culture in the New World, 1880–1950'. In Susan Braunstein and Jenna Weissman Joselit, eds., *Getting Comfortable in New York: The American Jewish Home, 1880–1950*, 20–73. New York.

——1994. *The Wonders of America: Reinventing Jewish Culture, 1880–1950*. New York.

ZEITLIN, STEVEN J. 1994. 'Conserving our Cities' Endangered Spaces'. In Mary Hufford, ed., *Conserving Culture: A New Discourse on Heritage*, 215–28. Urbana.

——and ILANA HARLOW. 2001. *Giving a Voice to Sorrow: Personal Responses to Death and Mourning*. New York.

PART IV
Ritual Performance

TWELVE

Are You Just What You Eat? Ritual Slaughter and the Politics of National Identity

SANDER L. GILMAN

YOU ARE WHAT YOU EAT. Eat organically, eat naturally, eat healthily, eat fat-free, eat high-fibre, eat low-carb, eat fair-traded, eat slowly (or, at least, eat slow food), and you are by definition a better person than those who do not. The conventions of diet remain, anthropologist Mary Douglas reminds us, one of the central means of creating categories of social inclusion and exclusion (1975: 249–75). From the nineteenth century to the twenty-first, for example, the debates about Jewish and Muslim ritual slaughtering practices were and are a litmus test for the potential or actual integration of these religious communities into a secularized, post-Enlightenment Europe. You are quite literally what you eat.

In the nineteenth century this was a particularly troubling question, especially in *fin-de-siècle* 'human science', as was stated in the subtitle to Friedrich Nietzsche's *Ecce Homo*: 'How one becomes what one is' (1983: 52). Jews of the time lived in terror, even greater than Nietzsche's, of the inevitability of becoming what they were said to be. What one ate was central: 'how to nourish yourself so as to attain your maximum of strength'. Nietzsche's view was that what one eats makes one what one is:

> But as to German cookery in general—what has it not got on its conscience! Soup before the meal (still called *alla tedesca* in the sixteenth century Venetian cookbooks); meat cooked till the flavor is gone, vegetables cooked with fat and flour; the degeneration of pastries into paper-weights! Add to this the utterly bestial postprandial habits of the ancients, not merely of the ancient Germans, and you will begin to understand where German intellect had its origin—in a disordered intestinal tract . . . German intellect is indigestion; it can assimilate nothing. (1983: 56)

What one must do is to have 'selectivity in nutriment'. You are what you eat, but in the nineteenth century, with the rise of nationalism, your political identity was also the result of what you ate, as Nietzsche noted. And if you eat food that reveals you to be cruel and foreign and unassimilable, you will be treated as if you were cruel and foreign and unassimilable. For the Jews of the nineteenth century this debate about diet was focused on the process of ritual slaughter, or *Schächten* (German)/*sheḥitah* (Hebrew). A contemporary secular Jewish source describing *shehitah* stresses the painlessness of the act in spite of the physical torment the animals seemingly experience:

Through bending the head backward the throat is exposed. Then a lightning-fast cut across the throat using a long, razor-sharp knife that cuts the softer parts of the throat through to the backbone. A huge amount of blood flows in thick streams from the severed veins and arteries, especially from the jugular. Because of the shock to the nerves as well as the sudden halting of blood to the brain there is immediate unconsciousness. The animal remains immobile until after about three-quarters of a minute a purely mechanical autonomous reflex causes more or less powerful muscular reactions in the unconscious animal. Within 2 to 3 minutes these give way to the death cramps. ('Schächten' 1927–30: 134–5)

The intense debate in the nineteenth century about *shehitah* is closely associated with European arguments about decorum and health.[1] Food and health were intimately linked and correct preparation of food reflected social decorum as well as political identity.

One needs to stress that both Jewish ritual slaughter as well as the response to it shift over time and from geographical context to geographical context. Such procedures reflect not only subtle (and sometimes less subtle) changes in ritual interpretation but also the cultural context in which they take place. The expansion and contraction of the Ottoman Empire, the proximity to Islamic practices, and the changes in Christian (Catholic and Protestant) attitudes towards Jewish rituals all had an impact on those practices. Thus the nineteenth-century debates altered the understanding in which slaughter was carried out: the changes among Christians and Jews were the direct result of the overall acceptance of ideas of hygiene that echo in the debates about the ritual even in the twenty-first century.

In the 'age of progress', as the mid to late nineteenth-century period was labelled by European and American politicians as well as intellectuals, Jews figured as representatives of a lack of progress (or 'modernization' and 'civilization', coding for contemporary industrial society) because of fidelity to the ancient, superstitious past.[2] This past and its rituals had to be made to conform with modern notions of hygienic practice or they had to be abandoned. Thus in 1906, as part of the 'pure food and drugs' reform in the United States, a new requirement was introduced of 'hoisting and shackling' conscious animals prior to their being slaughtered rather than slaughtering them on the ground so as to prevent contamination by the blood of previously slaughtered animals. Half a century later this practice was outlawed as inhumane in the United States by the Humane Slaughter Act of 1958. Only unconscious animals could be so slaughtered. Kosher slaughter in 1906 moved to the use of shackling and hoisting for conscious animals with the rationale that it solved the problem of the exposure of animals to blood. Kosher and hygienic. In 1958 kosher slaughterers were exempted from the 'hoisting and shackling' provision once it was required that the animals be stunned before hoisting as it was seen to be impossible to recon-cile the idea of a conscious animal being hoisted and shackled with the claims of humane slaughter. As a result, by 1963 kosher slaughterers in the United States had developed alternative means of keeping animals upright (unhoisted) and 'calm' prior to slaughter. Kosher and humane. Between 1906 and 1963 kosher slaughter responded to American notions of hygiene and animal rights by chang-ing its practices and attitudes as well as by explaining traditional practices in the light of new demands (Dorff and Roth 2002).

What is striking to us today is that the procedure for ritual slaughter is the same for Jews as it is for Muslims. Both slaughter only conscious animals and allow them to bleed out. Both have strict rules as to who can slaughter (though Muslims allow the consumption of meat slaughtered by Jews if a Muslim is not available). Both link ritual slaughter with the divine rules of daily life. But the general association of such procedures with health also remains a part of the claim of religion on the status of science in modernity. Even today Muslims asso-ciate the ritual with the rules of Western hygiene, as the Mufti Ebrahim Desai at a meat safety seminar recently stated: 'Blood contains organisms, which are responsible for various diseases' (Desai 2007). Such arguments were initially made in the construction of national identity around the concept of hygiene. Learning the rules of hygiene meant simultaneously learning the rules of decorum. 'Clean is healthy is proper' was a sign of the good citizen.

In Switzerland the selfsame rules of social decorum led to the nineteenth-century prohibition against kosher slaughter and against the Muslim practice (dhabiha) that results in halal meat ('kosher' is a broader category than simply meat, as is 'halal', but both apply to slaughtered meat as well). This prohibition remains in effect today. Shehitah was banned by the Nazis with the Law on the Slaughtering of Animals ('Gesetz über das Schlachten von Tieren') of 21 April 1933; it was sporadically permitted after 1945 through exceptions, which were only made part of the legal code in 1997. Since the Nazis were interested in winning the hearts and minds of Mohammad Amin al-Husayni, the Mufti of Jerusalem, and his Muslim SS legion, Islamic practices never came directly under attack. Indeed, the perceived flexibility of their rituals was contrasted with the obduracy of the Jews. After the war Muslim slaughter was outlawed in Ger-many until 1979 and even today is only tolerated but not sanctioned (Jentzsch 1998; Judd 2007). These prohibitions impact on Jews and Muslims in oddly similar ways in the light of Western responses to slaughter. Very different is the debate, on the other hand, about how the meat should be used: whether in traditional dishes or in a Big Mac (see Hess 2002).

The debate about ritual slaughter did not focus on what was eaten but on how the animal was slaughtered. The most widely read fin-de-siècle work on public health in German was by Ferdinand Hueppe, who held the chair of hygiene in Prague from 1889. His discussion of animal slaughter begins with a diatribe against ritual slaughter (1899: 275–7). For him, slaughter must occur in a manner that does not violate 'our moral feelings'. Animals should be anaesthetized or at least stunned before slaughter. 'From the ethical standpoint *shehitah* must be halted, because it is the crudest and most disgusting method . . . [I]n *shehitah* the cramps as the animal bleeds to death are so horrible that any feeling human being who has once seen it must turn from such primitive and disgusting techniques with abhorrence' (1899: 275). According to Hueppe, the hygienic claim that meat that has been bled is healthier is false; in fact, 'such meat is of lower quality'. *Shehitah* is unjustifiable in 'our climate and cultural conditions'. Only the Jews, who 'naturally' belong in a foreign space and have a different culture, would advocate such a procedure. Thus the charges of cruelty, brutality, and indifference to suffering are lodged against the Jews in the light of their ritual practice of *shehitah*.

The social response to the ritual slaughter of animals by Jews is itself brutal and direct.[3] The anti-cruelty forces in Europe and America teamed up closely with the antisemites, who saw everything associated with the Jews as an abomination, to label this form of slaughter cruel and barbaric. In Germany as early as the first Congress for the Protection of Animals (1860) there was a strong attack on ritual slaughter. This was in the light of contemporary views such as that of Arthur Schopenhauer, who saw in the Jews' refusal to use 'humane' methods of slaughter such as 'chloroform' a sign of the 'unnatural separation' of human beings from the animal world that he attributed to the spirit of Judaism (2000: 375). Such attacks were always accompanied by comments linking *shehitah* with other forms of Jewish 'brutality'. In 1885, the campaign against ritual slaughter in Great Britain led the Lord Mayor of London to comment that the obsession with this Jewish practice recalled the ritual murder accusations from the time of Chaucer (Külling 1977: 249–385). It is of little surprise that the so-called ritual murder accusation, resurrected after the initial Damascus libel of 1840, centred on the representation of *shehitah* as the ritual for also slaughtering young women. The fantasy murder in Arnold Zweig's 1914 play, *Ritual Murder in Hungary*, is carried out by the local kosher butcher (*Schächter*), who, according to the suborned witness, 'cut her throat with the big calf knife and the others caught her blood in large, silver bowls' (Zweig 1914: 76–7). This reference reflects the intense debate at the turn of the century about *shehitah* as closely associated with the charges of ritual murder and illness. There seemed to be a clear line leading from Chaucer's account of Little St Hugh of Lincoln to the Tiszaeszlár blood libel affair in Hungary in 1882–3 about which Zweig wrote.

In the 1883 meeting of Congress for the Protection of Animals in Vienna, the argument was made that the defence of ritual slaughter, or at least lack of condemnation thereof, was a sign that the Jews controlled the political process in Europe. The nineteenth-century 'Jewish lobby' was seen to restrict any objection to ritual slaughter through its economic power. Yet in 1892 a law against *shehitah* was passed in Saxony, and by 1897 there was a clear link between such attacks and the anti-vivisection movement, as the cruellest physicians were reputed to be Jews (see Ritvo 1987).[4] Over and over again it was argued that Jewish cruelty, especially to the most powerless of beings, was a sign of the innate nature of the Jews and of their alienation from anything resembling Western and modern morality.

Indeed, the great German socialist leader Karl Liebknecht denounced the right-wing attacks on ritual slaughter on the floor of the Reichstag on 24 April 1899 as a further attempt to defame the Jews, and a colleague of his in the same debate simply labelled these attacks 'antisemitic desires'. Liberal newspapers such as the *Berliner Tageblatt* in 1893 called those campaigning against ritual slaughter 'pure antisemites'. *Die Nation* in 1894 observed that 'the cry against the so-called *Schächten* belongs to the best-loved sports of the modern persecutor of the Jews' (von Schwartz 1905: 21). It is no accident that the most repulsive antisemitic film of the Third Reich, Fritz Hippler's *The Eternal Jew* (1940), concludes with a scene of ritual slaughter, as conclusive evidence of the Jew's inhumanity (see Ahren et al. 1990; Welch 1983).

A typical text from this tradition is Ernst von Schwarz's 1905 monograph against the ritual slaughter of animals. Schwarz begins by defending himself against the charge that he is simply an antisemite. He cites his Jewish landlord and his Jewish doctor as proof of his fairness, and claims that the anti-cruelty forces are not antisemitic. Nonetheless, like many intellectuals of his day, he pinpoints Jewish practices such as ritual slaughter as the barrier between Jews and their Christian neighbours: 'Nothing is so disposed to increase the divide between Christians and Jews, and to make Judaism be felt as a foreign element, than to demand the ability to do what is morally and legally forbidden to Christians' (1905: 21). But Jews, in their egoism, insist on their right to be different and still be part of the body politic.

This reaction had its origin in nineteenth-century debates about the meanings associated with food and food preparation in both religious and secular settings. For the campaign against ritual slaughter was paralleled by both the religious restructuring of biblical views of food taboos as well as the growing importance of the notion of food hygiene as reflected in the work of scientists such as Ferdinand Hueppe. Ellen White (1827–1915), the founder of the Seventh-Day Adventist Church, propagated a dietary philosophy as part of her reconstruction of a Sabbatarian dietary code (White 1946). She aimed at cultivating and preparing Christian souls for the Second Coming. She wrote, 'I was informed that the inhabitants of earth had been degenerating, losing their strength and comeliness. Satan has the power of disease and death, and with every age the effects of the curse have been more visible and the power of Satan more plainly seen' (1946: 184). In 1864 her husband, the Reverend James White, became ill, and White nursed him back to health using vegetarian principles, which were seen as fulfilling the ritual obligations of the Bible. In 1866 they founded the Western

Health Reform Institute at Battle Creek, Michigan, which became the centre for late-nineteenth-century diet reform in the United States. White simply reversed the claims about original sin and the eating of the forbidden fruit in the Garden of Eden: 'God gave our first parents the food He designed that the race should eat. It was contrary to His plan to have the life of any creature taken. There was to be no death in Eden. The fruit of the trees in the garden was the food man's wants required', she wrote in 1864 (1946: 111). Again, in 1902, she warned against the diseased nature of modern food: 'Flesh was never the best food; but its use is now doubly objectionable, since disease in animals is so rapidly increasing' (1946: 19). White's teachings were characteristic of the American health reform movement's emphasis on temperance and abstemious living (see Rosenberg 2003).

Such health views about consuming meat, reflecting the debates about ritual slaughter, were often presented within a biblical context. The German health faddist Moriz Schnitzer also gave his hygienic, vegetarian regime biblical underpinnings: 'Moses led the Jews through the desert so that they might become vegetarians in these forty years' (quoted in Karl 1991: 270). But it was clear that such a position avoided the condemnation of ritual slaughter through the substitution of vegetarianism for any consumption of meat, no matter how slaughtered. Since vegetarianism in its Continental and British forms was excessively animal-rights oriented, this revision of the notion of the appropriate reading of biblical admonitions concerning food taboos managed to avoid the debate while arguing for the inherently healthy nature of a 'biblical' diet. These answers to the debates about kosher slaughter are echoed in the code of twenty-first-century vegans.

Perhaps the most extraordinary exchange concerning the claim about the healthy nature of biblical (i.e. Jewish) food taboos took place in 1874, in the prestigious Philadelphia *Medical and Surgical Reporter*, where Madison Marsh, a physician from Port Hudson, Louisiana, argued that Jews had a much greater tolerance for disease than the general population. The Jew, he wrote, 'enjoy[s] a wonderful national immunity', because 'his constitution has become so hardened and fortified against disease by centuries of national calamities, by the dietetics, regimen and sanitas of his religion, continuing for consecutive years of so many ages' (1874: 343). A month after this report was published, it was answered in detail by Ephraim M. Epstein of Cincinnati, a Jewish physician who had earlier practised in Vienna and in Russia. He rebutted Marsh's argument point by point. First, Jews had no immunity to diseases, including the kind long associated with Jewish religious practices: 'I am sure I have observed no Jewish immunity from any diseases, venereal disease not excepted' (Epstein 1874: 440). Second, Jews did not have 'superior longevity', nor any advantage because of their diet or thanks to their practice of circumcision. However, Jews did possess a quality lacking in their Christian neighbours: what put them at less risk was their network of support, their 'close fraternity'; 'one Jew never forsak[es] the material welfare of his brother Jew, and he knows it instinctively' (1874: 441). It was simply the 'common mental construction' of the Jew that preserved his health. Finally, such health as the Jews possessed was due to 'the constitutional stamina that that nation inherited from its progenitor, Abraham of old, and because it kept that inheritance undeteriorated by not intermarrying with other races' (1874: 441). Jewish religious practices provided the key to a fabled Jewish health.

American Jewish religious leaders strongly agreed with the hygienic rather than the social argument. Rabbi Joseph Krauskopf informed his Reformed congregation in Philadelphia,

Eminent physicians and statisticians have amply confirmed the truth: that the marvelous preservation of Israel, despite all the efforts to blot them out from the face of the earth, their comparative freedom from a number of diseases, which cause frightful ravages among the Non-Jewish people, was largely due to their close adherence to their excellent Sanitary Laws. Health was their coat of mail, it was their magic shield that caught, and warded off, every thrust aimed at their heart. Vitality was their birthright . . . Their immunity, which the enemy charged to magic-Arts, to alliances with the spirits of evil, was traceable solely to their faithful compliance with the sanitary requirements of their religion. (1889: 7)

This view became the commonplace explanation for continuing religious practices such as ritual slaughter.

Here we see the struggle to understand the special (here in a positive sense) nature of Jewish difference: is it the practice (which anyone can copy, even the Seventh-Day Adventists) or is it the biological inheritance (which no one has but the Jews)? In *The Jews: A Study of Race and Environment* (1911; German translation 1913) Maurice Fishberg introduces his own argument that the traditional hygienic virtues of Jewish law and family life enable Jews to have a lower incidence of illness only through their inheritance of historically acquired characteristics:

[T]hat it is not a racial trait is seen from the fact that in the United States the number of Jewish consumptives is growing to an alarming extent. Racial immunities are not lost by a residence for a few years in a new country, or by a change of milieu for one generation . . . Nor can we attribute it to the ritual inspection of meat practiced by the Jews, because in western countries, where they are not loath to consume meat not prepared according to the dietary laws, their tuberculosis mortality is lower than in the East, where they are very strict in this regard. They are better adapted to city life and overcrowding by a long sojourn in the Ghetto, and by a process of natural selection there were [sic] eliminated most of those who were predisposed to tuberculosis, thus giving them an advantage. (Fishberg 1911: 529)

As late as 1940 Emil Bogen presented a summary essay on the 'strikingly lower death rate' among Jews for tuberculosis. An American Jewish physician writing in the one short-lived American Jewish medical journal, he was constrained to argue against any 'mysterious genetic or acquired constitutional cellular or humoral, immunological mechanism', and preferred to look at the lifestyle defined by Jewish ritual. He stressed the 'Jewish diet . . . rich in protein and calories', which deterred the 'initial breakdown and progression' of tuberculosis (1940: 123–4). Is it what the Jews eat or is it their special nature, or is there really no difference between Jews and others in terms of the impact of food?

Central to the ritual of *Schächten* is the purification of the animal's carcass by the removal of its blood through the act of slaughter (see Garçia-Ballester 1991; Sackmann 1988). The religious argument is that the Jews (beginning with the biblical admonition in Genesis 9: 4) were forbidden to eat blood. In the course of the late nineteenth century this ritual argument was given hygienic content: the refusal of the Jews to consume blood was a sign of the 'hygienic' importance of ritual slaughter in the preservation of human life, especially its protection against tuberculosis (Lochmann 1969, 1992; Schliesser 1974).

The hygiene argument is summarized in a statement made in 1889 by Henry Behrend in the British periodical *The Nineteenth Century*.[5] Writing in the wake of the extraordinary popular response to Robert Koch's discovery of the tubercular bacillus in 1882, Behrend argued that the present state of scientific knowledge demanded that diseased meat be withheld from human consumption. This was very much in line with the general shift from treatment to prevention that took place in the 1880s (Guerrand 1984). Scientists were confident that they knew the etiology of tuberculosis and similar infectious diseases (such as anthrax) and were therefore able to state without doubt how they could be passed on to human beings. Infected meat 'is not only deprived of most of its nutritive qualities, but is capable of communicating its specific malady to man, when taken as food' (Behrend 1889: 410). The effects of the disease could be seen in the slaughtered animal, as the Sheriff-Principal of Glasgow commented: 'The presence of the agent of the disease must precede the visible results of its action; indeed, the present case affords an illustration of the danger of inferring, from the absence of symptoms visible to the unaided eye, that the disease is localized' (Behrend 1889: 411). In July 1888 the International Congress of Tuberculosis in Paris stressed the dangers of eating infected meat. The assumption at the time was that there was an absolute association between the consumption of tainted meat and the acquiring of tuberculosis, which would then be 'transmitted to their unborn children' (Behrend 1889: 412). Thus the eating of such meat affected not only the present generation but all future generations.

Behrend rests his argument on two scientific premises: one is that there is an absolute 'identity of human and bovine tuberculosis', and the other is that tuberculosis is communicable to man 'from the flesh of affected cattle' (1889: 413). This disease, Behrend claims, quoting a Dr Klein from the Brown Institution, 'is communicable by ingestion' (1889: 416). Thus the 'comparative immunity from the tubercular diathesis' of the Jews can be explained by their dietary laws (1889:

418). Behrend's authorities support him in this matter. In 1885, Noël Guéneau de Mussy spoke before the Academy of Medicine in Paris about the 'vitality of the Jewish race' depending on 'the care exercised by them in the selection of their food supply' (Behrend 1889: 418). This is evidenced especially in the relatively low rate of infant mortality among the Jews, particularly in Germany (Behrend 1889: 419–20).

A belief in the continuity from Judaism to modern science underpins much of this argumentation. For Behrend, Moses becomes the first bacteriologist on the model of Koch and Pasteur:

The idea of parasitic and infectious maladies, which has conquered so great a position in modern pathology, appears to have greatly occupied the mind of Moses, and to have dominated all his hygienic rules. He excludes from the Hebrew diet animals particularly liable to parasites; and as it is in the blood that the germs or spores of infectious disease circulate, he orders that they must be drained of their blood before serving for food . . . What an extraordinary prescience! The contagion of tuberculosis has been proved only during the last few years; its transmissibility by food is not yet universally recognized, though the experiments of M. Chauveau render it almost certain; yet the law of Israel, thousands of years in advance of modern science, has inscribed in its precepts these ordinances, preventive of the malady. (Behrend 1889: 417)

Both Jewish and Christian advocates of ritual slaughter took up this argument. At the Sanitary Congress at Brighton in 1881, a Dr Carpenter commented, 'obedience to the sanitary laws laid down by Moses is a necessary condition to perfect health, and to a state that shall give us power to stamp out zymotic diseases. If these laws were observed by all classes, the zymotic death-rate would not be an appreciable quantity in our mortality list' (quoted in Wolf 1884: 250). The British Jewish anthropologist Lucien Wolf commented in 1884 that it was because of the 'legalism' of the Jews, so disparaged by the antisemites of the day, that Moses 'the lawgiver was not unmindful of the probable unwholesomeness' of animals declared to be not for consumption by Jews and especially that 'the use of blood is emphatically and repeatedly forbidden' (1884: 246–7). The claim, made by physicians as well as the lay public, was that the Jews, through their religious practices, were following a basic model of hygiene, under the rubric that 'we may go to Moses for instruction in some of the best methods in hygiene', as William Osler wrote in 1914 (1884: 729). Even the opponents of ritual slaughter, such as Ernst von Schwartz, had to agree that 'Moses was the great, wise reformer and hygienist' (1905: 37). But they disagreed that ritual slaughter was Mosaic and therefore divinely inspired; instead they considered it rabbinic.

The image of Moses as 'a super-eminent, specially evolved and Divinely-led genius' also serves as the theme of Alexander Rattray's study of 'divine hygiene' (1903: i. 250–3). His view is that the Bible is a 'deep mine of most important medico-hygienic information', and he seeks 'to prove that this is directly or indirectly Divine' (1903: i. 227). For all of Rattray's attention to the biblical admonitions concerning food, he mentions ritual slaughter to stress that the removal of blood preserves meat. This approach curtailed the discussion of ritual slaughter as divinely inspired, while emphasizing the potential benefits of ritually slaughtered flesh. Jews used the argument to defend *sheḥitah*; their opponents labelled it as an invention of the Jews, not of the divinely inspired Moses.

By the early twentieth century the question of ritual practices had come to define Jewish identity in an odd and disturbing manner. Sigmund Freud in *Totem and Taboo* (1913) made claims about the nature of religious practice in general and the 'code du totémisme' which he saw as determining it. 'Ritual sacrifice' with its fetishization of the totemic animal was central to this belief system (Freud 1955–74: xii. 100). 'Individual taboo prohibitions of this very kind' were a form of 'taboo sickness', an 'obsessional sickness'. They were irrational in that 'they are forcibly maintained by an irresistible fear' (1955–74: xii. 25). But it was only much later that Freud revealed the Jewish underpinnings of his claims about the totemic nature of sacrifice. In *Moses and Monotheism* (1939) he commented on the obsessive nature of ritual practice after Moses:

During the centuries since then they had become merged with the people or with the priesthood, and it had become the main function of the priests to develop and supervise the ritual, and besides this to preserve the holy writ and revise it in accordance with their aims. But was not all sacrifice and all ceremonial at bottom only magic and sorcery, such as had been unconditionally rejected by the old Mosaic teaching? (Freud 1955–74: xxiii. 50)

Modern Jews in the model of Moses, however, had to confront these claims and follow 'the Prophets, who tirelessly preached the old Mosaic doctrine—that the deity disdained sacrifice and ceremonial and asked only for faith and a life in truth and justice (Ma'at)' (Freud 1955–74: xxiii. 50). This was the pattern of reform that Freud saw as defining Jewish character: the rejection of the frozen, meaningless fetishization of ritual and the ability (which Freud saw in himself) to question tradition. It was the overcoming of ritual slaughter which was Jewish, not the ritual itself.

Sheḥitah was seen by non-Jews as a reflex of the Jewish soul as well as part of a pattern of Jewish illness. In Thomas Mann's *The Magic Mountain*, the figure of Leo Naphta, whom the protagonist Hans Castorp meets in the tuberculosis sanatorium at Davos, is immediately revealed to the reader as a Jew by his 'corrosive ugliness': 'Everything about him was sharp: the hooked nose dominating his face, the narrow, pursed mouth, the thick, beveled lenses of his glasses in their light frame, behind which were a pair of pale-gray eyes—even the silence he preserved, which suggested that when he broke it, his speech would be incisive and logical' (Mann 1982 [1924]: 372). Naphta's background reveals all the connections between the Jew, ritual murder, and *sheḥitah*. Mann believed strongly in the inheritance of family characteristics and in degeneracy as the explanation of individual pathology.[6] For him, the Jew was the exemplary case and the ritual butcher the Jew's best representation.

Leo, or as he was then called, Leib Naphta, came from the eastern reaches of the Austrian empire, from the Galician–Volhynian border, where his father Elie was a *shoḥet* (ritual slaughterer). Mann's description of the act of *sheḥitah* plays on the stereotype of the Jew as a 'brooding and refining spirit':

Standing near the victim, which was hobbled and bound indeed, but not stunned, he would lift the mighty slaughter-knife and bring it to rest in a deep gash close to the cervical vertebra; while the assistant held the quickly filling basins to receive the gushing, steaming blood, and the child looked on the sight with that childish gaze that often pierces through the sense into the essential, and may have been in an unusual degree the gift of the starry-eyed Elie's son. He knew that Christian butchers had to stun their cattle with a blow from a club before killing them, and that this regulation was made in order to avoid unnecessary cruelty. Yet his father, so fine and so intelligent by comparison with those louts, and starry-eyed as never one of them, did his task according to the Law, striking down the creature while its senses were undimmed, and letting its life-blood well out until it sank. The boy Leib felt that the stupid *goyim* were actuated by an easy and irreverent good nature, which paid less honour to the deity than did his father's solemn mercilessness; thus the conception of piety came to be bound up in his mind with that of cruelty, and the idea of the sacred and the spiritual with the sight and smell of spurting blood. (1982 [1924]: 440–1)

This is a more or less standard representation of ritual slaughter, but Mann, never one to leave well alone, provides us with the mythic continuum on which this spiritual type must be placed. For Elie Naphta is also a 'familiar of God, a Baal-Shem or Zaddik, a miracle man' who can cure 'a woman of a malignant sore, and another time a boy of spasms, simply by means of blood and invocations'. The word 'blood' seems to signify the blood gathered by the *shoḥet* during the ritual slaughter; indirectly, it refers to the race of the Jews, to their blood. Continuing this line of associations, in the very next sentences Mann describes Elie Naphta's eventual fate: 'But it was precisely this aura of an uncanny piety, in which the odour of his blood-boltered calling played a part, that proved his destruction. There had been the unexplained death of two gentile boys, a popular uprising, a panic of rage—and Elie had died horribly, nailed crucifix-wise on the door of his burning home.' Here the set of associations seems to be complete: ritual slaughter, the physiognomy and psyche of the Jew, the Jew who cures through blood, and the ritual murder accusation, which ends in the death of the Jew crucified as a Jew.

An argument has been made that after the Holocaust the focus on ritual slaughter in Germany (and the rest of Europe) moved from the rhetoric of anti-semitism to that of animal rights (Jentzsch 1998). In point of fact, these two views were and remain linked. The Nazi view was that the ritual practices of the Jews revealed their inherently inhumane nature; the advocates of animal rights (above those of human beings as members of a religious community) argue that anyone (including the Jews) who would violate the explicit rights of an animal is inhumane. Talal Asad has noted that 'for a long time now the law has been concerned to penalize "unjustifiable" pain and distress in animals'. Today he sees a shift towards the 'normalization' of 'desirable conduct', which is merely another way of defining 'decorum' (2003: 156–7). Placing the rights of animals above those of human beings strikes me as a continuation of the older position clothed in a new, more politically correct rhetoric. On 15 January 2002 the Constitutional Court in Karlsruhe dismissed a suit advocating a ban on ritual slaughter in Germany. On 17 May 2002 the members of the German Bundestag, the lower house of parliament, voted 543 to 19 to amend the nation's constitution to include rights for animals. This was echoed by a two-thirds affirmation in the Bundesrat, the upper chamber. The proposed law amended Article 20a of German Basic Law, which requires the state to protect human dignity and now reads, 'The state takes responsibility for protecting the natural foundations of life and animals in the interest of future generations'. This echoed the inclusion of animal rights in the constitution of three of the new German states, *Neue Bundesländer*, as well as of the city-state of Berlin. Shortly thereafter an advertisement supported by the most vociferous anti-vivisection organization, Der Bundesverband Menschen für Tierrechte, and by members of the Constitutional Court, appeared in a number of German papers asking for support in a court case to ban the ritual slaughter of animals as a violation of their newly acquired civil rights. Ritual slaughter is primarily defined, even in this day of a heightened awareness of Islam, as function of the Jewish community.

In Germany the claims for the 'human' rights of animals facing ritual slaughter could never use the rhetoric of the Holocaust. However, they do parallel the 'Holocaust on your plate' argument of the American People for the Ethical Treatment of Animals (PETA) from 2003, stating that 'the victimization of Jews, Gypsies, homosexuals, and others characterized as "life unworthy of life" during the Holocaust parallels the way that modern society abuses and justifies the slaughter of animals' (PETA Media Center 2007). The rhetoric of human rights and genocide is extended to the actions of the Jews in a turn-about more than a little reminiscent of the rhetoric of the time used against the Israeli government as the 'new Nazis'. No greater attack on the character of the Jews can be made than to label ritual slaughter as violating human rights. The irony is that after the founding of the United Nations in 1945, Rabbi Isaac Lewin (representing Agudat Yisrael[7]) argued that it was rather the right to a Jewish burial and to *sheḥitah* that needed to be defended (Lewin 1964).

And yet there seems to be an answer to the continued condemnation of ritual slaughter in the late twentieth-century elevation of 'kosher' to the status of organic or healthy. Ironically the boom in the sale of kosher food (which only means ritually supervised) in the United States today has much the same rationale. As one hot dog maker's advertisement has it, kosher food answers to a higher authority—but it also carries with it the promise of better eating. As reported in London's *Guardian*,

What kosher-certifying enhances today is 'economic vigour'. Out of a market of $500 billion, US food manufacturers sell more than $170 billion worth of kosher-certified products each year . . . Whenever a company makes a food line kosher it sees a jump in its market share. And for Nestlé or Nabisco or Best Foods or General Mills, even a fraction of a percentage point may translate into millions of dollars.[8]

Kosher has become interchangeable with organic and is therefore deemed healthy —a claim which anyone raised on traditional east European cooking will be happy to correct. Ritual slaughter as a sign of Jewish cruelty disappears as a problem in this context. Perhaps this will be an answer to the uniqueness of ritual slaughter for Muslims and Jews in a future Europe?

The debate about the meaning of ritual slaughter continues in a world now attuned to the claims of 'animal rights' and to a heightened anxiety about Islam. In the post-9/11 context these debates take on a furious tone exactly at the same moment when 'kosher' has come to be more or less accepted as a positive factor. In Australia, where the debates about terror and immigration have focused on Muslims as much as in Europe and in the United States, there is a call for the elimination of the 'form of halal ritual slaughter of sheep for export, whereby the sheep's throats are cut and they are allowed to bleed to death. They are conscious throughout'. An editorial for the Melbourne newspaper *The Age* declared such ritual slaughter an example of 'blatant and unacceptable brutality'.[9] This let loose a broadside of attacks on Muslim practices and the local 'Muslim organization that oversees halal meat certification in Australia said it accepted the slaughter of animals with electrical stunning, as Muslims had to obey the law of the land wherever they live.'[10]

But, of course, Orthodox Jews could not agree with this claim: 'Kosher Australia defended the Jewish method of slaughter without prior stunning as humane and said it was unacceptable to stun animals first as they were often killed by the stunning.' It was the Muslims who followed the decorum of Australian society:

The Australian Federation of Islamic Councils halal services manager, Mohamed Rahman, said Muslims in Australia had no issue with animals being unconscious when they were slaughtered. He took a swipe at the Jewish slaughter methods for kosher food. 'According to Islam, we have to respect the law of the country,' he said. 'But for kosher, they don't accept anything which is stunned.'[11]

He was immediately answered by Rabbi Mordechai Gutnick, the rabbinic administrator of Kosher Australia and president of the Organization of Rabbis in Australasia, who said that 'the Jewish method of slaughter was not cruel'.[12] The idea that kosher is 'cool' seems not to have permeated the Australian debate, which now centres on Jewish–Muslim conflicts about which religious practice is more attuned to Western values.

Indeed, the debate has focused on whether Islamic principles, unlike those of the Jews, allowed the stunning of animals before slaughter. In certain diaspora contexts Islamic ritual had agreed to such a compromise (which had pleased the British fascists such as Arnold Leese in the 1930s) but the meat slaughtered in Australia was intended for shipment to Islamic nations in the Middle East, which would not accept meat so slaughtered as halal. In the United Kingdom about 90 per cent of halal meat is produced from animals that are stunned before they are butchered. This is seen by the opponents of traditional slaughtering as a sign of the

widespread acceptance of the practice within the Muslim community. Similarly, many people within the Jewish community do not support slaughter without prestunning. Many Muslims and Jews are also vegetarian, indicating that the consumption of meat slaughtered in any particular fashion is not central to their religious beliefs. Banning slaughter without prestunning would not stop people from following the religious faiths of their choosing.[13]

In general the answer seems to be that of Ellen White: it was not part of God's original plan for man to eat animals.

Could halal become the next 'organic' for Europeans? Certainly at the moment, as Olivier Roy notes, there is a greater demand for Western-style food to be made from halal meat than for the rejection of McDonald's in favour of traditional food, whatever that might mean (2004: 48). The general tendency in diaspora communities is to want access to the modern fast-food culture. This has created a natural alliance between old adversaries such as Muslims and Hindus and new ones such as Jews and Muslims. In nation-states where such coalitions are not desirable or necessary, there has been a general condemnation of fast food as a sign of the West. As one neo-fundamentalist leader stated in Pakistan: 'This is forbidden—the Kentucky chicken and the McDonald burger is forbidden for Muslims. There are people present here who can make such foods, which are better than this McDonald burger and Kentucky chicken. Why should we allow from abroad these things?' (Roy 2004: 272). Such attitudes still seem to be marginal to the Western experience, which may over time reject McDonald's, but through the rhetoric of health or anti-globalization.

In 2002 the Meat and Livestock Commission in the United Kingdom encouraged British farmers to diversify into the thriving halal meat sector as Muslim families in Britain consume 20 per cent of all the lamb and mutton eaten in the country while constituting only about 5 per cent of the population (BBC News 2002). In addition the market for halal Christmas turkeys, perhaps the ultimate multicultural animal, has exploded in the UK (BBC News 2001). The turkeys are prepared Tandoori style, without, I am sure, the traditional brussels sprouts. Can ritual be given new meanings within a diasporic community without being reduced to 'kosher-style' or 'halal-style', as hasidic mysticism has been reduced to Madonna wearing a bracelet amulet? Fareena Alam asks whether Islam in Britain should always be reduced to 'beards, scarves and halal meat'. She bemoans this reduction to the 'ethical vagaries of ritually slaughtered meat' (2003). For Muslims, an alternative to the tradition of sacrificing a ram on Eid al-Adha (Feast of the Sacrifice) has been created on a website where one can sacrifice virtual rams. This is a direct response to charges of inhumaneness lodged against Islamic religious practices both within and outside the Muslim community. Can it be a further sign of alternative practices developing within Islam?

Is not the claim of cultural integration at least partly the decorum of the table: that eating certain foods in certain ways makes people better and more moral? Are foodways and morality not both worlds in which the claims of difference are claims of not just inferiority but of inhumaneness? Food and acceptance are often paired in Western culture, and nowhere more than in the world of Jews and Muslims in the Western diaspora.

Notes

1   See *Auszüge* 1887; Bauwerker 1882; Bilberfeld 1911; Board of Deputies 1925, 1926; Friedman 1904; Galandauer 1933; Gilman 2005; Hildesheimer 1905, 1908; Kayserling 1867; Komite 1894; Landsberg 1882; Liebling 1900; Vialles 1994; Weichmann 1899; Wood 1925.

2   See Kautsky 1914; Kingsley 1885: 472; Pennell 1892; see also Bronner 1998: 132–8; Cohen and Cohen 2008; Friesel 2008; Gilman 2008.

3   See Breuer 1992; Grandin 1990; Klug 1989a, 1989b; Kushner 1989; Metcalf 1989.

4   Two questions that are reflected in the antisemitic rhetoric against ritual slaughter and that also turned into aspects of the debate about vivisection are the irrationality of the anti-vivisectionist and the notion of 'sacrifice'. See Buettinger 1993 and Lynch 1988.

5   The importance of this essay must not be underestimated. It is cited as the epigraph to the pro-*Schächten* pamphlet 'Herrn Otto Hartmann in Cöln und sein Kampf gegen die Schlachtweise der Israeliten ... von einem Collegen' (1889).

6   A most incisive psychoanalytical reading of this fascination is given in Lubich 1993.

7   Agudat Yisrael was founded in 1912 in Upper Silesia (now Poland) as an Orthodox movement (and then party) opposed to secular Zionism.

8   See 'A Kosher Knosh Explosion', *Guardian*, 8 Jan. 2005, p. 25.

9   See 'Protecting Animals, a Measure of our Humanity', editorial, *The Age* (Melbourne), 3 Aug. 2007, p. 12.

10   Ibid.

11   Ibid.

12   Ibid.

13   See 'In God's Name—Religious Slaughter in the UK',<http://www.viva.org.uk/cam paigns/ritual_slaughter/index.htm>, accessed 4 Aug. 2009.

References

AHREN, YIZHAK, STIG HORNSHOJ-MOLLER, and CHRISTOPH B. MELCHERS. 1990. *Der ewige Jude: Wie Goebbels hetzte: Untersuchungen zum nationalsozialistischen Propagandafilm*. Aachen.

ALAM, FAREENA. 2003. 'Are We Just What We Eat?', *Guardian*, 15 June, <http://www.guardian.co.uk/world/2003/jun/15/race.religion>, accessed 4 Aug. 2009.

ASAD, TALAL. 2003. *Formations of the Secular: Christianity, Islam, Modernity*. Stanford, Calif.

Auszüge aus den Gutachten der hervorragendsten Physiologen und Veterinärärzte über das 'Schächten'. 1887. Frankfurt am Main.

BAUWERKER, C. 1882. *Das rituelle Schächten der Israeliten im Lichte der Wissenschaft*. Kaiserslautern.

BBC News. 2001. 'Demand Grows for Halal Turkeys'. BBC News website, 24 Dec., <http://news.bbc.co.uk/1/hi/uk/1724177.stm>, accessed 4 Aug. 2009.

——2002. 'Farmers Urged to Go Halal'. BBC News World Edition website, 31 July, <http://news.bbc.co.uk/1/hi/uk/2163101.stm>, accessed 4 Aug. 2009.

BEHREND, HENRY. 1889. 'Diseases Caught from Butcher's Meat', *The Nineteenth Century*, 26: 409–22.

BIBERFELD, EDUARD. 1911. *Halsschnitt nicht Hirnertrümmerung*. Berlin.

Board of Deputies of British Jews. 1926. *Opinions of Foreign Experts on the Jewish Method of Slaughtering Animals*. London.

BOGEN, EMIL. 1940. 'Tuberculosis among the Jews', *Medical Leaves*, 3: 123–4.

BREUER, MORDECHAI. 1992. *Modernity within Tradition: The Social History of Orthodox Jewry in Imperial Germany*, trans. Elizabeth Petuchowski. New York.

BRONNER, SIMON J. 1998. *Following Tradition: Folklore in the Discourse of American Culture*. Logan, Ut.

BUETTINGER, CRAIG. 1993. 'Antivivisection and the Charge of Zoophil-Psychosis in the Early Twentieth Century', *Historian*, 55: 277–88.

COHEN, JEREMY, and RICHARD I. COHEN, eds. 2008. *The Jewish Contribution to Civilization: Reassessing an Idea*. Oxford.

DESAI, MUFTI EBRAHIM. 2007. 'The Ritual Islamic Slaughter'. Madrassah In'aamiyyah website, <http://www.al-inaam.com/library/rslaughter.htm>, accessed 4 Aug. 2009.

DORFF, RABBI ELLIOT N., and RABBI JOEL ROTH. 2002. 'Shackling and Hoisting'. Dr Temple Grandin's webpage, <http://www.grandin.com/ritual/conservative.jewish.law.html>, accessed 5 Aug. 2009.

DOUGLAS, MARY. 1975. *Implicit Meanings*. London.

EPSTEIN, EPHRAIM M. 1874. 'Have the Jews any Immunity from Certain Diseases?', *Medical and Surgical Reporter*, 30: 440–2.

FISHBERG, MAURICE. 1911. *The Jews: A Study of Race and Environment*. New York.

FREUD, SIGMUND. 1955–74. *Standard Edition of the Complete Psychological Works of Sigmund Freud*, ed. and trans. James Strachey. 24 vols. London.

FRIEDMAN, AARON ZEBI. 1904. *Tub Taam Or a Vindication of the Jewish Mode of Slaughtering Animals for Food Called Shechitah*, trans. Laemlein Buttenwieser. New York.

FRIESEL, EVYATAR. 2008. 'The "Return of the Jews to History": Considerations about an Ideological Concept'. In Lauren B. Strauss and Michael Brenner, eds., *Mediating Modernity: Challenges and Trends in the Jewish Encounter with the Modern World*, 133–42. Detroit.

GALANDAUER, BELA. 1933. *Zur Physiologie des Schachtschnittes: ist das Schächten eine Tierquälerei?* Berlin.

GARÇIA-BALLESTER, LUIS. 1991. 'Dietetic and Pharmacological Therapy: A Dilemma among 14th-Century Jewish Practitioners in the Montpellier Area', *Clio Medica*, 22: 23–37.

GILMAN, SANDER. 2005. 'The Problem with Purim: Jews and Alcohol in the Modern Period', *Leo Baeck Institute Year Book*, 50: 215–31.

——2008. 'Are Jews Musical? Historical Notes on the Question of Jewish Musical Modernism'. In Philip V. Bohlman, ed., *Jewish Musical Modernism: Old and New*, pp. vii–xvi. Chicago.

GRANDIN, TEMPLE. 1990. 'Humanitarian Aspects of Shehitah in the United States', *Judaism*, 39: 436–46.

GUERRAND, ROGER-HENRI. 1984. 'Guerre à la tuberculose!', *Histoire*, 74: 78–81.

Herrn Otto Hartmann in Köln und sein Kampf gegen die Schlachtweise der Israeliten . . . von einem Collegen. 1889. Frankfurt.

HESS, JONATHAN M. 2002. *Germans, Jews, and the Claims of Modernity.* New Haven.

HILDESHEIMER, HIRSCH. 1905. *Das Schächten.* Berlin.

——ed. 1908. *Neue Gutachten über das jüdische-rituelle Schlacht-verfahren (Schächten).* Berlin.

HOELZEL, ALFRED. 1990. 'Thomas Mann's Attitudes to Jews and Judaism: An Investigation of Biography and Oeuvre', *Studies in Contemporary Jewry*, 6: 229–53.

HUEPPE, FERDINAND. 1899. *Handbuch der Hygiene.* Berlin.

HUMPHREYS, PETER. 1989. 'The *Magic Mountain*—A Time Capsule of Tuberculosis Treatment in the Early Twentieth Century', *Bulletin of the Canadian History of Medicine*, 6: 147–63.

JENTZSCH, RUPERT. 1998. 'Das rituelle Schlachten von Haustieren in Deutschland ab 1933'. Ph.D. diss., Tierärztliches Hochschul Hanover.

JUDD, ROBIN. 2007. *Contested Rituals: Circumcision, Kosher Butchering, and Jewish Political Life in Germany, 1843–1933.* Ithaca, NY.

KARL, FREDERICK ROBERT. 1991. *Franz Kafka, Representative Man.* New York.

KAUTSKY, KARL. 1914. *Rasse und Judentum.* Stuttgart.

KAYSERLING, MEYER. 1867. *Die rituale Schlachtfrage oder ist Schächten Thierquälerei?* Aarau.

KINGSLEY, JOHN STERLING, ed. 1885. *The Standard Natural History*, vi: *The Natural History of Man.* Boston.

KLUG, BRIAN. 1989a. 'Overkill: The Polemic against Ritual Slaughter', *Jewish Quarterly*, 34: 38–42.

KLUG, BRIAN. 1989b. 'Ritual Murmur: The Undercurrent of Protest against Religious Slaughter of Animals in Britain in the 1980s', *Patterns of Prejudice*, 23: 16–28.

Komite zur abwehr antisemitischer Angriffe, ed. 1894. *Gutachten über das Jüdisch-Rituelle Schlachtverfahren ('Schächten')*. Berlin.

KRAUSKOPF, JOSEPH. 1889. *Sanitary Science: A Sunday Lecture*. Philadelphia.

KÜLLING, FRIEDRICH. 1977. *Bei uns wie überall? Antisemitismus*. Zurich.

KUSHNER, ANTONY. 1989. 'Stunning Intolerance: A Century of Opposition to Religious Slaughter', *Jewish Quarterly*, 36: 16–20.

LANDSBERG, WILHELM. 1882. *Das rituelle Schächten der Israeliten im Lichte der Wahrheit*. Kaiserslautern.

LEESE, ARNOLD. 2002 [1940]. *The Legalised Cruelty of Shechita: The Jewish Method of Cattle-Slaughter*. London.

LEWIN, ISAAC. 1964. *On the History of Agudat Yisrael* [Tsu der geshikhte fun agudas yisroel]. New York.

LIEBLING, U. 1900. 'Das rituelle Fleischbeschau', *Österreiche Monatsschrift für Tierheil-kunde*, 12: 2241–50.

LLORENTE, L. E. MONTIEL. 1980. 'La ciencia medica en *La montana magica* de Thomas Mann', *Asclepio*, 32: 271–85.

LOCHMANN, E. H. 1969. 'Folgenschwere Irrtümer bei der Beurteilung tuberkulöser Schlachtrinder', *Archiv für Lebensmittelhygiene*, 20: 155–8.

——1992. 'Zur lebensmittelrechtlichen Beurteilung tuberkulöser Schlachtrinder im ausgehenden 18. Jahrhundert—Zugleich eine Studie zur Stellung des Tierarztes im öffentlichen Dienst jener Zeit', *Deutsche Tierarztliche Wochenschrift*, 99: 345–6.

LUBICH, FREDRICK A. 1993. 'Thomas Manns *Der Zauberberg*: Spukschloß der Großen Mutter oder die Männerdämmerung des Abendlandes', *Deutsche Vierteljahrsschrift für Literaturwissenschaft und Geistesgeschichte*, 67: 729–63.

LYNCH, MICHAEL E. 1988. 'Sacrifice and the Transformation of the Animal Body into a Scientific Object: Laboratory Culture and Ritual Practice in the Neurosciences', *Social Studies of Science*, 18: 265–89.

MANN, THOMAS. 1982 [1924]. *The Magic Mountain*, trans. H. T. Lowe-Porter. New York.

MARSH, MADISON. 1874. 'Jews and Christians', *Medical and Surgical Reporter*, 30: 343–4.

METCALF, MICHAEL F. 1989. 'Regulating Slaughter: Animal Protection and Anti-semitism in Scandinavia, 1880–1941', *Patterns of Prejudice*, 23: 32–48.

NIETZSCHE, FRIEDRICH. 1983. *Ecce Homo*, trans. R. J. Hollindale. Harmondsworth.

OSLER, WILLIAM. 1914. 'Israel and Medicine', *Canadian Medical Association Journal*, 4: 729–33.

PENNELL, JOSEPH. 1892. *The Jew at Home: Impressions of a Summer and Autumn Spent with Him*. New York.

PETA MEDIA CENTER. 2007. 'PETA's "Holocaust on Your Plate" National Tour Comes to New York', <http://www.peta.org/mc/NewsItem.asp?id=3021>, accessed 12 Oct. 2007.

RATTRAY, ALEXANDER. 1903. *Divine Hygiene: Sanitary Science and Sanitariness of the Sacred Scriptures and Mosaic Code*, vol. i, pp. 200–53. London.

RITVO, HARRIET. 1987. *The Animal Estate: The English and Other Creatures in the Victorian Age.* Cambridge, Mass.

ROSENBERG, CHARLES, ed. 2003. *Right Living: An Anglo-American Tradition of Self-Help Medicine and Hygiene.* Baltimore.

ROY, OLIVIER. 2004. *Globalised Islam: The Search for the New Ummah.* London.

SACKMANN, M. 1988. 'Fleischhygienische Verordnungen im Alten Testament', *Deutsche Tierartzliche Wochenschrift*, 95: 451–3.

SAUERESSIG, H. 1974. 'Literatur und Medizin. Zu Thomas Manns Roman *Der Zauberberg*', *Deutsche Medizinische Wochenschrift*, 99: 1780–6.

'Schächten.' 1927–30. In Georg Herlitz and Bruno Kirschner, eds., *Jüdisches Lexikon*, 4(2), 134–7. Berlin.

SCHLIESSER, T. 1974. 'Die Bekämpfung der Rindertuberkulose—"Tierversuch" der Vergangenheit', *Praxis der Pneumologie*, 28 (supplement): 870–4.

SCHOPENHAUER, ARTHUR. 2000. *Parerga and Paralipomena: A Collection of Philosophical Essays*, ed. E. F. J. Payne, vol. ii, pp. 324–95. Oxford.

VIALLES, NOËLIE. 1994. *Animal to Edible*, trans. J. A. Underwood. Cambridge.

VON SCHWARTZ, ERNST. 1905. *Das Betäubungslose Schächten der Israeliten.* Konstanz.

WEICHMANN, FRIEDRICH. 1899. *Das Schächten (das rituelle Schlachten bei den Juden).* Leipzig.

WELCH, DAVID. 1983. *Propaganda and the German Cinema 1933–45.* Oxford.

WHITE, ELLEN. 1946. *Counsels on Food and Diet.* Washington, DC.

WOLF, LUCIEN. 1884. 'What Is Judaism? A Question of To-Day', *Fortnightly Review*, ns, 36: 237–56.

WOOD, THOMAS BARLOW. 1925. *The Jewish Method of Slaughtering Animals for Food.* London.

ZWEIG, ARNOLD. 1914. *Ritualmord in Ungarn. Jüdische Tragödie in fünf Aufzügen.* Berlin.

THIRTEEN

The Bureaucratization of Ritual Innovation: The Festive Cycle of the American Soviet Jewry Movement

SHAUL KELNER

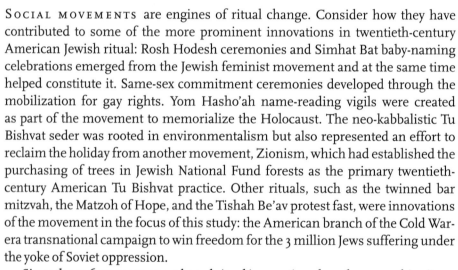

SOCIAL MOVEMENTS are engines of ritual change. Consider how they have contributed to some of the more prominent innovations in twentieth-century American Jewish ritual: Rosh Hodesh ceremonies and Simhat Bat baby-naming celebrations emerged from the Jewish feminist movement and at the same time helped constitute it. Same-sex commitment ceremonies developed through the mobilization for gay rights. Yom Hasho'ah name-reading vigils were created as part of the movement to memorialize the Holocaust. The neo-kabbalistic Tu Bishvat seder was rooted in environmentalism but also represented an effort to reclaim the holiday from another movement, Zionism, which had established the purchasing of trees in Jewish National Fund forests as the primary twentieth-century American Tu Bishvat practice. Other rituals, such as the twinned bar mitzvah, the Matzoh of Hope, and the Tishah Be'av protest fast, were innovations of the movement in the focus of this study: the American branch of the Cold War-era transnational campaign to win freedom for the 3 million Jews suffering under the yoke of Soviet oppression.

Since the 1960s, movement-based ritual innovations have become ubiquitous in American Judaism. The proliferation of cause-oriented seders is indicative. In 1968 a pioneering 'symbolic seder for Soviet Jews' was conducted on the streets of Manhattan, the first of many that would be held over the course of two decades.[1] A year later, in the basement of an African American church in Washington, DC, Arthur Waskow gave ritual expression to the politics of the New Left in his famous Freedom Seder. Within two years of Waskow's seder, a haggadah with feminist themes had been created in the Pacific Northwest, and by 1974 the practice of women's seders had been established in major Jewish population centres on both coasts. Since then, the list of cause-oriented niche seders has expanded to include environmentalist seders, Stonewall seders for gay rights, and vegetarian seders for 'liberated lambs', to name but a few. Meanwhile, readings and rituals have been created for insertion into home seders by supporters of the Israeli peace movement and by opponents of human trafficking, of South African apartheid, and of the various genocides of the past two decades (Staub 2002: 163–7; Zylberberg 2006: 52–3, 117).

How are we to account for the fact that so much ritual innovation has taken place in so many different movements and in so many similar yet diverse ways during the short span of time from the late 1960s to the present? How, in other words, should scholars interested in the revisioning of Jewish ritual account for the meteoric rise, in late twentieth-century American Judaism, of instances of ritual revisioning attached to political causes?

At present, the dominant paradigm for thinking about these questions emerges from scholarship on Jewish feminism. Studies of ritual innovation in this context have emphasized its roots in the movement's content, namely, Jewish feminism's focus on critiquing and reforming a patriarchal Jewish religion (Grant 2007; Myers 2007; Ochs 2007a, 2007b). We could generalize from the Jewish feminist case to argue that in identity movements that make Judaism the target of their change efforts, ritual revisioning should be understood as an end in itself. Certainly, part of the reason that we have seen the proliferation of movement-based ritual innovations over the past half-century is that movements that are explicitly concerned with identity work (including the movement to give religious affirmation to the life experiences of gays and lesbians, and the campaigns to instil an environmental habitus or various forms of a social justice habitus) have increased in number, size, and strength.

Yet to say that some movements make ritual revisioning an end in itself is hardly to answer our question. Such an explanation speaks only to movements of a certain type, and, more importantly, it neglects questions of process. To the extent that analysts have contemplated the processes of ritual creation in Jewish feminism, they have generally identified the locus of innovation in the unleashing of creativity among newly empowered individuals who have come 'to see themselves as having the agency to dream up new or refreshed rituals' (Ochs 2007a: 43). Thrust to the margins in such readings, however, is the consideration of the collective, institutionalized processes that have been crucial in structuring ritual production.[2]

The development of a calendrical cycle of protest rituals in the American movement to free Soviet Jews serves is a case in point whose examination will enable us to focus needed attention on the role of social movement organizations in the proliferation of cause-based ritual revisioning. This will reveal a process of innovation that was as much a product of institutional learning as of individual creativity, and that was driven as much by organizational routines as by activists' ideologies. Social movement organizations were much more than popularizers of new rituals. They functioned in a profound way as key sites of knowledge production where activists revisioned not merely particular rites but the entire category of ritual altogether. It was through the strategic, tactical, and operational work of movement organizations that activists clarified and refined their burgeoning realization that Jewish rituals were objects that could and should be revisioned for use as agents of political mobilization.[3]

Ultimately, it was the creation of a new understanding of ritual that made the proliferation of its movement-based innovative application possible. The reason was simple: the ability to put ritual to political use depended first and foremost on the ability to conceive of it as a thing to be put to political use. Although we might take this for granted today, it is precisely the generation of this knowledge that needs to be examined, for the 'discovery' of ritual as an instrument represented an innovation in its time.

This way of thinking about ritual did not exist fully formed prior to its use. Jews had been playing with the plasticity of ritual for generations, sometimes to make political statements,[4] but these piecemeal acts did not come anywhere near the systematic and even bureaucratized efforts in which twentieth-century activists in the American Soviet Jewry movement scrutinized ritual after ritual to identify ways whereby each could be moulded into a means of mass mobilization. There had, of course, been revolutionary groups in the past that had worked systematically to develop political ritual. The French republicans and the Bolsheviks, with their new calendars and holidays, are perhaps the best known. The Zionists, with their socialist revisioning of the Jewish agricultural festivals and their nationalist reinterpretation of Hanukah, may have been the most familiar to the American Jewish activists I study here. These historical precedents do not imply an unbroken chain of transmission, however, and it seems difficult to argue that the American Jewish activists' awareness of the instrumental potential of rituals was simply the application of a timeless, universal knowledge. Rather, I will present evidence of a process of unfolding in which knowledge about ritual developed gradually over a period of several years, beginning in the mid-1960s as American Jewish activists experimented with mobilization tactics, refined them, and extended them.

Ritual as an Instrument

Any satisfactory attempt to account for the extensive ritual creativity within American Judaism over the past half-century must confront the phenomenon's roots in politicized movements for social change. Yet canonical approaches to the interpretation of ritual are of little help in this. Anthropologists and sociologists typically treat ritual as a summarizing and encapsulating cultural performance that they can use as a key 'to unlock the unconscious workings of a culture' (Markowitz 1988: 129–30). This sort of interpretative approach will tell us little, however, about the dynamics of ritual innovation among self-aware political actors who quite consciously manipulate cultural symbols and practices as a means of accomplishing clearly defined political goals. This genre of ritual creation began emerging in force during the 1960s, and characterizes much of American Jewish ritual revisioning to the present day. Consider, for example, two of the holiday-centred campaigns and cause-oriented rituals of the new millennium's first decade: the production by Jewish Funds for Justice, in 2007, of 'Are Our Doors Still Open?' immigration-rights posters for hanging in American sukkahs, and the Coalition on the Environment and Jewish Life's promotion, in the same year, of a 'Light Among the Nations' bulb-changing Hanukah ceremony to install environment-friendly compact fluorescents.[5] Ritual innovations such as these begin as more or less systematically planned tactics of strategic mobilization. It is not ritual as a creation of the soul striving for expression, but ritual instrumentalized, deployed by Jewish social movement organizations as a means of accomplishing the indispensable but prosaic tasks of recruiting participants, building commitment, and garnering public attention.

This is not to say that the rituals hold no emotional or symbolically resonant meaning for those whom they engage. Indeed, even as activists think of the category of ritual in instrumental terms, they may well recognize that the deeper value of movement-initiated rituals derives from their ability to advance the more profound cultural work of imagining and realizing new socio-political identities.[6] Cultural analysts would probably deem this aspect of movement rituals to be the most worthy of study because it engages the question of what the rituals mean to the people who enact them, and thereby conforms to common presuppositions that ritual matters because it somehow expresses a social groups' core values. Yet it would be a mistake to dismiss the instrumental uses or relegate them to second-class status for being 'merely technical'. On the contrary, the introduction of a means–end calculus that treats ritual as something to be applied instrumentally to accomplish even the seemingly mundane tasks of raising awareness and recruiting adherents is the unique insight that distinguishes movement-based ritual innovation as a separate category. It is this conscious, systematic, deliberate instrumentalization that demands an accounting, so at odds is it with standard paradigms that understand ritual only as cultural performance, so crucial is it for changes afoot in contemporary American Judaism, and so problematic does it become for those who would apply it.

The problems are inherent. The power of ritual as a vehicle for political mobilization derives from its capacity to reframe the definitions of a situation, to take what might otherwise be thought of as secular politics and to generate a sense that there is transcendent meaning in the political act (Kelner 2008; Prell 2007; Szerszynski 2002). Yet the revisioning of Jewish rituals for conscription into the service of a cause always threatens to proclaim itself a profanation, simply because it entails the transformation of an end in itself into a means to some other end. The deployment of ritual therefore inevitably runs the risk of undermining the notion of sanctity that is the very source of its utility to those who would deploy it.

Of all the American Jewish social movements that have revisioned ritual into a strategic resource for use in political mobilization, the one in which this strategy has appeared at its most routinized, systematized, and bureaucratized—that is, the one in which the means–end calculus underlying the expressive practice has been the least obscured, and therefore the one that most clearly exposes the potentially 'profaning' character of the enterprise—has been the American branch of the transnational movement to redeem Soviet Jews, referred to here as the American Soviet Jewry movement (ASJM).

Active from 1963 to 1991, the ASJM became well known for its flurry of activity surrounding Passover. The movement adopted the Exodus story as its core metaphor, analogizing the plight of the Jews under the Kremlin to the plight of the Hebrews under Pharaoh, and invoking the exodus of the ancient slaves as a prefiguration of the hoped-for exodus of the Jewish victims of Soviet communism. Hence the movement's *cri de cœur*, 'Let my people go!' Connecting movement themes with the symbols, practices, and narrative of the Festival of Freedom, activists staged protest seders outside Soviet diplomatic offices, added a 'matzoh of hope' to home seders, marched through metaphorical Red Seas in Passover demonstrations, and more. In so far as they successfully negotiated the tensions inherent in the instrumentalization of ritual, they helped legitimize protest on behalf of oppressed Jews by framing it as consonant with, and even mandated by, traditional Jewish principles.

In spite of the attention that the American Soviet Jewry movement lavished on Passover, it was not the only holiday that it put to use for mobilization purposes. By 1968, four years after the first ASJM advocacy groups had been established in the United States, bureaucratized movement organizations were advocating in writing that the Jewish holiday calendar be employed to structure the campaign into an annual cycle with seasonal rhythms that would ebb and flow and allow the movement to sustain interest through recurring variations on its themes. The institutions that made these recommendations also acted to carry them out. The processes that occurred in the ASJM can be found in other Jewish movements of the same era, including feminism, but in the activism for Soviet Jews they were rationalized and institutionalized to a much greater degree than in the other movements.

After briefly introducing the American branch of the transnational mobilization for Soviet Jews, I will turn to an examination of the movement's use of the Jewish holiday calendar to structure its annual cycle, addressing the various ritual innovations that emerged out of this. My analysis highlights four action plans prepared by ASJM co-ordinating bodies from 1968 to 1981, all of which made concrete recommendations for structuring movement activities according to the rhythm of the Jewish ritual calendar, and all of which exemplify the organizational processes that led to the institutionalization of ritual innovation within the movement. I then draw out the implications of this to offer an explanation for the rapid expansion of cause-oriented rituals in late twentieth-century American Judaism. At the centre of this account will be the issue of knowledge production, and the revisioning this entailed, not only of the known object, ritual, but also of the knowing subjects, American Jews themselves.

Historical Background: American Jews and the Transnational Mobilization for Soviet Jewry

The persecution of Soviet Jews was unlike the Nazi persecution in that it did not seek physical annihilation through mass slaughter. Rather, the USSR pursued an insidious policy of cultural genocide that combined discrimination against Jewish citizens with an evisceration of the institutional framework necessary for sustaining their culture. Jewish leadership was eliminated through harassment, arrest, and sometimes assassination. Schools, synagogues, seminaries, theatres, publishing houses, and newspapers were shut down entirely, save for the token few that were left to facilitate the regime's surveillance of the Jewish population and to refute accusations of official antisemitism. Judaism itself was subjected to vilification in state-run media, workplaces, and schools. The possession of religious artefacts and Yiddish books was treated as anti-Soviet activity and made grounds for arrest, as was the teaching of Hebrew. Although Soviet Jews could not express their Jewishness, neither could they escape it. Anti-Jewish restrictions, not openly declared as such, limited their access to the educational system and their advancement in the workplace. They were trapped in this discriminatory environment by tight controls on emigration. Those who nevertheless sought to leave the USSR often found that this brought the weight of the Soviet bureaucracy down upon them, costing them their jobs, their homes, and more.

The movement first to ameliorate the condition of Soviet Jews and later to free them was transnational in character. It had three branches: one among Jews in the USSR itself, one in Israel, where in the 1950s a clandestine government agency, Nativ, was established to work on the Soviet Jews' behalf, and one in the countries of the Western diaspora. A Nativ operation named Bar, headed by Nehemiah Levanon (who would later take the helm of Nativ), was charged with setting in motion the campaign in the West. There had been little sustained action there prior to the 1960s, but Bar's work in Europe and North America helped to raise awareness of the issue and also to prompt the creation of organizations like the American Jewish Conference on Soviet Jewry. The AJCSJ was established by twenty-four prominent American Jewish organizations in April 1964 as an ad hoc co-ordinating body. The Conference's day-to-day activities were run out of the offices of the National Jewish Community Relations Advisory Council (NJCRAC; another umbrella organization which co-ordinated Jewish communal positions on public policy matters), under the direction of staffers Henry

Siegman (1964–5), Albert Chernin (1965–8), and Abraham Bayer (1968–71). In 1971 the AJCSJ was reorganized as the National Conference for Soviet Jewry (NCSJ), this time with its own budget, offices, and full-time staff, including executive director Jerry Goodman (1971–89).[7]

In a conflict over goals and tactics, the 'establishment' AJCSJ and NJCRAC were almost immediately pitted against 'grassroots' organizations that were then forming in North America. The New York-based Student Struggle for Soviet Jewry (SSSJ), which introduced the ritualized forms of protest that the AJCSJ would later advocate, was launched, also in April 1964, by a British immigrant named Jacob Birnbaum (Orbach 1979: 22–35). He argued that 'a "Conference" could not be a substitute for a great international struggle'.[8] Other grassroots organizations were created by local activists in Cleveland, Los Angeles, San Francisco, south Florida, and Washington, DC. These banded together in 1970 to create the Union of Councils for Soviet Jews (UCSJ), under the leadership of Louis Rosenblum. Over the next twenty years, the UCSJ expanded its membership to include over thirty affiliated councils in the United States, Canada, Europe, Israel, and, towards the end of the Gorbachev years, the Soviet Union (Naftalin 1999: 230, 234). Other groups, such as the Thirty-Fives in the United Kingdom and Canada, also played a prominent role in grassroots action.

In the late 1960s, as Soviet Jews themselves became more vocal in opposing the Kremlin's anti-Jewish policies, the mobilization in North America and Europe followed suit. Mass demonstrations that had drawn tens of thousands in the 1960s began drawing hundreds of thousands in the 1970s. Three world conferences on Soviet Jewry brought activists together in Brussels and later in Jerusalem. The movement also began experiencing important successes. It saw the Soviet government relax emigration restrictions from 1971 to 1974, and commute the death sentences handed down to the Jewish defendants in the Leningrad hijacking show trials. The United States Congress passed legislation in 1975 making American trade concessions dependent on freedom of exit for Soviet Jews (Lazin 2005). Eventually, this helped the campaign achieve its goals of freedom of Jewish cultural expression and freedom of exit. During and after the series of events that culminated in the 1991 collapse of the Soviet Union, over one million Jews left the USSR and its successor states. Approximately three-quarters of these emigrants settled in Israel.[9]

Mobilizing the Jewish Calendar

Ritual transformation was occurring in the American Soviet Jewry movement almost from the outset. It figured prominently in the April 1965 Jericho March held in Manhattan by the Student Struggle for Soviet Jewry. Passover would begin less than two weeks later, but SSSJ chose not to employ the symbolism of that holiday. Preferring Joshua to Moses, it placed seven rabbis, robed in prayer shawls and carrying Torah scrolls, and seven students with shofars at the front of a crowd of 3,000. The seven shofars were sounded seven times. Then the demonstrators proceeded to encircle the Soviet UN mission.[10] The Passover Youth Protest/ Geulah (Redemption) March, sponsored by a twenty-two-group coalition in New York a year later and involving 12,000 participants, mixed its ritual metaphors, combining 'Jericho-style' encircling with a 'symbolic re-enactment of the Crossing of the Red Sea' and the kindling of an eternal flame.[11] Such Passover demonstrations appropriated a hodgepodge of Jewish ritual practices from traditional contexts, and recombined them syncretistically with elements common in Western political demonstrations.

Between 1965 and 1967, festival-related campaigns across the United States had been organized to coincide with Passover, Hanukah, and Simhat Torah. For Passover 1966, the American Jewish Conference on Soviet Jewry launched its Matzoh of Oppression campaign. This was reintroduced as the Matzoh of Hope a year later, after 'a technical subcommittee' decided that 'changing circumstances', such as the increased availability of matzah in the Soviet Union, warranted a more forward-looking name.[12] Through synagogue bulletins, advertisements in the New York Times, and radio spots featuring the well-known Jewish American film actor Edward G. Robinson, the AJCSJ urged American Jews to introduce into their Passover seders a new ritual in which they would set aside an extra matzah to recall the plight of the Jews of the USSR. An accompanying booklet was produced, of which almost 1 million copies were circulated.[13] During Hanukah in 1965, the SSSJ marked the opening of its winter campaign with a Menorah March, in which a 12 ft × 8 ft, 200 lb Hanukah candelabrum was paraded at the front of a torchlit procession.[14] For its part, the AJCSJ prepared a statement similar to that of the Matzoh of Hope to be read when lighting Hanukah candles at home.[15] The first Simhat Torah demonstrations held outside the USSR were organized in 1967 in two American cities. Two years later they were being conducted in forty-nine cities in the United States, in seven cities in Canada, and also in London and Buenos Aires.[16]

What distinguished the ASJM's revisioning of Jewish ritual was not simply the fact that its activists had used these holidays for instrumental ends, but that in so doing they gradually realized that the Jewish ritual calendar could serve as a mechanism for structuring the campaign along a pattern of cyclical, rather than linear, time. As this realization took hold, organizations that had conducted ad hoc holiday-related activities during the early years began calling for a systematized approach that was, at least in theory, to be co-ordinated horizontally across the movement's organizations and integrated vertically into a coherent annual campaign cycle.[17] The use of the Jewish calendar helped establish the temporal rhythm of the movement's efforts. It provided seasonally variable thematic links that helped sustain interest by keeping the movement fresh and topical. Further, it lent credence to the notion, also conveyed through each individual ritual adaptation, that the mobilization was not simply political in character but was, more broadly, an expression of Jewish religious values. The movement thus helped construct an American Jewish mode of acting in and on the world—that is, a subjectivity—that defined ethnic activism as an act of transcendent significance and of sacred Jewish affirmation (Kelner 2008).

Beginning in the late 1960s and continuing throughout the 1980s, written calls to adopt a comprehensive approach to holiday-related campaigns appeared in the programmatic statements of national and local organizations. Meeting in New York City in April 1968 for its biennial conference, the umbrella AJCSJ adopted eighty-seven recommendations for mobilizing various constituencies. Addressing first the mobilization of the Jewish community, the document opened with the pronouncement that 'Special efforts should be made to *project a long-range calendar* for community action to be concerted as part of overall national demonstrations.' The first four recommendations used the holiday cycle to define the movement's calendar structure. Simhat Torah 1968 was to be a time for mass demonstrations of solidarity with Soviet Jewish youth, including 'Hakafot, when feasible out in the street'. Passover 1969 was to be greeted with a 'massive' automobile caravan as well as vigils, protest seders, and the Matzoh of Hope. The High Holy Days were to be treated as occasions for reciting a special prayer for Soviet Jewry. Hanukah would inaugurate a week of activities including some associated with Human Rights Day, 10 December, the anniversary of the United Nations' ratification of the Universal Declaration of Human Rights.[18]

By 1971 the elaboration of a movement calendar structured around the Jewish holiday cycle had achieved greater sophistication. In that year two organizations, one local and one national, recommended action plans that itemized their suggested activities holiday by holiday. In both instances, the legacy of the AJCSJ was in evidence. The Philadelphia Jewish Community Relations Council (PJCRC), which produced one of the action guides, was headed at the time by Albert Chernin, who had left his position as head of the AJCSJ in July 1968 to assume the directorship of the PJCRC (the production of the guide itself was most likely under the purview of the PJCRC professional then responsible for the Soviet Jewry campaign, Maurice Corson, a Conservative rabbi). At the National Jewish Community Relations Advisory Council, which produced the other programme guide, AJCSJ director Abraham Bayer continued to serve as the contact person on Soviet Jewry issues even after the disbanding of the AJCSJ.

Many of the recommendations in the action calendars circulated by the PJCRC and by the NJCRAC had already been implemented. These co-ordinating agencies were attempting to compile and synthesize information about what was being done, and then systematize and extend it for broader use. This was indicative of their general approach to the utilization of holiday rituals, which emphasized the diffusion of others' innovations more than innovation of their own. Especially at the national level, the establishment umbrella organizations tended not to develop independent ideas for holiday programmes (the AJCSJ's Matzoh of Hope being an important exception). Rather, they served as clearing-houses, using their power as information brokers to collect and disseminate information about creative programming in local communities (often initiated by grassroots groups), and using their position of authority to encourage the replication of these programmes elsewhere. This approach still persisted a decade later when, in 1981, the NJCRAC and the AJCSJ's successor, the National Conference on Soviet Jewry, collaborated on another holiday-based mobilization calendar.[19]

The Holiday Cycle of the Protest Movement for Soviet Jewry

Reviewing the four mobilization calendars of the AJCSJ, PJCRC, NJCRAC, and NCSJ alongside other documentary records of holiday-related protests enables us to sketch the ritualized protest cycle that American Soviet Jewry movement organizations used to structure their activities into a predictable, recurring annual campaign.

The Days of Awe

In spite of the importance of Passover in ASJM campaigns, and despite the fact that the first day of the month of Nisan, during which Passover falls, is traditionally counted as one of the four New Year's Days in the Jewish calendar, none of the four action plans treated the spring season as the starting point for the movement's annual cycle. Instead, their holiday-based calendars all began with Rosh Hashanah. Philadelphia's JCRC suggested that the *seliḥot* period of penitential prayer that leads up to the High Holidays be used for dedicating special programmes to the plight of Soviet Jewry. However, it did not specify what these might be or how they might relate to themes associated with the *seliḥot* prayers.[20] Suggested ritual adaptations for Rosh Hashanah and Yom Kippur (always treated as a unit) began with the call for special prayers and sermons. A typical example of such a prayer is found in a small blue card printed in Hebrew and English for Yom Kippur in 1971 by the Baltimore Committee for Soviet Jewry. Invoking the *Eleh ezkerah* martyrology traditionally recited on the Day of Atonement, the prayer 'recall[s] our heroes and martyrs of old, saintly men and women of our people who gave their lives for sanctification of Thy Name', and prays 'on behalf of their modern counterparts, our valiant brothers and sisters residing within the Soviet Union'.[21]

The call for prayers and sermons is perhaps not surprising in light of the central place synagogue worship plays in the observance of the Days of Awe. Even so, the holidays are not devoid of ritualized practices involving material culture. One of the striking things about the ASJM's High Holiday campaigns is the absence, at least in these instances, of a specific call to revision its traditional shofar rituals. Considering that the shofar had already been widely deployed in street protests, one wonders whether this absence was the result of a conscious decision (which could imply contestation surrounding the use of ritual as a mobilization device) or a failure of imagination.

Although it did not co-opt the material culture of the synagogue service, the ASJM did attempt to politicize the practice of sending New Year's greeting cards before Rosh Hashanah (on this custom, see Joselit 1994: 247–52). Grassroots groups like the UCSJ and the SSSJ, local establishment organizations like the Jewish federations in Springfield, Massachusetts, and Washington, DC, and national umbrella organizations like the AJCSJ all engaged in producing and disseminating holiday greeting cards to be mailed to Jews in the Soviet Union. The iconography on the cards referred to Zionism, Jewish historical consciousness and pride, and Holocaust memory. One card reproduced the 1958 'Israel liberata' state medal next to the ancient Roman 'Judaea capta' coin whose imagery it reversed (notably, however, it changed the Latin phrase 'Israel liberata' to 'Judaea renata', presumably less of an affront to the anti-Zionism of Soviet authorities). Another displayed the Arch of Titus beside the Hebrew words *am yisra'el ḥai* ('the Jewish people lives'). Some displayed portraits of prominent Zionist and non-Zionist Jewish men, such as Herzl, Disraeli, Peretz, Einstein, Spinoza, and Bialik. Others evoked places such as the Western Wall and Babi Yar. Then there were those that opted for more universalistic iconography, such as a dove, suggesting peace.[22]

The greeting cards often came with pre-printed texts in Russian, Hebrew, and English. Others, blank on the inside, were distributed in packets that contained an insert listing suggested messages and showing how to write them in Hebrew and Cyrillic characters. All of these typically included New Year's greetings and a generalized message of Jewish solidarity and support:

L'Shanah Tovah Tikatavu!
Happy New Year!
From the Jews of the U.S.A.
To the Jews of the U.S.S.R.
We have not forgotten you.
And we will not forget you![23]

Ḥazak, ḥazak veniṯḥazek
[Be strong, be strong, and we will grow stronger][24]

Cards were available for purchase from ASJM organizations, which also made recommendations about how they should be used. An August 1970 AJCSJ memo encouraging member organizations to purchase cards in bulk or produce their own noted that the likelihood of a response was minimal and that whether the cards would be delivered was 'impossible to predict', but that nevertheless, 'we feel the project can have merit' as long as certain caveats were borne in mind:

(a) That no cards be sent to private individuals in the Soviet Union who are not personally known to the sender.

(b) Messages should not be political and certainly not anti-Soviet.

(c) Cards should have art which portray [sic] themes of Jewish culture and education—items unavailable to Jews in the Soviet Union.[25]

The AJCSJ's concern that sending cards to individual Soviet Jews might mark them for government persecution led it to recommend that greeting cards be sent only to synagogues, and accordingly it provided the addresses of these institutions. Taking the view that the practice could serve not only an expressive purpose for American Jews, but also an instrumental goal for their Soviet Jewish recipients, the grassroots Union of Councils would later recommend that the Rosh Hashanah greetings be sent specifically to individual refuseniks, arguing that 'your card will afford them some measure of protection, since the Soviets hesitate to persecute those widely known to people in the Western world'. Intended to be received by individuals, the cards they produced included Jewish holiday calendars and the Hebrew alphabet with the names of the letters transliterated into Cyrillic characters along with a pronunciation guide.[26]

Sukkot and Simhat Torah

Programme guides made few suggestions for the systematic adoption of the rituals and material culture of Sukkot, although some demonstrators in an October 1969 SSSJ rally in New York marched with the palm branches of the *lulav* in hand.[27] Rather, the major effort of the autumn (Tishrei) holiday cycle was focused on Simhat Torah. The choice of this holiday as the centre of activity came neither from its themes nor from its place in American Jewish culture. Rather, it was a result of the transnational character of the movement. Simhat Torah had been a time of Jewish self-assertion in the USSR since at least the 1950s, both in the synagogues and in the gulags. By the mid-1960s, it had become a rallying point for the rising Jewish national movement there, particularly among the youth (Ro'i 1991). Aware of the role the holiday was assuming inside the Soviet Union, activists throughout the West began conducting Simhat Torah rallies of their own as an expression of solidarity. As mentioned, the first of these took place in the United States in 1967 and the practice quickly spread around the world. In Britain, *The Times* offered a colourful, albeit orientalized, report of the 1968 London rally, conveying some of the flavour of the ritualized protests that had quickly become the norm for Simhat Torah rallies.

A sinuous torchlit procession, led by a man bearing a trumpet of rams horn [sic], wound its spectacular way through London late last night to the Soviet Embassy. Naked flames shook their fire into the night sky of Notting Hill . . . Outside the Embassy, the man blew a mighty 10 second blast on the Shofar, the trumpet which is as old as Abraham and which Joshua used to blow down the walls of Jericho; a high pitched eerie Old Testament noise, wild and shrill . . . The demonstrators stood in silent vigil and then doused their torches into blackness as a gesture of bitterness that the flame of Jewishness can only burn in Russia on one evening in the year. (Howard 1968)

As the use of the shofar waned in later years, the ritualized dimensions of Simhat Torah protests were increasingly confined to the holiday's traditional practice of *hakafot* (parading and dancing with the Torah scrolls). An AJCSJ publicity booklet celebrating the 1969 Simhat Torah demonstrations included photographs of protestors dancing with Torah scrolls in London and Montreal, as well as in Harrisburg, Pennsylvania, and Portland, Oregon. Calls for special *hakafot* and *aliyot* (blessings over the Torah reading) appeared in the action programmes of the AJCSJ, NJCRAC, and PJCRC, often specifying that these were to be dedicated to Soviet Jewish youth.[28] Whereas the Passover mobilization emphasized exodus from oppression, and the Rosh Hashanah activities revolved around the theme of remembrance, the Simhat Torah rituals focused on solidarity, youth, and the choice of vocal public activism over quiet diplomacy.

Hanukah

When suggesting ways to enlist Hanukah in the Soviet Jewry cause, the commissions and committees disseminating programme plans identified four aspects of the holiday suitable for co-option: its temporal structure, its temporal proximity to another commemoration, its presumed themes, and its ritual practices. 'The week long celebration . . . is an opportunity for a week of community programming', an NJCRAC memo declared in 1981. Philadelphia's JCRC had made a similar point a decade earlier: 'Each night a section of the city might sponsor a special program on the theme of Soviet Jewry.' Although Passover and Sukkot also lasted eight days, no such recommendations were made in those instances.[29] One could speculate that this was because the temporal rhythm of Hanukah was perceived differently from the rhythms of the other two holidays. In the case of Passover and Sukkot, the *yom tov–ḥol hamo'ed–yom tov* (festival–intermediate day–festival) bookend structure divided the eight days of the holiday into three multi-day periods (or two, if the second *yom tov* was not observed, as was common among non-Orthodox Jews).[30] By contrast, aside from the addition of the 'Sheheḥeyanu' prayer at candle-lighting on the first night of Hanukah, there was no distinction in Jewish law that would establish a different status for the various days of the holiday. Hanukah time was of a uniform rather than heterogeneous character. Moreover, the traditional Hanukah practice of candle-lighting served as a way of counting the eight-day passage of this uniform time. The combination of lit candles and empty spaces (or unlit candles) in the menorah each night marked both the time that had passed and the time that remained. Conceiving of Hanukah as a sequence of eight distinct but otherwise equivalent days, movement activists recommended an eight-day sequence of programming.

I should add a point of clarification. The failure of ASJM activists to treat Sukkot and Passover like Hanukah and to portray them as opportunities for eight-day campaigns only implies that these holidays *were not* so conceived, not that they *could not* be so conceived. In fact, the conception of mobilizable time that guided the ASJM's approach to Hanukah was later applied to Sukkot by the Jewish feminist movement. It too drew upon a traditional ritual practice that established the experience of time within the holiday. Sukkot's *ushpizin* ritual of symbolically welcoming a different male biblical hero into the sukkah each day as a guest overlaid the holiday's otherwise tripartite temporal rhythm with an eight-day linear flow. Co-opting this practice, the feminist movement introduced an *ushpizot* ritual, whose honoured guests would be great Jewish women, a different one each day (Kustanowitz 1999).

In addition to recommending eight days of events, the ASJM's suggestions for the utilization of Hanukah also built on the proximity of another commemorative occasion, Human Rights Day. The advocacy of a strong international human rights regime had become a cornerstone of the foreign policy conducted by American Jewish non-governmental organizations (NGOs) at the United Nations and in other international forums (Galchinsky 2007). Because these NGOs were also involved in the domestic coalitions working on behalf of Soviet Jews, the movement's attention to Human Rights Day was in large measure a reflection of the pre-existing organizational cultures of the AJCSJ's constituent agencies. In the minds of activists, the proximity of Human Rights Day to Hanukah 'extend[ed] the possibilities for programs'.[31] Specific linkages could be highlighted from year to year as the situation warranted. For example, in 1968, the AJCSJ called on its members to hold a 'special Sabbath for Soviet Jewry' on the weekend of 13–15 December 'to inaugurate a week of activity . . . geared to Hanukah and Human Rights Day . . . Such activity should remind the public of [Soviet Premier Aleksey] Kosygin's unfulfilled promise of December 3, 1966 on family reunion.' By linking Hanukah with Human Rights Day, not only could the movement engage American Jews but it could also make a more universalistic appeal to other communities.[32]

The recommendations for holiday-related activities were also guided by particular notions of Hanukah's themes. 'This holiday offers many opportunities to relate to the problem of Soviet Jewry inasmuch as it marks the flight [*sic*] for religious freedom', the PJCRC's programme guide announced.[33] The fighting aspect of the Soviet Jewish cause was alluded to in the Freedom Lights rally at Madison Square Garden in 1971, where 20,000 people participated and where actor and stage personality Theodore Bikel performed some of the resistance songs that were circulating among Soviet Jews at the time (Spiegel 1971). The chronicling of specific acts of Soviet discrimination against the Jewish religion was a regular feature of speakers' addresses at Hanukah rallies. But in contrast to Passover's narrative, which strongly constrained how the movement framed the Soviet

Jewish plight in the mobilization efforts surrounding that holiday, the Hanukah story functioned as a much looser organizing framework. Calls for emigration went hand in hand with calls for free religious expression. Moreover, the Hanukah narrative was supplemented by other orienting metaphors. For instance, a 1966 Hanukah rally in New York veered sharply away from an exclusive focus on the notion of a Maccabean fight for religious freedom. Organizers chose not only to invoke as an interpretative frame the UN's Human Rights Day (which had fallen one day earlier) but also to appropriate the African American experience— both slavery and the civil rights movement—as an additional guiding metaphor. They decided to hold the rally of 3,000 participants in Cooper Union Hall, where Lincoln had called for an end to slavery in his 'Right Makes Might' speech. Martin Luther King Jr. addressed the assembled participants via telephone, telling them that 'a denial of human rights anywhere is a threat to man everywhere' (*Commentator* 1966; Spiegel 1966b, 1971).

Hanukah's traditional ritual practices surrounding candle-lighting provided cultural material that could be and was transformed into vehicles of protest. The march to Cooper Union Hall included the SSSJ's giant menorah being borne on a platform carried by six men. The Madison Square Garden rally involved the lighting of a menorah and the singing of the liturgical poem 'Ma'oz tsur'. The AJCSJ prepared a text similar to that of the Matzoh of Hope to be read in homes and synagogues when kindling the holiday lights. The NJCRAC attempted to popularize the practice of maintaining an unlit menorah to symbolize the inability of Soviet Jews to observe the holiday freely. Philadelphia's Jewish Community Relations Council recommended that synagogues mail menorahs to synagogues in the USSR. It also suggested that they 'erect electric torches that would be lit outside their buildings on a permanent (or temporary) basis as a reminder of the plight of Soviet Jews'. Interestingly, there were few if any suggestions for ritual adaptations involving other Hanukah practices like playing with a *dreydl*, eating fried foods, and exchanging gifts. Only the menorah rituals were revisioned to any significant extent.[34] Notwithstanding all of these proposed or enacted menorah-centred activities, ritual innovations tended to play only a supporting role in Hanukah protest events. Geared towards a universalistic appeal and non-Jewish constituencies more than any of the other Jewish holiday campaigns, Hanukah protests were more likely to emphasize speeches by politicians, civil rights leaders, and Christian clergy than the deployment of Jewish ritual practices in the public square.[35]

The Tenth of Tevet and the Fifteenth of Shevat

When the authors of the programme guides moved forward from Hanukah in their holiday-based calendars, they skipped directly to Tu Bishvat, overlooking the fast of the Tenth of Tevet. But even this little-appreciated day of commemoration did not go entirely unexploited. Across the Atlantic, it too was enlisted to support the Soviet Jewish cause. In December 1970, shortly after the Soviet government imposed a death sentence on the defendants in the Leningrad hijacking trials, Britain's chief rabbi Immanuel Jakobovits declared the Tenth of Tevet to be a 'day of intercession for Soviet Jewry' (*The Times* 1970). Still, the winter fast did not become an enduring red-letter day on the movement's mobilization calendar. For that matter, neither did Tu Bishvat. Reference to this holiday was absent from the NJCRAC's and AJCSJ's programme guides. The PJCRC devoted only one sentence to it: 'This holiday of Jewish Arbor Day can be used to commemorate Soviet Jews by the planting of trees in Israel in their honor.'[36] Zionism and the struggle to free Soviet Jewry, which converged in so many other ways, did so here, too, in this variation on the JNF-inspired holiday ritual.

Purim

Like Passover and Hanukah, Purim's historical narrative of redemption from oppression served as a cognitive frame through which the plight of Soviet Jews could be interpreted, and by which the contemporaneous situation could be presented as evidence of the enduring validity of paradigmatic Jewish myth. The PJCRC saw in the story of Mordecai and Esther an 'obvious link to Soviet Jews', and suggested that this be 'portrayed by staging carnivals which link the theme of Soviet Jewry to the plight of the Jews in the days of Haman'. There was no indication, at least in the PJCRC's mobilization calendar, that a carnival in and of itself could be used to signify the Kafkaesque character of the Soviet Jewish situation. Rather, the focus remained squarely on the equation with the narrative of the book of Esther and on the instrumental potential for using the carnival as a fundraising tool.[37]

Considering that Jews have a long history of using Purim plays, or *purim-shpiln*, to make timely comments on the politics of the day, it is not surprising that these annually changing rituals found their way into the ASJM's repertoire. Activists used *purimshpiln* to present the situation of Soviet Jews as the contemporary manifestation of a transcendent mytho-historical paradigm.[38] One SSSJ play, *The Megillah of Anatoly Sharansky*, placed Brezhnev in the role of Haman, Avital Sharansky in the role of Esther, and her husband, the famous refusenik Anatoly, in the role of Mordecai—here Esther's lover, not her uncle:

Now it came to pass in the days of King Kremlin, this is King Kremlin who ruled over a hundred and seven and twenty nationalities from the steppes of the Ukraine to the labor camps of Siberia . . .

There was a certain Jew in the capital of Shushan-Moscow, whose name was Mordecai-Anatoly . . . who had been separated from Jerusalem by the cruel and arbitrary decrees of Nebuchadnezzar-OVIR [the Soviet visa office], who had declared that Mordecai-Anatoly somehow possessed secrets of the king . . .

But Haman-Brezhnev . . . created false charges and had Mordechai-Anatoly sentenced to the worst dungeons in the kingdom.

Esther-Avital [said to King Kremlin] . . . 'If you wish détente with the neighboring kingdoms, then you will stop our adversary . . . the wicked Haman-Brezhnev!'

The Megillah of Anatoly Sharansky, performed in 1981, concluded with words that seem striking in retrospect: 'And Mordecai-Anatoly rose unto an advisor to the Prime Minister of Israel, seeking the good of his people and speaking peace to all mankind.'[39]

Passover

Following the well-established tradition of reframing Passover to speak to contemporary political identities (Balin 1999; Gereboff 2003; Kelner 2008; Shuldiner 1999), the spring festival of freedom quickly emerged as the centrepiece of the ASJM's holiday cycle. As Passover-related actions have already been discussed at several points in the previous pages, here I will only note that the use of this festival's rituals tended to be of two types: one brought protest out of the streets and into the home, such as the Matzoh of Hope campaign described above, and the other brought rituals out of the home and into the streets. The most common instances of this second approach were the syncretistic Passover marches described earlier and the so-called Freedom seders. First conducted in 1968, these ceremonies repositioned the Passover meal as a form of street theatre intended to communicate different messages to several different target audiences including the Soviet government, American public opinion, and the American Jewish protestors themselves.[40] Freedom seders were often conducted outside Soviet diplomatic offices. Adapting phrasings from the Haggadah, these protest rituals involved the display of traditional Passover symbols and the recitation of texts that related these to the plight of Soviet Jews. They declared matzah 'the bread of affliction which our ancestors ate in the land of Egypt, and cannot eat in the land of Russia'.[41] Of the bitterness symbolized by *maror* (bitter herbs) they said that 'to Anatoly Sharansky, now in the solitary confinement cells of the Perm labor camp, it's real indeed. As we taste the bitter herbs, his entire life is bitterness.'[42]

Shavuot and the Ninth of Av

Even after the flurry of activism and ritual innovation that accompanied the Passover festival, activists were still urged to do more. The Shavuot custom of the all-night study session, or *tikun leil shavuot*, was invoked to promote the holiday as a time for teach-ins about Soviet Jewish history, culture, and oppression. Also recommended were 'other campus or school related activities appropriate to the traditional devotion of this holiday to study'.[43] The fast of the Ninth of Av fared somewhat better than the fast of the Tenth of Tevet in the consciousness of ASJM activists. The SSSJ made recurring use of Tishah Be'av protest fasts, particularly as a way of highlighting the plight of refuseniks like Anatoly Sharansky.[44]

The Philadelphia JCRC suggested that this day of lamentation could be used to 'commemorate destruction of synagogues in the Soviet Union'.[45]

The AJCSJ, which so often served as a clearing-house for information about local community programming, began recommending the use of Tishah Be'av after it learned of planned protest fasts in Denver and Washington, DC, in 1970. 'Those interested in conducting similar programs will find the enclosed format, schedule of preparations and program of the Denver Committee of assistance', the AJCSJ wrote to its members in late July, leaving insufficient time to organize similar programmes that year but perhaps planting a seed for the future. Denver's multi-day public fast, held on the grounds of the Colorado State Capitol, included speeches, sympathy statements by Christian clergy, study sessions, a commemoration of the anniversary of Stalin's 12 August 1952 execution of prominent Yiddish writers, and a religious service for Tishah Be'av.[46]

The Bureaucratization of Ritual Revisioning

The rhetorical context and style of the programme guides reveal a paradigm of ritual revisioning very different from that emphasized in treatments of feminist ritual creation. Ritual innovations in the ASJM sprang only secondarily from a desire to give public affirmation to a set of value commitments. Their main impetus was the realization that revisioned rituals could be tactically useful in the effort to mobilize the public, to frame issues, and to garner attention. This is not to say that the ceremonies were devoid of expressive function, as we will see. This dimension was hardly in evidence, however, in the texts of the programme guides produced by the AJCSJ, PJCRC, NJCRAC, and NCSJ.

The discovery of ritual as an instrument, and the resultant ability to make revisioning more a tactical than an expressive act may seem both ironic and problematic, inasmuch as it takes that which is typically valued as an end in itself and reconfigures it as a means to an end. Yet evidence that such a discovery indeed occurred—certainly at the level of tacit, practical knowledge and sometimes even at the level of discursive awareness—is found in the very model of ritual innovation that the ASJM applied. This model was not one of devolution of power to creative free agents. Rather, it was a systematized approach that made ritual innovation an object of collective processes of bureaucratic administration. To see this one need only look at the desacralized, utilitarian treatment of ritual in those quintessential bureaucratic products, the organizational memos that were the ASJM programme guides.

Although the guides recommended that Jews engage in activities like special Passover seders and revisioned Hanukah candle-lighting ceremonies, these were only a small part of longer documents that detailed precisely tailored mobilization tactics for a variety of specific constituencies:

Essay contests on the plight of Soviet Jewry should be encouraged for students in Jewish religious schools.

The International Affairs Committee of the AFL-CIO should be encouraged to issue an annual report and survey on world human rights which would give special emphasis to Soviet Jewry.

The Voice of America should continue to be made aware of the value of its presenting, on a sustained basis, various aspects of American Jewish life in its interpretation of the United States as a pluralistic society.[47]

Embedded among the recommendations for mobilizing the labour movement, the academic community, Christian clergy, and others, the call to develop a calendar of Jewish holiday protest was deprived of any special status and was presented as just one more tactic in the movement's diverse and well-stocked arsenal.

The tendency to limit the value of ritual to its ability to serve as an instrument of mobilization was also revealed in language: Tu Bishvat 'can be *used* to commemorate Soviet Jews'. Tishah Be'av 'can be *used* to commemorate destruction of synagogues in the Soviet Union'.[48] The High Holy Day period '*affords an opportunity* to mobilize'.[49] Hanukah, too, '*offers many opportunities* to relate to the problem of Soviet Jewry', as does Passover, which '*offers a wonderful opportunity* to invite in neighboring churches'.[50]

These 'opportunities' for 'using' holidays were presented together as a group, typically in chronological order, which further defined the language of the ASJM's ritual transformation as a strategic rhetoric. Holidays were not considered in isolation or in an ad hoc manner. Rather, each holiday—with its unique narrative hook, adaptable rituals, and opportunity for engaging people in collectively performed actions—was presented as one element of an integrated campaign that would stretch across the calendar year and recur in an annual cycle. To ensure that the point was not lost on those using the programme guides, the authors made this explicit, referring to the lists as 'calendar programs', introducing them with the observation that 'Holidays throughout the year provide opportunities for meaningful expressions on behalf of Soviet Jewry', and recommending that 'each Jewish community develop a calendar providing for the following occasions to be marked by appropriate activities'.[51]

In the suggestion that a calendar of movement activities be developed by 'each Jewish community', we can see yet another way in which the ASJM's revisioning of ritual was shaped by an instrumental orientation. Not only did the authors of the programme guides recommend that holiday-related campaigns be integrated vertically in time, forming a planned sequence of activities that would recur year after year; they also implied that there was value in co-ordinating these actions horizontally across the independently operating communities and organizations. By co-ordination I do not mean control or uniformity. Programme guides consistently spoke of suggestions and recommendations. The PJCRC's guide introduced its list of holiday programmes by noting that 'These ideas are illustrative and congregations are encouraged to develop their own creative approaches in relation to the holiday observances'.[52] Still, the act of producing such documents indicated an awareness that some commonality of practice among the movement's constituent actors could redound to the benefit of the Soviet Jewish cause.

The co-ordination of holiday-related campaigns ended up serving the movement in many ways. Perhaps the least important of these was that in activities where the number of people involved would materially affect the nature of the protest, such as the mailing of Rosh Hashanah greeting cards to Jews in the Soviet Union, it broadened the base of participation. More crucially, co-ordination enhanced the solidarity of the protestors, uniting geographically separated activists into a national movement culture. It multiplied the public relations value of the local actions, repositioning each one as part of a national (and sometimes even global) protest activity. At the same time, it communicated to key target audiences such as the US and Soviet governments that the movement was national (or international) in scope, well co-ordinated, and therefore not to be easily ignored. Within the ASJM itself, co-ordination helped to institutionalize holiday protests as a standard part of the tactical repertoire, a form of routinization that reduced the non-material costs associated with tactical planning and the mobilization of constituents. It also strengthened the position of agencies like the AJCSJ and NCSJ, whose *raison d'être* was to promote and guide a co-ordinated national campaign.

Profaning the Sacred or Sanctifying the Profane?

Itemized in passive-voice bureaucratese under agency letterhead and nestled among suggestions for recruiting labour unions and government radio, the recommendations of programme guides for ritual revisioning appeared as sterile instructions, one set of tools among many to be applied rationally to attain strategic ends. Absent from these memos was any indication that this revisioning project had dimensions that transcended the utilitarian. That such dimensions existed is undeniable. Indeed, they were integral both to ASJM activists' rationales for deploying ritual and to their ability to do so successfully. Yet even with this, the notion that revisioning might be governed even in part by instrumental considerations had the potential to make such a use of ritual problematic both for those deploying it and for those whom it was designed to engage. The desacralization inherent in any 'tactical revisioning' represents an internal contradiction in the practice, which threatens to undermine its very rationale. Desacralization denudes the rituals of the aura of sanctity that is the source of their power as symbols of protest and as motivational agents. Desacralized, ritual innovation risks becoming counter-productive and demobilizing if the application of a means–end calculus to ritual is perceived as an act of bad faith.

If Soviet Jewry movement activists needed an object lesson in the critical reception of movement-based ritual innovation, they need only have looked to the outcry against Arthur Waskow's 1969 interracial Freedom Seder, which was denounced by opponents of the New Left as a profanation of the holy Passover rite (Staub 2002: 172–5, 192). This denunciation, however, had more to do with conservative opposition to the particular political stance Waskow was adopting in his seder than with a principled rejection of the political use of ritual altogether. ASJM activists never faced similar condemnation. Their use of ritual enjoyed widespread support among Jewish religious conservatives and politically cautious establishment bureaucracies as well as among the Jewish youth counterculture.[53]

Although the breadth of support for the movement was such that it did not face serious charges of inappropriately politicizing ritual, an implicit recognition of the profaning potential inherent in a utilitarian treatment was evident in the self-imposed constraints that delimited the boundaries of ASJM revisioning. The programme guides collected and disseminated many creative ideas for adapting Jewish ritual to advance the Soviet Jewish cause, but even so, they avoided suggesting changes that would violate halakhah (Jewish law). Speaking of the protest rituals developed in his particular organization, former SSSJ national chairman Rabbi Avraham (Avi) Weiss acknowledged these self-imposed boundaries. 'We were very careful, you know', he said. 'We were careful when we were using the name of God, *berakhot* [blessings], [and the like].'[54]

To succeed as a tactic of Jewish mobilization, the political deployment of sacred rituals had to maintain and preferably reaffirm a notion of their sacred character. What the organizations' action guides did not convey would have to emerge from the protestors' actions themselves. It was an indicator of the success of the ASJM's deployment of ritual that acts like blowing shofars, donning prayer shawls, and fasting in public to oppose the oppression of Soviet Jews became, for many, assertions of faith in the transcendent meaning of the political act. Recalling the 1965 Menorah March with its 12-foot-tall Hanukah candelabrum leading the way, former SSSJ national co-ordinator Glenn Richter described how the protestors saw their own actions. 'When we marched with that big heavy menorah through Central Park, from the West Side to the East Side over to the Soviet mission, even though we were *ḥalashing* [straining] under that big heavy menorah, but to us that menorah really meant something. The lights of the menorah really meant the lights of freedom.'[55]

Particularly in the SSSJ, which more than other ASJM organizations used a religious discourse to frame the Soviet Jewish cause, activists construed their actions not as a politicization of ritual, which would profane the sacred, but as a ritualization of protest, which would sanctify the political. In Weiss's words,

[If someone were to say] 'How could you use ritual in this way?' or 'It's a desecration of the ritual', my position is [that] it was a sanctification of the ritual . . . To me it was the real deal because on Passover, for example, the goal is not just to retell but to re-enact. Well! It doesn't get more powerful than this! . . . There was a special Matzah or a special empty seat. It was powerful stuff . . . We began to interpret ritual. We began to read into this a tremendous amount of meaning. The goal of ritual is not to be static.[56]

Outside the SSSJ as well, the organizers of ritualized protests understood that it was the protestors' attitude to action, the motivational states guiding them as they engaged in the ritualized protests, that would either profane the sacred or sanctify the profane. '[I]t is most important that the students conduct themselves with utmost propriety', the planners of a 1966 Passover rally in New York told the youth movement leaders who would be chaperoning their charges. '*They should see these two hours of march and rally as a solemn redemptive act by free American Jews on behalf of their muted brethren.*'[57]

In this call to view protest as 'a solemn redemptive act', we can recognize that the discovery of tactical ritual deployment entailed not only a concern for the actions of Jews' bodies but also for the frameworks of thought that shaped the understanding of these actions in Jews' minds. Alongside the expressly instrumental rhetoric of the programme guides, there existed an alternative discourse that mitigated the demystifying excesses of the former. In this other discourse, prominent in the SSSJ but not limited to it, the deployment of rituals was understood not only as a tactic but simultaneously as the realization of an imperative to action inherent in the rituals themselves. Even as activists were thinking of how ritual could be used, they were to understand this not as an act of exploitation but as an act of renewal and rejuvenation.

As a result of this, any distinction we might try to make between expressive and instrumental action, or between cultural performance and strategic tactic, breaks down, for what the movement was constructing was a particular subjectivity. The orientation that understood the effort to redeem Soviet Jews as a sacred Jewish act implied the choice of ritual as a tactic to express this understanding. At the same time, the use of ritual as a tactic—its actual deployment in practice by embodied actors—constructed the subjectivity that could understand protest on behalf of Soviet Jews as an act of transcending significance. By representing their plight through the ritual cycle of the Jewish calendar, the ASJM integrated the unfolding situation into a timeless Jewish cosmology.

The Mobilizing Gaze

The rapid spread of cause-oriented rituals in American Judaism in the late twentieth century was linked not only to new understandings of what ritual could be, but also to new understandings among American Jews of who they were and how they should relate to ritual.[58] Ritual had long been the subject of religious discourse, but suddenly American Jews were able to make it the subject of a strategic discourse—that is, they were able to begin conceiving of ritual not only as a sacred act to be performed in the context of religious observance but also as a useful instrument to be deployed in the context of political mobilization. For this shift to happen, American Jews had to posit three things simultaneously: themselves as political actors whose task was to mobilize the public for political action, American Jewry as a public to be mobilized, and the mobilization of the public as an effective and legitimate form of democratic political action.

In the 1960s, broader trends in American society were making it easier to do this. The civil rights, anti-war, and other social movements of the day were precipitating changes in the conception of democratic politics and of citizens' roles as political actors. These changes moved the notions of democratic citizenship away from a model of participation solely as individuals within the institutionalized frameworks of civil society. They revived an alternative model of democratic participation in which citizens became political actors by joining forces in collective action to initiate change from both inside and outside the established decision-making frameworks.

The ascendancy of extra-institutional collective action in conceptions of democratic participation simultaneously repositioned citizens as masses to be mobilized and reconstituted political organizations as agents of mass mobilization. The organizations working in the American movement to free Soviet Jews were part and parcel of this broader shift in American political culture. They understood the core of their mission to be the mobilization of American Jews,[59] which was seen as the crucial first step in a long causal chain whereby the social movement organizations would prompt American Jewish citizens to engage in a sustained campaign to influence their government to apply pressure on the Soviet government to change its policies toward Soviet Jews (Klein Halevi 2004: 42). The notion that American Jews needed to be mobilized—that is, that sustained collective action by Jewish citizens was a legitimate and effective form of political participation, but that it would not emerge or maintain itself, nor remain strategically focused, on its own—justified the movement organizations' assumption of the role of mobilizer.

Having identified the goal of mobilizing the masses of American Jews, and having appropriated the right to do so, the organizational vanguard of the American Soviet Jewry movement applied to its environment a 'mobilizing gaze'.[60] This can be defined as the act of looking at objects, practices, and symbols to determine if and how they can be used to influence the behaviour of others. The word 'mobilizing' carries a dual connotation, inasmuch as the initial object of the gaze (here, ritual) is both mobilized and mobilizing. Such a gaze is an imperial one: in the ASJM, it subjected venerated cultural forms and respected institutions to a revaluation in light of their potential to serve as instruments of mass mobilization. It enabled civic organizations such as the AJCSJ and NJCRAC to penetrate the religious and domestic spheres and to exercise power over synagogue worship and home ritual observance. Most importantly, it was continually extending its reach into new territories.

Once activists began thinking in terms of an annual campaign cycle, which, as noted, was early in the movement's history, they began directing their mobilizing gaze not only at Jewish holidays but also at anniversaries in Soviet Jewish history. The best known of these was the so-called Night of the Murdered Poets, the anniversary of Stalin's execution of members of the Jewish intelligentsia on 12 August 1952, and a 'symbol of Jewish cultural genocide in the Soviet Union. The yahrzeit has become a time for rallies and educational programs in support of the cultural rights of Soviet Jews.' The birthdays and the anniversaries of the arrests of well-known refusenik prisoners of conscience were also used to help structure the movement's annual cycle.[61]

The mobilizing gaze was also applied to non-Jewish calendars. As noted, the AJCSJ and NJCRAC emphasized the UN's Human Rights Day in their recommendations for the winter campaign. The SSSJ turned the Soviet Union's own holidays against the regime, regularly demonstrating on May Day and on the anniversary of the Bolshevik Revolution. In one such protest, activists attempted to deliver a birthday cake to the Soviet UN Mission decorated with the words 'Let My People Go' (Klein Halevi 2004: 42). American holidays were mined for metaphors, symbols, and rituals that could be deployed. Among other things, this led SSSJ activists to gather in front of the Aeroflot offices in New York City one sunny October afternoon in 1977. 'With black candles, white robes, prayershawls, rams' horns and incantations', they conducted a Hallowe'en exorcism of the '*dybbuk* of anti-semitism which has possessed the very soul of the Kremlin'.[62] Other calendars, such as the academic calendar, were also used in structuring the protest cycle: 'To emphasize the denial of Jewish education in the Soviet Union special ceremonies might be conducted at the opening of the school year at Jewish seminaries . . . References to the plight of Soviet Jewry should be included in the graduation exercises.'[63]

The imperial reach of the mobilizing gaze extended from the Jewish ritual calendar to encompass not only other calendars, but also Jewish rituals not associated with the annual holidays. After a decade of co-opting festivals, ASJM activists realized that life-cycle events could be put to similar use. Perhaps the best-known ritual innovation in this genre is the UCSJ-inspired custom of bar and bat mitzvah twinning, which began in the mid-1970s and continued throughout the following decade (Harrison 2001: 77–8). The practice, which infused political content into a domesticated and commercialized celebration of American adolescence (Joselit 1994: 89–105), was described by a zealous boy in his 1982 bar mitzvah speech as follows:

I am fighting anti-Semitism by twinning my bar-mitzvah. This is sharing my bar-mitzvah with a boy in the U.S.S.R. who cannot have one due to the anti-Semitism in the Russian government. I am twinning with a boy named Leonid Barros. I have sent letters to him and have sent him a tape of our Torah and Haftorah portions. The Russian government censors all mail so by writing to Leonid I help show his government that we are aware of their anti-Semitism and what they are doing to their Jews.[64]

From its first ad hoc deployment of Jewish rituals and symbols in outdoor rallies in the early 1960s, the mobilizing gaze had, by the end of the decade, enabled ASJM activists to appropriate the Jewish ritual cycle as a means of structuring an annually recurring mobilization campaign. The gaze continued to extend outwards, bringing Soviet Jewish and American civil calendars under its purview as well. By the mid-1970s, it was appropriating non-calendrical life-cycle rituals and reconfiguring them to serve the Soviet Jewish cause. The dynamic created by the ASJM's application of the mobilizing gaze propelled the enterprise of movement-based ritual revisioning forward and helped set the stage for the revisioning projects undertaken in other American Jewish social movements as well. Although the specific protest rituals of the campaign to free Soviet Jewry lost their justification and fell into disuse with the successful conclusion of the movement, the mobilizing gaze pioneered by the ASJM endures as one of the movement's lasting achievements.

Conclusion

In recent decades American Judaism has seen a veritable explosion of ritual revisioning tied to a growing variety of political and social causes. The appearance in such a brief period of time of so many adaptations (often similar, such as the plethora of cause-oriented seders) suggests that we are not witnessing independently emerging phenomena, but the diffusion of a social practice. We might speak of a field of American Jewish social movements that links the various organizations and their activists in mutual observation, dialogue, and sometimes participation. The American movement to free Soviet Jewry played a pioneering role in this field. Along with Jewish feminism and the New Left, it helped to launch the contemporary wave of mobilization through ritual.

The ASJM's contribution was different from that of the other movements in two important ways. The first was a matter of timing and scope. It engaged large numbers of American Jews at the earliest stages of the development of cause-oriented ritual revisioning. In the mid-1960s it was involving tens of thousands of demonstrators in ritualized protest marches in cities across the United States. Beginning in 1966, the support of national agencies, denominational umbrella organizations, local synagogues, and other groups helped the ASJM's first major home ritual, the Matzoh of Hope, engage an even greater proportion of the American Jewish population. Although the ASJM was not the only American Jewish movement developing such tactics, it was the first of its time to do so on a mass scale, and as such it played a highly visible popularizing role.

Perhaps most important, the ASJM made a seminal contribution to the developmental course that the practice of ritual revisioning was to take: the movement's activists quickly transformed ritual innovation from an ad hoc tactic to an organizing principle for structuring Jewish activism. They accomplished this by applying a mobilizing gaze within the framework of organizations that were bureaucratized to a greater or lesser degree. The rationalizing dynamic inherent both in their gaze—what I termed its imperial character—and in the bureaucratic quest for routinization, efficiency, and economy of scale took the initial insight that Jewish ritual could be deployed in order to mobilize Jews, and carried it closer to its logical conclusions. From the realization that Passover could be drafted in the service of the cause came the awareness that Hanukah could, too. And if Hanukah, then Simhat Torah and Tishah Be'av and indeed the entire holiday cycle, which could then be used to structure the movement's annual calendar. And if the Jewish holiday cycle could, then so could the Jewish life cycle, and on and on. If an innovation was developed in one community, due note of this would be taken by central agencies which would then compile and disseminate the information so that it might be replicated widely. The result of this process was rich with paradox and irony, for it took the dynamics of rationalization and bureaucratization that had been associated with the disenchantment of the world and used them precisely to the opposite effect.

In this marriage of tactical mobilization and organizational process, the ASJM established a paradigm of movement-based ritual revisioning which was different from the model of individual self-empowerment emphasized in the scholarship on American Jewish feminism. An awareness of the existence of this alternative paradigm enables us to see the project of feminist ritual innovation in a new light, for it has been decidedly present there, too. One brief example should suffice to make this point. In 1994 a women's organization, Ma'yan, sought to popularize the two-decades-old practice of feminist seders. It therefore began sponsoring them annually, drawing 20,000 attendees over ten years and reaching even more through the Haggadot and CDs it produced as part of the initiative. In 2005 the *New York Times* reported on Ma'yan's decision to cease holding the seders. The strategic thought underlying the decision was clear: "'Indeed, Ma'yan is giving up running the feminist seders because it has accomplished what it set out to do: create change," said Eve Landau, the director of Ma'yan. "Our goal is to be a catalyst," Ms. Landau said. "We can give it up because it has become mainstream"' (Nussbaum Cohen 2005).

This is not to deny the role that individual self-empowerment has played in feminist ritual innovation or in that in other contemporary Jewish social movements. More complete accounts, however, will have to bring to the fore the interaction of emergent grassroots creativity with what has heretofore remained on the margins of analysis, namely, the co-ordinated efforts of social movement organizations. These efforts, rooted in a politics of mass mobilization, have been central to the proliferation of movement-based ritual revisioning in late twentieth-century American Judaism. They show every sign of remaining so in the years to come.

Acknowledgements

My gratitude goes to Marcy Brink-Danan, Riv-Ellen Prell, Eviatar Zerubavel, James Jasper, Larry Isaac, Holly McCammon, Richard Lloyd, George Sanders, and participants in the Robert Penn Warren Center for the Humanities' and Curb Center for the Arts' Culture Workshop at Vanderbilt University for helpful comments on earlier drafts, to Ellen Bayer, Jenny Bayer, Jacob Birnbaum, Cindy Chazan, Maurice Corson, Gillian Lindt, Aaron Panken, and Mala Tabory, and to Adina Anflick, Shuli Boxer Rieser, Jennifer Anna, and the other staff at the American Jewish Historical Society, Center for Jewish History, and Yeshiva University archives. This essay is dedicated to the memory of Abraham Bayer.

Abbreviations

AB	Abraham Bayer's personal papers, New York
AJCSJ	American Jewish Conference on Soviet Jewry
ASJM	American Soviet Jewry movement
JB	Jacob Birnbaum's personal papers, New York
NCSJ	National Conference on Soviet Jewry
NJCRAC	National Jewish Community Relations Advisory Council
NYYCSJ	New York Youth Conference on Soviet Jewry
PJCRC	Philadelphia Jewish Community Relations Council
SSSJ	Student Struggle for Soviet Jewry
UCSJ	Union of Councils for Soviet Jews

Notes

1   Alvin Boretz, 'A Symbolic Seder for Soviet Jewry: Passover—1970—A Protest for Freedom', NCSJ/I-181/1/6; Spiegel 1968.

2   Notable exceptions are Prell's ethnographic treatment of the creation of worship services in a 1970s *ḥaburah* (1989), and Nadell's discussion of the implications of female rabbinic ordination on the proliferation of Jewish feminist ritual (2007).

3   The notion that social movements are agents of knowledge production is at the centre of Eyerman and Jamison's approach to the study of social movements (1996). Their perspective substantially informs my own.

4   See, for example, the socialist Passover Haggadot and the attendant discussion in Shuldiner 1999: 119–40, 155–96.

5   See Coalition on the Environment and Jewish Life, 'CFL Installation Ceremony for Hanukkah 5767', <http://www.coejl.org/~coejlor/climatechange/cflhanukkah.pdf>, accessed 19 Sept. 2007; Jewish Task Force for Comprehensive Immigration Reform, 'What's at Stake? Sukkot Immigration Pledge', <http://ga6.org/campaign/sukkot_immigration_pledge/explanation >, accessed 19 Sept. 2007.

6   On the role of social movements in the creation of new identities, see Eyerman and Jamison 1996. In the case of Jewish feminism, this theme is well treated in Prell 2007b.

7   For a history of the transnational movement, see Peretz 2006. On the AJCSJ, see Chernin 1999.

8   Letter from Jacob Birnbaum to J. J. Goldberg, New York, 13 July 2002 (JB).

9   National Conference on Soviet Jewry, 'N.C.S.J. Statistics', <http://www.ncsj.org/stats.shtml>, accessed 20 Sept. 2007.

10   Jacob Birnbaum, 'The Story of "Operation Jericho" (April 4th–May 20th, 1965)', n.d. (JB); '"Jericho March" Held on East Side near Russian Mission', *New York Times*, 5 Apr. 1966; Spiegel 1966a.

11   NYYCSJ, 'Minutes of Youth Directors' and Youth Representatives' Meetings', 8 Mar. 1966 (SSSJ/2/3); 'Outline: Leil Shimurim All Night Vigil, Geulah March And Rally' (SSSJ/2/3); *Queens College Hillel Newsletter*, Mar. 1966 (SSSJ/2/3); Glenn Richter, 'Geulah March for Soviet Jewry' (SSSJ/2/3); Spiegel 1966c.

12   Memo from Rabbi Israel Miller, Chairman, to Member Organizations of the AJCSJ, Re: 'Matzoh of Hope', New York, 15 Mar. 1967 (NCSJ/I-181/1/2).

13   Ibid.; 'A Passover Plea for Soviet Jews', *New York Times*, 20 Mar. 1966.

14   Letter from Jacob Birnbaum to Abraham J. Heschel, New York, 22 Nov. 1965 (JB); *Commentator* 1966; Spiegel 1965.

15   Letter from Albert D. Chernin to Rabbi Israel Miller, New York, 2 Apr. 1968, Re: Summary of Conference Activity, p. 6 (NCSJ/I-181/1/4).

16   AJCSJ, 'Simchat Torah 1969', p. 2 (NCSJ/I-181/1/6).

17   AJCSJ, 'Programmatic Recommendations Adopted by the Biennial', New York, 7–8 Apr. 1968 (NCSJ/I-181/1/4); PJCRC, 'Guide to Action', Philadelphia, Pa., 1971 (AB) (hereafter PJCRC 1971); NJCRAC, 'Joint Program Plan for Jewish Community Relations 1971–72', New York, 1971 (AB) (hereafter NJCRAC 1971); Memo from Jacqueline K. Levine to International Commission, 14 June 1981, Re: 'Draft Outline Proposed Program Manual for Soviet Jewry, a joint project of the NJCRAC and the National Conference on Soviet Jewry', (AB) (hereafter NJCRAC/NCSJ 1981).

18   AJCSJ, 'Programmatic Recommendations Adopted by the Biennial', New York, 7–8 Apr. 1968 (NCSJ/I-181/1/4), emphasis added.

19   PJCRC 1971; NJCRAC 1971; NJCRAC/NCSJ 1981.

20   PJCRC 1971.

21   Baltimore Committee for Soviet Jewry, 'Prayer for Soviet Jewry: Yom Kippur 5732', Baltimore, Md., 1971 (AB).

22   UCSJ, 'Greeting Cards for Soviet Jews', n.d. (NCSJ/I-181/69/16); SSSJ, 'May the Coming Year See the Redemption of Soviet Jewry', SSSJ greeting card, n.d. (JB); Soviet Jewry Committee of the Springfield, Mass. Jewish Federation, Rosh Hashanah greeting cards, 1974 (AB); Memo from Rabbi Herschel Schachter to Conference Membership and Community Leadership, 21 Aug. 1970, Re: 'Sending Greeting Cards to Soviet Synagogues' (NCSJ/I-181/1/6).

23   Schachter to Conference Membership and Community Leadership, 21 Aug. 1970 (NCSJ/I-181/1/6).

24   UCSJ, 'Greeting Cards for Soviet Jews', n.d. (NCSJ/I-181/69/16).

25   Schachter to Conference Membership, 21 Aug. 1970 (NCSJ/I-181/1/6).

26   UCSJ, 'Greeting Cards for Soviet Jews', n.d. (NCSJ/I-181/69/16).

27   The *lulav* is a bundle of three different tree branches: palm, myrtle, and willow. Shaking it together with a citrus fruit forms a part of the Sukkot ritual. On the Sukkot rally, see AJCSJ, 'Simchat Torah 1969', p. 5 (NCSJ/I-181/1/6).

28   AJCSJ, 'Simchat Torah 1969', p. 5 (NCSJ/I-181/1/6); AJCSJ, 'Programmatic Recommendations Adopted by the Biennial', New York, 7–8 Apr. 1968 (NCSJ/I-181/1/4); PJCRC, 1971; NJCRAC 1971; NJCRAC/NCSJ 1981.

29   NJCRAC/NCSJ 1981; PJCRC 1971.

30   The first two and last two days of Passover and Sukkot are considered in Jewish law to be *yom tov* (festival days). This entails restrictions on work, travel, and the use of technology, and the recitation of special prayers in the synagogue. On the intermediate days of these holidays, known as *ḥol hamo'ed*, these restrictions and additional prayers do not apply.

31   NJCRAC/NCSJ 1981.

32   AJCSJ, 'Programmatic Recommendations Adopted by the Biennial', New York, 7–8 Apr. 1968, p. 1 (NCSJ/I-181/1/4).

33   PJCRC 1971.

34   Spiegel 1966b, 1971; Letter from Chernin to Miller, 2 Apr. 1968, p. 6 (NCSJ/I-181/1/4); NJCRAC/NCSJ 1981; PJCRC 1971.

35   Memo from Albert D. Chernin to Membership of AJCSJ, New York, 21 Dec. 1966, and enclosure 'A Day of Dedication for Soviet Jewry' (NCSJ/I-181/1/2).

36   PJCRC 1971.

37   PJCRC 1971.

38   *Purimshpiln* representing the tensions of Soviet Jewish life were also popular among refuseniks in the USSR. It is unclear whether the practices there and in the West informed one another (Genzeleva 2005).

39   SSSJ, 'The Megillah of Anatoly Sharansky', 19 Mar. 1981 (SSSJ/23/17).

40   Alvin Boretz, 'A Symbolic Seder for Soviet Jewry' (NCSJ/I-181/1/6).

41   SSSJ, 'SSSJ Freedom Seder 1982/5742 *Hagadah*' 4 Apr. 1982 (SSSJ/24/12).

42   SSSJ, 'Freedom Seder', press release, 27 Mar. 1981 (SSSJ/23/19).

43   NJCRAC/NCSJ 1981; PJCRC 1971.

44   SSSJ, 'Tisha B'av for Anatoly Sharansky', press releases, 15 and 24 July 1977 (SSSJ/19/18).

45   PJCRC 1971.

46   Letter from Abraham J. Bayer to Conference Membership and Community Leadership, 31 July 1970, Re: News and Actions, and enclosure, 'Committee of Concern for Soviet Jewry: Fast for Freedom, August 9–10–11, 1970' (NCSJ/I-181/1/6).

47   AJCSJ, 'Programmatic Recommendations Adopted by the Biennial', New York, 7–8 Apr. 1968, pp. 3, 5, 6 (NCSJ/I-181/1/4).

48   PJCRC 1971, emphasis added.

49   NJCRAC/NCSJ 1981, emphasis added.

50   PJCRC 1971, emphasis added.

51   NJCRAC 1971; PJCRC 1971; NJCRAC/NCSJ 1981.

52   PJCRC 1971.

53   On the particularly prominent role played by Modern Orthodox Jews in the creation and popularization of ASJM protest rituals, see Ferziger 2006 and Kelner 2008.

54   Avraham Weiss, interview with author, 28 Apr. 2006.

55   Glenn Richter, interview with author, 27 July 2006.

56   Avraham Weiss, interview with author, 28 Apr. 2006.

57   NYYCSJ, memo to youth directors, emphasis in original (SSSJ/2/3).

58   The notion that the knowing subject and known object are mutually constituted in a historically specific manner is developed throughout Foucault's oeuvre. A concise statement of this approach is found in Foucault 1979: 27–8.

59   The decision to cast mobilization in unabashedly particularist terms, laden with traditional Jewish religious symbolism, also bespeaks an important baby-boom-era critique of earlier assimilationist models of Americanization. On the implications of this for twentieth-century American Jewish political culture, see Kelner 2008. On its implications for American Modern Orthodoxy, see Ferziger 2006.

60   On the notion of the 'gaze', see Foucault 1973. Foucauldian purists will object that I deviate from his use by not limiting it to a literal visual engagement with a physical object.

61   NJCRAC/NCSJ 1981.

62   SSSJ, 'Exorcism—Soviet Jewry Style!', press release, 28 Oct. 1977 (SSSJ/20/2).

63   AJCSJ, 'Programmatic Recommendations Adopted by the Biennial', New York, 7–8 Apr. 1968, p. 2 (NCSJ/I-181/1/4).

64   Bar mitzvah speech of Saul Jacob Kelner, Manalapan, NJ, 23 Oct. 1982. Personal papers of the author.

References

Primary Sources

Abraham Bayer's personal papers, New York (AB)

Center for Russian Jewry—Student Struggle for Soviet Jewry, 1962–1990, Yeshiva University Archives, New York.

Jacob Birnbaum's personal papers, New York (JB)

National Conference on Soviet Jewry, Records, 1964–1979, Record Group I-181, American Jewish Historical Society, Center for Jewish History, New York

Other Sources

BALIN, CAROLE B. 1999. 'The Modern Transformation of the Ancient Passover Haggadah'. In Paul F. Bradshaw and Lawrence A. Hoffman, eds., *Passover and Easter: Origin and History to Modern Times*. Notre Dame, Ind.

CHERNIN, ALBERT D. 1999. 'Making Soviet Jews an Issue: A History'. In Murray Friedman and Albert D. Chernin, eds., *A Second Exodus: The American Movement to Free Soviet Jews*. Hanover, NH.

Commentator. 1966. 'Menorah March During Hanukkah Sets Off New Campaign in Soviet Jewry Struggle', 18 Jan.

EYERMAN, RON, and ANDREW JAMISON. 1996. *Social Movements: A Cognitive Approach*. University Park, Pa.

FERZIGER, ADAM. 2006. '"Outside the Shul": The American Soviet Jewry Movement and the Rise of Solidarity Orthodoxy (1964–1986)'. Paper presented at the conference 'Orthodoxy in the 20th Century', University of Scranton.

FOUCAULT, MICHEL. 1973. *The Birth of the Clinic: An Archaeology of Medical Perception*. London.

——1979. *Discipline and Punish: The Birth of the Prison*, trans. Alan Sheridan. New York.

GALCHINSKY, MICHAEL. 2007. *Jews and Human Rights: Dancing at Three Weddings*. Lanham, Md.

GENZELEVA, RITA. 2005. 'Moskovskiye i leningradskiye purimshpili 1970–1980-ch godov: problema mezkulturnych svyazey'. In K.Y. Burmistrov, ed., *Paralleli: russko-yevreyskiy istoriko-literaturniy i bibliograficheskiy almanach*. Moscow.

GEREBOFF, JOEL. 2003. 'One Nation, with Liberty and Haggadahs for All'. In Jack Kugelmass, ed., *Key Texts in American Jewish Culture*. New Brunswick, NJ.

GRANT, LISA D. 2007. 'Finding her Right Place in the Synagogue: The Rite of Adult Bat Mitzvah'. In Riv-Ellen Prell, ed., *Women Remaking American Judaism*. Detroit, Mich.

HARRISON, ANDREW. 2001. *Passover Revisited: Philadelphia's Efforts to Aid Soviet Jews 1963–1998*. Madison, NJ.

HOWARD, PHILIP. 1968. 'Jews in Protest March', *The Times*, 16 Oct.

KELNER, SHAUL. 2008. 'Ritualized Protest and Redemptive Politics: Cultural Consequences of the American Mobilization to Free Soviet Jewry', *Jewish Social Studies*, 14(3): 1–37.

KLEIN HALEVI, YOSSI. 2004. 'Jacob Birnbaum and the Struggle for Soviet Jewry', *Azure* (Spring): 27–57.

KUSTANOWITZ, ESTHER D. 1999. 'Ushpizot', *JOFA Journal*, 1(4): 3.

LAZIN, FRED A. 2005. *The Struggle for Soviet Jewry in American Politics: Israel versus the American Jewish Establishment*. Lanham, Md.

MARKOWITZ, FRAN. 1988. 'Rituals as Keys to Soviet Immigrants' Jewish Identity'. In Jack Kugelmass, ed., *Between Two Worlds: Ethnographic Essays on American Jewry*. Ithaca, NY.

MYERS, JODY. 2007. 'Phasing In: Rosh Hodesh Ceremonies in American Jewish Life'. In Riv-Ellen Prell, ed., *Women Remaking American Judaism*. Detroit, Mich.

NADELL, PAMELA S. 2007. 'Bridges to "a Judaism Transformed by Women's Wisdom": The First Generation of Women Rabbis'. In Riv-Ellen Prell, ed., *Women Remaking American Judaism*. Detroit.

NAFTALIN, MICAH H. 1999. 'The Activist Movement'. In Murray Friedman and Albert D. Chernin, eds., *A Second Exodus: The American Movement to Free Soviet Jews*. Hanover, NH.

NUSSBAUM COHEN, DEBRA. 2005. 'Feminist Seders Now Their Own Tradition', *New York Times*, 16 Apr.

OCHS, VANESSA L. 2007a. *Inventing Jewish Ritual*. Philadelphia.

——2007b. 'Miriam's Object Lesson: Ritualizing the Presence of Miriam'. In Riv-Ellen Prell, ed., *Women Remaking American Judaism*. Detroit, Mich.

ORBACH, WILLIAM W. 1979. *The American Movement to Aid Soviet Jews*. Amherst, Mass.

PERETZ, PAULINE. 2006. *Le Combat pour les Juifs soviétiques: Washington–Moscou–Jérusalem, 1953–1989*. Paris.

PRELL, RIV-ELLEN. 1989. *Prayer and Community: The Havurah in American Judaism*. Detroit, Mich.

——2007a. 'Introduction: Feminism and the Remaking of American Judaism'. In ead., ed., *Women Remaking American Judaism*. Detroit, Mich.

——ed. 2007b. *Women Remaking American Judaism*. Detroit, Mich.

RO'I, YAACOV. 1991. *The Struggle for Soviet Jewish Emigration 1948–1967*, ed. Stephen White. Cambridge.

SHULDINER, DAVID P. 1999. *Of Moses and Marx: Folk Ideology and Folk History in the Jewish Labor Movement*. Westport, Conn.

SPIEGEL, IRVING. 1965. '1,000 Here Protest Russian Treatment of Jews', *New York Times*, 20 Dec.

——1966a. '3,000 Here Protest Soviet Curb on Jews: "Jericho March" Held on East Side Near Russian Mission', *New York Times*, 5 Apr.

——1966b. 'Soviet Curbs on Jews Protested', *New York Times*, 12 Dec.

——1966c. 'Students Rally Here to Protest Suppression of Jews in Soviet [*sic*]', *New York Times*, 9 Apr.

——1968. 'Passover Seder is Held Here for Jews of Soviet [*sic*]', *New York Times*, 11 Apr.

——1971. 'A Hanukkah Rite Attracts 20,000', *New York Times*, 14 Dec.

STAUB, MICHAEL E. 2002. *Torn at the Roots: The Crisis of Jewish Liberalism in Postwar America*. New York.

SZERSZYNSKI, BRONISLAW. 2002. 'Ecological Rites: Ritual Action in Environmental Protest', *Theory, Culture and Society*, 19(3): 51–69.

The Times. 1970. 'Israelis Hold Silent Protest', 30 Dec.

WEISSMAN JOSELIT, JENNA. 1994. *The Wonders of America: Reinventing Jewish Culture, 1880–1950*. New York.

ZYLBERBERG, SONIA. 2006. 'Transforming Rituals: Contemporary Jewish Women's Seders'. Ph.D. diss., Concordia University.

FOURTEEN

New Israeli Rituals: Inventing a Folk Dance Tradition

NINA S. SPIEGEL

IN THE SUMMER OF 1944, during the final four years of the British Mandate of Palestine before the establishment of the State of Israel, a national folk dance festival was organized at Kibbutz Dalia, a collective agricultural settlement located in the Jezreel Valley.[1] Dancers and spectators arrived from all over the Yishuv (the Jewish settlement in Palestine) to participate in the festival and to share in what would prove to be a defining moment in the creation of Israeli folk dance. By nationalizing and institutionalizing the Israeli folk dance movement, the festival was a watershed event that solidified a space for this genre in the emerging nation.

The development of a folk dance style was connected to the Zionist goal of producing a new Jewish culture and new traditions to celebrate the emerging society. Zionist theory negated Jewish life in the diaspora (*shelilat hagolah*) and called for the construction of a 'new Jew' in all spheres of life, seeking to transform the way Jews looked, acted, thought, and spoke. To that end, the Yishuv residents searched to find innovative forms of expression in language and the arts that would articulate the new life, referring to these developments as Hebrew culture. They transformed ancient Hebrew into a modern language that could be used in daily life and created national theatre, music, dance, and visual art. They also sought to develop folk forms, particularly in music through the creation of folk songs, and in dance.

The Dalia Festival was initiated and organized by Gurit Kadman, or Gert Kaufmann as she was then known. Born in Leipzig, Germany, she had been influenced by the Wandervogel youth movement and its popular 'return to nature' ideology. Begun in Germany before the First World War, the movement aimed to connect youth with nature and to build anti-bourgeois feeling by promoting folk expressions such as song and dance. It had an influence on the Zionist youth movements in Germany, and Kadman brought this sensibility with her when she emigrated to Palestine in 1920 (Kadman 1969: 8). Drawing on concepts of romantic nationalism, she strongly believed that the Jews in Palestine needed to develop a national folk dance along the lines of national folk dances in Europe if they were to create a new nation.

The first Dalia folk dance festival was a great success, held under the auspices of the Inter-Kibbutz Music Committee, the cultural department of the Histadrut,[2] and Kibbutz Dalia. Not only did the festival generate tremendous enthusiasm, inspiring its participants to create and learn new Israeli folk dances, but it also resulted in important institutional developments, including the establishment in 1945 of the Israel Folk Dance Committee that became part of the Cultural Department of the Histadrut.[3] Following this period of extensive dance activity and organization, a second festival was held at the kibbutz in 1947, also directed by Kadman. These first two Dalia festivals during the period of the British Mandate of Palestine set the stage for three additional dance events at the kibbutz after the establishment of the state: in 1951, 1958, and 1968.

The initial Dalia festivals of the 1940s illustrate the invention of an Israeli national tradition. Historian Yaacov Shavit has referred to Yishuv celebrations as 'official folk culture' because the creators were identified, the event was carefully orchestrated, and the Yishuv was not a nation-state (Shavit 1996; Shavit and Sitton 2004: pp. xii–xiii). The creation of both a national folk dance form and a festival represents the paradoxes and dilemmas intrinsic to this process. Since folk dance usually evolves organically over time, transmitted in a community from generation to generation, the notion of developing new, original folk dances on a national scale appeared to be a contradiction. But for leaders of the dance movement, 'folk' was important to convey the sense, if not the practice, of a common culture or community at the grassroots that formed the basis of the nation. Invoking 'folk' to suggest the connections of the dance to tradition, even if it was choreographed, implied the rootedness of a distinctive group in the land. The rhetorical combination of a new form of dance and old traditions corresponded to the Zionist conception of a modern state constructed on the site of ancient Jewish settlement.

Because it embodied a variety of central Zionist goals, folk dance aligned seamlessly with the Zionist ethos. It was an integral part of the emerging civil religion, representing the secular Zionist aim of connecting to Jewish traditions while simultaneously breaking away from religious practice. Many folk dances were based on themes from the Bible and from Jewish holidays, thus linking them to Judaism. At the same time, secular Zionists, and in particular the dominant socialist Zionists, altered Jewish holidays, celebrating them in new ways that suited their goals and ideals (Liebman and Don-Yehiya 1983). Dance in particular became a secular ritual with ideological underpinnings. According to Charles Liebman and Eliezer Don-Yehiya, 'The most striking feature common to all the transformed rituals was the involvement of all the participants in song and dance, which became a functional equivalent of public prayer' (1983: 48).

Folk dance also answered the Zionist call for the creation of a new Jew in a new Jewish body. With their strong, upright, and energetically moving bodies, the folk dancers represented an image that was fundamentally different from the Zionist portrayal of diaspora Jews as passive and weak, and of their bodies as shackled, helpless, and effeminate (Gilman 1991). The labour Zionist ethos calling for a physical and spiritual connection to the land was also evident in the way that folk dances were performed—outside, in nature, often with bare feet or wearing light sandals. The lack of a barrier between the dancer and the earth denoted deep roots in the land. Because folk dance could locate itself among the different important strains of Zionism, it intersected with a variety of streams within the budding Israeli society and served the goals of the burgeoning culture.

The Dalia festivals inspired debates about the interpretation and celebration of Judaism in the emerging state. The Yishuv sought to develop a culture that was rooted in the Jewish past and would therefore be viewed as 'authentic', yet simultaneously aimed to separate from the past and produce new customs. This quest for authenticity represented the paradox of invented traditions, as a newly constructed culture could not simultaneously be old (Hobsbawm 1983).

The creation of folk dance was an integral part of the effort to find new ways of observing Judaism. The concept of dancing in a pageant as a way of celebrating traditional Jewish holidays, or of dancing to music on the sabbath, was viewed by the choreographers as an appropriate way of interpreting and maintaining Judaism. For the Orthodox community, however, these forms challenged traditional religious norms. Especially conspicuous in the relationship of dance to religion was the staging of the first two festivals on the sabbath. By the second festival, the Orthodox protested at this timing, and a conflict between the religious and secular communities was unleashed. The debate focused not only on how to observe Jewish tradition, but also on who had the authority to dictate public guidelines for the practice of Judaism in a Jewish state.

As the Dalia festivals occurred during and shortly after the Second World War and the Holocaust, there was much disagreement about the propriety of holding a celebration at this juncture, given the overwhelming number of Jews who had perished in the Holocaust. The events embodied defiance: they showcased the 'new Jewish body' and represented Hebrew strength precisely at a time when Jews were being annihilated. This bold stance became an important part of the new tradition.

Creating a Folk Dance Festival

The emergence of the Dalia Festival was an integral component of the development of new ritual celebrations in the Yishuv. The first festival in the summer of 1944 took place after two related occasions in the spring of that year: a festival of musical choirs at Kibbutz Ein Harod and a Shavuot festival at Kibbutz Dalia.

Gurit Kadman had already been active in the arena of folk dance in Palestine in the early 1940s. Like many others working in dance in this period, Kadman was familiar with the work of Rudolph von Laban and his creation of movement choirs, in which large groups of people, often amateurs, performed together with the intention of building community through dance. The holiday pageants created in the kibbutzim from the 1920s to the 1940s, designed to celebrate the ancient Jewish agricultural festivals, were replete with folk songs and dances informed by Laban's ideas of using dance to foster community (Ashkenazi 1992: 26, 73–6). Kadman was also a close friend of Gertrud Kraus, the pre-eminent modern dancer who had emigrated to Palestine from Vienna in 1935. Kraus, who was very close to the Kaufmann/Kadman family,[4] assisted Kadman with the direction of the first three Dalia festivals. She had also worked with Laban in the 1920s in Vienna and Austria (Ashkenazi 1992: 74).

Before the first Dalia Festival, in 1929 and 1931 Kadman had organized two folk dance festivals at Ben Shemen, a youth village. These events had showcased mostly European dances.[5] In the early 1940s she taught folk dance at Hapo'el, the sports association of the 'Hebrew worker', as well as at the Seminar Hakibutsim (Kibbutz Teachers' Seminary) in Tel Aviv (Friedhaber 1985, 1992; Ingber 2000).

In early 1944 Dr Yeshayahu Shapira, one of the leaders of the Inter-Kibbutz Music Committee, asked Kadman (then Kaufmann) if she would organize a folk dance component for the end of the festival of choirs. It was scheduled to take place in April that year at Kibbutz Ein Harod during the holiday of Passover. Kadman was intrigued by Shapira's suggestion and in February 1944 she invited thirty people who were active in dance in different parts of the country to a meeting in her Tel Aviv home. To her great amazement, all thirty invitees attended. They decided to tour the country to take an inventory of what was being danced at the time, and Kadman collected twenty-two dances, many of which came from the immigrants' different countries of origin. These findings surprised Kadman and encouraged her to move forward with the idea of creating a folk dance festival, but she decided not to plan it as part of the festival of choirs, mostly because of the lack of time to prepare. However, Shapira's request had instilled the idea in her and she decided instead to organize a folk dance festival separately at another point (Friedhaber 1985, 1992; Ingber 2000; Kadman 1969).[6]

In the spring of 1944 Ilza Gutman (Filtz), a student of Kadman's in the Seminar Hakibutsim in Tel Aviv, asked her to choreograph a dance pageant at Kibbutz Dalia for the celebration of the festival of Shavuot at the kibbutz (Friedhaber 1994: 32; Ingber 2000; Kadman 1969). The kibbutz members were creating new ways of observing a traditional Jewish holiday in a non-traditional manner: they employed dance in all their innovative celebrations. Each year three kibbutzim— Dalia, Ein Hashofet, and Ramat Hashofet—would celebrate Shavuot together at one location, and in 1944 it was Kibbutz Dalia's turn to host the event (Ashkenazi 1992). Like many of the kibbutzim at the time, they focused on the agricultural component of the holiday: the offering of the first fruits, or *bikurim*, mentioned in the Bible.

Kadman was at first reluctant to travel to the kibbutz. Athough Dalia is geographically near Tel Aviv, the roads leading there were not yet paved and, as a result, it was a six-hour journey. Ultimately, she agreed and choreographed a pageant entitled *Megilat rut* ('the story of Ruth'), based on the biblical book traditionally read in the synagogue on this holiday (*Mishmar*, 31 May 1944: 2).

While visiting the kibbutz, Kadman realized that the site could serve as an ideal venue for furthering folk dance. She recognized that the kibbutz could connect the people with the land and nature, a key component of labour Zionist ideology. She also fell in love with the natural setting of Kibbutz Dalia, which featured an outdoor stage with a view of the hills behind and space on the ground for an audience in front. Shaped in the form of a U by white columns adorned with vines, the stage was referred to by Kadman by the ancient Greek word 'pergola', denoting a type of garden gazebo (Kadman 1969: 11). She was convinced that she had found the perfect place for a dance festival.

Kadman moved forward with her idea of developing a folk dance festival, and only two months later the first Dalia Festival took place on Friday and Saturday 14–15 July 1944. The event included dancing, singing, workshops, and discussion; it also featured opening and closing performances. Approximately 1,000 guests participated in the festival, and about 3,500 attended the final performance on Saturday evening (*Palestine Post*, 17 July 1944: 3). The unpaved roads to the kibbutz did not seem to deter the guests and the approximately 200 dancers from coming from all over the country (Ingber 1974: 8). Like Kadman, the journalists also appreciated the beautiful natural landscape and pergola. The *Palestine Post* reported:

> The settlement of Dalia, situated in the mountains of Ephraim and overlooking the Carmel Range, provided a magnificent site for the festival. A pagoda fashioned of living stone columns was the background of the ample stage. The large audience was comfortably accommodated on chairs and hay-bales and enthusiasm did not wane although the packed programme began at 6 o'clock and finished after midnight.[7]

The guests at the first Dalia Festival included well-known composers as well as concert dancers such as Gertrud Kraus, Devorah Bertonov, Yardena Cohen, and Baruch Agadati.[8] This event set the format for future festivals at Kibbutz Dalia: a meeting of dancers in which they taught their dances to one another, followed by a public performance for spectators along with a pageant performed by the members of Kibbutz Dalia (Friedhaber 1985: 29–33). Kadman scheduled a time both for teaching dances and for discussing the project itself. Her intention was to generate a community of dancers and actively engage participants in the mission (Kadman 1969).

In 1944 the aim of the festival was to bring together people who were working in folk dance as they conceived it. The goal was both to take stock of what was being danced in the Yishuv at the time and to show new dances and inspire fur-

Figure 14.1 Folk dance group performing at the Kibbutz Dalia Festival, 20 June 1947. Note the pergola stage. *Photo: Zoltan Kluger. Reproduced by courtesy of the Israeli Government Press Office*

ther creations. By the 1920s and 1930s, many agricultural settlements as well as urban communities had begun to develop new dances in celebration of traditional Jewish festivals. Dancers, choreographers, and teachers such as Yardena Cohen, Rivka Sturman, Lea Bergstein, Sara Levi-Tanai, and Gurit Kadman had been working in this arena before the 1944 Dalia Festival.[9] This gathering, however, was the fundamental event that changed the course of folk dancing in the emerging nation.

Dalia 1944 showcased the new fledgling Israeli dances as well as those that were already familiar in the Yishuv at the time, including some from Jewish diaspora communities and from European cultures. At the closing performance on Saturday night, thirty dances were performed by approximately fourteen groups. Kadman opened and concluded the show with creations from kibbutz holiday pageants based on traditional Jewish sources. The evening opened with 'Hallel', a dance by Yardena Cohen based on her choreography for the Shavuot (Bikurim) pageant at Kibbutz Ein Hashofet, and alluding to the songs of praise that are part of the daily and holiday liturgy (Friedhaber 1994: 29, 39). 'Hallel' was followed by *Megilat rut*, the full pageant created by Kadman for Shavuot earlier that year and performed by members of Kibbutz Dalia. The programme closed with another pageant based on the Bible: *Shir hashirim* (The Song of Songs), choreographed by Sara Levi-Tanai previously that year for the celebration of Passover at Kibbutz Ramat Hakovesh (Friedhaber 1994: 34).

Between presentations based on biblical stories, Kadman organized the rest of the programme in a pattern moving from old to new to international. Thus the new Israeli folk dances were presented in the centre of the show. She divided the event into several sections. First, there were dances created for the joint school of the kibbutzim at Ein Harod and Tel Yosef—this part included the performance of dances such as 'Maḥol hagoren' and 'Rikud habe'er', crafted by the soon to be famous folk dance choreographer Rivka Sturman. Another section was built around Jewish and European folk dances from the diaspora that were familiar in the Yishuv, such as a *sherele, cherkessias, krakoviak*, and *polkas*. A third part featured new creations including 'Mayim, Mayim', a *debka* (Arab dance), and a suite in Yemenite style. This segment was followed by the performance of a Yemenite troupe from Tel Aviv and Rishon Letsiyon, directed by Saadia Damari and Rachel Nadav, the principal dancer in Rina Nikova's Yemenite Ballet troupe. Finally, the section of European folk dances included Scandinavian, old English, Moldavian, and Czech dances.[10]

Connecting to Jewish Festivals

In order to link the Dalia Festival more closely with the Jewish holidays, there were attempts to hold the event in conjunction with a specific Jewish festival. The founders also realized that since these days were already demarcated in the calendar for celebration, this connection could help to ensure the continuation of the dancing festivities. In an internal meeting of the cultural division of the Histadrut, Nahum Banari described the efforts to connect the Dalia Festival of 1947 to a Jewish festival: 'To the heart of the matter—we had the idea in the beginning to connect the dance festival to a date that matched the Hebrew calendar, either Lag Ba'omer or Tu Be'av.[11] It's good to have a set date for gatherings like this, so that it will turn into a folk tradition.'[12]

Yom-Tov Levinski, editor of the festival anthology, thought that Tu Be'av, the ancient holiday of love, was the most appropriate time for holding the dance festival:

If only the custom of our forefathers were known to the organizers of the folk dancing gathering at Dalia . . . they would organize the great and lofty gathering at Tu Be'av . . .

They would bring back from antiquity the crown of the folk holiday. . . They would have revived our ancient holiday of dances, the holiday of equality and love, unity and brotherhood . . . The gathering of folk dances at Dalia would have become a national new-old holiday.[13]

The commentator Dan B. Amos also thought that the value of the dance festival would increase if it were connected to a traditional holiday. In a statement reflecting the dual value system of socialist Zionism, Amos pronounced: 'But also in a big artistic assembly like this, it would be better to put it into the framework of a holiday, like the Bikurim [Shavuot] or 1 May, or connected to a day of remembrance of the events in our renewed lives in the land' (*Mishmar*, 29 June 1947: 2).

Initially, the Dalia Festival of 1947 was scheduled for July 1946. The date had to be changed due to political circumstances: two weeks before the festival was scheduled to take place, on 29 June 1946, the British launched a two-week search for Jewish underground leaders and arms in response to the underground (Haganah) blowing up ten of the eleven bridges connecting Palestine with surrounding countries. The aim of the Haganah in this period was to thwart British immigration restrictions directed at Jews. In retaliation, the British established a curfew for the entire population and began their most intensive search operation to date among the Jews in Palestine on the day referred to by the Yishuv as the Black Sabbath. They arrested approximately 3,000 people, including many of the young people who would have participated in the festival (Friedhaber 1994: 45; Kadman 1969: 14; Sachar 2007: 265; Segev 2000: 475–6). As a result of the postponement, the festival was rescheduled for Lag Ba'omer in May 1947 but ultimately took place on 20 and 21 June 1947.[14]

The dances created for the 1947 festival were divided into two categories: folk dances and festive dances, the latter to be performed at different Jewish holiday celebrations. In contrast to the numerous international dances at the 1944 festival, there was a concerted effort to show only Israeli ones in 1947. The closing performance consisted of two sections of folk dance and two of festive dance. The folk dances included, among others: 'Hora Agadati' by Baruch Agadati; 'Hey Harmonikah' by Rivka Sturman; 'The Dance of Ovadiah' and a fisherman's dance by Yardena Cohen; and a *hora* by Gurit Kadman. The section devoted to festive dances included works for a variety of Jewish holidays such as Tu Bishvat, Shavuot, and Sukkot, and for talmudic celebrations such as the festival of the vineyards and Tu Be'av. The dances were choreographed by Yardena Cohen, Tova Cymbal, Rivka Sturman, Lea Bergstein, and Gurit Kadman among others. The well-known dance 'Mayim, Mayim' was also shown: it celebrated finding water at a specific kibbutz, though some connected it to the ancient *simḥat beit hasho'evah* ceremony or the 'joy of water-drawing', a celebration held in Temple times during the festival of Sukkot. This festive section even included a new dance choreographed for the socialist holiday of May Day.[15]

Many believed that the effort to create festive dances was crucial. At the Histadrut's cultural division meeting in 1947, Baruch Shwartz voiced his belief in the importance of creating this new form of expression for the Jewish holidays: 'I especially appreciate dance that is connected to a holiday. We are searching for a form for our holidays, and this is one of the fine forms. We will shorten our solemn speeches and will gradually include a festive ceremony that speaks more to the heart and also better educates the masses.' In the same meeting, Ya'akov Uri also expressed his belief in the necessity of developing the festive dances because he thought they would serve an important function in the refashioning of Jewish holiday celebrations: 'There needs to be more and more emphasis on holiday dances. This is what is essential for us. Folk dances—how fine. But our holiday is missing dance and this is what needs to be filled.'[16]

Both the types of dance that were to be created—whether festive or folk—and the direction in which the movement should develop were contested. The timing of the festival in general was also a point of contention.

Dancing Defiance

Gurit Kadman believed that it was important to convene a dance festival even during the Holocaust. Of course, not everyone agreed about the wisdom of holding festivities at this time.[17] Although Kadman received much criticism for planning the events, which were considered disrespectful to the memory of the dead, she felt that, in spite of the tragedy, it was important to celebrate.[18] Regarding the Dalia Festival of 1944, Kadman stated, 'It was during World War II and I was told I was crazy to plan something like that, but my opinion has always been that people need time to be joyous so I went ahead with the plans' (quoted in Ingber 1974: 8).

The title for the first festival encapsulated the atmosphere and Kadman's intention: it was nicknamed the Davka Festival. The Hebrew word *davka* does not have an exact English translation; it loosely means 'in spite of' and is generally used for emphasis. It is described by sociologist Oz Almog: 'The *davka* spirit is one of defiance, disobedience, standing one's ground, doing things out of spite and stubbornness' (Almog 2000: 114). Talking about her decision to hold the Dalia Festival, Kadman recalled:

Many warned us about the action that we were about to do, that indeed these were the days of the Second World War (1944), when the terrible scope of the Holocaust of European Jewry was beginning to be revealed. They asked us: how is it possible to arrange a gathering of dances at a time like this? But our answer was: '*Davka* (in spite of it all) now', and the word *davka* was chosen as the symbol of the gathering, according to the words of A. D. Gordon: 'If the whole world hits me and attacks me—I will *davka* burst out in dance.' (Kadman 1969: 12)[19]

In addition, Gertrud Kraus choreographed a piece entitled *Davka* that influenced Kadman and that was performed at the closing show of the festival (Ingber 2000).

The 1944 gathering represented the defiant nature of the Jews of the Yishuv, affirming life in the face of tragedy. It conveyed a message that *davka* in these times it was necessary to rejoice.

In the daily newspaper *Mishmar* in 1944 Mordechai Amitai agreed that convening a dance festival at this time was appropriate:

Dance in these days—can it be? No—not a play of dances for display, not a celebration that bursts forth in days of mourning, but a piece of the unforgettable experiences of a people that includes the wishes of generations, sorrow and grief, happiness and rebellion. And the gathering did not come but to serve as a guide to all who strive to develop the movements of the body into a precious human expression. These hours will serve us as hours that renew our existence and renew our strengths. (19 July 1944: 2)

Dancing was not viewed as peripheral, but was rather envisioned as a form of resistance and even as generating the renewal of the Jewish people. Those who saw the importance of holding a dance festival at this time also viewed the festivals at Dalia as a demonstration of their strength and as a symbol of the new society. As Shlomo Tenai stated in *Ha'aretz*, it was a 'demonstration of the strength of the renewed Hebrew life' (22 June 1947: 1).

These different views about the propriety of convening a dance festival at such a time were also expressed over the second Dalia Festival in 1947. After that event the well-known journalist Uri Keysari wrote an article in the daily newspaper *Yediot aharonot* entitled 'Dalia Danced at Dalia . . .' which captured the divergence of opinions between the older and younger generations about this issue. In his typical ironic style, Keysari wrote of a young girl named Dalia returning from the dance festival at Kibbutz Dalia, expressing the wonderful and exciting quality of the event that was so far removed from all of the worries of the Yishuv. Of course the young girl's name, just as that of the kibbutz, is a reference to nature (the dahlia flower), thereby giving importance to the land and its growth. In contrast to those who opposed the festival, young Dalia was strongly in favour. She tried to convince Keysari of the importance of the festival; he responded, in a patronizing tone:

of course, of course—I said to her—you are right, Dalia. We need to continue! All of the loudspeakers, all of them, in chorus, announce the need, this necessity, and therefore there is no reason to convince you. You're going to Dalia—to dance. This is a historical event . . . No. You are correct and not me. We need to continue . . . to continue! To shout in such a loud voice that we are continuing, that maybe, in the end, the world will also believe that we are continuing . . . to burst—but to continue . . . It is incumbent upon us to continue. (*Yediot aharonot*, 27 June 1947: 2)

For young Dalia, the dance festival had an important *davka* quality, showing the world that the Jews were alive and were building a new life. She further responded to Keysari's concerns over holding a dance event at this time:

Yes, yes! I know . . . the Yishuv is always worried . . . but would we help it if we sat shiva [Jewish mourning custom] and said lamentations? . . . do we need to wear sackcloth and be alone? Surely it is impossible to mourn for twelve months. True, we were exterminated, we were hit; true, to this day they hate us, they are hostile to us, they torture and chase after us, but a demonstration of strength like that shown at Dalia amplifies our strength, emphasizes our strength, our will to live. We are continuing and will continue. (*Yediot aharonot*, 27 June 1947: 2)

She emphasized the need to demonstrate Jewish strength and to celebrate even in these hard times. Keysari was not against the event, but he questioned the timing in his response to Dalia's defiant comments:

And then I said, all of this is well and nice. Dalia was a celebratory project, nice and charming. It is possible that a great Hebrew art will develop from Dalia . . . I would only be happier if the Yishuv danced at Dalia after the commission left,[20] after the *aliyah* of those held in Cyprus[21] . . . after the elimination of the camps in Europe[22] . . . because I would want the people of Israel to dance not before it exists, but rather after it is revived . . . Dalia didn't agree: 'You wouldn't understand this', she said. And I saw in her the face of a reckless youth, without patience, but so dear! (*Yediot aharonot*, 27 June 1947: 2)

For Keysari, holding the event during such tense political times was problematic. His debate with the symbolic young Dalia illustrates not only the difference of opinion between the generations, but also the opposition between the view that it was inappropriate to hold a festival at that time and the notion that it was critical to celebrate and to demonstrate the Yishuv's strength precisely at that juncture.

While Kadman moved forward with the plans in spite of the timing, she incorporated Holocaust remembrance into the 1947 festival: its closing ceremony began with a memorial to Holocaust victims in a pageant called *Vayehi or* ('And there was light'), performed by members of Kibbutz Dalia. They recited Hebrew poetry (by Shlonsky), spoke about remembrance, marched up a hill carrying torches, and lit a large memorial flame, an eternal light that burned throughout the night (Kadman quoted in Ingber 1974: 10). This commemoration—considered a focal point of the event—was followed by the entrance of groups of dancers.

Creating Tradition through Political Defiance

In addition to occurring in the aftermath of the Holocaust, two years after the Allied forces defeated Hitler, Dalia 1947 took place not long before the birth of the state, a time when the Jewish community in Palestine was ardently seeking to gain independence from the British. In February 1947 the British announced that they were relinquishing the Mandate, and a UN special committee on Palestine (UNSCOP) was appointed to determine a political solution for the country. It was in the summer of that year that the second Dalia Festival took place.

During this time of great political uncertainty, despite a British-imposed curfew where no one could travel after sunset, 25,000 people from both village and city—according to *Ha'olam hazeh* (26 June 1947: 9), approximately 5 per cent of the Jewish population of Palestine—travelled on unpaved roads to take part in the event.[23] The 1947 Dalia Festival represented a defining moment in the development of Israeli culture: it illustrated how folk dance was already becoming central to the public expression of national sentiment in the Yishuv. Like the first festival, it too contained a *davka* element—this time of political defiance.

This festival received extensive press coverage. The *Palestine Post* reported: 'For a week in advance a "Dalia Dance" madness seemed to infect Tel Aviv as well as the other towns and villages. Nobody remembered anything quite like it. From noon on Friday the little village in the Ephraim mountains became a Mecca, vehicles streaming up the mountain road in an orderly unbroken ribbon' (22 June 1947: 3). There were roughly 500 dancers from eighteen different groups, and even representatives of the UN Special Committee were present as guests at the event.[24]

The 1947 festival also created a new participatory tradition. Gurit Kadman was astounded that people were undeterred by the British-imposed curfew. She described the scene at the public performance:

This was the time of the curfew imposed by the British Mandate authorities in 1947. There were incidents of gunfire and with all our asking for one night free of the curfew, it didn't come. We were not allowed to be on the roads from sunset to sunrise. What would we do with the thousands who would surely come to Dalia? We decided to enlarge the facilities—there was a natural amphitheatre on the land of the kibbutz formed by the hills . . . We were prepared for about 8,000 spectators. Before the public performance 500 folk dancers from all over the country came to participate in two days and two nights of continuous dancing. On the third night, despite the curfew, we had the public performance, attended by more than three times as many people as we had expected. The 25,000 were squeezed into the hillside for the nonstop programme that had to last all the night long. There was no place for them all to move to, nor was there the possibility of making an intermission in the programme, for I had gotten a note backstage from the kibbutz that they feared a landslide if such a large group left their seats. (quoted in Ingber 1974: 9–10)

Because the curfew was not lifted for the night, people were forced to stay on and the closing performance had to last the whole night through, instead of until twelve or one, as had been planned. Thus, thanks to the political circumstances in 1947, a new tradition was invented. Perhaps because staying awake all night ritually bonded subsequent participants to this defiant moment and to the importance of continuing to celebrate Jewish strength, in later years it became part of the Dalia event.

Dancing the New Jewish Body

Both developing and presenting the 'new Jewish body' were central components of the national goals to revitalize Jewish life and alter the image of the Jew in the Yishuv. Physical activities were nurtured and encouraged in order to achieve these goals, and folk dance fell directly into this category.

The idea of re-creating the Jewish body originated from European circles and was espoused in particular by the ideologist Max Nordau. In 1898 at the Second Zionist Congress in Basel, Nordau called for the creation of a 'muscle Jewry'. In order for Jews to counter the image of being weak and feminized, and to re-create themselves fully, he claimed that they needed to become physically strong, a quality which was associated with, and promoted, a hypermasculine image. These notions had their origin in the German Physical Culture Movement (Turnen/Körperkultur) that began in the early nineteenth century and that placed an emphasis on the connection between the body and the mind. A healthy body, in this view, was intimately linked to a healthy spirit (Hart 2007; Krüger 1996: 410; Presner 2007; Stanislawski 2001).

The strong and vibrant dancing bodies at Dalia were seen as a sign that the 'new Jew' was breaking away from diaspora life. Representing socialist Zionist ideals of equality, women and men danced together in contrast to the separation of genders in Orthodox Judaism. As one commentator proclaimed after the second Dalia Festival: 'Indeed the collective folk dance and the free whistling are loyal evidence that a new generation is rising in the homeland, disconnected and free from the chains of the old Diaspora.'[25] These dancing bodies were also interpreted as a signal that the Jews were capable of creating a new state and a new society. Defending the importance of representing Jewish strength, in part via a strong body, this commentator proclaimed: '*Davka* in front of the members of the research commission [of the UN] we will show that we are strong in our spirits, in our bodies, and strong in our decisions.'[26]

Images at the time further represented and celebrated the new Jewish body. Photographs of the festival in newspapers, posters, and pamphlets showed vibrant, upright young people dancing exuberantly on the outdoor stage at Dalia. The scene was sunny and beautiful. The smiling dancers appeared festive and jubilant; they were energetic and buoyant. They were also connected to the land, and often adorned with flowers in their hair and on their costumes, or carrying flowers or leaves.

Drawing on the labour Zionist notion that living and working the land would transform the Jews, one writer remarked on the appearance of the dancers, illustrating his assumption that growing up in Palestine had changed their bodies: 'The human material was excellent. It was simply a joy to see the young generation that had grown up in the land. Straight bodies, tall, flexible, filled with tension and expression. Joy of life is stirring in them' (*Davar*, 27 June 1947: 4).

Figure 14.2 Folk dancing during the Kibbutz Dalia Festival, 20 June 1947. Note the vigorous and energetic movement in these various circles of the *hora*. *Photo: Zoltan Kluger. Reproduced by courtesy of the Israeli Government Press Office*

Creating a Nation of Dancers

The very notion of developing a national folk dance tradition stood as a challenge to the notion that Jews did not dance. It also served to differentiate between the 'new Jew' in Palestine and the 'old Jew' of the diaspora whose image was sedentary. Since the project of constructing a new Jew was tied to the goal of building a nation, the idea of creating a country of dancers was seen as fitting into this objective. Besides staging the event, Kadman thus sought to establish a community of dancers at the Dalia Festival. At the second Dalia, Avraham Levinsohn, the director of the cultural division of the Histadrut, proclaimed in a memorable phrase that rhymed in Hebrew: 'there is no unity without dance' (*ein likud beli rikud*: *Devar hashavua*, 26 June 1947: 13).

Dancers and journalists alike remarked on the ritual formation of community out of dance. Gurit Kadman claimed that the '25,000 people of Israel were as a family for one night' (*Mishmar*, 4 July 1947: 5). A journalist cited the Bible when he wrote: 'The great experience at the gathering was not the programme but the audience . . . *Mah tov umah na'im shevet aḥim gam yaḥad* [How good and how pleasant it is that brothers dwell together; Ps. 33: 1]. The masses that participated in the gathering will never forget it' (*Davar*, 27 June 1947: 4). The author, signed

'Sh. Nosa', emphasized the building of community when he claimed in his article in *Ha'aretz* that those who attended, even if not dancing, felt they were 'among a big family of dancers' (27 June 1947: 4).

The goal of nation-building was further enhanced by the collective singing of 'Hatikvah', the as yet unofficial national anthem. Starting off the opening performance, 'Hatikvah' was central to the communal experience according to news accounts (*Ha'aretz*, 22 June 1947: 1). In their issues of 22 June 1947, *Yediot aḥaronot* noted that 30,000 people sang it together, while *Ha'aretz* emphasized the importance of 'Hatikvah' and its place in the national experience. Thus, the audience was united by both music and dance, which served to solidify the ritual nature of the event.

Dance was viewed as a means of building both social and political bonds. In an internal meeting of the cultural division of the Histadrut, Banari discussed the ways in which folk dance fostered social cohesion:

> This is an important tool for social unity . . . What it [sport] lacks is found in folk dance, which unites, and still contains movement and pleasant rhythm, bringing aesthetic enjoyment both to the participant and to the viewer. It also has an element of enthusiasm that is connected to lovely music. It is not by chance that the hasidic movement elevated dance to a high level as it connected the great masses to the teaching of *ḥasidut*, without their knowing the depth of its teaching.[27]

In the hasidic movement dance was used for spiritual purposes: to bring people closer to God. Banari here suggested that dance has a profound ritual power that should be used to foster social unity in the emerging Jewish state.

Commentators noted the diversity of groups dancing and the fact that many political rivals, such as socialist and revisionist Jews, danced side by side. 'Sh. Shriah' commented on the ability of dance to unify the people. He noted: 'The answer was given, at the end of the evening, by the public itself. When the programme was over, people from the audience went up on the stage and danced. And the excitement was so great that Lipa Livyatan, the ardent revisionist, danced until he lost consciousness on the stage of a Hashomer Hatsa'ir kibbutz' (*Ha'olam hazeh*, 26 June 1947: 9).[28] The social ideals of the kibbutz were thus embodied in the festivals.

Creating a Folk Dance Form: The Inherent Paradox

The idea of 'creating' a folk dance form represented a paradox. This inherent contradiction raised the question of authenticity: how does a people create folk dance, when the very concept implies its gradual development among 'the folk'? This issue was addressed by the well-known poet and critic Leah Goldberg in her article about the first Dalia Festival in *Mishmar* on 23 July 1944: 'they showed the dances and with them the basic question was also shown: the question of the dance of a nation in particular, and the question of folklore in general: is it possible to create folk art not in the natural-historical path, but out of a wish and direct cultivation?'

The festival also raised the question of who constitutes 'the folk'. One concern was that the Jews in Palestine, even those who lived in agricultural settlements, were not the typical uneducated folk or peasants rooted in one place from which folk culture presumably emerges, but were instead educated people, often viewing themselves as members of the intelligentsia. An author in the *Davar* newspaper noted the problem: 'The village folklore in the world was created from the enclosed and conservative village. Our villagers are not enclosed and are not conservative; they are intelligentsia. They go to the theatre and to dance recitals' (27 June 1947: 4). Similarly, Goldberg thought that the Jews of Europe were neither a village nor a dancing people:

In our discussion of the folk dance we refer in general, and principally, to dances of village people who are rooted in the ground . . . But we are a nation that is hurried in movement and uprooted. We are not only not 'a dancing people' by nature, but more than that: we are a people who have lacked the earthly and village happiness . . . that healthy eroticism and the dance from which it arises. (*Mishmar*, 23 July 1944)

Moreover, according to its classic definition, folk dance should be created by the people, not by an individual choreographer. Unlike many other folk dance forms where there is a repertoire of steps and movements that can be danced to a variety of tunes, Israeli folk dance was choreographed primarily with specific steps and patterns for particular songs. Each dance had a set structure which was intended to be danced to its designated music, raising the question of whether an organized or formalized tradition could contain the kind of variation and spontaneity associated with folk culture.

Although Israeli folk dance did not emerge via the same route as many other national folk forms, it was used to serve the same purpose: to create a sense of community and collective identity.

Connecting to the Jewish Tradition

One of the most significant questions the festival organizers grappled with was that of developing a 'Hebrew-style' dance. The choreographers turned to the Bible as a key source of inspiration and investigated biblical references to dance. In ancient Jewish history, dance had been connected with life-cycle events and festivals. The ancient Israelites danced ritually in victory celebrations, in prayer, and in mourning. For example, Moses' sister Miriam danced with timbrels at the Sea of Reeds to celebrate the exodus from Egypt (Exod. 15: 20) and King David danced before the Ark of the Covenant (2 Sam. 6: 14, 16).

The Yishuv choreographers tried to incorporate biblical stories and influences into the new dances in order to assert their ancient and presumed genuine nature. They borrowed not only the content but also the concept of dance as ritual from biblical times. Although they attempted to revive actual ancient Israelite dances, there was no record of what these looked like. Avraham Levinsohn, the director of the cultural division of the Histadrut, addressed this problem when he said, 'While there is a tradition for literature, painting, sculpture, architecture, music, and other forms of art, there are no signposts yet regarding the ancient Hebrew dance' (*Palestine Post*, 22 June 1947: 3). Dr Chaim Gamzu also spoke of the difficulty of attempting to revive something of which there were no records. Addressing 'the renaissance of the dance', he claimed: 'And indeed we have hardly any memory, any document, any record, or witness to how our forefathers danced. And here we can ask a question: how can we revive something for whose material reality we have no recognizable signs?' (*Ha'aretz*, 27 June 1947: 9).

This question of how to re-create the ancient dances was a significant issue discussed and debated at Dalia. Despite the lack of knowledge of Israelite dance in biblical times, leaders of the folk dance movement sought nonetheless to recapture its symbolic nature. The *Palestine Post* reported:

It must be remembered that this was far more than just a night's entertainment. In the field of dancing there is a definite search for national expression. The question is primarily, 'Exactly how did Miriam dance with her timbrels in Biblical days?' and on the basis of that, to build the modern dance with roots in the past and branches developing into the future. (22 June 1947: 3)

'Sh. Shriah' also remarked that the dancers themselves participated in the debates about how to create Hebrew dance: 'And all day they took part in arguments . . . on the subject: what is the folk dance, and what is the original Hebrew dance?' (*Ha'olam hazeh*, 26 June 1947: 9).

Leah Goldberg addressed the issue of creating a new form from what she considered a blank slate, representing her view that the Jews were not a dancing people: 'It is not easy to revive a folklore that is dying because of historical developments, but it is much more difficult . . . to create something new from nothing. And it is mainly us, the Jews, who stand before this question' (*Mishmar*, 23 July 1944).

The dancers, choreographers, and commentators viewed the Dalia festivals as the beginning of the project of creating a new style and a new repertory, and ritually associating dance with Jewish life in the emerging modern state. The *Palestine Post* remarked that they were embarking on the search for a Hebrew style: 'It is too early to say that we have found the style, but there is a beginning. The future generation will dance—dance without questions or problems or searching. Today we are building the foundation of the Hebrew dance' (22 June 1947: 3). Similarly, Goldberg noted the difficulties of the project, and particularly the challenges of creating a unique style:

And from here is the beginning of the path to the second aim, the very difficult one, the very problematic one, an aim that, if it will be achieved, will not be achieved until after many years, and it is possible that only the children after us will enjoy its fruits: the creation of a style of the dance of the country. Style is not created in an arbitrary way, style is dependent not on the wishes of individuals, and not on the desirable aims of entire groups—it is always and forever the result of historical development. (*Mishmar*, 23 July 1944)

Goldberg thus viewed the attempts to create a Hebrew style as problematic, since, in her opinion, it needed to develop over time.

Connecting to Jewish Communities

As part of their search for connection with Jewish tradition, the choreographers and dancers examined the dances of two religious Jewish communities: the hasidim of eastern Europe and the Yemenite Jews. Leah Goldberg and the well-known dancer Devorah Bertonov both noted that hasidic dance was absent from the programme in 1944. Goldberg thought that hasidic dancing was 'in its essence closer to the type of mystical ecstatic dancing than to folk dancing in its general structure' and concluded that it was therefore inappropriate for folk dances (*Mishmar*, 23 July 1944). Devorah Bertonov, on the other hand, thought that the new Israeli dance would represent a hybrid mix of hasidic and Yemenite dances. She stated:

Our folk dance is still in its formation . . . Let's say it won't be a bridge between Russian dance and Arab dance, but the blending of hasidic dance (it's a great shame that this dance was not shown in the gathering) and Yemenite dance. From the Yemenite it will receive the burning syncopation, from the hasidic—the 'craziness', the drunkenness of the dance; and it will be Erets Yisra'eli because the builders and their children will dance it. (*Davar*, 21 July 1944)

Like Bertonov, Nahum Banari thought that the dances of the hasidim and of the Yemenites should be an essential source of inspiration for Israeli folk dances. He made his point at the Histadrut cultural division's internal meeting:

With the widening of the activity in this area we need to worry about one more thing: more Eastern-Jewish colour. Most of the people who work among us in this area are from the schools of western Europe. They grasp Jewish dance from hearing and from artistic intuition, but it is not in their blood. Therefore we need to bring in more and more people from the East, who, if they feel the rhythm more, will express the Eastern movement that lives in their blood, that they know still from the home, from dances of the hasidim and from weddings. We need to learn Yemenite movement.[29]

Banari's and Bertonov's comments represent the widely held opinion that the best solution, as with the creation of theatrical dance, was to develop a mix between 'East' and 'West' (Spiegel 2000). Gurit Kadman also wanted to find folk dance which represented such an amalgamation (*Yediot aharonot, La'ishah*, 25 June 1947).

In the Yishuv many seemed to assume that Yemenite dancing possessed authentic Jewish qualities. This attitude was epitomized by Leah Goldberg when she said: 'Real folklore is found only in the eastern communities [*edot hamizrah*]; even though it is not of the village, in any event it has a primitive and elementary quality that arose from a non-cut-off tradition, from celebrations of life events.' Yet she was still uncertain if it could be an appropriate basis for Israeli folk dance: 'But between this dance and us . . . lies a chasm, and even if it were possible to use these Yemenite dances . . . for the revival of our dances—most of us are not able to dance them in their essence, in a natural way, simple, as a folk dance would be danced in general' (*Mishmar*, 23 July 1944). She ultimately concluded that Yemenite dance was not a fitting starting place for folk dance, but was rather a suitable source of inspiration for concert dance: 'A difficult and complicated question is, will this pure folklore be used as a basis for our folk dances? It appears to me not—but . . . it can be used to enrich without limits the artistic choreography in our country and to make it original, interesting, special' (*Mishmar*, 26 July 1944).

These discussions reflect the self-conscious debates around the development of a folk dance form. Also embedded in them are conceptions of the definition of this genre, namely, dances that could be performed 'naturally' or spontaneously. This delineation was tied to notions of East and West: a folk dance was seen as a dance that should be inherent to the popular experience and it was viewed as distinctly Ashkenazi. While these conversations reflect a range of views about the suitability of Yemenite dance for the newly emerging Israeli form, its influence was present from the inception of the folk dance movement and played a strong role throughout its development.

Connecting to Arab Culture and Dancing Coexistence

The creators of Israeli folk dance were also influenced by Arab dances in Palestine that they viewed as rooted in the experience of living in the land. As connection to the land was a central tenet of Zionist ideology, Arab dance suited the aspiration to create a form that would be Middle Eastern with a strong connection to the local environment. Incorporated into many Israeli dances were elements of the Arab *debka*, a line dance in which men stand shoulder to shoulder, stamping on the earth in varied rhythms (Kaschl 2003).

Yet because the idea was to create folk dance that was Jewish, some questioned the use of Arab dances. Banari believed that the influence of the 'Eastern' Jewish communities had to be greater in the new dances. He thought that the non-Jewish Arab dances did not appropriately represent the emerging Israeli dance. In an internal Histadrut cultural division meeting, he claimed: 'I don't know if the movement and the rhythm of the Arab *debka* fits our dances. It has a particular nature, more desert-like; even though it looks good on the dancing Arab, indeed when our youth dance it, it loses its originality and there is some kind of an imitation in it that is inconsistent with our nature.'[30]

Banari's impression that Arab dances did not represent 'true' Israeli folk dances illustrated one of the dilemmas of the East–West negotiation. His opinion was disputed and, in fact, the Arab *debka* did become an integral part of the emerging Israeli folk dances.

In addition to a range of different segments of Yishuv society dancing together at Dalia (such as socialists and revisionists), Arabs and Jews also danced together in 1947. Gurit Kadman later reflected on the participation of Arabs at the event. As discussed earlier, because the British curfew had not been lifted, the performance scheduled to end at midnight had to last the whole night. Kadman felt the pressure of trying to fill the programme until sunrise and was pleased, relieved, and moved by the participation of Arab dancers. She described the scene as follows:

Despite the tension in the country that the British used in order to impose the curfew, three groups of Arabs and Druze came and performed on the stage one after the other. And once they start they cannot stop, that is the character of Arab dances. They warmed up and performed for a full hour, and I was so happy because this filled a full hour of this dangerous programme. And our people were standing about and clapped and danced along with them. And this was a picture of peace and tranquillity that did not match the picture of tension that the British spoke of.[31]

Shimon Filtz, a member of Kibbutz Dalia, also commented on the unusual occurrence of Arabs and Jews dancing together at this political moment:

Here we also mention the performance of our neighbours . . . More than the influence of the *debka* was the influence of the performance by Arabs. In my opinion, there were many dances that had great artistic value. But the participation of Arabs in this scene, at this time, and in this place, isn't this worthy of special attention beyond all the artistic points? Indeed, it was the performance of the Arabs that was so central and not the dances. (*Mishmar*, 3 July 1947: 2)

The combined *horas* of Arabs and Jews at this event, as well as the *debka* performances of the neighbouring Arab communities, were viewed by the press at the time as significant and memorable components of the 1947 festival.[32] At such a politically tense juncture, the notion of Arabs and Jews dancing together symbolically presented an image of peace and coexistence.

Conclusion

The Dalia festivals were seen as national achievements, became a source of national pride, and played a vital role in the emergence of a distinct Israeli culture and identity. In addition to being recognized as a national form of expression, folk dancing became ritualized in Israeli life. Both within the emerging state and abroad, it was considered a characteristic quality of the new Israeli and became a form of identification with the land and the community.

At the same time that the Dalia festivals celebrated the new society, they also unleashed debates between the religious and secular segments of the Yishuv. The secular community was pleased with the success of the event, and for them a Jewish dance festival that occurred on the sabbath was in keeping with Jewish tradition. However, in the aftermath of the 1947 festival the religious community protested that the event had been held on the sabbath, and used this occasion to express its concern over the future of Judaism and the development of Jewish culture in the Yishuv.

At this juncture, close to statehood, the internal politics of building a Jewish state became an even more central element of the debate. The second Dalia Festival took place in a period of fervent discussions about the future of religion in Israel.[33] An agreement between the Jewish Agency, the formal body representing the Jews in Palestine, and Agudat Yisrael, the anti-Zionist ultra-Orthodox political party, was signed in the summer of 1947. The document, which became the basis of the status quo agreement on religion in the State of Israel, was sent to the world headquarters of Agudat Yisrael on 19 June 1947, the day before the second Dalia Festival opened. The agreement was vague, but the sabbath was delineated as the formal day of rest in the emerging state (Kolatt 1998: 295).

The sabbath controversy surrounding the 1947 Dalia Festival reflected the internal politics of building a new state where each party and political view sought to claim its own place. As the society solidified, the Orthodox community's insistence on the public abiding by the rules of Jewish law intensified. In the aftermath of the second Dalia Festival the Orthodox leadership attacked the very nature of the emerging Israeli secular culture. Whereas the more secular Jews were seeking to create an Israeli culture that was influenced by Jewish tradition through performative and artistic rituals, religious Jews assumed that the Jewish religion was Israel's culture. While the dispute itself remained unresolved in 1947, future Dalia festivals were no longer held on the sabbath. Thus, the contestation over the celebration of Judaism in the budding state directly affected the timing of future folk dance festivals. Unwittingly, another custom was created, based on the religious–secular debate.

Future Dalia festivals were to be conducted outdoors, with both opening and closing public performances taking place on a stage. Established in an act of political defiance during the British curfew in 1947, the practice of dancing throughout the night would continue thereafter. In fact, the successor to the Dalia festivals, the annual Karmiel Dance Festival that began in 1988 in celebration of the fortieth anniversary of the establishment of the state, follows the same guidelines. While it has several differences from its predecessor at Dalia, the Karmiel

Festival, held in the summer in the Galilee town of Karmiel, has maintained the tradition of outdoor performances and all-night dancing, preserving the ritual connection to land and nature.

Other traditions also continue: the name of the choreographer is noted and dances are choreographed to specific songs. Several of the folk dances that were developed for the first two Dalia festivals are still a part of the repertoire of Israeli folk dance. The process of creating folk dances, a paradox that was initially addressed and viewed as a potential detriment in the 1940s, has now been both embraced and embedded as the 'tradition' for the form. In contemporary Israeli society, folk dances are avidly choreographed for newly composed songs, and the names of their creators are disseminated alongside the movements. It is common for these choreographers to travel the world, teaching their dances.

Moreover, the self-conscious way in which Israeli folk dance developed has been instilled as a tradition in the country's contemporary folk dance movement, whose leaders continue to discuss and review which dances are the most 'Israeli' and most suitable to the form. In addition, the annual Karmiel Dance Festival includes a competition to select the best 'Israeli' dance created in the preceding year.

Thus, both the festival and the folk dance form, while undergoing numerous changes since the 1940s, have remained an integral part of contemporary Israeli culture. These creations, which were developed consciously and defiantly, have now become symbols embedded in Israeli national custom, and are viewed as having always been in existence: the quintessential hallmark of an invented tradition.

Acknowledgements

I am particularly grateful to Ayalah Kadman Goren who has generously spent countless hours with me, conversing and dancing. Her spirit, experiences, and life's work embody the passion of the foundational period of the Israeli folk dance movement and she has given me priceless insights into this era. This piece has also benefited significantly from Judith Brin Ingber's valuable comments.

Notes

1   Kibbutz Dalia was established in 1939 as a Hashomer Hatsa'ir kibbutz. While there are numerous transliterations of its name, I have selected this spelling based on the version used by the kibbutz on its website.

2   The Histadrut (General Federation of Labourers in the Land of Israel) was founded in 1920, with important social and cultural functions besides being a labour union.

3   In addition, in April 1945, Gurit Kadman organized the first leadership course for folk dance leaders and teachers at the Kibbutz Teachers' Seminary in Tel Aviv (Hermon 1981: 113–14). See also Ayalah Dan-Caspi's interview with her, 11 Feb. 1981.

4   Ayalah Kadman Goren, interview by author, New York, 1 Aug. 2005.

5   A few Arab *debkas* were also featured. In addition, for the second festival in 1931, Kadman included the 'Hora Agadati' that had been created in the Yishuv (Ingber 2000: 40–1).

6   Kadman later reflected that it was fortuitous that she had declined to organize the dance component for the festival of choirs because during the rehearsal the stage broke with 1,000 people standing on it. Although they held the festival regardless, they would not have been able to dance on a broken stage. See Ayalah Dan-Caspi's interview with Kadman, 11 Feb. 1981.

7   The superb nature of the natural amphitheatre was also commented upon in the press reports of the 1947 festival. See *Ha'olam hazeh*, 26 June 1947, p. 9; *Ha'aretz*, 27 June 1947, p. 9; *Davar*, 27 June 1947, p. 4; *Davar*, 3 July 1947.

8   It is not clear which of the Orenstein dancers (Margalit, Shoshana, or Yehudit) attended. The composers included, among others, Girosov, Ben-Chaim, Nardi, and Yizhar (*Davar*, 25 July 1944). It was also noted in the press—and viewed as a shame—that the Ben Shemen students were not able to attend the festival due to illness. See for instance *Mishmar*, 23 July 1944.

9   See Friedhaber 1994; Goren 1983; Ingber 1974; Manor 1978; Roginsky 2006; Sharett 1988; Spiegel 2000.

10   Programme of the Dalia Dance Festival, 1944. The piece entitled 'Hallel' is not documented in the programme. For a fuller discussion of the dances, see Ashkenazi 1992; Cohen 1963; Friedhaber 1994; Ingber 1974 and 2000; Kadman 1969. It was also noted in the press that couples dances were popular at the festival in 1944, an aspect that is beyond the scope of this piece but should be the topic of further study. See for instance *Mishmar*, 23 July 1944.

11   Lag Ba'omer is a minor holiday that falls between Passover and Shavuot in the spring, and Tu Be'av is a minor holiday in the summer. Both are characterized by rejoicing, music, and dance.

12   Bulletin of the Cultural Centre of the Histadrut, Aug. 1947, Lavon Institute.

13   *Davar* 1947, undated, Dalia Archives.

14   Notes of Committees in the Bulletin of the Cultural Centre of the Histadrut, 1946–7, Lavon Institute.

15   Programme of the Dalia Dance Festival, 1947.

16   Bulletin of the Cultural Centre of the Histadrut, Aug. 1947, Lavon Institute.

17   Avraham Levinsohn and Chaim Freedman, directors of the cultural and educational centre of the Histadrut, were against holding the festival at that time. Although they later became supporters of the festival and of the burgeoning folk dance movement, they tried to persuade Kadman to delay the event in 1944 (Friedhaber 1994: 37, 40). Regarding Avraham Levinsohn, see also Ingber 2000.

18   Folk dancer and folk dance choreographer Zev Havatzelet wrote an article in 1945 addressing the issue of dancing during this period. See *Mishmar*, 22 July 1945.

19   A. D. Gordon was a Zionist philosopher, considered to be the father of labour Zionism. Zvi Friedhaber notes that this line of his was influenced by the words of poet Mordechai Warshavsky (1994: 37).

20 He is referring to the United Nations Special Committee on Palestine, UNSCOP, that arrived in May 1947 to try and find a solution to the future of Palestine after the British had announced they would end the Mandate.

21 A reference to Jewish refugees who were prevented from entering Palestine by the British and held in British detention camps in Cyprus.

22 A reference to displaced persons camps after the Second World War.

23 The number of participants in different newspaper accounts ranged from 20,000 to 25,000 to 30,000 people.

24 *Yediot aḥaronot*, 22 June 1947; *Haboker*, 22 June 1947: 4.

25 *Or hayom*, 27 June 1947, Dalia Archive.

26 Ibid.

27 Bulletin of the Cultural Centre of the Histadrut, Aug. 1947, Lavon Institute.

28 It seems that 'Sh. Shriah' was Shriah Shapiro, who wrote art reviews in the *Palestine Bulletin* and the Hebrew press.

29 Bulletin of the Cultural Centre of the Histadrut, Aug. 1947, Lavon Institute.

30 Ibid.

31 Ayalah Dan-Caspi's interview with Gurit Kadman, 11 Feb. 1981.

32 *Davar*, 22 June 1947, p. 1; *Kol ha'am*, 6 July 1947. Members of the UN praised the Arab participation.

33 While the 1944 Dalia festival also took place on the sabbath, there was no religious protest or unrest over this event, probably because it was a smaller festival and it did not take place in the period of discussions about the future of religion in the emerging state.

List of Interviewees

YARDENA COHEN, interviewed by author, Haifa, 2 Aug. 1998

AYALAH KADMAN GOREN, interviewed by author, Jerusalem, 13 July 1998 and 8 Apr. 1999; New York, 1 Aug. 2005

GURIT KADMAN, interviewed by Ayalah Dan-Caspi, Oral History Archives of the Histadrut, 11 Feb. 1981

SARA LEVI TANAI, interviewed by author, Tel Aviv, 26 Apr. 1999

RAHEL NADAV, interviewed by author, Tel Aviv, 11 May 1999

References

Archival and Library Collections in Israel

Dalia Archive, Kibbutz Dalia

Dance Library of Israel, Tel Aviv

Jewish National and University Library, Jerusalem

Lavon Institute, Tel Aviv

Steven Spielberg Jewish Film Archive, Jerusalem

Wingate Institute, Netanya

Videos

Lea Bergstein. Dance Library of Israel, H-360, H-378

Yardena Cohen. Dance Library of Israel, H-723, H-323

Documentary of Gurit Kadman. Dance Library of Israel, H-138

Gurit Kadman. Dance Library of Israel, H-317

Gertrud Kraus. Dance Library of Israel, H-65, H-181

Other Sources

ALMOG, OZ. 2000. *The Sabra: The Creation of the New Jew*. Berkeley, Calif.

ANDERSON, BENEDICT. 1991. *Imagined Communities: Reflections on the Origin and Spread of Nationalism*. London.

ARONOFF, MYRON J. 1991. 'Myths, Symbols, and Rituals of the Emerging State'. In Laurence J. Silberstein, ed., *New Perspectives on Israeli History: The Early Years of the State*, 175–92. New York.

ASHKENAZI, RUTH. 1992. *The Story of the Folk Dances at Dalia* [Sipur meḥolot ha'am bedalyah]. Haifa.

BAHAT-RATZON, NAOMI, ed. 1999. *Barefooted: Jewish-Yemenite Tradition in Israeli Dance* [Beregel yeḥefah: masoret yehudei teiman bemaḥol beyisra'el]. Tel Aviv.

BALDWIN, P. M. 1980. 'Liberalism, Nationalism, and Degeneration: The Case of Max Nordau', *Central European History*, 13: 99–120.

BOHLMAN, PHILIP V. 1992. *The World Centre for Jewish Music in Palestine, 1936–1940*. New York.

BOYARIN, DANIEL. 1997. *Unheroic Conduct: The Rise of Heterosexuality and the Invention of the Jewish Man*. Berkeley, Calif.

BUTLER, JUDITH. 1990. 'Performative Acts and Gender Constitution: An Essay in Phenomenology and Feminist Theory'. In Sue-Ellen Case, ed., *Performing Feminisms: Feminist Critical Theory and Theatre*, 270–82. Baltimore.

——1999. *Gender Trouble: Feminism and the Subversion of Identity*. New York.

COHEN, YARDENA. 1963. *The Drum and the Dance* [Hatof vehamaḥol]. Tel Aviv.

——1976. *The Drum and the Sea* [Hatof vehayam]. Tel Aviv.

ESHEL, RUTH. 1991. *Dancing with the Dream: The Development of Artistic Dance in Israel,1920–1964* [Lirkod im haḥalom: reshit hamaḥol ha'omanuti be'erets yisra'el 1920–1964]. Tel Aviv.

EVEN-ZOHAR, ITAMAR. 1996. 'The Emergence of a Native Hebrew Culture in Palestine: 1882–1948'. In Jehuda Reinharz and Anita Shapira, eds., *Essential Papers on Zionism*, 727–44. New York.

FRIEDHABER, ZVI. 1984. *Dance in Israel* [Hamaḥol be'am yisra'el]. Tel Aviv.

——1985. 'The First Folk Dance Festival at Dalia in 1944', *Israel Dance*, 29–33.

——1987-8. 'The Development of Folk Dance in Israel', *Israel Dance*, 33–9.

——1989. *Gurit Kadman: Mother and Bride* [Gurit kadman: em vekalah]. Haifa.

——1992. 'From Ben Shemen to the First Dance Festival in Kibbutz Dalia in 1944' (Heb.), *Rokedim*, 13: 12–15.

——1994. *Let Us Go Out Dancing: On the History of Folk Dances in Israel* [Hava netse bimeholot: lekorot rikudei am beyisra'el]. Tel Aviv.

——1995. 'Pioneers Of Expressionism', *Israel Dance*, 50–3.

GILMAN, SANDER L. 1985. *Difference and Pathology: Stereotypes of Sexuality, Race, and Madness*. Ithaca, NY.

——1991. *The Jew's Body*. New York.

GOREN, YORAM. 1983. *Fields Were Dressed in Dance* [Sadot lavshu mahol]. Ramat-Yohanan.

HART, MITCHELL B. 2007. *The Healthy Jews: The Symbiosis of Judaism and Modern Medicine*. New York.

HERMON, SHALOM. 1981. 'The Development of Folkdance in Modern Israel: From the Beginnings to the Establishment of the State of Israel (1882–1948)'. In *Physical Education and Sport in Jewish History and Culture: Proceedings of an International Seminar in Netanya, Israel, July 1981*, 109–14. Netanya.

HIRSCHBERG, JEHOASH. 1995. *Music in the Jewish Community of Palestine 1880–1948*. Oxford.

HOBSBAWM, ERIC. 1983. 'Introduction: Inventing Traditions'. In Eric Hobsbawm and Terence Ranger, eds., *The Invention of Tradition*, 1–14. Cambridge.

INGBER, JUDITH BRIN. 1974. 'Shorashim: The Roots of Israeli Folk Dance', *Dance Perspectives* (Autumn): 1–59.

——1995. 'The Priestesses', *Dance Chronicle*, 18: 453–65.

——2000. 'Vilified or Glorified? Views of the Jewish Body in 1947', *Jewish Folklore and Ethnology Review*, 20: 39–58.

KADMAN, GURIT. 1969. *Dancing Nation* [Am roked]. Tel Aviv.

——1982. *Dances of the Ethnic Communities of Israel* [Rikudei edot beyisra'el]. Givatayim.

KASCHL, ELKE. 2003. *Dance and Authenticity in Israel and Palestine*. Leiden.

KEALIINOHOMOKU, JOANN. 1983. 'An Anthropologist Looks at Ballet as a Form of Ethnic Dance'. In Roger Copeland and Marshall Cohen, eds., *What Is Dance?*, 533–50. Oxford.

KOLATT, ISRAEL. 1998. 'Religion, Society, and State in the National Home Period'. In Shmuel Almog, Jehuda Reinharz, and Anita Shapira, eds., *Zionism and Religion*, 273–301. Hanover, NH.

KRÜGER, MICHAEL. 1996. 'Body Culture and Nation Building: The History of Gymnastics in Germany in the Period of its Foundation as a Nation-State.' *The International Journal of the History of Sport*, 13: 409–17.

LABAN, RUDOLF. 1975. *A Life for Dance*. London.

LEVINE, LAWRENCE W. 1988. *Highbrow Lowbrow: The Emergence of Cultural Hierarchy in America*. Cambridge, Mass.

LIEBMAN, CHARLES S., and ELIEZER DON-YEHIYA. 1983. *Civil Religion in Israel*. Berkeley, Calif.

MANNING, SUSAN. 1993. *Ecstasy and the Demon: Feminism and Nationalism in the Dances of Mary Wigman*. Berkeley, Calif.

MANOR, GIORA. 1978. *The Life and Dance of Gertrud Kraus* [Hayei hamahol shel gertrud kraus]. Tel Aviv.

PRESNER, TODD. 2007. *Muscular Judaism: The Jewish Body and the Politics of Regenera-tion*. London.

ROGINSKY, DINA. 2006. 'Orientalism, the Body, and Cultural Politics in Israel: Sara Levi Tanai and the Inbal Dance Theater', *Nashim*, 11: 164–97.

SACHAR, HOWARD M. 2007. *A History of Israel: From the Rise of Zionism to our Time*. New York.

SEGEV, TOM. 2000. *One Palestine, Complete: Jews and Arabs under the British Mandate*. New York.

SHAHAR, NATAN. 1993. 'The Eretz Israeli Song and the Jewish National Fund'. In Ezra Mendelsohn, ed., *Studies in Contemporary Jewry*, ix: *Modern Jews and their Musical Agendas*, 78–91. New York.

SHAPIRA, ANITA. 1997. 'The Origins of the Myth of the "New Jew": The Zionist Variety'. In Jonathan Frankel, ed., *Studies in Contemporary Jewry*, xiii: *The Fate of the European Jews, 1939–1945: Continuity or Contingency?*, 253–68. New York.

SHARETT, RENA. 1988. *Arise, Brother* [Kumah eḥa]. Tel Aviv.

SHAVIT, YAACOV. 1996. 'Supplying a Missing System—Between Official and Unofficial Popular Culture in the Hebrew National Culture in Eretz-Israel' (Heb.). In Binyamin Ze'ev Kedar, ed., *Studies in the History of Popular Culture* [Hatarbut ha'amamit: kovets meḥkarim], 327–45. Jerusalem.

——and SHOSHANA SITTON. 2004. *Staging and Stagers in Modern Jewish Palestine: The Creation of Festive Lore in a New Culture, 1882–1948*. Detroit, Mich.

SHAY, ANTHONY. 2002. *Choreographic Politics: State Folk Dance Companies, Representa-tion and Power*. Middletown, Conn.

SÖDER, HANS-PETER. 1990. 'A Tale of Dr. Jekyll and Mr. Hyde? Max Nordau and the Problem of Degeneracy'. In Rudolf Käser and Vera Pohland, eds., *Disease and Medi-cine in Modern German Cultures*, 56–70. Ithaca, NY.

SPENCER, PAUL. 1985. *Society and the Dance*. Cambridge.

SPIEGEL, NINA S. 2000. 'Cultural Formulation in Eretz Israel: The National Dance Competition of 1937', *Jewish Folklore and Ethnology Review*, 20: 24–38.

STANISLAWSKI, MICHAEL. 2001. *Zionism and the Fin de Siècle: Cosmopolitanism and Nationalism from Nordau to Jabotinsky*. Berkeley, Calif.

ZERUBAVEL, YAEL. 1995. *Recovered Roots: Collective Memory and the Making of Israeli National Tradition*. Chicago.

Contributors

Simon J. Bronner is Distinguished University Professor of American Studies and Folklore at the Pennsylvania State University, Harrisburg, where he is lead scholar of the campus's Holocaust and Jewish Studies Center. He is the author and editor of over thirty books including, most recently, *Greater Harrisburg's Jewish Community* (2010), *The Meaning of Folklore* (2009), *Killing Tradition: Inside Hunting and Animal Rights Controversies* (2008), *Encyclopedia of American Folklife* (2006), and *Manly Traditions: The Folk Roots of American Masculinities* (2005). He edits the Jewish Cultural Studies series for the Littman Library of Jewish Civilization and the Material Worlds series for the University Press of Kentucky. He leads the Jewish Folklore and Ethnology section of the American Folklore Society and was elected a Fellow of the American Folklore Society. He has received the Mary Turpie Prize from the American Studies Association and the Wayland D. Hand Prize and Peter and Iona Opie Prize from the American Folklore Society for his scholarship and educational leadership.

Alanna E. Cooper is a cultural anthropologist whose work deals with Jews of Muslim lands. She was visiting scholar at Boston University in 2010, and previously has held research fellowships at Harvard University's Center for the Study of World Religions at the University of Massachusetts, Amherst, and the University of Michigan's Frankle Institute of Judaic Studies. Her recent publications include 'Rituals in Flux: Courtship and Marriage among Bukharan Jews', published in Ingeborg Baldauf (ed.), *Bukharan Jews in the 20th Century* (2008), and 'Remember Home and Exile: Memoirs of Jews of Muslim Lands', in *AJS Perspectives* (2007).

Jean R. Freedman teaches history and women's studies at Montgomery College in Rockville, Maryland. Her book *Whistling in the Dark: Memory and Culture in Wartime London* (1999) examines the relationship between popular culture and political ideology in London during the Second World War, with particular emphasis on the experience of Jews, women, and the working class. She has served as an oral historian and oral history consultant for many organizations, including the Jewish Museum of Maryland, the Jewish Women's Archive, and the Jewish Historical Society of Memphis and the Mid-South. At Montgomery College she has organized and directed a Holocaust commemoration ceremony, and wrote and edited material for the photographic exhibition 'Portraits of Life: Student Experiences'. She has received grants from the Mellon Foundation, the Indiana University Graduate School, and the Indiana University's Center on Global Change and World Peace.

Sander L. Gilman is Distinguished Professor of the Arts and Sciences at Emory University, where he also serves as Director of the Psychoanalytic Studies Program. Before going to Emory in 2005, he was the founding director of the Program in Jewish Studies at the University of Illinois in Chicago. He is the author or editor of over eighty books, including *Multiculturalism and the Jews* (2006), *Jewish Frontiers: Essays on Bodies, Histories, and Identities* (2003), *Smart Jews: The Construction of the Idea of Jewish Superior Intelligence* (1996), *Jews in Today's German Culture* (1995), and *The Jew's Body* (1991). He has received many awards for his work, including the Berlin Prize from the American Academy in Berlin, Fellow of the Royal Society of Medicine (London), Distinguished Humanist Award from the Melton Center for Jewish Studies at Ohio State University, and the Alexander von Humboldt Research Prize from the Humboldt Foundation. He has served as president of the Modern Language Association, as editor of the Jewish Writing in the Contemporary World series for the University of Nebraska Press, and as co-editor of Studies in the Culture of Psychiatry and Psychoanalysis for Cornell University Press, and of the Johns Hopkins Jewish Studies series.

Harvey E. Goldberg is Emeritus Sarah Allen Shaine Chair in Sociology and Anthropology at the Hebrew University of Jerusalem. His work has focused on the cultural history of Jews in North Africa, on religious and ethnic identities in Israel, and on the interfaces between anthropology and Jewish studies. He has been Visiting Professor at the University of California, Berkeley, and at Boğaziçi University, Istanbul; Visiting Lecturer at the École des Hautes Études en Science Sociale, Paris, and Fellow at the Oxford Centre for Hebrew and Jewish Studies and at the Center for Advanced Judaic Studies at the University of Pennsylvania. His books include *Jewish Life in Muslim Libya: Rivals and Relatives* (1990), *Sephardi and Middle Eastern Jewries* (1996), *The Life of Judaism* (2001), *Jewish Passages: Cycles of Jewish Life* (2003), and *Perspectives on Israeli Anthropology* (with Esther Hertzog, Orit Abuhav and Emanuel Marx, 2010). He is also co-editor of Indiana University Press's series in Sephardi and Mizrahi studies.

Jillian Gould is Assistant Professor at the Department of Folklore at Memorial University of Newfoundland. Her research specialities include Jewish culture, ageing, foodways, and public folklore, interests reflected in the articles 'Candy Stores and Egg Creams' in *The Jews of Brooklyn* (2002) and 'Blueberry Buns: History, Community, Memory' in *Material History Review* (2003). Her dissertation, 'Heimish and Home-ish' (2009), analyses the various ways in which the inhabitants of a Jewish assisted-living residence in Toronto create a sense of home within an institutional context. She won the American Folklore Society's Raphael Patai Prize in Jewish Folklore and Ethnology in 2009 for the essay that was revised for this volume. In the public sector she has worked as an oral historian for the Ontario Jewish Archives Small Jewish Communities project (2007), and as the education co-ordinator/museum educator for the Eldridge Street Project (now Museum at Eldridge Street) (1998–2001).

Michael Hoberman is Associate Professor of English and Folklore at Fitchburg State University (USA). He has also taught at Utrecht University in the Netherlands as Fulbright Professor of American Studies. He is the author of *Yankee Moderns: Folk Regional Identity in the Sawmill Valley of Western Massachusetts, 1890–1920* (2000) and *How Strange It Seems: The Cultural Life of Jews in Small-Town New England* (2008). His third book, forthcoming from the University of Massachusetts Press, is *New Israel/New England: Jews and Puritans in Early America*. He was a 2008/9 recipient of a National Endowment for the Humanities Long-Term Research Fellowship at the Massachusetts Historical Society.

Agnieszka Jagodzińska is Assistant Professor in the Department of Jewish Studies at the University of Wrocław, Poland. She is the author of *'Pomiędzy': Akulturacja Żydów Warszawy w drugiej połowie XIX wieku* ['In-Between': Acculturation of Warsaw Jews in the Second Half of the Nineteenth Century] (2008) and articles on Jewish cultural studies in *East European Jewish Affairs, Jews in Russia and Eastern Europe, Pinkas, Gal-Ed, Studia Judaica*, and *Polin*. She has received scholarships from the Hebrew University, Jerusalem; the British government (Chevening Scholarship); the Center for the Study of the Culture and History of East European Jewry, Vilnius; the De Brzezie Lanckoroński Foundation, and others. Currently she is working on the topic of English Christian missions to the Polish Jews.

Shaul Kelner is Assistant Professor of Sociology and Jewish Studies at Vanderbilt University. He is the author of *Tours that Bind: Diaspora, Pilgrimage, and Israeli Birthright Tourism* (2010), which won the Jordan Schnitzer Book Award from the Association for Jewish Studies. His writings have appeared in numerous journals, including *Sociology of Religion, Jewish Social Studies, Israel Studies*, and *Social Forces*. He was a Fellow of the Institute for Advanced Studies at the Hebrew University of Jerusalem, Senior Research Associate at Brandeis University's Cohen Center for Modern Jewish Studies, and chair of the Social Sciences, Anthropology, and Folklore Division of the Association for Jewish Studies.

Irit Koren received her doctorate in gender studies from Bar-Ilan University. Her research focuses on the intersection of socio-anthropology with Jewish studies, gender studies, and Israeli society. She recently concluded an appointment as the Visiting Aresty Scholar for 2008/9 at the Allen and Joan Bildner Center for the Study of Jewish Life at Rutgers University. Previously she was a postdoctoral Fellow at the Institute for Israel and Jewish Studies at Columbia University. She is the author of *Aron betokh aron* [Closet Within a Closet: Stories of Religious Homosexuals] (2003) and *You Are Hereby Renewed Unto Me: Orthodox Women*

Challenge the Wedding Ritual (2010). She has received fellowships from the Memorial Foundation for Jewish Culture; the Hadassah-Brandeis Institute, and Bar-Ilan University's Fanya Gottesfeld Heller Center for the Study of Women in Judaism. In 2007 she received the American Folklore Society's Raphael Patai Prize in Jewish Folklore and Ethnology for the essay that was revised for this volume.

Gail Labovitz is Associate Professor of Rabbinics at the American Jewish University, where she teaches rabbinic literature and Jewish law for the Ziegler School of Rabbinic Studies. Her book *Marriage and Metaphor: Constructions of Gender in Rabbinic Literature*, was published in 2009. Before going to the AJU she served as a senior research analyst for the Feminist Sexual Ethics Project at Brandeis University and as co-ordinator of the Jewish Feminist Research Group, a project of the Women's Studies Program at the Jewish Theological Seminary of America, and in 2002 was a recipient of a research award from the Hadassah International Research Institute on Jewish Women at Brandeis University. She serves as the co-chair of the Women's Caucus of the Association for Jewish Studies, and is the founder and co-ordinator of the Dr Elka Klein Memorial Travel Grant.

Vanessa L. Ochs is Associate Professor in the Department of Religious Studies and Program in Jewish Studies at the University of Virginia. She is the author of *Inventing Jewish Ritual* (2007), winner of a National Jewish Book Award. Her other books include *Sarah Laughed* (2008), *The Jewish Dream Book* (with Elizabeth Ochs, 2003), *The Book of Jewish Sacred Practices* (edited with Irwin Kula, 2001), *Words on Fire: One Woman's Journey into the Sacred* (1999), and *Safe and Sound: Protecting Your Child in an Unpredictable World* (1995). She is currently writing *The Passover Haggadah: A Biography* for Princeton University Press. Her body of work also includes journalism, fiction, reviews, and works for the theatre. She was awarded a Creative Writing Fellowship by the National Endowment for the Arts, and a research fellowship at the Frankel Institute at the University of Michigan.

Hagar Salamon is the head of the Jewish and Comparative Folklore program and the Africa Unit at the Harry S. Truman Research Institute for the Advancement of Peace, both at the Hebrew University of Jerusalem. Focusing mainly on Ethiopian Jews and Israeli folklore, her research fields include ritualistic and symbolic expressions of inter-group relations, racial perceptions, and life stories. She is the author of *The Hyena People: Ethiopian Jews in Christian Ethiopia* (1999), editor of *Ethiopia: Jewish Communities in the East in the Nineteenth and Twentieth Centuries* (2007), and a co-editor of *Jerusalem Studies in Jewish Folklore* (Hebrew University, Jerusalem). She has received fellowships from the Fulbright Foundation, the Memorial Foundation for Jewish Culture, and the Shain Center for Research in the Social Sciences at the Hebrew University.

Rachel Sharaby is a lecturer in sociology at the Academic College of Ashkelon and at the Interdisciplinary Social Sciences Department at Bar-Ilan University. Her research deals with immigration, syncretism, and the encounter between traditional and modern communities in Israeli society. She is the author of *The Spanish Community in Jerusalem at the Height of the Ottoman Period* (1989) and *Sinkretizm and vehistaglut: hamifgash bein kehilah masoratit levein ḥevrah sotsiyalistit* [Syncretism and Adjustment: the Encounter between a Traditional Community and a Socialist Society] (2002), and *Ḥag hamimunah: mehaperiferiyah el hamerkaz* [The Mimouna Holiday: From the Periphery to the Centre] (2009). She has published articles in numerous sociological and Jewish studies journals, including *Journal of Israeli History*, *Nashim*, the *Journal of Feminist Studies in Religion*, *International Migration*, and *Social Compass*. She has received support for her work from the Schnitzer Foundation for Research on Israeli Economy and Society and the Research Authority of Ashkelon Academic College.

Nina S. Spiegel is Assistant Professor of History and Jewish Studies at American University. She holds a Ph.D. in history from Stanford University. Her research includes the exploration of modern Jewish culture in Israel and America, with a focus on public culture, dance, museums, and the construction of memory. Her forthcoming book examines the formation of an Israeli culture during the British Mandate of Palestine, while uncovering its connection to the country's social and political dynamics. In 2004 she earned an honourable mention for the Raphael Patai Prize in Jewish Folklore and Ethnology for her article on the 1937 National Dance Competition in Mandate Palestine published in *Jewish Folklore and Ethnology Review* in 2000. Additionally she was elected to serve on the board of directors of the Congress on Research in Dance from 2004 until 2007.

Seth Ward is Academic Professional Lecturer in Religious Studies at the University of Wyoming (UW), where he also leads the UW study abroad programme in Israel. He previously taught at the University of Denver, where he directed the Institute for Islamic–Judaic Studies, and he continues to be a Research Associate of the Institute for the Study of Israel in the Middle East at the Graduate School of International Studies at the University of Denver. He served as a Wyoming Council for the Humanities Forum presenter, lecturing throughout the state on religion and the Middle East. He is the editor of *Convenant and Chosenness in Judaism and Mormonism* (2001) and has published religious and Jewish studies in *Modern Judaism*, *Shofar*, the *Journal of Near Eastern Studies*, and the *Journal of Ecumenical Studies*.

Index